# Communication Yearbook 26

# Communication Yearbook 26

## WILLIAM B. GUDYKUNST
### EDITOR

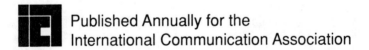

Published Annually for the
International Communication Association

LAWRENCE ERLBAUM ASSOCIATES, PUBLISHERS

2002    Mahwah, New Jersey                                    London

P
87
.C5974
V 26
August, 2002

Lawrence Erlbaum Associates, Inc., Publishers
10 Industrial Avenue
Mahwah, NJ 07430

Library of Congress:
ISSN: 0147-4642
ISBN: 0-8058-4437-6 (hardcover)

Cover design by Kathryn Houghtaling-Lacey

Books published by Lawrence Erlbaum Associates are printed on acid-free paper, and their bindings are chosen for strength and durability.

Printed in the United States of America
10  9  8  7  6  5  4  3  2  1

*Managing Editor:*     Barbara Stooksberry, ICA Headquarters
*Production Editor:*   Shannon Smithson

# CONTENTS

**Editor's Introduction**                                          xi
 *William B. Gudykunst*

**1. Comprehending Speaker Meaning**                                 2
 *Thomas Holtgraves*

**2. Understanding Family Communication Patterns**                  37
 **and Family Functioning: The Role of Conversation**
 **Orientation and Conformity Orientation**
 *Ascan F. Koerner and Mary Anne Fitzpatrick*

**3. Affection in Interpersonal Relationships:**                    70
 **Not Just a "Fond and Tender Feeling"**
 *Sue D. Pendell*

**4. Audience Activity and Passivity**                             116
 *Paul Power, Robert Kubey, and Spiro Kiousis*

**5. The Political Role and Influence of Business**                160
 **Organizations: A Communication Perspective**
 *Bruce K. Berger, James K. Hertog, and Dong-Jin Park*

**6. Emotional Intelligence as Organizational Communication**      202
 *Debbie S. Dougherty and Kathleen J. Krone*

**7. Professionalism and Social Responsibility:**                  230
 **Foundations of Public Relations Ethics**
 *Lois A. Boynton*

**8. Climate of Opinion, *Kuuki*, and Democracy**                  266
 *Ito Youichi*

**9. Ideology and the Study of Identity**                          298
 **in Interethnic Communication**
 *Young Yun Kim*

**10. Telehealth, Managed Care, and Patient-Physician:**           326
 **Communication: Twenty-first Century Interface**
 *Ruth M. Guzley, Norah E. Dunbar, and Stephanie A. Hamel*

**11. Lifespan Communication**                                     366
 *Jon F. Nussbaum, Loretta L. Pecchioni,*
 *Doreen K. Baringer, and Amanda L. Kundrat*

**Author Index**                                                390

**Subject Index**                                               408

**About the Editor**                                            422

**About the Contributors**                                      423

# THE INTERNATIONAL COMMUNICATION ASSOCIATION

The International Communication Association (ICA) was formed in 1950, bringing together academics and other professionals whose interests focus on human communication. The Association maintains an active membership of more than 3,000 individuals, of whom some two thirds are teaching and conducting research in colleges, universities, and schools around the world. Other members are in government, law, medicine, and other professions. The wide professional and geographic distribution of the membership provides the basic strength of the ICA. The Association is a meeting ground for sharing research and useful dialogue about communication interests.

Through its divisions and interest groups, publications, annual conferences, and relations with other associations around the world, the ICA promotes the systemic study of communication theories, processes, and skills. In addition to *Communication Yearbook,* the Association publishes the *Journal of Communication, Human Communication Research, Communication Theory, A Guide to Publishing in Scholarly Communication Journals*, and the *ICA Newsletter.*

For additional information about the ICA and its activities, visit online at www.icahdq.org or contact Michael L. Haley, Executive Director, International Communication Association, 1730 Rhode Island NW, Suite 300, Washington, DC 20036 USA; phone (202) 530-9855; fax (202) 530-9851; email: ica@icahdq.org.

Editors of the *Communication Yearbook* series:

Volumes 1 and 2, Brent D. Ruben
Volumes 3 and 4, Dan Nimmo
Volumes 5 and 6, Michael Burgoon
Volumes 7 and 8, Robert N. Bostrom
Volumes 9 and 10, Margaret L. McLaughlin
Volumes 11, 12, 13, and 14, James A. Anderson
Volumes 15, 16, and 17, Stanley A. Deetz
Volumes 18, 19, and 20, Brant R. Burleson
Volumes 21, 22, and 23, Michael E. Roloff
Volumes 24, 25, and 26, William B. Gudykunst

# INTERNATIONAL COMMUNICATION ASSOCIATION
## EXECUTIVE COMMITTEE

**President and Chair**
Cindy Gallois, *University of Queensland*

**President-Elect**
Jennings Bryant, *University of Alabama*

**President-Elect Select**
Robert T. Craig, *University of Colorado*

**Immediate Past President**
Joseph N. Cappella, *University of Pennsylvania*

**Past President**
Linda Putnam, *Texas A&M University*

**Finance Chair**
Howard Giles (ex-officio), *University of Southern California, Santa Barbara*

**Executive Director**
Michael L. Haley (ex-officio), *ICA Headquarters*

**Associate Executive Director**
Robert L. Cox (ex-officio), *ICA Headquarters*

## BOARD OF DIRECTORS

**Members-at-Large**
Sandra Ball-Rokeach, *University of Southern California*
Daniel Hallin, *University of California, La Jolla*
Cees Hamelink, *University of Amsterdam*

**Student Members**
Kristine Nowak, *University of Connecticut*
Jody Waters, *University of Texas at Austin*

**Division Chairs and Vice Presidents**
Information Systems
Mark Hamilton, *University of Connecticut*

Interpersonal Communication
Laura Stafford, *Ohio State University*

Mass Communication
Kasisomayajula Viswanath, *National Cancer Institute*

Organizational Communication
Patrice M. Buzzanell, *Purdue University*

Intercultural/Development Communication
Richard L. Wiseman, *California State University, Fullerton*

Political Communication
Steve Reese, *University of Texas at Austin*

Instructional & Developmental Communication
Jake Harwood, *University of Kansas*

Health Communication
Kim Witte, *Michigan State University*

Philosophy of Communication
Toby Miller, *New York University*

Communication & Technology
Joseph Schmitz, *University of Tulsa*

Popular Communication
Sharon R. Mazzarella, *Ithaca College*

Public Relations
Bonita Dostal Neff, *Valparaiso University*

Feminist Scholarship
Carolyn M. Byerly, *University of Maryland*

Language & Social Interaction
Stuart Sigman, *Emerson College*

Communication Law & Policy
Louise Benjamin, *University of Georgia*

**Special Interest Group Chairs/Heads**
Visual Communication
Ann Marie Barry, *Boston College*

Gay, Lesbian, Bisexual, & Transgender Studies
David Gleason, *Nickelodeon*
Sue Lafky, *University of Iowa*

## CONSULTING EDITORS

The following scholars made this volume of *Communication Yearbook* possible. The editor thanks them for their assistance in reviewing one or more manuscripts.

# EDITOR'S INTRODUCTION

*C*OMMUNICATION *Yearbook* is devoted to publishing state-of-the-art literature reviews in which authors critique and synthesize a body of communication research. This volume continues the tradition of publishing critical, integrative reviews of specific lines of research. This volume also includes senior scholars' reviews of their lines of theory and research. I had hoped to include reviews of research published in languages other than English, but no complete manuscripts were submitted.

Thomas Holtgraves summarizes his research on the comprehension of speaker meaning. His research suggests that the comprehension of conversational implicatures is influenced by the relative status of the participants, the conventionality of the utterance, and the type of implicature (i.e., generalized vs. particular). Holtgraves also argues that face management influences the comprehension of conversational implicatures because it is a major factor motivating individuals to speak indirectly. He integrates cross-cultural research on conversational constraints and indirectness with his line of research.

Ascan Koerner and Mary Anne Fitzpatrick examine their research on family communication patterns. They argue that conversation orientation and conformity orientation are two dimensions that influence family communication patterns. Koerner and Fitzpatrick summarize research on the development of the Revised Family Communication Pattern (RFCP) instrument and discuss how the RFCP can be used to create a typology of families. They then link conversational and conformity orientations and the family typology to family functioning (e.g., conflict management, speech acts used in the family).

Sue Pendell looks at the concept of affection. She reviews research on affection and its role as a dimension of interpersonal relationships. Pendell looks at the wide range of behaviors considered affectionate, summarizes theories that can be used to explain affectionate communication, and how affection has been measured.

Paul Power, Robert Kubey, and Spiro Kiousis examine how the major theoretical perspectives used in the study of mass communication view the activity and passivity of audiences. They present intellectual histories of the major perspectives (e.g., "bullet" theories, critical theory, cultivation theory, uses and gratifications) and isolate the position each perspective takes on audience passivity.

Bruce Berger, James Hertog, and Dong-Jin Park summarize research on the role of communication in "profit-seeking organizations' influence on public policy," especially the federal legislative process. They isolate a set of propositions that can be used as hypotheses to examine the influence of businesses on other aspects of the policy-making process (e.g., the federal executive branch, state or local policy making).

Debbie Dougherty and Kathleen Krone look at the role of emotional intelligence in organizational communication. They present a communication model of emotional intelligence then use this model to integrate previous research on emotions in organizations.

Lois Boynton argues that professionalism and social responsibility are the foundation of ethics in public relations. She examines the historical roots of professionalism and social responsibility in the field of public relations and links these concepts to public relations practitioners' ethical decision making.

Youichi Ito summarizes his work on climate of opinion, *kuuki*, and democracy. *Kuuki* is a Japanese, Chinese, and Korean concept suggesting a climate of opinion where there is social or political pressure for the participants to conform. Ito examines historical examples of *kuuki* and explains the conditions that lead to the emergence of *kuuki*. He also presents ways that *kuuki* can be measured.

Young Kim examines how ideology influences the study of identity in interethnic communication. She isolates areas of disagreement among "traditional" (e.g., those using social scientific approaches) and "nontraditional" (e.g., critical theorists) researchers with regard to the conceptualization and measurement of identity in studying interethnic communication. Kim's analysis sheds light on the "place of personal ideologies and politics in social research."

Ruth Guzley, Norah Dunbar, and Stephanie Hamel examine the role of technology in the physician-patient relationship. They look at how telemedicine, email, and the Internet influence communication between physicians and patients. Given the limited research to date, Guzley et al. provide suggestions for future research in this area.

Jon Nussbaum, Loretta Pecchioni, Doreen Baringer, and Amanda Kundrat examine research on communication across the lifespan. They summarize research regarding changes in "cognition/social cognition, language development, communication competence, [and] relationship change across the lifespan." Nussbaum et al. present a perspective designed "to capture age-related, intraindividual change" that researchers can use to study communication across the lifespan.

The chapters in this volume should be of interest to a large number of communication scholars. The chapters cover research from several different areas of research in the field, and they will be useful to researchers in a variety of the ICA's divisions and interest groups.

Before concluding, I want to thank the people who made this volume possible. The volume would not exist in its present form without the authors' contributions and the reviewers' suggestions for improving the chapters. The School of Communications and the Department of Speech Communication at California State University, Fullerton provided release time for me to work on *Communication Yearbook*. Finally, I want to thank Shannon Smithson for excellent work in copyediting and preparing this volume for publication.

*Bill Gudykunst,*
*Laguna Beach, CA*

# CHAPTER CONTENTS

• The Gricean Model                                              4

• Face Management and Reply Interpretation                       5
  *Preference Organization and Reply Comprehension*             *10*

• Processing Conversational Implicatures                        12
  *Generalized Implicatures*                                    *14*
  *Particularized Implicatures*                                 *17*
  *Conventionality*                                             *19*
  *Status and Interpretation*                                   *20*

• Coordinating Perspectives in the Communication                22
  of Speaker Meaning

• Individual and Cultural Variability in Processing              25
  Speaker Meaning

• Unintended Inferences                                         27

• Conclusion                                                    29
  *Potential Limitations and Future Directions*                *31*

• Notes                                                         31

• References                                                   32

# 1 Comprehending Speaker Meaning

THOMAS HOLTGRAVES
*Ball State University*

This paper reviews research on the comprehension of speaker meaning. The starting point for this review is Grice's (1975) theory of conversational implicature, an extremely heuristic approach but one that is incomplete in several respects. The present review centers on the processes that are involved in the generation of conversational implicatures, and the specific inferences that recipients will tend to generate. In terms of processing, research suggests that the comprehension of implicatures varies as a function of implicature type (particularized vs. generalized), utterance conventionality, and relative status. For particularized implicatures (e.g., violations of the relevance maxim) the specific implicature that is generated is based on a process whereby the recipient reasons about why the violation occurred. Because face management is a major motive for speaking indirectly, it will play a parallel role in the interpretation of speaker meaning. Individual, cultural, and perspective differences in the interpretive process, and the possibility that conversational maxims may provide a framework for understanding the generation of unintended inferences, are considered as well.

S peaker meaning—what a speaker means with an utterance at the time the utterance is used—is central to understanding language use (Clark, 1985). Yet speaker meaning has traditionally not been a focus of study in linguistics and psycholinguistics. Instead the emphasis has been on word meaning and sentence meaning. Understanding speaker meaning is particularly difficult because speakers rarely say exactly what they mean, and hearers rarely interpret utterances on a strictly literal basis. In other words, people often speak indirectly. Note that indirect meanings are neither rare nor deviant forms of communication (Gibbs, 1994a). Hence, a fundamental problem for language researchers is to understand exactly how speakers are able to convey, and hearers are able to interpret, indirect meanings. Although there is some debate about the status of literal (or direct) versus nonliteral (or indirect) meaning (e.g., Dascal, 1987; Gibbs,

AUTHOR'S NOTE: Much of the research described in this chapter was supported by grants for the National Science Foundation, National Institute of Mental Health, and Ball State University Office of Research and Sponsored Programs.

Correspondence: Thomas Holtgraves, Department of Psychological Science, Ball State University, Muncie, IN 47306; email: 00t0holtgrav@bsu.edu.

1984), most researchers agree the distinction is an important and valid one. The debate over literal versus nonliteral meaning really boils down to considerations of cognitive processing, research that will be discussed in detail in this paper.

We have conducted research on various aspects of speaker meaning over the past 15 years, with a particular emphasis on indirect communication (Holtgraves, 2001a). The two major goals of this research program have been to understand why people speak indirectly, and how recipients process utterances with potential indirect meanings. The former issue has been studied in terms of face management (Goffman, 1967) and politeness theory (Brown & Levinson, 1987) and has been summarized and reviewed elsewhere (e.g., Holtgraves, 2001b). It is the second issue—how indirect utterances are processed—that I focus on in this paper. Note, however, that the first issue—why people speak indirectly—is not totally ignored. This is because understanding how people comprehend indirect meanings involves a consideration of how and why people speak indirectly in the first place.

In the first section of this chapter, I outline the major framework for explaining how indirect meanings are comprehended—Grice's (1975) model of conversational implicature. The rest of this paper then focuses on certain problematic aspects of this model (and extensions of it) that have been investigated empirically. These issues center on the specific implicatures that people generate and the cognitive processes involved in their generation.

## THE GRICEAN MODEL

The starting point for most attempts to explain the comprehension of indirect meaning is Grice's (1975) theory of conversational implicature; in the psycholinguistics literature this has become known as the standard model (e.g., Gibbs, 1994b; Glucksberg, 1991). Grice argued that it is possible to communicate indirect meanings because interlocutors abide by what he termed the cooperative principle (CP). The CP states that one should: "Make your conversational contribution such as is required, at the stage at which it occurs, by the accepted purpose or direction of the talk exchange in which you are engaged" (p. 45). This general requirement is further specified in terms of the following four conversational maxims:

1. *Quantity*—Make your contribution as informative as required (i.e., do not be either overinformative or underinformative).
2. *Quality*—Try to make your contribution true; one for which you have evidence.
3. *Manner*—Be clear. That is, avoid ambiguity, obscurity, and so forth.
4. *Relation*—Make your contribution relevant for the exchange.

It is usually the case that people will mutually assume adherence to the CP and maxims, and this assumption serves as a frame for interpreting a speaker's utterances. That is, speakers' utterances will be interpreted as if they were clear, relevant, truthful, and informative. For example, saying, "Can you pass the salt?" at the dinner table is a violation of the relation maxim (i.e., in this context, inquiring into another's ability to pass the salt would not be a relevant contribution). But because the hearer assumes the speaker is being relevant, she will search for an ulterior meaning and interpret the utterance (i.e., generate a conversational implicature) in such a way so as to maintain adherence to the conversational maxims.

The "pass the salt" example is an instance of an implicature that arises to preserve adherence to a specific conversational maxim. Additionally, speakers will sometimes intentionally flout or violate a maxim, in which case it is simply not possible for the hearer to assume the speaker is adhering to the maxims. For example, abrupt topic changes ("I really think the Cubs will win the pennant.") in response to personal questions ("How did you do on that history exam?") function as relevance violations, and convey much more than their strictly literal meaning (possible gloss: I didn't do well on the exam.). In this case, it is obvious the speaker is not complying with the relation maxim. Still, the hearer will usually assume overall cooperativeness on the part of the speaker and generate a conversational implicature that makes sense of the violation.

Overall, Grice's (1975) theory has been enormously popular; it has influenced research not only on language use but also research on social reasoning in general (e.g., Schwarz, 1996). Although there are clearly problems with this approach, some of which will be noted below, it has provided an important framework for investigating many aspects of how people produce and understand speaker meaning. In our research we have investigated several issues raised by Grice's theory of conversational implicature. The first issue deals with the specific interpretations assigned to violations of the relation maxim.

## FACE MANAGEMENT AND REPLY INTERPRETATION

Given that a maxim violation has been recognized and hence that the recipient realizes the speaker is conveying a nonliteral meaning, what specific nonliteral meaning will be generated? This is not trivial; there are, in theory, an infinite number of implicatures a recipient might generate. Grice (1975) was not particularly clear in this regard. He argued that the implicature would be one that made the utterance a cooperative response, one that would "fit" in the conversation. This makes perfect sense, but in many instances there are numerous possible interpretations that would fit in the conversation; the theory narrows down these possibilities but it does not specify exactly how an utterance will be interpreted. Of course it is impossible to specify precisely, in advance, how an utterance will be interpreted. Still, it seems likely that additional interpretive constraints could be developed. In our research we have focused on violations of the relation maxim and how face management (Goffman, 1967) may play a role in their interpretation.

Utterances violating the relation maxim are utterances that are not relevant, at the surface level, for the conversational exchange. The concept of relevance is somewhat ambiguous and its manipulation tricky. However, some headway can be made with the use of tightly constrained adjacency pairs (Schegloff & Sacks, 1973) such as questions and replies. In this case, replies that do not provide a literal answer to the preceding question can be considered violations of the relation maxim.

To investigate relevance violations we constructed scenarios such as the following.

Bob and Al are students in the same history class and Bob has just given a presentation in this class. The following exchange then takes place:

Bob: What did you think of my presentation?

Al: It's hard to give a good presentation.

How is Al's reply to be interpreted? Obviously he is asserting the belief that the act of giving a class presentation is difficult. But most people would probably conclude that he really means something more, the most likely interpretation being that he did not like the presentation. How was this interpretation arrived at? Technically, Al's reply violates the relation maxim; it does not provide (at the surface level) the information requested by Bob. I assume that the recipient of such a reply will construct an inference that represents an attempt to explain why the relevance violation occurred. This assumption is consistent with attribution research demonstrating that people attempt to explain why unexpected or unscripted actions occurred (e.g., Hastie, 1984). It is also consistent with text processing research (e.g., Singer, Halldorson, Lear, & Andrusiak, 1992) demonstrating that readers generate causal inferences as a means of achieving coherence in their representation of a text (a property of text that is similar to the conversational requirement of relevance), and with Graesser, Singer, and Trabasso's (1994) model of text comprehension that is based on a search after meaning (i.e., readers' representations are influenced by their attempts to understand why something is mentioned in the text).

Although there are no doubt many reasons why people might violate the relation maxim and speak indirectly (e.g., see Roberts & Kreuz, 1994), a fundamental motivation for indirectness is face management. According to Brown and Levinson (1987), indirectness is an important mechanism for conveying politeness, and all politeness is motivated by concerns for managing "face." The essence of politeness is the performance of a face-threatening act in a manner that simultaneously attends to the face needs of the interactants. For example, people frequently perform requests indirectly (e.g., Could you open the door?) rather than directly (e.g., Open the door); in this way they attend to the face of the recipient by symbolically lessening the implied imposition of the act. Research has documented that indirectness (as a form of politeness) is motivated by face management concerns (R. Brown & Gilman, 1989; Clark & Schunk, 1980; Holtgraves & Yang, 1990, 1992; Kim, Shin, & Cai, 1998), and that the manner in which specific acts are performed is responsive to the specific face-threat inherent in that act (Wilson, Aleman, & Leatham, 1998). Importantly, this relationship has been found for replies to personal information questions; people will be indirect and violate the relevance maxim as a means of managing face (Bavelas, Black, Chovil, & Mullet, 1990), and replies that do this are perceived as more polite (Holtgraves, 1986).

Almost all research on Brown and Levinson's (1987) model has focused on how speakers' produce polite remarks; there has been virtually no research on how face management might impact the manner in which a recipient interprets a speaker's remark. But there is a straightforward extension here. Because face management is a major reason for violating Gricean conversational maxims, it is reasonable to assume that when faced with such a violation hearers will consider the possibility that the speaker is trying to engage in face management. This recognition then can serve as the basis for generating an interpretation of what the speaker actually means with an utterance. This reasoning seems very likely to occur for replies to personal questions. So, when Al replies "It's hard to give a good presentation," in response to Bob's request for feedback, Bob is likely to infer that Al is engaging in face management. Now, because it is a negative opinion about Bob's presentation that would be face-threatening in this situation, the most likely inference is that Al does not have a positive opinion of the presentation. If the information was positive, there would usually be no need to violate the relation maxim; a positive opinion would not be face-threatening. The claim, then, is that in these situations relevance violations will be interpreted as conveying nonliteral meanings, and that because it is negative information that would be most face-threatening in these situations, the most likely interpretation is that the speaker is conveying negative information. It is important to note that it is not being claimed that all relevance violations will be interpreted as conveying negative information. Rather, the claim is that they will be interpreted as conveying negative information if it is negative information that is face-threatening.

We have found support for this reasoning in several experiments (Holtgraves, 1998a). In the first experiment, we had participants read brief descriptions of situations, each followed by a question-reply exchange. Two types of situations were created, an "opinion" situation in which the requested information pertained to the person asking the question (e.g., "What did you think of my presentation?"), and a self-disclosure situation in which the requested information pertained to the recipient of the question (e.g., "How did you do on the chemistry test?").[1] The reply always violated the relation maxim, either by completely changing the topic or by providing an excuse for why the requested information might be negative. The information requested by the questions was described in the scenario as being either positive, negative, or no information was given. Sample scenarios are presented in Table 1.

In the first experiment, participants were asked to interpret each reply, and to indicate their degree of confidence in their interpretation. Their interpretations were coded in terms of whether they were literal or indirect, and if the latter, whether the interpretation was positive, negative, or neutral. Obviously, participants should interpret the replies as conveying negative information when they are told that the requested information is negative (the negative information condition in Table 1). When no information is provided (the no information condition in Table 1), however, participants could infer a number of different things (e.g., that the information is negative, that it's positive, that the speaker is not really giving an opinion at all, etc.). However, if participants attempt to uncover a reason for the relevance violation, and if a major reason for violating the relevance maxim is to manage face, and if (as in the present situations) it is negative information that is face-threatening, then participants should be most likely to infer that the information is negative. That is exactly what happened. Participants were far more likely to interpret the replies as conveying negative information than positive or neutral information. More importantly, they were just as likely to interpret the replies as conveying negative information when no information was provided (62.2%) as when they were told explicitly that the requested information was negative (66.4%).

A second experiment tested this logic further. The same materials were presented to participants on a computer screen and the time taken for them to comprehend the replies was recorded. After reading the replies, participants also indicated whether an indirect interpretation was a reasonable interpretation of the preceding reply (the indirect interpretation target in Table 1). When the vignette makes clear that the requested information is positive (the positive information condition), then the comprehension of relevance violations should become quite difficult and time consuming because there is no apparent reason for the violation. In contrast, in the no information and negative information conditions, the hearer can reasonably assume the existence of face management as a reason for the violation. Consistent with this logic, participants took far longer to comprehend replies in the positive information condition (2766 ms) than in the no information (2281 ms) and negative information (2263 ms) conditions. Importantly, the difference between the latter two conditions was not significant. Judgment speeds for the interpretations paralleled these results. Participants were far slower at judging the indirect interpretation in the positive information condition (2791 ms) than in the negative (2147 ms) and no information (2090 ms) conditions.

These results provide support for the idea that the specific interpretation given to a relevance violation is guided by beliefs about the reason for the violation. Again, it is not being claimed that relevance violations will always be interpreted

TABLE 1

Sample Experimental Materials From Holtgraves (1998a, 1999)

---

*Opinion*

---

Nick and Paul are taking the same history class. Students in this class have to give a 20-minute presentation to the class on some topic.

*No information:* Nick gave his presentation and then decided to ask Paul what he thought of it.
*Negative information:* Nick gave his presentation and it was truly terrible. He decides to ask Paul what he thought of it.
*Positive information:* Nick gave his presentation and it was excellent. He decides to ask Paul what he thought of it.

> Nick: What did you think of my presentation?
> Paul: It's hard to give a good presentation. (excuse)
> Paul: I hope I win the lottery tonight. (topic change)

*Indirect interpretation target:* I didn't like your presentation. (Experiment 2, Holtgraves, 1998a; Experiments 1–3, Holtgraves, 1999)
*Neutral target:* I gave her roses for Valentine's Day. (Experiments 1–3, Holtgraves, 1999)

---

*Self-Disclosure*

---

Jim is in seventh grade. Report cards were due today and Jim's mother is curious about how well he did.

*No information:* Jim just got home from school and his mother met him at the door.
*Negative information:* Jim is having a bad semester and flunking several classes. Jim just got home from school and his mother met him at the door.
*Positive information:* Jim is having a great semester and getting "As" in all but one class. Jim just got home from school and his mother met him at the door.

> Mom: How were your grades this semester?
> Jim: I don't think the teacher grades fairly. (excuse)
> Jim: It snowed very hard last night. (topic change)

*Indirect interpretation target:* My grades aren't very good. (Experiment 2, Holtgraves, 1998a; Experiments 1–3, Holtgraves, 1999)
*Neutral target:* His wallet was stolen. (Experiments 1–3, Holtgraves, 1999)

---

as conveying negative information, only that if face management is recognized as a motivation for the violation, then the utterance will tend to be interpreted as conveying face-threatening information. Occasionally it might be positive information that is face-threatening. For example, imagine a conversation between two siblings, Mark and John, in which Mark always outperforms John in school, much to John's chagrin. Mark is aware of John's feelings and generally tries to manage John's face. Now, when John asks Mark how he did on his chemistry test, and Mark fails to answer directly (e.g., "Let's go get a pizza."), John will probably interpret the reply as conveying positive information (i.e., He did well on his exam.) rather than negative information. In this context it is positive information that may be face-threatening, and so the reply will tend to be interpreted as conveying positive information.

Do people automatically generate indirect interpretations of relevance violations when they comprehend the utterance, or are these interpretations constructed in a post hoc manner only when people are asked to generate them? In the two experiments described above, participants were explicitly asked to interpret the replies (Experiment 1) or to judge the adequacy of interpretations of the replies (Experiment 2). It is possible, then, these our results reflect a post-hoc judgment process rather than on-line comprehension. We conducted additional experiments to examine this issue (Holtgraves, 1999; experiments 1–3).

In these experiments, participants were presented materials similar to those used in earlier research (Holtgraves, 1998a). Participants first read a (no information) scenario, question, and reply on a computer screen, and then performed a sentence verification task. For this task a string of words appeared on the screen and participants were asked to indicate, as quickly as possible, whether or not the word string formed a sentence. Sometimes the target string was an indirect interpretation of the reply; other times it was a neutral string that was not related to the reply (see the indirect interpretation and neutral targets in Table 1). A pretest was conducted to select indirect and neutral target strings that were equal in comprehension difficulty. If there is any activation of the indirect meaning when a reply is comprehended, then sentence verification judgments for the indirect interpretation targets should be faster than for the control sentence (a priming effect). This is exactly what happened. Participants were significantly faster at verifying sentences that were indirect interpretations of the reply than they were at verifying matched control sentences. This effect occurred for excuses (Experiment 1) and topic changes (Experiment 2). Importantly, it did not occur when the scenarios were altered so that the reply did not violate the relation maxim. Finally, this priming effect is not the result of the indirect targets being more related to the preceding vignette than the control targets. This possibility was eliminated in a third experiment in which participants read only the scenario and question (and not the reply). Under these conditions the priming effect did not occur, suggesting that it is the comprehension of the reply in the context of the preceding question that activates an indirect reading; facilitation of the indirect target is not a result of the indirect targets being more related to the context than the neutral targets. Taken together, these results demonstrate that the indirect meaning of a relevance violation is activated when the utterance is comprehended; it is not simply the result of a postcomprehension judgment process.

## Preference Organization and Reply Comprehension

Our research on reply interpretation demonstrates that people are actively interpreting what a speaker means with an indirect reply (Holtgraves, 1998a,

1999). That is, in these instances comprehension involves a reasoning process of some sort (more detail regarding the exact nature of this process is provided below). Of course language use always occurs in a context and so any features of the context that are relevant for this reasoning process should play a role in comprehension. Thus, if face management is recognized as the motive behind a relevance violation, then any contextual information suggesting that face management processes are operative should facilitate recognition of an indirect (face-threatening) meaning. We have investigated this issue by examining the impact of dispreferred markers on the comprehension of indirect replies.

A question-reply sequence is an adjacency pair (Schegloff & Sacks, 1973), and as such a reply (the second pair part) is expected given the occurrence of the question (the first pair part). As with all adjacency pairs, however, there is a range of possible second pair parts that could occur, and these alternatives are not equal; some are preferred, others are dispreferred. Dispreferred turns are turns that are marked (in the linguistic sense) in some way; preferred turns are unmarked. A common means of marking dispreferred turns is with a delay, a delay that will often include prefaces such as "well," "yes, but," (with disagreements), and apologies or accounts (with request refusals). In contrast, preferred turns are quick, simple, and direct.

In our research we have focused on "well" as a marker of dispreferred turns. In general, the occurrence of "well" at the beginning of an utterance can be interpreted as indicating that the speaker is engaging in face management (Jucker, 1993). To refuse a request, decline an offer, and so on are threatening to the other person's face, and the dispreferred marker "well" helps soften this threat (Holtgraves, 1992). Moreover, as discourse analysts have argued, discourse markers such as "well" should signal to the recipient that the remark underway is indirect and needs to be interpreted within a context that is not immediately apparent (Jucker, 1993; Lakoff, 1973). Because of this, the occurrence of the dispreferred marker "well" in a reply should facilitate recognition of a face-threatening interpretation of that reply.

To examine this issue we modified the materials used in our earlier studies of indirect replies (Holtgraves, 1998a, 1999). The major change was to manipulate whether the indirect reply contained a "well" marker. One half of the time it did (e.g., "Well, I think it's hard to give a good presentation.") and one half of the time it did not (e.g., "I think it's hard to give a good presentation."). In Experiment 1, participants read the scenario, question, and reply on a computer screen, and then judged the adequacy of a potential interpretation of the reply. For the critical trials the interpretation was always a face-threatening paraphrase of the reply (e.g., "I didn't like your presentation."). As expected, face-threatening interpretations of the replies were more quickly verified when the reply contained a "well" preface (1534 ms) than when it did not (1632 ms).

It is possible that the facilitation observed in Experiment 1 occurred because participants were asked to judge the meaning of the reply. A second experiment

was conducted, using a more on-line measure, in order to determine if this facilitation occurs automatically. Participants in this experiment viewed the same
materials as before, and one half of the time the reply contained a "well" preface
and one half of the time it did not. However, rather than providing a judgment
regarding the meaning of the reply, participants performed a timed sentence verification task after reading the reply. On the critical trials, the to-be-judged target
string was either a face-threatening interpretation of the reply (the paraphrases
used in the first experiment) or an unrelated sentence. As in our previous research
(Holtgraves, 1999), there was a substantial priming effect; verification speeds
were much faster for the indirect (face-threatening) targets (1425 ms) than for the
matched neutral targets (1690 ms). More importantly, however, this priming
effect was significantly greater when the reply contained the "well" marker (a
322 ms difference) than when it did not contain the marker (a 206 ms difference).
These results suggest that the impact of a "well" marker on comprehension is
fairly immediate, its presence facilitates the comprehension of indirect meanings
when they reply is comprehended.

It seems likely that other markers of dispreferred turns will play a role in
comprehension similar to that played by a "well" preface. There is some preliminary evidence that they do. In an earlier study (Holtgraves, 1998b; Experiment
3) we had participants listen to (rather than read) question-reply exchanges. In
some conditions the reply was briefly delayed (2 sec). Brief delays are a common
means of marking a turn as dispreferred, and in this condition participants were
faster at comprehending the reply, relative to replies that were not preceded by a
brief delay. A delay, similar to a "well" marker, serves to mark the turn as dispreferred, and hence facilitate recognition of a likely indirect reading. Taken
together, these studies demonstrate clearly the role played by paralinguistic and
noncontent features of talk in the comprehension of speaker meaning. This is an
important avenue for future investigation as relatively little research has examined the impact of nonverbal and paralinguistic behaviors on the comprehension
of speaker meaning.

## PROCESSING CONVERSATIONAL IMPLICATURES

A second major issue that we have pursued concerns the cognitive processes
involved in the comprehension of speaker meaning. The primary issue here is
whether the Gricean model is an accurate description of how people interpret
instances of nonliteral meaning. In general, the Gricean model (or standard pragmatic view) assumes that addressees: (a) always first recognize the literal meaning of an utterance prior to comprehending the indirect meaning, (b) search for
an indirect interpretation only after deciding that the literal reading is defective
(i.e., it violates a conversational maxim), and (c) generate additional inferences
in order to comprehend the utterance (Gibbs, 1994b; Glucksberg, 1991).

There is some support for certain aspects of this model, primarily the claim that both the literal and nonliteral meanings of indirect requests are activated. For example, Clark (1979) demonstrated that when people respond to indirect requests for information (e.g., "Can you tell me what time you close?"), they frequently address both the literal meaning (i.e., do you have the ability to tell me when you close) and the indirect meaning (tell me what time you close) of the request (e.g., "Sure, 8 p.m."). The "sure" is directed toward the literal meaning and hence suggests that both the literal meaning and the indirect meaning of the utterance has been recognized.

Second, research on politeness also provides indirect evidence that people recognize the literal meaning of many indirect utterances. This is because the politeness of an utterance is based on the remark's literal rather than indirect meaning. For example, "Could you shut the door?" is more polite than "I want you to shut the door," even though both are indirect requests to shut the door. There is fairly extensive research demonstrating that the perceived politeness of requests is influenced by variations in literal wording (Clark & Schunk, 1980; Holtgraves & Yang, 1990, 1992). There must be some awareness of the literal meaning if politeness judgments vary in this way.

Third, there is also some evidence that people encode the specific wording of an utterance when that wording varies in politeness (Holtgraves, 1997a). In these studies, people spontaneously remembered the politeness wording of utterances at better than chance levels. Even when they did not remember the exact wording they did seem to retain some gist of the politeness of the utterance. For example, if people had heard "I'd like you to read the list," they were more likely to recall an equally polite form (e.g., "Could you read the list?") rather than an impolite form (e.g., "Read the list."). These results also suggest some activation of literal meaning.

The problem with this research is that it is not direct evidence; there is no evidence regarding the actual cognitive operations involved in the comprehension of requests. For example, it is possible that the politeness of a request is recognized simultaneously with (rather than prior to) the recognition of the conveyed, or indirect, meaning. Furthermore, it is conceivable that some wordings have conventionalized politeness values that determine perceived politeness without any activation of the literal meaning of the remark. For example, "Can you X?" forms might be conventionally more polite than "I want you to X" forms. It is possible that this difference in wording could affect perceived politeness without any activation of the literal meaning of the utterance.

More direct tests of this model have been provided by psycholinguists who have examined in detail the processing of figures of speech. In general, this research has not supported Grice's (1975) model. For example, consider the claim that a nonliteral meaning is the result of an inference process. An inference process is time consuming and so people should take longer to comprehend figures of speech than their direct equivalents. However, numerous studies have demonstrated that an inference process is not required for these forms. People simply do not take more time to understand the meaning of figurative expressions (e.g., "He spilled the beans.") than they do equivalent literal expressions (Gibbs, 1980; Ortony, Schallert, Reynolds, & Antos, 1978).

Moreover, in the standard pragmatic view, activation of the literal meaning of a remark is obligatory and must occur prior to the (optional) recognition of the nonliteral, or figurative meaning. But research indicates that for many figures of speech, the literal and figurative meanings are assessed simultaneously, and in some cases even in a reversed order. For example, several studies have demonstrated that the nonliteral meaning of a figure of speech is activated even when the literal meaning is acceptable in context (Gildea & Glucksberg, 1983; Glucksberg, Gildea, & Bookin, 1982; Keysar, 1989). Sometimes, people recognize the literal meaning only after first considering and then rejecting the nonliteral meaning, the reverse of the predicted ordering (Keysar, 1994a). In terms of requests, Gibbs (1983) has demonstrated that certain conventional indirect requests are idiomatic and comprehended without activation of their literal meaning.

Finally, most interpretations of Grice's model claim that once a literal meaning has been rejected, it will no longer play a role in determining the meaning of an utterance. But this too appears not to be the case. Rather, the literal meaning of the words in a metaphor can continue to influence the manner in which the metaphor is interpreted (Cacciari & Glucksberg, 1994; Titone & Connine, 1994).

There is mixed evidence here: politeness research (indirectly) supports Grice's model, but the majority of psycholinguistic research contradicts it. An important fact to recognize is that there are many different ways to convey indirect meanings, with corresponding differences in how those meanings are processed. Note in this regard that psycholinguistic research has focused on a narrow range of utterance types, primarily figures of speech (which are highly idiomatic) and conventional requests (which are also highly idiomatic). In our research we have examined the processing of various utterance types that have not been extensively investigated in the past. In doing so we have focused on: (a) generalized implicatures, (b) particularized implicatures, (c) conventionality, and (d) the role speaker status.

## Generalized Implicatures

Of particular importance for processing models is Grice's (1975) distinction between generalized and particularized implicatures. The basic difference between the two is that generalized implicatures are context independent; they can arise without reference to the context. Particularized implicatures, on the other hand, are context dependent; their computation requires a consideration of the utterance in terms of a context, most notably the prior discourse context. Because of their independence from the context, generalized implicatures will usually not require a Gricean inference process for the recognition of speaker meaning. Particularized implicatures, on the other hand, will often involve an inference process of some sort.

Much of the figurative language examined in prior psycholinguistic research appears to involve generalized implicatures. For example, most metaphors and idioms seem to be interpretable independent of any discourse context. Regardless of the context, people will usually interpret "He spilled the beans" as meaning "He revealed a secret." Support for this comes from the fact that the nonliteral meaning of many metaphors is not optional; even when the context supports a literal reading, the nonliteral meaning is still activated (Gildea & Glucksberg, 1983; Glucksberg et al.,1982; Keysar, 1989; but see Levinson, 2000 for an alternative view).

It is not only metaphors and idioms that produce generalized implicatures. In fact, there is a very large class of utterance forms that possess preferred interpretations regardless of the context in which they are used. Scalar implicatures (e.g., some, few) are common and generally result in what Levinson (2000) refers to as Q-implicatures. For example, "Some of the students attended class" implies that not all of the students attended class. Note that this is an implicature because the sentence would be true even if all of the students attended class. Other examples of generalized implicatures include sentences such as "Mark has three children" and "Harry tried to play the stock market." The former yields the inference that Mark has no more than three children (even though the sentence would be true if Mark did have more than three children) and the latter the inference that Harry failed at playing the stock market (again, even though the sentence would be true had he been successful). Empirical evidence regarding the manner in which these forms are comprehended is lacking. Conceptually, however, their preferred meanings should be recognized directly (e.g., Levinson, 2000).

Our research has focused on one specific type of generalized implicature, but one that is extremely broad—the illocutionary force of an utterance. This research is based on Austin's (1962) and Searle's (1969) theory of speech acts. Although speech act theory is limited in several ways (some of which will be noted below), it does have the advantage of providing a framework for examining language use as intentional action. In this view, conversational utterances involve the simultaneous performance of multiple acts: a locutionary act (i.e., propositional meaning), an illocutionary act (i.e., the force associated with the use of the utterance in a specific context), and a perlocutionary act (i.e., the effects on the recipient of the performed speech act). It is the illocutionary act that most closely captures the nature of the speaker's intention in producing a particular conversation turn. For example, when Bob says to Andy "I definitely will do it tomorrow," in many contexts this utterance will have the illocutionary force of a promise. (Note that the terms speech act and illocutionary force are used here interchangeably, and both are to be distinguished from the illocutionary point [e.g., directive, commissive, etc.] of an utterance.)

Although speech act theory has continued to develop in philosophy and linguistics, many of its propositions have not been empirically examined. The most basic question is simply whether the comprehension of conversation utterances involves recognition, at some level, of the speech act performed with the utterance. For example, when Bob says to Andy, "I definitely will do it tomorrow," does Andy's comprehension of Bob's utterance involve recognition that Bob is performing a promise? Surprisingly there has been little research conducted on this topic. There is some evidence that readers of sentences that describe actions will sometimes misremember the actions in terms of the speech acts that were performed (Schweller, Brewer, & Dahl, 1976). There is some evidence that the comprehension of certain speech acts (e.g., promise) involves the recognition of the components (e.g., speaker desire and ability) underlying illocutionary force (Amrhein, 1992).

Note that with the exception of performative utterances (e.g., I order you to shut the door) speech acts are usually implicit and not literally present in the utterance that performs the act (e.g., "I'll definitely do it tomorrow" does not contain the speech act verb "promise"). In this case, speech act recognition would seem to represent an inference of sorts. Note, in this regard, that text processing researchers have demonstrated that readers must make many inferences in order to comprehend a text (though the nature and extent of that inferencing is open to debate; e.g., McKoon & Ratcliff, 1992; Graesser, Singer, & Trabasso, 1994). In general, readers generate inferences that allow them to understand why something is happening in the text such as inferences regarding an actor's superordinate goals (Dopkins, Klin, & Myers, 1993) or emotional reactions (Gernsbacher, Goldsmith, & Robertson, 1992). In a different domain, Uleman (1987) and others (e.g., Uleman, Han, Roman, & Moskowitz, 1996; Whitney & Williams-Whitney, 1990) have demonstrated that readers automatically generate dispositional inferences about a person when comprehending descriptions of that person's behavior, the dispositional inference serving as an explanation for why the behavior occurred. In a similar manner, then, the illocutionary force of an utterance can be viewed as representing the "why" behind the occurrence of a particular utterance; the remark is being uttered in order to perform a particular act. The reason Andy says, "I'll definitely do it tomorrow" to Bob is in order to perform a promise. Hence, Bob's representation of Andy's remark may include the inference that his remark constitutes a promise.

Consistent with this logic, we have found preliminary evidence for the on-line activation of illocutionary force (Holtgraves & Ashley, 2001). In these studies we used a recognition probe reaction time procedure (Experiments 1 and 2) and a lexical decision task (Experiments 3 and 4) to investigate whether illocutionary force is activated during comprehension. The speech acts we used in these studies were chosen from the list of illocutionary verbs developed by Searle and Vanderveken (1985) and represented four of their five illocutionary points: expressives (apologize, thank), assertives (brag, agree, accuse, remind, blame), directives (warn, beg, encourage), and commissives (threaten, invite).

We had participants read scenarios that were followed by a short conversational exchange (see Table 2). On critical trials the final remark of the exchange either performed a specific speech act (e.g., "remind" as in Table 2) or did not perform this particular speech act. After reading the final remark, participants were asked to indicate whether or not a probe word (e.g., remind) had literally appeared in the last remark that they read. If comprehension of an utterance involves activation of its illocutionary force, then when the probe represents the speech act just performed, participants' ability to verify that the probe had not been literally present should be slowed. That is, activation of the speech act term should interfere with performance on this task. For example, participants should be slower at verifying that "remind" had not literally been present in the remark "Don't forgot to go to your dentist appointment today" than in the (control) remark "I'll bet you forgot to go to your dentist appointment today."

This is exactly what happened. In Experiments 1 and 2 participants were significantly slower at making this judgment (and made significantly more errors) when the probe represented the speech act performed with the prior remark than when it did not. This suggests that comprehension of the target utterance involved recognition of its illocutionary force. We then conducted two conceptually similar experiments using a lexical decision task. Participants read the same materials as before. However, the task following the target utterance was to decide whether a string of letters constituted a word (the lexical decision task). Sometimes the string represented the speech act performed with the utterance and sometimes it did not. If comprehension involves activation of illocutionary force, then with this task participants should be faster (rather than slower as in Experiments 1 and 2) when the to-be-judged string represents the speech act performed with the utterance. Again, the data were quite consistent with the idea that speech act recognition is involved in the comprehension of conversation utterances: Lexical decision times were faster when the target string represented the speech act performed with the prior remark than when it did not.

Although the results of these illocutionary force activation studies are clear, there are many unresolved issued that we are currently pursuing. For example, is speech act recognition unique to conversation utterances or does it occur also for textual descriptions of utterances? For example, does reading the sentence "Frank told Mark he would definitely do it tomorrow" involve activation of the speech act verb "promise" in the same way as reading the utterance "I definitely will do it tomorrow"? What type of process is involved in speech act recognition? Although a Gricean inference process is probably not involved, exactly how are such interpretations generated?

Particularized Implicatures

In contrast to generalized implicatures (e.g., metaphors and idioms), particularized implicatures have received much less empirical attention. One type of

TABLE 2
Sample Scenario and Speech Act Manipulation
From Holtgraves and Ashley (2001)

---

Jenny and Emily had been close friends since grade school. Now they were rooming together at
    college.
Emily was very forgetful.
Today, Jenny was sure Emily *didn't remember* (had forgotten) her dentist appointment.
Jenny: *Don't forget* (I'll bet you forgot) to go to your dentist appointment today.
*Probe:* remind

---

NOTE: The speech act version contained the italicized material; the control version was created by replacing the
italicized material with the material in parentheses.

utterance that should frequently yield particularized implicatures is violations of
the relation maxim, such as the indirect replies described above (Holtgraves,
1998a, 1999, 2000). Indirect replies should generally yield particularized implicatures because their interpretation is dependent on the prior discourse context,
a context that is continually changing. In our research we have found that particularized implicatures, unlike generalized conversational implicatures, do
require an inference process for comprehension, much along the lines suggested by Grice (1975). In these studies (Experiments 4–6; Holtgraves, 1999) we
used both reading times and sentence verification procedures to investigate this
issue. In two of these experiments, participants read versions of the question-
reply materials described earlier. After indicating comprehension of the reply,
they performed a timed sentence verification task. On critical trials the target
string of words was either a literal interpretation of the reply or a neutral sentence
matched with the literal interpretation in terms of comprehension difficulty. For
most of the reply types, participants were significantly faster at verifying the literal interpretations than matched controls (one particular reply type did not
demonstrate this pattern, a finding to be discussed below). Unlike comprehension of metaphors and other generalized implicatures, these results are consistent
with the standard pragmatic view that the literal meaning of an indirect utterance
will be activated during the comprehension process. In another experiment we
timed how long it took participants to read the reply as a function of whether the
preceding context activated or did not activate an indirect (face-threatening)
reading of the reply. Participants took significantly longer to read the replies
when the indirect meaning was activated than when it was not. This too demonstrates that these types of particularized implicatures require a Gricean inference
process for comprehension.

So, very clearly this research suggests that particularized implicatures involve
a relatively time-consuming inference process; generalized implicatures probably do not (although the exact nature of the processes involved in their recognition is as yet not well understood). Note that the particularized-generalized dis-

tinction is not a property of utterances per se, but rather a property of the manner in which an utterance is used. As a result, some utterances may yield both particularized and generalized implicatures. That is, idioms, metaphors, and so on might yield both generalized and particularized implicatures when they occur as replies to questions. For example, imagine Frank asking Bob if he should apply for a job with Bob's firm, and Bob replies "My job is a jail." Now, Frank will probably recognize the metaphorical meaning of the remark; that is, Bob believes his job is very confining (a generalized implicature). But it is also quite likely that Frank will construct a particularized implicature, a belief that Bob is advising him that he would not enjoy working for Bob's firm. This particularized implicature is a function of the metaphor serving as a reply to a question.

## Conventionality

Another factor influencing the comprehension of speaker meaning is whether the form of the utterance represents a conventional means for performing a speech act. In general, a conventional means for performing a speech act means that the literal meaning of the utterance is pro forma, not to be taken seriously (Clark, 1985). Most discussions of conventionality have focused on requests. Although there is some disagreement regarding this issue, conventional indirect requests generally have the following features: (a) They can be performed by asserting or questioning the felicity conditions that underlie requests, (b) The utterance contains the request-based propositional content (e.g., "shut the door" in "Could you shut the door?"), and (c) The preverbal insertion of "please" is allowed (e.g., "Could you please shut the door?"). Research demonstrates that people are relatively unlikely to respond to the literal meaning of conventional indirect requests (Clark, 1979). More importantly, their indirect meanings are recognized in a direct fashion, without need for a time-consuming inference. For example, in two priming studies Gibbs (1983) found that indirect requests activated the conveyed, indirect meanings but not the literal meanings, suggesting that for these requests comprehension does not involve an initial recognition of the literal meaning of the request.

All other indirect requests that do not meet these criteria can be regarded as nonconventional indirect requests, and there are a lot of them. Unfortunately, little is known about the forms they can take. One possible form has been termed a negative state remark (Holtgraves, 1994). This type of request is based on the following principle: A speaker can perform a request by asserting (or questioning) the existence of a negative state (or a state that the hearer can infer is negative) if there is some action that the hearer can perform in order to alter the negative state. This principle yields indirect requests such as "It's warm in here" or "I'm thirsty" to request another to open a window or get one a drink, respectively. Note that these forms do not contain the directive propositional content, cannot take "please," and are not related (at least directly) to the underlying felicity conditions.

In a series of studies, we examined the processing of conventional and non-conventional (negative state) indirect requests using both a reading time and priming procedure methodology (Holtgraves, 1994). The results were very clear. Consistent with Gibbs (1983), conventional indirect requests were comprehended quickly, without any recognition and subsequent rejection of the literal meaning of the utterance. In contrast, under certain conditions negative state remarks did involve an inference process; processing was relatively time-consuming and did involve activation of the literal meaning of the utterance. This inferential processing occurred, however, only when the scenario interactants were equal in status, suggesting that even nonconventional forms can be recognized directly depending on the context, a point to be discussed below.

Finally, although conventionality has been pursued primarily in terms of requests, it may be possible to extend the logic of conventionality to certain responses to requests. Consider how requests for action can be conventionally performed. There exists a set of preconditions (e.g., hearer's ability and willingness)·that underlies the successful performance of a request (e.g., Searle, 1975), and these preconditions can be questioned as a means of performing a conventional indirect request. This common strategy produces requests such as "Can you open the window?" (questions hearer's ability). Because requests project to the next turn, these conditions should remain relevant for that turn (Clark, 1985). Consequently these preconditions can be denied as a means of indirectly refusing to comply with the request. Hence, one can indicate refusal by asserting a lack of ability (e.g., "I can't reach it.") or willingness (e.g., "I opened it the last time."). As a conventional means for refusing a request, the refusal implied with these utterances should be relatively apparent; the asserted lack of ability constitutes the refusal. In our research we have found this to be the case (Experiment 5, Holtgraves, 1999). When replies to requests for action were conventionally performed with an asserted lack of ability they were recognized directly and without need of a time-consuming inference process.

Status and Interpretation

Status (or power) is a feature of the discourse context that has been demonstrated to play a very clear role in language production. In general, the greater the status of the recipient, the greater the likelihood that polite (or indirect) request forms will be used (Brown & Levinson, 1987; Holtgraves & Yang, 1990, 1992). Because of its role in language production, it seems likely that speaker status will play an important role in comprehension. Our research suggests that it does. For example, in our research on the processing of conventional and nonconventional indirect requests (Holtgraves, 1994), the status of the speaker moderated the effects of request conventionality. For conventional indirect requests, the status of the speaker did not affect comprehension; these forms were recognized quickly and directly, without any type of inference process. In contrast, the comprehension of nonconventional forms was affected by the status of the speaker.

Participants were faster at comprehending these forms when the speaker was higher rather than equal in status to his conversation partner. In addition, priming experiments demonstrated that both the literal and the indirect meanings were activated for these forms when the speaker was equal status; this did not occur when the speaker was high status. These results thus demonstrate that a Gricean inference process appears to be required for the comprehension of nonconventional forms when performed by an equal status speaker, a process that was not necessary when the speaker was high status.

Similar to face management, speaker status is a feature of the social context that impacts both utterance production and utterance comprehension. But exactly how does status play a role in the comprehension of requests? There are at least two possibilities. The first possibility is that knowledge that a speaker is high status may circumvent the need for an inference process, a directive interpretation may be activated prior to any activation of the literal meaning of the utterance. Thus, when a speaker is high status, a recipient may be inclined to interpret the speaker's utterances, a priori, as directives (cf., Ervin-Tripp, Strage, Lampert, & Bell, 1987). The finding that an inference process is not required for nonconventional indirect requests when the speaker is high status supports this possibility (Holtgraves, 1994). Additional empirical support for this idea is provided by a priming study we conducted demonstrating that directive readings can be activated based solely on the status of the speaker (Experiment 4; Holtgraves, 1994). Participants in this study first read descriptions of situations in which speaker status was varied, and then made sentence verification judgments of targets that either were or were not possible directives in each situation. The requests themselves were not presented. When the speaker was high status, sentence verification times were significantly faster for directives than for related control targets (i.e., a priming effect), and this effect did not occur when the speaker was equal status. In short, speaker status alone (without the utterance) was sufficient for priming a directive interpretation.

A second possibility is that knowledge that a speaker is high status can facilitate an inference process if one is required. Rejection of the literal meaning of an utterance depends, in part, on the possibility that there are alternative interpretations of the utterance (e.g., Sperber & Wilson, 1986). People who are high status have the right to issue directives, and hence there exists possible directive interpretations of their utterances. The existence of these interpretations, then, increases the likelihood that the literal meaning will be rejected. Moreover, given that the literal meaning is rejected, knowledge that the speaker is high status can increase the likelihood that a directive interpretation will be adopted.

Regardless of how speaker status impacts the comprehension of speaker meaning, other research we have conducted suggests that speaker status can influence long-term memory for a speaker's remarks. In several experiments we had participants read or listen to dialogues in which we manipulated the ostensible status of one of the speakers (Holtgraves, Srull, & Socall, 1989). In these experiments there was a tendency for the utterances of high status speakers to be recalled as being more assertive (direct) than the same remarks uttered by an equal status speaker. These results are consistent with our research demonstrating the impact of speaker status on comprehension (high speaker status prompts a directive reading, a reading that is then retained in long-term memory). However, we have conducted additional studies demonstrating that, at times, if the wording of an utterance is at odds with normative expectations, these wordings will tend to be remembered well. In one experiment (Experiment 3, Holtgraves, 1997a) we gave participants a surprise memory test for the experimenter's instructions. The ostensible status of the experimenter was manipulated (high status professor vs. equal status undergraduate research assistant) as was the politeness (or directness) of his utterances. On subsequent memory tests, participants were more likely to remember the polite remarks of the high status speaker and the impolite remarks of the equal status speaker. In this situation, it is utterances violating normative expectancies that receive additional processing and hence are remembered relatively well.

## COORDINATING PERSPECTIVES IN THE COMMUNICATION OF SPEAKER MEANING

Perspective taking is crucial for language use (e.g., Brown, 1965; Clark, 1985; Krauss & Fussell, 1991; Mead, 1934; Pearce, 1994; Rommetviet, 1974). To successfully comprehend a speaker's utterance requires the recipient to have some sense of the speaker's perspective in producing that utterance. Conversely, the speaker must have some sense of the recipient's perspective in order to design an utterance that will be comprehended successfully. Perspective taking is required for all levels of language use, but would seem to be particularly important for the recognition of speaker meaning. To successfully use an indirect expression, for example, requires the speaker to have some sense of how the recipient will interpret the utterance, and for the hearer to take the speaker's perspective in producing this particular utterance. Note how Grice's (1975) theory of conversational implicature requires perspective taking. Consider, for example, the quantity maxim, or stipulation that one's conversational contribution should be as informative as required. Obviously, adherence to this principle requires an assessment of what one's interlocutor "knows"; one can't be appropriately informative without an assessment of the recipient's knowledge. People are sensitive to this; the explanations they give to others vary as a function of what they believe their audience knows (Slugoski, Lalljee, Lamb, & Ginsburg, 1993).

But perspective taking is not perfect. Research suggests that interactants often exhibit an egocentric bias; they produce and interpret (at least initially) utterances from their unique perspective, without taking into account the perspective of their interlocutors. One model that makes explicit the egocentric nature of perspective taking is Keysar's perspective adjustment model (1998; Keysar, Barr, Balin, & Paek, 1998). This model focuses on both the addressee, and the role of perspective taking in message interpretation (Keysar et al., 1998), as well as the speaker and the role of perspective taking in message formulation (Horton & Keysar, 1996). Regarding the addressee, Keysar's model assumes that recipients first interpret a remark without considering the speaker's perspective, and hence the initial, default interpretation is an egocentric interpretation. These egocentric interpretations are assumed to be fast and effortless and what the processing system does best. However, people are not completely unaware of the speaker's perspective and they sometimes do take it into account. This occurs during what Keysar refers to as an adjustment process, a process that attempts to correct the initial egocentric interpretation. Unlike the initial egocentric interpretation, the adjustment process is slow and effortful.

Research has supported various aspects of Keysar's model. For example, people demonstrate a transparency of meaning effect (Keysar & Bly, 1995); a tendency to believe that the idiomatic meaning of certain expressions is more transparent than the meanings really are. If a person has come to believe that an expression has a particular meaning, she may assume others will arrive at the same meaning and in this way fail to consider the possibility of alternative interpretations of the expression. Similar results have been found for the interpretation of potentially sarcastic expressions (Keysar, 1994b). Participants in these studies tended to endorse interpretations of utterances based on information unavailable to the intended addressee. For example, when indicating how they thought an addressee would interpret Mark's utterance regarding a recent dining experience ("Marvelous, simply marvelous"), participants were likely to infer a sarcastic reading if they knew Mark had a negative dining experience, even though the intended recipient of the remark had no knowledge of Mark's dining experience. In other words, participants generally failed to correctly take the addressee's perspective into account when interpreting these utterances. Instead, they used their own egocentric perspective.[2]

Egocentric tendencies in communication appear to be fairly widespread. For example, research has demonstrated that recollections of episodes of embarrassment (Kowalski, 2000) and teasing (Sharkey, Kim, & Diggs, in press) are influenced by whether one adapts the perspective of victim or perpetrator. Overall, then, a person's conversational goal or agenda may blind them to the possibility that their interlocutors have different goals or agendas (Russell & Schober, 1999). Hence, speakers may assume they mean one thing without considering how the hearer might interpret it differently, and hearers may assume the speaker means one thing without considering how he may have meant something else. So, even though theories of communication suggest that perspective taking underlies successful communication (e.g., Brown, 1965; Clark, 1985; Krauss & Fussell, 1991; Mead, 1934; Pearce, 1994; Rommetviet, 1974), it is possible that hearers and speakers will systematically diverge in their interpretations.

This raises the issue of whether the comprehension of indirect meaning might vary as a function of perspective. In our earlier studies (Holtgraves, 1998a, 1999, 2000) participants were asked to read and interpret replies from the perspective of the recipient of the reply, and there was a strong tendency for them to interpret relevance violations as conveying face-threatening information (i.e., a negative opinion or disclosure). From the recipient's perspective, interpreting the reply as conveying negative information makes sense. This person has asked for the opinion, and failing to obtain a direct and relevant reply, should assume that the requested information is negative. If the information was positive, the speaker would have said so. However, these participants may have been engaged in means-end reasoning (Levinson, 2000). That is, they interpreted a relevance violation (the means) as reflecting face concerns (the end), and hence they interpreted the replies as indirectly conveying negative (i.e., face-threatening) information. Logically, of course, this is fallacious (affirming the consequent in deductive logic). That is, the means (a relevance violation) may occur for reasons other than face management. Consider a relevance violation in response to a request for an opinion. Perhaps the speaker's opinion was not well-formed, or was ambiguous, or perhaps it did not even exist, or was one that the speaker would prefer not to convey. All of these possibilities could be handled with a relevance violation, an utterance that functions to avoid providing a specific opinion rather than conveying a negative one. As a result, a speaker's intention in producing a relevance violation could sometimes be at odds with the recipient's interpretation of the same utterance.

To test this possibility we asked participants to interpret replies from either the perspective of the recipient of the reply, or from the perspective of the speaker, the person who produces the reply (Holtgraves, 2002). The materials for these experiments were adapted from those used in earlier work on the role of face management in reply comprehension (Holtgraves, 1998a, 1999). If perspective taking is perfect, then, one would expect perspective to matter little in how an utterance is interpreted. If meaning simply resides in an utterance, then speakers and hearers should agree quite readily in what is being communicated. Our results suggest otherwise. In three experiments, participants were far more likely to interpret relevance violations as conveying a negative opinion or disclosure when they assumed the perspective of the hearer than when they assumed the perspective of the speaker. This effect occurred for both excuses and topic changes, and for requests for opinions and requests for disclosures. Also, it made no difference whether participants were informed that the requested information was negative. Nor did it make any difference that participants alternated assuming the perspective of the speaker and hearer, a design that should have sensitized them to the possibility that they were interpreting the replies one way when they took the speaker's view and another way when they took the hearer's perspective. Despite these various features of the design, in the end replies were more likely to be interpreted as conveying negative information when participants took the hearer's perspective than when they took the speaker's perspective.

This research, then, suggests that there may be a systematic, interpretive bias built into the hearer and speaker roles. The tendency for hearers to interpret relevance violations as conveying negative information is consistent with our earlier research (Holtgraves, 1998a, 1999, 2000). Because indirect replies are frequently used as a means of managing face, and because interactants are generally aware that this is the case, recipients should interpret the relevance violation as conveying face-threatening information (a negative opinion or disclosure). That is exactly what happened in this research. But indirect utterances are inherently ambiguous and open to multiple interpretations. The means-ends reasoning used by a recipient to recover a face-threatening interpretation can yield errors. In other words, relevance violations can mean many things. From the speaker's perspective, a relevance violation may be a means of signaling an unwillingness to provide the requested information. Hence, speakers may not believe that they are communicating negative information, but instead communicating an unwillingness to convey an opinion or disclosure.

## INDIVIDUAL AND CULTURAL VARIABILITY IN PROCESSING SPEAKER MEANING

One of the major criticisms of Grice's (1975) model, as well as related approaches such as speech act theory (Searle, 1969) and politeness theory (Brown & Levinson, 1987), has been that it is not cross-culturally valid. Consider, for example, Grice's (1975) quantity maxim. In a well-known paper, Keenan (1976) argued that people in Malagasy routinely withhold information from one another (information is a culturally prized commodity), an action that is in clear violation of the quantity maxim. Because of this, violations of the quantity maxim in Malagasy do not usually result in conversational implicatures (as presumably would be the case in most other cultures). There is a more general criticism here. It has been suggested that Grice's view, with its emphasis on individual autonomy, has relevance only in Western cultures (Fitch & Sanders, 1994). For example, Rosaldo (1982), in her analysis of Llongot speech acts, argues that directives in that culture are not particularly face threatening, referencing as they do group membership and responsibility rather than individual wants and desires. Hence, directives in that culture will usually not be performed indirectly.

It is clearly possible that the maxims people follow in communicating cooperatively may vary over cultures, reflecting, perhaps, differences in what is regarded as rational interaction. Note, however, that even if there are cultural differences in this regard, it will not alter the basic Gricean insight that if a person believes a maxim has been violated, then some interpretive work will be undertaken. Nor will they alter Grice's fundamental point that conversational maxims (whatever they may look like) serve as a basis for rational interaction, and hence as a framework for interpretation.

Still, it is clearly important to determine the specific content of conversation maxims and how they might vary over cultures. We have explored this issue in various ways. One research line has been to examine overall cultural differences in the tendency to interpret utterances indirectly. This research has been guided by the cultural dimensions of individualism and collectivism (Triandis, 1995). In general, collectivism entails a relatively greater concern for the needs, feelings, and wants of one's in-groups; it represents a relatively greater concern for the face of in-group members (Ting-Toomey, 1988). These broad cultural syndromes have been demonstrated to be related to different communication styles (Gudykunst et al., 1996; Kim et al., 1996). Our interest has been in cultural variability in indirectness. Because one of the major means for attending to face is indirectness (Brown & Levinson, 1987), it seems reasonable that indirectness will be more common in collectivist cultures than individualistic cultures. We have examined this using the conversational indirectness scale (CIS; Holtgraves, 1997b). The CIS is a 19-item self-report measure assessing both an interpretation dimension (the extent to which a person looks for indirect meanings in the remarks of others) and a production dimension (the extent to which a person phrases his or her remarks indirectly). Our initial research demonstrated that this is a reliable and valid measure of these two dimensions. For example, people scoring high on the interpretation dimension are more likely to recognize indirect meanings, and to be significantly faster at doing so, than people scoring low on this dimension (Experiment 6, Holtgraves, 1997b).

To examine cultural variability we translated the CIS into Korean and administered it to a sample of students at Korean universities. Factor analyses of the scores from this sample were highly similar to the factor analytic results based on a sample of U.S. American students. Accordingly, we compared the two samples in terms of their scores on the CIS. Overall, Korean students scored significantly higher on both the interpretation dimension (53.26 vs. 43.62) and production dimension (42.37 vs. 33.61). These results provide some support for the notion that people in collectivist cultures tend to produce and look for indirect meanings to a greater extent than people in individualistic cultures. Recently, Hara and Kim (2001) have demonstrated that these broad cultural differences may be partly explained in terms of differing self construals. Specifically, they found that individuals with interdependent self construals were more likely to speak and interpret indirectly than were people with independent self construals. Of course, not all collectivist and individualistic cultures are alike (e.g., Kashima et al., 1995), and cultural differences in indirectness reflect only average differences. People in all cultures will vary the politeness (and thus the indirectness) of their remarks as a function of the context. In fact, this may reflect another dimension of cultural variability: people in collectivist cultures are more sensitive and responsive to the context than are people in individualistic cultures (Gudykunst, Yoon, & Nishida, 1987; Holtgraves & Yang, 1992; Triandis,

Bontempo, Villareal, Asai, & Lucca, 1988).

A second way in which we have explored cultural variability is in terms of differences regarding which maxims are likely to result in conversational implicatures (Holtgraves & Drozd, 1998). Participants in this study were students at Ball State University who were either from an individualistic culture (the United States) or collectivist culture (East and Southeast Asia). Participants read scenarios and corresponding target utterances and then chose which of three possible interpretations (one literal interpretation and two indirect interpretations) best captured the speaker's meaning in each situation. For all but one type of utterance, East and Southeast Asian participants were more likely to interpret utterances indirectly than were the U.S. American participants, a finding that is consistent with research demonstrating that collectivists tend to be more indirect than individualists. However, this pattern was reversed for violations of the quality maxim: East and Southeast Asians were less likely to interpret these utterances indirectly than were the U.S. American participants. Although these findings are preliminary, they do suggest that it is too simplistic to view collectivists as more indirect than individualists. Instead, there may be cultural and individual variability in interpretation as a function of how the indirect meaning is conveyed (and no doubt as a function of many other differences as well). This is clearly an important avenue for future research.

## UNINTENDED INFERENCES

Speaker meaning is generally viewed as intentional. More specifically, it is viewed as an intention that is intended to be recognized, what Grice (1957) referred to as a reflexive intention or what speech act theorists refer to as illocutionary force (Austin, 1962). All of the meanings considered so far in this chapter are of this sort. But language use in context is an extremely rich source of information regarding the motives, intentions, and personality of one's interlocutors, and these effects need not be conveyed intentionally. They are impressions "given off" rather than impressions "given" (Goffman, 1959), or in speech act theory, perlocutionary effects rather than illocutionary forces. This feature of language use is clearly under researched. We have attempted to make some headway here by applying the Gricean conversational framework to the generation of unintended inferences.

Our approach has been to assume that hearers who recognize the violation of a conversational maxim will first attempt to discern an indirect meaning that was intended to be communicated. On occasion, however, it may not be possible to construct an intended meaning with any degree of certainty. However, because conversationalists have a strong drive to make the remarks of others understandable, there will be an attempt to derive some type of explanation for the violation, even if only that the speaker was simply not paying attention. Consider violations of the quantity maxim, or stipulation that one should be appropriately informative. Gruenfeld and Wyer (1992) have demonstrated that under certain conditions denials of propositions generally believed to be false can boomerang and actually increase belief in the denied proposition. According to these authors, statements that are obviously false represent violations of the quantity maxim; the information they convey is generally known and hence the statements are redundant. Because of their redundancy, recipients of such statements must construct a scenario explaining why the statement is being made. One possibility (though certainly not the only one) is that there must be some doubt about the truth in the denied proposition.

In some ways this effect is reminiscent of Richard Nixon's 1973 "I am not a crook" speech. During a press conference that year, Richard Nixon proclaimed his innocence of any financial wrongdoing by denying that he was a crook. By most accounts he was very defensive and extremely talkative during the session. The impact of his denials on public opinion was negative; rather than influencing people to believe he was not a crook, the denials had the opposite effect. Why? One possibility is that by denying any wrongdoing he was in effect violating the quantity maxim by being overinformative. The reasoning here is somewhat akin to a "methinks he doth protest too much" effect. He must be trying to hide something, or he would not engage in such vigorous denials.

There is, however, a difference between the Nixon denials and the denials read by participants in the Gruenfeld and Wyer (1992) study. In the latter case the source of the denial was a newspaper rather than a speaker making a denial about his own behavior. In Nixon's case, of course, the denials pertained to the source of the denial. Obviously Nixon did not intend for his denials to boomerang; his intention was for people to believe them. So why did his denials boomerang? It appears that in certain contexts violations of the quantity maxim can undermine confidence in the literal meaning of a speaker's utterances.

We tested this general idea by having participants read courtroom testimony in which the defendant sometimes violated the quantity maxim and provided more information than was required by the prosecutor's question (Holtgraves & Grayer, 1994). For example, when asked whether he was insured as a driver, the defendant in the over informative condition replied ("Yes, I've never lost my insurance because of speeding tickets."). In this case the defendant provided more information (by mentioning speeding tickets) than was required by the yes-no question. Now, it would be difficult for a hearer to infer an intended indirect meaning with this remark. So, in order to make sense of the remark, participants generated inferences about the speaker's motive (e.g., that he was trying to convey a favorable image), personality (that he was nervous and anxious), and guilt (he was judged guilty more often than the defendant in the control condition). Importantly, these results did not represent an overall negative evaluation of a speaker who was overly informative. For example, the overly informative defendant was not perceived as any less intelligent or competent than a defendant who was not overly informative. Thus, the perceptions that were affected by this manipulation appear to be based on perceivers' reasoning about why the speaker made these remarks.

What these and other studies (e.g., Davis & Holtgraves, 1984) suggest is that perceptions of speakers may be part of a general process whereby people attempt to understand the meaning of another's utterances. If a hearer (or overhearer) notices a maxim violation, the overarching question becomes one of understanding why the speaker is making this utterance in this context. Why is he being redundant (quantity maxim violation) or evading the question (relation maxim violation) or being unclear (manner maxim violation), and so on? If an intended meaning can not be constructed, then a fall back position for recipients is to generate unintended inferences in order to make sense of the violation. It is in this way that the Gricean framework may prove useful for understanding the comprehension of both intended and unintended meaning.

## CONCLUSION

Speakers are trying to do things with their words, and one of the most important things they are trying to do is to get their recipients to recognize just what it is that they are doing with their words. Understanding speaker meaning—a speaker's communicative intention—is central to understanding language use. In this paper I have reviewed some of our attempts to empirically investigate how people recognize speaker meaning. Our starting point—as it is for many researchers in this domain—is Grice's (1975) theory of conversational implicature, a theory proposing that we recognize many indirect meanings based on our noticing, and then reasoning about, the violation of a conversational maxim.

Our focus has been on the specific inferences that recipients generate and the cognitive processes involved in their generation. Grice (1975) was relatively unclear regarding the specific inferences that hearers will generate when they recognize the violation of a maxim. But to the extent that a violation is intentionally communicative, then recognition of the motive for violating the maxim should aid in the recovery of the specific meaning that the speaker is intending to convey. Because face management is frequently a motive for speaking indirectly, recipients can use their recognition of this motivation as a means of generating an indirect reading of the reply (Holtgraves, 1998a, 1999). Note that this illustrates a basic and pervasive phenomenon: variables that play a role in language production will play an important role in language comprehension. Face management clearly plays a role in production, as many studies of politeness and indirectness have demonstrated. Our research makes clear that it also plays a crucial role in comprehending a speaker's indirect remarks.

Of course speaker meaning can be ambiguous. What a recipient recognizes as an intended meaning need not necessarily be what the speaker intended to have recognized. Means-end reasoning is not foolproof. Although inferring that a relevance violation constitutes an attempt at face management will often result in an accurate interpretation of a speaker's meaning, it does not necessarily guarantee it. Relevance violations can occur for reasons other than face management, and because of this, speakers and hearers may diverge in how utterances of this sort might be interpreted (Holtgraves, 2002).

People may also misinterpret one another, not because of biases associated with adopting the perspective of the speaker or the hearer, but simply because of individual and cultural variability in the tendency to speak and interpret indirectly (Holtgraves, 1997b). There appear to be consistent individual differences in this regard, and such differences can have an obvious impact on communicative success. People (and cultures) who differ dramatically in their tendencies to speak and interpret indirectly will frequently miss the intended meanings of each others' remarks. A person who tends to look for indirect meanings in the remarks of others will find them—even if they are not there. Of course, one who interprets directly will frequently miss the intended, indirect meanings conveyed by others.

Our other major concern has been with specifying exactly how speaker meaning is recognized. It appears, as suggested by Grice (1975), that there are different means for conveying implicatures, and by extension, different processes involved in their recognition. Foremost here is the distinction between generalized and particularized implicatures. Violations of the relation maxim—indirect replies, for example—usually produce particularized implicatures. Their recognition involves a relatively time-consuming inference process whereby the initial literal meaning is activated and then rejected in favor of an indirect meaning. Particularized implicatures are extremely sensitive to the context; in fact, relevance violations are defined by the relationship between an utterance and the context.

Of course not all conversational implicatures involve this type of reasoning process. In fact, generalized implicatures appear not to involve such a process, as psycholinguistic research on the processing of figurative language has demonstrated. Metaphors, idioms, illocutionary force, Q-implicatures, and so on, all represent instances in which a preferred reading of an utterance will be generated regardless of the context within which the utterance is used. Although a time-consuming inference process is not required for comprehending generalized implicatures, the manner in which these implicatures are generated remains largely an unknown process, a process that is deserving of subsequent empirical investigation.

The particularized generalized implicature categorization is not mutually exclusive. An utterance may convey both an idiomatic meaning (a generalized implicature) as well as a meaning that must be computed on the spot (a particularized implicature). Nor is this distinction a property of utterances per se. The exact same utterance can produce a generalized implicature in one context and a particularized implicature in another context. For example, a negative state remark will be recognized directly (a generalized implicature) if the speaker is relatively high status, but will require an inference process (a particularized implicature) if the speaker is not high in status.

## Potential Limitations and Future Directions

Several potential limitations of the present approach should be noted. First, in the majority of our comprehension studies, participants are asked to interpret or comprehend the utterances of people who are engaged in a conversation. In effect, we are examining how observers comprehend the utterances of other conversationalists. Are those comprehension processes different from those of people who are actually involved in a conversation? It is difficult to tell, and as such, this must be regarded as a potential limitation of our research. Currently we are attempting to develop a technique that will allow us to examine the on-line comprehension processes of people who are actually involved in a verbal interaction.

Second, the stimulus materials in most of our studies were constructed specifically for use in our experiments, rather than being remarks that someone actually said. Our focus has been on theory testing, a concern that we believe justifies the construction of utterances so as to test a particular hypothesis. But this too should be regarded as a potential limitation, and one that we are currently attempting to overcome. For example, we are currently conducting research in which we ask participants to indicate how they would perform various speech acts in certain situations. These utterances will then be used as the stimuli in a series of subsequent studies examining the on-line activation of illocutionary force.

Finally, there is the question of whether speaker meaning—because it is so contextualized and idiosyncratic—can ever really be studied apart from its occurrence in a conversation. Obviously we assume that speaker meaning can be studied experimentally. Our guiding assumption in this regard has been that people bring to any verbal encounter certain reasoning abilities, in addition to knowledge regarding how conversations work, that allows them to produce and comprehend conversational utterances. Further, these capacities must exist independently of any particular conversation and thus it should, in principle, be possible to study these processes under controlled laboratory conditions. Obviously the particulars of any verbal interaction will play a role in comprehension, but the manner in which they do so may be quite general.

## NOTES

1. In general, we have not found meaningful differences between these two types of situations, both in this study and in others as well. Accordingly, in this paper the differences between opinions and disclosures are not discussed.

2. It should be noted that there is some debate about whether these results truly reflect a transparency of intention. Gerrig, Ohaeri, and Brennan (2000) have argued that Keysar's materials were biased toward sarcastic readings; in their research they found sarcastic interpretations to be just as likely when no information was provided as when participants were given negative information. But such a finding does not really explain why participants interpreted utterances differently as a function of privileged information (Keysar, 2000). At this point the issue is an open one.

## REFERENCES

Amrhein, P. C. (1992). The comprehension of quasi-performative verbs in verbal commitments: New evidence for componential theories of lexical meaning. *Journal of Memory and Language, 31,* 756–784.

Austin, J. L. (1962). *How to do things with words.* Oxford, UK: Clarendon Press.

Bavelas, J. B., Black, A., Chovil, N., & Mullet, J. (1990). *Equivocal communication.* Newbury Park, CA: Sage.

Brown, P., & Levinson, S. (1987). *Politeness: Some universals in language usage.* Cambridge, UK: Cambridge University Press.

Brown, R. (1965). *Social psychology.* New York: The Free Press

Brown, R., & Gilman, A. (1989). Politeness theory and Shakespeare's four major tragedies. *Language in Society, 18,* 159–212.

Cacciari, C., & Glucksberg, S. (1994). Understanding figurative language. In M. A. Gernsbacher (Ed.), *Handbook of psycholinguistic research* (pp. 447–478). San Diego, CA: Academic Press.

Clark, H. H. (1979). Responding to indirect speech acts. *Cognitive Psychology, 11,* 430–477.

Clark, H. H. (1985). Language use and language users. In G. Lindzey & E. Aronson (Eds.), *The handbook of social psychology* (3rd ed., Vol. 2, pp. 179–232). Reading, MA: Addison-Wesley.

Clark, H. H., & Schunk, D. (1980). Polite responses to polite requests. *Cognition, 8,* 111–143.

Dascal, M. (1987). Defending literal meaning. *Cognitive Science, 11,* 259–281.

Davis, D., & Holtgraves, T. (1984). Perceptions of unresponsive others: Attributions, attraction, understandability, and memory for their utterances. *Journal of Experimental Social Psychology, 20,* 383–408.

Dopkins, S., Klin, C., & Myers, J. L. (1993). Accessibility of information about goals during the processing of narrative text. *Journal of Memory and Language, 19,* 70–80.

Ervin-Tripp, S., Strage, M., Lampert, M., & Bell, N. (1987). Understanding requests. *Linguistics, 25,* 107–143.

Fitch, K. L., & Sanders, R. E. (1994). Culture, communication, and preferences for directness in expression of directives. *Communication Theory, 4,* 219–245.

Gernsbacher, M. A., Goldsmith, H. H., & Robertson, R. R. (1992). Do readers mentally represent characters' emotional states? *Cognition and Emotion, 6,* 89–112.

Gerrig, R. J., Ohaeri, J. O., & Brennan, S. E. (2000). Illusory transparency revisited. *Discourse Processes, 29,* 137–159.

Gibbs, R. W. (1980). Spilling the beans on understanding and memory for idioms. *Memory & Cognition, 8,* 449–456.

Gibbs, R. W. (1983). Do people always process the literal meaning of indirect requests? *Journal of Experimental Psychology: Learning, Memory, and Cognition, 9,* 524–533.

Gibbs, R. W., Jr. (1984). Literal meaning and psychological theory. *Cognitive Science, 8,* 225–304.

Gibbs, R. W., Jr. (1994a). *The poetics of mind.* Cambridge, UK: Cambridge University Press.

Gibbs, R. W., Jr. (1994b). Figurative thought and figurative language. In M. A. Gernsbacher (Ed.), *Handbook of psycholinguistic research* (pp. 411–446). San Diego, CA: Academic Press.

Gildea, P., & Glucksberg, S. (1983). On understanding metaphor: The role of context. *Journal of Verbal Learning and Verbal Behavior, 22,* 577–590.

Glucksberg, S. (1991). Beyond literal meanings: The psychology of allusion. *Psychological Science 2,* 146–152.

Glucksberg, S., Gildea, P., & Bookin, H. (1982). On understanding nonliteral speech: Can people ignore metaphors? *Journal of Verbal Learning and Verbal Behavior, 21,* 85–98.

Goffman, E. (1959). *The presentation of self in everyday life.* Garden City, NY: Doubleday Anchor.

Goffman, E. (1967). *Interaction ritual: Essays on face to face behavior.* Garden City, NY: Anchor Books.

Graesser, A. C., Singer, M., & Trabasso, T. (1994). Constructing inferences during narrative text comprehension. *Psychological Review, 101,* 371–395.

Grice, H. P. (1957). Meaning. *Philosophical Review, 67,* 377–388.

Grice, H. P. (1975). Logic and conversation. In P. Cole & J. Morgan (Eds.), *Syntax and semantics 3: Speech acts* (pp. 41–58). New York: Academic Press.

Gruenfeld, D. H., & Wyer, R. S., Jr. (1992). Semantics and pragmatics of social influence: How affirmations and denials affect beliefs in referent propositions. *Journal of Personality and Social Psychology, 62,* 38–49.

Gudykunst, W., Matsumoto, Y., Ting-Toomey, S., Nishida, T., Kim, K. S., & Heyman, S. (1996). The influence of cultural individualism-collectivism, self construals, and individual values on communication styles across cultures. *Human Communication Research, 22,* 510–543.

Gudykunst, W., Yoon, Y. C., & Nishida, T. (1987). The influence of individualism-collectivism on perceptions of communication in in-group and out-group relations. *Communication Monographs, 54,* 295–306.

Hara, K., & Kim, M. S. (2001, May). *The effect of self construals on conversational indirectness.* Paper presented the annual conference of the International Communication Association, Washington, DC.

Hastie, R. (1984). Causes and consequences of causal attributions. *Journal of Personality and Social Psychology, 46,* 44–56.

Holtgraves, T. M. (1986). Language structure in social interaction: Perceptions of direct and indirect speech act and interactants who use them. *Journal of Personality and Social Psychology, 51,* 305–314.

Holtgraves, T. M. (1992). The linguistic realization of face management: Implications for language production and comprehension, person perception, and cross-cultural communication. *Social Psychology Quarterly, 55,* 141–159.

Holtgraves, T. M. (1994). Communication in context: Effects of speaker status on the comprehension of indirect requests. *Journal of Experimental Psychology: Learning, Memory, and Cognition, 20,* 1205–1218.

Holtgraves, T. M. (1997a). Politeness and memory for the wording of remarks. *Memory & Cognition, 25,* 106–116.

Holtgraves, T. M. (1997b). Styles of language use: Individual and cultural variability in conversational indirectness. *Journal of Personality and Social Psychology, 73,* 624–637.

Holtgraves T. M. (1998a). Interpreting indirect replies. *Cognitive Psychology, 37,* 1–27.

Holtgraves, T. M. (1998b, July). *Interpreting indirect replies.* Paper presented at the annual conference of the International Communication Association, Jerusalem, Israel.

Holtgraves, T. M. (1999). Comprehending indirect replies: When and how are their conveyed meanings activated. *Journal of Memory and Language, 41,* 519–540.

Holtgraves, T. M. (2000). Preference organization and reply comprehension. *Discourse Processes, 30,* 87–106.

Holtgraves, T. M. (2001a). *Language as social action: Social psychology and language use.* Mahwah, NJ: Erlbaum.

Holtgraves, T. M. (2001b). Politeness. In W. P. Robinson & H. Giles (Eds.), *The new handbook of language and social psychology* (pp. 341–355). Chichester, UK: Wiley.

Holtgraves, T. M. (2002). *Conversational perspective taking: Diverging assumptions of speakers and hearers.* Manuscript submitted for publication.

Holtgraves, T. M., & Ashley, A. (2001). Comprehending illocutionary force. *Memory & Cognition, 29,* 83–90.

Holtgraves, T. M., & Drozd, B. (1998, May). *Cross-cultural differences in conversational interpre-*

*tation*. Paper presented at the annual conference of the Midwestern Psychological Association, Chicago, IL.

Holtgraves, T. M., & Grayer, A. R. (1994). I am not a crook: Effects of denials on perceptions of a defendant's guilt, personality, and motives. *Journal of Applied Social Psychology, 24,* 2132–2150.

Holtgraves, T. M., Srull, T. K., & Socall, D. (1989). Conversation memory: Effects of speaker status on memory for the assertiveness of conversation remarks. *Journal of Personality and Social Psychology, 56,* 149–160.

Holtgraves, T. M., & Yang, J. N. (1990). Politeness as an universal: Cross-cultural perceptions of request strategies and inferences based on their use. *Journal of Personality and Social Psychology, 59,* 719–729.

Holtgraves, T. M., & Yang, J. N. (1992). The interpersonal underpinnings of request strategies: General principles and differences due to culture and gender. *Journal of Personality and Social Psychology, 62,* 246–256.

Horton, W. S., & Keysar, B. (1996). When do speakers take into account common ground? *Cognition, 59,* 91–117.

Jucker, A. H. (1993). The discourse marker well: A relevance-theoretical account. *Journal of Pragmatics, 19,* 435–452.

Kashima, Y., Yamaguchi, S., Kim, U., Choi, S., Gelfand, M. J., & Yuki, M. (1995). Culture, gender, and the self: A perspective from individualism-collectivism research. *Journal of Personality and Social Psychology, 69,* 925–937.

Keenan, E. O. (1976). The universality of conversational implicature. *Language in Society, 5,* 67–80.

Keysar, B. (1989). On the functional equivalence of literal and metaphorical interpretation in discourse. *Journal of Memory and Language, 28,* 375–385.

Keysar, B. (1994a). Discourse context effects: Metaphorical and literal interpretations. *Discourse Processes, 18,* 247–269.

Keysar, B. (1994b). The illusory transparency of intention: Linguistic perspective taking in text. *Cognitive Psychology, 26,* 165–208.

Keysar, B. (1998). Language users as problem solvers: Just what ambiguity problem do they solve? In S. Fussell & R. Kreuz (Eds.), *Social and cognitive approaches to interpersonal communication* (pp. 175–200). Mahwah, NJ: Erlbaum.

Keysar, B. (2000). The illusory transparency of intention: Does June understand what Mark means because he means it? *Discourse Processes, 29,* 161–172

Keysar, B., Barr, D. J., Balin, J. A., & Paek, T. (1998). Definite reference and mutual knowledge: A processing model of common ground in comprehension. *Journal of Memory and Language, 39,* 1–20.

Keysar, B., & Bly, B. (1995). Intuitions of the transparency of idioms: Can one keep a secret by spilling the beans? *Journal of Memory and Language, 34,* 89–109.

Kim, M. S., Hunter, J. E., Miyahara, A., Hovarth, A., Bresnahan, M., & Yoon, H. (1996). Individual- vs. cultural-level dimensions of individualism and collectivism: Effects on preferred conversational styles. *Communication Monographs, 63,* 28–49.

Kim, M. S., Shin, H. C., & Cai, D. (1998). Cultural influences on the preferred forms of requesting and re-requesting. *Communication Monographs, 65,* 47–66.

Kowalski, R. (2000). "I was only kidding!": Victims' and perpetrators' perceptions of teasing. *Personality and Social Psychology Bulletin, 26,* 231–241.

Krauss, R. M., & Fussell, S. R. (1991). Perspective taking in communication: Representations of others' knowledge in reference. *Social Cognition, 9,* 2–24.

Lakoff, R. (1973). Questionable answers and answerable questions. In B. B. Kachru (Ed.), *Issues in linguistics: Papers in honor of Henry and Renee Kahane* (pp. 453–467). Chicago: University of Illinois Press.

Levinson, S. C. (2000). *Presumptive meanings*. Cambridge, MA: MIT Press.

McKoon, G., & Ratcliff, R. (1992). Inferences during reading. *Psychological Review, 99,* 440–466.

Mead, G. H. (1934). *Mind, self, and society.* Chicago: University of Chicago Press.

Ortony, A., Reynolds, R., Schallert, D., & Antos, S. (1978). Interpreting metaphors and idioms: Some effects of context on comprehension. *Journal of Verbal Learning and Verbal Behavior, 16,* 465–477.

Pearce, W. B. (1994). *Interpersonal communication: Making social worlds.* New York: HarperCollins.

Roberts, R. M., & Kreuz, R. J. (1994). Why do people use figurative language? *Psychological Science, 5,* 159–163.

Rommetviet, R. (1974). *On message structure: A framework for the study of language and communication.* New York: Wiley.

Rosaldo, M. Z. (1982). The things we do with words: Llongot speech acts and speech act theory in philosophy. *Language in Society, 11,* 203–237.

Russell, A. W., & Schober, M. F. (1999). How beliefs about a partner's goals affect referring in goal-discrepant conversations. *Discourse Processes, 27,* 1–33.

Schegloff, E., & Sacks, H. (1973). Opening up closings. *Semiotica, 8,* 289–327.

Schwarz, N. (1996). *Cognition and communication: Judgmental biases, research methods, and the logic of conversation.* Mahwah, NJ: Erlbaum.

Schweller, K., Brewer, W., & Dahl, D. (1976). Memory for illocutionary forces and perlocutionary effects of utterances. *Journal of Verbal Learning and Verbal Behavior, 15,* 325–337.

Searle, J. R. (1969). *Speech acts.* Cambridge, UK: Cambridge University Press.

Searle, J. R. (1975). Indirect speech acts. In P. Cole & J. Morgan (Eds.), *Syntax and semantics 3: Speech acts* (pp. 59–82). New York: Academic Press

Searle, J. R. (1979). *Expression and meaning.* Cambridge, UK: Cambridge University Press.

Searle, J. R., & Vanderveken, D. (1985). *Foundations of illocutionary logic.* Cambridge, UK: Cambridge University Press.

Sharkey, W. F., Kim, M. S., & Diggs, R. C. (in press). Intentional embarrassment: A look at embarrassors' and targets' perspectives. *Personality and Individual Differences.*

Singer, M., Halldorson, M., Lear, J. C., & Andrusiak, P. (1992). Validation of causal bridging inferences in discourse understanding. *Journal of Memory and Language, 31,* 507–524.

Slugoski, B., Lalljee, M., Lamb, R., & Ginsburg, G. P. (1993). Attributions in conversational context: Effects of mutual knowledge on explanation giving. *European Journal of Social Psychology, 23,* 219–238.

Sperber, D. & Wilson, D. (1986). *Relevance.* Cambridge, MA: Harvard University Press.

Ting-Toomey, S. (1988). Intercultural conflict styles. In Y. Y. Kim & W. B. Gudykunst (Eds.), *Theories in intercultural communication* (pp. 213–238). Beverly Hills, CA: Sage.

Titone, D. A., & Connine, C. M. (1994). Comprehension of idiomatic expressions: Effects of familiarity and literality. *Journal of Experimental Psychology: Learning, Memory and Cognition, 20,* 1126–1138.

Triandis, H. (1995). *Individualism & collectivism.* Boulder, CO: Westview Press

Triandis, H., Bontempo, R., Villareal, M., Asai, M., & Lucca, N. (1988). Individualism and collectivism: Cross-cultural perspectives on self-ingroup relationships. *Journal of Personality and Social Psychology, 54,* 323–333.

Uleman, J. S. (1987). Consciousness and control: The case of spontaneous trait inferences. *Personality and Social Psychology Bulletin, 13,* 337–354.

Uleman, J. S., Han, A., Roman, R. J., & Moskowitz, G. B. (1996). On-line evidence for spontaneous trait inferences at encoding. *Personality and Social Psychology Bulletin, 22,* 377– 394.

Whitney, P., & Williams-Whitney, D. L. (1990). Toward a contextualist view of elaborative inferences. In A. C. Graesser & G. H. Bower (Eds.), *Inferences and text comprehension* (pp. 279–293). San Diego, CA: Academic Press.

Wilson, S. R., Aleman, C. G., & Leatham, G. B. (1998). Identity implications of influence goals: A revised analysis of face-threatening acts and application to seeking compliance with same-sex friends. *Human Communication Research, 26,* 64–96.

# CHAPTER CONTENTS

• Dimensions of Family Communication                                      38
   *Conversation Orientation*                               39
   *Conformity Orientation*                                  39
   *Conversation Orientation, Conformity Orientation,*       40
   *and Family Functioning*
   *Family Communication Patterns and Cognitive Structures*  41

• The Revised Family Communication Pattern Instrument                     42
   *Family Types*                                            44
   *Family Types and Marital Types*                          45

• Family Communication Patterns and Outcomes for Families                46
   *Behavioral Outcomes*                                     47
   *Psychosocial Outcomes*                                   52

• Methodological Issues                                                   54
   *The Correlation of Conversation Orientation*             54
   *and Conformity Orientation*
   *Different Perspectives on Family Communication*          56
   *by Family Members*
   *Continuous Dimensions and Discrete Family Types*         57
   *Classification Based on Small and None Representative Samples*  60
   *Validity of the RFCP*                                    60

• Conclusion                                                              62

• Appendix                                                                66

• References                                                              67

# 2 Understanding Family Communication Patterns and Family Functioning: The Roles of Conversation Orientation and Conformity Orientation

ASCAN F. KOERNER
*University of Minnesota-Twin Cities*

MARY ANNE FITZPATRICK
*University of Wisconsin-Madison*

Family communication behavior and family beliefs about how family members should communicate with one another are closely related and combine to create family communication patterns. Two dimensions that determine family communication patterns are conversation orientation and conformity orientation. In this chapter, we discuss theoretical and practical issues relating to these two dimensions and the family typology that is based on them. First, the dimensions are discussed and a resulting family typology is introduced. Then, we discuss the instrument to measure family communication patterns, the Revised Family Communication Patterns instrument (RFCP), and review research that links conversation orientation and conformity orientation and the resulting family types to different behavioral and psychosocial outcomes of family functioning in the areas of conflict and conflict resolution, speech act production, and the socialization of children. Following this discussion, we address a number of methodological considerations regarding the RFCP and its use in family research. Finally, we evaluate the roles of family communication patterns in family functioning and individuals' success in their relationship and suggest directions for future research.

The family has long been regarded as among the most interesting and influential human systems, and nowhere is its influence on individual behaviors more profound than in the area of communicative behaviors (Berger & Luckmann, 1967; Burleson, Delia, & Applegate, 1995; Fitzpatrick & Ritchie, 1993; McLeod & Chaffee, 1972; Reiss, 1981; Ritchie & Fitzpatrick, 1990). Particularly Reiss (1981) has argued strongly that families are characterized by uniquely shared world views, as well as by value and belief systems that define

Correspondence: Ascan F. Koerner, Department of Communication Studies, 225 Ford Hall, 224 Church St. S E, Minneapolis, MN 55455; email: koern011@umn.edu.

families within their social environment. These value and belief systems have far-reaching consequences for how family members perceive their social environment and their family's place in it, and, as a consequence, how they communicate within and outside the family. How families communicate, however, is not only interesting on its own right, but the ways in which families communicate have important implications for the psychological well-being of family members and their social functioning (Noller & Fitzpatrick, 1993).

Family communication is characterized by clearly discernible patterns and forms. An analysis of family communication reveals that families develop and sustain a variety of different communication patterns. One way to address this variability theoretically is to create a typology of families. Communication scholars who propose typologies of families hold some axioms in common. First, although these perspectives acknowledge an enormous variability among families, the typologies are based on the premise that within any given sample of families, there are a few basic, identifiable types. Second, these approaches systematically categorize some aspect of family functioning. This categorization is accomplished by proposing central dimensions of family life. Third, although the primary function of all typologies is description, typologies can also serve to predict, to explain, and to prescribe. Indeed, the real value of a family typology for communication scholars lies not in its descriptive power, but in its ability to systematically associate family types with a variety of important family processes and outcomes (Christensen & Arrington, 1987).

In this chapter, we discuss a family typology that is based on two central dimensions of family communication. These dimensions, labeled conversation orientation and conformity orientation, respectively, play a crucial role in family functioning and form the template for a typology of families that is capable of predicting and explaining a number of behavioral and psychosocial outcomes for families. After a thorough discussion of the dimensions and the resulting typology, we introduce a reliable and easily administered measure of family communication patterns, the Revised Family Communication Pattern instrument (RFCP). We then review some of the research involving family communication patterns to present the reader with an overview of the breadth of the areas of family communication and functioning that are influenced by families' conversation orientation and conformity orientation. We conclude by arguing that conversation orientation and conformity orientation have proved to be influential explanatory variables in family communication that are easily assessed with the Revised Family Communication Pattern instrument and that we expected to play an increasingly important role in the study of family communication.

## DIMENSIONS OF FAMILY COMMUNICATION

Two fundamental dimensions that both distinguish how families communicate and that have been associated with various functional consequences for families are conversation orientation and conformity orientation (Fitzpatrick & Ritchie, 1994; Ritchie & Fitzpatrick, 1990).

## Conversation Orientation

The first fundamental dimension of family communication is conversation orientation. It is defined as the degree to which families create a climate in which all family members are encouraged to participate in unrestrained interactions about a wide array of topics. In families on the high end of this dimension, family members freely, frequently, and spontaneously interact with each other, spend large amounts of time in interactions, and discuss a substantial range of topics. That is, these families spend a lot of time talking to each other and family members share their individual activities, thoughts, and feelings with each other. Actions or activities that the family plans to engage in as a unit are discussed with all family members and family decisions are made together. Conversely, in families at the low end of the conversation orientation dimension, family members interact less frequently with each other and discuss only few topics openly with one another. There is little exchange of private thoughts, feelings, and activities. In these families, activities that families engage in as a unit are not usually discussed in great detail, nor is everybody's input sought in family decision making.

Associated with high conversation orientation is the belief that open and frequent communication is essential to an enjoyable and fruitful family life. Families holding this view value the exchange of ideas, and parents holding this belief see frequent communication with their children as the main means to educate and to socialize them. Conversely, families low in conversation orientation believe that open and frequent exchanges of ideas, opinion, and values are not necessary for the function of the family in general, and for the children's education and socialization in particular.

## Conformity Orientation

The other important dimension of family communication is conformity orientation. Conformity orientation refers to the degree to which family communication stresses a climate of homogeneity of attitudes, values, and beliefs. Families on the high end of this dimension are characterized by interactions that emphasize a uniformity of beliefs and attitudes. Their interactions typically focus on conformity, conflict avoidance, and the interdependence of family members. In intergenerational exchanges, communication in these families reflects obedience to parents and to other adults. Conversely, families on the low end of the conformity orientation dimension are characterized by interactions that focus on heterogeneous attitudes and beliefs, and the individuality and independence of family members. In intergenerational exchanges, communication reflects the equality of all family members; that is, children are usually involved in decision making.

Associated with high conformity orientation is the belief in what might be called a traditional family structure. In this view, families are cohesive and hierarchical. That is, family members favor their family relationships over relationships external to the family and they expect that resources such as space and money are shared among family members. Families high in conformity orientation believe that individual schedules should be coordinated among family members to maximize family time, and they expect family members to subordinate personal interests to those of the family. Parents are expected to make the decisions for the family, and the children are expected to act according to their parents' wishes. Conversely, families low in conformity orientation do not believe in a traditional family structure. Instead, they believe in less cohesive and less hierarchically organized families. Families on the low end of the conformity dimension believe that relationships outside the family are as important as family relationships. They also believe that families should encourage the personal growth of individual family members, even if that leads them to develop strong relationships outside the family system. These families believe in the independence of family members, they value personal space, and they subordinate family interests to personal interests.

Conversation Orientation, Conformity Orientation, and Family Functioning

Conversation orientation and conformity orientation are dimensions that underlay and define family types because they are central to family functioning. Their centrality and influence on family functioning have been discussed by various communication scholars, although not necessarily under the same labels. For example, recognizing the importance of family conformity, Noller (1995), in her discussion of the socializing functions of parent-adolescent communication, argued that how families balance adolescent children's desires for autonomy and interdependence with parents' desires for control determines the effectiveness of the families' socialization of their children. Specifically, Noller found that how families manage conformity correlates with adolescents' identity formation, their self-esteem, their problem-solving, and their decision making. Similarly, conformity orientation in families also is central to Baumrind's (1971a, 1971b) seminal typology of parenting styles. According to Baumrind, authoritarian parents require the most conformity from their children, authoritative parents require less conformity, and permissive parents require the least conformity. Baumrind found that these differences in parenting were predictive of how well the children developed social responsibility and of their academic and social achievements. Finally, in their discussion of the socialization of person- versus position-centered communication, Burelson, Delia, and Applegate (1995) also recognized the central role played by parents' conformity orientation, expressed through their regulative and disciplining messages, for how well children come to self-regulate and for how well they relate to their peers.

Conformity in families, however, is not the only communication variable affecting family functioning addressed by these scholars. In fact, they all found that the communication orientation in the form of openness and supportiveness of the communication between parents and children also affects family functioning. For example, Noller (1995) in her discussion of adolescents' socialization, noted that supportive communication from parents is about equally important to adolescents' socialization as are the issues of independence and autonomy. Similarly, parental support also plays an important role in differentiating Baumrind's (1971a, 1971b) parenting styles. According to Baumrind, permissive parents are the most supportive, authoritative parents are somewhat less supportive, and authoritarian parents are the least supportive in their communication with their children. Finally, Burelson et al. (1995) associated more extensive and involving parent-child interactions with a person-centered communication style and with an increased social and cognitive development of children.

As these examples show, both conversation orientation and conformity orientation have successfully been used to describe and to explain family communication patterns and to predict their effects on important outcomes for parents and children. The effects of conversation orientation and conformity orientation have been investigated independently from one another, as well as in combination. They have not been used by these scholars, however, to create a typology of families. That notwithstanding, results from these investigations suggest that a family typology that is based on these two fundamental dimensions of family communication patterns should be able to explain and to predict important functional outcomes for families and for individual family members.

## Family Communication Patterns and Cognitive Structures

As the preceding discussion of conversation orientation and conformity orientation has indicated, we argue that beliefs that family members have about family communication and the actual communicative behaviors they engage in within their families are closely intertwined. In light of this intertwinement, one might even argue that to distinguish between them is more of theoretical than practical relevance. Our making this distinction in the preceding section was motivated by our concern to distinguish between the directly observable (e.g., behaviors indicating conformity and conversation orientation) and the not directly observable aspects of family communication patterns (e.g., beliefs relevant to conversation orientation and conformity such as beliefs in traditional family structures and in the importance of communicating within families).

It should be clear from this discussion that we do not suggest a causal relationship between beliefs and behaviors; rather we see them both as different manifestations of the same phenomenon. In other words, we conceptualize family communication patterns as encompassing both beliefs and behavior, which we understand to be interdependent. By interdependent, we mean that neither beliefs nor behaviors are primary in causation; rather, each impacts the other and, in turn, is itself impacted by the other. Thus, we do not assume an extremely psychological position that regards behavior as entirely dependent on cognitive processes, nor do we assume an extremely sociological position that regards cognition as mere reflections of social processes. Rather, we consider both behavior and cognition to be equivalent components of family communication patterns.

Our theoretical position not withstanding, in the operationalization of family communication patterns in the RFCP instrument discussed in the following section, we are more interested in respondents' recollections of their families' outward behavior than their recollections of their families' beliefs. The main reason for us to rely on recollections of communication behavior is our experience that persons are more capable to respond reliably about their own and their family members' behaviors than about their own and their family members' beliefs. In order to report on beliefs, which are not directly observable, respondents would need to make inferences and to speculate, at least as far as the beliefs of other family members are concerned.

## THE REVISED FAMILY COMMUNICATION PATTERN INSTRUMENT

The instrument we use to measure conversation orientation and conformity orientation is the Revised Family Communication Pattern instrument (Fitzpatrick & Ritchie, 1994; Ritchie, 1991; Ritchie & Fitzpatrick, 1990). The RFCP is a self-report questionnaire asking respondents to agree or disagree with 26 statements (using 7-point scales) about their families' communication (Appendix). It is based on McLeod and Chaffee's (1972) Family Communication Pattern (FCP) instrument, but represents an advancement over the FCP because it better labels and operationalizes the underlying dimensions of conversation orientation and conformity orientation (Fitzpatrick & Ritchie, 1994; Ritchie & Fitzpatrick, 1990), which in the FCP were labeled concept-orientation and socio-orientation, respectively. Like the FCP, the items of the RFCP focus on the interactions between parents and children rather than the interactions among the children or among the parents, because it is during these intergenerational exchanges that parents socialize their children and define the very concept of family communication. Unlike the FCP, however, the RFCP focuses more closely on the actual communication that occurs between parents and children, and it focuses less on the interactions' consequences for information processing.

The focus of the original FCP on information processing can be explained by the history of the instrument and the purpose for which it was designed. McLeod and Chaffee (1972) were scholars of mass communication who developed the FCP to assess the influence that family communication has on how families as a unit construct social reality in general, and how children use external information in that process, in particular. Consequently, McLeod and Chaffee were most concerned with understanding family communication patterns in terms of their influences on children's information processing, rather than understanding it in terms of its behavioral features. This also explains why McLeod and Chaffee labeled the two dimensions concept-orientation and socio-orientation, respectively. The label concept-orientation indicates that the ideas and concepts discussed have a greater influence on children's information processing and subsequent decision making, whereas the label socio-orientation indicates that social roles and relationships have a greater influence on children's decision making. In the RFCP, which was developed with a greater concern for the behavioral features of family communication and its psychosocial outcomes, these dimensions are called conversation orientation and conformity orientation, respectively. The label conversation orientation indicates the concern for open discussion of ideas between parents and children, and the label conformity orientation indicates the concern for children's agreement with their parents.

In addition to relabeling the underlying dimensions of the original FCP, Fitzpatrick and Ritchie's (1994, Ritchie & Fitzpatrick, 1990) revision of the FCP also included a rewording of the 11 original items of the FCP to reflect the new focus on a wider range of communication behaviors and the addition of 15 items to the instrument to increase the reliability and validity of the two scales. Thus, the revision of the FCP has had a number of positive conceptual and practical outcomes for the instrument and for the scholars using it. First, it significantly widened the scope of the instrument by shifting the focus away from information processing to a wider range of communicative behaviors occurring during family interactions. Second, it significantly increased the reliability and thus the validity of the instrument, because there are now more items that are worded to apply to the broader contexts and with greater concern for internal consistency (Ritchie & Fitzpatrick, 1990). Third, the revision increased the conceptual clarity of the dimensions underlying family communication patterns, which were now labeled according to how they are expressed in communicative behavior rather than according to how they impact information processing.

A final advancement of the RFCP over the FCP was that the RFCP was written and administered in two different versions. The version for parents assesses the parents' perception of their families' communicative behaviors, whereas the children's version assesses family communication from the children's perspective. For example, a question assessing conversation orientation for parents, "I encourage my child to challenge my ideas and beliefs," in the children's version is phrased, "My parents encourage me to challenge their ideas and beliefs." Assessing all family members' perceptions of family communication is necessary to gain a more valid description of family communication patterns because individual family members are often biased in how they perceive family communication patterns based on their family role (Ritchie & Fitzpatrick, 1990). Thus one encounters validity problems with the FCP because it privileges the parents' perceptions over those of the children or vice versa, and the original FCP has justly been criticized for ignoring the possibilities of biased perceptions and reporting of family communication.

Family Types

Both the FCP (McCleod & Chaffee, 1972) and the RFCP (Fitzpatrick & Ritchie, 1994; Ritchie & Fitzpatrick, 1990) can be used to classify families as belonging into one of four types, each characterized by specific family schemata associated with their own communicative behaviors of parents and children and with their own socialization outcomes for children.

*Consensual families.* Families high in both conversation and conformity orientation are labeled *consensual.* Their communication is characterized by a tension between pressure to agree and to preserve the existing hierarchy within the family, on the one hand, and an interest in open communication and in exploring new ideas, on the other hand. That is, parents in these families are very interested in their children and what the children have to say, but at the same time also believe that they should make decisions for the family and for the children. They resolve this tension by listening to their children and by spending time and energy in explaining their decisions to their children in the hope that their children will understand the reasoning, beliefs, and values behind the parents' decisions. Children in these families usually learn to value family conversations and adopt their parents' values and beliefs. In regard to influence, they are most likely to be persuaded by messages that are consistent with their parents' beliefs and values, and they tend to resist messages that deviate from their parents' stated positions or values.

*Pluralistic families.* Families high in conversation orientation but low in conformity orientation are labeled *pluralistic.* Communication in pluralistic families is characterized by open, unconstrained discussions that are open to and involve all family members. Parents in these families do not feel the need to be in control of their children or to make all their decisions for them. This parental attitude leads to family discussions where opinions are evaluated based on the merit of the arguments that support them rather than on which family members support them. That is, parents are willing to accept their children's opinions and to let them participate equally in family decision making. Children of these families learn to value family conversations and, at the same time, learn to be independent and autonomous, which fosters their communication competence and their confidence in their ability to make their own decisions. As a consequence, in their information processing and decision making, children of pluralistic families are influenced most by messages that are based on rational arguments.

*Protective families.* Families low on conversation orientation but high on conformity orientation are labeled *protective.* Communication in protective families is characterized by an emphasis on obedience to parental authority and by little concern for conceptual matters or for open communication within the family. Parents in these families believe that they should be making the decisions for their families and their children, and they see little value in explaining their reasoning to their children. Children in protective families learn that there is little value in family conversations and to distrust their own decision making ability. As a consequence, they are easily influenced and persuaded by outside authorities, independent of argument quality.

*Laissez-faire families.* Families low in both conversation orientation and conformity orientation are labeled laissez-faire. Their communication is characterized by few and usually uninvolving interactions among family members that usually concern only a limited number of topics. Parents in laissez-faire families do believe that all family members should be able to make their own decisions, but unlike parents in pluralistic families, they have little interest in their children's decisions, nor do they value communicating with them. Most members of laissez-faire families are emotionally divorced from their families. Children of these families learn that there is little value in family conversation and that they have to make their own decisions. Because they do not receive much support from their parents, however, they come to question their decision-making ability. Consequently, in their information processing and decision making, they are often influenced by peers and other external sources.

Family Types and Marital Types

Because parents, at least initially, have greater influence on family communication than their children and because family relationships most often develop from marital or similar dyadic relationships, how the parents communicate with each other should have a great influence on how families communicate. Consequently, there should be a positive correlation between marital and family communication, and, by extension, between marital types and family types if both typologies are based on similar communication behaviors and belief systems. Investigating such a connection, Fitzpatrick and Ritchie (1994) have linked the RFCP family typology to Fitzpatrick's (1988) typology of marriages.

Based on theoretical and empirical research of people's marital beliefs and behaviors, Fitzpatrick (1988) identified three distinct types of married people, which she labeled as *traditional, independent,* and *separate.* These three marriage types are defined by three different dimensions of marital relationships relevant to communicative behavior that can be measured with the relational dimension inventory (RDI): ideology (conventional vs. nonconventional), interdependence (interdependent vs. independent), and communication (avoidance vs. engagement of conflict). Although these three dimensions yield eight theoretical marital types (2 x 2 x 2 = 8), in her research Fitzpatrick (1988) showed that in actuality, most persons fall in only the three marital types labeled traditional, independent, and separate. Fitzpatrick's research further showed that in about two thirds of all marriages, both partners are of the same married type, resulting in marriages of pure types. In about one third of marriages, however, partners are of dissimilar marital types, resulting in mixed type marriages.

Among mixed type marriages, the type combining a separate husband with a traditional wife is the most frequent one.

*Traditional* couples hold conventional ideological values about marital relationships (e.g., the wife adopts the husband's last name, infidelity is unacceptable), are interdependent (e.g., share time, space, and companionship), and describe their communication as nonassertive but engage in, rather than avoid, marital conflicts about important issues. *Independent* couples hold nonconventional values about marital relationships (e.g., marriage should not constrain individual achievement, wives keep their own name), exhibit a high degree of sharing and companionship while maintaining separate time schedules and physical space (e.g., spouses have their own individual bathrooms and offices), and also tend to engage in, rather than avoid, marital conflict. *Separate* couples hold conventional values about relationships and families, but at the same time value individual freedom over relational maintenance, have significantly less companionship and sharing, and describe their communication as persuasive and assertive, yet avoid rather than engage in open marital conflict.

Recognizing the similarities between these marital beliefs and the beliefs associated with the family types, Fitzpatrick and Ritchie (1994) investigated the relationships between marital types and family types. Based on questionnaires completed by 169 family triads (father, mother, one child) that contained the RFCP for all family members and Fitzpatrick's RDI for the parents, Fitzpatrick and Ritchie were able to establish clear links between the marital types and the family types. In regard to the underlying dimensions, family members of families headed by traditional or separate parents described their families as high in conformity orientation, and members of families headed by traditional and independent parents described their families as high in conversation orientation. In other words, consensual families are most likely to be headed by parents that fall into Fitzpatrick's traditional category. Parents heading pluralistic families are likely to be of Fitzpatrick's independent type. Protective families are likely to be headed by parents of Fitzpatrick's separate type, and parents heading laissez-faire families are likely to be separate/independent or of another mixed type of Fitzpatrick's typology. Spouses in mixed couples define their marriages differently along the dimensions of ideology, interdependence, and conflict engagement, which makes it difficult for parents to agree even on fundamental values and beliefs associated with their families and to form cohesive family units.

## FAMILY COMMUNICATION PATTERNS
## AND OUTCOMES FOR FAMILIES

Our own research and that of our colleagues has demonstrated the influence of family communication patterns on various outcomes for families, such as conflict and conflict resolution (Koerner & Fitzpatrick, 1997a), children's future romantic relationships (Koerner & Fitzpatrick, 1997b), speech act production in families (Koerner, 1995; Koerner & Cvancara, in press) the utilization of social self-restraint and social withdrawal behaviors (Fitzpatrick, Marshall, Leutwiler & Krcmar, 1996), the enactment of family rituals (Baxter & Clark, 1996), and the relationship between parent's work place communication and family communication (Ritchie, 1997). This research has utilized family communication patterns to address a number of interesting questions regarding the communicative behavior of families and its consequences for the functioning of families and of individual family members. These questions can be roughly divided into two areas. The first area deals with the interaction process. Here research has focused on the communicative behaviors associated with family communication patterns. The second area addresses psychosocial outcomes associated with family communication patterns for families and individual family members.

Behavioral Outcomes

A number of studies investigating the influence of conversation orientation and conformity orientation on family behaviors have focused on describing how families express their communication orientations in their behaviors (see Table 1). The goal of these studies was to come to a fuller understanding of how the conversation orientation and conformity orientation operate and the functions they serve. In two studies involving more than 80 families who produced more than 30,000 speech acts, Koerner (1995; Koerner & Cvancara, in press) investigated the influence of conformity orientation on individual speech acts.

*Conformity orientation and self-orientation in family conversations.* In the first study, 31 families with adult children were recruited at a small, religious college in a large Midwestern city educating mostly nontraditional students, many of them single mothers. Participants were asked to bring to the laboratory whomever they considered as belonging to the family, resulting in a very diverse sample. The average number of participants per family was 3.9 and ranged from 2 (1 parent and 1 child) to 8 (2 parents and 6 children). The majority of the families were single-parent (18) and one family was headed by a lesbian couple. In all, 39 daughters and 21 sons participated in the study, as well as 12 fathers and 32 mothers ($N = 106$).

We asked these families to discuss issues that had recently led to disagreements between parents and children and to try to come to a solution for the conflict. These conversations were videotaped for 15 minutes and transcribed for further analysis using Stiles's (1992) verbal response mode (VRM). The VRM classifies individual speech acts along three binominal dimensions that are anchored by "speaker" versus "other": source of experience (SE; i.e., whose experience is the speech act about), presumption of experience (PE; i.e., whose experience does the speaker presume to share), and frame of reference (FR; i.e., the viewpoint from which the speech act is evaluated). The classification along

TABLE 1
Family Types and Communication Behaviors During Normal Conversation and During Conflict

| Consensual | Pluralistic |
|---|---|
| Family conversation | Family conversation |
| medium persuasiveness$_a$ | high persuasiveness$_a$ |
| good conflict management$_a$ | good conflict management$_a$ |
| more ego-support$_a$ | more ego-support$_a$ |
| more advice$_b$ | less advice$_b$ |
| more interpretation$_b$ | less interpretation$_b$ |
| more questions$_b$ | more questions$_b$ |
| less confirmations$_b$ | more confirmations$_b$ |
| less reflections$_b$ | more reflections$_b$ |
| | |
| Interpersonal conflict | Interpersonal conflict |
| less avoidance$_d$ | less avoidance$_d$ |
| more venting$_d$ | less venting$_d$ |
| more resisting$_c$ | less resisting$_c$ |
| more negativity$_c$ | less negativity$_c$ |
| medium positivity$_c$ | high positivity$_c$ |
| medium complementariness$_c$ | low complementariness$_c$ |
| medium aggressiveness$_c$ | low aggressiveness$_c$ |

| Protective | Laissez-faire |
|---|---|
| Family conversation | Family conversation |
| medium persuasiveness$_a$ | low persuasiveness$_a$ |
| less conflict management$_a$ | less conflict management$_a$ |
| less ego-support$_a$ | less ego-support$_a$ |
| more advice$_b$ | less advice$_b$ |
| more interpretation$_b$ | less interpretation$_b$ |
| more questions$_b$ | more questions$_b$ |
| less confirmations$_b$ | more confirmations$_b$ |
| less reflections$_b$ | more reflections$_b$ |
| | |
| Interpersonal conflict | Interpersonal conflict |
| more avoidance$_d$ | more avoidance$_d$ |
| more venting$_d$ | less venting$_d$ |
| more resisting$_c$ | less resisting$_c$ |
| more negativity$_c$ | less negativity$_c$ |
| low positivity$_c$ | medium positivity$_c$ |
| high complementariness$_c$ | medium complementariness$_c$ |
| high aggressiveness$_c$ | medium aggressiveness$_c$ |

NOTE: a = (Fitzpatrick & Koerner, 1996); b = (Koerner & Cvancara, in press); c = (Koerner & Fitzpatrick, 1997b); d = (Koerner & Fitzpatrick, 1997a).

these three dimensions yields eight different types of speech acts: self disclosure (SE = self; PE = self; FR = self); edification (self, self, other); advisement (self, other, self); confirmation (self, other, other); question (other, self, self); acknowledgement (other, self, other); interpretation (other, other, self); and reflection (other, other, other).

The analysis of the 12,522 speech acts produced by the 31 families showed that conformity orientation was positively correlated ($r = .34$) with a self-orientation for the frame of reference and that families high in conformity orientation produced more advice, interpretation, and questions than families low in conformity orientation. Conversely, families low in conformity orientation produced more speech acts coded as confirmation, reflection, and acknowledgement than families high in conformity orientation. No effects were observed for the conversation orientation of families.

Because of the particular nature of the sample in the first study, which raised questions about the validity of the analysis and the generalizability of the findings, we replicated the first study on a larger and more representative sample with a narrower definition of family. The sample was randomly selected from a list of all families with children in the middle schools of a medium-sized Midwestern city. For the purpose of this study, we defined family as a two-parent household, where the two adults were married for more than one year. Moreover, we only invited the two parents and one child in middle school to participate in the study, even in cases where families had more than one child. Of the families randomly selected, more than 70% of the families that qualified agreed to participate, yielding a sample of 50 families, 26 with boys and 24 with girls.

The procedure and data analysis mirrored that of the first study. The analysis of the 17,724 speech acts produced by the families in their discussion of family conflicts mostly supported the findings of the first study. Again, conformity orientation in families was positively correlated ($r = .29$) with self orientation in frame of reference. Also supported were the findings from Study 1 that families high in conformity orientation produce more advice and questions and fewer confirmations than families low in conformity. The findings that families high in conformity also produce more interpretations and fewer reflections did not receive statistically significant support in the replication, although the correlations were in the same directions. New findings in Study 2 were that conformity orientation in families was associated with more self-disclosure and less edification. We also observed some interesting interactions of family conformity orientation with the sex of the child, which indicated to us that families with sons are more stereotypical in their implementation of conformity orientation than families with daughters.

Combining the findings of these two studies, results indicate that in their conversations, families high in conformity orientation (i.e., consensual and protective families) exhibit more regulatory behaviors and less confirming behaviors than families low in conformity orientation (i.e., pluralistic and laissez-faire). In addition, families high in conformity orientation also exhibit much less empathy and perspective taking than families low in conformity orientation. This is not an unexpected finding, because conformity to family norms (i.e., parental norms) does not require family members to be empathetic or to really understand the internal life of individual family members. The knowledge of family norms and rules is sufficient for families to exhibit conformity. What these findings reinforced, then, is that family conformity does not imply closeness or cohesion in families. Rather, conformity has clear coercive characteristics in most families. The fact that conversation orientation of families did not interact with conformity orientation in regard to these outcomes suggests that even in families where parents communicate with their children about their reasons for demanding conformity, conformity is nonetheless coercive in its expression and explanation alone does not aid the development of empathy. In other words, even rational justifications by parents for why they require their children's compliance with their decisions does not do much to change the coercive discourse associated with high conformity orientation.

*Family types and conflict.* In another set of studies, Koerner and Fitzpatrick (1997a, 1997b) investigated the influence of family communication patterns on how families interact during conflict, what type of conflict styles and coping behaviors children learn from their families of origin, and how they apply it to their own romantic relationships in the future.

The first study involved the conflict behavior of 35 Midwestern families. Because we were interested in an ecologically valid sample, families were again asked to bring all persons they consider to be members of the family to the laboratory, resulting in the participation of 25 families headed by two parents in heterosexual relationships and 10 families headed by single mothers. In all, 35 mothers, 25 fathers, 26 sons, and 30 daughters participated. After the families had a family discussion about a recent conflict they had experienced, family members individually completed questionnaires containing, among other measures, the RFCP and a measure of the conflict coping strategies avoidance, seeking social support, and venting negative feelings (Patterson & McCubbin, 1991).

Results showed statistically significant positive correlations between conformity orientation of families and both conflict avoidance ($\beta = .21, p < .05$) and the venting of negative feelings ($\beta = .36, p < .01$). We interpreted these results to show that families high in conformity orientation experience both the pressure to avoid violating a family norm against engaging in conflict and a certain level of hostility that results from a number of unresolved conflicts (Segrin & Fitzpatrick, 1991). Conversation orientation of families was statistically significantly negatively correlated with conflict avoidance ($\beta = -.31, p < .01$), and positively correlated with seeking social support ($\beta = .41, p < .01$). We interpreted these results to show that conversation orientation of families extends to conflict interactions as well as to positive family interactions. In addition, the firm belief in the value of interpersonal communication also enables members of these families to seek and to obtain social support from outside their families. Based on these observations, we concluded that conversation orientation in families leads children to acquire better conflict communication skills and more tools to mitigate the negative consequences of interpersonal conflict.

In regard to family types, these results showed that consensual families avoid small conflicts but engage in important confrontations and that their conflict interactions are generally positive and supportive. Nonetheless, their conflicts were also characterized by instances of negative affect. Members of consensual families, however, are able to obtain outside support in conflict situations, which often helps them to mitigate the negative effects of their expressed hostility. Of all family types, pluralistic families have the easiest time with conflict and experience it most often. They regard conflict as a normal and expected part of their family life and willingly engage in it. As a result, they are skillful in their conflict behaviors and their conflict interactions are the most positive and supportive ones of all family types. Members of these families do seek outside support and are able to obtain it, aiding them even more in avoiding any potentially negative consequences of family conflict. In stark contrast to pluralistic families, protective families have the most difficulties with family conflict, although they usually are quite successful in avoiding conflict altogether. However, when conflict happens, it is experienced as threatening to the family and family members exhibit both low skills in conflict resolution and a high degree of verbal aggressiveness in their interactions. The negative consequences of these behaviors are compounded by the unwillingness and inability of family members to seek and to obtain social support outside the family. In contrast to the volatile conflict of protective families, the conflict on laissez-faire families is much less dramatic. Although not as active in avoiding conflict as protective families, the lack of involvement with their families leads members of laissez-faire families to avoid most conflict interactions. In cases where conflict proves unavoidable, the conflict does not lead to a lot of verbal aggression. Because family members do not easily obtain social support, however, laissez-faire families do experience some of the negative consequences of conflict.

In our second study investigating the links between family types and conflict (Koerner & Fitzpatrick, 1997b), we were interested in how adult children of different family types communicate during conflict in their romantic relationships. Participants were 260 undergraduate students recruited from several introductory communication courses at a large Midwestern university who, at the time of the study, were individually involved in a dating or marital relationship. The mean age of the 156 female and 104 male participants was 21.5 (range 18–32 years). Participants were seated separately in cubicles and individually responded to questionnaires containing the RFCP and Christensen and Sullaway's (1984) Communications Patterns Questionnaire (CPQ). The CPQ is a self-report instrument that assesses the symmetry and the complementarity of communication behaviors during conflict episodes such as demanding, withdrawing, avoiding, aggressing, and resisting.

The data thus obtained was analyzed using multiple linear regression and MANOVA. Results showed that for young adults in their romantic relationships, the conformity orientation of their families of origin was associated with mutual negative behavior and greater unilateral resistance in their conflicts with romantic partners. Also associated with the conformity orientation of their families of origin were less mutual positive behaviors, more complementary behaviors, and more avoiding and aggressive behaviors in their conflicts with romantic partners.

The observed effects of conformity orientation, with the exception of avoidance which was a direct function of conversation orientation, were amplified by the families' of origin conversation orientation. That is, participants originating from consensual families, which are high in both conformity orientation and conversation orientation, reported less mutually positive behaviors, more complementary behaviors, more aggressive behaviors and less conflict avoidance in their conflicts with their romantic partners than participants originating from protective families, which are high in conformity orientation but low in conversation orientation. Similarly, participants originating from pluralistic families, which are low in conformity orientation but high in conversation orientation, had more mutually positive behaviors, less complementary behaviors, less aggressive behaviors, and less conflict avoidance in their conflicts with their romantic partners than participants originating from laissez-faire families, which are low in conformity orientation and low in conversation orientation.

Psychosocial Outcomes

In addition to behavioral outcomes, research has also shown the influence of family communication patterns on psychosocial outcomes. Because researchers who used McLeod and Chaffee's (1972) original conceptualization of family communication patterns were mainly interested in how families process information from their environment, the influence of families' conversation orientation and conformity orientation on information processing is comparably well understood (for a summary, see Fitzpatrick & Ritchie, 1994). Essentially, children of families high in conversation (concept) orientation are more influenced by the quality of an argument (i.e., structure and quality of supporting evidence), whereas children of families high in conformity (socio) orientation are more influenced by the social status of the message source.

*Anxiety and depression.* Other psychosocial outcomes, however, are less well researched, but there is evidence that family communication patterns exert substantial influence on a variety of important psychosocial outcomes. For example, in our study of family type and conflict discussed earlier (Koerner & Fitzpatrick, 1997a), we found that conformity orientation is negatively correlated with depression, which we interpreted as the result of the greater salience of discrepancies between one's actual-self and one's ideal-self for members of families low in conformity orientation. Low conformity orientation encourages family members to define themselves independently from their families and thus to compare their actual-self to their ideal-self, whereas high conformity orientation encourages family members to define themselves in terms of their family membership, thus encouraging family members to compare their actual-self to their ought-self. According to self-discrepancy theory (Higgins, 1987), discrepancies between the actual-self and ideal-self are associated with depression, whereas discrepancies between the actual-self and the ought-self are associated with anxiety.

*Communication apprehension.* Depression and anxiety, however, are not the only psychological outcomes linked to family types. In their investigation of family communication patterns and communication apprehension, Elwood and Schrader (1998) found that conversation orientation was negatively correlated with communication apprehension across several private and public communication contexts, and that there was a curvilinear correlation between conversation orientation and communication apprehension for families low, moderate, and high in conformity orientation, respectively.

*Resiliency.* In our (Fitzpatrick & Koerner, 1996) review of literature regarding family communication and children's resiliency, we found that family communication patterns impact children's resiliency against negative environmental influences in three ways. First, different family types model different interaction strategies for their children. As a result, depending on family type, children internalize different communication behaviors, some of which are more strongly correlated with resilience than others. Generally speaking, high conversation orientation in families is associated with children's resiliency regardless of context. The impact on resiliency of children's behavior associated with conformity orientation, however, is highly context dependent. For example, in situations where the influence of an authority figure is positive, conformity orientation is associated with resiliency, whereas in situations where the influence of an authority figure is negative, conformity orientation is associated with lower resiliency.

Second, different family types hold different expectations for behavior and differ in their willingness and their means of enforcing these expectations. As a consequence, children differ in their expectations of how others should behave, their reactions to expectation violations, and their ability to learn from others how to behave. Generally speaking, children of families high in conversation orientation have better developed communication and problem solving skills, which allow them to negotiate their roles and expectations with others, making it more likely that these children function well in difficult environments. Also generally speaking, high conformity orientation has the opposite effect on children's ability to deal with others' expectations. Usually, children of these families are less flexible and cannot adapt very well to changing situations. Consequently, they do not deal well with novel and challenging situations and are less resilient than children that are more flexible and that can better adapt to novel situations.

Finally, families of the four family types also differ in their impact on their children's integration with their peers. That is, children of different family types differ in respect to their social skills, their ability to adapt to different social situations, and their ability to solicit help and assistance from their social environment. Usually, high conversation orientation of families is a benefit in this regard, because it allows children to develop the communication skills necessary to develop good relationships with their peers. The effects of conformity orientation are less clear. On the one hand, families high in conformity orientation often succeed in teaching their children the rules and norms of society and the behavior expected of them, which facilitates their children's peer relationships. On the other hand, peers might expect different behaviors, and then high conformity orientation is counterproductive in peer relationship. All in all, the evidence in regard to children's resilience suggests that children of consensual and pluralistic families are most likely to be resilient to stressors external to the family. If the stressors originate with the parents, however (e.g., abuse or alcoholism), children of pluralistic and laissez-faire families are more resilient than children of consensual and protective families.

## METHODOLOGICAL ISSUES

There are a number of methodological choices and trade-offs confronting theorists attempting to categorize families based on family members' reports on their own and their family members' communicative behavior. In this section, we discuss some of the major methodological issues we have confronted in our research on family communication patterns from both the practical and the theoretical perspectives. We begin by discussing the frequently found negative correlation between conversation orientation and conformity orientation. Then, we discuss the complex issues that arise from the potential biases in family members' perceptions of their family's communication patterns based on their own roles in the families. We then address issues relating to the dichotomization of continuous variables and to the classification of families based on small and not-representative samples. A discussion of the reliability and validity of the RFCP concludes this section.

### The Correlation of Conversation Orientation and Conformity Orientation

Conversation orientation and conformity orientation are conceptually distinct but not necessarily independent dimensions of family interaction. That is, although the conversation orientation of family is different from a family's conformity orientation, most studies using the RFCP have found small- to medium-sized negative correlations between conversation orientation and conformity orientation across families. In other words, although there are certainly families that are either high in both conversation orientation and conformity orientation or low in both, more frequently families that are high in conversation orientation tend to be low in conformity orientation and families that are high in conformity orientation tend to be low in conversation orientation.

One possible explanation for the negative correlation between conversation orientation and conformity orientation can be found in contemporary American cultural values. Most Americans value open communication in their interpersonal and familial relationships (Bellah, Madsen, Sullivan, Swidler, & Tipton, 1985), and there has been a historical trend away from authoritarian to more egalitarian parenting. As a consequence, the more a family corresponds with the cultural norm, the more likely it is that it is high in conversation orientation while being low in conformity orientation. That is, the negative correlation between conversation orientation and conformity orientation is partly the result of cultural forces.

Not all of the negative correlation between conversation orientation and conformity orientation, however, can be attributed to larger cultural factors. There are pragmatic considerations that also suggest a small negative correlation between the two dimensions as well. One pragmatic reason is that flatter hierarchical structures in groups generally require more communicative exchanges between group members. A consequence of this requirement is that whereas families high in conformity orientation, which are typically hierarchically organized, can function with minimal communication between family members, families low in conformity orientation, which typically are not hierarchically organized, cannot.

For example, for a family high in conformity orientation to make a decision does not require any interaction among family members beyond the head informing the family of the decision, because the head of the family can make that decision unilaterally. For a family low in conformity orientation, however, making a decision requires at the very least that all family members state their opinion on the issue, meaning that at least some communication will have to take place. Consequently, even if family members in low conformity families do not value communication per se (i.e., laissez-faire families), to function they must engage in communication to a greater extent than high conformity families that do not value communication (i.e., protective families). Because in the RFCP, conversation orientation is largely operationalized in terms of observable communicative behavior, families low in conformity orientation are necessarily somewhat higher in conversation orientation than families high in conformity orientation. Thus, for pragmatic reasons alone, one would expect conversation orientation and conformity orientation to be somewhat negatively correlated.

Regardless of its causes, the negative correlation between conversation orientation and conformity orientation has a few implications for data analysis that need to be considered by researchers using the RFCP. First, researchers using the RFCP to categorize individuals or families into family types based on the median split technique will find that they inflate the number of those family types where conversation orientation and conformity orientation are negatively correlated (i.e., pluralistic and protective families) and deflate the number of families where conversation orientation and conformity orientation are positively correlated (i.e., consensual and laissez-faire families). These unequal cell sizes in 2x2 ANOVAs can lead to incorrect significance tests, although most modern statistical analysis software such as SPSS or SAS automatically adjust their significance tests for unequal cell sizes.

For researchers using more powerful statistical methods such as multiple linear regression or structural equation modeling, the negative correlation between conversation orientation and conformity orientation presents the problem of multicollinearity. Although the problem of multicollinearity is fundamentally not solvable, researchers can mitigate the problems multicollinearity by analyzing the $R$-change statistic when conversation orientation and conformity orientation are entered as a block into the regression equation, and by treating the analysis of the main effects of the individual dimensions as analyses of covariance, where the other dimension is the covariate.

### Different Perspectives on Family Communication by Family Members

That family members of the same family have different perceptions of their families and their families' communicative behaviors is neither a surprising nor a new insight. In the area of family communication, for example, it has been discussed in terms of a shared versus a nonshared family communication environment for siblings. Nonetheless, the differences in how individual family members perceive and describe their families' communication patterns poses both theoretical and practical challenges for family researchers. These challenges are particularly visible to users of the RFCP because it was specifically designed to measure the perceptions of all family members.

Essentially, the problem is that when family members have divergent perceptions about their families' communication patterns, but the researcher is interested in categorizing the family to use it as unit of analysis, family classification becomes difficult. Without a compelling theoretical reason to privilege any family member's perception, the most sensible approach seems to be to take all family members' perspectives into account and to use family averages to classify families. This approach, however, rests on the theoretical assumptions that individual family members' perceptions are all equally valid and unbiased assessments of family communication patterns. As social scientist, we have to realize that this assumption is problematic.

Specifically, there is compelling empirical evidence that persons' perceptions of their families depend at least in part on their own family role (Fitzpatrick & Ritchie, 1994). Fitzpatrick and Ritchie reported data from a random survey of 328 families that indicated, for example, that mothers report their families to be much more conversation oriented than other family members, and that sons report their families to be much higher in conformity orientation than other family members (see Table 2). As a consequence, if simply the raw scores of family members are averaged, families with sons will score higher on conformity orientation than families with daughters, and families without mothers will score lower on conversation orientation.

One solution to this problem is to first transform individuals' scores on conversation orientation and conformity orientation to family role $z$-scores. To compute family role $z$-scores, one first computes the means for conversation orientation and conformity orientation for each family role. Then, for both conversation orientation and conformity orientation, one subtracts the family role means from the individual scores on the two variables and, finally, divides the difference by the standard deviations of the family role means. These $z$-scores have the property of expressing family members' perceptions of their families without any bias due to family role. That is, family scores computed based on these $z$-scores are comparable with one another, even if the composition of families is different. In addition, the $z$-score transformation also normalizes the distribution of the variables, which is beneficial for most statistical analyses. Consequently, in our research, we prefer to compute family types based on standardized scores of conformity and conversation orientation.

Family role standardization as described above removes one source of systematic bias in how family members perceive and report on their family communication patterns and increases the percentage of agreement among family members regarding their family type (Koerner & Fitzpatrick, 1997a). Standardization, however, is not the only way to address family members' divergent perspectives on family communication patterns, especially if the divergent perspectives of family members themselves are of theoretical interest. In those instances, a cluster analytical strategy that groups families together that are similar in their constellations (e.g., both parents are high in conversation and conformity orientation, and the child is high on conversation but low on conformity) might be more fruitful. Using such an approach, Ritchie and Fitzpatrick (1990) arrived at a seven family type solution that included pure protective and pluralistic family types, and five mixed types. The problem with this approach, however, is that it requires large samples, which makes it unpractical for many family researchers. In addition, without strong theoretical bases, such cluster solutions are often difficult to interpret. Finally, we found in our own research that in most cases, family members do agree largely on their perceptions of family communication patterns. Consequently, for most researchers just interested in family types who have no particular interest in investigating the effects of divergent perceptions of family members, a cluster analytical approach might prove too cumbersome to be advantageous. For researchers, however, to whom the analysis of divergent perceptions is relevant, cluster analysis might prove very beneficial.

## Continuous Dimensions and Discrete Family Types

The use of continuous dimensions such as conversation orientation and conformity orientation to create distinct family types is problematic for both conceptual and pragmatic reasons. Conceptually, to separate groups along characteristics that are continuous is always problematic because in most cases, such dividing lines are at least somewhat arbitrary. Very few people, for example,

TABLE 2
Population Means and Standard Deviations in Reported Conversation
Orientation and Conformity Orientation as a Function of Family Role Based
on a Large, Random Sample

| Family role | Conversation orientation | | | Conformity orientation | | |
|---|---|---|---|---|---|---|
| | Mean | SD | N | Mean | SD | N |
| Father | 3.65 | .41 | 211 | 2.68 | .45 | 211 |
| Mother | 3.92 | .48 | 283 | 2.62 | .44 | 283 |
| Son | 3.57 | .48 | 157 | 3.03 | .59 | 157 |
| Daughter | 3.68 | .54 | 151 | 2.85 | .56 | 151 |
| Total | 3.74 | .48 | 802 | 2.76 | .52 | 802 |

NOTE: Adapted from Fitzpatrick & Ritchie, 1994.

would argue that a man who at 5'2" is classified as short is fundamentally different from as man who at 5'3" is classified as of normal height, or that there
really is a difference between a child who with an IQ of 150 is classified as
extremely gifted and a child who with an IQ of 149 is only classified as gifted.
This problem of unclear and arbitrary separation of cases that are very similar is
amplified by classification systems that have only few broadly defined categories, such as high or low in conformity orientation. Thus, it appears that for
conceptual reasons alone, conceptually continuous variables should be measured
and operationalized as being continuous as well.

Pragmatically, to ordinalize continuous variables also creates problems for
researchers. Ordinalization of continuous variables decreases their statistical
power, and, even more important, potentially obfuscates more complex, nonlin-
ear relationships between these variables and other variables. Dichotomous variables, for example, can only have linear relationships with other variables. In
addition, the majority of statistical techniques using dichotomous independent
variables are only special cases of more general statistical techniques that use
continuous variables. For example, ANOVA is a special case of multiple linear
regression (Cohen & Cohen, 1983). It is therefore generally more useful for
researchers to use continuous variables in their statistical analyses, because to
ordinalize otherwise continuous variables is not only unnecessary, but in many
cases even detrimental to the statistical analysis.

The above argument notwithstanding, there is one very good reason to ordinalize continuous variables. If two or more independent variables consistently
interact with one another in their relationships with dependent variables, it makes
sense to ordinalize these variables and to use them to create a typology. In such
a case, simple bivariate relationships are less meaningful than the interaction of
the independent variables in their relationships with the dependent variables, and
a typology makes the interpretation of these interactions much easier. As a result,

the loss of information due to the ordinalization of continuous variables is compensated for by the gain of information from the consistent consideration of the interaction between independent variables that a typology affords. Statistically, such conceptual ordinalization is not necessarily a problem either, as long as the statistical techniques employed use continuous variables in their analysis, such as regression analysis (Cohen & Cohen, 1983). Even if statistical techniques are used that do treat such variables as ordinal (i.e., ANOVA), the loss of statistical power is often outweighed the gain in conceptual understanding.

In regard to family communication patterns, the research we reviewed thus far has shown that the two independent variables of conversation orientation and conformity orientation that define the family typology of the RFCP consistently interact with one another. Consequently, dichotomizing them to create the family typology is justified in this case. The influence that conversation orientation has on family communication is in many respects dependent on the conformity orientation of families. Similarly, the influence that conformity orientation has on family communication also depends on the conversation orientation of families. That is, for most aspects of family communication, the influence of one variable cannot be fully appreciated without considering how the family scores on the other. This creates a situation where each of the independent variables has to be discussed at different levels of the other, which in effect creates the typology. Ultimately then, the family typology created by the RFCP is not so much the result of an unwarranted ordinalization of two continuous variables, but one of conceptual and empirical necessity.

Conversation orientation and conformity orientation, however, do not always interact for all dependent variables (i.e., Koerner, 1995; Skinner & Slater, 1995). In such cases, an ordinalization of the variables makes less sense and analyses should treat both variables as continuous, both conceptually and statistically. It is important, however, to use the other family dimension as a covariate in such cases to obtain estimates of the direct and undiluted effects on the dependent variables. Both conversation orientation and conformity orientation have great influence on family communication. Because they are negatively correlated, any correlation of one of the two dimensions with a dependent variable will contain variance that is shared with the other dimension, unless this is statistically controlled for by using the other dimension as a covariate.

These infrequent instances in which conversation orientation and conformity orientation do not interact with one another in their influence on dependent variables, however, do not pose a serious threat to our family typology, as long as the majority of important outcome variables is predicted by the interaction between conversation orientation and conformity orientation. As one can observe in the research reviewed earlier in this chapter, there are some dependent variables for families that are predicted by only one of the dimensions with no interaction with the other dimension. For most dependent variables, however, the interaction exists, ultimately validating the family typology and making it meaningful.

## Classification Based on Small and None Representative Samples

In cases where a classification of families is desirable, another problem that family researchers often face is that their samples are small and often not very representative of the population at large. When families of these samples are classified based on the median split technique, any bias in the sample leads to a biased classification. For example, if researchers were to collect data from a community where the majority of families are either consensual or protective, the median split technique would wrongly classify a large number of these families as pluralistic and laissez-faire. Researchers can avoid this pitfall of small and not representative samples by basing their classification on established population means rather than the medians of their particular sample. Fortunately, Fitzpatrick and Ritchie's (1994) study involving 802 individuals from 328 families that were randomly selected from a all families with children in the public school system of a mid-sized Midwestern city provides good estimates of the true population means (see Table 2). Thus, we would advise researchers using small samples, samples drawn from untypical populations, and samples that were not randomly selected to classify the families in their samples based on the population means reported by Fitzpatrick and Ritchie (1994) rather than based on the median split technique.

## Validity of the RFCP

Reliability is a precondition for validity, and both scales of the RFCP have proved their reliability in many studies. Of the two scales, the conversation orientation subscale has consistently shown a higher reliability, with a mean reliability of alpha = .89 (range = .84–.92). The conformity orientation subscale has proved to be equally consistent in its reliability, although at a somewhat lower mean of alpha = .79 (range = .73–.87). These estimates are based on the last five published studies using the RFCP. In a study that specifically investigated the test-retest reliability of the two scales, Fitzpatrick and Ritchie (1994) reported test-retest reliability coefficients for parents and children of three different age groups after a three week period as close to 1 for conversation orientation and between .73 and .93 for conformity orientation. Based on these results, it appears safe to assert that the RFCP produces reliable measurements of conversation orientation and conformity orientation.

Although reliability is usually regarded as a necessary condition for validity, reliability alone is not sufficient to establish the validity of a measurement. In addition to a measurement's reliability, Kerlinger (1986) suggested three additional criteria to establish a measurement's validity: content validity, criterion-related validity, and construct validity. According to Kerlinger, an instrument is said to have content validity if the measurement assesses the whole breadth of the theoretical construct and if there is a close correspondence between the theoretical construct and its indicators. In the case of the RFCP, both scales ask respondents to indicate the frequency of certain behaviors of their families that correspond closely to the theoretical constructs of conversation orientation and conformity orientation. In addition, these scales also cover the full range of behaviors associated with these two communication orientations. Consequently, the RFCP has content validity.

Criterion-related validity refers to the correlations a measure has with measures of other concepts that theoretically should correlate positively or negatively with the concept measured. In other words, one assumes a measure is valid if the measure has correlations with the measures of other concepts that correspond to the theoretical correlations between the concepts. For example, if we have theoretical reasons to believe that conversation orientation should negatively correlate with conflict avoidance, we would assume that measures of conversation orientation and conflict avoidance are valid if they indeed have the negative correlation predicted by theory. A caveat is that if researchers were to establish criterion validity by observing the same correlations they use to test hypotheses, they would fall victim to tautological reasoning (i.e., I supported my predictions, therefore my measures are valid; and I failed to support my predictions, therefore my measures are invalid). Kerlinger (1986) therefore suggested establishing criterion validity through a measure's correlations with measurements of other concepts that are not central to the theoretical model tested in a particular study.

In the case of the RFCP, the family types and the dimensions underlying the family typology have shown that they correlate with measures of theoretically related constructs. Fitzpatrick and Ritchie (1994) have shown that the RFCP dimensions correlate with the dimensions of the old Family Communications Pattern instrument (McLeod & Chaffee, 1972) and with scores on Fitzpatrick's Relational Dimension Inventory (Fitzpatrick, 1988). High correlations between the dimensions of the FCP and the dimensions of the RFCP alone do not establish the validity of the RFCP, of course. After all, all 11 original items of the FCP are still part of the 26 items of the RFCP, and even though they were in some cases substantially reworded, one would expect scales that contain identical and very similar items to correlate. What the high correlations do show, however, is that the revisions did not change the essential content of the scales, that is, they measure very similar concepts.

That Fitzpatrick and Ritchie (1994) found the theoretically predicted correlations between family communication patterns and parents' scores on the RDI is more significant support for the criterion-related validity of the RFCP. The RDI and the RFCP measure very different types of behavior and contain very different items. Consequently, any correlation between the scales can only be due to a correlation between the concepts that the two instruments measure. Similarly strong evidence for criterion-related validity, however, comes from a number of studies that have successfully employed the RFCP in research and correlated the dimensions to a variety of measures of other concepts. Because these studies often found the theoretically predicted correlations between the RFCP and the measures of other concepts, they provide strong evidence for the criterion-related validity of the RFCP. It is just too unlikely that these theoretically predicted correlations would have been observed in so many cases if the RFCP would not validly measure the concepts it supposes to measure.

Construct validity of a measure is the final of Kerlinger's (1986) three criterions for a measure's validity and refers to the extent to which the measure is based on theory and the measure's observed correlations are explained by theory. In other words, the construct validity of a measure is high if the concept it measures is part of a coherent and convincingly presented theoretical model that goes beyond the mere definition of its concepts. As was the case with the two forms of validity discussed earlier, the evidence of the construct validity of the RFCP is cumulatively provided by the sum total of the research conducted using the RFCP rather than by one specific finding. The RFCP and its two scales have been theoretically derived and are based on the large research tradition involving the FCP and family research that has looked at very closely related constructs. Consequently, the RFCP has a strong theoretical foundation, and the mechanisms by which conversation orientation and conformity orientation exert their influence on family communication and its outcomes are usually well explicated and fit into the larger picture of family communication that has emerged from research based on a variety of theoretical models and approaches. Because of this, it appears that there is good evidence for the construct validity of the RFCP. Ultimately, however, it will be the scientific community that, through its acceptance or rejection of the RFCP and the theory behind it, will pass judgment on the validity of the RFCP.

## CONCLUSION

In this chapter, we have presented the case for examining the variability of family life in terms of family communication behaviors and beliefs that family members hold about conversation orientation and conformity orientation in their families. We have discussed the RFCP as the instrument to measure conversation orientation and conformity orientation in families, and we addressed a number of practical issues relating to the use of the RFCP in the study of family communication. We have presented evidence that suggests that the resulting family typology is capable of describing and explaining family communication behaviors and a wide range of relevant outcomes for families and for individual family members. Some of these outcomes are closely linked to family communication behaviors, and others go far beyond that what we customarily associated with, and explain by, family communication behaviors.

The typology based on family communication patterns describes families in a clear and consistent manner that is related to other attempts to classify various aspects of the family, but that also goes beyond that what was achieved previously. For example, in her classic paper, Baumrind (1971a, 1971b) describes three major types of parenting styles based on observations of parents with four-year-old children that fit nicely with our typology of family communication patterns. Her authoritative parents (moderately controlling but highly supportive) are similar to parents in consensual families, for they direct the activities of the child but allow a reasonable give-and-take as they explain the reasons behind their various suggestions or decisions regarding their children's behaviors. Baumrind's authoritarian parents are similar to parents in protective families. They issue orders and demand compliance from the children without giving the children very much of an explanation for their demands and without caring much for their children's input on the issues. Baumrind's permissive parents are similar to parents in pluralistic families. Permissive parents are very supportive of their children and require little compliance from their children and make few demands. There is no description of a fourth type of parenting that would correspond to parents in laissez-faire families. From our knowledge of family types, however, it is easy to predict that these parents are similar to Baumrind's permissive parents, although without being as supportive of their children.

Despite this conceptual overlap, the descriptions and predictions possible in the family communication patterns paradigm, however, allows for replication and extension in a manner not possible with purely descriptive systems such as Baumrind's (1971a, 1971b) typology of parenting styles. For example, family communication patterns have been shown to be predictive of a variety of communication behaviors as diverse as self-orientation at the level of individual speech acts (Koerner & Cvancara, in press) and conflict coping strategies in future romantic relationships of adult children (Koerner & Fitzpatrick, 1997b). The dimensions and the family types of the RFCP predict how families interact during conflict episodes (Koerner & Fitzpatrick, 1997a), as well as how individuals and families respond to stressor within and outside the family (Fitzpatrick & Koerner, 1996). Particularly noteworthy is the ability of the typology to predict actual sequences of communicative behaviors, such as withdraw-demand patterns in conflict interactions (Koerner & Fitzpatrick, 1997b) or different family types' responses to self-disclosure (Koerner, 1995). That is, because the model of family communication patterns is based as much on theoretical as on empirical evidence, it is linked to much more than just the communication behaviors it describes.

The typology of family communication patterns has prescriptive power in that it can differentiate among various positive and negative outcomes for individuals and families. The designation of health and pathology, however, is a minefield that must be negotiated carefully. We have had some success in relating the types to the incidence of depression and conflicts (Koerner, 1995), but only a good deal of future research on a wide variety of populations across ethnic, racial and class lines can confirm the typology's success in that realm.

By considering cognition and behavior simultaneously, the model of family communication patterns also address issues of *intersubjectivity* and *interactivity*, which Fitzpatrick and Ritchie (1993) identified as core theoretical issues for the understanding of human communication in general, and family communication in particular. Intersubjectivity refers to the sharing of cognition (i.e., participants have identical or at least very similar beliefs, attitudes, etc.) among participants in a communicative event, whereas interactivity refers to the communicative process of symbol creation and interpretation (Fitzpatrick & Ritchie, 1993). Thus, for families, interactivity refers to the ways in which families maintain their own structures through patterns of the family members' responses to each others' communicative acts. Because family communication takes place simultaneously within the social unit of family and between the individual family members who can also be considered independent cognitive units, both intersubjectivity and interactivity are of interest to scholars of family communication. Consequently, an adequate theoretical model of family communication must account for both intersubjectivity and interactivity. That is, it must contain a cognitive element that accounts for intersubjectivity, and a social element that explains how family members create, shape, and maintain the social unit through their responses to each other's actions.

Accounting for both intersubjectivity and interactivity in one theoretical model is a greater challenge than it appears from the outside, because interactivity does not necessarily imply intersubjectivity. In fact, even if absolutely no intersubjectivity is assumed, interactivity will be high if individuals (a) base their own actions on their predictions of other individuals' actions and (b) alter those predictions according to their observations of what other individuals actually do (Fitzpatrick & Ritchie, 1993). In other words, although interactivity requires cognitive representations of others (including their behavior, motives, responses, etc.), these representations do not necessarily have to be shared with the others to be functional, as long as the cognitive representations lead to comparable predictions of the others' behaviors. For example, the parents might believe that they punish their child because she endangered herself by staying out beyond her curfew, whereas the child believes she is punished for breaking the parents' order. This lack of intersubjectivity must not mean that families cannot function properly, because it does not lead the parents and her daughter to different expectations and behaviors (i.e., the child accepting the punishment from the parents). Thus, interaction alone does not presuppose intersubjectivity. It is only when cognition and behavior are truly interdependent, as we propose they are in the model of family communication patterns, that interactivity can explain intersubjectivity.

In light of the obvious advancement that the theoretical model of family communication patterns represent in the area of family communication, there are many more opportunities for future research utilizing the theoretical model and the RFCP. Among the many areas that have not been investigated from the perspective of family communication patterns but where we think that such an investigation would generate interesting results are sibling relationships, interactions in blended and other nontraditional families, and cross-cultural comparisons of families, to name just a few.

Two different but interrelated topics form the template for our own future research. First, we will continue to develop different methodological techniques to study the systematic variations in family communication. We have had some success in developing interaction scenarios to present to children too young or otherwise unable to read in order to identify their family type (Fitzpatrick, Marshall, Leutwiler, & Krcmar, 1996), and we are also working on identifying representative examples from popular culture that can aid respondents in identifying their family types. In addition, we are working on interactive and World-Wide-Web-based versions of the RFCP. In an initial study, we were able to obtain data from families in Singapore and Indonesia through these means. Clearly, the opportunity to study families world wide relatively simply and inexpensively presents a great opportunity.

Second, we will further examine the issue of intersubjectivity and shared meaning in families. Specifically, we will try to answer the question whether the four types of family communication patterns actually reflect some type of family communication schemata as we proposed here and elsewhere (see, Koerner & Fitzpatrick, in press), or whether they are the result of some other processes. A closely related question that we will pursue regards the extent to which meaning is shared in families and how the extent of shared meaning affects the nature of family communication and other, related processes. Hypotheses that we will be testing in this regard are that the greater the sharing of meaning, the less the need for explicit verbal communication on relevant topics, because speakers and listeners have less need to elaborate and to explain themselves to each other when the schema is shared. In addition, we would also expect that the greater the sharing of the schema, the less the need family members have to consider alternative views. That is, shared schemas lead to reduced amounts of communication, while increasing its efficiency.

Understanding communication in the family is central to explaining the postmodern family, and research in the area of family communication has made tremendous strides in understanding and explaining family communication. The model of family communication patterns as measured by the RFCP has guided our own research and that of our colleagues and has produced some very impressive results that greatly have aided our understanding of families and their communication. In our experience, the family typology represents a powerful tool in predicting and explaining the dynamic process of human communication, and we expect it to be useful for a long time to come.

# APPENDIX

## The Revised Family Communication Pattern Instrument (Children's Version)

*Conversation orientation*

1) In our family we often talk about topics like politics and religion where some persons disagree with others.
2) My parents often say something like "Every member of the family should have some say in family decisions."
3) My parents often ask my opinion when the family is talking about something.
4) My parents encourage me to challenge their ideas and beliefs.
5) My parents often say something like "You should always look at both sides of an issue."
6) I usually tell my parents what I am thinking about things.
7) I can tell my parents almost anything.
8) In our family we often talk about our feelings and emotions.
9) My parents and I often have long, relaxed conversations about nothing in particular.
10) I really enjoy talking with my parents, even when we disagree.
11) My parents encourage me to express my feelings.
12) My parents tend to be very open about their emotions.
13) We often talk as a family about things we have done during the day.
14) In our family, we often talk about our plans and hopes for the future.
15) My parents like to hear my opinion, even when I don't agree with them.

*Conformity orientation*

1) When anything really important is involved, my parents expect me to obey without question.
2) In our home, my parents usually have the last word.
3) My parents feel that it is important to be the boss.
4) My parents sometimes become irritated with my views if they are different from theirs.
5) If my parents don't approve of it, they don't want to know about it.
6) When I am at home, I am expected to obey my parents' rules.
7) My parents often say things like "You'll know better when you grow up."
8) My parents often say things like "My ideas are right and you should not question them."
9) My parents often say things like "A child should not argue with adults."
10 ) My parents often say things like "There are some things that just shouldn't be talked about."
11) My parents often say things like "You should give in on arguments rather than risk making people mad."

## The Revised Family Communication Pattern Instrument (Parent's Version)

*Conversation orientation*

1) In our family we often talk about topics like politics and religion where some persons disagree with others.
2) I often say things like "Every member of the family should have some say in family decisions."
3) I often ask my child's opinion when the family is talking about something.
4) I encourage my child to challenge my ideas and beliefs.
5) I often say things like "You should always look at both sides of an issue."

6) My child usually tells me what s/he is thinking about things.
7) My child can tell me almost anything.
8) In our family we often talk about our feelings and emotions.
9) My child and I often have long, relaxed conversations about nothing in particular.
10) I think my child really enjoys talking with me, even when we disagree.
11) I encourage my child to express his/her feelings.
12) I tend to be very open about my emotions.
13) We often talk as a family about things we have done during the day.
14) In our family, we often talk about our plans and hopes for the future.
15) I like to hear my child's opinion, even when s/he doesn't agree with me.

*Conformity orientation*

1) When anything really important is involved, I expect my child to obey me without question.
2) In our home, the parents usually have the last word.
3) I feel that it is important for the parents to be the boss.
4) I sometimes become irritated with my child's views if they are different from mine.
5) If I don't approve of it, I don't want to know about it.
6) When my child is at home, it is expected to obey the parents' rules.
7) I often say things like "You'll know better when you grow up."
8) I often say things like "My ideas are right and you should not question them."
9) I often say things like "A child should not argue with adults."
10 ) I often say things like "There are some things that just shouldn't be talked about."
11) I often say things like "You should give in on arguments rather than risk making people mad."

# REFERENCES

Baumrind, D. (1971a). Current patterns of parental authority. *Developmental Psychology, 4*(1, part 2), 1–103.

Baumrind, D. (1971b). Harmonious parents and their preschool children. *Developmental Psychology, 4*(1, part 1), 99–102.

Baxter, L. A., & Clark, C. L. (1996). Perceptions of family communication patterns and the enactment of family rituals. *Western Journal of Communication, 60,* 254–268.

Bellah, R. N., Madsen, R., Sullivan, W. M., Swidler, A., & Tipton, S. M. (1985). *Habits of the heart.* New York: Haper & Row.

Berger, P., & Luckmann, T. (1967). *The social construction of reality.* New York: Anchor Books.

Burleson, B. R., Delia, J. G., & Applegate, J. L. (1995). The socialization of person-centered communication: Parents' contributions to their children's social-cognitive and communication skills. In M. A. Fitzpatrick & A. Vangelisti (Eds.), *Explaining family interactions* (pp. 34–76). Thousand Oaks, CA: Sage.

Christensen, A., & Arrington, A. (1987). Research issues and strategies. In T. Jacob (Ed.), *Family interaction and psychopathology* (pp. 259–296). New York: Plenum.

Christensen, A., & Sullaway, M. (1984). *Communication patterns questionnaire.* Unpublished manuscript, University of California, Los Angeles.

Cohen, J., & Cohen, P. (1983) *Applied multiple regression/correlation analysis for the behavioral sciences* (2nd ed.). Hillsdale, NJ: Erlbaum.

Elwood, T. D., & Schrader, D. C. (1998). Family communication patterns and communication apprehension. *Journal of Social Behavior and Personality, 13,* 493–502.

Fitzpatrick, M. A. (1988). *Between husbands and wives: Communication in marriage.* Newbury Park, CA: Sage.

Fitzpatrick, M. A., & Koerner, A. F. (1996, July). *Family communication schemata and social functions of communication*. Paper presented at the International Research Colloquium on Communication Research, Moscow, Russia.

Fitzpatrick, M. A., Marshall, L. J., Leutwiler, T. J., & Krcmar, M. (1996). The effect of family communication environments on children's social behavior during middle childhood. *Communication Research, 23*, 379–406.

Fitzpatrick, M. A., & Ritchie, L. D. (1993). Communication theory and the family. In P. G. Boss, W. J. Doherty, W. R. Schumm, & S. K. Steinmetz (Eds.), *Sourcebook of family theories and methods: A contextual approach* (pp. 565–585). New York: Plenum Press.

Fitzpatrick, M. A., & Ritchie, L. D. (1994). Communication schemata within the family: Multiple perspectives on family interaction. *Human Communication Research, 20*, 275–301.

Higgins, E. T. (1987). Self-discrepancy: A theory relating self and affect. *Psychological Review, 94* (3), 319–340.

Kerlinger, F. N. (1986). *Foundations of behavioral research* (3rd ed.). Fort Worth, TX: Harcourt Brace Jovanovich.

Koerner, A. F. (1995, November). *Family communication patterns: Differences in collectivistic and individualistic families*. Paper presented at the annual conference of the Speech Communication Association, San Antonio, TX.

Koerner, A. F., & Cvancara, K. E. (in press). The influence of conformity orientation on communication patterns in family conversations. *Journal of Communication*.

Koerner, A. F., & Fitzpatrick, M. A. (1997a). Family type and conflict: The impact of conversation orientation and conformity orientation on conflict in the family. *Communication Studies, 48*, 59–75.

Koerner, A. F., & Fitzpatrick, M. A. (1997b, May). *You never leave your family in a fight: The impact of families of origins on conflict-behavior in romantic relationships*. Paper presented at the annual conference of the International Communication Association, Montreal, Canada.

McLeod, J. M., & Chaffee, S. H. (1972). The construction of social reality. In J. Tedeschi (Ed.), *The social influence process* (pp. 50–59). Chicago: Aldine-Atherton.

Noller, P. (1995). Parent-adolescent relationships. In M. A. Fitzpatrick & A. Vangelisti (Eds.), *Explaining family interactions* (pp. 77–111). Thousand Oaks, CA: Sage.

Noller, P., & Fitzpatrick, M. A. (1993). *Communication in family relationships*. Englewood Cliffs, NJ: Prentice Hall.

Patterson, J. M., & McCubbin, H. I. (1991). A-COPE: Adolescent coping orientation for problem experiences. In H. I. Hamilton & J. M. McCubbin (Eds.) *Family assessment inventories for research and practice* (2nd ed., pp. 234–250). Madison: University of Wisconsin.

Reiss, D. (1981). *The family's construction of reality*. Cambridge, MA: Harvard University Press.

Ritchie, D. L. (1991). Family communication patterns: An epistemic analysis and conceptual reinterpretation. *Communication Research, 18*, 548–565.

Ritchie, D. L. (1997). Parents' workplace experiences and family communication patterns. *Communication Research, 24*, 175–187.

Ritchie, L. D., & Fitzpatrick, M. A. (1990). Family communication patterns: Measuring interpersonal perceptions of interpersonal relationships. *Communication Research, 17*, 523–544.

Segrin, C., & Fitzpatrick, M. A. (1991). Depression and verbal aggressiveness in different marital couples. *Communication Studies, 43*, 79–91.

Skinner, E. R., & Slater, M. R. (1995). Family communication patterns, rebelliousness, and adolescent reactions to anti-drugs PSAs. *Journal of Drug Education, 25*(4), 343–355.

Stiles, W. B. (1992). *Describing talk: A taxonomy of verbal response modes*. Newbury Park, CA: Sage.

# CHAPTER CONTENTS

• Affection Plays a Significant Role in Interpersonal          72
   Relationships

• Affection Is an Underlying Dimension of Interpersonal          73
   Relationships

• Affection Is the Need for Positive Regard From Another          74
   and the Feeling of Positive Regard for Another,
   Communicated Through Affectionate Behaviors, Found
   in Relationships Ranging From Acquaintance to Intimate

• Affectionate Behaviors Are Many and Varied          80

• Six Major Factors Influence Affectionate Communication          81

• Both Biology and the Environment Influence          91
   the Development of Affectionate Communication Patterns

• Social Exchange Theories Help Explain the Process          94
   of Affectionate Communication

• Affection Has Been Measured as a Need or Behavior          95

• Conclusion          103

• Appendix          104

• References          106

# 3 Affection in Interpersonal Relationships: Not Just "A Fond or Tender Feeling"

SUE D. PENDELL
*Colorado State University*

Affection is the need for positive regard from another and the feeling of positive regard for another, communicated through affectionate behaviors, that occurs in relationships ranging from acquaintance to intimate. It plays a significant role in child development, parenting, couple relationships, adult well-being, and elder health. It is crucial to our existence and an underlying dimension of interpersonal relationships. This essay reviews the extensive literature on affection, looking at the importance of affection and its place as a dimension of relationships. It provides a definition of affection, discusses how affection relates to associated concepts, summarizes the wide range of behaviors classified as affectionate, considers the factors influencing affectionate communication, traces the development of affectionate communication patterns in individuals, summarizes theories that help explain affectionate communication, and examines instruments used to measure affection. It concludes with suggestions for expanding our knowledge of the process of affectionate communication.

Recent research in several disciplines indicates the importance and role of affection in interpersonal relationships. In communication, affection has been related to warmth as a social emotion (Andersen & Guerrero, 1998), studied in relation to liking (Floyd & Burgoon, 1999; Floyd & Voloudakis, 1999; Morman & Floyd, 1998), examined as part of the experience of intimacy (Marston, Hecht, Manke, McDaniel, & Reeder, 1998), discussed as an interpersonal communication motive (Rubin & Martin, 1998), and included in a developmental model of intimacy (Solomon, 1997). In family and human development, researchers have examined adolescent affection (Eberly & Montemayor, 1998, 1999), studied caregiver affection (Mill & Romano-White, 1999), investigated perception of parental acceptance-rejection including affection (Kuterovac-

AUTHOR'S NOTE: The author would like to thank Peter Andersen and the reviewers for their assistance.

Correspondence: Sue D. Pendell, Department of Speech Communication, 209 Eddy, Colorado State University, Fort Collins, CO 80523-1783; email: Sue.Pendell@colostate.edu.

Jagodic & Kerestes, 1997), examined the effects of affection on help and support in families (Parrott & Bengtson, 1999), looked at the role of affection in relation to filial piety (Koyano, 1996; Sung, 1998), examined the influence of Alzheimer's disease of a spouse on affection and sexuality in couples (Wright, 1998), and found affection to be a crucial dimension of positive parenting (Russell, 1997). In psychology, affection has been investigated in terms of reciprocity (Gaines, 1997), gender differences in love (Murstein & Tuerkheimer, 1998), intimacy and need fulfillment in couple relationships (Prager & Buhrmester, 1998), public displays of affection (Regan, Jerry, Narvaez, & Johnson, 1999), and as part of a model of social well-being that includes affection as an instrumental goal (Ormel, Lindenberg, Steverink, & Verbrugge, 1999). Even popular writing considers variations on ways to communicate affection (Kelleher, 1998; Mathias-Riegel, 1999).

## AFFECTION PLAYS A SIGNIFICANT ROLE IN INTERPERSONAL RELATIONSHIPS

Evidence for the importance of affection is overwhelming in child development, parenting, couple relationships, adult well-being, and elder health. Research on the development of children concludes that affection, or its lack, has an impact particularly on self-esteem and the ability to demonstrate caring and affection (Castiglia, 1999). Research on neonatal handling suggests that physical affection with young children helps them develop into well-adjusted adults (Sapolsky, 1997). Affection is especially important for the healthy development of children (Barber & Thomas, 1986; Compton & Niemeyer, 1994; Mackinnon, Henderson, & Andrews, 1993; Oatley & Jenkins, 1996; Oliver, Raftery, Reeb, & Delaney, 1993; Prescott, cited in Wallace, 1981; Twardosz & Nordquist, 1983; Vega et al., 1996; and Villard, 1976), and the importance of affection for children is further emphasized by the National Association for the Education of Young Children's accreditation standards, which include consideration of caregivers' warmth (Mill & Romano-White, 1999, p. 157). Affection even has been called the "key to socialization" (Oatley & Jenkins, 1996, p. 290).

Affection is integral to a successful parent-child relationship (Barber & Thomas, 1986; Floyd & Morman, 1998; MacDonald, 1992; Parrott & Bengtson, 1999; Prescott & Wallace, 1978; Quinn, 1983; Rubin & Martin, 1998; Russell, 1997; Villard, 1976) and the most important interactional type affecting the relationship of couples (Dainton, 1994, 1998; Parrott & Bengtson, 1999). It is related to marital adjustment (Spanier, 1976; Waring, McElrath, Lefcoe, & Weisz, 1981) and marital satisfaction (Liederman, 1991; Schultz & Schultz, 1987; Stuart, 1989; Thomas-Brown, 1996; Villard, 1976). Also, there is a link between affection and satisfaction in groups (Anderson & Martin, 1995; Rubin & Martin, 1998; Schutz, 1958) and organizational commitment (Rubin & Martin, 1998).

In adults, affection contributes to psychological well-being (Downs & Javidi, 1990; Green & Wildermuth, 1993; Prager & Buhrmester, 1998; Rubin & Martin,

1998; Villard, 1976), self-esteem (Barber & Thomas, 1986; Roberts & Bengtson, 1996), interpersonal competence and relationship satisfaction (Oliver, 1981; Rubin & Martin, 1998; Rubin, Perse, & Barbato, 1988), and the ability to build and maintain intimate relationships (Bell & Healey, 1992; Dainton, Stafford, & Canary, 1994; Knapp & Vangelisti, 1996). In elders, affection is associated with greater life satisfaction and more interpersonal interaction (Barbato & Perse, 1992; Downs & Javidi, 1990), psychological well-being (Quinn, 1983), and satisfactory relationships with caregivers (Parsons, Cox, & Kimboko, 1989). Mathias-Riegel (1999) reports that affectionate behavior is more crucial to elders' happiness than sex (p. 48). Lack of affection can lead to depression (Mackinnon et al., 1993; Oliver et al., 1993; Vega et al., 1996), loneliness (Downs & Javidi, 1990), and dysfunctional relationships (Prescott & Wallace, 1978).

In sum, affection is crucial to our emotional, mental, and physical health and our relationships. It enables positive parenting and child development, helps us to be well-adjusted individuals, and draws us together creatively in cooperation. It makes us secure, confident, competent, and happy adults.

## AFFECTION IS AN UNDERLYING DIMENSION
## OF INTERPERSONAL RELATIONSHIPS

Consistently, affection is found to be an underlying dimension of interpersonal relationships. Oatley and Jenkins (1996) argue that there are two fundamental facts or modes of social interaction, two dimensions "that allow us to locate ourselves at any moment in interpersonal geography" (p. 286): affection/status (cooperation with and acceptance of another) and aggression/dominance/power (controlling another). They describe these as the "fundamental explanatory concepts in understanding human interaction" (p. 286). Gaines (1996) says, "Two major psychological axes—the tendency to give affection to others and the tendency to give respect to others—have been identified by a number of researchers as underlying general patterns of interpersonal behavior" (p. 244). According to MacDonald (1992), "the dimension of parent-child warmth has emerged independently in several factor-analytic studies of parenting performed over the last 35 years" (p. 754). Warmth in these studies is empirically defined as high affection, positive reinforcement, responsiveness, and acceptance, the opposite of hostility, rejection, and coldness (p. 754).

Research on people's conceptions of the similarities and differences in social relationships yields two primary dimensions of relationships: affection and control (Fiske, 1991, p. 36). Affection is also called friendliness, solidarity, affiliation, sociability, and intimacy, and it has two poles: cooperative and friendly versus competitive and hostile, warm-agreeable versus cold-quarrelsome, or devoted-indulgent/cooperative-helpful/friendly versus rancorous-sadistic/antagonistic-harmful/hostile (p. 36). In a summary of research on interpersonal models to 1980, Oliver (1981) says, "there is strong empirical evidence that interpersonal behavior can be considered in terms of a two-dimensional model . . . 'Dominance-Submission' and 'Affection-Hostility'" (p. 16). After summarizing the findings of 23 reviews and studies of interpersonal behavior, Millar, Rogers-Millar, and Villard (1978) say, "a common conclusion has been that major portions of interpersonal behavior fall along one of two dimensions: control (dominance/submission) and affection (emotional closeness/farness)" (pp. 2–3). Villard (1976) cites 20 studies that identify the control and affection dimensions of relationships (pp. 4–5).

In a study of marital relationships, Huston and Vangelisti (1991) found three types of socioemotional behavior including affection, sexual interest, and negativity (p. 721). According to Schutz (1958), "every individual has three interpersonal needs: inclusion, control, and affection" (p. 13), and the existence of these three needs is supported by a large number of studies of interpersonal behavior (p. 34). Rubin et al. (1988) found support for Schutz's Fundamental Interpersonal Relations Orientation (FIRO) theory of inclusion, control, and affection (p. 620), although Fisher, Macrosson, and Walker (1995), in a factor analysis of FIRO-B data obtained from teams as well as a review of other factor analyses, reformulated Schutz's (1958) constructs of inclusion and affection into warmth (p. 203). Warmth, they say, appears to equate with affiliation but is not the same as intimacy (p. 203).

In a review of the literature concerning why people communicate, Rubin et al. (1988) found offering affection to others to be one of 18 motives identified from television-viewing and the interpersonal literature. Their study found that affection as a motive accounted for 11.5% of the total variance of why their respondents communicated with each (p. 615). In their classic article, Burgoon and Hale (1984) synthesized an extensive amount of literature to arrive at a set of 12 "conceptually distinct dimensions" of relational communication, including affection-hostility (p. 193). Clearly, affection is a key component of interpersonal relationships. The lack of consistency in labeling the affection dimension likely is related to the inconsistency in definitions of affection and its associated terms.

AFFECTION IS THE NEED FOR POSITIVE REGARD FROM ANOTHER, AND THE FEELING OF POSITIVE REGARD FOR ANOTHER, COMMUNICATED THROUGH AFFECTIONATE BEHAVIORS, FOUND IN RELATIONSHIPS RANGING FROM ACQUAINTANCE TO INTIMATE

Although the term *affection* often is used in a limited way, the literature shows it is actually an extensive concept involving components of need, feeling, and behavior, related to other concepts including affinity, altruism, caring, immediacy, intimacy/closeness, liking, ritual, social support, and warmth.

Affection Is a Human Need

Affection as a concept has considerable overlap with Maslow's belongingness and love need (Ormel et al., 1999; Knapp & Vangelisti, 1996). Maslow (1987) defines that need as "giving and receiving affection" (p. 20), the need to relate to other people, for companionship and association with others. Similarly, Prager and Buhrmester (1998), in a cluster analysis of human needs, classified affection/love as a communal need, satisfied through interaction and partnership with another (p. 441). Schutz (1958) discusses affection as an interpersonal need, defined behaviorally as establishing and maintaining satisfactory relations with others and defined at the level of the self-concept as the feeling that the self is lovable (p. 20). Rubin and Martin (1998) say it is "the need to achieve or maintain mutual support of and connection with others" (p. 293), based in the need for affiliation with love as the goal (pp. 290–291).

Affection Is a Feeling

Affection frequently is defined as a feeling or emotion (Floyd & Voloudakis, 1997; Oatley & Jenkins, 1996; Schutz, 1992; Twardosz & Nordquist, 1983), the emotional acceptance of another (Foa & Foa, 1974; Gaines, 1996), and being able to love another (Schutz, 1958). Even dictionaries define affection as a fond and tender feeling toward another (Morris, 1969; *Webster's New Collegiate*, 1979). As a feeling, it is an internal emotional experience.

Affection Involves Positive Regard

This internal emotional experience of affection is perhaps best described as one of positive regard (Castiglia, 1999; Floyd & Morman, 1998; Huston & Vangelisti, 1991), a concept popularized by Rogers (1951, 1959) as a key component of his humanistic approach to interpersonal communication (Cissna & Anderson, 1990, pp. 134, 136–137). "Positive regard means to feel the other is of value, and to communicate an acceptance of the other" (Cissna & Anderson, 1990, p. 136); it is "to experience one-self as making a positive difference in the experiential field of another" and to be experienced by another as making a positive difference in her or his experiential field (Rogers, 1959, p. 208). Affection, then, is both the need for acceptance and confirmation from another and the feeling of acceptance and confirmation for another.

Affection Is Communicated Through Behavior

Affection also involves the expression of feelings; that is, it is communicated through behavior (Castiglia, 1999; Floyd & Morman, 1998; Floyd & Voloudakis, 1997; Liederman, 1991; Ormel et al., 1999; Twardosz & Nordquist, 1983), so affectionate communication is a set of behaviors through which the feeling or experience of affection is revealed. If an affectionate feeling is present but no affectionate behavior is used, then the communication of affection has not occurred (Twardosz & Nordquist, 1983).

Because communicating affection involves revealing personally private information about feelings to another, it constitutes self-disclosure (Derlega, Metts, Petronio, & Margulis, 1993; Villard, 1976), with self-disclosure's inherent risks as well as rewards. These risks include the relational partner misinterpreting the affectionate behavior (Floyd & Morman, 2000; Villard & Whipple, 1976); the interpretation of the behavior as inappropriate for the relationship, the context/situation, or other factors (Floyd & Morman, 1997; Floyd & Morman, 2000); violation of personal expectations (Floyd & Voloudakis, 1997); lack of reciprocity (Floyd & Burgoon, 1999); setting up an expectation the relational partner may not want to or cannot meet (Floyd & Burgoon, 1999; Derlega et al., 1993); hurting the other person (Derlega et al., 1993); and a perception of ulterior motives (i.e., deception, manipulation, or another negative purpose; Booth-Butterfield & Trotta, 1994; Derlega et al., 1993). These risks may result in the relational partner giving the information to people we don't know or like (Derlega et al., 1993); avoiding or not liking us anymore (Derlega et al., 1993); ridiculing, rejecting, or exploiting us (Derlega et al., 1993); or we may be embarrassed, hurt, or lose face (Floyd & Burgoon, 1999). Ultimately, the relationship may suffer or terminate. Consequently, a communicator weighs the rewards of relationship development and maintenance as well as personal development against the risks of relationship deterioration and possible termination as well as personal damage in deciding whether or not to communication affection.

In addition to the communication of affection being a type of self-disclosure, self-disclosure is a type of affectionate communication. As such, it can be genuine or apparent (Miller & Steinberg, 1975). Genuine self-disclosure occurs when people provide information they consider personally private, that is, information they do not share with most people, for reasons of personal or relational growth (p. 321). Apparent self-disclosure, on the other hand, occurs when people provide information that others might consider personally private but the discloser does not, that is, information they are willing to disclose to almost anyone but most people are not (p. 321). In addition, apparent self-disclosure is manipulative; it may be to shock, embarrass, hurt, secure an advantage, elicit personal information, and so forth (p. 321). The key to distinguishing whether an instance of self-disclosure is genuine or apparent is whether or not the information would generally be considered appropriate or inappropriate to disclose, given the relationship between the people involved and the context/situation (pp. 321–322). Clearly, affectionate behavior, as self-disclosure, can be genuine or apparent.

Similarly, LaFrance and Mayo (1978) discuss how "people both express inner states *and* manage their behavior in order to *appear* to be feeling certain things [italics added]" (p. 32). They label the former *representation* and the latter *presentation*. Representation includes genuine expression of affection; presentation includes apparent expression of affection in a performance, "an arrangement and appearance designed to be seen" (p. 32). Genuine expression of affection also falls into Patterson's (1988) function of intimacy expression, whereas apparent expression of affection is presenting an image, that is, self-presentation or relationship presentation (p. 48). Patterson (1988, p. 54) gives the example of a quarreling couple who hold hands and smile while at a social gathering to give the audience the impression of relational harmony, rather than actually expressing affection to each other (intimacy expression) or showing off who they are with to increase their positive face (relationship presentation).

### Affection Occurs in Interpersonal Relationships

Affection occurs particularly but not exclusively in relationships that are closer and more intimate (Andersen, 1999; Ormel et al., 1999; Prager, 1995; Twardosz & Nordquist, 1983). Schutz (1958) defines affection as establishing and maintaining satisfactory relations with others and says that "affection always refers, to a two-person (dyadic) relation" (p. 20). Millar et al. (1978) say that affection exists within a relational system (p. 11).

### Affection Is Related to a Number of Other Interpersonal Concepts

The term "affection" is used synonymously with, considered characteristic of, or defined by other terms including affinity, altruism, caring, immediacy, intimacy/closeness, liking, ritual, social support (including comforting behaviors), and warmth.

*Affinity* is defined as liking and feeling positive toward someone, as is the feeling component of affection, and its strategies include several that overlap with behaviors that communicate affection (Richmond, Gorham, & Furio, 1987). *Altruism* is "cooperative, constructive, and felicitous social behavior" (Oliver, 1981, p. 4), which includes affection, the "acceptance of and care for others" (p. 4). *Caring* is used to define affection and vice versa (Mackinnon et al., 1993; Parker, Tupling, & Brown, 1979; Rubin et al., 1988), although caring, as a feeling, appears closer in meaning to affinity, whereas affection also includes a behavioral component (Rubin et al., 1988).

*Immediacy's* relationship to affection is complex. Knapp and Vangelisti (1996) define immediacy as the degree of liking between communicators and list immediacy behaviors that are synonymous with affectionate behaviors (p. 71). To Andersen (1999), immediacy involves warmth, closeness, and involvement with others (p. 187), which could be a definition of affection, and his list of immediacy behaviors includes affectionate behaviors (pp. 190–203). Floyd and Voloudakis (1997) define responses to affectionate behavior as including immediacy and report that when confederates in an experiment increased their affectionate behavior they significantly increased their immediacy (p. 23). Burgoon, Buller, and Woodall (1996) consider immediacy behaviors as particularly significant to communication of affection (pp. 324–326). If immediacy indicates a degree of liking, then affection would be felt and communicated when immediacy is high, so the terms may be synonymous. Immediacy may be conceptualized as behaviors that communicate attraction, interest, liking, and affection, so immediacy overlaps with but is not isomorphic with affection.

Like immediacy, *intimacy* has a complicated relationship with affection. For Reis (1990), intimacy is an interpersonal process in which an individual feels understood, validated, and cared for by another (p. 16). Andersen (1999) defines intimacy as warm, involving behaviors, interactions, experiences and relationships (p. 219), particularly close relationships. Canary and Emmers-Sommer with Faulkner (1997) describe intimacy as the expression of thought, emotion, and behavior, requiring time, routine access, and psychological closeness (pp. 49–51), used to move a relationship toward more complete communication (p. 48). As with definitions of affection, definitions of intimacy include closeness, but intimacy seems to occur only after a certain level of closeness occurs (Noller & Fitzpatrick, 1993; Prager & Buhrmester, 1998; Solomon, 1997), whereas affection can occur at low levels of closeness (i.e., with an acquaintance). Indeed, Parks and Floyd (1996) say that "closeness appears to be a broader, more inclusive term" than intimacy (p. 103), with intimacy involving more closeness, that is, intimacy is a more intense form of closeness (p. 85). Closeness refers to the emotional distance in a relationship (Derlega et al., 1993; Floyd & Voloudakis, 1997; Knapp & Vangelisti, 1996; Millar et al., 1978; Schutz, 1958; Villard, 1976; Waring & Reddon, 1983) and is used synonymously with affection, although you can feel affection for someone to whom you are not particularly close. So affection would be a characteristic of closeness but not vice versa. Prager's (1995) model of relational intimacy includes affection as a relationship factor, and Waring, Tillman, Frelick, Russell, and Weisz (1980) report that expression of affection is an important aspect of intimacy (p. 471); they later say that affection, along with support, defines intimacy (Waring et al., 1981, p. 172). We might say that intimacy is a state or stage of close relationships that includes affection, but affection is not limited to intimate relationships.

*Liking*, or "general favorability," is considered an index of affection (Pearce, Wright, Sharp, & Slama, 1974; Sprecher, 1987). Interestingly, love is rarely used as a synonym for affection, although Rubin et al. (1988) define affection as the need to love and be loved by others (p. 605), and Metts and Bowers (1994) classify affection as a variant of love (p. 510), but most reserve the term love for a more intense and special emotion.

*Rituals* are "stylized, repetitive, communicative enactments that pay homage to a valued object, person, or phenomenon" (Bruess & Pearson, 1997, p. 25). The description of rituals as being significant, patterned, occurring in all types of relationships, and creating intimacy, as well as the examination of types of rituals in marriages and friendships, show considerable overlap with affectionate communication. Although Bruess and Pearson (1997) specify affection as one type of intimacy expression (p. 36), most of the rituals they delineate communicate affection. In sum, affectionate communication appears to be ritualistic, but all rituals do not necessarily appear to be affectionate communication.

*Social support,* when defined as conveying assistance in situations involving distress (Albrecht, Burleson, & Goldsmith, 1994), includes affectionate communication as well as instrumental and emotional support and appears limited to specific types of affectionate behaviors (e.g., helping, comforting, caring for, and aiding others; Albrecht et al., 1994; Vaux, 1988). Comforting behaviors, according to Dolin and Booth-Butterfield (1993), are a specific type of social support, "actions directed at managing the emotional distress of others" (Burleson, 1994a, p. 135), and helping, caring for others, and so forth, would be other specific types of social support. However, Barnes and Duck (1994) argue that social support is basic and ongoing in relationships and not limited to specific situations; if social support is defined as actions that "indicate liking, caring, and concern for their recipient; signal interest; and tacitly send a message that the provider regards the recipient as special and important" (Burleson, Albrecht, Goldsmith, & Sarason, 1994, p. xiv), then social support is synonymous with affection (e.g., expressing love, concern, empathy; listening; praising; physical presence; Burleson, 1994b).

Finally, *warmth,* according to Andersen and Guerrero (1998) and MacDonald (1992), is not the same as affection, although it is related. MacDonald (1992) defines affection as purposive behaviors that result in pleasure (pp. 757–758) but goes on to argue that, whereas affection as an emotion undoubtedly is positive, the behaviors themselves may be negative, such as discipline and authoritarian behaviors. He says that warmth, conceptualized as a positive social reward system, is the positive end of a continuum of which hostility is the negative end, but affection may be communicated by behaviors not considered warm. However, the term affection is also used synonymously with warmth (DePaulo & Coleman, 1987; Knapp & Vangelisti, 1996; Oatley & Jenkins, 1996), and Fisher et al. (1995), from a meta-analysis of factor analyses of FIRO-B data, say that warmth appears to equate with affection (p. 203).

Other lay terms synonymous with affection include appreciation, empathy/sympathy, fondness, friendliness, partiality/favor, tenderness/kindness, and many others.

Affection is an extensive concept. It occurs in relationships that range from less close to more close to intimate. It characterizes social support, but social support can exist without affection. It is a positive emotion, similar to warmth in a relationship, but its behaviors may appear negative. Perhaps affection is best thought of as overlapping with immediacy, intimacy, rituals, social support, warmth, and so forth, so that sometimes affection is synonymous with each of these other concepts, and sometimes it is separate. Defining affection as "the need for positive regard from another and the feeling of positive regard for another, communicated through affectionate behaviors, found in relationships ranging from acquaintance to intimate" provides an organizing framework for consideration of affection in its numerous aspects.

## AFFECTIONATE BEHAVIORS ARE MANY AND VARIED

Although human beings may blush with modesty, embarrassment, or shame, they usually do not physically brighten in color to communicate affection as seahorses do. Yet their affectionate behaviors are many and varied. Since the term affection is used synonymously with caring, intimacy, liking, warmth, and many others, the number and range of behaviors considered affectionate is vast.

The nonverbal communication of affection can be organized by the traditional systems or forms of nonverbal cues (Andersen & Guerrero, 1998). Affectionate touching is the most frequently mentioned affectionate behavior. It is "generalized in the sense that the positive feelings are directed toward another person *qua* person and are not tied to a specific situation" (Jones & Yarborough, 1985, p. 39); that is, affectionate touch does not have a specific other meaning and is not tied to situational demands as other types of touch are. Afifi and Johnson (1999) classify affectionate touch into three categories: moderately intimate—arm around shoulder, leaning body on body, caressing face or hair, linking arms; intimate—arm around waist, hugging, kissing on cheek, physically leading someone to a particular location; and very intimate—holding hands, leaning head against head; plus handshakes, mock attacks, pats/rubs, kissing on the mouth, and hand-to-hand. Handshakes seem to call for a fourth category, perhaps nonintimate. Seemingly, all types of affectionate behavior can be classified on a continuum from nonintimate to very intimate.

A second way of categorizing affectionate behaviors is as resources, material or symbolic commodities transmitted through interpersonal behavior (Foa & Foa, 1974, p. 36). According to resource theory, these include love—feeling affection and caring for, enjoying being with the other; status—importance, ability, admiration and respect; information—facts, opinions, advice; money; goods—merchandise, products; and services—doing something for the other.

A third set of categories involves relational currencies, the "processes by which individuals exchange affection and caring for one another" (Villard, 1976, p. 16), that include intimate and economic forms of exchange commodities (Villard & Whipple, 1976). Intimacy currencies, likely based on the idea of intrinsic rewards, include overt communication of affection involving a level of physical or psychological identity (Villard, 1976, p. 17) in which the meaning is intrinsically coded (Villard & Whipple, 1976, p. 141). For Villard, intimacy currencies include aggression, sexuality, self-disclosure, physical touch, and facial affect displays. Economic currencies, likely based on extrinsic rewards, involve symbolic communication of affection in which the behavior involves the individual's time and energy in which the meaning is extrinsically coded (Villard & Whipple, 1976, p. 142). Economic currencies include access rights, money, favors, and gifts.

A wide range of behaviors are considered affectionate, and these behaviors can be considered as three general types: nonverbal, verbal, and patterns of nonverbal and verbal together (see Appendix).

## SIX MAJOR FACTORS INFLUENCE AFFECTIONATE COMMUNICATION

Six major factors appear to influence affectionate communication, that is, the expression of affection: (a) the communicator, (b) the relational partner, (c) the compatibility of affection exchange and the reciprocity in the relationship, (d) the nature of the relationship, (e) the context or situation, and (f) the culture. These factors are not mutually exclusive, nor may they be exhaustive.

### Communicator

Affectionate communication is influenced by the communicator through personal style, mood, motivational state, goal, and the idiosyncratic characteristics of age, ethnic origin, health/disability, role, sex/gender, and socioeconomic class.

*Personal style.* Personal style is "the medium that we as individuals select to communicate our feelings about others and, conversely, the way we allow others to communicate their feelings about us" (Villard, 1976, p. 144). Our personal style depends on our culture, our upbringing/parents' behaviors/parental interaction, and our personality dimensions and traits. Personality is described by how we characteristically act over time and across situations (Oatley & Jenkins, 1996); MacDonald (1992) says that "individual differences in attraction to the rewards of intimacy and affection are viewed as a personality dimension" (p. 759). One personality trait, agreeableness, is close to the concept of affection (Oatley & Jenkins, 1996, p. 218). A related personality trait is extraversion, which includes warmth, gregariousness, and the tendency to positive emotions (Oatley & Jenkins, 1996, p. 218). Gunn (1995) found that people who preferred extraversion and feeling on the Myers-Briggs Type Indicator tended to score high on expressed and wanted affection on the FIRO-B scale; introverted scores were related to low affection scores, and thinking types also tended to be low on expressed and wanted affection (pp. 132–133). Gaines (1996) found that affectionate behaviors are predicted by individuals' "affection-giving traits" (p. 251). An affectionate personal style, therefore, appears to be characterized by agreeableness, extraversion, and feeling.

*Mood.* Mood, unlike personality dimensions/traits, is an internal, temporary state of mind or feeling. As it does for warmth (Andersen & Guerrero, 1998, p. 321), mood is likely to influence an individual's communication of affection and vice versa; however, no direct evidence exists about the association.

*Motivational state.* Motivational state activates the human affectional system to search for pleasurable affective responses (Foa & Foa, 1974, p. 125; MacDonald, 1992, p. 758). Rubin et al. (1988) found that offering affection to others was one of 18 communication motives (p. 615), and Rubin and Martin (1988) report that people with a need for intimacy communicate more for affection than those with a need for seclusion (p. 296).

Four motivational states for affection are described by Schutz (1958): (a) "deficient—indicating that the individual is not trying directly to satisfy the need" (p. 25), which he calls "underpersonal" (p. 30); (b) "excessive—indicating that the individual is constantly trying to satisfy the need" (p. 25), which he calls "overpersonal" (p. 31); (c) "ideal—indicating satisfaction of the need " (p. 25), which he calls "personal" (p. 31), and (d) "pathological" (p. 25). Related research by Rosenfeld and Frandsen (1972) shows that reticent students, to a greater degree than nonreticent students, want more affection then they express (p. 300), and Rubin and Martin (1998) report that high communication apprehensives (CAs) are less likely to communicate for affection than low CAs (p. 294). In a study of computer-mediated communication (CMC) as an alternative to face-to-face communication (FtF), Flaherty, Pearce, and Rubin (1998) found that low CMC apprehensives seek FtF interactions more for affection than do high CMC apprehensives (p. 262). In addition, Powell and Bock (1975) found that students attempt to make their expressed affection consistent with their wanted affection (pp. 129–130). People with a high motivation for affection are more likely to use other-involvement and positive self-image affinity-seeking strategies, positive humor in conversation, talk about many topics but at a less personal level, and disclose more about low intimacy topics, whereas those with a low motivation for affection use rational compliance-gaining strategies, according to Rubin and Martin (1998, pp. 296–297).

Villard and Whipple (1976) argue that, historically, when people were motivated primarily by the need for physiological security, the focus of their relationships tended to be economic, so affection was communicated using economic currencies. As physiological needs became routinely satisfied, and the media offered a diversity of "identities" previously not available, affection became communicated more frequently using intimacy currencies (pp. 156–160). This implies that economically disadvantaged people would use economic currencies to communicate affection, whereas the more economically advantaged would have the opportunity and means (primarily media) to develop their individual identities and be more likely to use intimacy currencies.

In sum, individuals who have more need for intimacy, are nonreticent, and low communication apprehensive are more likely to communicate for affection, and the level of physiological security, as a motivator, may influence the ways in which people communicate affection.

*Goal.* The communicator's goal for an interaction also influences the communication of affection. These goals usually are referred to in the literature as functions (Burgoon et al., 1996, p. 19). All communication serves a function or is goal driven; the same communicative behavior may serve more than one function, and the same function can be accomplished in a number of ways (Afifi & Johnson, 1999, p. 19). Although functions frequently are discussed in regards to nonverbal behavior, they apply to verbal behavior as well. Affectionate communication can serve a number of functions: expressing intimacy, expressing emotion, presenting the self and impression formation, presenting an image of a relationship, relational communication and relationship management, social influence, and deception (Andersen, 1999; Burgoon et al., 1996; Patterson, 1988).

*Idiosyncratic characteristics.* In addition to the influence of personal style, mood, motivational state, and goal on the communicator's affectionate behaviors is the influence of idiosyncratic characteristics including age, ethnic origin, health/disability, role, sex/gender, and socioeconomic class.

Age has been found to be positively related to affection; that is, the older the respondents the more likely they reported communicating for reasons of affection (Downs & Javidi, 1990; Rubin & Martin, 1998; Rubin et al., 1988). However, across age, lovers' expressions of affection were found by Reeder (1996) to significantly decline, unrelated to the length of the relationship (p. 325). Floyd (1996a) found that "older adults cited shared perceptions and memories as a component of closeness significantly more often than did adolescents and more often than did those in their early 20s" (p. 381). Older adults have more perceptions and memories to share, so they may be more likely to communicate affection in that way than younger adults. Murstein and Tuerkheimer (1998) found that men in the oldest age group of their study scored higher on the physical release motive for sex than those in the youngest age group; men in the intermediate age group scored higher on affection-closeness, but those in the youngest age group described their motive for sex as relatively intermediate between affection-closeness and physical release (p. 447). McCabe (1987) found no age differences in the level of affection wanted or experienced during dating (p. 23). Eberly and Montemayor in 1998 found that 6th graders were more affectionate than 8th graders or 10th graders, who did not differ from each other (p. 416), but in 1999 found that children reported less affectionate behavior toward their parents during early and middle adolescence (i.e., 6th and 8th grades) than in later adolescence (10th grade; p. 226). Evidence suggests that there may be changes in reasons for and types of communication of affection as one gets older, but at this point the nature of the relationship of age and affection is unclear.

The arguments of Gaines (1997) and Wood (1998) that there are ethnic patterns of affectionate communication are supported by the results of Regan et al.'s (1999) study of public displays of affection among Latino and Asian heterosexual couples. Ethnic differences are, of course, grounded in cultural distinctions, which the literature suggests is a major variable in communication of affection.

Health/disability influences an individual's affectionate communication. Children with developmental disabilities may not receive as much affection from parents and caregivers as normally developing children and may be less responsive to affectionate behavior from others (Compton & Niemeyer, 1994, pp. 70–71), and chronically ill adolescents, compared to healthy adolescents, have been found to experience less affection in their friendships (Schmidt & SeiffgeKrenke, 1996, p. 155). Wright (1998) found that expressions of affection declined for couples with an Alzheimer's disease afflicted spouse, but affection increased significantly after the ill spouse was placed in a nursing home (p. 167). Leiber, Plumb, Gerstenzang, and Holland (1976) found that affectionate feelings and behavior of cancer patients and their spouses remained unchanged or increased after chemotherapy began (p. 386). Poor health and disability may lead to the experience of less affection, particularly on the part of children.

A role consists of learned actions performed by an individual in a specific situation based on her definition of the situation. The role an individual plays at any given time is constrained by behaviors considered by others appropriate for that role. Individuals in formal role relationships, those relationships extensively constrained by externally imposed rules, are likely to communicate and experience less affection than those in more personal role relationships.

Both differences and similarities in the communication of affection have been observed based on sex and gender. Castiglia's (1999) review found differences in expressions of physical affection for fathers and mothers with daughters and sons (pp. 35–36). Eberly and Montemayor (1998), Barber and Thomas (1986), and Noller (1978) also found sex differences in affection between children and parents. Bakken and Romig (1992) found gender differences in adolescents' ranking of the importance of affection to interpersonal relationships. Swain (1989) traces gender differences in intimacy behaviors to the different worlds in which boys and girls are raised; he says that what he calls the masculine style of intimacy comes from the physical-activity oriented outside environment that is the male world.

Literature on interpersonal communication motives shows that women communicate more for affection than men (Rubin & Martin, 1998, p. 295). Wood's (1998) review of the literature found that women communicate affection through being with others, giving attention to others, and talking, whereas men communicate affection through doing things with and for others (pp. 150–151). Many of Floyd's findings (1995, 1996a, 1997a, 1997b, Floyd & Parks, 1995; Parks & Floyd, 1996) have shown that women express affection more frequently than men, and men express affection in more covert ways. Shuntich and Shapiro (1991) found that male-male pairs are less affectionate than female-female and mixed-sex dyads (p. 297); Derlega, Lewis, Harrison, Winstead, and Costanza (1989) found that males use less affectionate touch in public than females (p. 85), and Hollender, Dowdy, & Kourany (1979) found that women generally preferred being held and men preferred holding (p. 121). Owen (1987) found that females are reactive and males proactive in saying "I love you" first (p. 22), and Barbato and Perse (1992) and Rubin et al. (1988) found that women were more likely than men to report communicating affection. Swain (1989) concludes that men and women have different styles of intimacy (active vs. verbal), and "each sex tends to overlook, devalue, and not fully comprehend the other sex's style of expressing care" (p. 78). However, he says that men and women can "cross over" and use both active and verbal styles and that both styles appear to be necessary for healthy lives (p. 85). Wallace (1981) found that females said they both gave and received more affection in the family of origin as compared with males, and this difference continues in their current experience (pp. 298–299); according to Wallace (1981), these responses indicate "traditional, stereotypical sex role scripting" (p. 299). Kotulski (1996) concludes that sex-role socialization profoundly influences the affectionate behaviors of a couple (p. 2).

However, in a meta-analysis of over 200 studies on self-disclosure, a type of affectionate communication, Dindia and Allen (1992) reported that sex differences in self-disclosive behavior are slight although women disclose more than men (p. 110). Pearce et al. (1974) found that affection did not correlate more strongly with self-disclosure for males than females (p. 10). Liederman (1991) found that wives and husbands in happily married couples have different affectional desires but concludes, from her survey of the literature on affection and sexuality, that the evidence suggesting "women are more interested in the affectional and sensual aspects of sexuality, whereas men are more interested in genital sex" (p. 24) comes largely from unmarried samples, whereas studies using married or both single and married samples find that "gender differences in sexual affection are less dramatic, if present at all" (p. 25). Snell (1986, 1989) found that, although women perceived themselves as less inhibited than men in terms of affection and reported that they engaged in fewer behaviors associated with inhibited affection, both women and men said that inhibited affection was not characteristic of their behavior (p. 757).

Also arguing for similarities, Murstein and Tuerkheimer (1998) found that, contrary to earlier findings, there was no significant difference between the total sample of women and men in motive for sexual intercourse (affection-closeness vs. physical release) and that Rubin's (1970) Love Scale did not differentiate between men and women (p. 435). Solomon (1997) found no sex differences in the association of affection with date request explicitness (p. 112). Floyd's work has not found consistent sex differences in communicating closeness (Floyd, 1996b, 1997a, 1997b), and Gaines (1996) found that "gender-role compliance was not significant as a predictor of men's or women's affectionate or respectful behaviors" (p. 251; see also Gaines, 1994). Botkin, Townley, and Twardosz (1991) found that preschool children's affectionate behavior was not gender typed (p. 281), and McCabe (1987) found no sex differences in the level of affection wanted or experienced during dating (p. 23).

In sum, although there are apparently sex/gender differences in the ways in which affection is communicated, there are not differences in motive for affection nor feeling of affection.

"Socioeconomic class is another group influence on our rules for caring," according to Wood (1998, p. 152), and Cancian's (1989) work suggests that, historically, people from different classes may have communicated affection in different ways, a possibility supported by Villard and Whipple (1976, pp. 156–160). Wallen (1989), in a response to work by Buss (Buss & Barnes, 1986) on economics and mate selection, provides additional evidence for individuals' consideration of financial prospects in mate selection, along with good looks, chastity, ambition, and preferred age difference (p. 37). She points out, however, that Buss does not include emotional variables, such as affection, in his model (p. 38). Therefore, in terms of socioeconomic class, economic status particularly appears to influence how we communicate affection and to whom.

## Relational Partner

As each person in a relationship is influenced differently by individual elements, each will have different needs and feelings and use different behaviors in communicating affection. According to Villard and Whipple (1976, p. 154), we can interpret another's communication of affection through the frequency with which an affectionate behavior is used. Relative to an individual's tendency to be affectionate, if a particular behavior is used frequently and in many relationships, it probably is not intended to communicate a great deal of affection; if it is used rarely and only in a limited number of relationships, it probably is intended to communicate a high level of affection. If a currency is never used, it has no value. Villard and Whipple (1976) base this conclusion on the economic principle that "people generally value those things which are rare" (p. 154). Therefore, individuals communicate affection differently based on the affectionate behaviors they value.

## Compatibility and Reciprocity

If two people's rules for sending and receiving messages of affection do not correspond, according to Knapp and Vangelisti (1996), then there will be misperception of what constitutes communication of affection. In addition, although messages of affection may be communicated in ways on which two people agree, these rules may hurt the relationship. An example they give is when a husband can't lose weight, although he needs to, because he eats the big meals his wife has lovingly prepared for him (p. 330).

*Compatibility.* "Compatibility is a property of a relation between two or more persons . . . that leads to mutual satisfaction of interpersonal needs and harmonious coexistence" (Schutz , 1958, p. 105). Schutz (1958) describes three types of compatibility. First, "interchange compatibility" is compatibility based on similarity in amount exchanged—high-interchange includes those who prefer a high level of affection exchange; low-exchange includes those who want little or no affection exchange (pp. 106-107). Second, "originator compatibility" is compatibility based on complementarity—one gives and the other receives; and third, reciprocal compatibility occurs when the behavior of one equals the wanted behavior of the other and vice versa (p. 107). The potential for misunderstanding occurs when the individuals in a relationship use incompatible affectionate behaviors to communicate (Villard & Whipple, 1976). When one person uses an affectionate behavior the other does not value, the other may feel that no affection has been communicated. "Different people have different ways of telling each other how they feel about one another, ways that are perhaps so fundamentally different that misunderstanding is almost inevitable" (Villard & Whipple, 1976, p. 162). Only if differences in affectionate behaviors are identified and a mutually agreeable system of affection exchange negotiated can individuals accurately interpret their relational partner's communication of affection.

*Reciprocity.* A balance of giving and receiving needs to occur for a relationship to succeed, so we consider what the other can offer us as well as what we can offer the other (Foa & Foa, 1974, p. 241), and what we prefer to offer the other is influenced by what they offer us (p. 217). Uehara (1995) says the evidence suggests that "people feel obligated to return benefits they receive from others, appear to be more psychologically and emotionally averse to overbenefiting then underbenefiting from social support interactions, and tend to avoid placing themselves in the position of 'overbenefitors'" (p. 483). From a moral perspective, people interpret reciprocations flexibly depending upon "the degree of interpersonal trust and the specific norms and expectations associated with specific categories of social relationships and social networks" (p. 498), and "people's considerations of reciprocity in actual interactions may have as much or more to do with moral obligations as with self-interested concerns" (p. 498). These patterns of reciprocity are referred to as "enmeshment," the total set of behaviors used to communicate love in a relationship. Marston and Hecht (1999) argue that the behaviors do not have to match; rather, one partner has to receive love from the other's behaviors. When both partners' behaviors are interpreted as loving, love is sent and received in a relationship (p. 288; see also Turner, Foa, & Foa, 1971). For affection exchange in a relationship to be functional, the individuals involved must have a balance of giving and receiving acceptable to both, though not necessarily equal in amount nor identical in kind.

## Nature of the Relationship

Much of the behavior that occurs in a relationship is based on the unique properties of the relationship itself, so the nature of the relationship influences the communication of affection that goes on within it (Gaines, 1994, 1995; Haslam, 1995; Villard & Whipple, 1976). The nature of the relationship includes at least three elements: relationship type, related to relationship level, and the sex composition of the relationship.

*Relationship type.* Relational types differ in expression of affection, according to Fitzpatrick and Best (1979, p. 175), and there are two types of relationships based on their determinates: attachments and affiliations (Weiss, 1998). *Attachments* are characterized by a primarily emotional component involving feelings of security and two primarily cognitive components involving the parent whose presence fosters security and the child who is made secure (p. 675).

Three kinds of attachment relationships maintained by adults are (a) the pair-bond relationship in which "the self and other each are interpreted as both beneficiary and provider of secure bases" (p. 676); (b) the parental relationship in which the self is the provider and other is the beneficiary (pp. 676–677); and (c) the guidance-obtaining relationship in which the other is the provider and the self is the beneficiary (pp. 676–677). *Affiliations* are characterized by a sense of alliance based on common interest. Affiliations include (a) friendships in which the relationship itself is beneficial to both parties and entirely voluntary; (b) work relationships in which the participants contribute to a shared goal, and the relationship ends when the goal is achieved; and (c) kinships in which participants belong to the same family group with a concomitant obligation to assist the other if needed (p. 678). Further distinctions between attachments and affiliations include (a) attachments are exclusive; affiliations involve numerous relationships, with associated issues; (b) attachments are basically permanent, affiliations temporary; (c) ending attachments produces grief—"a condition of persisting inconsolable and painful distress" (p. 680)—whereas ending affiliations may produce regret or sorrow but not grief; (d) attachments are maintained through the bond itself, affiliations often are maintained due to threat of negative perception by others; and (e) lack of attachments may lead to loneliness characterized by feelings of emptiness and "a vigilance that can be both fearful and hopeful" (p. 681), whereas the lack of affiliations may lead to loneliness characterized by "feelings of marginality, unacceptability to others, isolation, and boredom" (p. 681).

*Relationship level.* Affection exchange is characteristic of both attachments and affiliations, but the affectionate communication that occurs differs depending upon the level of the relationship (Andersen & Guerrero, 1998; Foa & Foa, 1974). Gaines (1996) argues that "what distinguishes behavior in close relationships from behavior in all other forms of human interaction is the preponderance of affection-giving (or denying) and respect-giving (or denying) behaviors" (pp. 242–243). Solomon (1997) found that when affection is present in early stages of a relationship, date request explicitness is avoided, but when affection is present in later stages of a relationship, explicitness is used (p. 110). Although Floyd and Morman (1997) found that the level of relational closeness did not effect perceptions of appropriateness of communicating affection (p. 284), the comparison was limited to platonic friendship versus full biological, nontwin siblings. However, Morman and Floyd (1998) did find that affectionate communication is considered more appropriate among brothers than among male friends (p. 877). Although all types of relationships can involve communication of affection, affection exchange appears more likely to occur in closer relationships, and certain affectionate behaviors may be more appropriate at certain levels of relationships.

*Sex composition of relationship.* "Regardless of relationship type, men and women generally reciprocate affection to a significant degree" (Gaines, 1996, p. 244). However, women and men seem to communicate affection differently depending upon whether the relationship is same-sex or opposite-sex (Floyd,

1997a; Swain, 1989), and some affectionate behaviors such as words and physical contact seem to be considered more appropriate in opposite-sex relationships than in same-sex relationships (Floyd & Morman, 1997, p. 289). Shuntich and Shapiro (1991) found "that male-male pairs were significantly less affectionate than female-female pairs or mixed-sex dyads" (p. 297), but their definition of affection was limited to compliments and direct statements of caring. Swain (1989) found that men felt more at ease and relaxed with male friends than with female friends (p. 75) and so felt more comfortable communicating their closeness in male-male relationships (p. 76). As with sex/gender differences, the influence of sex composition of the relationship on the communication of affection in the relationship is unclear, although the type and amount of affectionate behavior apparently differ depending upon sex composition.

## Context or Situation

Context, situation, or what Foa and Foa (1974) call "the environment" surrounds the exchange of intimacy behaviors, and certain situations are more conducive to intimacy than others (Andersen & Guerrero, 1998). This conclusion applies to affectionate communication as well. Morman and Floyd (1998) found that affectionate communication was more appropriate in emotionally charged contexts than emotionally neutral ones and more appropriate in public situations than private ones (p. 877). Bell and Healey (1992) found that idioms used to communicate affection were more likely to be used in private than in public (p. 328). According to Foa and Foa (1974), the appropriateness of the environment is one of two conditions affecting the exchange of resources (p. 125; the other is the motivational state of the potential exchangers), and properties affecting the environment include time for processing input, delay of reward, and optimum group size (pp. 166–168).

Schutz (1958) describes two types of affection exchange situations: high affection exchange situations involve many close, personal feelings and occur in close relationships, and low affection exchange situations are those in which expression of close, personal feelings generally is considered inappropriate (p. 158). The type of situation in which affection exchange occurs also is related to the channel of communication, and Westmyer, DiCioccio, and Rubin (1998) found that the preferred channels for both appropriately and effectively giving and receiving affection were, in order, face-to-face, telephone, letter, voice-mail, email, and fax (p. 43). Overall, situations that appear to be more appropriate for the communication of affection include those that are personal, private, emotionally charged, unhurried, and face-to-face.

## Culture

The final factor influencing affectionate communication is culture (Castiglia, 1999). Public displays of affection (limited to touching behaviors) are greater among Latino heterosexual couples than among Asian heterosexual couples

(Regan et al., 1999, p. 1202), and touch scores were found to be significantly lower for Asian dyads than for Caribbean-Latin, Northern European, or U.S. American dyads (McDaniel & Andersen, 1998, p. 66). Rubin and Martin (1998) say that people in Mexico report communicating less for affection than those in the United States (p. 298), although motives for communicating are consistent within cultures (p. 299). McDaniel and Andersen (1998) conclude that culture has a central affect on communicative behavior (p. 68), a conclusion supported by Lustig and Koester's (1999) interpretation of Hall's (1966a, 1966b) writings on high and low contact cultures.

Although some emotions, including affection, may be universal, Oatley and Jenkins (1996) argue that their occurrence and emphasis is culturally specific. According to Triandis (1995), exchange relationships tend to be different in collectivist versus individualist cultures, with people in collectivist cultures exchanging love, status, and services whereas people in individualist cultures exchange money, goods, and information (pp. 156–157). Gaines (1997) says that we must consider communalism as a cultural influence on behavior as well (p. 360); communalism is the one-on-one focus of an individual on her or his significant other, the value attached to being in a relationship with a specific person (p. 358). It is differentiated from collectivism in that collectivism is "an orientation toward one's socially defined ingroup" (p. 359). Communalism is important in understanding why we initiate and not just respond to affectionate behavior (p. 361).

Although warmth is present in relationships cross-culturally, its patterning varies widely (MacDonald, 1992, p. 754). Affectional currency exchange is influenced by what is viewed culturally as appropriate, including "some general cultural guidelines that specify not only the appropriateness of certain interpersonal behaviors or currencies, but also allude to the esteem or priority in which the culture holds these behaviors" (Villard & Whipple, 1976, pp. 143–144). These rules or expectancies are patterns of behavior that Burgoon (1995) calls "socially normative," that is, "applicable to an entire speech community or subgroup" (p. 195). In interaction, behaviors are evaluated for their desirability, and cultures differ in the extent to which a behavior must vary in order to constitute a violation (p. 200). Responses to expectancy violations differ among cultures as well. Therefore, culture affects not only what behaviors we use to communicate affection but also how we respond to those behaviors from others.

Affection is a universal emotion, but which behaviors are appropriate for whom and in what context, as well as sanctions for violation of appropriateness rules, differ depending upon the culture. The dimensions of collectivism/individualism and communalism appear to influence a specific culture's communication of affection.

Culture is the final major factor that influences how an individual communicates affection. The others are the communicator, including elements of personal style, mood, motivational state, goal, and idiosyncratic characteristics, the relational partner, the compatibility of affection exchange and the reciprocity in the relationship, the nature of the relationship, and the context or situation. The influence of these factors is grounded in the development of our patterns of affectionate communication.

## BOTH BIOLOGY AND THE ENVIRONMENT INFLUENCE THE DEVELOPMENT OF AFFECTIONATE COMMUNICATION PATTERNS

The development of affectionate communication patterns has both a biological/genetic basis and a social/environmental one. Biology and experience both affect us by altering the synaptic organization of the brain (LeDoux, 1998, p. B8), and our behavior is a product of both our evolved psychological mechanisms and environmental influences (Buss, 1994, p. 17). According to Oatley and Jenkins (1996), although affection (among other interpersonal factors) has a genetic basis, only between 20% and 50% of the variation in people's behavior is accounted for by these genetic factors, and genetic influences are built upon by experience and culture (pp. 216–217).

### Biological/Genetic Basis

Our evolved psychological mechanisms are the internal processes that tell us what adaptive problem we are facing and transform information into action to solve the problem (Buss, 1999, p. 9). Intimate relationships, pair bonding, and affection are basic human biological adaptations evolved for the purposes of reproduction and protecting the young (MacDonald, 1992, p. 755), and the impulse for caring is biologically programmed in human beings (Gaylin, 1976, p. 13). According to Gray (1991) and Beatty, McCroskey, and Heisel (1998), affectionate communication is not a personality trait but a set of learned behaviors possibly influenced by the biologically determined individual differences in approach-avoidance patterns that are part of temperament (see Bates, 1989). Beatty et al. (1998) say that "the neurological networks involved in approach and avoidance patterns . . . are evident in infancy and continue developing until late adolescence, which accounts for observations of social approach and avoidance soon after birth" (p. 208). In fact, de Bono and Bargmann (1998), in a study of the nematode *C. elegans*, found that a specific type of social behavior (communal feeding vs. solitary foraging) is due to natural variation in npr-1, "a predicted G protein-coupled receptor in the NPY receptor family" (p. 679). They argue that, due to the presence of such neuropeptides in the human brain, "changes in neuropeptide pathways could be a widespread mechanism for generating natural variation in behavior" (p. 687), specifically social behavior.

Biologically the behavior patterns related to communication of affection are grounded in temperament, the characteristic patterns of emotional reactions, biologically based, present early in life, and relatively stable across time and situations (Bates, 1994; Strelau & Angleitner, 1991). Scholars differ on whether temperament has what is referred to as the "Big Five" factors—extraversion, agreeableness, conscientiousness, neuroticism, and openness; or three basic dimensions—activity, emotionality, and sociability (Strelau & Angleitner, 1991, p. 304). Bates (1994) refers to three dimensions of temperament: (a) negative emotionality/affectivity, including fearfulness, anxiety/tension, inhibition, dysphoria, negative mood, and difficultness; (b) positive emotionality/affectivity, including enthusiasm, excitement, happiness, sociability, and activity level; and (c) impulsive, unsocialized sensation seeking/constraint versus impulsiveness, including resistance to control (p. 4). However, he goes on to state that the full range of temperament variables may not be well described in only three dimensions (p. 5). Positive emotionality is related to sociability, "appreciation of the company of other people, in the form of responsive interchange" (Bates, 1994, p. 16), clearly including the communication of affection.

## Social/Environmental Basis

In addition to the biological basis of affectionate communication in temperament and sociability, a social/environmental basis exists. The biological/genetic basis provides the outlines and initial parameters of the individual's response to social/environmental conditions. These social/environmental conditions are shaped through modeling and interaction. Landau (1989) found that affectionate responses first appeared at seven months of age (p. 59); Cummings, Zahn-Waxler, & Radke-Yarrow (1981) found that by approximately one year of age children are aware of others' affectionate interactions and likely to evidence an emotional reaction to them (p. 1281).

A number of studies document the influence of affection in the family on children and adults. Parrott and Bengtson (1999) found that affection in parent-child relationships is associated with giving and receiving various forms of help and support (p. 73). In a study of the relationship of parental behavior and personality variables of young adults, Kuterovac-Jagodic and Kerestes (1997) found that father's warmth and affection predicted extroversion (p. 477). Roberts and Bengtson (1996) conclude that "the quality of affective ties to parents during the transition to adulthood has long-term significance for self-esteem among offspring" (p. 96). Silverstein, Parrott, and Bengtson (1995) found that affection between middle-aged children and their elderly parents is the factor that most motivates daughters to provide support for their parents (p. 465).

There is extensive support for the affectional climate in the family of origin as the basis for current affectionate behavior and attitudes (Wallace, 1981, p. 305), and attitudes toward affection are related to early parental affectionate behavior (Hyson et al., 1986, p. 5). A number of scholars agree that children imitate the affectionate behavior of their parents and caregivers (Castiglia, 1999; Oatley & Jenkins, 1996; Schutz, 1958). Acker and Marton (1984) found that a combination of modeling and practice of affectionate behaviors increased subsequent affectionate behaviors (p. 255); Cummings et al. (1981) reported that children frequently modeled the affectionate behaviors they observed (p. 1281). Koblinsky and Palmeter (1984) found that greater exposure to a mother's expression of sexual affection toward her spouse was associated with a daughter's more positive attitudes toward speaking affectionately to men (p. 32).

In addition to modeling, interaction influences the development of affectionate behaviors in children. When we interact with others we learn which emotions are appropriate, when they are appropriate, and which ones will help us accomplish our goals, and we develop patterns in emotional responding that affect us throughout our lives (Oatley & Jenkins, 1996, p. 208). Morris and Smith (1980) found that children prefer to be physically closer to an adult who shows them affection than to one who does not (p. 155). Botkin et al. (1991) found support for socialization in regards to affection in a study examining affectionate behavior in girls and boys 3 to 6 years old (p. 281). In a discussion of the development of social support patterns in individuals, Albrecht et al. (1994) say that "the communication practices of parents play the central role in the child's development of an attachment style and working models of social relationships" (p. 430).

Affectional bonds are based on the attachment individuals have for each other (Bowlby, 1979) but are not the same as attachments (Gaylin, 1976; Oatley & Jenkins, 1996; Twardosz & Nordquist, 1983). Attachment occurs among all primates, but only some species form affectional bonds (Oatley & Jenkins, 1996). MacDonald (1992) says, "While the function of the attachment system is to provide security in the face of threat, the human affectional system functions to facilitate cohesive, psychologically rewarding family relationships and paternal investment in children" (p. 753). The two systems operate together, but affection influences aspects of a child's development other than just attachment style (Oatley & Jenkins, 1996, p. 201). In addition, caregivers can be attached but show little affection (Oatley & Jenkins, 1996, p. 201), although infants who experience affectionate care likely will experience more security than those who experience hostile care (Twardosz & Nordquist, 1983, p. 136).

Attachments are the intense, enduring relationships formed with specific others and characterized by the desire to remain close to the other (Bowlby, 1979; Twardosz & Nordquist, 1983), and attachment behaviors are the behaviors that bring two people together. Attachment theory explains that attachment is crucial to the development of a "healthy" personality and the formation of the "self" (Gaylin, 1976; Lopez, 1995), and attachment patterns develop in early childhood (usually by 12 months) from interaction (usually with more than one person, and not necessarily with the person who provides the most physical care, although this usually is the case; Twardosz & Nordquist, 1983, p. 138). The greater the attachment behavior in the caregiver the more securely attached the infant will be; although some infants may be adverse to certain forms of attachment behavior. Securely attached infants are more likely to explore, comply with maternal requests, respond positively both to being held and being put down, engage in more "sinking in" when being held, and engage in more active contact with the caregiver (Twardosz & Nordquist, 1983, p. 138). The more attached as a child, the more compliant and curious and the better at problem solving and social interaction with peers an individual is as she or he gets older (Twardosz & Nordquist, 1983, p. 141). In a review of attachment theory, Lopez (1995) reports that the quality of early attachment relationships is related to subsequent adult attachment styles and competencies, although he says that healthy adult attachments can moderate problems from insecure childhood attachments (pp. 406–407). Simon and Baxter (1993) discuss the relevance of attachment style to adult personal relationships, particularly to relationship outcomes, and the findings of their study support the influence of attachment style on maintenance strategies in adult, romantic relationships. Specifically, they found that people with a secure attachment style use more prosocial maintenance strategies (p. 416). Lopez (1995) reports that differences in adult attachment style are linked to variations in adult affect regulation and social competence.

The naive theory of affection also helps explain the role of affection in attachment. The naive theory of affection is the belief held by children that affection is limited in amount (Castiglia, 1999, p. 35). This belief may lead to a child resenting or being jealous of the attention and affection given to one or more sibling because she or he sees them as rivals for the limited amount of affection the parent has to give. Usually adults are viewed as sources of affection, whereas children see other children as recipients of, and therefore rivals for, affection from adults. Castiglia (1999) concludes that research supports the naive theory of affection, with children perceiving "a diminished supply of affection because affection was given to someone else" (p. 35).

Although the development of affectional communication patterns is grounded in basic human biological adaptation and individual temperament, social and environmental conditions shape these patterns through modeling and interaction. Initially, the types of behavior people perceive as affectionate will be those they associated with secure, caring relationships as infants and at various growth stages. In adults, secure attachments provide the framework for positive relationships in which affection is communicated.

## SOCIAL EXCHANGE THEORIES HELP EXPLAIN THE PROCESS OF AFFECTIONATE COMMUNICATION

Attachment theory provides a grounding for why individuals experience and communicate affection as they do, and several social exchange theories help explain how affectionate communication functions in our personal relationships.

Social exchange theory itself explains affectionate communication as a transfer of the resource of affection to the relational partner in order to receive affection from the relational partner (Knapp & Vangelisti, 1996; Roloff, 1981; Villard, 1976). Functional relationships follow the norm of reciprocity, with the amount and type of affection communicated being satisfactory to each individual involved, although not necessarily the same (Uehara, 1995). Based on resource theory, affection is a commodity exchanged through interpersonal communication (Foa & Foa, 1974). It can be in the form of love, status, information, money, goods, or services. It ranges from individualized to generalized in terms of giver and receiver and concrete to symbolic in expression. To succeed, affection exchange must be perceived as fair by those involved in the relationship. According to social production function theory, affection is an instrumental goal in the attainment of self-esteem and social well-being and is accomplished through intimate relationships and emotional support (Ormel et al., 1999). People choose their means of communicating affection based on relationship costs and benefits, the relational partner, and the context or situation.

Communicating affection, based on interaction adaptation theory, involves individuals adapting to the necessities of an interaction based on their predictions about the interaction and their goals and preferences for the interaction as well as on the relational partner's affectionate behaviors (Burgoon, Stern, & Dillman, 1995; Floyd & Burgoon, 1999). The resulting affectionate behaviors should be equivalent and mutually exchanged. Finally, expectancy violations theory helps explain why people respond the way they do to others' use of specific types of affectionate communication (Burgoon, 1991, 1995). When people's expectations for appropriate affectionate behavior are violated, they react negatively. In addition, one reason people use the types of affectionate communication they do may be because they do not want to violate their relational partner's expectations.

## AFFECTION HAS BEEN MEASURED AS A NEED OR BEHAVIOR

As defined, affection is the need for positive regard from another and the feeling of positive regard for another, communicated through affectionate behaviors, that occurs in relationships ranging from acquaintance to intimate. Corresponding ways to measure affection have focused on need or behavior, although not on feeling. Each instrument measures somewhat different needs and behaviors, and no instrument is inclusive of the numerous ways of expressing affection.

### Affection Measured as a Need

Need for affection has been measured as part of an Affection and Autonomy Index by Oliver (1981) using a 5-point Likert scale construction, subdividing affection into three categories—history, situation, and attitude. Her scales to define Affection and Autonomy were developed using adjectives from the Gough-Heilbrun Adjective Check List (Gough & Heilbrun, 1965). The questionnaire has 75 items of which 33 loaded on the six factors from the Affection Index. She reports the scales have content and construct validity (pp. 180–181) and acceptable reliability (p. 187). In her research, the history subscale of the affection index was the most powerful measure of affection (p. 186), although the history and situation subscales correlated significantly and positively (p. 96).

The Affectional Environment in the Family of Origin (AEFO) measure, constructed by Wallace (1981), uses nine items that assess affectional history with one's parents from the Somatosensory Index of Affection (Prescott & Wallace, 1978) plus items from the Affectional History Questionnaire (AHQ) derived from Leiber et al. (1976). Items from the AHQ ask about parents showing affection by hugging or kissing you, telling you, doing things for you, and giving you presents, with similar questions for the respondent's close friends and relatives (Wallace, 1981, p. 297). Additional affectionate behaviors from the AHQ include shaking hands, holding the other, making physical contact, and sexual intercourse. A factor analysis of the AEFO items on affectional history yielded nine factors, with the first two factors, which accounted for the majority of the variance, including mainly the items about hugging and kissing. Other than face and concurrent validity, Wallace provides no information on the validity and reliability of the measure.

The Somatosensory Index of Human Affection was developed by Prescott and Wallace (1978) "to evaluate the role of pain and pleasure in human development and their relationship to social, sexual, cultural and moral values and behaviors" (p. 233). Questions focus upon parent-child relationships, sexual values and behaviors, drug and alcoholic behaviors, and moral values. The questionnaire has 104 items rated 1–6 from *strongly agree* to *strongly disagree*. According to Wallace (1981), nine items assess the respondent's affectional history with her or his parents, for example: "My father (mother) did not hug and kiss me a lot" (p. 297). Four additional items from the Somatosensory Index of Human Affection relate to affection, two each for touch and sexual activity. The authors provide no information regarding reliability and validity.

The Parental Bonding Instrument (PBI) was developed by Parker et al. (1979) to measure parental care and overprotection, the two principal source variables of parental contributions to bonding (p. 2). The Likert-type scales can be used separately or together (p. 7). The "care-indifference/rejection" dimension consists of 12 items and accounted for 28% of the total variance in factor structure in their study (p. 3). It includes speaking with a warm and friendly voice, helping, being affectionate, talking things over, smiling, praising, and other items. According to Parker et al. (1979), "on measurements of reliability and validity the scales appear to be acceptable, and are independent of the parent's sex" (p. 9). Mackinnon et al. (1993) report that "a growing body of evidence indicates that the PBI has excellent psychometric properties and that scores on its scales relate to actual parental behavior" (p. 135).

In addition to analyzing affectional history as a way of establishing need for affection, researchers also look at affection related to motives and traits. Rubin et al. (1988) found that affection as a motive included helping, letting others know I care about their feelings, thanking them, showing encouragement, and being concerned. Their Interpersonal Communication Motives (ICM) scale has 28 items measuring the six motives for interpersonal communication, including affection. Rubin et al. (1988) provide evidence for the convergent validity of the ICM scale.

Finally, Gaines (1996) used an 8-item version of the Interpersonal Adjective Scale (IAS; Wiggins, 1979; Wiggins, Trapnell, & Phillips, 1988) designed to measure individuals' affection-giving and respect-giving traits. Two items of the IAS are positively keyed for affection: warm and agreeable, and two items are negatively keyed: cold and quarrelsome (Gaines, 1996, p. 248). The scale asks respondents the extent to which each item is descriptive of themselves on a 9-point Likert scale. Factor analysis yielded one factor with the four affection items; reliability analysis was acceptable (p. 248). In addition, respondents self-reported affection-giving traits were highly correlated with their affectionate behavior as reported by their partners (p. 258).

Affection Measured as Behavior

A number of instruments measure self-reported affectionate behavior in adults. The Affectionate Communication Index (ACI; Floyd & Morman, 1998) has three factors that accounted for 53.8% of the variance in their study. The factors are nonverbal expressions of affection, verbal expressions of affection, and social supportiveness (pp. 150–151). Results of one study indicated that "the verbal and nonverbal subscales [of the ACI] successfully predicted nonverbal immediacy and that all three subscales successfully predicted nonverbal expressiveness" (p. 157). According to the authors, the ACI is grounded in native experience, demonstrates convergent and discriminant validity and internal and test-retest reliability, and discriminates between affectionate and nonaffectionate relationships (p. 152). However, as the authors also point out, due to limitations in the process of development, the scale may be focused more on romantic affection and may be more appropriate for younger respondents (p. 159).

Floyd (1997a) reports the development of an 13-item scale measuring overt behaviors focusing on affectionate words, active physical contact, and passive physical contact, which come from Twardosz, Schwartz, Fox, & Cunningham (1979), with specific verbal and nonverbal behaviors from other sources. A pilot study tested face validity by asking respondents if they saw any of the listed behaviors as not affectionate behaviors; all behaviors were perceived as affectionate. Floyd (1997a) also reports using Foa & Foa's (1974) affection subscale of the Role Behavior Test; since the two subscales are love and status, he may mean the love subscale items.

The Love, Sex, and Intimacy Questionnaire was developed by Kotulski (1996) to examine the sexual and affectionate behavior of heterosexual and lesbian couples. The section on expression of affection includes 46 items that suggest ways to express affection, to which subjects respond using a 5-point Likert scale. In addition to expression of affection, the section on frequency of sexual behaviors asked about four behaviors involving "non-genital affection" such as holding hands (p. 46). No information regarding reliability and validity is provided.

Dainton et al. (1994) used eight statements regarding routine physical affection and five statements regarding satisfaction with physical affection to measure physical affection with a romantic partner using a Likert scale. The authors note that the physical affection satisfaction measure may be biased toward sexual satisfaction (p. 92). The scale apparently is reliable, but no information regarding its validity is provided.

Shuntich and Shapiro (1991) developed a list of statements to measure verbal forms of affection, which they define as the "type of statement when said to another person will tend to make the other person feel pleasant" (p. 285), specifically compliments and direct statements of caring. Direct statements of caring were ranked higher in intensity and in agreement as to type than compliments in one of their studies. Support for the validity of the statements was observed in two studies (p. 283).

The behavioral tendency of inhibited affection is included in Snell's (1989) Masculine Behavior Scale (MBS). The items included in this subscale focus on time devoted to close relationships, level of involvement in relationships, and telling others about feelings of affection. Previously, Snell (1986) included a similar inhibited affection subscale in his Masculine Role Inventory (MRI). According to the author, both the MBS and the MRI demonstrated adequate reliability and validity.

Current Affectional Experience (CAE) in romantic relationships is measured using 12 items, six asking about the respondent's behavior and six about the partner's behavior (Wallace, 1981). Behaviors are limited to hugging/holding, sexual intercourse, physical closeness, kissing, giving presents, and telling. The CAE items apparently come from the Somatosensory Index of Affection (Prescott & Wallace, 1978); no information regarding the reliability and validity of the CAE measure is reported.

Villard (1976) developed a questionnaire with 12 intimacy items and 12 economic items based on his conceptualization of affection/caring. He argues for its content validity based on social exchange theory (p. 132) and the relevance of the items as demonstrated by participant responses to whether or not the behaviors are used to show affection and caring in respondent marriages (p. 133). Construct validity was based on a factor analysis (p. 133); reliability was measured as internal consistency, and the resulting moderate reliability coefficients were attributed to the small number of items being compared (p. 139). Factor analysis showed seven dimensions of affection exchange: self-disclosing, sexual, aggressive, demonstrative, helping, gift giving, and access (p. 136).

Two instruments measure self-reported affectionate behavior in children. The

Adolescent Prosocial Behavior Inventory (APBI) was developed by Eberly and Montemayor (1998) to assess the diversity and frequency of adolescents' prosocial behavior toward each parent. The APBI has 30 items that fall into two factors: affection with 19 items, such as saying "I love you," giving a compliment, and giving a hug, and helpfulness with 11 items, such as doing the dishes, making one's bed, and straightening up the house (p. 413). For the parent survey, the parent circles the number (0 to 5) that best represents how often the adolescent did the particular activity or behavior for the parent in the past week; for the adolescent survey, the adolescent circles the number that best represents how often they did the behavior for the parent in the past week. The APBI has a consistent factor structure, content validity, convergent validity, and divergent validity, and the authors conclude that it has "demonstrated adequate psychometric strength indicating that adolescents' prosocial behavior toward parents was measured" (p. 423).

The Sibling Relationship Inventory (SRI) was developed by Boer, Westenberg, McHale, Updegraff, & Stocker (1997). The SRI has a three dimensional factor structure: affection, hostility, and rivalry (p. 851). The affection scale items include taking care of the sibling, sharing secrets, and so forth. Scale intercorrelations in the two studies showed that affection and hostility are unipolar dimensions of the sibling relationship, rather than two extremes of one continuum, and rivalry is a separate dimension, modestly related to hostility (p. 856). The authors found adequate internal consistency, satisfactory test-retest reliability, and promising convergent and discriminant validity for the SRI (p. 851) and conclude that it "provides a reliable impression of the way children perceive their behavior and feelings in the sibling relationship during middle childhood. A particular strength of the SRI is its applicability with children as young as 6–9 years of age" (p. 857).

Finally, although no instrument to measure observed behaviors in adults has been found, several measure observed behaviors in children. Twardosz et al. (1979) developed a system to measure affectionate behavior using four categories: smiling and laughing, affectionate, active affectionate physical contact, and passive affectionate physical contact. Two additional categories were included for other types of social behavior that typically occur during adult-child and child-child interactions: speech and other social interactions. A seventh category, leveling, was scored only for adults when they were sitting, kneeling, or otherwise in a posture that would bring them closer to the height of the children. The system was developed based on informal observations of adult-child interactions and past research and evaluated using videotapes of care giver-child interactions in day-care settings. Results support the reliability and validity of the measuring system (Mill & Romano-White, 1999, p. 162; Twardosz et al., 1979, p. 177).

In a study of children's affectionate communication, Noller (1978) defined affectionate behavior a priori as "interactive behavior that would normally be regarded as affectionate (e.g., kissing, cuddling, hugging)" (p. 317). The other behaviors she observed, referred to as interaction, including holding hands, touching, patting on the head, patting on the bottom, waving, calling goodbye, and talking, but it is unclear if any of these were included as affectionate behavior or if affectionate behavior was included in interaction. Interrater reliability was acceptable and was the same for the interaction measure and the affection measure.

### Affection Measured as Need and Behavior

Four instruments combine self-report measures of need with behavior. The FIRO-B, the Fundamental Interpersonal Relations Orientation-Behavior, was developed by Schutz (1958) to measure the three interpersonal needs of inclusion, control, and affection. FIRO-B contains two scales measuring behavior and need in the affection area: "expressed behavior of the self" and "behavior wanted from others toward self." The scales include general statements about friendly, close, and personal relationships. Schutz presents a great deal of evidence that the FIRO-B scales have content, concurrent, predictive, and construct validity and are reliable based on internal consistency and intercorrelation (pp. 66–80).

The Affectional Needs and Behavior Scale (ANBS) was developed by Leiber et al. (1976) to measure affectional needs, customary modes of expressing those needs, and changes in affectional needs and behaviors, among other areas. Items include frequency of actual behavior, desire for frequency of behavior, and change in actual behavior and desire for behavior for feeling affectionate, amorous, and protective; sexual intercourse; nonsexual/other physical closeness, and talking. Items are rated on a 5-point scale indicating frequency or intensity of response. No information is provided regarding validity and reliability.

The Affectional Interaction Scale (AIS) was developed by Liederman (1991) as a measure of behavioral affectional interaction for use with married couples. It consists of 25 physical and verbal/supportive affectionate behaviors that assess the amounts of affection desired, received, and given as well as affectional satisfaction and give-and-take in both sexual and nonsexual contexts on a 9-point Likert scale. Affectional satisfaction is the difference between amount of affection desired and received; give-and-take is the difference between the affection given and received (pp. 41–42). She found that the AIS has high temporal stability, high internal consistency, good concurrent validity, and good discriminative ability (p. 77).

Haslam (1995) developed items corresponding to the features of Foa and Foa's (1974) four resource classes: love, information, status, and services. Love and status items had the highest loadings, although information loadings were also high. According to Haslam's analysis, the items in status overlap love; those in information overlap status, and those in services overlap information (pp. 220–221). Consequently, the items appear to be measuring the same factor and doing so with internal consistency (p. 220).

Instruments That Include Affection Items

A number of other instruments include items that measure affection. The Waring Intimacy Questionnaire (WIQ; Waring, 1979; Waring & Reddon, 1983) measures eight components of marital intimacy, each with 10 items, including affection, or "the degree to which feelings of emotional closeness are expressed by the couple" (p. 53). The WIQ scales "are minimally redundant, highly reliable, relatively free from response bias, and free from sexual bias" (p. 56). In addition, convergent and discriminant item validity have been shown, and comparison across diverse samples indicates the constructs are stable (Reddon, Patton, & Waring, 1985, p. 242). Results show that "the WIQ consists of eight distinct components of intimacy that can be distinguished from each other, as well as from social desirability" (p. 241). According to Reddon et al. (1985), "the 40-item summary index provides a good basis for a short form assessment of total intimacy with little loss in terms of validity" (238).

The 32-item Dyadic Adjustment Scale (DAS) was developed by Spanier (1976) for assessing the quality of marriage and similar dyads. The Affectional Expression subscale includes four items: demonstrations of affection, sex relations, being too tired for sex, and not showing love. The DAS and its subscales are reported to have content, criterion, and construct validity (pp. 22–23) and high reliability (p. 24).

The Role Behavior Test was developed by Foa and Foa (1974) to analyze a person's exchanges of love and status with another person in a specific role relationship, such as wife-husband (pp. 391–396). Six items each examine giving status to the other, giving love to the other, taking love from the other, and taking status from the other. Gaines (1996) reports that factor analysis yielded one underlying factor for affection, and reliability was acceptable (p. 250).

Foa and Foa (1974) also constructed the Social Interaction Inventory for Exchanges of Giving (SIIEG), which is "designed to record preferences for receiving a certain resource in return for the resource given by the subject to the other" (p. 398). The inventory includes each resource class five times, each time described by a different statement (p. 398). The Social Interaction Inventory for Exchanges of Taking is identical to the SIIEG except that it records exchanges of taking rather than giving (p. 406).

Rubin (1970) developed a 13-item Love Scale and a 13-item Liking Scale to measure the attitudes of love and liking. The conception of love, as defined by the Love Scale, includes three components: affiliative and dependent need, predisposition to help, and an orientation of exclusiveness and absorption. The conception of liking, as defined by the Liking Scale, includes two components: favorable evaluation and respect for the target person and perception that the target is similar to oneself. Rubin (1970) states that the Love Scale measures romantic love (p. 265), yet he found that respondents loved their same-sex friends (p. 268), indicating that the scale measures love as a broader conception than just romantic. In addition, correlations between scores on the Love and Liking Scales were relatively high, indicating a conceptual overlap between the two scales. Validity of the Love Scale was assessed in a questionnaire study and a laboratory experiment and was confirmed (p. 265). Liederman (1991) used Rubin's (1970) Liking Scale to measure affection, and she argues, based on evidence from additional research, that the Liking and Love Scales measure different phenomena (p. 43). Dainton et al. (1994) say the Love Scale measures compassionate love rather than passion (p. 95).

Three instruments that measure immediacy include items that can be considered as measuring affection. The Behavioral Indicants of Immediacy Scale (BII) measures nonverbal immediacy behaviors including the affectionate behaviors of eye contact, touch, smiles, and spending time talking (Andersen, Andersen, & Jensen, 1979). This 20-item scale uses a Likert-type format to ask respondents to evaluate a relational partner's nonverbal immediacy behaviors in terms of how "usual" these behaviors are. Alpha reliability in a recent study that used an 18-item slightly modified version of the scale was .82 (Andersen, Guerrero, Buller, & Jorgensen, 1998, p. 514). The scale has factorial, content, face, and predictive validity (Andersen et al, 1979, p. 162).

The Dimensions of Relational Message Themes (Burgoon & Hale, 1987) was developed to measure the fundamental themes of relational communication posited by Burgoon and Hale (1984). It is a 30-item Likert-type scale incorporating eight themes including immediacy/affection, which Burgoon and Hale (1984) define as attraction and liking. Based on a number of studies, the instrument has strong predictive validity and good reliability (Burgoon & Hale, 1987, p. 40).

The Verbal Approach/Avoidance Survey was developed by Mottet and Richmond (1998) as part of a reconceptualization of the construct of verbal immediacy. The survey has 14 items, to which respondents indicate how frequently they use each of the verbal approach/avoidance strategies (p. 34). Three items involve affection. Reliability as reported is good (pp. 37–38), and evidence is presented for construct validity (p. 29).

Finally, whereas Mehrabian's (1966; Wiener & Mehrabian, 1968) immediacy scale was developed to assess verbal immediacy, that is, the degree of directness and intensity in a message (Mehrabian, 1966, p. 28), it might be adapted to measure the affection one feels for another. According to Mehrabian (1966), more immediate statements refer to an object in its entirety versus to a part or aspect of the object, directly relate to the speaker versus being related to another object, refer to a direct relationship between the communicator and the object versus reducing the involvement of the two, contain a direct relationship versus a mediated relationship between the communicator and the object, and make an explicit statement of relationship versus an implied one (pp. 31–32). Hence, in the following pairs of statements, the first would be more immediate or indicate more affection than the second: I love Krista; I love Krista's sense of humor. Kim is my daughter; Kim and I are members of the same family. I talked to Kurt yesterday; I talked to my children yesterday. I visited Kersten; I visited Kersten's house. Mom needs my help; Mom needs help. Although the immediacy scale apparently is problematic both in conceptualization and use (see Mottet & Richmond, 1998, pp. 26–27), it may provide a beginning for the development of a measure of verbal expression of affectionate feeling.

In sum, a number of instruments measure affection, but each defines affection differently and measures different components of the affection process. Most are self-report measures for adults, and some include affection as part of a broader concept. Since each was constructed to examine the specific interests of the researcher and none surveys the range of affectionate needs, feelings, and behaviors, building on previous research that used these instruments is problematic.

## CONCLUSION

This essay has examined the concept of affection in interpersonal relationships—its importance, definition, and place as a dimension of relationships as well as behaviors characterized as affectionate, factors influencing affectionate communication, development of affectionate patterns, theories explaining the communication of affection, and ways to measure affection. Obviously, affection cannot be thought of as just a fond and tender feeling.

Considering its importance in human development and well-being, affection has received relatively little emphasis and little systematic investigation over the years, particularly in the discipline of communication. This overview of what we know about affection begins the process of synthesizing our knowledge of this key dimension of relationships. To continue the synthesis, we must use a consistent definition of affection and examine the components of that definition: need, feeling, and behavior, to understand how each works, how they are associated with each other, and how they function in all types of relationships. To accomplish the synthesis, we must develop and validate a standard set of measuring instruments and use those instruments systematically in future research. In addition, we must examine the process of the communication of affection from both individual and relational perspectives, investigating the numerous influences on that process across cultures. Given our emphasis on the control dimension of relationships over the years, likely grounded in our rhetorical heritage and emphasis on persuasive processes, the time has come to grant the affection dimension of relationships the attention it deserves.

# APPENDIX

Affectionate Behaviors

*Nonverbal*

Touching (Acker, Acker, & Pearson, 1973; Barber & Thomas, 1986; Burgoon, 1991; Harrison-Speake, & Willis, 1995; Jones & Yarborough, 1985; Marston, Hecht, & Robers, 1987; Monsour, 1992; Noller & Fitzpatrick, 1993; Prager, 1999; Prager & Buhrmester, 1998; Salt, 1991; Schoenhofer, 1989; Villard & Whipple, 1976)

Handshakes (Afifi & Johnson, 1999)

Friendly roughhousing/mock aggression/mock assault/mock attacks/playful wrestling (Afifi & Johnson, 1999; Kelleher, 1998; Twardosz, Botkin, Cunningham, Weddle, Sollie, & Shreve, 1987; Twardosz, Schwartz, Fox, & Cunningham, 1979; Villard & Whipple, 1976)

Pats/rubs/caresses (Afifi & Johnson, 1999; Acker & Marton, 1984; Jones & Yarborough, 1985; Landau, 1989; Schoenhofer, 1989; Twardosz & Nordquist, 1983; Twardosz et al., 1987; Walters, Pearce, & Dahms, 1957)

Kissing (Afifi & Johnson, 1999; Acker & Marton, 1984; Barber & Thomas, 1986; Boer, Westenberg, McHale, Updegraff, & Stocker, 1997; Jones & Yarborough, 1985; Landau, 1989; Noller & Fitzpatrick, 1993; Oliver, 1981; Wallace, 1981; Walters et al., 1957)

Holding hands (Afifi & Johnson, 1999; Acker & Marton, 1984; Boer et al., 1997; Burgoon, 1991; Twardosz et al., 1987)/hand squeezes (Prager & Buhrmester, 1998)

Shaking hands (Burgoon, 1991; Wallace, 1981)

Picking up (Acker et al., 1973; Barber & Thomas, 1986)

Lifting leg (Acker et al., 1973)

Hugging [body-to-body contact, usually with immediate disengagement (Acker & Marton, 1984, p. 260)] (Barber & Thomas, 1986; Boer et al., 1997; Hollender, Dowdy, & Kourany, 1979; Hyson, Whitehead, & Prudhoe, 1986; Jones & Yarborough, 1985; Landau, 1989; Noller & Fitzpatrick, 1993; Oliver, 1981; Twardosz & Nordquist, 1983; Wallace, 1981; Walters et al., 1957)

Cuddling/holding [supporting recipient in arms with gentle body-to-body contact, usually with no immediate disengagement (Acker & Marton, 1984, p. 260)] (Hollender et al., 1979)

Snuggling [leaning into or resting against the recipient without arm involvement (Acker & Marton, 1984, p. 260)] (Twardosz & Nordquist, 1983)

Fondling [digital manipulation of part of the recipient's body (Acker & Marton, 1984, p. 260)] (Walters et al., 1957)

Gently bouncing up and down in lap (Acker & Marton, 1984)

Gently cleaning (Acker & Marton, 1984)

Caring for an imagined injury (Acker & Marton, 1984)

Picking up (Barber & Thomas, 1986)

Lap sitting (Hyson et al., 1986; Twardosz & Nordquist, 1983; Twardosz et al., 1987).

Proxemic behaviors

Physical closeness (DeVito, 1992; Morris & Smith, 1980; Noller & Fitzpatrick, 1993)

Oculesic behaviors

Mutual eye contact (Andersen & Guerrero, 1998; Kellerman, Lewis, & Laird, 1989; Marston et al., 1987; Noller & Fitzpatrick, 1993)

Prolonged & focused eye contact (DeVito, 1992; Palmer & Simmons, 1995; Twardosz & Nordquist, 1983)

Kinesic behaviors

Smiling (Andersen & Guerrero, 1998; Marston et al., 1987; Palmer & Simmons, 1995; Twardosz & Nordquist, 1983; Twardosz et al., 1987)

Facial pleasantness (Noller & Fitzpatrick, 1993; Wilkinson, 1996)

Head nodding (Palmer & Simmons, 1995)
Forward lean (Palmer & Simmons, 1995)
Object-focused gestures (Palmer & Simmons, 1995)
Leveling [sitting, kneeling or using a posture to come closer to the height of the other (Twardosz et al., 1979)]
Outstretched arms (Wilkinson, 1996)
Vocalic behaviors
Speaking tenderly (DeVito, 1992)
Increased talk rate (Palmer & Simmons, 1995)
Moderate amounts of talk (Palmer & Simmons, 1995)
Positive affective tone (Prager & Buhrmester, 1998)
Laughing (Twardosz & Nordquist, 1983; Walters et al., 1957)
Chronemic behaviors
Spending time together (Andersen & Guerrero, 1998)
Being on time (Knapp & Vangelisti, 1996)
Objects
Gifts (Knapp & Vangelisti, 1996; Lemieux, 1996; Noller & Fitzpatrick, 1993; Twardosz & Nordquist, 1983; Villard & Whipple, 1979; Wallace, 1981), including specific objects such as rings (Scarisbrick, 1993)
Money (Villard & Whipple, 1979)
Dress (Marston et al., 1987)
Other Nonverbal Behaviors
Pretend feeding (Acker & Marton, 1984)
Making oneself as attractive as possible (DeVito, 1992)
General exuberance (Wilkinson, 1996)

*Verbal Expressions*

Compliments/praises
General [such as "you look nice" (Acker et al., 1973)] (Boer et al., 1997; Oliver, 1981; Twardosz & Nordquist, 1983; Twardosz et al., 1987; Walters et al., 1957)
Specific [such as "what pretty eyes" (Acker et al., 1973)]
Positive reinforcement (Oliver, 1981)
Direct emotional expressions [words used to directly communicate positive feelings, such as "I love you" (Acker et al., 1973)] (Andersen & Guerrero, 1998; Bell & Healey, 1992; Marston et al., 1987; Monsour, 1992; Noller & Fitzpatrick, 1993; Twardosz & Nordquist, 1983; Twardosz et al., 1987; Wallace, 1981; Wilkinson, 1996)
Teasing/friendly insults [framing a potentially negative statement as humor or play (Alberts, Kellar-Guenther, & Corman, 1996, p. 337] (Andersen & Guerrero, 1998; Bell & Healey, 1992; Bell, Buerkel-Rothfuss, & Gore, 1987; Kelleher, 1998; Noller & Fitzpatrick, 1993; Powers & Glenn, 1979)
Self-disclosure (Andersen & Guerrero, 1998; DeVito, 1992; Floyd, 1996b; Monsour, 1992; Noller & Fitzpatrick, 1993; Oliver, 1981; Prager & Buhrmester, 1998; Sprecher, 1987; Villard & Whipple, 1979; Wood & Inman, 1993), including sharing feelings (Oliver, 1981; Wood & Inman, 1993) and sharing secrets (Boer et al., 1997; DeVito, 1992)
Verbal immediacy, including use of first-person pronouns (Andersen & Guerrero, 1998)
Personal forms of address (Bell et al., 1987; DeVito, 1992; Noller & Fitzpatrick, 1993; Twardosz et al., 1987), including nicknames (Andersen & Guerrero, 1998)
Assurances [emphasizing positive feelings about the relationship (Andersen & Guerrero, 1998)]
Politeness (DeVito, 1992)
Sexual invitations (Bell et al., 1987)
Joking (Swain, 1989)

*Patterns of Nonverbal and Verbal Expression of Affection*

General support (Barber & Thomas, 1986; Marston et al., 1987; Monsour, 1992)

Taking care of (Boer et al., 1997; Twardosz et al., 1987), including feeding (Twardosz et al., 1979)

Helping (Barber & Thomas, 1986; Boer et al., 1997; Oliver, 1981; Twardosz et al., 1979; Wood & Inman, 1993; Walters et al., 1957)

Teaching (Barber & Thomas, 1986; Boer et al., 1997)

Doing favors for/granting privileges to (Boer et al., 1997; Marston et al., 1987; Noller & Fitzpatrick, 1993; Swain, 1989; Twardosz & Nordquist, 1983; Villard & Whipple, 1979; Wallace, 1981; Weinberg, 1994; Wilkinson, 1996; Wood, 1998; Wood & Inman, 1993)

Sharing things, i.e., objects (Boer et al., 1997; Twardosz & Nordquist, 1983; Walters et al., 1957)

Trying to make other feel better when hurt or upset (Boer et al., 1997)

Sharing interests/showing interest in other's interests (Barber & Thomas, 1986; Noller & Fitzpatrick, 1993; Oliver, 1981)

Being there/being dependable, loyal, trustworthy (Barber & Thomas, 1986; Marston et al., 1987; Oliver, 1981)

Giving encouragement (Noller & Fitzpatrick, 1993)

Companionship/being with (Barber & Thomas, 1986; Wood, 1998)

Sharing activities/experiences/accomplishments (Barber & Thomas, 1986; DeVito, 1992; Floyd, 1995, 1996b; Lemieux, 1996; Monsour, 1992; Noller & Fitzpatrick, 1993; Swain, 1989; Wood & Inman, 1993)

Talking with ( Barber & Thomas, 1986) and listening to (Oliver, 1981; Prager & Buhrmester, 1998)

Working hard for someone (Knapp & Vangelisti, 1996)

Cooking for someone/eating someone's cooking (Knapp & Vangelisti, 1996; Wilkinson, 1996)

Negotiating/talking things out (Marston et al., 1987; Twardosz et al., 1987); compromising (Walters et al., 1957)

Future commitment (Marston et al., 1987)

Communicating (Marston et al., 1987; Oliver, 1981; Twardosz et al., 1987; Wilkinson, 1996), including notes, cards, letters (Marston et al., 1987) and telephone calls (Knapp & Vangelisti, 1996)

Sex (Marston et al., 1987; Monsour, 1992; Noller & Fitzpatrick, 1993; Prager, 1999; Villard & Whipple, 1979; Wallace, 1981)

"Tolerating the less pleasant aspects of the other" (Noller & Fitzpatrick, 1993, p. 88 )

Not fighting (Oliver, 1981)

Not comparing negatively to others, not criticizing, minimizing the faults (DeVito, 1992; Oliver, 1981)

Physical punishment /discipline (MacDonald, 1992; Wallace, 1981)

Trust (Monsour, 1992)

Being compliant/accepting [conforming to another's request (Walters et al, 1957)]

# REFERENCES

Acker, L. E., & Marton, J. (1984). Facilitation of affectionate-like behaviors in the play of young children. *Child Study Journal, 14*(4), 255–269.

Acker, L. E., Acker, M. A., & Pearson, D. (1973). Generalized imitative affection: Relationship to prior kinds of imitation training. *Journal of Experimental Child Psychology, 16,* 111–125.

Afifi, W. A., & Johnson, M. L. (1999). The use and interpretation of tie signs in a public setting: Relationship and sex differences. *Journal of Social and Personal Relationships, 16*(1), 9–38.

Albrecht, T. L., Burleson, B. R., & Goldsmith, D. (1994). Supportive communication. In M. L. Knapp & G. R. Miller (Eds.), *Handbook of interpersonal communication* (2nd ed., pp. 419–449). Thousand Oaks, CA: Sage.

Alberts, J. K., Kellar-Guenther, Y., & Corman, S. R. (1996). That's not funny: Understanding recipients' responses to teasing. *Western Journal of Communication, 60*(4), 337–357.

Andersen, J. F., Andersen, P. A., & Jensen, A. D. (1979). The measurement of nonverbal intimacy. *Journal of Applied Communication Research, 7,* 153–180.

Andersen, P. A. (1999). *Nonverbal communication: Forms and functions.* Mountain View, CA: Mayfield.

Andersen, P. A., & Guerrero, L. K. (1998). The bright side of relational communication: Interpersonal warmth as a social emotion. In P. A. Andersen & L. K. Guerrero (Eds.), *Handbook of communication and emotion: Research, theory, applications, and contexts* (pp. 303–329). San Diego, CA: Academic Press.

Andersen, P. A., Guerrero, L. K., Buller, D. K., & Jorgensen, P. F. (1998). An empirical comparison of three theories of nonverbal immediacy exchange. *Human Communication Research, 24,* 501–535.

Anderson, C. M, & Martin, M. M. (1995). The effects of communication motives, interaction involvement, and loneliness on satisfaction—A model of small groups. *Small Group Research, 26*(1), 118–137.

Bakken, L., & Romig, C. (1992). Interpersonal needs in middle adolescents: Companionship, leadership and intimacy. *Journal of Adolescence, 15,* 301–316.

Barbato, C. A., & Perse, E. M. (1992). Interpersonal communication motives and the life position of elders. *Communication Research, 19*(4), 516–531.

Barber, B. K., & Thomas, D. L. (1986). Dimensions of fathers' and mothers' supportive behavior: The case for physical affection. *Journal of Marriage and the Family, 48,* 783–794.

Barnes, M. K., & Duck, S. (1994). Everyday communicative contexts for social support. In B. R. Burleson, T. L. Albrecht, & I. G. Sarason (Eds.), *Communication of social support: Messages, interactions, relationships, and community* (pp. 175–194). Thousand Oaks, CA: Sage.

Bates, J. E. (1989). Concepts and measures of temperament. In G. A. Kohnstamm, J. E. Bates, & M. K. Rothbart (Eds.), *Temperament in childhood* (pp. 3–26). Chichester, UK; New York: Wiley.

Bates, J. E. (1994). Introduction. In J. E. Bates & T. D. Wachs (Eds.), *Temperament: Individual differences at the interface of biology and behavior* (pp. 1–14). Washington, DC: American Psychological Association.

Beatty, M. J., McCroskey, J. C., & Heisel, A. D. (1998). Communication apprehension as temperamental expression: A communibiological paradigm. *Communication Monographs, 65,* 197–219.

Bell, R. A., & Healey, J. G. (1992). Idiomatic communication and interpersonal solidarity in friends' relational cultures. *Human Communication Research, 18,* 307–335.

Bell, R. A., Buerkel-Rothfuss, N. L., & Gore, K. E. (1987). "Did you bring the yarmulke for the Cabbage Patch Kid?" The idiomatic communication of young lovers. *Human Communication Research, 14,* 47–67.

Boer, F., Westenberg, P. M., McHale, S. M., Updegraff, K. A., & Stocker, C. M. (1997). The factorial structure of the Sibling Relationship Inventory (SRI) in American and Dutch samples. *Journal of Social and Personal Relationships, 14*(6), 851–859.

Booth-Butterfield, M., & Trotta, M. R. (1994). Attributional patterns for expressions of love. *Communication Reports, 7*(2), 119–129.

Botkin, D., Townley, K. F., & Twardosz, S. (1991). Children's affectionate behavior: Gender differences. *Early Education and Development, 2*(4), 270–286.

Bowlby, J. (1979). *The making & breaking of affectional bonds.* London: Tavistock/Routledge.

Bruess, C. J. S., & Pearson, J. C. (1997). Interpersonal rituals in marriage and adult friendship. *Communication Monographs, 64,* 25–46.

Burgoon, J. K. (1991). Relational message interpretations of touch, conversational distance, and posture. *Journal of Nonverbal Behavior, 15*(4), 233–259.

Burgoon, J. K. (1995). Cross-cultural and intercultural applications of expectancy violations theory. In R. L. Wiseman (Ed.), *Intercultural communication theory (International and Intercultural Communication Annual, 19,* pp. 194–214). Thousand Oaks, CA: Sage.

Burgoon, J. K., & Hale, J. L. (1984). The fundamental topoi of relational communication. *Communication Monographs, 51*(3), 193–214.

Burgoon, J. K., & Hale, J. L. (1987). Validation and measurement of the fundamental themes of relational communication. *Communication Monographs, 54*, 19–41.

Burgoon, J. K., Buller, D. B., & Woodall, W. G. (1996). *Nonverbal communication: The unspoken dialogue* (2nd ed.). New York: McGraw-Hill.

Burgoon, J. K., Stern, L. A., & Dillman, L. (1995). *Interpersonal adaptation: Dyadic interaction patterns*. Cambridge, UK: Cambridge University Press.

Burleson, B. R. (1994a). Comforting messages: Features, functions, and outcomes. In J. A. Daly & J. M. Wiemann (Eds.), *Strategic interpersonal communication* (pp. 135–161). Hillsdale, NJ: Erlbaum.

Burleson, B. R. (1994b). Comforting messages: Significance, approaches, and effects. In B. R. Burleson, T. L. Albrecht, & I. G. Sarason (Eds.), *Communication of social support: Messages, interactions, relationships, and community* (pp. 3–28). Thousand Oaks, CA: Sage.

Burleson, B. R., Albrecht, T. L., Goldsmith, D. J., & Sarason, I. G. (1994). The communication of social support. In B. R. Burleson, T. L. Albrecht, & I. G. Sarason (Eds.), *Communication of social support: Messages, interactions, relationships, and community* (pp. xi–xxx). Thousand Oaks, CA: Sage.

Buss, D. M. (1994). *The evolution of desire: Strategies of human mating*. New York: Basic Books.

Buss, D. M. (1999). Evolutionary psychology: A new paradigm for psychological science. In D. H. Rosen & M. C. Luebbert (Eds.), *Evolution of the psyche* (pp. 1–33). Westport, CT: Praeger.

Buss, D. M., & Barnes, M. (1986). Preferences in human mate selection. *Journal of Personality and Social Psychology, 50*(3), 559–570.

Canary, D. J., & Emmers-Sommer, T. M., with Faulkner, S. (1997). *Sex and gender differences in personal relationships*. New York: Guilford Press.

Cancian, F. M. (1989). Love and the rise of capitalism. In B. J. Risman & P. S. Schwarts (Eds.), *Gender in intimate relationships* (pp. 12–25). Belmont, CA: Wadsworth.

Castiglia, P. T. (1999). Growth and development: Affectionate behavior. *Journal of Pediatric Health Care, 13*, 34–36.

Cissna, K. N., & Anderson. R. (1990). The contributions of Carl R. Rogers to a philosophical praxis of dialogue. *Western Journal of Speech Communication, 54*, 125–147.

Compton, M. V., & Niemeyer, J. A. (1994). Expressions of affection in young children with sensory impairments: A research agenda. *Education and Treatment of Children, 17*(1), 68–85.

Cummings, E. M., Zahn-Waxler, C., & Radke-Yarrow, M. (1981). Young children's' responses to expressions of anger and affection by others in the family. *Child Development, 52*, 1274–1282.

Dainton, M. (1994). *An examination of routine and strategic interactions in maintained marital relationships*. Unpublished doctoral dissertation, The Ohio State University, Columbus.

Dainton, M. (1998). Everyday interaction in marital relationships: Variations in relative importance and event duration. *Communication Reports, 11*(2), 101–109.

Dainton, M., Stafford, L., & Canary, D. J. (1994). Maintenance strategies and physical affection as predictors of love, liking, and satisfaction in marriage. *Communication Reports, 7*(2), 88–98.

de Bono, M., & Bargmann, C. I. (1998). Natural variation in a neuropeptide Y receptor homolog modifies social behavior and food responses in *C. Elegans. Cell, 94*, 679–689.

Derlega, V. J., Lewis, R. J., Harrison, S., Winstead, B. A., & Costanza, R. (1989). Gender differences in the initiation and attribution of tactile intimacy. *Journal of Nonverbal Behavior, 13*(2), 83–96.

Derlega, V. J., Metts, S., Petronio, S., & Margulis, S. T. (1993). *Self-disclosure*. Newbury Park, CA: Sage.

DePaulo, B. M., & Coleman, L. M. (1987). Verbal and nonverbal communication of warmth to children, foreigners, and retarded adults. *Journal of Nonverbal Behavior, 11*(2), 75–88.

DeVito, J. A. (1992). *The interpersonal communication book* (6th ed.). New York: HarperCollins.

Dindia, K., & Allen, M. (1992). Sex differences in self-disclosure: A meta-analysis. *Psychological Bulletin, 112*(1), 106–124.

Dolin, D. J., & Booth-Butterfield, M. (1993). Reach out and touch someone: Analysis of nonverbal comforting responses. *Communication Quarterly, 41*(4), 383–393.

Downs, V. C., & Javidi, M. (1990). Linking communication motives to loneliness in the lives of older adults: An empirical test of interpersonal needs and gratifications. *Journal of Applied Communication Research, 18*(1), 32–48.

Eberly, M. D., & Montemayor, R. (1999). Adolescent affection and helpfulness toward parents: A 2-year follow-up. *Journal of Early Adolescence, 19*(2), 226–248.

Eberly, M. B., & Montemayor, R. (1998). Doing good deeds: An examination of adolescent prosocial behavior in the context of parent-adolescent relationships. *Journal of Adolescent Research, 13*(4), 403–432.

Fisher, S. G., Macrosson, W. D. K., & Walker, C. A. (1995). FIRO-B: The power of love and the love of power. *Psychological Reports, 76,* 195–206.

Fiske, A. P. (1991). *Structures of social life: The four elementary forms of human relations: Communal sharing, authority ranking, equality matching, market pricing.* New York: Free Press.

Fitzpatrick, M. A., & Best, P. (1979). Dyadic adjustment in relational types: Consensus, cohesion, affectional expression, and satisfaction in enduring relationships. *Communication Monographs, 46*(3), 167–178.

Flaherty, L. M., Pearce, K. J., & Rubin, R. B. (1998). Internet and face-to-face communication: Not functional alternatives. *Communication Quarterly, 46*(3), 250–268.

Floyd, K. (1995). Gender and closeness among friends and siblings. *Journal of Psychology, 129,* 193–202.

Floyd, K. (1996a). Brotherly love I: The experience of closeness in the fraternal dyad. *Personal Relationships, 3,* 369–385.

Floyd, K. (1996b). Communicating closeness among siblings: As an application of the gendered closeness perspective. *Communication Research Reports, 13*(1), 27–34.

Floyd, K. (1997a). Communicating affection in dyadic relationships: As an assessment of behavior and expectancies. *Communication Quarterly, 45*(1), 68–80.

Floyd, K. (1997b). Knowing when to say "I love you": As an expectancy approach to affectionate communication. *Communication Research Reports, 14*(3), 321–330.

Floyd, K., & Burgoon, J. K. (1999). Reacting to nonverbal expressions of liking: A test of interaction adaptation theory. *Communication Monographs, 66,* 219–239.

Floyd, K., & Morman, M. T. (1997). Affectionate communication in nonromantic relationships: Influences of communicator, relational, and contextual factors. *Western Journal of Communication, 61*(3), 279–298.

Floyd, K., & Morman, M. T. (1998). The measure of affectionate communication. *Communication Quarterly, 46*(2), 144–162.

Floyd, K., & Morman, M. T. (2000). Reacting to the verbal expression of affection in same-sex interaction. *Southern Communication Journal, 65*(4), 287–299.

Floyd, K., & Parks, M. R. (1995). Manifesting closeness in the interactions of peers: A look at siblings and friends. *Communication Reports, 8*(2), 69–76.

Floyd, K., & Voloudakis, M. (1997, November). *Affectionate behavior in adult platonic friendships: Interpreting and evaluating expectancy violations.* Paper presented at the conference of the Speech Communication Association, Chicago.

Floyd, K., & Voloudakis, M. (1999). Affectionate behavior in adult platonic friendships: Interpreting and evaluating expectancy violations. *Human Communication Research, 25,* 341–369.

Foa, U. G., & Foa, E. B. (1974). *Societal structures of the mind.* Springfield, IL: Thomas.

Gaines, S. O., Jr. (1994). Exchange of respect-denying behaviors among male-female friendships. *Journal of Social and Personal Relationships, 11,* 5–24.

Gaines, S. O., Jr. (1995). Classifying dating couples: Gender as reflected in traits, roles, and resulting behavior. *Basic and Applied Social Psychology, 16,* 75–94.

Gaines, S. O., Jr. (1996). Impact of interpersonal traits and gender-role compliance on interpersonal resource exchange among dating and engaged/married couples. *Journal of Social and Personal Relationships, 13*(2), 241–261.

Gaines, S. O., Jr. (1997). Communalism and the reciprocity of affection and respect among interethnic married couples. *Journal of Black Studies, 27*(3), 352–364.

Gaylin, W. (1976). *Caring.* New York: Knopf.

Gough, H. G., & Heilbrun, A. B., Jr. (1965). *The adjective check list manual.* Palo Alto, CA: Consulting Psychologist Press.

Gray, J. A. (1991). The neuropsychology of temperament. In J. Strelau & A. Angleitner (Eds.), *Explorations in temperament* (pp. 105–128). New York: Plenum.

Green, V. A., & Wildermuth, N. L. (1993). Self-focus, other-focus, and interpersonal needs as correlates of loneliness. *Psychological Reports, 73,* 843–850.

Gunn, G. W., Jr. (1995). *An assessment of the relationship between the Myers-Briggs Type Indicator and the Fundamental Interpersonal Relationship Orientation—Behavior Scale.* Unpublished doctoral dissertation, University of North Carolina, Chapel Hill.

Hall, E. T. (1966a). A system of the notation of proxemic behavior. *American Anthropologist, 65,* 1003–1026.

Hall, E. T. (1996b). *The hidden dimension.* Garden City, NY: Doubleday.

Harrison-Speake, K., & Willis, F. N. (1995). Ratings of the appropriateness of touch among family members. *Journal of Nonverbal Behavior, 19*(2), 85–100.

Haslam, N. (1995). Factor structure of social relationships: An examination of relational models and resource exchange theories. *Journal of Social and Personal Relationships, 12*(2), 217–227.

Hollender, M. H., Dowdy, S., & Kourany, R. K. (1979). The wish to be held and hold in couples. *Journal of Clinical Psychiatry, 40*(3), 121–123.

Huston, T. L., & Vangelisti, A. L. (1991). Socioemotional behavior and satisfaction in marital relationships: A longitudinal study. *Journal of Personality and Social Psychology, 61*(5), 721–733.

Hyson, M. C., Whitehead, L. C., & Prudhoe, C. M. (1986). *Influence on attitudes toward physical affection between adults and children.* Urbana, IL: ERIC.

Jones, S. E., & Yarborough, E. (1985). A naturalistic study of the meanings of touch. *Communication Monographs, 52,* 19-56.

Kelleher, K. (1998, January 8). From boys to bash brothers: Friendly assault a sure sign of male bonding. *Denver Post,* pp. 1E, 3E.

Kellerman, J., Lewis, J., & Laird, J. D. (1989). Looking and loving: The effects of mutual gaze on feelings of romantic love. *Journal of Research in Personality, 23*(2), 144–161.

Knapp, M. L., & Vangelisti, A. L. (1996). *Interpersonal communication and human relationships* (3rd ed.). Boston: Allyn & Bacon.

Koblinsky, S. A., & Palmeter, J. G. (1984). Sex-role orientation, mother's expression of affection toward spouse, and college women's attitudes toward sexual behaviors. *The Journal of Sex Research, 20*(1), 32–43.

Kotulski, D. (1996). *The expressions of love, sex, and intimacy in lesbian and heterosexual couples: A feminist inquiry.* Unpublished doctoral dissertation, California School of Professional Psychology, Berkeley/Alameda.

Koyano, W. (1996). Filial piety and intergenerational solidarity in Japan. *Australian Journal on Ageing, 15*(2), 51–56.

Kuterovac-Jagodic, G., & Kerestes, G. (1997). Perception of parental acceptance-rejection and some personality variables in young adults. *Drustvena Istrazivanja, 6*(4–5), 477–491.

LaFrance, M., & Mayo, C. (1978). *Moving bodies: Nonverbal communication in social relationships.* Monterey, CA: Brooks/Cole.

Landau, R. (1989). Affect and attachment: Kissing, hugging, and patting as attachment behaviors. *Infant Mental Health Journal, 10* (1), 59–69.

LeDoux, J. E. (1998, December 11). Nature vs. nurture: The pendulum still swings with plenty of momentum. *Chronicle of Higher Education,* B7 & B8.

Leiber, L., Plumb, M. M., Gerstenzang, M. L., & Holland, J. (1976). The communication of affection between cancer patients and their spouses. *Psychosomatic Medicine, 38*(6), 379–389.

Lemieux, R. (1996). *Behavioral indicators of intimacy, passion, and commitment in young versus mature romantic relationships: A test of the triangular theory of love.* Unpublished doctoral dissertation, University of Georgia, Athens.

Liederman, G. (1991). *Gender differences in affectional interaction of happily married husbands and wives.* Unpublished master's thesis, Concordia University, Montreal, Canada.

Lopez, F. G. (1995). Contemporary attachment theory: An introduction with implications for counseling psychology. *Counseling Psychologist, 23*(3), 395–415.

Lustig, M. W., & Koester, J. (1999). *Intercultural communication* (3rd ed.). New York: Longman.

MacDonald, K. (1992). Warmth as a developmental construct: An evolutionary analysis. *Child Development, 63*(4), 753–773.

Mackinnon, A., Henderson, A. S., & Andrews, G. (1993). Parental "affectionless control" as an antecedent to adult depression: A risk factor refined. *Psychological Medicine, 23,* 135–141.

Marston, P. J., & Hecht, M. L. (1999). The nonverbal communication of romantic love. In L. K. Guerrero, J. A. DeVito, & M. L. Hecht (Eds.), *The nonverbal communication reader* (2nd ed., pp. 284–289). Prospect Heights, IL: Waveland.

Marston, P. J., Hecht, M. L., Manke, M. L., McDaniel, S., & Reeder, H. (1998). The subjective experience of intimacy, passion, and commitment in heterosexual loving relationships. *Personal Relationships, 5*(1), 15–30.

Marston, P. J., Hecht, M. L., & Robers, T. (1987). "True love ways": The subjective experience and communication of romantic love. *Journal of Personal and Social Relations, 4,* 387–407.

Maslow, A. H. (1987). *Motivation and personality* (3rd ed.). New York: Harper & Row.

Mathias-Riegel, B. (1999 September–October). Intimacy 101: A refresher course in the language of love. *Modern Maturity, 46–49,* 84.

McCabe, M. P. (1987). Desired and experienced levels of premarital affection and sexual intercourse during dating. *Journal of Sex Research, 23*(1), 23–33.

McDaniel, E., & Andersen, P. A. (1998). International patterns of interpersonal tactile communication: A field study. *Journal of Nonverbal Behavior, 22*(1), 59–73.

Mehrabian, A. (1966). Immediacy: An indicator of attitudes in linguistic communication. *Journal of Personality, 34*(1), 26–34.

Metts, S., & Bowers, J. W. (1994). Emotion in interpersonal communication. In M. L. Knapp & G. R. Miller (Eds.), *Handbook of interpersonal communication* (2nd ed., pp. 508–541). Thousand Oaks, CA: Sage.

Mill, D., & Romano-White, D. (1999). Correlates of affectionate and angry behavior in child care educators of preschool-aged children. *Early Childhood Research Quarterly, 14*(2), 155–178.

Millar, F., Rogers-Millar, L. E., & Villard, K. L. (1978). *A proposed model of relational communication and family functioning.* Paper presented at the conference of the Central States Communication Association, Chicago.

Miller, G. R., & Steinberg, M. (1975). *Between people: A new analysis of interpersonal communication.* Chicago: Science Research Associates.

Monsour, M. (1992). Meanings of intimacy in cross- and same-sex friendships. *Journal of Social and Personal Relationships, 9,* 277–295.

Morman, M. T., & Floyd, K. (1998). "I love you, man": Overt expressions of affection in male-male interaction. *Sex Roles, 38*(9/10), 871–881.

Morris, E. K., & Smith, G. L. (1980). A functional analysis of adult affection and children's interpersonal distance. *The Psychological Record, 30,* 155–163.

Morris, W. (Ed.). (1969). *American Heritage dictionary of the English language.* Boston: American Heritage

Mottet, T. P., & Richmond, V.P. (1998). An inductive analysis of verbal immediacy: Alternative conceptualization of relational verbal approach/avoidance strategies. *Communication Quarterly, 46*(1), 25–40.

Murstein, B. I., & Tuerkheimer, A. (1998). Gender differences in love, sex, and motivation for sex. *Psychological Reports, 82*(2), 435–450.

Noller, P. (1978). Sex differences in the socialization of affectionate expression. *Developmental Psychology, 14*(3), 317–319.

Noller, P., & Fitzpatrick, M. A. (1993). *Communication in family relationships.* Englewood Cliffs, NJ: Prentice Hall.

Oatley, K., & Jenkins, J. M. (1996). *Understanding emotions.* Cambridge, MA: Blackwell.

Oliver, J. M., Raftery, M., Reeb, A., & Delaney, P. (1993). Perceptions of parent-offspring relationships as functions of depression in offspring: "Affectionless control," "negative bias," and "depressive realism." *Journal of Social Behavior and Personality, 8*(3), 405–424.

Oliver, R. L. (1981). *Measures of affection and autonomy defined by a theory of culture.* Unpublished doctoral dissertation, University of California-Irvine.

Ormel, J., Lindenberg, S., Steverink, N., & Verbrugge, L. M. (1999). Subjective well-being and social production functions. *Social Indicators Research, 46*(1), 61–90.

Owen, W. F. (1987). The verbal expression of love by women and men as a critical communication event in personal relationships. *Women's Studies in Communication, 10,* 15–24.

Palmer, M. T., & Simmons, K. B. (1995). Communicating intentions through nonverbal behaviors: Conscious and nonconscious encoding of liking. *Human Communication Research, 22,* 128–160.

Parker, G., Tupling, H., & Brown, L. B. (1979). A parental bonding instrument. *British Journal of Medical Psychology, 52,* 1–10.

Parks, M. R., & Floyd, K. (1996). Meanings for closeness and intimacy in friendships. *Journal of Social and Personal Relationships, 13*(1), 85–107.

Parrott, T. M., & Bengtson, V. L. (1999). The effects of earlier intergenerational affection, normative expectations, and family conflict on contemporary exchanges of help and support. *Research on Aging, 21*(1), 73–105.

Parsons, R. J., Cox, E. O., & Kimboko, P. J. (1989). Satisfaction, communication and affection in caregiving: A view from the elder's perspective. *Journal of Gerontological Social Work, 13*(3/4), 9–20.

Patterson, M. L. (1988). Functions of nonverbal behavior in close relationships. In S. W. Duck (Ed.), *Handbook of personal relationships: Theory, research, and interventions* (pp. 41–56). Chichester, UK: Wiley.

Pearce, W. B., Wright, P. H., Sharp, S. M., & Slama, K. M. (1974) Affection and reciprocity in self-disclosing communication. *Human Communication Research, 1,* 5–14.

Prager, K. J. (1995). *The psychology of intimacy.* New York: Guilford Press.

Prager, K. J. (1999). Nonverbal behavior in intimate interactions. In L. K. Guerrero, J. A. DeVito, & M. L. Hecht (Eds.), *The nonverbal communication reader* (2nd ed., 298–304). Prospect Heights, IL: Waveland.

Prager, K. J., & Buhrmester, D. (1998). Intimacy and need fulfillment in couple relationships. *Journal of Social and Personal Relationships, 15*(4), 435–469.

Prescott, J. W., & Wallace, D. (1978). Role of pain and pleasure in the development of destructive behaviors: A psychometric study of parenting, sexuality, substance abuse and criminality. In *Invited papers of the colloquium on the correlates of crime and the determinates of criminal behavior* (pp. 229–279). McLean, VA: Mitre Corporation.

Powell, J. L., & Bock, D. G. (1975). The impact of public speaking and interpersonal communication courses on inclusion, control and affection. *Central States Speech Journal, 26,* 126–132.

Powers, W. G., & Glenn, R. B. (1979). Perceptions of friendly insult greetings in interpersonal relationships. *Southern Speech Communication Journal, 44,* 264–274.

Quinn, W. H. (1983). Personal and family adjustment in later life. *Journal of Marriage and the Family, 45*(1), 57–73.

Reddon, J. R., Patton, D., & Waring, E. M. (1985). The item-factor structure of the Waring Intimacy Questionnaire. *Educational and Psychological Measurement, 45*(2), 233–244.

Reeder, H. M. (1996). The subjective experience of love through adult life. *International Journal of Aging & Human Development, 43*(4), 325–340.

Regan, P. C., Jerry, D., Narvaez, M., & Johnson, D. (1999). Public displays of affection among Asian and Latino heterosexual couples. *Psychological Reports, 84,* 1201–1202.

Reis, H. T. (1990). The role of intimacy in interpersonal relations. *Journal of Social and Clinical Psychology, 9*(1), 15–30.

Richmond, V. P., Gorham, J. S., & Furio, B. J. (1987). Affinity-seeking communication in collegiate female-male relationships. *Communication Quarterly, 35*(4), 334–348.

Roberts, R. E. L., & Bengtson, V. L. (1996). Affective ties to parents in early adulthood and self-esteem across 20 years. *Social Psychology Quarterly, 59*(1), 96–106.

Rogers, C. R. (1951). *Client-centered therapy.* Boston: Houghton Mifflin.

Rogers, C. R. (1959). A theory of therapy, personality, and interpersonal relationships as developed in the client-centered framework. In S. Koch (Ed.), *Psychology: A study of science (vol. 3), Formations of the person and social context* (pp. 184–256). New York: McGraw-Hill.

Roloff, M. E. (1981). *Interpersonal communication: The social exchange approach.* Beverly Hills, CA: Sage.

Rosenfeld, L. B., & Frandsen, K. D. (1972). The "other" speech student: An empirical analysis of some interpersonal relations orientations of the reticent student. *Communication Education, 21*(4), 296–302.

Rubin, R. B., & Martin, M. M. (1998). Interpersonal communication motives. In J. C. McCroskey, J. A. Daly, M. M. Martin, & M. J. Beatty (Eds.), *Communication and personality: Trait perspectives* (pp. 287–307). Cresskill, NJ: Hampton Press.

Rubin, R. B., Perse, E. M., & Barbato, C. A. (1988). Conceptualization and measurement of interpersonal communication motives. *Human Communication Research, 14*, 602–628.

Rubin, Z. (1970). Measurement of romantic love. *Journal of Personality and Social Psychology, 16*(2), 265–273.

Russell, A. (1997). Individual and family factors contributing to mothers' and father's positive parenting. *International Journal of Behavioral Development, 21*(1), 111–132.

Salt, R. E. (1991). Affectionate touch between fathers and preadolescent sons. *Journal of Marriage and the Family, 53*, 545–554.

Sapolsky, R. M. (1997 September 12). The importance of a well-groomed child. *Science, 277*, 1620–1621.

Scarisbrick, D. (1993). *Rings: Symbols of wealth, power and affection.* New York: Abrams.

Schmidt, C., & SeiffgeKrenke, I. (1996). Perceptions of friendships and family relations in chronically ill and healthy adolescents: Quality of relationships and change over time. *Psychologie in Erziehung und Unterricht, 43*(2), 155–168.

Schoenhofer, S. O. (1989). Affectional touch in critical care nursing: A descriptive study. *Heart and Lung, 18*(2) 146–154.

Schultz, N. C., & Schultz, C. L. (1987). Affection and intimacy as a special strength of couples in blended families. *Australian Journal of Sex, Marriage & Family, 8*(2), 66–72.

Schutz, W. (1992). Beyond FIRO-B—Three new theory-derived measures—Element B: Behavior, Element F: Feelings, Element S: Self. *Psychological Reports, 70*, 915–937.

Schutz, W. (1958). *FIRO: A three-dimensional theory of interpersonal behavior.* New York: Rinehart.

Shuntich, R. J., & Shapiro, R. M. (1991). Explorations of verbal affection and aggression. *Journal of Social Behavior and Personality, 6*(2), 283–300.

Silverstein, M., Parrott, T. M., & Bengtson, V. L. (1995). Factors that predispose middle-aged sons and daughters to provide social support to older parents. *Journal of Marriage and the Family, 57*(2), 465–475.

Simon, E. P., & Baxter, L. A. (1993). Attachment-style differences in relationship maintenance strategies. *Western Journal of Communication, 57*, 416–430.

Snell, W. E., Jr. (1986). The Masculine Role Inventory: Components and correlates. *Sex Roles, 15*(7/8), 443–455.

Snell, W. E., Jr. (1989). Development and validation of the Masculine Behavior Scale: A measure of behaviors stereotypically attributed to males vs. females. *Sex Roles, 21*(11/12), 749–767.

Solomon, D. H. (1997). A developmental model of intimacy and date request explicitness. *Communication Monographs, 64*(2), 99–118.

Spanier, G. (1976). Measuring dyadic adjustment: New scales for measuring the quality of marriage and similar dyads. *Journal of Marriage and the Family, 38*, 15–28.

Sprecher, S. (1987). The effects of self-discloser given and received on affection for an intimate partner and stability of the relationship. *Journal of Social and Personal Relationships, 4*(2), 115–127.

Strelau, J., & Angleitner, A. (1991). Temperament research: Some divergences and similarities. In J. Strelau & A. Angleitner (Eds.), *Explorations in temperament: International perspectives on theory and measurement* (pp. 1–12). London: Plenum.

Stuart, B. J. (1989). *Gender differences in marital satisfaction.* Unpublished doctoral dissertation, University of Utah, Salt Lake City.

Sung, K. T. (1998). An exploration of actions of filial piety. *Journal of Aging Studies, 12*(4), 369–386.

Swain, S. (1989). Covert intimacy: Closeness in men's friendships. In B. J. Risman & P. Schwartz (Eds.), *Gender in intimate relationships* (pp. 73–86). Belmont, CA: Wadsworth.

Thomas-Brown, A. M. (1996). *The relationship of interpersonal needs for control and affection to marital satisfaction: A study of dual-career black and white couples.* Unpublished doctoral dissertation, George Washington University, Washington, D.C.

Triandis, H. C. (1995). *Individualism & collectivism.* Boulder, CO: Westview Press.

Turner, J. L., Foa, E., & Foa, U. (1971). Interpersonal reinforcers: Classification, interrelationship and some differential properties. *Journal of Personality and Social Psychology, 19*(2), 170–177.

Twardosz, S., Botkin, D., Cunningham, J. L., Weddle, K., Sollie, D., & Shreve, C. (1987). Expression of affection in day care. *Child Study Journal, 17*(2), 133–151.

Twardosz, S., & Nordquist, V. M. (1983). The development and importance of affection. *Advances in Clinical Psychology, 6,* 129–168.

Twardosz, S., Schwartz, S., Fox, J., & Cunningham, J. L. (1979). Development and evaluation of a system to measure affectionate behavior. *Behavioral Assessment, 1,* 177–190.

Uehara, E. S. (1995). Reciprocity reconsidered: Gouldner's "Moral Norm of Reciprocity" and social support. *Journal of Social and Personal Relationships, 12*(4), 483–502.

Vaux, A. (1988). *Social support: Theory, research, and intervention.* New York: Praeger.

Vega, B. R, Canas, F., Bayon, C., Franco, B., Salvador, M., Graell, M., & SantoDomingo, J. (1996). Interpersonal factors in female depression. *European Journal of Psychiatry, 10*(1), 16–24.

Villard, K. L. (1976). *Affection exchange in marital dyads.* Unpublished doctoral dissertation, Michigan State University, East Lansing.

Villard, K. L., & Whipple, L. J. (1976). *Beginnings in relational communication.* New York: Wiley.

Wallace, D. H. (1981). Affectional climate in the family of origin and the experience of subsequent sexual-affectional behaviors. *Journal of Sex and Marital Therapy, 7*(4), 296–306.

Wallen, K. (1989). Mate selection: Economics and affection. *Behavioral and Brain Sciences, 12*(1), 37–38.

Walters, J., Pearce, D., & Dahms, L. (1957). Affectional and aggressive behavior of preschool children. *Child Development, 28*(1), 15–26.

Waring, E. M. (1979). *Waring Intimacy Questionnaire (Form 90).* Kingston, Ontario, Canada: Queen's University, Department of Psychiatry.

Waring, E. M., & Reddon, J. R. (1983). The measurement of intimacy in marriage: The Waring Intimacy Questionnaire. *Journal of Clinical Psychology, 39,* 53–57.

Waring, E., McElrath, D., Lefcoe, D., & Weisz, G. (1981). Dimensions of intimacy in marriage. *Psychiatry, 44,* 169–175.

Waring, E. M., Tillman, M. P., Frelick, L., Russell, L., & Weisz, G. (1980). Concepts of intimacy in the general population. *Journal of Nervous and Mental Disease, 168*(8), 471–474.

Wiener, M, & Mehrabian, A. (1968). *Language within language: Immediacy, a channel in verbal communication.* New York: Appleton-Century-Crofts.

Weinberg, D. J. (1994). *Reciprocity reconsidered: Motivations to give and return in the everyday exchange of favors.* Unpublished doctoral dissertation, University of California at Berkeley.

*Webster's New Collegiate Dictionary.* (1979). Springfield, MA: G. & C. Merriam.

Weiss, R. S. (1998). A taxonomy of relationships. *Journal of Social and Personal Relationships, 15*(5), 671–683.

Westmyer, S. A., DiCioccio, R. L., & Rubin, R. B. (1998). Appropriateness and effectiveness of communication channels in competent interpersonal communication. *Journal of Communication, 48*(3), 27–48.

Wiggins, J. S. (1979). A psychological taxonomy of trait-descriptive terms: The interpersonal domain. *Journal of Personality and Social Psychology, 37*(3), 395–412.

Wiggins, J. S., Trapnell, P., & Phillips, N. (1988). Psychometric and geometric characteristics of the revised interpersonal adjective scales (IAS-R). *Multivariate Behavioral Research, 23*, 517–530.

Wilkinson, C. A. (1996). Expressing affection: A vocabulary of loving messages. In K. M. Galvin & P. Cooper (Eds.), *Making connections* (pp. 150–157). Los Angeles: Roxbury.

Wood, J. T. (1998). *But I thought you meant...: Misunderstandings in human communication.* Mountain View, CA: Mayfield.

Wood, J. T., & Inman, C. C. (1993). In a different mode: Masculine styles of communicating closeness. *Journal of Applied Communication Research, 21*(3), 279–295.

Wright, L. K. (1998). Affection and sexuality in the presence of Alzheimer's disease: A longitudinal study. *Sexuality and Disability, 16*(3), 167–179.

# CHAPTER CONTENTS

| | |
|---|---|
| • The Problem | 118 |
| *Is Audience Involvement Active?* | *118* |
| *Is Audience Consensus Passive?* | *119* |
| | |
| • The Passive Audience | 124 |
| *Theories of the Sign* | *124* |
| *Stimulus-Response Approaches ("Bullet"* | *125* |
| *or "Hypodermic" Theories)* | |
| *The Payne Fund Studies and Children* | *126* |
| *The Frankfurt School and Critical Theory* | *128* |
| *Cultivation Theory* | *129* |
| *Spiral of Silence* | *129* |
| | |
| • The Active Audience | 130 |
| *The Bureau of Applied Social Research* | *130* |
| *Uses and Gratifications* | *132* |
| *Poststructuralist Influence* | *135* |
| *The Birmingham School, Cultural Studies,* | *136* |
| *and Reader Response Theory* | |
| | |
| • The Active/Passive Audience | 138 |
| *Psychophysiological Approaches* | *138* |
| *Cognitive and Psychological Approaches* | *140* |
| *Technology and Culture* | *142* |
| *Agenda-Setting Theory* | *145* |
| | |
| • Discussion | 146 |
| | |
| • Method and Conceptual Bias | 150 |
| | |
| • The Need for Synthesis | 152 |
| | |
| • References | 153 |

# 4 Audience Activity and Passivity: An Historical Taxonomy

PAUL POWER
*Rutgers University*

ROBERT KUBEY
*Rutgers University*

SPIRO KIOUSIS
*Iowa State University*

The primary theoretical research perspectives that have informed the field of mass communication over the past 70 years are examined with regard to what each perspective has explicitly stated or implied about whether audiences and audience members are active or passive. We see these audience conceptualizations as central to longstanding debates on the power of the media. The article describes each perspective, offers an historical, intellectual genealogy, and attempts to categorize each, in terms of its views on audience activity and passivity. The authors suggest that the interaction of opposing philosophical and methodological traditions can give rise to integration and synthesis that will be productive in future theorizing and research on audiences and the many issues raised by the debate over activity and passivity.

*The most dramatic change in general communication theory during the last forty years has been the gradual abandonment of the idea of a passive audience, and its replacement by the concept of a highly active, highly selective audience, manipulating, rather than being manipulated by the message* (Schramm, 1971, p. 8).

The debate over audience activity/passivity has not been laid to rest with Schramm's observation above. Schramm did, however, recognize that the communication studies literature acknowledged intervening variables in the process of communication, in a step away from the view that, "communication was seen as a magic bullet that transferred ideas or feelings or knowledge or motivations almost automatically from one mind to another" (p. 8; see also

Authors' Note: The authors wish to acknowledge the helpful comments of Steve Chaffee and Ted Glasser on an early draft of this article, as well as anonymous reviewers whose comments strengthened the paper.

Correspondence: Paul Power, 12 Redspire Drive, Union, NJ 07083; email: ppower@scils.rutgers.edu.

Klapper, 1960). As it applies to the mass media, the "magic bullet" theory contrasts sharply with the view of individual audience members as active and goal-directed, using the media and its messages toward their own interests and motives (Katz, Blumler, & Gurevitch, 1974). Thus we have the polarities: a passive audience, victimized by the initiators of media messages; an active, goal-directed audience of individuals using the media to their own advantage. Our purpose in this essay is to organize, review, and trace the evolution of various audience conceptualizations with respect to the active/passive issue, an issue that remains central to the longstanding debate over the extent—the very existence—of media effects. The subject is important to communication researchers because of potential social consequences. The idea of passivity is viewed, in itself, as an audience effect that, in turn, clears the way for social lethargy, manipulation by media messages, vulnerability to media content with its attendant likelihood of acting out in terms of sex and violence, and other potential negative effects (Bryant & Zillmann, 1994; Klapper, 1960). Although the issue is presented in terms of polarities, we find that our discipline has been brought to a level of understanding through the way the various paradigms within communication studies relate to one another, frequently overlapping as well as standing in opposition. We define audience activity/passivity in terms of various views of whether the media facilitate or impede our ability to think critically, freely interpret media messages, and form opinions and value judgments about what we are receiving through the media.

## THE PROBLEM

### Is Audience Involvement Active?

In soap operas, regular viewers are often said to become involved in a "parasocial interaction" (Horton & Wohl, 1956), as if they were watching people they truly know and care about. The scenario raises questions of identification—the extent to which viewers imagine themselves as certain characters and think of themselves as carrying out a character's actions—and involvement—the psychological effect of the perceived reality of a depicted situation, and the need to react to it (Jo & Berkowitz, 1994). "No! Don't go home with him," a viewer exclaims out loud, urging the character behind the television glass not to make the same mistake every other woman over the past three years has made on this particular program. We know from self-reports that viewers occasionally talk to people on the screen, shake their heads in dismay, or reel back in their chairs in reaction to a fictional character's error in judgement or to the gaff of a politician. So, too, in much drama and suspense viewing—or listening in the case of the nearly lost art of radio drama—do audience members become so involved as to lose track of time, growing physically tense at moments of high intrigue, laughing and crying from one moment to the next.

But the question remains as to whether such moments of high involvement denote audience activity or passivity, or how the viewer responds intellectually to the underlying ideology embedded in the drama. On first blush, many viewers would conclude that such intense engagement connotes heightened audience activity. After all, the deeply involved audience member appears to be marshaling all available attention to each moment, to every word spoken, to each small and nuanced nonverbal expression of the face, whether viewing television, a movie, or reading descriptions on a printed page. Whether it's a boxing fan watching a successful flurry of punches thrown by a favorite fighter on TV or a romance reader sharing a moment of rapture with the book's heroine, the concentration and psychological involvement can be considerable. How could this be construed as anything but audience activity?

## Is Audience Consensus Passive?

Would millions of new viewers, year in and year out, become enamored of certain movies and certain scenes in certain movies if they had wildly different or even substantially different responses? We believe the answer is no. At the end of *Casablanca,* Rick (Bogart) and Louis (Rains) walk off together into the mist, "La Marseillaise" rises in volume and viewers are vicariously proud of Bogey's selfless sacrifice of Ilsa (Bergman) to Victor Laszlo (Henreid) and the heroic cause they all now share. Of course, there may be resistant or alternative readings that critique the scene as sexist because Bergman chooses to abdicate all autonomy to Bogart; and contemporary Nazi sympathizers may read the scene differently, as they cannot share the political goals of the heroes, but these readings are surely few and far between. Too few theories of the audience adequately account for such facts of audience response. The strength of the audience's reaction and its relative uniformity must mean that the screenplay, the direction, the acting, and the production elements have somehow brought most viewers to nearly the same point simultaneously.

At moments such as these, should the audience be seen as actively engaged by virtue of involvement in the plot and identification with the film's characters, or should the audience be seen as having given over some measure of individual control over its interpretative process and emotional reaction to the scene? If audience members are "carried away" or "swept away" by a film, as is often reported, is the audience member still active? The language suggests otherwise. If the director and the text are now "in control," does this mean that the audience has lost a measure of control? Surely, part of the filmgoing (and TV viewing and book reading) experience is based in giving over to the text one's attention in order to be entertained. Is it an act of conscious will on the part of the audience member to suspend disbelief, or is that something that skilled writers, directors, and actors must earn, in time, as the story unwinds? Haven't we all had the experience of imbibing in some media story, prepared to dislike it or being skeptical as to whether we will, only to find that the story sweeps us away? Clearly, if the storytellers err by, for example, having a character begin to do things or behave in ways that are out of character isn't it the case that many in the audience will no longer be able to continue to suspend disbelief? Isn't this one of the hallmarks of successful storytelling, a fictional world that rings true?

The answer to these questions is, it depends. It depends on the observer's point-of-view, on what scholarly research position is being taken, and on how different schools of thought conceptualize the audience. We will organize and review the numerous approaches to, and definitions of, audience activity and passivity in the following pages. We expect that what will emerge is part taxonomy and part genealogy. Table 1 lists the major approaches to media studies that are covered in this paper, and specifies whether researchers in the paradigm tend to focus more on analysis of media texts (i. e. studies that focus on books, television, movies etc., "as a more or less well-made artifact, [which] contains a set of meanings that can be articulated adequately by a trained critic" [Radway, 1983, p. 54]), audience studies, media institutions, or technologies. The third column of the table specifies where each paradigm locates the production of meaning or power, a key to whether a passive or active view of the audience is taken. Finally, the table summarizes the way each approach conceptualizes the audience with respect to the active/passive issue.

The organization of the paper is to separate the active and passive audience conceptualizations within media studies, and place each within a chronological time frame, pointing to the principal scholarly traditions that influenced their development. Figure 1 depicts such chronology, and points to the influential scholarly traditions.

First, we will address those views that primarily see the audience as *passive* receptors. We begin with a brief discussion of structural semiotics, which we believe influenced much of the literature that characterizes the audience as passive. These views include so-called "bullet" theories, the Payne Fund studies, the Frankfurt School and critical theory, cultivation theory, and the spiral of silence. We will then review the schools of thought where the *dominant* view is that of an active audience: the "adult discount"; the Bureau of Applied Social Research (Limited Effects) and Uses and Gratifications; the Birmingham School, cultural studies, and reader response theory. We need to emphasize that we are categorizing each paradigm according to its dominant view because we will point out where, in spite of strong leaning in one direction or another, there are allowances for the contrary view. After that, we will examine paradigms that remain ambiguous on the issue, yet nevertheless contribute to the debate. Included here are views of the role of communication technology in society, views that emerge from the field of psychology, both psychophysiological and cognitive, and agenda-setting theory. The meanings explored are not all-inclusive, although we tried to include the lion's share of work that testifies to the issue, nor exhaustive across all media or audience types. "Media," for some authors, applies only to television, or newspapers, and "audience" for some authors applies only to discrete segments of the population. Despite these difficulties, we have endeavored to

TABLE 1
Taxonomy of Major Approaches to Media Studies

| Major approaches | Research focus | Locus of meaning/power | Audience conceptualization |
|---|---|---|---|
| Structural semiotics | Text | Powerful text; one-to-one correspondence between signifier & signified, based on culture | Individuals are passive receptors |
| S-R approaches "bullet" & "hypodermic" theories | Text | Powerful text | Passive mass; each media message is presumed to have the same effect on all members of the audience |
| Payne Fund studies | Text<br>Audience | Influential text<br>Mature individuals | Segmented by age & educational level—passive at the low end; active as individuals learn to separate fact & fiction, and appreciate the art of media production |
| Frankfurt school Critical theory | Media institutions | Text | Undistinguished passive mass, differentiated from a minority elite layer of society |
| Two-step flow & limited effects | Audience | Community | Pluralist mass, segmented by SES factors and community influence; actively select media that reinforce existing beliefs & attitudes |
| Uses & gratifications | Audience | Individual | Individuals who select and interpret messages according to personal needs and wants |
| Psychophysiological | Audience | Physical features of media | Physical organism that involuntarily responds to features of media, with allowances for active information processing |

*(continued)*

TABLE 1 continued

| Major approaches | Research focus | Locus of meaning/power | Audience conceptualization |
|---|---|---|---|
| Birmingham school Cultural studies | Text & audience | Localized audiences | Audience members decode media messages according to available cultural codes |
| Reader response reception analysis | Text & audience | Audience within a cultural community | Interpretive communities actively construct meaning from media texts |
| Technological perspective | Media | Specific technologies | Alternatively, a passive mass and individuals who interpret messages within localized cultural influences |
| Cognitive/psychological | Audience | Individuals & mediating factors | Although cognitive abilities enable audience members to actively interpret messages based on individual schemata, individuals may adopt a passive viewing mode |
| Poststructural semiotics | Text | Audience extracts meaning from polysemic signifiers based on available inventory of meanings | Individuals are active interpreters of meaning |
| Agenda setting | Text | Text/audience | Passive mass audience is subject to what the media determine are subjects for discourse, but the theory allows for some influence by the public on its agenda |
| Cultivation theory | Text | Text | Passive homogenous mass constructs reality around media representations |
| Spiral of silence | Text | Text | Passive mass who receive and repeat dominant media views |

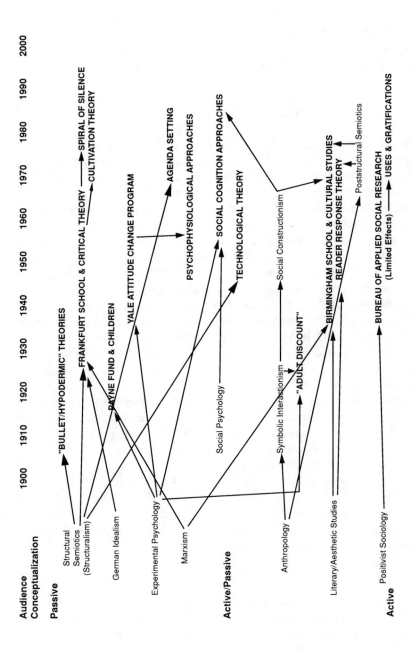

**Figure 1.** Chronology of the appearance of media studies paradigms, with reference to scholarly influences. Major media studies approches are in upper case bold type; influential scholarly traditions are in regular type.

formulate general working statements for each major approach. It is important to note that when we address activity and passivity, we are referring to the audience conceptualization from within the paradigm under discussion, and not from the perception of its critics or others outside the paradigm. Throughout, we keep Schramm's (1971) observation, at the top of this paper, in mind as a sort of working hypothesis to determine if, over time, the concept of a highly selective, active audience prevails over that of the audience as passive receptors.


## THE PASSIVE AUDIENCE

We will not attempt to trace the roots of the present issue to the Enlightenment, but we point to the influence of enlightenment rationalist thinking that brought us to the nineteenth century and the emergent complexities from the technological innovations of that century. More to the point, as the Industrial Revolution altered human relations, the development of the behavioral sciences with logical empiricist epistemological underpinnings laid the groundwork for a direct cause and effect (stimulus-response) view of communication (Fromkin, 1998; Giddens, 1971, 1974; McGuire, 1996; Williams, 1974). The constitutive elements of the "discursive formation" (Foucault, 1972) of the nineteenth century included a view of society as a monolithic mass (Curran, Gurevitch, & Woollacott, 1982/1995). The concept of the "passive audience," was crystallized in this view of mass society, "one of the keys to the social and psychological meaning of modern life in America" (Mills, 1956, p. 304). For Mills, it is a society in which few voices speak to many, with no opportunity to answer back; opinion is controlled by authorities that control the channels of communication; and supposed "public" institutions in fact reduce the autonomy of individuals in a democratic society. Addressing the concern of social observers for the negative effects of mass communication, Klapper (1960) defines audience passivity: "The critics typically speak of a possible or even a probable widespread atrophy of creative and critical powers, a socially general lethargic compliance, and a predominantly dependent and passive pattern of behavior" (p. 235).

During the nineteenth century, the influence of the beginnings of "positivist sociology" as coined by Auguste Comte (Giddens, 1974) and the experimental psychology of Wilhelm Wundt (McGuire, 1996) in turn, influenced Pavlov's work in classical conditioning. Contemporary with Pavlov's work was Ferdinand Saussure's work in semiotics and linguistics.

### Theories of the Sign

Saussure's theory of linguistics and semiotics dates from the first decade of the twentieth century. Saussure's theory opened discourse on the relation between language, thought, culture, and society, and the questions raised have emerged in a wide range of intellectual inquiries into the locus of the production of meaning and the locus of power. These issues have a perspectival bearing on the active/passive issue in media studies as Saussure (1996) described a psychophysiological (brain-to-brain) process where two or more people participate in a circuit wherein mental facts (signifieds) are converted into sounds (signifiers) that reach the ear of the auditor where the process is reversed to create an image in the auditor's brain. Saussure is explicit on the active/passive issue—meaning is produced in the mind of the message initiator as the circuit is divided into, "an active and a passive part: everything that goes from the associative center of the speaker to the ear of the listener is active, and everything that goes from the ear of the listener to his associative center is passive" (p. 42). We put these Saussurian views at the foundation of so-called "bullet" or "hypodermic" theories of media influence. Linguistic theory laid the foundation for structuralism, and later poststructuralism in inquiring, "Does language act as a vehicle for thought or does it actually determine the nature of thought?" (Cobley, 1996, p. 1).

Cinema studies is firmly rooted in structuralism—Browne's (1996) focus on a scene from the movie *Stagecoach* exemplifies the writings in *Screen* magazine. He specifies the cinema producer as the producer of meaning, and he describes a scene in which cinematic framing and sequencing inscribe the spectator in the text and produce the desired audience effect—in this case empathy for one character's humiliation, and repudiation of another's prejudice as unjust. Eco's (1979) study of James Bond novels suggests how fixed and consistent narrative elements often please the reader by confirming expectations that the reader comes to know in a particular formula and genre. Structural semiotics plays a critical role in how advertisers target their primary audience. According to Levy (1986) the primary source of meaning is the product as symbol: "The function of advertising is to symbolize the statuses and aspirations of human identities; and that is how it is interpreted by consumers" (p. 215). Nadin and Zakia (1994) outline techniques wherein advertising mediates between the object to be sold, its representation, and the consumer. Accordingly, the advertisement will be interpreted as a sign in a process (semiosis) that starts with the identification of the object advertised. The audience is seen as passive because certain "iconic" characteristics are believed to generate predictable responses from consumers, for instance an elevated face symbolizes sophistication.

As we shall see, structural linguistics gave rise to the poststructural view and a gradual shift in the locus of the production of meaning, wherein the locus of power moved from the message initiator to the auditor. But for now, let us consider the coincidence of Saussure's linguistic theory and the way Pavlov's work in classical conditioning apparently influenced communication studies. It took an event as major as the Great War to make the coincidence clear.

Stimulus-Response Approaches ("Bullet" or "Hypodermic" Theories)

In the view of some, formal "bullet theories," at least in name, never actually existed (Chaffee & Hochheimer, 1982). We speculate that the term, "bullet theory" was coined to follow Lasswell's quote of the U.S. military's view of propaganda: "Armies fight as the people think.... Thoughts are Bullets" ("Propaganda in its Military and Legal Aspects" in Lasswell, 1927, p. 214). In his World War I propaganda studies, Lasswell asserted, "propaganda is one of the most powerful instrumentalities in the world" (1927, p. 220). The model postulated that each media message (stimulus) influenced each audience member in approximately the same manner (response; McQuail, 1994), and "all subjects will receive some critical feature of the message (the magic bullet) that will change them in the same way" (DeFleur & Dennis, 1981, p. 502). A direct effects model such as this clearly implies text as the locus of the production of meaning and the audience as a passive receptor, and simple S-R approaches did influence many thinkers' assumptions. For example, Lippmann (1971), writing in 1921 in a vein that was consistent with the propaganda studies, told of the power of the written word to create "pseudo-environments" and steer public opinion by triggering images of heroes and demons, victories and defeats.

Although we have been unable to locate the genesis of the term "hypodermic needle" with respect to media studies, we speculate that the expression emerged from its complement, the "inoculation" effect (Lumsdaine & Janis, 1953), which posits that if a person is exposed to the negative side of an argument, and, then subsequently exposed to the presentation of opposing arguments in the counterpropaganda, he is less likely to be influenced by them. Even though this view continues to focus on the power of the message, we can see that it makes allowances for the activity of the audience in evaluating and resisting an argument. Current research continues to maintain the efficacy of inoculation in counterpersuasion. For example, in a recent experiment probing the role of threat and involvement in inoculation, Pfau et al. (1997) found that "inoculated subjects are less influenced by subsequent attacks than controls, regardless of whether the treatments contained the same or different content as the corresponding attack message" (p. 189).

Through the first decades of the twentieth century, the principal medium of mass communication was the press, as radio was in its infancy. This period was also the dawn for a new medium, the talking motion picture, which would cause concern among scholars as to the influence it would wield.

The Payne Fund Studies and Children

In 1929, only 2 years after audiences first heard Al Jolson in *The Jazz Singer,* the Motion Picture Research Council, in response to a popular concern for the negative effects of movies, commissioned the Payne Fund studies of radio, motion pictures, and reading in relation to children and youth. The project consisted of twelve independently conducted studies that were published separately and summarized in a monograph by W. W. Charters (1933), the chairman of the project. Among the component studies were content analyses, studies of children's attendance at motion pictures, studies of the physical and emotional

effects of movies, and studies of the effects of movies on social attitudes and conduct. The project ultimately concluded, 65 years ago, that the movie was a deci-
sively powerful medium, and the young, passive recipients relatively powerless:

> We see that as an instrument of education it [the motion picture] has unusual power to impart
> information, to influence specific attitudes towards objects of social value, to affect emotions
> in either gross or microscopic proportions, to affect health in a minor degree through sleep
> disturbance, and to affect profoundly the patterns of conduct of children. (Charters, p. 43)

Although the focus of these studies was the effect of media on children, they
also alluded to the way adults would deal with the power of the media. Within
the Payne Fund studies, the concept of the "adult discount" emerged from the
respective analyses of Dale (1935/1970) and Blumer (1933/1970). They maintained that children's acceptance of what they see on the screen as true, correct,
proper, and right, and their intense "emotional possession" is displaced by the
adult discount. This is developed through response to the attitudes of older
groups, the conviction that movies are not true to life, and instruction about
movies. In a conclusion that many contemporary media literacy teachers subscribe to, Charters (1933) reported both Dale's and Blumer's contention:
"Detachment comes with learning how movies are made, how effects are
secured, what to look for in pictures, what makes pictures artistically good or
bad" (p. 43). The adult discount offers an early view of an "active" process,
summed up simply as the ability of audience members to resist incoming media
messages. The Payne studies can be seen, therefore, as representing an empirical
move away from the presumed strict dogma of "bullet" theory. The view of a
specific audience segment as more active helps confirm Schramm's (1971)
observation that the "active" conceptualization began in the early 1930s.

Following the first radio broadcast in 1920, radio's growth was rapid and by
1938, 86% of U.S. families had radios. The concepts of audience reception that
we have discussed thus far, which basically viewed the audience as a passive
mass, were prelude to what we consider to be the epicenter of media studies. In
the United States, the principal influences emerged from the oppositional views
of two groups in residence at Columbia University during the 1940s: On the one
hand were the German-Jewish exiles, later known as the Frankfurt School,
whose work was based in the European interpretive tradition, who viewed the
massification of culture as degrading; on the other was the Bureau of Applied
Social Research, working in the American empiricist tradition, who saw the massification of culture as democratizing. Further, the work of Hovland and his associates at Yale University served as the springboard for much work in the psychology of audience reception. In Britain, in the 1950s, a tradition emerged from
the Birmingham Center for Contemporary Cultural Studies that, in a sense,
mediated the passive audience view of the Frankfurt School and the active audi-

ence view of the Bureau of Applied Social Research. At Columbia, Lazarsfeld's focus on media effects, and Adorno's concern with the study of mass culture, appeared to constitute a favorable working relationship. However, their efforts to work together resulted in something of a rivalry—a standoff between the European interpretive tradition and American logical empiricism (Jay, 1973).

## The Frankfurt School and Critical Theory

The Frankfurt School philosophy, influenced by the phenomenological sociology of the German Idealists and Marxism, was grounded in the antimodernist fear of the oppression of technology, and the attendant belief that positivist epistemology, particularly when applied to mass culture, was used to control beliefs, attitudes, and behavior. The consumer of the culture product is not required to make an intellectual contribution because everything is set out in the presentation of the product. The merging of culture and entertainment results in a confusion of the two, and the emphasis on amusement desensitizes the individual to what may be serious (Horkheimer & Adorno, 1944/1972). The audience's tastes and expectations were largely molded by the reiterative flow of stereotypical plots and characters, and through the mass media the culture reproduces itself.

Frankfurt scholar Leo Lowenthal (1961) examined how a passive audience was manipulated by the establishment to adhere to capitalistic goals and ideas through popular culture texts, and Herbert Marcuse (1964) solidifies the Frankfurt view of the passive audience by reasoning that the "unification of opposites" in society makes it implausible to rebel against it. As a result, the audience becomes "one-dimensional." Any illusion that the mass media are impartial or separate participants in our culture makes us all the more vulnerable to media messages, particularly advertising.

The Frankfurt School view was clearly one of a passive audience, grounded as it was in the mass society/mass culture paradigm. However, the Frankfurt School's audience conceptualization made a distinction between the undistinguished masses and a layer of elite, knowledgeable individuals (Adorno, 1976). These elites were capable of making discriminating judgments and did not give themselves over to the stereotypes that the cultural institutions dished up, as did the masses who were in need of escape from performing alienating labor at work. In the view of Habermas (1962/1989), a latter day Frankfurt scholar, the massification of media resulted in a public sphere in which members of society are consumers of culture and information. Although drawing on his Frankfurt School roots, Habermas acknowledges the Katz and Lazarsfeld (1955) view of interpersonal influence on public decisions (Habermas, 1962/1989), but he does not accept the idea of an active audience that is impervious to influence. The media "become instrumental in the creation of public spheres capable of serving authoritarian or emancipatory interests" (Habermas, 1985, p. 142). This last idea is one of the connecting points between critical theory in the Frankfurt School tradition and cultural studies, which will be discussed later.

Later critical theory in media studies adds the Gramscian concept of hegemony to the Frankfurt School view. The term "hegemony," adapted from Gramsci's view of how dominant classes could rule without employing force, is used "to describe any aspect of a culture, ideology, or set of practices through which elites impose their views and establish the legitimacy of their power and privilege over nonelites" (Mukerji & Schudson, 1991). Kellner (1995) reflects such a view of the "media culture," in which "images, sounds and spectacles help produce the fabric of everyday life, dominating leisure time, shaping political views and social behavior, and providing the materials out of which people forge their very identities" (p. 1). "The concern is for the dominant messages embedded in the pleasant disguise of fictional entertainment, and the concern of the researcher is often that the control of these messages is, more than anything else, a complex sort of political control" (Newcomb & Hirsch, 1994, p. 504). The audience is viewed as passive with the establishment operating in hegemonic keys embedded in reiterative formats, genres, settings and character types, slants, and solutions (Gitlin, 1985, 1994).

## Cultivation Theory

The Frankfurt School notion of the "one dimensional" audience is discerned in cultivation theory as developed by George Gerbner and his associates (Gerbner, Gross, Morgan, & Signorielli, 1980). For Gerbner, power and meaning reside in the text. The passive audience (particularly heavy television viewers) gradually comes to hold a homogeneous view of reality as depicted on television rather than real life (Gerbner, Gross, Morgan, & Signorielli, 1994; Signorielli, 1990). "Television viewing cultivates 'mainstream' conceptions of life and society. That is, groups that differ (either positively or negatively), come to share a more homogenous view of the world" (Gerbner et al., 1980, p. 11). Certain variables, such as personal interaction, parental coviewing patterns, orientations toward television, integration with peer or family group, and direct experience may provide the individual with the means of resisting cultivation. But, to the extent that television is a socializing agent, cultivation theorists point to strong evidence of mainstreaming and "resonance"—that is, when "cultivation is enhanced among those for whom a certain issue has special salience" (Morgan & Signorielli, 1990, p. 26). Thus, an observed cultivation effect for violence would be hypothesized to be greater among people living in crime-ridden areas than among those residing in safe neighborhoods.

A form of mainstreaming is seen in a paradigm that emerged in the 1970s that Anderson (1996) places in the structuralist-functionalist school of sociology on a branch that includes Lasswell's and Wright's definitions of the functions of media, with a tip of the hat to Lippmann's and Park's early work in journalism.

## Spiral of Silence

Noelle-Neumann's (1984) "spiral of silence" theory posits strong media effects owing to the media's primary role in establishing popular opinion.

Individuals who are in disagreement with those opinions are reluctant to express their own opinion, and suppress their views, which then results in the appearance of even greater support for the view originally espoused by the media. Thus, the theory argues that individuals with unpopular opinions are rendered politically passive in the face of media opposition. Individuals holding the majority opinion are themselves passive in that they adhere to the dominant view. They could be seen as playing an active role in bullying the minority members into silence. However, Noelle-Neumann's view is that these people are largely repeating the messages sent by media, and in this sense, are passive.

## THE ACTIVE AUDIENCE

The concept of the active audience is not one born of the twentieth century. In 1808, Goethe wrote in Faust that "Each loves the play for what he brings to it." By 1916, Hugo Munsterberg (1916) had already appropriated the psychoanalytic term "projection" to help explain the film viewers' intense absorption in what were then called "photoplays." The development of projective tests in psychology in the 1930s, notably the Rorschach and Thematic Apperception Tests (TAT), also assumed that individuals saw very different things in ambiguous inkblots, photos, and drawings. We noted the Payne Fund Studies' recognition of audience activity in the adult discount. But the full series of studies was not completed, having been interrupted by World War II. For Biocca (1988), the concept of the active audience as a focus of study was "born of the inability to find and measure convincing evidence of mass 'hypodermic' effects" (p. 57). Levy and Windahl (1985) define audience activity as:

> a voluntaristic and selective orientation by audiences toward the communication process. In brief, it suggests that media use is motivated by needs and goals that are defined by audience members themselves, and that active participation in the communication process may facilitate, limit, or otherwise influence the gratifications and effects associated with exposure. (p. 110)

Thus we return to where we left off earlier, in our discussion of the work that emerged from the groups at Columbia in the 1940s and 1950s.

### The Bureau of Applied Social Research

Shortly after the formation of Princeton's Office of Radio Research, a radio event provided an unexpected experimental situation—the Halloween broadcast of Orson Welles' Mercury Theatre production of *War of the Worlds*. The opportunity was embraced by Hadley Cantril (1940) with the assistance of Hazel Gaudet and Herta Herzog. Cantril reports that an estimated six million people were tuned to the broadcast, and at least a million were frightened or disturbed by it. He ascribed the phenomenon to individual standards of judgment with psychological, cultural, and educational roots that enabled individuals to interpret a specific event. This work did not address the matter of the active audience per se, however it did raise questions about the supposed "mass effect" of the media, which struck a chord that was resonant throughout the work of the Bureau. Subsequently, Lazarsfeld and Merton (1948) dismissed the idea of powerful media effects—"the social role played by the very existence of the mass media has been commonly overestimated" (p. 98). A frequently cited example that supports the contention of the media's lack of power to alter attitudes is the Mr. Biggott case (Kendall & Wolf, 1949/1979), which found that individuals' biases will guide their interpretation of propagandist material.

Lazarsfeld and Merton (1948) list three conditions to prove propaganda effective: little or no opposition, canalization of preexisting behavior patterns or attitudes, and supplementation through personal contacts. "As a result of this three-fold situation, the present role of mass media is largely confined to peripheral social concerns and the mass media do not exhibit the degree of social power commonly attributed to them" (p. 117). The final condition, supplementation through personal contacts, we now know as the "two step flow" communication theory, which was introduced in the account of Lazarsfeld's Erie County study (Lazarsfeld, Berelson, & Gaudet, 1944), wherein the media's role in a political campaign was the subject. Indicative of a selective/active audience, the researchers concluded that individuals choose to expose themselves to propaganda with which they agree, and that attitudes are reinforced in contacts with other members of their group.

Lazarsfeld and Merton (1948) distinguished between audience activity in the sense of critical thinking, and activity in the sense of political or social action. They note that the flood of information via the media leaves little time for social action and the active listener/reader becomes a passive participant, a phenomenon they call the "narcotizing dysfunction":

> The interested and informed citizen can congratulate himself on his lofty state of interest and information and neglect to see that he has abstained from decision and action. In short, he takes his secondary contact with the world of political reality, his reading and listening and thinking, as a vicarious performance. He comes to mistake knowing about problems of the day for doing something about them. His social conscience remains spotlessly clean. He is concerned. He is informed. And he has all sorts of ideas as to what should be done. But after he has gotten through his dinner and after he has listened to his favorite radio programs and after he has read his second newspaper of the day, it is really time for bed. (p. 106)

As for the formative roots of the Bureau of Applied Social Research, we must consider Lazarsfeld's grounding in quantitative marketing methodologies at the University of Vienna, combined with Stanton's interest, as director of research at CBS, in maximizing audience size (Schramm, 1997). Much of the Bureau's work focused on creating classifications of media content and audience segments (Lazarsfeld & Stanton, 1949/1979). For example, Lazarsfeld and Dinerman's (1949/1979) segmentation of the morning radio audience, and Berelson's (1949/1979) delineation of individuals' use of newspapers added to active audience conceptualizations, and established the basis for the uses and gratifications model for audience analysis.

## Uses and Gratifications

The assumptions of the uses and gratifications approach are clearly stated in Katz, Blumler, and Gurevitch (1974): "The audience is conceived of as active. . . . In the mass communication process much initiative in linking need gratification and media choice lies with the audience member" (p. 21). The approach gains theoretical coherence through the adjunct of expectancy-value theory (Palmgreen & Rayburn, 1985), which postulates a functional relationship between gratifications sought from media exposure and "the beliefs (expectations) that audience members hold about media sources and the affective evaluations they attach to media attributes" (p. 63). Audience members are characterized as active consumers searching for messages that suit their own needs and rejecting those that do not. Rosengren (1974) outlines a uses and gratifications paradigm that spells out the interrelationships between basic individual biological and psychological needs, social institutions, media consumption, gratifications, and effects (presented here in simple prose form):

> Certain basic human needs of lower and higher order under interaction with differential combinations of intra- and extra-individual characteristics and also with the structure of the surrounding society, including media structure, result in differential combinations of individual problems; the combination of problems and solutions constituting differential motives for attempts at gratification-seeking or problem-solving behavior, resulting in differential patterns of actual media consumption and differential patterns of other behavior, both behavior categories giving differential patterns of gratifications or non-gratifications and, possibly, affecting the individual's combination of intra- and extra-individual characteristics as well as, ultimately, the media structure and other social, political, cultural and economic structures in society. (p. 270)

However, Blumler (1979) eschews the notion of "grand theory" with respect to uses and gratifications, noting (as to audience "active-ness") the need to

> distinguish and dimensionalise some of the different senses in which audience members could be active. One approach to this task might differentiate forms of 'active-ness' likely to manifest themselves at different moments in a temporally ordered mass communication sequence: before exposure; during consumption; and after the media experience as such has been terminated." (p. 14)

Levy and Windahl (1985) incorporate this into a two-dimensional typology, with Blumler's temporal considerations along one dimension, and qualitative orientation (selectivity, involvement, and utility) along the other. They further recommend, as a step toward addressing activity-type interrelationships empirically, combining two or more activity types. In their example, preexposure selectivity and involvement during exposure are combined: A high reading on both dimensions results in "motivated gratification seeking," "an especially active orientation" (p. 118); high preexposure selectivity and low involvement produces "topic ritualism," "consumption of media content in a habitual, relatively noninvolved fashion" (p. 119); at the intersection of low selectivity and high involvement is "indiscriminate involvement . . . a theoretically interesting activity subtype that raises the possibility of audience members who actively process and relate to almost any type of media content" (p. 119); low readings on both dimensions indicate "time passing . . . a comparatively inactive orientation" (p. 119).

Levy and Windahl (1985) state that there is evidence that links audience gratifications to various effects, such as agenda-setting, which will be discussed further below, and media dependency. Media dependency theory (Ball-Rokeach & DeFleur, 1976), specifies an active audience that turns to the media to fulfill various information needs:

> For example, one form of dependency is based on the need to understand one's social world; another type of dependency arises from the need to act meaningfully and effectively in that world; still a third type of dependency is based on the need for fantasy-escape from daily problems and tensions. The greater the need and consequently the stronger the dependency in such matters, the greater the likelihood that the information supplied will alter various forms of audience cognitions, feelings, and behavior. (p. 6)

The authors, however, distinguish media dependency theory from uses and gratifications: "Proponents of the uses and gratifications approach examine how audiences use the media to gratify similar information needs but do so by taking the audience as the focal point of analysis, not the interrelationships between audience, media and society" (p. 8).

A clear construct of uses and gratifications is seen in Bryant and Zillmann (1984), which studies the polarities of boredom and stress and the influence of these states on the selection of exciting versus relaxing television programming. The study found a positive correlation between the bored state and the selection of exciting programs; however, there was a balance of selections among the stressed individuals. These results were reflections of the individual's beliefs concerning the appropriate remedy for their state. To the extent that television viewing is regarded as therapeutic relief for an emotional or psychological state, it is assumed here that the greater the degree of the state, the greater the measure of therapeutic viewing.

Rubin (1984), following Windahl's finding—that viewers tended toward one of two types of viewing: instrumental, defined as goal-directed media use to gratify informational needs or motives; and ritualized, habitualized use, driven by diversionary needs or motives—found a positive correlation between age and instrumental viewing, and negative correlation between education level and ritualized viewing. Significant relationships were found between level of viewing and diversionary viewing. With respect to the uses and gratifications model, it can be said that audience activity is a concept that varies according to utility, intentionality, and selectivity. Rubin proposed that to understand the uses and gratifications of the media it is necessary to appreciate the social context of audience television viewing behavior. In support of that idea, Peterson (1992) found a correspondence between low status occupations and Rubin's characteristics of ritualistic viewers. Although Peterson's purpose focused on tastes in music, the article presents tabulated results that indicate that individuals in those occupations were more likely to be viewers of three or more hours of television per day. Albarran and Umphrey (1993), in a step toward understanding the social, psychological, and cultural origins of television viewing, found that Whites more typically answered to Rubin's typology of instrumental and ritualistic television use, whereas Blacks' motivations for viewing were of a more entertainment/diversionary nature than Whites' or Hispanics', as Hispanics preferred information-based programs.

As technology has advanced, uses and gratifications has frequently been invoked to gain understanding of the uses of various devices and their social impact. For example, Ferguson and Perse (1993) challenged the idea of a passive audience on a multichannel landscape, noting that, "individual factors representing levels of audience activity accounted for more of the variance in MCR [mindful channel repertoire] than audience availability factors and nearly as much variance as media factors" (p. 42). Similarly, Youn (1994) determined that viewers are more likely to view programs of their preference in a multichannel universe than in a broadcast-only one. As to the ubiquitous remote control device, Ferguson (1994) found extremely high remote control flipping frequency, and Weimann (1995) makes the distinction, based on maturity of the technology, between remote control use as a commercial avoidance tool (as in Israel, where multiple channels recently became available) and its use for grazing to see what's on (as in the U.S.).

As computers have become more of a factor, and Internet use has risen, much of the social research in computer use, convergence, and interactivity combines uses and gratifications with diffusion theory. For example, Atkin, Jeffres, and Neuendorf (1998) found some support for an early adopter profile of Internet users, but no support for the hypothesis that Internet users have a greater desire to fulfill various communication needs than nonadopters. Perse and Dunn (1998) found an early adopter effect, with no displacement of media use, as early adopters tended to be light television viewers, and continued to be heavier users of print media. Integrating a uses and gratifications approach, the authors found that computers were not mentioned frequently by their respondents to fill communication needs. Rather, computers were used to pass time, consistent with ritualistic use of media. Among non-users, they found little utility in computers, a fact that explains relatively slow diffusion.

The uses and gratifications perspective altered mass communication study, particularly in the United States, championing an empowered audience—one that could make its own choices. Active audiences control their own fates, thus offering new topics for researchers to investigate. There was a shift away from thinking of the audience as an undifferentiated mass to its being understood more in terms of audience segments defined by demographics, attitudes, and tastes. Rejection of the view of society as a passive mass was also found in a tradition that traces its roots to Britain in the late 1950s. Before turning to the position of the Birmingham School and related views, we will make a brief stop at a semiotic turn that influenced media studies post-1960s and had particular relevance to the way cultural studies developed.

Poststructuralist Influence

Although it has been criticized as rationalist, determinist, and reductionist, structuralism is recognized as a step in a direction away from logical empiricism, providing a springboard for poststructuralist, interpretive social science, in which "understanding any action is analogous to textual interpretation. This means that the intelligibility of any action requires reference to its larger context, a cultural world" (Rabinow & Sullivan, 1979, p. 13). This interpretive turn in the study of social phenomena has given rise to the concept of multiple readings of a text and a shift in emphasis from the power of the text to the power of the reader (Lyotard, 1993).

Poststructuralists do not flatly reject the basic tenets of structural linguistics, but rather build upon them. For example, while referring to structuralist norms, Derrida (1993) works toward the decentering of structures. As the center orients and organizes the coherence of a system, it permits freeplay of the structure's elements inside the total form, but does not allow for substitution of contents, elements, or terms. It is, so to speak, the immutable taken for granted. A basic tenet of structural linguistics is that the relationship between signifieds and signifiers is based on the difference of signifiers, and there is a privileged significance to the chosen signifier. Derrida claims that the choice is a matter of deference: "There is thus no ground, in the incessant play of *differance* that constitutes language, for attributing a decidable meaning, or even a finite set of determinately multiple meanings to any utterance we speak or write" (Abrams, 1993). As we see structural linguistics give rise to the poststructural view, we see a gradual shift in the locus of the production of meaning, and the locus of power from the message initiator to the auditor, a shift that is evident in the views that emerged from the Birmingham School.

The Birmingham School, Cultural Studies, and Reader Response Theory

The Birmingham Center for Contemporary Cultural Studies, under Richard Hoggart, Raymond Williams, and Stuart Hall, although asserting an active audience view, somewhat akin to that of uses and gratifications, also claimed the same interdisciplinary intellectual roots as the Frankfurt School. "British and American cultural studies, as well as the critical studies of the Frankfurt School, all have representatives of the trapped despair, dangerous change, and cautious utopian optimism that colors cultural constructionism" (Anderson, 1996). Frankfurt School critical theory and cultural studies are set apart by the Frankfurt School tendency "to see mass culture as a homogenous and potent form of ideological domination" (Kellner, 1997, p. 17) as opposed to the cultural studies view that group identity is the key to the way individuals "resist dominant forms of culture and identity, creating their own styles and identities" (p.17).

At the outset of Hoggart's (1971) collection of essays, *On Culture and Communication*, we get the impression that he is about to make a case for audience passivity—"Most of the signals we pick up, especially when we are in our own society, we pick up without knowing it" (p. 13). However, he goes on to strike a chord that is resonant throughout Birmingham School thought and later cultural studies work—that the taken for granted signals become a filter through which we interpret our experiences. Although cultural studies steer away from the notion of direct media effects—"We should beware of leaping from content analysis to effects and of assuming any direct and mechanistic connection between media and social behavior" (Hall & Whannel, 1964, p. 33)—it likewise turns away from the uses and gratifications conceptualization of the active audience. Indeed, for Stuart Hall, interpretation must come before any impact is possible:

> Before this message can have an "effect" (however defined), satisfy a "need," or be put to a "use," it must first be appropriated as meaningful discourse and be meaningfully decoded. It is this set of decoded meanings which "have an effect," or influence, entertain, instruct or persuade. (Hall, 1980, p. 130)

Cultural studies views the audience as active, but within the constraints of a dominant, localized sphere. Hall posits a model wherein the television program is represented as meaningful discourse with two "meaning structures," the production structure where meaning is constructed, or coded, and the reception side where decoding takes place. Where structure 1 and structure 2 are not symmetrical, variant interpretations will be made. Interpretations are made according to the cultural codes that are available to the individual, and the availability of such codes are grounded in social status and education (Morley, 1992). Cultural studies draws on Volosinov's (1996) poststructuralist concept of polysemy, a challenge to the Sausurrian notion of one-to-one correspondence between signified and signifier—"There is no reason for saying that meaning belongs to a word as such. In essence, meaning belongs to a word in its position between speakers; that is meaning is realized only in the process of active, responsive understanding" (p. 82). This is not to say that texts are open to any interpretation:

> We must attend to the way in which the broadcasters, constrained as they are by their desire to communicate "effectively," are bound to attempt to provide "direction" or "closures" within the structure of the message, which attempt to establish one of the several possible readings as the "preferred or dominant reading". . . . However we must not assume that these strategies of closure are necessarily effective. It is always possible to read against the grain, as it were, to produce an interpretation which goes against the grain of that "preferred" by the program discourse. (Morley, 1992, pp. 83–84)

As Hoggart and Williams laid the foundations of cultural studies in Britain, in America, J. L. Austin's speech-act theory placed the locus of meaning "outside the formal structure of the communication, and into an analysis of situation" (Cobley, 1996, p. 18). Austin's theory stimulated debate among an international cast of linguists and literary theorists from which emerged Stanley Fish's Austinian reader response theory. Fish (1996) distinguished between what is "given" in the text and the set of assumptions that determine what is "supplied" by the reader. The reader interprets "by virtue of his membership in a community of interpretation" (p. 422). Fish's concept of a community of readers (although Fish's "readers" were a community of literary scholars [Radway, 1991]) was very much consistent with the Birmingham concept of the active audience and has influenced cultural studies writing (Ang, 1985; Carey, 1975; Lewis, 1991; Lull, 1990; Radway, 1984). Audiences are made up of groups of individuals who belong to "interpretive communities"—women romance novel readers, punk rock fans, soap opera viewers. They actively construct meaning from media texts. For Fiske (1986), for example, the "text" can only exist in the reader's or viewer's experience. Meaning is, "created through the interplay of text and audience . . . this interplay is powerfully influenced by the discourse that audiences bring to their media consumption" (Curran, 1996, p.152). Ang (1996) states, "Reception analysis has intensified our interest in the ways in which people actively and creatively make their own meanings and create their own culture, rather than passively absorb pregiven meanings imposed upon them" (p. 136).

Returning now to the starting premise of the paper, it is clear that Schramm's (1971) observation—that the prevailing view of the audience as a passive mass had been replaced by that of an active audience conceptualization—was valid at the time of his writing. Uses and gratifications had ascended to the position of the dominant paradigm in media studies, having replaced so-called "bullet" and "hypodermic" theories. The Birmingham scholars had added to the idea of the audience as active interpreters of media messages. However, we have also seen continued reference to a passive audience in later critical theory, cultivation theory, and the spiral of silence. We want to bring into the discussion some important literatures that, although ambiguous or bimodal with respect to the active/passive issue, contribute importantly to the debate.

## THE ACTIVE/PASSIVE AUDIENCE

As we have indicated, the Frankfurt School and the Bureau of Applied Social Research represented opposing approaches to sociological study. For the other powerful American influence on mass communication studies of the 1950s, we turn to the psychological branch of the genealogical tree. Hovland's Attitude Change program tracks back to Wilhelm Wundt's experimental psychology of the late nineteenth century, through the social psychology of William McDougall and E. A. Ross in the early twentieth century, and more directly the hypothetico-deductive method of Clark Hull (McGuire, 1996).

### Psychophysiological Approaches

"The audience of persuasive communication was conceptualized by Hovland as a passive receiver of the information contained in the message" (McGuire, 1996, p. 55). The work of Hovland and his associates served as a springboard for much work in the psychology of audience reception and, for the most part, psychophysiological approaches characterize the audience, following Hovland, as passive. Audience reactions to media are predicated on specific formal features of the media and are played out in pupil dilation, brain waves, sweat gland activity, and the orienting reflex (Krugman, 1986; Lang, 1995; Lang, Greenwald, Bradley, & Hamm, 1993; Singer, 1980). These reactions are generally conceived as being outside the control of audience members ("automaticity of viewing") as we are naturally "programmed," or "prewired" through evolution and genetics to respond in certain ways. The psychophysiological approach is represented in recent studies that have led researchers to conclude that "individual reactions with computers, television, interfaces, and other communication technologies are fundamentally social and natural, just like interactions in real life" (Reeves & Nass, 1995, p. 3). Audience members cannot actively choose how they will respond to certain aspects of media. Rather, they respond as they do because their responses are grounded in nature and physiology. Some important examples of these grounded responses are "attentional inertia" and the "orienting reflex." Anderson and Burns (1991) elucidate the former with television viewing as "an underlying change in attentional state as a look is maintained such that the viewer becomes increasingly engaged" (p. 6). Singer (1980) explains the "orienting reflex" as a programmed human reaction to pay attention to anything unusual or surprising:

The TV set, and particularly commercial television with its clever use of constantly changing short sequences, holds our attention by a constant sensory bombardment that maximizes orienting responses. . . . We are constantly drawn back to the set and to processing each new sequence of information as it is presented. . . . The set trains us to watch it. (pp. 50–51)

EEG evidence indicates that some "formal features" of television (zooms, pans, rapid cutting, etc.) do command involuntary responses and that they very probably "derive their attentional value through the evolutionary significance of detecting movement" (Reeves et al., 1986, p. 271). EEG studies have also indicated that reading requires more eye-movement and active left-brain processing whereas the perception of images seems to coincide with more right-brain activity of low involvement owing to a motionless or focused eye, as in most TV viewing (Krugman, 1986; Mulholland, 1973). It may well be that eye movement is a surprisingly important factor in understanding some of the experiential differences among television viewing, reading, and other media experience. Reading, by its nature, requires constant, active eye movements. Watching a movie on a large screen may also involve some active searching and scanning. But with most TV viewing there is relatively little eye movement because of the relatively small screen, and this fact alone may explain some reduction in active concentration and intentional control. As technology advances, HDTV (high definition television) provides a wider aspect ratio and higher resolution than analog sets, thus allowing viewers to sit closer to the screen without noticing imperfections in the image. Interestingly, that will make for more eye movement and a kind of greater viewer activity (Kubey & Csikszentmihalyi, 1990).

Within the psychophysiological approaches, there is a recognition that certain factors are in line with activity:

Rather the view is of an organism that is actively approaching each new situation, already anticipating certain consequences, prepared to screen out as much irrelevant information as possible, searching for information that will mesh with previous plans and expectations, and, at the same time, attracted by moderate degrees of novelty to engage in further exploration. (Singer, 1980, p. 34)

The simple fact that the audience is processing information necessarily causes it to be in some sense active because of the processing itself—or in the attendant striving to make the information intelligible. Although these processes may appear to differ in nature and scope from those in uses and gratifications or cultural studies, a degree of cognitive agency is implied and points to audience activity, albeit not at a conscious level—however, let us be clear that much of the "activity" in uses and gratifications and cultural studies conceptualizations need not be entirely conscious or consciously directed. The difference lies in an activity born of brain processes in the psychophysiological approach versus activity grounded in preference and opinion, as in uses and gratifications, or in attitude, sensibility, and politics (race, gender, and class) as in cultural studies.

Geiger and Newhagen (1993) suggest that attention is both automatic and controlled. Audience members are active insofar as certain messages are pursued over others depending upon preconceived expectations, but in doing so, cognition necessarily relies on "schema or what might be called 'preparatory plans,' (or 'flexible and adaptive knowledge structures') based of course, on previous experiences about what may be expected in a situation [parentheses added]" (Singer, 1980, p. 34). How truly hard-wired are schemata is still open for debate and research, but psychology has advanced to the point where it is accepted that cognitive structures, that is schemata, are built, and it is very hard indeed to imagine how they do not rely in some way on the anatomy and physiology of the brain. However, what is too often lost in such conundrums is that nature or nurture is the wrong question. An informed, unified conceptualization recognizes nature and nurture. The "neuroplasticity" of the brain can no longer be ignored by those who would only look at nurture. Cognition, and much of what flows from cognition, must be seen as necessarily grounded in the stuff of the brain, but we now know that the brain also builds itself through experience and past predilection and cognition. Thus, a pure "nature" view is as obsolete as that of pure "nurture."

Such merged positions have actually been with us for some time, whether we return to Kant's advance beyond the one-sidedness of the rationalists and empiricists, Piaget's genetic epistemology, or the various studies showing that the brain uses multiple pathways in its searching, retrieving, and linking processes (see, for example, Collins & Quillian, 1969). In summary, some psychophysiological researchers lean toward passive or automatic processing, whereas others see the audience as both active and passive, not because they lack consensus so much as because of a recognition of two interdependent processes. This is different from those approaches where the audience is more typically categorized as either active or passive.

Cognitive and Psychological Approaches

Social cognition theory and research focus on the knowledge that people have acquired, and their cognitive mapping and sense making processes in regard to the social worlds they inhabit. The intellectual roots of social cognition are in the constructivist approach to communication and psychology and in the symbolic interactionist view that has long and correctly argued that peoples' understandings necessarily constitute their reality. By extension, social cognition is also grounded in basic tenets and findings of Gestalt psychology, dating back now nearly 70 years, that showed how human cognition typically seeks coherence and wholeness from the particular (Kohler, 1930). Cognitive developmental theory as developed by Piaget has also contributed substantially to a more comprehensive understanding of how our perception of reality gets built dynamically through the interrelated cognitive processes of assimilation and accommodation. Meaning and knowledge are constructed, and in showing us how this is done by the youngest of children, Piaget helped advance the wisdom of merging the rationalist and empiricist arguments in epistemology and theories of the mind.

In cognitive psychology, and particularly in the area of social cognition, much work has been done on how people selectively interpret, decode, process, and make sense of what they experience. The idea of interpretive heuristics is central in social cognition and has to do with the accessibility and primacy of existing cognitions and schemata and the salience of "texts" to these, especially as each relates to social phenomena and social judgment. Social cognition studies examine how social knowledge is constructed and represented in the mind and how these representations then inform our understanding of subsequent social information we encounter. One of many examples is work that shows how people characteristically misapprehend social reality, for example, the likely risks of different potential threats, due to the combined salience and availability of schemata and media produced information (Fiske & Taylor, 1984; Tversky & Kahneman, 1973). In a step beyond the more simple cultivation theory view, an heuristic processing model has begun to take us further inside the "black box" of the mind by showing us how different social-psychological processes and related processing strategies moderate cultivation effects (Shrum, 1995, 1996). Cognitive developmental theory showed us that the mind's representations of reality do not occur in some random unpredictable way. Our understandings are very much anchored—just as we would argue are media related constructions of meaning—in the worlds outside our cognitive apparatus, but also in the nature of how the brain and mind work and assimilate those worlds.

Social cognition can also house the "elaboration likelihood" model of Petty and Cacioppo (1986), especially as their findings speak to the active-passive debate in that the differential processing of persuasive messages is understood to vary in effectiveness owing to whether the messages go through central route versus peripheral processing. Their findings show that arguments for a particular position are much more likely to be effective and resistant to counter argument if the recipients of messages go through a process of self-generating relevant arguments on the way to their eventual position. This is what is meant by elaboration, and it is seen as the "central" route to persuasion. Peripheral route processing involves the weighing of source credibility and related affective associations and contextual cues. Generally, central processing is seen as involving a more active and conscious process whereas peripheral processing is seen as being more passive, but in different circumstances and conditions these distinctions are not so clean or clear.

With regard to general television viewing, such distinctions are perhaps seen more clearly in the experiments of Langer and Piper (1988) wherein viewers who were asked to watch television more "mindfully" (central route processing) performed better on measures of creativity and flexibility after viewing than those who viewed as they might normally (peripheral route processing). Here, we should also point to the recognition, as discussed earlier within the uses and gratifications approach, that there are arguably at least two important and substantially different factor-analyzed types of television use, instrumental (information seeking) and ritualized (Rubin, 1984). Like Langer and Piper (1988), Kubey and Csikzsentmihalyi's (1990) findings of high degrees of passivity reported during TV viewing in four different nations and of a so-called cognitive and affective "passive spillover effect" in their U.S. subjects after television viewing have suggested that the viewing state, at least as they conceptualized it and as it occurs most of the time, may be a rather passive one. Similar findings of less creative and imaginative thinking in many viewers and increased aggressiveness in children in a small Canadian community previously deprived of television due to poor reception are in line with the view that audiences are often made more passive by viewing and that most television viewing does not involve or require much higher order thinking (Williams, 1986). Subsequent theorizing applying various psychological processes beyond cognition, including operant conditioning, the modulation of affect, and how substance dependencies develop have been recently presented to explain why in the view of many psychologists so much television viewing is ritualized, relatively passive, habit forming, and a deeply ingrained part of people's daily routines (Kubey, 1996b; McIlwraith, Jacobvitz, Kubey, & Alexander, 1991).

Continuing with our taxonomy, the cognitive approaches can be seen as viewing individuals as both active and passive. Audience members are active insofar as it is assumed there is a constant building up and accommodation of existing schemata to new information and understandings. However, there is also a clear recognition that the nature of human cognition is such that accessible understandings do not always readily change or assimilate new information perfectly and thus, in an almost mechanical way, we are all prone to knee-jerk sorts of reactions and erroneous conclusions based on existing understandings and in these instances, a fair amount of mental processing is shallow, routine, and unconscious. Thus, audience members' mental processes at times might also be seen as reactive and passive, responding without autonomy, agency, or real awareness to certain bits of mediated information and the formal features of a medium. Let us be clear that we are not saying that errors in thought must denote passivity as no doubt one could be actively processing and still misconstrue. Suffice it to say that it has often been the errors in thinking that cognitive developmental and social cognitive studies have used to illustrate various limitations on thinking, perception, and decision making.

## Technology and Culture

The underlying theme of the discourse on communication technology and its relation to culture and society, rooted in structuralism, is that the structure of technology governs the structure of thought. The work of economist and historian Harold Innis (1950/1972; 1951/1995) laid much of the foundation for this discourse as he lamented civilization's passing from an oral tradition to mechanized media. In his view the flexibility of the oral tradition stimulated discourse, and contributed to the growth of democracy; the rigidity of print media constrains the free flow of ideas, and its mechanization and massification resulted in monopolies of knowledge:

> The conditions of freedom of thought are in danger of being destroyed by science, technology, and the mechanization of knowledge, and with them, Western civilization. . . . The passive reading of newspapers and newspaper placards and the small number of significant magazines and books point to the dominance of conversation by the newspaper and to the pervasive influence of discontinuity, which is, of course, the characteristic of the newspaper, as it is of the dictionary. (Innis, 1951/1995, pp. 190–192)

Marshall McLuhan (1964) continued Innis' evolutionary view of communication, bridging from the mechanical age to the electronic age, asserting "The mark of our time is its revulsion against imposed patterns" (p. 21). He distinguished between a hot medium, "one that extends one single sense in 'high definition'" (p. 36) (i.e., low in participation) and a cool medium, high in participation because information must be filled in by the audience. "The past mechanical time was hot, and we of the TV age are cool" (p. 40). For McLuhan, whereas radio is a hot medium, television is a cool medium, the viewer actively stitching together the low definition, scattered dots that make up the TV image into a "mosaic" in order to receive the television picture. McLuhan's view of television audience activity seems somewhat convoluted as he explains that because of the participatory nature of the television image, television producers steer away from controversial material so as not to stimulate social disturbance, and when television is "hotted up by dramatization and stingers, it performs less well because there is less opportunity for participation" (1964, p. 271). This point is perhaps best explicated by Postman (1985, 1992) who maintains that television is not merely an add-on to already existing media, but the contemporary paradigm for discourse. Its structure, consisting of quick takes, bite-size news pieces, and constant commercial interruption, serves to deactivate thinking.

Whereas McLuhan's ideas have been discounted by some scholars (Rosenthal, 1969), other views focus on the continuing evolution of media technology (Negroponte, 1995; Poole, 1973), and McLuhan is frequently invoked (e.g., Neuman, 1991; Tapscott, 1998) with respect to the evolution from passive to active modes of participation with emerging technologies. It is argued frequently in the popular press that technological innovation has (Wright, 1995) and will (Abramson, 1992; Fineman, 1997; Gilder, 1994) lead to a more participatory democracy. Abramson, for example, describes several hopeful techniques that would ensure that the new electronic media promote democratic processes through sustained discussion.

Following McLuhan, for Meyrowitz (1985) it is not so much the sensory impact of a medium or the power of the medium's message that affects behavior, but, "the reorganizing [of] the social settings in which people interact and . . . weakening [of] the once strong relationship between physical place and social 'place'" (p. ix). Integrating McLuhan with Goffmann's dramaturgic ideas about front and back-stage, Meyrowitz sees social change resulting from the nature of technology and the new situation of individuals otherwise separated by time and distance receiv-ing the same information. As a result, what may traditionally be "backstage" behavior for a member of the family or group is now frontstage, on view for all. Women can see into men's worlds and vice versa; children see the adult world; we all see into more of the politician's backstage world than the politician would wish. It has been pointed out (Kubey, 1992) that Meyrowitz's is also a homoge-nization theory, similar to Gerbner's, where people become more alike through media exposure, and not because they intended to. But Meyrowitz also concludes that television explains much activism among women, minorities, and other groups. By TV causing the backstage that separates one group from another to fall away, equality movements are born. So, as with McLuhan, Meyrowitz, by turns, can be understood as seeing the audience as both passive and active.

Carey (1989) incorporates the Innis/McLuhan historical view that changes in communication technology affect structural changes in society, the Birmingham view of the influence of local culture, and the Chicago School's symbolic inter-actionism to arrive at the view that national media diminish the influence of local culture. That is not to say that individual agency is lost, but that the individual's frame of cultural reference is altered. In concentrating media power

> what they monopolize is not the body of data itself but the approved, certified, sanctioned, official mode of thought—indeed, the definition of what it means to be reasonable. And this is possible because of a persistent confusion between information and knowledge. . . . Knowledge is, after all, paradigmatic. It is not given in experience as data. There is no such thing as information about the world devoid of conceptual systems that create and define the world in the act of discovering it. (pp. 194–195)

In summary, there is no singular audience conceptualization among those who write about technology and culture. Rather, we can separate the commentary on technology into two views, frequently articulated by authors with feet in both camps. On the one hand, what we shall call the structural view conceptualizes the audience in terms of the homogenized masses who are subject to the hegemonic signs and symbols of a small, controlling class; on the other hand is a democra-tizing poststructural view in which individuals across all social classes may share in the same cultural experiences, and may provide their own interpretations according to their own cultural schema. Raymond Williams (1974) of the Birmingham School articulated these two potentialities:

> Over a wide range from general television through commercial advertising to centralised information and data-processing systems, the technology that is now or is becoming available can be used to affect, to alter, and in some cases to control our whole social process (p. 151).
> ... In the young radical underground, and even more in the young cultural underground, there is a familiarity with media, and an eager sense of experiment and practice, which is as much an effect as the more widely publicized and predicted passivity. (p. 133)

## Agenda-Setting Theory

In its classic definition, agenda setting theory holds that media transmit issue salience to audience members (Funkhouser, 1973; McCombs & Shaw, 1972). That is, the hierarchy of issue importance in the media corresponds to the hierarchy of issue importance for the public. If abortion, welfare, and unemployment dominate the content of media, they will also be the most crucial issues in public opinion. At first blush, agenda setting appears to classify easily in our taxonomy under the passive category, with the locus of control seeming to lie with the media. Indeed, the literature supports the hypothesis that media coverage leads to increased issue salience for voters. However, salience transferral is not the only dimension of the process as agenda setting does not occur consistently at the same level on all individuals and for all issues. It is necessary to differentiate between public, policy, and media agendas, understanding these groups are continuously vying for public opinion (Dearing & Rogers, 1996). In the opinion of some, the audience is construed as active in that the media agenda is influenced by public opinion and, in turn, influences the policy agenda of elite decision makers. Gans (1989), for example, has explicated how policy makers are constrained by what they believe silent bystanders (the mass public) will or will not accept. Wanta (1997), calling for a natural bridge between agenda setting and uses and gratifications research (see also McCombs & Weaver, 1985), concludes variables such as age, education, attitude, and motivations for media use are highly associated with agenda setting susceptibility. Further, empirical investigations reveal that the type of issue covered, source, and external political conditions play a significant role in issue salience (Iyengar, 1987; Lasorsa & Reese, 1990; Page, Shapiro, & Dempsey, 1987).

However, current work has not abandoned the idea of strong cognitive media effects. The new "second level agenda setting" research posits that media not only transfer issue agendas to the public, but "attribute" agendas as well (McCombs & Estrada, 1997). Issue frames, related issues, affective responses, and so forth all comprise the agenda of attributes that is conveyed to the public (Ghanem, 1997). Thus, the media not only tell us what to think about, but how to think about it. The evolution of second level analyses have begun to consider alternative objects as well as political images (e.g., Roberts, 1997). In brief, we can state that agenda setting falls into both categories because it argues for strong media effects, but acknowledges several contingent conditions and intervening variables that mediate influence. Thus, agenda setting portrays the audience as more active than the stimulus-response and cultivation models, but not to the same extent as uses and gratifications or cultural studies.

## DISCUSSION

To reiterate, views rooted in structural linguistics have given rise to interpretive, poststructuralist theory, which shifts the emphasis from message to audience as the locus of the production of meaning and the locus of power. The shift lends substance to Schramm's (1971) observation that there is an overall trend toward active audience conceptualization, as well as a tendency to allow for audience activity within paradigms that view the audience as passive receptors. However, there remains little question that numerous media products masterfully direct each audience member's attention and thinking such that millions of people in the same nation and culture, and sometimes throughout the world, respond very similarly, at least to portions of content, if not to an entire story. Where Liebes and Katz (1990) see audience activity in the different responses, culture to culture, to the same television program, *Dallas*, we see a more constrained reception process (Kubey, 1996a) in the uniformity of response within each culture. Katz (1996) reports that new Russian arrivals to Israel "saw an ideological threat in the program, and argued that the doctrine of the unhappy rich is an ideological manipulation," whereas such readings of *Dallas* "are roundly denounced by the Americans who refused to see any message at all in the program" (p. 18). Frankfurt School theorists would see the "American" reading as politically passive, with audience members unable to even consider a different or resistant reading when it is offered to them. Passivity for the Frankfurt School means something rather different than those who think in terms of uses and gratifications, and these are different once again from the psychophysiological.

The problem is not simple. This is seen clearly when we return to the problem of deep engagement and involvement. Over 80 years ago, Hugo Munsterberg (1916) was among the first to formally think about how projection and identification might help us better understand the nature of the moviegoer's experience. Applying psychoanalytic theory helps us recognize that possibly the more psychologically relevant material that an audience member brings to a film or TV program, the more that audience member may identify with and project his emotions onto particular characters and plot developments. But insofar as projection and identification are often largely or entirely unconscious processes, and at least in traditional psychoanalytic theory do not involve awareness by the ego (the idea of a conflict-free sphere of ego activity and "regression in the service of the ego" awaited the development of ego psychology in the 1950s), there may be at work a fascinating dialectic wherein the more the filmgoer brings to the film the more he or she can become potentially involved and absorbed and, in one sense, rendered passive. The more there is to identify with, the more difficult it may become for some viewers to distance themselves from the experience, at least at the moment of viewing, and perhaps afterward. Thus, for those approaches that invoke individual choice and consciousness as hallmarks of audience activity, we here have a thorny problem of the highly absorbed viewer, conceivably being more passive, in one sense than the viewer who does not resonate to the same story and forever stays one or more steps removed from the plot and the intentions of the director to involve the viewer. In this sense, the least engaged viewer could be deemed the most active.

There is a cognitive studies corollary for this interesting dialectical possibility. Consider Anderson, Alwitt, Lorch, and Levin's (1979) description and observations of "attentional inertia": "the longer people look at television, the greater is the probability that they will continue to look" (p. 339). They go on to describe children's bodies relaxing, their heads dropping forward, and their mouths opening. However, a few years later Anderson and Lorch (1983) hypothesized that this "inertia" may be indicative of increased "cognitive engagement." Biocca (1988) asserts that Anderson and Lorch's "attentional cues" are the result of media socialization, and addresses the matter of preconscious, "priming" effects (see also Jo & Berkowitz, 1994), which moderate the idea of the active audience:

> Meaning in television may be the final product of a complex interaction of message form and content, contextual and situational factors, as well as the semiotic competence of the viewer, sociopsychological construction of the viewers' semantic associations, and, finally, idiosyncratic processing dispositions. (p. 65)

Here, again, we see the importance of research techniques that will illuminate what actually occurs inside the mind and brain, as "attentional inertia" has more often been equated with the anecdotal mindless and passive "zombie stare" reportedly observed in young viewers, but Anderson and Lorch suggest it may indicate a viewer who is truly absorbed. In contradiction, EEG studies show more alpha waves, indicating lower cortical arousal, coinciding with prolonged viewing (Mulholland, 1973; Reeves et al., 1986). This is in line with self-report findings from Kubey and Czikszentmihalyi's (1990) subjects that the more people view, the more passivity they report.

Munsterberg (1916), writing as much about films as plays, well captured the yin-yang of activity-passivity in his perceptive accounts of audience involvement. Munsterberg realized that the viewer is at once actively involved, but simultaneously suggestible and thus "stirred up," led and "drawn" by the play or film. We have taken the liberty of inserting parenthetically the letters "a" for

"active" and "p" for "passive" at the end of each phrase below to demonstrate
that both are clearly operative in this account. For Munsterberg, images and
scenes:

> Must have a meaning for us [a], they must be enriched by our own imagination [a], they must
> awaken the remnants of earlier experiences [a, p], they must stir up our feelings and emotions
> [p], they must play on our suggestibility [p], they must start ideas and thoughts [a, p], they
> must be linked in our mind with the continuous chain of the play [a], and they must draw our
> attention constantly to important elements of the action [p]. (p. 72)

In contrasting plays with films, which he called "photoplays," Munsterberg
well captures how the film, because of its nature, is better able to control the
attention of the audience member than the play where the audience can more
actively choose to attend to a particular part of the stage. For Munsterberg, in
film, the viewer is more at the mercy of the content, of the medium itself:

> Our whole attention can now be focused in the play of the face and hands. . . . Everything is
> condensed, the whole rhythm is quickened, a great pressure of time is applied, and through
> that the accents become sharper and the emphasis more powerful for the attention. We might
> sit though the photoplay with the voluntary attention of watching the pictures with a scientif-
> ic interest in order to look up some new fashions. . . . But none of these aspects has anything
> to do with the photoplay. If we follow the play in a genuine attitude of theatrical interest, we
> must accept those cues for our attention which the playwright and the producers have pre-
> pared for us. (pp. 80–81)

Here Munsterberg sees the audience member as virtually having to follow the
lead of the storyteller (uses and gratifications will argue that this is still active
because the viewer chose to let himself follow). The very fact that the pace of
audience experience is set by the creators in such media as film, TV, and radio
makes for a less idiosyncratic and active experience generally than that compared to what happens during the reading of a book where the pace is almost
entirely set by the reader (Kubey, 1996a). Print relies on abstract signs and symbols and must be reconstituted by the reader in ways not required by film or television where much, or everything, is directly given both visually and aurally.
Thus, the experience of readers will be more idiosyncratic than that of viewers
of television or film where the main characters, their vocal characteristics, and
the settings they inhabit must necessarily be experienced in more uniform ways
precisely because much more detailed information is given. Where less is given,
as in print, the individual imaginative propensities of the reader are given much
freer reign. Readers unexposed to the film versions of *Gone With the Wind* or *The
Bridges of Madison County* will each construct for themselves slightly different,

but highly idiosyncratic, images of what Rhett Butler and Robert Kincaid look
and sound like. This is not so for the film viewer, and indeed, few readers of the
novel, if first exposed to the film, can get Clark Gable or Clint Eastwood out of
their minds.

Humans seek and appreciate coherence and consistency, both basic tenets of
Gestalt psychology and social cognitive understanding of human psychology.
Even in ostensibly implausible plots such as those in much situation comedy
whether it be *I Love Lucy, The Beverly Hillbillies,* or *Seinfeld,* there are episodes
where we buy in completely to the ridiculous world portrayed—at least for a
time. However, in an occasional episode, the writing, direction, and acting somehow fail to cohere, verisimilitude is lost, and suddenly the pleasurable gestalt of
that other world is gone and the episode is a comparative failure, certainly not a
classic one. So, too, in science fiction, suspense thrillers, and most all of drama.

There appears, then, to be much greater precision and predictability in audience responses than many active audience conceptualizations allow for or can
conceive of as presently constituted. Of course there are stories that are quite
open to multiple readings, where audience members do exert more autonomy and
control and, shall we say, "activity," but although it is not currently popular to
say so, it is our view that more often than not, the popular entertainments of the
past half-century, the movies, books, and television episodes returned to time and
again and rediscovered by newly appreciative audiences year after year are those
creations that necessarily—at least at this stage in the history of mass audiences—offer the more closed readings. Whereas Fiske (1986) and others argue
that widely popular texts must be more open in nature in order to garner huge
appreciative audiences rendering multiple interpretations, we would argue just
the opposite. *E.T., It's a Wonderful Life, The Cosby Show, The Honeymooners,*
and *Independence Day* are successful and popular because they manage to reliably take vast audiences to the same points and places, cognitively, emotionally,
and experientially. In these instances, we wonder whether audience members are
nearly so autonomous or active in their agency as many theorists would claim or
like to believe.

Ignoring and neglecting to appreciate how different media, genres, formulas,
and specific media products provoke in audiences similar and predictable
responses contributes to an undeveloped state in much media studies scholarship.
Were the field to begin to point to certain facts about the nature of media impact
and audience engagement, and were these phenomena to be described and understood, then perhaps media studies would become more disciplinary than is currently the case. If we cannot point to how certain techniques bring about certain
effects in certain types of audience members under different circumstances, then
a portion of what our field might rightly strive toward understanding will continue to go undeveloped. To not appreciate that there are more and less effective,
persuasive, compelling, and meaningful ways that communication gets done or
that stories are told loses sight of what should be an important concern in media

studies, and seems to us to also contribute to the view that no stories or movies or books or techniques or artists are any better than any other because there either are no standards, or that necessarily all such standards are socially constructed. How could it be otherwise? Social construction need not mean that there are not facts about how and why different media evoke in people certain responses, or why one film or TV program elicits more suspense or racism in viewers than another film or TV program. Such facts grow out of the nature of how social structure and human beings function in relation to the products of culture

## METHOD AND CONCEPTUAL BIAS

As we stated earlier in this paper, we contend that the various positions with respect to audience activity/passivity depend largely on the observer's point of view and on what scholarly position is being taken. Reference to Table 1 reveals evidence that those traditions that view the audience as passive tend to focus on media texts. That is, researchers who work in those paradigms analyze language, and visual and audio signs and symbols, and draw inferences as to the effects of media communication (Krippendorff, 1980).

On the other hand, we believe that much of the reconceptualizations of the audience as active over the past 70 years have been warranted and have helped bring about more sophisticated and complex understandings to a field of study that clearly needed it. However, we wish to consider the possibility that particular conceptual and methodological orientations may have increased the likelihood that researchers either conclude that audiences are active or passive, or that they find what they are looking for.

The first type of bias is that simply brought about as a result of some investigators wanting only to examine the active end of the active-passive spectrum, as in uses and gratifications. This is evident in Katz's (1996) explicit declaration that "what interests us, however, is not what people take from television but what they put into it" (p. 11). Such an approach that chooses to focus on audience activity while ignoring the "effects" can only reify an active audience view. Katz has wondered why some studies of the television audience do not find the high level of activity and engagement that he and his colleagues have found: "Audiences dress up to watch; they prepare their hearts—for the moon landings, for Kennedy's funeral, for the Pope in Poland, for Sadat in Jerusalem" (p. 16). But as has been raised elsewhere, Katz's "examples come from once-in-a-lifetime—or once in many a lifetime events: the moon landing and an Egyptian leader visiting Israel. . . occurred *only once in recorded history*" (Kubey, 1996a, p. 193), and so it is not hard to imagine why Katz would conclude that his viewers are very active indeed.

Second, although those employing traditional quantitative methods in studies of the audience are often criticized for the limiting and distorting nature of their research techniques, the more qualitative and interpretive modes favored in cultural studies are themselves not without potentially distorting method reaction effects. Some cultural studies practitioners are well aware of this. Ian Ang (1985), for example, argues that a viewer's immediate experience of a television program may differ substantially from the much more cerebral and logical explanations offered to researchers. Audience members who are interviewed may tend "to construct a more critical reading than they might do otherwise" (Wren-Lewis, 1983, p. 196). In other words, elaborated meaning may largely be produced once viewers are asked to reconstruct their experiences (Fry, Fry, & Alexander, 1988).

Third, traditional experimental laboratory studies, as in the psychological approaches, will tend to elicit more activity in audience members than passivity. Some of the low concentration and passive viewing that is said to accompany television viewing is a function of the relaxed ways in which people view in the privacy of their own homes, their bodies often splayed on couches, watching for 3–5 hours at a time. Contrast that with a research subject being ushered into a sterile room in a university building, asked by a graduate assistant or professor to sit and watch a particular program, or set of video images. Even if the protocol doesn't ask for the research subject to answer direct questions about what has been viewed it is probable that subjects will watch the material with greater attention and with different goals in mind than were they at home—perhaps reasonably expecting that they will be questioned or tested after viewing. Even well-intentioned attempts by experimentalists to simulate the home viewing situation still must, by definition, result in an artificial setting, and certainly the nature of viewing will be affected. In short, there are many more reasons to believe that the laboratory will increase viewer activity than increase passivity.

Perse (2001), in a chapter on learning, has codified the issue. Stating, "Most considerations of media effects imply that, somehow, media content is learned and becomes the basis for knowledge, attitudes, and action" (p. 131), she goes on to specify models that incorporate active or passive theories of learning: "Active learning theories fall within two models of media effects: the conditional model or the cognitive-transactional model. . . . the main focus of the passive approach is media content variables and they fall under the direct and cumulative effects model" (p. 132).

Active approaches to learning from the media include both conditional and cognitive models. Learning from different media may be conditional on aspects of the audience, such as prior knowledge, age, and cognitive abilities. Learning involves creating new schemas or linking newly encountered information to existing schemas. Passive approaches are more media content centered. The focus is on using media content to attract the involuntary attention of the audience. . . . Passive approaches also suggest media content that will focus on things that people are interested in—such as sex appeal, celebrities, and so on. This media centered approach assumes that people need to be pushed to pay attention to media content. (p. 163)

Our view is that better accommodation among different approaches should be the direction for much future theorizing and research on audiences and the many issues raised by the debate over activity and passivity.

## THE NEED FOR SYNTHESIS

Just as in the psychophysiological section we pointed to the much needed synthesis in understanding that nature and nurture are interdependent phenomena, certainly when it comes to brain and behavior, and that most any either/or position is mistaken from the outset, so too do we believe that in some instances, the movement toward active audience conceptualizations has gone too far in neglecting the power and limitations of both text and social structure. As Sonia Livingstone (1990) puts it, "If we see the media or life events as all-powerful creators of meaning, we neglect the role of audiences; if we see people as all-powerful creators of meaning, we neglect the structure of that which people interpret" (p. 23).

Keeping with our view that better accommodation among different approaches should be the direction for much future theorizing and research on audiences and the many issues raised by the debate over activity and passivity, we also wish to point to areas where we believe integration and synthesis might prove particularly productive. We see various syntheses possible and concur with Livingstone (1990) that perhaps the most promising would be between the social cognition and cultural studies approaches where "a cognitive theory of viewers' interpretations" would be developed (p. 24). The sorts of questions that such a theory might answer would include "what do viewers find salient, how are they selective, how do they integrate 'new' programme information with 'old' social knowledge, how do they differentiate among messages, how perceptive are they of underlying messages?" (p. 24).

Instead of maintaining the usual polarization between different "camps" or, as disturbing, the complete neglect by one group of the other's work—the near complete talking past one another—we advocate drawing from the strengths and relevant theorizing and observations of various approaches. Altogether ignoring how meaning is constructed is as unproductive as ignoring the text or focusing only on audience members' interpretations. "The important question concerns the interrelation between the two: how do people actively make sense of structured texts and events; how do texts guide and restrict interpretations" (Livingstone, 1990, p. 23). Developments in social cognition in concert with understandings arising out of the cultural approaches can help advance the field and potentially begin to bring some greater clarity and fruitful research directions to address current dilemmas. Nor can we ignore the psychophysiological and traditional uses and gratifications and critical studies approaches either.

As a field, we should be well beyond the notion that people can and will make any interpretation of a given text. Developments in cultural studies over the past fifteen years have increasingly recognized that social structure does place restraining limits both on texts and the likely and available interpretations. This is a positive sign that more accommodation between cognitivists and those doing psychological work on the media and cultural and critical studies scholars is possible.

## REFERENCES

Abrams, M. L. (1993). *A glossary of literary terms* (6th ed.). New York: Harcourt Brace.

Abramson, J. B. (1992, October). *Democratic designs for electronic town meetings.* Paper prepared for a conference on Electronic Town Meeting, the Aspen Institute Wye Center, Queenstown, MD.

Adorno, T. W. (1976). Television and the patterns of mass culture. In H. Newcomb (Ed.), *Television: The critical view* (pp. 239–259). New York: Oxford University Press.

Albarran, A. B., & Umphrey, D. (1993). An examination of television motivations and program preferences by Hispanics, Blacks, and Whites. *Journal of Broadcasting and Electronic Media, 37,* 95–103.

Anderson, D. R., Alwitt, L. F., Lorch, E. P., & Levin, S. T. (1979) Watching children watch television. In G. Hale & M. Lewis (Eds.), *Attention and the development of cognitive skills* (pp. 331–361). New York: Plenum.

Anderson, D. R., & Burns, J. (1991). Paying attention to television. In J. Bryant & D. Zillmann (Eds.), *Responding to the screen: Reception and reaction processes* (pp. 3–25). Hillsdale, NJ: Erlbaum.

Anderson, D. R., & Lorch, E. P. (1983). Looking at television: Action or reaction? In J. Bryant & D. R. Anderson (Eds.), *Children's understanding of television: Research on attention and comprehension* (pp. 1–33). New York: Academic Press.

Anderson, J. A. (1996). *Communication theory: Epistemological foundations.* New York: Oxford University Press.

Ang, I. (1985). *Watching* Dallas. London: Verso.

Ang, I. (1996). *Living room wars: Rethinking media audiences for a postmodern world.* London: Routledge.

Atkin, D. J., Jeffres, L. W., & Neuendorf, K. A. (1998). Understanding internet adoption as telecommunications behavior. *Journal of Broadcasting & Electronic Media, 42*(4), 475-490.

Ball-Rokeach, S. J., & DeFleur, M. L. (1976). A dependency model of mass-media effects. *Communication Research, 3*(1), 3–21.

Berelson, B. (1949/1979). What "missing the newspaper" means. In P. F. Lazarsfeld & F. N. Stanton (Eds.), *Communication research 1948–1949* (pp. 111–129). New York: Arno Press.

Biocca, F. A. (1988). Opposing conceptions of the audience: The active and passive hemispheres of mass communication theory. *Communication yearbook 11* (pp. 51–80).

Blumer, H. (1933/1970). *Movies and conduct.* New York: Arno Press.

Blumler, J. G. (1979). The role of theory in uses and gratifications studies. *Communication Research, 6*(1), 9–36.

Browne, N. (1996). The spectator in the text: The rhetoric of *Stagecoach.* In P. Cobley (Ed.), *The communication theory reader* (pp. 331–351). London: Routledge.

Bryant, J., & Zillmann, D. (1984). Using television to alleviate boredom and stress: Selective exposure as a function of induced excitational states. *Journal of Broadcasting, 28,* 1–20.

Bryant, J., & Zillmann, D. (1994). *Media effects: Advances in theory and research.* Hillsdale, NJ: Erlbaum.

Cantril, H. (1940). *The invasion from Mars: A study in the psychology of panic.* Princeton, NJ: Princeton University Press.

Carey, J. (1975). A cultural approach to communication. *Communication, 2,* 1–22.

Carey, J. W. (1989). *Communication as culture: Essays on media and society.* New York: Routledge.

Chaffee, S. H., & Hochheimer, J. L. (1982). The beginnings of political communication research in the U.S.: Origins of the limited effects model. In E. M. Rogers & F. Balle (Eds.), *The media revolution in America and Europe* (pp. 263–283). Norwood, NJ: Ablex.

Charters, W. W. (1933). *Motion pictures and youth.* New York: Macmillan.

Cobley, P. (Ed.). (1996). *The communication theory reader.* London: Routledge.

Collins, A. M., & Quillian, M. R. (1969). Retrieval time from semantic memory. *Journal of Verbal Learning and Verbal Behavior, 8,* 240–247.

Curran, J. (1996). Rethinking mass communication. In J. Curran, D. Morley, & V. Walkerdine (Eds.), *Cultural studies and communications* (pp. 119–165). London: Arnold.

Curran, J., Gurevitch, M., & Woollacott, J. (1982/1995). The study of the media: Theoretical approaches. In M. Gurevitch, T. Bennett, J. Curran, & J. Woollacott (Eds.), *Culture, society and the media.* London: Routledge.

Dale, E. (1935/1970). *The content of motion pictures.* New York: Macmillan.

Dearing, J. W., & Rogers, E. M. (1996). *Communications concepts 6: Agenda-setting.* London: Sage.

DeFleur, M. L. & Dennis, E. E. (1981). *Understanding mass communication.* Boston, MA: Houghton Mifflin.

Derrida, J. (1993). Structure, sign, and play in the discourse of the human sciences. In J. Natoli & L. Hutcheon (Eds.), *A postmodern reader* (pp. 223–242). Albany: State University of New York Press.

Eco, U. (1979). *Role of the reader: Explorations in the semiotics of texts.* Bloomington, IN: Brooks/Cole.

Ferguson, D. A. (1994). Measurement of mundane TV behaviors: Remote control device flipping frequency. *Journal of Broadcasting & Electronic Media, 38,* 35–47.

Ferguson, D. A., & Perse, E. M. (1993). Media and audience influences on channel repertoire. *Journal of Broadcasting & Electronic Media, 37,* 31–47.

Fineman, H. (1997, January 27). Who needs Washington? *Newsweek* (pp. 50–52).

Fish, S. (1996). Why no one's afraid of Wolfgang Iser. In P. Cobley (Ed.), *The communication theory reader* (pp. 407–425). London: Routledge.

Fiske, J. (1986). Television: Polysemy and popularity. *Critical Studies in Mass Communication, 3,* 391–408.

Fiske, S. T., & Taylor, S. E. (1984). *Social cognition.* New York: Random House.

Foucault, M. (1972). *The archaeology of knowledge & the discourse on language.* (A. M. Sheridan Smith, Trans.). New York: Pantheon Books.

Fromkin, D. (1998). *The way of the world: From the dawn of civilization to the eve of the twenty-first century.* New York: Knopf.

Fry, D., Fry, D. H., & Alexander, A. (1988, May). *The relative importance of primary and secondary contexts in the constitution of textual meaning.* Paper presented at the annual conference of the International Communication Association, New Orleans, LA.

Funkhouser, G. R. (1973). The issues of the sixties: An exploratory study in the dynamics of public opinion. *Public Opinion Quarterly, 37,* 62–75.

Gans, H. (1989, Spring). Bystanders as opinion makers: A bottoms-up perspective. *Gannett Center Journal, 3,* 97–104.

Geiger, S., & Newhagen, J. (1993). Revealing the black box: Information processing and media effects. *Journal of Communication, 43*(4), 42–50.

Gerbner, G. L., Gross, L., Morgan, M., & Signorielli, N. (1980). The mainstreaming of America: Violence profile no.11. *Journal of Communication, 28*(3), 10–29.

Gerbner, G., Gross, L., Morgan, M. & Signorielli, N. (1994). Growing up with television: The cultivation perspective. In J. Bryant & D. Zillmann (Eds.), *Media effects: Advances in theory and research* (pp. 17–42). Hillsdale, NJ: Erlbaum.

Ghanem, S. (1997). Filling in the tapestry: The second level of agenda-setting. In M. McCombs,

D. L. Shaw, & D. Weaver (Eds.), *Communication and democracy* (pp. 3–14). Mahwah, NJ: Erlbaum.

Giddens, A. (1971). *Capitalism and modern social theory: An analysis of the writings of Marx, Durkheim and Max Weber.* Cambridge, UK: Cambridge University Press.

Giddens, A. (Ed.). (1974). *Positivism and sociology.* London: Heinemann.

Gilder, G. (1994). *Life after television: The coming transformation of media and American life.* New York: W. W. Norton.

Gitlin, T. (1985). *Inside prime time.* New York: Pantheon.

Gitlin, T. (1994). Prime time ideology: The hegemonic process in television entertainment. In H. Newcomb (Ed.), *Television: The critical view* (5th ed., pp. 516–536). New York: Oxford University Press.

Habermas, J. (1962/1989). *The structural transformation of the public sphere: An inquiry into a category of bourgeois society.* Cambridge, MA: MIT Press.

Habermas, J. (1985). Questions and counterquestions. In R. Bernstein (Ed.), *Habermas and modernity* (pp. 192–216), Cambridge, MA: Polity Press.

Hall, S. (1980). Coding and encoding in television discourse In S. Hall, D. Hobson, A. Love, & P. Willis (Eds.), *Culture, media, and language* (pp.197–208). London: Hutchinson.

Hall, S., & Whannel, P. (1964). *The popular arts.* New York: Pantheon Books.

Hoggart, R. (1971). *On culture and communication.* New York: Oxford University Press.

Horkheimer, M., & Adorno, T.W. (1944/1972). *Dialectic of enlightenment.* New York: Herder & Herder.

Horton, D., & Wohl, R. R. (1956). Mass communication and parasocial interaction: Observations on intimacy at a distance. *Psychiatry, 19,* 215–229.

Innis, H. (1950/1972). *Empire and communications.* Toronto, Canada: University of Toronto Press.

Innis, H. (1951/1995). *The bias of communication.* Toronto, Canada: University of Toronto Press.

Iyengar, S. (1987). Television news and citizens' explanations of national affairs. *American Political Science Review, 81,* 815–831.

Jay, M. (1973). *The dialectical imagination: A history of Frankfurt School and the Institute of Social Research 1923–1950.* Boston: Little, Brown.

Jo, E., & Berkowitz, L. (1994). A priming effect analysis of media influences: An update. In J. Bryant & D. Zillmann (Eds.), *Media effects: Advances in theory and research* (pp. 43–60). Hillsdale, NJ: Erlbaum.

Katz, E. (1996). Viewers work. In J. Hay, L. Grossberg, & E. Wartella (Eds.), *The audience and its landscape* (pp. 9–21). Boulder, CO: Westview Press.

Katz, E., Blumler, J., & Gurevitch, M. (1974). Utilization of mass communication by the individual. In J. Blumler & E. Katz (Eds.), *The uses of mass communications: Current perspectives on gratifications research* (pp. 19–32). Beverly Hills, CA: Sage.

Katz, E., & Lazarsfeld, P. F. (1955). *Personal influence.* New York: Free Press.

Kellner, D. (1995). *Media culture: Cultural studies, identity and politics between the modern and the postmodern.* London: Routledge.

Kellner, D. (1997). Critical theory and cultural studies: The missed articulation. In J. McGuigan (Ed.), *Cultural methodologies* (pp. 12–41). London: Sage.

Kendall, P. L., & Wolf, K. M. (1949/1979). The analysis of deviant cases in communications research. In P. F. Lazarsfeld & F. N. Stanton (Eds.), *Communication research 1948–1949.* New York: Arno Press.

Klapper, J. T. (1960). *The effects of mass communication.* New York: Free Press.

Kohler, W. (1930). *Gestalt psychology.* London: Bell & Sons.

Krippendorff, K. (1980). *Content analysis: An introduction to its methodology.* Newbury Park, CA: Sage.

Krugman, H. (1986). Low recall and high recognition in advertising. *Journal of Advertising, 15,* 79–86.

Kubey, R. (1992). A critique of *No Sense of Place* and the homogenization theory of Joshua

Meyrowitz. *Communication Theory, 2,* 259–271.

Kubey, R. (1996a). On not finding media effects: Conceptual problems in the notion of an "active" audience (with a reply to Elihu Katz). In J. Hay, L. Grossberg, & E. Wartella (Eds.), *The audience and its landscape* (pp. 187–205). Boulder, CO: Westview Press.

Kubey, R. (1996b). Television dependence, diagnosis, and prevention: With commentary on video games, pornography, and media education. In T. MacBeth (Ed.), *Tuning in to young viewers: Social science perspectives on television* (pp. 221–260). Newbury Park, CA: Sage.

Kubey, R., & Csikszentmihalyi, M. (1990). *Television and the quality of life: How viewing shapes everyday experience.* Hillsdale, NJ: Erlbaum.

Lang, P. J. (1995). The emotion probe: studies of motivation and attention. *American Psychologist, 50,* 372–385.

Lang, P. J., Greenwald, M. K., Bradley, M. M., & Hamm, A. O. (1993). Looking at pictures: Affective, facial, visceral, behavioral reactions. *Psychophysiology, 30,* 261–273.

Langer, E., & Piper, A. (1988). Television from a mindful/mindless perspective. In S. Oskamp (Ed.), *Television as a social issue* (pp. 247–260). Newbury Park, CA: Sage.

Lasorsa, D. L., & Reese, S. D. (1990). News source use in the crash of 1987: A study of four national media. *Journalism Quarterly, 67*(1), 60–71.

Lasswell, H. D. (1927). *Propaganda technique in the world war.* New York: Knopf.

Lazarsfeld, P. F., Berelson, B., & Gaudet, H. (1944). *The people's choice.* New York: Duell, Sloan, & Pearce.

Lazarsfeld, P. F., & Dinerman, H. (1949/1979). Research for action. In P. F. Lazarsfeld & F. N. Stanton (Eds.), *Communication research 1948–1949* (pp. 73–110). New York: Arno Press.

Lazarsfeld, P. F., & Merton, R. (1948). Mass communication, popular taste and organized social action. In L. Bryson (Ed.), *The communication of ideas* (pp. 95–118). New York: Cooper Square.

Lazarsfeld, P. F., & Stanton, F. N. (Eds.). (1949/1979). *Communication research 1948–1949.* New York: Arno Press.

Levy, M. R., & Windahl, S. (1985). The concept of audience activity. In K. E. Rosengren, L. A. Wenner, & P. Palmgreen (Eds.), *Media gratifications research: Current perspectives* (pp. 109–122). Beverly Hills, CA: Sage.

Levy, S. J. (1986). Meanings in advertising stimuli. In J. Olson & K. Sentis (Eds.) *Advertising and consumer psychology.* New York: Praeger.

Lewis, J. (1991). *The ideological octopus.* London: Routledge.

Liebes, T., & Katz, E. (1990). *The export of meaning: Cross-cultural readings of "Dallas."* New York: Oxford University Press.

Lippmann, W. (1971). The world outside and the pictures in our heads. In W Schramm & D. F. Roberts (Eds.), *The process and effects of mass communication* (rev. ed., pp. 265–286). Urbana: University of Illinois Press.

Livingstone, S. M. (1990). *Making sense of television: The psychology of audience interpretation.* New York: Pergamon Press.

Lowenthal, L. (1961) The triumph of mass idols. In L. Lowenthal (Ed.), *Literature, popular culture, and society* (pp. 109–136). Englewood Cliffs, NJ: Prentice Hall.

Lull, J. (1990). *Inside family viewing: Ethnographic research on television's audiences.* London: Routledge.

Lumsdaine, A. A., & Janis, I. L. (1953, Fall). Resistance to "counterpropaganda" produced by one-sided and two-sided "propaganda" presentations. *Public Opinion Quarterly,* 311–318.

Lyotard, J. (1993). Excerpts from "The postmodern condition: A report on knowledge." In J. Natoli & L. Hutcheon (Eds.), *A postmodern reader* (pp. 71–90). Albany: State University of New York Press.

Marcuse, H. (1964). *One dimensional man.* Boston: Beacon Press.

McCombs, M., & Estrada, G. (1997). The news media and the pictures in our heads. In S. Iyengar &

R. Reeves (Eds.), *Do the media govern?* (pp. 237–247). London: Sage.

McCombs, M. E. & Shaw, D. L. (1972). The agenda setting function of the press. *Public Opinion Quarterly, 36,* 176–87.

McCombs, M., & Weaver, D. H. (1985). Toward a merger of gratifications and agenda-setting. In K. E. Rosengren, L. A. Wenner, & P. Palmgreen (Eds.), *Media gratifications research: Current perspectives* (pp. 95–108). Newbury Park, CA: Sage.

McGuire, W. J. (1996). The Yale communication and attitude-change program in the 1950s. In E. E. Dennis & E. Wartella (Eds.), *American communication research: The remembered history* (pp. 39–60). Mahwah, NJ: Erlbaum.

McIlwraith, R. D., Jacobvitz, R. S., Kubey, R., & Alexander, A. (1991). Television addiction: Theories and data behind the ubiquitous metaphor. *American Behavioral Scientist, 35,* 104–121.

McLuhan, M. (1964). *Understanding media: The extensions of man.* New York: McGraw Hill.

McQuail, D. (1994) *Mass communication theory: An introduction.* London: Sage.

Meyrowitz, J. (1985). *No sense of place: The impact of electronic media on social behavior.* New York: Oxford University Press.

Mills, C. W. (1956). *The power elite.* New York: Oxford University Press.

Morgan, M., & Signorielli, N. (1990). Cultivation analysis: Conceptualization and methodology. In N. Signorielli & M. Morgan (Eds.), *Cultivation analysis: New directions in media effects research* (pp. 13–34). Newbury Park, CA: Sage.

Morley, D. (1992). *Television, audiences, and cultural studies.* London: Routledge.

Mukerji, C., & Schudson, M. (1991). *Rethinking popular culture: Contemporary perspectives in cultural studies.* Berkeley: University of California Press.

Mulholland, T. (1973). Objective EEG methods for studying covert shifts of visual attention. In F. G. McGuigan & R. A. Schoonauer (Eds.), *The psychophysiology of thinking* (pp. 109–151). New York: Academic Press.

Munsterberg, H. (1916). *The photoplay: A psychological study.* New York: Appleton.

Nadin, M., & Zakia, R. (1994). *Creating effective advertising using semiotics.* New York: Consultant Press.

Negroponte, N. (1995). *Being digital.* New York: Vintage Books.

Neuman, W. R. (1991). *The future of the mass audience.* Cambridge, UK: Cambridge University Press.

Newcomb, H., & Hirsch, P. M. (1994). Television as a cultural forum. In H. Newcomb (Ed.), *Television: The critical view* (5th ed., pp. 503–515). New York: Oxford University Press.

Noelle-Neumann, E. (1984). *The spiral of silence: Public opinion—our social skin.* Chicago: University of Chicago Press.

Page, B. I., Shapiro, R. Y., & Dempsey, G. R. (1987). What moves public opinion? *American Political Science Review, 81,* 23–34.

Palmgreen, P., & Rayburn, II, J. D. (1985). An expectancy-value approach to media gratifications. In K. E. Rosengren, L. A. Wenner, & P. Palmgreen (Eds.), *Media gratifications research: Current perspectives.* Beverly Hills, CA: Sage.

Perse. E. M. (2001). *Media effects and society.* Mahwah, NJ: Erlbaum.

Perse, E. M., & Dunn, D. G. (1998). The utility of home computers and media use: Implications of multimedia and connectivity. *Journal of Broadcasting & Electronic Media, 42,* 435–456.

Peterson, R. A. (1992). Understanding audience segmentation: From elite and mass to omnivore and univore. *Poetica, 21,* 243–258.

Petty, R. E., & Cacioppo, J. T., (1986). *Communication and persuasion: Central and peripheral routes to attitude change.* New York: Springer.

Pfau, M., Tusing, K. J., Koerner, A. F., Lee, W., Godbold, L. C., Penaloza, L. J. Yang, V. S., & Hong, Y. (1997). Enriching the inoculation construct: The role of critical components in the process of resistance. *Human Communication Research, 24,* 187–215.

Poole, I. (1973). *Talking back: Citizen feedback and cable technology.* Cambridge, MA: MIT Press.

Postman, N. (1985). *Amusing ourselves to death: Public discourse in the age of show business.* New York: Penguin Books.

Postman, N. (1992). *Technopoly: The surrender of culture to technology.* New York: Knopf.

Rabinow, P., & Sullivan, W. M. (1979). The interpretive turn: Emergence of an approach. In P. Rabinow & W. M. Sullivan (Eds.), *Interpretive social science: A reader* (pp. 1–21). Berkeley: University of California Press.

Radway, J. (1983). Women read the romance: The interaction of text and context. *Feminist Studies, 9*(1), 53–78.

Radway, J. (1984). *Reading the romance novel.* Chapel Hill: University of North Carolina Press.

Radway, J. (1991). Interpretive communities and variable literacies: The functions of romance reading. In C. Mukerji & M. Schudson (Eds.), *Rethinking popular culture: Contemporary perspectives in cultural studies* (pp. 465–486). Berkeley: University of California Press.

Reeves, B., & Nass, C. (1995). *New media, old brains.* Unpublished manuscript, Stanford University.

Reeves, B., Thorson, E., Rothschild, M., McDonald, D., Hirsch, J., & Goldstein, R. (1986). Attention to television: Intrastimulus effects of movement and scene change on alpha variation over time. *International Journal of Neuroscience, 27,* 241–255.

Roberts, M. (1997). Political advertising's influence on news, the public and their behavior. In M. McCombs, D. L. Shaw, & D. Weaver (Eds.), *Communication and democracy* (pp. 85–98). Mahwah, NJ: Erlbaum.

Rosengren, K. E. (1974). Uses and gratifications: A paradigm outlined. In J. G. Blumler & E. Katz (Eds.), *The uses of mass communications: Current perspectives on gratifications research* (pp. 269–286). Beverly Hills, CA: Sage.

Rosenthal, R. (1969). *McLuhan: Pro and con.* New York: Penguin.

Rubin, A. (1984). Ritualized and instrumental television viewing. *Journal of Communication, 34,* 67–77.

Saussure, F. (1996). The object of linguistics. In P. Cobley (Ed.), *The communication theory reader* (pp. 37–47). London: Routledge.

Schramm, W. (1971). The nature of communication between humans. In W. Schramm & D. Roberts (Eds.), *The process and effects of mass communication* (pp. 3–53). Urbana: University of Illinois Press.

Schramm, W. (1997). *The beginnings of communication study in America: A personal memoir.* Thousand Oaks, CA: Sage.

Shrum, L. J. (1995). Assessing the social influence of television: A social cognition perspective on cultivation effects. *Communication Research, 22,* 402–429.

Shrum, L. J. (1996). Psychological processes underlying cultivation effects: Further tests of construct assessibility. *Human Communication Research, 22,* 482–509.

Signorielli, N. (1990). Television's mean and dangerous world: A continuation of the cultural indicators perspective. In N. Signorielli & M. Morgan (Eds.), *Cultivation analysis: New directions in media effects research* (pp. 85–106). Newbury Park, CA: Sage.

Singer, J. L. (1980). The power and limitations of television: A cognitive-affective analysis. In P. H. Tannenbaum (Ed.), *The entertainment functions of television* (pp. 31–65). Hillsdale, NJ: Erlbaum.

Tapscott, D. (1998). *Growing up digital: The rise of the net generation,* New York: McGraw-Hill.

Tversky, A., & Kahneman, D. (1973) Availability: A heuristic for judging frequency and probability. *Cognitive Psychology, 22,* 207–232.

Volosinov, V. N. (1996). Toward a Marxist philosophy of language. In P. Cobley (Ed.), *The communication theory reader* (pp. 70–87). London: Routledge.

Wanta, W. (1997). *The public and the national agenda.* Mahwah, NJ: Erlbaum.

Weimann, G. (1995). Zapping in the Holy Land: Coping with multi-channel TV in Israel. *Journal of Communication, 45*(1), 96–102.

Williams, R. (1974). *Television: Technology and cultural form.* New York: Schocken Books.

Williams, T. M. (Ed.). (1986). *The impact of television: A natural experiment in three communities.* New York: Academic Press.

Wren-Lewis, J. (1983). The encoding/decoding model: Criticism and redevelopments for research on decoding. *Media, Culture, and Society, 5,* 197–198.

Wright, R. (1995, January 23). Hyperdemocracy. *Time,* 15–21.

Youn, S. (1994). Program type preference and program choice in a multichannel situation. *Journal of Broadcasting & Electronic Media, 38,* 465–475.

# CHAPTER CONTENTS

• The Literature: Political Science Perspectives                           163
   *Contending Political Theories*                                         *163*

• The Literature: Communication Perspectives                              167
   *The Policy Process in Cultural Context*                                *169*
   *Identifying Social Issues and Influencing Agendas*                     *172*
   *Framing: The Symbolic Construction of Public Policy Issues*            *173*
   *Managing Issues and Public Policy Involvement*                         *176*

• Propositions Regarding Economic Power and Political Influence           179
   *Strategy Propositions*                                                 *179*
   *Tactics Propositions*                                                  *181*
   *Outcome Propositions*                                                  *185*

• Suggestions for a Communication Research Agenda                          187
   *Focus on Business Groups*                                              *187*
   *The Importance of Framing*                                             *188*
   *The Concept of Influence*                                              *190*

•References                                                                191

# 5 The Political Role and Influence of Business Organizations: A Communication Perspective

**BRUCE K. BERGER**
*University of Alabama*

**JAMES K. HERTOG**
*University of Kentucky*

**DONG-JIN PARK**
*University of Alabama*

Relationships between economic power and political influence have long been of interest to scholars in several disciplines. Despite an extensive literature and rich theorizing on the topic, however, we still know little about how economic producers attempt public policy influence and the extent to which they may be successful. In this chapter, the authors argue that a communication perspective on the public policy process sheds new light on relationships between business organizations and political influence. Drawing from the political science, agenda-setting, framing, and issues management literatures, three interrelated communication processes that bear heavily on public policy formation are elaborated—issue selection, issue framing, and issue management. The literatures are critically reviewed and then integrated in a series of 36 propositions regarding what we think we know about the communication strategies and tactics business actors employ in the policy process and the conditions in which such approaches may yield favorable outcomes. A framework for future communication research studies is presented in the form of a business model of political influence. The model highlights complex communicative aspects of policy making and a multifaceted concept of influence in public policy formation.

T he political role of business, and the extent to which profit-seeking organizations influence public policy, are crucial and sharply contested topics among scholars in a number of disciplines, including political science, mass communication, business management, and public relations. Some scholars consider business participation in policy formation to be "normal" in a demo-

---

Correspondence: Bruce K. Berger, Department of Advertising and Public Relations, College of Communication, Box 870172, University of Alabama, Tuscaloosa, AL; email: berger@apr.ua.edu.

*Communication Yearbook 26*, pp. 160–200

cratic process that invites and involves competition for political attention from diverse groups. Others view economic producers as enjoying resource and cultural advantages in the development of social policy that distort or even undermine democratic processes.

Although a wide range of scholars have generated an extensive literature on the topic, our understanding of the relationships between economic power and political influence in American democracy is "theory rich and data poor" (Arnold, 1982). Empirical data regarding business influence on public policy are limited and ambiguous. We still know relatively little about: (a) the communication strategies and tactics economic producers employ in the policy process, (b) whether or not their influence attempts produce "favorable" outcomes, and, if they do, (c) the circumstances or conditions most likely to yield such outcomes.

To help address such issues, we seek to accomplish four goals in this chapter. First, we review more than 300 articles and books from the political science, agenda-setting, framing, and issues management literatures in order to summarize and map progress on the topic. Because of the enormity of the literature—more than 1,000 books and articles in various disciplines—we draw primarily from commonly referenced works that specifically examine economic producers.

Second, we call attention to communicative aspects of business interaction in the policy process. By doing so, we wish to bring a unique and more comprehensive perspective to the topic. As part of this process, we critically analyze the theoretical and methodological adequacy of the literature. Third, we present a series of 36 propositions regarding the policy involvement of economic producers. Here we integrate the literatures and draw some tentative conclusions concerning what we think we know about the strategies and tactics business actors use in the policy process and the circumstances that may produce favorable outcomes for such actors. Finally, we propose a research framework for future studies—a business model of political influence combining agenda-setting and framing analyses with research on the policy process.

The role of communication in policy making is rarely examined (Baumgartner & Leech, 1998; Cobb & Elder, 1981; Nimmo & Sanders, 1981; Stone, 1989). If one conceives of the legislative policy process as a form of social communication, as we do, this oversight is indeed troubling. In essence, democratic government is a porous system wherein various groups engage in symbolic conflict over social issues, resources, and values. Communication processes are the foundation of policy engagement and competition. We examine three interrelated communication processes—issue identification, issue framing, and issue management—that bear heavily on policy formation. Our review highlights these processes and the techniques economic producers employ in their attempts to influence policy outcomes.

Due to the size of the literature, we limit our review in several ways. First, we focus on the federal legislative process, the area of the most significant literature on this topic. Laws, orders, and regulations emanating from Executive or Judicial offices are not examined, despite their importance. Nor do we review business policy involvement at state or local levels, where much policy activity occurs. Principles identified in this review can serve as hypotheses to be tested in other public policy-making institutions. Finally, though we focus on business organizations, we recognize the importance of many actors in the process, including policy makers, nonbusiness advocates, media organizations, and the general public. The interactions of these groups render the policy-making process a dynamic and unpredictable one. To understand the actions of economic actors in this process, we address the actions of other actors on occasion.

A brief note on terms is in order. Our focus is on for-profit corporations, which we refer to as "business," "economic producers," and "business political actors." We avoid using "corporation" or "corporate actor" because such terms may characterize nonbusiness groups that are united or incorporated into one political action body. Our terms also reflect a range of business policy participation, including individual companies; trade, industry, or special policy associations; and business-led coalitions. At the federal level, economic producers increasingly participate not as individual producers, but through such collectivities (Salisbury, 1984).

## THE LITERATURE: POLITICAL SCIENCE PERSPECTIVES

As Getz (1997) has demonstrated, multiple theoretical perspectives offer insights into the political actions of economic producers. Getz' review identified interest group, collective action, public choice, transaction cost, exchange, resource dependency, institutions, agency, and firm behavioral theories. As she indicates, however, many of these perspectives are concerned with identifying which firms participate in political action and why. In contrast, we are more concerned with how economic producers participate in policy formation—the communication strategies and tactics they use—and the apparent results of such influence attempts.

Thus, our review draws heavily from four literatures, each of which contributes to our understanding of relationships between economic power and political influence. In this section, we review the political science literature, concentrating on theories concerning business and government and on interest-group studies. In the subsequent section, a communication perspective on business influence and public policy is presented. We use the agenda-setting, framing, and issues management literatures to elaborate three interrelated communication processes that we believe significantly shape public policy formation in this country.

### Contending Political Theories

Political scientists have long been intrigued with, and divided over, relationships between economic and political institutions. The issue goes to the heart of democratic theory, wherein governmental decisions and policies are seen to grow out of the public's identification and discussion of social issues and problems. No single interest or entity can dominate public decision making if a truly democratic system exists. In the twentieth century, however, concentrated economic power emerged as large, for-profit corporations came to dominate the economic landscape nationally and, more recently, globally. This evoked concerns in the early part of the century, and debates about the political role and influence of business have raged since in the forms of elitist versus pluralist theories, and, more recently, statist theories.

The elitist view has been the most consistent view (Berry, 1989). In this perspective, the overwhelming resource advantages and connections business enjoys lead to success in setting the national policy agenda, defining options, and producing compelling arguments for its positions. Early in the century, Beard (1913) argued that a wealthy and powerful elite influenced political decisions and suggested that the Constitution was designed to foster and protect the economic interests of this elite. Community power studies in the first half of the century often concluded that businesses controlled local policy agendas and decisions (Berry, 1989). At the national level, Mills (1956) concluded that an elite triad of business, political, and military leaders, linked by common social circles, education, group memberships, and ideologies, "ruled" policy choices.

In an early study of Washington-based lobbies, Herring (1967/1929) identified 530 associations and groups involved in lobbying. He argued that business was so heavily represented among such groups that it represented a "third house of Congress" (p. 41). Schattschneider (1935, 1960) found a similar overrepresentation of business interests in Washington, contending that the voices most often heard in policy debates were those of the wealthy, the upper class, and business representatives. A third major study of Washington lobbies (Schlozman & Tierney, 1986) found that 70% of Washington-based groups represented business.

At mid-century, the first of several variations of pluralist theory gained ascendancy, though the roots of group perspectives are found in the earlier works of Bentley (1935/1908) and Small and Vincent (1894). Pluralist scholars of the 1950s and 1960s viewed business as but one group, or set of groups, competing with many others for government attention and action in an open and dynamic policy process. The role of government was to listen to multiple voices, arbitrate conflicts, encourage compromise, and ultimately act for the "people." The power of business, pluralist scholars argued, was more imagined than real, businesses rarely achieved unity on issues, and the political process was fundamentally representative of all groups (Dahl, 1961, 1967; Epstein, 1969; Latham, 1952; McConnell, 1966; McFarland, 1969; Truman, 1951, 1968).

Interest group studies also proliferated in the period, focusing on the formation, roles, strategies, and tactics of interest groups, though not usually business groups (Baumgartner & Leech, 1998; Berry, 1977, 1989). Group studies waned in the late 1960s due to the influence of Olson's (1965) collective action theory and researcher disagreements over how to measure power and influence. Olson's theory highlighted the difficulties groups faced in organizing members and in engaging in concerted action. These difficulties, Olson said, prevent some groups from having an equal voice in policy debates, a conclusion that weakened the pluralist position.

Debates between elite and pluralist theorists continued. Pluralism of the 1950s and 1960s gave way to *plural elitism*, which describes policy arenas controlled by elites in *iron triangles* (Lowi, 1969; McConnell, 1966). The term describes relationships wherein groups like business or labor work with executive agencies and Congressional committees to "control" policy formation (Cater, 1964). Heclo (1978) later argued that iron triangles had been destabilized and replaced by *issue networks*, or loose networks linking interest groups, academics, policy makers, journalists, and policy research centers.

Marxist and class theorists also contributed to the debate in the 1970s, highlighting the influences of social, political, and economic structures on policy agendas and decisions. *Instrumentalists* (e.g., Miliband, 1969) argued that the State served the interests of a capitalist class whose members are closely tied to policy makers through common backgrounds, social circles, education, and ideologies. *Structuralists* such as Poulantzas (1973) contended that the systematic, functional relationships between the economy and the State produced a social cohesion necessary to the continued accumulation of capital, which supported both capitalists and the continued functioning of the State.

The concept of *countervailing group power* appeared in the 1980s, suggesting that business influence was balanced by the power of government agencies and large consumer groups (Berry, 1977; McFarland, 1976, 1984; Walker, 1983). Emerging statist theories posited that government officials and agency personnel make policy decisions independent of pressure groups and class influences. The state doesn't just respond to interest groups but is a powerful actor in its own right and exerts influence on policy making (Evans, Rueschemeyer, & Skocpol, 1985; Laumann & Knoke, 1987; Mitchell, 1997; Mucciaroni, 1995; Skocpol, 1988, 1992; Skocpol & Amenta, 1986). McFarland (1992) used *triadic power* (or *neopluralism*) to refer to such concepts of countervailing power. Government agencies, consumer power lobbies, and economic producers compete so that no single elite or entity dominates policy choices.

*Types of influence.* Political science researchers have devoted particular attention to two types of policy influence—lobbying and political action committee (PAC) contributions. Three qualitative studies of lobbying in the 1960s suggested that this approach was not particularly influential. Bauer, de Sola Pool, & Dexter (1963) concluded that business lobbying had little effect on trade policy because companies were divided over trade matters, and few companies actually participated in the policy process. Milbrath (1963) interviewed 101 Washington lobbyists and evaluated communication channels used by organizations to influence policy. The lobbyists indicated that personal presentation was the most effective form of communication, but Milbrath characterized lobbying work as informational, not influential. Scott and Hunt (1965) interviewed 34 Congressional representatives, who indicated that lobbyists were "cooperative" sources of information—they brokered information, not influence.

Campaign finance reform laws in 1971 and 1974 provided new databases regarding business lobbying and PAC expenditures, and researchers undertook a number of studies to assess the influences of these techniques on roll-call voting in Congress. The findings are inconsistent. Baumgartner and Leech (1998) analyzed 15 lobbying and 33 PAC studies and concluded that such influence attempts appeared to sometimes strongly affect voting, sometimes marginally, and sometimes not at all. Smith (1995) reviewed 35 PAC and 8 lobbying studies, most of them conducted in the 1980s, and reported similar inconsistencies.

Lobbying and PAC influences appear to vary by issue saliency, issue type, and other political contingencies (Cigler & Loomis, 1986; Frendreis & Waterman, 1985; Sabato, 1985, 1989; Smith, 1984, 1995). Studies are difficult to compare, however, because they present methodological deficiencies and often ignore real-world developments and other influence attempts (Baumgartner & Leech, 1998; Salamon & Siegfried, 1977; Smith, 1995).

Another technique of influence—coalition-building—has received limited research attention, despite its apparent increasing use by groups (Berry, 1977, 1989; Browne, 1988, 1990; Grefe & Linsky, 1995; Hojnacki, 1997; Hula, 1999; Megalli & Friedman, 1991). To assess why interest groups join coalitions, Hojnacki (1997) surveyed representatives of 172 Washington-based groups involved with five issues. She concluded that a group is unlikely to use coalition strategies when its interest is narrow and other potential groups appear to have little to contribute. Groups are more likely to join coalitions when they perceive strong opposition and when certain other groups in the potential coalition are considered critical to a successful policy outcome.

Hula (1999) studied the coalition strategies of 130 Washington representatives who actively lobbied in the 101st Congress and concluded that economic producers enjoy information and interlocking (network) relationship advantages in forming and effectively using coalitions. However, new technologies are leveling the playing field. Hula also found that groups often use collective strategies in support of policy-making influence but tend to act independently in election-influencing activities. Acting alone enhances an organization's political credentials.

According to elite theorists, the advantages economic producers enjoy lead to significant policy influence. These advantages include financial resources (Demaris, 1974; Domhoff, 1979, 1996; Dye, 1986; Harris, 1973; Korten, 1995); a pervasive capitalist ideology (Derber, 1998; Mitchell, 1997; Wilson, 1986); and established connections with each other through interlocking directorates, associations, and stock ownership, which create an inner circle of power (Domhoff, 1979, 1996; Jacobs, 1999; Kolko, 1962; Useem, 1980, 1984, 1985). Mizruchi (1992) concluded from his study of 57 *Fortune 500* firms that policy influence is an "inadvertent consequence of firms' standard operating procedures" (p. 49).

Such procedures and interfirm relations produce similar behaviors among economic producers, thereby unifying political behavior and influence.

To sum up, the political science literature contributes rich theorizing about the political role and influence of economic producers and provides some empirical data regarding the relationships between PACs and lobbying activities and policy outcomes. Elitist theories provide the most consistent strand, and studies demonstrate that business groups hold a strong advantage in terms of Washington-based lobbies and other policy-influencing resources (Domhoff, 1996; Herring, 1967/1929; Schattschneider, 1960; Schlozman & Tierney, 1987; Useem, 1984; Verba, Schlozman, & Brady, 1995). However, there is little direct evidence that business elites do influence policy (Berry, 1989; Tierney, 1992). What is more, public policy often runs counter to business interests.

A number of methodological difficulties have limited the scope and amount of empirical evidence on business influence over social policy. They include difficulties in conducting large-scale studies of business (Cigler, 1991; Wilson, 1986); limited access to economic producers (Vogel, 1996; Wilson, 1986); and few large-scale data sources (Cigler, 1991; Cigler & Loomis, 1986; Petracca, 1992). In addition, political science research has shifted its focus to elections, parties, and Executive and Judiciary offices (Baumgartner & Leech, 1998; Salisbury, 1994).

Perhaps the most central issue concerns the crucial concept of "influence." What stands for influence in public policy making? Is influence the ability to have one's interests reflected in new legislation? Is influence most effectively exercised in keeping unattractive policies from ever being considered? Even if one settles on a definition of influence, how can it be measured with so many variables in policy making? As Berry (1977, 1989) suggests, researchers have little alternative but to infer influence based on a policy actor's decision or behavior following a group's influence attempt. The shortcomings of this method of determining influence become apparent when we review the policy-making process from a communication perspective.

Finally, historical perspectives suggest that the political role and influence of business vacillates according to various socio-politico-economic factors in the democratic system (e.g., Galambos, 1975; Galambos & Pratt, 1988; Wiebe, 1995). Vogel (1996) contends there is no need to choose between pluralist and elitist paradigms—both are right and wrong, at times. The elitist perspective may have been more appropriate for the 1950s and 1960s, whereas the pluralist perspective may better characterize the late 1960s and 1970s.

## THE LITERATURE: COMMUNICATION PERSPECTIVES

Congress is an arena where groups cooperate, compete, debate, and use resources to shape policy. A diverse set of political actors operate in this dynamic environment, including policy makers, bureaucrats, interest groups (including business groups), policy experts, political parties, legal authorities, and social activists. Additionally, advocates can influence policy making at a number of different sites within Congress. Tactics and strategies are more or less effective depending upon the site. For example, one set of tactics may be most effective for influencing floor votes, a different set may hold sway in committee meetings, and yet others may best apply to one-on-one briefings and public hearings. Time is also a factor: actions taken at one point in the history of a bill may affect later choices, or an amendment attached at one point may end consideration of the bill later.

Groups use diverse communication strategies and tactics to influence policy formation. Strategies relate to the selection of communication goals, audiences, content, timing, intensity, and channels. Tactics may be used directly with policy makers, for instance, lobbying, PACs, and testimony, or indirectly in the forms of public relations actions, issue advertising, and grassroots campaigns. Nondirect policy communications in the form of organizational advertising, philanthropy, past actions, and reputation also may come into play.

In this section we examine three interrelated communication processes that bear heavily on public policy formation. When political actors engage in the policy arena, they engage primarily in these processes. The first process involves the selection or *identification* of certain social conditions as issues to be addressed by the public policy process and other conditions as nonissues and therefore not appropriate for government attention and action. The agenda-setting literature in mass and political communication is used to examine how social conditions are identified and moved (or not) to the policy agenda. Goals to be achieved in this process include getting issues on policy agendas or preventing issues from appearing or advancing on policy agendas at various sites in the policy arena.

A second, related process is concerned with the *framing* or definition of social conditions as social "problems." Political actors seek to control the rhetorical grounds on which social problems are debated. That is, they construct (relatively) coherent, organized frames that define or explain problems and promote particular remedies. Here we draw from framing studies in mass and political communication and social movement literatures.

The third, intertwined process, *issue management*, is concerned with how actors strategically and tactically attempt influence once specific policy issues have been engaged. This process focuses on the selection and application of various persuasive strategies and tactics to expand or reduce the scope of issue conflict, mobilize supporters, and sustain compelling arguments to achieve various influences in different policy sites. Here we draw from the issue management literature in the public relations and management disciplines.

By highlighting these communication processes, we begin to develop a multifaceted influence construct. In many political science studies, roll-call votes on agenda issues are where the "rubber meets the road," but there are many sites in the policy arena, and many points in issue life cycles, where political actors may exert influence of various types. For example, an editorial briefing may precipitate favorable issue publicity, constituent advertising may stimulate grassroots contacts with policy makers, or re-framing an issue might attract new adherents.

In short, political influences may be small or large, direct or indirect, and occur in many sites and at many times. This is an area where we believe communication scholarship can contribute important insights into policy formation. In the following section, we focus on these three communication processes and highlight various types of influence they suggest. We begin, however, with a brief examination of the cultural context within which the policy process takes place, arguing that this context often reinforces the policy communications of business.

## The Policy Process in Cultural Context

Culture determines business influence on public policy in a number of ways. First, culture legitimizes the existing social order. Most social theorists assign culture a significant role in legitimizing the basic economic and political structures of a society and the existing social hierarchy (Parsons, 1967). Critical scholars argue that the world view inherent in Western cultures promotes the interests of a powerful political and economic elite (Althusser, 1971; Hall, 1979, 1984; Mills, 1956). In Western cultures, representative democracy is presented as the ideal political structure. Members of society are constituted as "citizens" owing fealty to the system and enjoying a set of "rights" conferred upon them by the system, are called upon to actively engage the system to address and resolve social problems, and are admonished to accept and act in accordance with outcomes of the policy-making process (Hall, 1979, 1984).

The profit-based corporation, the dominant capitalist organization, is presented as the most "efficient" and "effective" means of promoting sanctified social values. A high level of cultural legitimacy confers standing and credibility upon business organizations. *Standing* refers to the right to be heard in public and policy arenas when matters touching upon the interests of economic political actors are taken up. *Credibility* refers to a presumption of the quality, truth, or special value of policy-related communications produced by business organizations. Groups challenging the current social distribution of values, especially those providing a radical critique of the political or economic structure, are often marginalized or delegitimated (Davis, 1995; Gitlin, 1980; Hertog & McLeod, 1995; McLeod & Hertog, 1999).

Second, culture structures the debate over social problems. A particular view of political and economic reality tends also to promote a particular set of social conditions as unacceptable and in need of address by government while interpreting other conditions as normal and outside the purview of government (Cobb & Elder, 1983; Hilgartner & Bosk, 1988). Bachrach and Baratz (1962) consider the ability to keep certain conditions off the social agenda—the "management of nondecisions"—one of the leading sources of social power.

Additionally, the grounds of policy debate are influenced by the larger cultural sphere (Bennett, 1980; Edelman, 1993). Members of a society share a set of presumptions, biases, beliefs, myths, and so on that, when brought to bear on social problems, suggest causal explanations, promote certain groups as sources and victims of the condition, outline moral implications and provide a legitimate set of potential cures (Entman, 1993; Hall, 1979, 1984). Thus, the existing culture sets limits on the topics and positions that can be discussed in policy arenas and weights the positions taken by contending groups as more or less compelling.

Third, culture provides the raw material for rhetorical conflict and compromise among interested groups. To convey their views to policy makers and other parties, political actors must draw on the "extant stock of meanings, beliefs, ideologies, practices, values, myths, narratives, and the like . . . which constitute the cultural resource base from which new cultural elements are fashioned" (Benford & Snow, 2000, p. 629). Bennett (1980) goes so far as to conclude that the success of politicians is more directly tied to their skillful use of powerful myths, values, and beliefs in American culture than to their ability to fashion objectively effective public policy.

Policy advocates can enhance their success by shaping coherent packages of information, myths, values, and stories to promote their positions (Ryan, 1991). Business advocates regularly call upon sets of cultural material relating to two major unified frames of understanding—liberal market economic theory and scientific/rational choice ideology. These two are so deeply imbedded in American culture that they can be applied to a wide array of policy fields and will automatically draw support and understanding among sections of the wider public and policy makers (Ellul, 1980; Hallin, 1985). Advocates challenging business positions must either adopt these same frames of understanding, and show how they are enhanced by policies at odds with those proposed by business, or they must promote values and beliefs at least as compelling as these in support of their challenge.

The source of system ideology is widely debated. Some have argued that significant conscious effort on the part of the powerful, especially government and business, is necessary to maintain a cultural system that supports its interests. In their "Propaganda Model" of the media, Edward Herman and Noam Chomsky identify five factors said to generate media content strongly supporting government and business power (Herman, 1996; Herman & Chomsky, 1988).

First, the media are owned and run as profit-making enterprises with owners having the right to fire those reporters or editors who generate content too critical of business, government or other groups favored by owners. In addition, media are controlled by their buying public—advertisers—who can, and occasionally do, place their ads in content that suits their political sensitivities and remove it from those they oppose. Third, the press depends most heavily upon government elites and, secondarily, business elites as sources for news coverage of public affairs. Fourth, right-wing media watch groups, often funded by business groups, regularly attack mainstream media interpretation of political events, pressuring the press to include conservative (business) voices and to limit liberal critique. Finally, the fifth filter—anticommunist ideology—originally proposed in 1988 appears to have declined in importance but is being replaced by a greater ideological salience of the belief in traditional liberal economic ideology. "There is now an almost religious faith in the market, at least among the elite, so that regardless of evidence, markets are assumed benevolent and non-market mechanisms are suspect" (Herman, 1996, p. 126).

Of course, the power of culture to determine policy outcomes in favor of the powerful is limited and temporary. Culture and language are always a site of struggle as consensus must continuously be produced and reproduced (Hall, 1984; Hallin, 1985). Nevertheless, existing culture appears to legitimize business organizations and spokespersons, to structure the ideological field in a manner conducive to the interests of economic producers, and to provide a number of myths, symbols, and values that economic political actors can use effectively in their attempts to influence public policy.

Identifying Social Issues and Influencing Agendas

All societies define certain social conditions and then select certain social problems and issues for policy attention and action (Cobb & Elder, 1983; Hilgartner & Bosk, 1988). Political actors who help set or build agendas influence policy formation, definitions, alternatives, and outcomes (Bachrach & Baratz, 1962, 1970; Berkowitz, 1992; Cobb & Elder, 1981, 1983; Gandy, 1982, 1992). Agenda research is prevalent in the mass and political communication literatures, and more than 350 agenda studies and articles have been completed (Dearing & Rogers, 1996). Several comprehensive reviews of agenda research exist and are not duplicated here (e.g., Dearing & Rogers, 1996; Kosicki, 1993; Protess & McCombs, 1991; Rogers & Dearing, 1988).

Agenda researchers examine interrelationships among media, public, and policy agendas within the larger socio-political environment. These relationships provide a framework for the agenda-setting process, "an ongoing competition among issue proponents to gain the attention of media professionals, the public, and policy elites" (Dearing & Rogers, 1996, p. 2). In this view, agenda-setting is a complex political process, involving interactions among agendas, political actors, influence attempts, and real-world developments (Danielian, 1992; Dearing & Rogers, 1996; Kosicki, 1993; Megwa & Brenner, 1988). Attempts to set and influence agendas are active forms of political participation (Garbrah-Aidoo, 1995), and the struggle among political actors over issue selection and definition is at the heart of the policy process (Godwin, 1992; Jones, 1994; Majone, 1989; Mucciaroni, 1995; Riker, 1993; Schattschneider, 1960).

The majority of agenda studies examine public agenda setting. Cohen (1963) first expressed the public-agenda-setting metaphor when he observed that the "press may not be successful much of the time in telling people what to think, but it is stunningly successful in telling its readers what to think about" (p. 13). McCombs and Shaw (1972) further developed the concept in their study of undecided voters and mass media coverage of five issues in the 1968 presidential election. Results of the study supported the basic hypothesis of public agenda setting: The pattern of news coverage influences public perceptions and opinions about what is important, and, in turn, public opinion influences policy choices and implementation. Media play a central role in democracy because they instigate public awareness and discussion of issues that may lead to policy attention and action (Dearing & Rogers, 1996).

The public agenda refers to that set of issues or problems, usually measured through public opinion or Most Important Problem surveys, identified by American citizens as being important social concerns requiring governmental attention. Many public agenda-setting studies have confirmed that the hierarchy of issues on the media agenda sets the issue hierarchy on the public agenda (Brosius & Kepplinger, 1990; Dearing & Rogers, 1996; Rogers & Dearing, 1988).

Political communication researchers have been more concerned with policy agenda studies, fewer in number, which examine the influences of many factors on the policy agenda. These include public opinion (Herbst, 1993; Lemert, 1981, 1992; Page & Shapiro, 1983), policy entrepreneurs (Kingdon, 1984; Riker, 1993; Walker, 1974), committee structures and protocols (Cobb & Elder, 1981, 1983; Kingdon, 1984; Shepsle & Weingast, 1987), and interest groups, as we saw in the political science literature. The dependent variable in such studies is the list of social issues to which policy makers are paying attention, or their issue agenda (Pritchard, 1992).

Media agenda studies, least common of the three, analyze influences on the media agenda by news sources, gatekeepers, elite media, economic factors, interest groups, and journalistic values and practices (Berkowitz, 1987; Berkowitz & Adams, 1990; Gans, 1979; Gitlin, 1980; Page, 1996; Tuchman, 1978). A number of studies show that government officials far outweigh other categories of press sources (Gans, 1979).

*Types of influence.* Economic producers attempt to influence agendas through diverse communication channels. The goals of such attempts are to place or advance issues on agendas, or to prevent their appearance or advance. Gandy (1982, 1992) argued that economic producers influence media, public, and policy agendas through *information subsidies*, or communications that "reduce the costs of gathering and processing information" (1982, p. 31). Policy actors "dominate the policy process in particular issue domains as a function of their ability to mobilize information resources in their own behalf" (1992, p. 136). Subsidies directed to policy makers include lobbying, testimony, "white papers," and research reports. Subsidies provided to media personnel include news releases, spokespersons, and satellite feeds. Public information subsidies appear in the forms of issue advertisements, speeches, or town-hall meetings.

News releases are the most common information subsidy provided by economic producers to media organizations. News releases may influence between

25–80% of news content (Cameron, Sallot, & Curtin, 1997; Cutlip, 1962). Blyskal and Blyskal (1985) suggested that as much as 50% of business news in *The Wall Street Journal* originates with business sources and subsidies. Grunig (1983) found that many Washington reporters were apathetic, responding only to public relations initiatives or indications of public interest in news topics and public hearings.

Duhe (1993) demonstrated that Monsanto information subsidies in the form of company experts and spokespersons influenced the media agenda for biotechnology stories and helped frame news coverage of biotechnology as both science and business, not as a risk. However, government-originated subsidies may be used more often than subsidies from other sources (Altheide, 1976; Gans, 1979; Morton, 1986). News reporters and editors increasingly use information subsidies due to growing economic constraints on media companies (Curtin, 1999).

Economic producers also attempt to influence policy makers and policy agendas with less direct techniques. For example, businesses may mobilize employees, retirees, shareholders, or other community groups in grassroots campaigns. Letters, emails, telegrams, and other forms of personal appeals from constituents may affect the policy maker's perceptions of an issue's importance. Such attempts are interpreted as forms of public opinion (Lemmert, 1981, 1992).

In summary, the agenda-setting literature emphasizes communicative aspects of the policy process in that policy issues are identified and socially constructed by policy actors (Cobb & Elder, 1981, 1983; Stone, 1989). Agenda studies also shed light on the dynamic interactions of political actors, agendas, and events. In this environment, economic producers and other actors attempt influence through multiple communication channels to gain the attention and support of policy makers, media professionals, and the public. Like the political science literature, however, many agenda-setting studies do not examine the role and involvement of business actors, often dealing instead with the influences of media and public agendas on policy agendas and outcomes.

Framing: The Symbolic Construction of Public Policy Issues

Most study of business influence in the policy process assumes clear and effective communication among activists, policy makers, and the public. Communication scholars consider the construction of meaning among contending groups to be far more problematic and ephemeral. The struggle over the symbolic construction of a social problem may, in the end, be far more important in determining social policy than is the debate over the relative merits of specific policy proposals (Bennett, 1980; Cobb & Elder, 1983; Entman, 1993; Hilgartner & Bosk, 1988).

Alongside their attempts to select issues for various agendas, political actors seek to construct a symbolic structure that explains the social problem in an advantageous manner. They draw from raw materials of the culture to define, explain, and provide context for their preferred social policy—to invest it with a particular set of meanings and to exclude those meanings that would undermine their position. Their ability to "frame" an issue in this way may be crucial to their success in the policy sphere (Benford & Snow, 2000; Cobb & Elder, 1983; Ryan, 1991).

Study of framing processes and effects has generated a significant literature across a number of disciplines in recent years (Benford & Snow, 2000; Hertog & McLeod, 2001; Reese, 2001). Entman (1993) is concerned with the political implications of frames:

> (Frames) define problems—determine what a causal agent is doing with what costs and benefits, usually measured in terms of common cultural values; diagnose causes—identify the forces creating the problem; make moral judgments—evaluate causal agents and their effects; and suggest remedies—offer and justify treatments for the problems and predict their likely effects. (p. 52)

Once a particular frame for approaching a social problem comes to dominate in the public or policy arena, options that do not fit within the frame will be excluded from discussion. Contending parties must either make their cases within this now-dominant terrain of meaning or attempt to reframe the issue. In their study of European Union environmental policy making, for example, Triandafyllidou and Fotiou (1998) found that "extreme" environmentalist groups—those whose policy proposals fell outside the accepted frame for sustainable growth—were effectively excluded from the policy debate. "Pragmatic" environmentalist groups gained access to the policy debate, but had to settle for minimizing environmental damage.

Despite the size of the literature—Benford and Snow (2000) counted nearly 250 references in the movement framing literature alone—little is known about the impact of framing on social policy. Little discussion of business framing of public problems could be identified in our review. Because of the critical importance of meaning-making in public policy formation, however, we speculate from some of the framing study in other contexts and with other groups.

In their review of the social movement framing literature, Benford and Snow (2000) identified three forms of framing. *Diagnostic frames* identify the nature of the problem and its sources. In the case of declining imports, for example, a business group might argue that high labor costs are the source of the problem. *Prognostic framing* "involves the articulation of a proposed solution to the problem" (Benford & Snow, 2000). Business groups often attempt to stave off government regulation of business as a proposed solution to public problems (Triandafyllidou & Fotiou, 1998). *Motivational framing* outlines a rationale for participant action and often highlights the severity of the problem or the immediate concern faced by the group.

Several features of collective action frames are thought to have a significant impact on their functioning and effectiveness (Benford & Snow, 2000). The first is the issue or topic they address. Each social problem has a history, set of actors, social conditions, and rhetorical field that is unique. A second consideration is the flexibility of the frame in accepting various interpretations, or in including potential supporters with varying dedication to its tenets. A third consideration is the "variation in interpretive scope and influence" among frames. "Master frames" are broad and general enough to make sense of significantly different social problems.

The cultural legitimacy of two master frames—scientific rationalization and market economics—provides business organizations an advantage in their framing activities (Bell, 1976; Ellul, 1980; Hallin, 1985). Industry sources can invoke these frames across a wide array of policy areas, be it environmental policy (Davis, 1995; Triandafyllidou & Fotiou, 1998), product safety regulations, employee health insurance coverage, or affirmative action.

Finally, the effectiveness or mobilization potency (resonance) of frames varies. Benford and Snow (2000) suggest the resonance of a frame is determined by its credibility and salience. *Credibility* is determined by the congruency between the group's articulated beliefs, claims, and actions; the apparent fit between the frame(s) and events in the world; and the perceived credibility of frame articulators. *Salience* to targeted audiences of the frame is based on (a) the importance of the frame's beliefs, values, and ideas to the lives of the targets of mobilization; (b) congruence of the frame with the personal, everyday experiences of these targets; and (c) the extent to which the frame aligns with cultural myths, ideology, master narratives, and so forth.

Frames develop both as a natural outcome of ongoing communication in a regularly interacting group and as the strategic product of communicators attempting to maximize their impact on social policy. Business advocates are likely to be in contact with one another, and a number of researchers have demonstrated the social as well as structural ties among business elites (Mills, 1956). In conversation and, possibly, business media, the development of sets of understandings, or ways of viewing the social world, likely develop and take hold (Weiss, 1974).

Frame sponsors attempt to construct frames in ways that encourage additional groups to support the sponsor's goals (Cobb & Elder, 1983). Davis (1995) recounted how both timber interests and environmentalists adjusted their framing practices to garner support from additional groups during their 10-year conflict over old growth logging in Oregon. Loggers originally tried to "contain" the issue by defining it as a local dispute over whether they would continue to have access to resources as they had historically. When environmentalists expanded their issue frames and gained sympathy and support from more diverse groups and even the national public, the loggers also expanded their frames and reached out to other groups for support. Timber interests eventually framed their position as preservation of families and communities and the need to halt environmentalist threats to free enterprise, property rights, and progress.

Research often examines the framing efforts of policy makers rather than those of business groups. Entman & Rojecki (1993) have argued that government elites have the greatest influence over media coverage of social problems and other governmental concerns such as foreign policy. They also found that despite overwhelming public support for a nuclear freeze, *The New York Times* and *Time* magazine tended to delegitimize the actions and character of freeze supporters while providing no significant critical frame to Reagan administration policy.

Research on press framing of social problems or activist groups also contributes significantly to our understanding of the influence of communication in policy making (Pan & Kosicki, 1993; Reese, 2001). This strand tends to find that press framing portrays competing policy preferences as clearer, simpler, and more extreme than they are, emphasizes conflict and violence, and treats the political conflict as a strategic game.

Most research on framing has focused on framing in the public arena rather than in the policy arena, that is, the symbolic construction of social problems located in media texts, movement brochures, and other "public" documents. However, public policy debate occurs partly in open committees, partly on the floor of Congress and importantly, partly behind closed doors. What is more, advantages in access appear to allow business groups to bring the attention of policy makers to conditions that have not been emphasized in public fora and preset the symbolic construction of those conditions as social issues, that is, to frame the issues before they are ever public issues in a relatively noncontested sphere. The ability to frame the debate early provides a powerful advantage in the realm of political meaning construction.

To conclude this section, the rhetorical contest among political actors to frame issues is a crucial communication process in the public policy arena. Existing culture may provide business groups with certain advantages in framing policy debate and structuring the discussion of policy options. However, a great deal more research into the frames and framing approaches used by business groups and other political actors is necessary to advance our understanding in this area.

## Managing Issues and Public Policy Involvement

W. Howard Chase first used the term "public issues management" in 1976 (Crable & Vibbert, 1985; Ewing, 1990) and subsequently detailed a five-step issues management (IM) process (Chase, 1984) that businesses can use to systematically manage involvement in the policy process. Chase, and many other theorists, define issues as points around which self-interests and conflicts develop. Issues are sometimes seen as broad categories of related problems, for instance, the environment or crime. But most researchers and policy studies are concerned with specific issues, often in bill form, which are up for debate and action (Kingdon, 1984), for instance, a proposed law or regulation affecting auto emission standards or funding for new anticrime measures.

Although economic producers have long been politically active, the IM process signaled an increasingly aggressive and organized approach to policy influence. Four developments in the 1960s spurred this approach: a sharp increase in the number of activist groups opposed to business, an increase in new regulations applied to business, declines in public confidence in business, and flat or declining business profits (Chase, 1984; Heath, 1997; McQuaid, 1981; Moore, 1980; Plotke, 1992; Silk & Vogel, 1976; Vogel, 1996).

Plotke (1992) argued that business executives mobilized in the 1970s to press for a new model of economic growth that would reduce regulations, limit social spending, and create a more favorable climate for business in Washington. Useem (1985) documented the formation of new business alliances during the same period. The Chamber of Commerce expanded rapidly in the late 1970s, the National Association of Manufacturers registered as a lobbying organization in 1975, and The Business Roundtable was founded in 1973 (Derber, 1998; Plotke, 1992; Shapiro, 1984). The development of these organizations helped to foster an "inner circle" of business leadership that lobbied policy makers on a regular basis (Useem, 1984).

The IM literature includes more than 250 articles and book chapters (Heath & Cousino, 1990), many of which are descriptive or self-reported case studies (Sanders, 1998). Most models prescribe a five-step IM process: issue monitoring, issue analysis and prioritization, formulation of communication strategies and plans, implementation of plans, and evaluation of results (Chase, 1984; Crable & Vibbert, 1985). Other research has examined how organizational members identify, evaluate, and prioritize strategic issues (Dutton, 1993; Dutton & Jackson, 1987; Dutton & Ottensmeyer, 1987). At least three studies suggest that about 75% of corporations use an IM process (Ewing, 1987; Hainsworth & Meng, 1988; Lusterman, 1987).

Political communication researchers Cobb and Elder (1983) highlighted the importance of issue characteristics and life cycles in policy development. They specified a policy-agenda-building model with four phases: issue initiation, specification, expansion, and entrance on to the policy agenda. Buchholz (1988) identified a three-stage issue cycle: a public opinion formation stage when issues emerge, a policy formulation stage when solutions are proposed and debated, and an implementation stage when policies are enacted. Hainsworth (1990) saw issues evolving through origin, development, expansion, and resolution cycles. Most theorists agree that early involvement with issues increases opportunities for influence or acceptable compromise.

IM theorists often present instrumental perspectives (Chase, 1984; Crable & Vibbert, 1985; Hainsworth & Meng, 1988; Jones & Chase, 1979; Renfro, 1993) or systems perspectives (Arrington & Sawaya, 1984; Dutton & Ottensmeyer, 1987; Heath, 1997). Heath espouses a normative framework within which IM processes and objectives incorporate concern for public interests and consensus-building dialogue between organizations and publics (Heath, 1988a, 1997; Heath & Cousino, 1990; Heath & Nelson, 1986). Preston and Post (1975) and Buchholz (1988, 1992) contend that market processes and public policy processes provide a framework to guide the behaviors of economic producers in achieving organizational and community goals.

*Types of influence.* The literature also describes the growth of communication channels used by economic producers to attempt policy influence. The number of business PACs rose from 89 in 1974 to more than 1,600 by 1985 (Morrison, 1986). Employees, shareholders, and retirees were increasingly mobilized into grassroots campaigns (Heath, 1997; Moore, 1980; Wilson, 1986). Businesses formed more coalitions and negotiated directly with activists (Heath, 1997; Greening, 1991; Sanders, 1998), and new public relations actions sought to influence media coverage of policy issues (Blyskal & Blyskal, 1985; Gandy, 1982, 1992; Waltzer, 1988).

Another technique of influence—issues or advocacy advertising—flourished in the 1970s and 1980s as some economic producers sought to balance what they perceived to be a critical and one-sided public discussion of business and the economic system (O'Toole, 1975). The ads were intended to influence public perceptions about issues important to economic producers (Sethi, 1976, 1977, 1987), and Mobil Oil's long-running campaign in national media against increased federal regulations is perhaps the best known example of such advertising (Schmertz, 1986). The extent to which issue ads influence public opinion, or the policy process, is unknown.

Salmon, Reid, Pokrywczynski, & Willet (1985) offered empirical evidence that messages in issue ads, compared to coverage in news stories, were more persuasive because ads were felt to be more informative and interesting. Coe (1983) found that many media and business executives rated issue ads as average or very good in exposing target audiences to key messages. Heath and Douglas (1986) reported that issue ads presented in print media may be more effective than those presented in television. An Opinion Research Corporation survey found that 90% of the public recalled seeing or hearing issue ads, and, as a result, 57% had changed opinions on issues (Ewing, 1982).

Other studies, however, found little success associated with the use of issue ads (Adkins, 1978; Coe, 1983; Fox, 1986; Sethi, 1977), and at least two areas require further study. First, most studies don't incorporate other techniques of influence that may be employed simultaneously with advertising, for instance, public relations initiatives. Second, little attention has been devoted to issue ads that are targeted to policy-maker constituents, rather than to larger public audiences.

Issue salience, characteristics, and life-cycle stages affect strategic and tactical choices. Van Leuven and Slater (1991) argued that public relations practitioners try to match influence channels (e.g., speeches, newsletters, position papers) and intensity of action to stages in issue life cycles and to publics according to the nature of each public's importance and involvement at each stage in the life cycle. In a study of *Fortune 500* companies, Ryan, Swanson, & Buchholz (1987) linked influence techniques with a three-stage policy cycle. Companies use annual reports, newsletters, and new releases to participate in public debate in the public opinion formation stage. In the policy formulation stage, companies direct PAC contributions and lobbying and coalition activities toward policy makers. In the implementation phase, companies choose whether or not to comply, litigate, or create new issues to attempt to ameliorate the effects of policies. Buchholz (1988) uses "goodness of fit" to describe the linking of issue stages and tactics.

Two reviews of case studies provide some evidence of the effectiveness of IM approaches. Bliss (1996) analyzed 16 case studies and concluded that economic producers that take proactive steps to work with activist groups often achieve common understanding and are satisfied with issue resolutions. Sanders (1998) found in his examination of 10 case studies that IM influences internal business policy decisions, and companies that use an IM approach are more likely to influence the policy agenda and outcomes than companies that do not. He also found that coalitions and grassroots campaigns may be the most effective influence techniques.

To conclude this section, the issues management literature adds other dimensions to our understanding of economic producers and the policy process. Perhaps most importantly, the literature (a) highlights the public policy process from the business perspective, (b) details issue life-cycles and characteristics, and (c) describes the communication strategies and tactics that economic producers use to attempt policy influence. However, the IM literature provides little empirical evidence of political influence, beyond self-reported case studies.

## PROPOSITIONS REGARDING ECONOMIC POWER AND POLITICAL INFLUENCE

In this section, we integrate the literatures and identify three types of propositions regarding what we think we know about economic power and political influence. We first identify propositions about business strategies, that is, what the literatures suggest about the strategic approaches of economic producers to policy involvement and formation. We then outline propositions regarding business tactics, highlighting communication channels and approaches. Following Berry (1977), a strategy is defined as a "broad plan of attack, or general approach," and a tactic is a "specific action taken to advocate certain questions" (p. 212). Finally, we address business outcomes, which refer to conditions wherein economic producers may be more likely to achieve influence or attain favorable outcomes. The propositions are drawn from theoretical insights and arguments, and, whenever available, qualitative or quantitative evidence.

### Strategy Propositions

1. Economic producers strategically invest resources in many communication roles and activities in their attempts to influence public policy agendas and outcomes (Berger, 1999; Domhoff, 1996; Dye, 1986; Eismeier & Pollock, 1988; Levitan & Cooper, 1984; Moore, 1980). Many researchers have noted that busi-

ness groups possess more resources and spend more on lobbying, advertising, and PAC contributions than other political actors. Businesses also invest heavily in less well-known policy-influencing communication networks and approaches:

a. Businesses maintain complex networks of professional specialists at the local, state, and federal levels to leverage information and influence. Investments in new technologies facilitate communication, mobilization, and issue monitoring activities among these networks. Economic producers may operate such political networks independently, participate in association efforts, join coalitions, or employ all three strategies (Bartlett, 1973; Berger, 1999; Elmendorf, 1988; McQuaid, 1981; Moore, 1980; Ryan et al., 1987; Schlozman & Tierney, 1986).

b. Economic producers use networks of interlocking relationships (directorates, stock holdings, associations, social circles) to exchange political ideas and intelligence (Domhoff, 1979, 1996; Dye, 1986; Jacobs, 1999; Levitan & Cooper, 1984; Useem, 1984).

c. Relationships with, and access to, bureaucrats and policy makers are nurtured, facilitating lobbying, advisory appointments, and invitations to testify at public hearings (Cobb & Elder, 1981, 1983; Domhoff, 1996; Levitan & Cooper, 1984; Mills, 1956; Useem, 1980, 1985).

d. "Built-in" supporters and constituents (employees, suppliers, shareholders, retirees) may be mobilized in grassroots actions. Here, business reputation and quality of interpersonal relationships with such individuals or groups, along with economic relationships, may facilitate political action (Chase, 1984; Elmendorf, 1988; Grefe & Linsky, 1995).

2. Savvy economic producers use a strategic issues management process to participate more effectively in public policy analysis, planning, and communication (Arrington & Sawaya, 1984; Buchholz, 1992; Chase, 1984; Dutton & Ottensmeyer, 1987; Ewing, 1990; Jones & Chase, 1979; Kasser & Truax, 1988). This process systematizes issue monitoring and analysis, enhances strategic business and communication planning, and may stimulate socially responsible actions.

3. Economic producers use inside strategies—lobbying campaigns, meetings with other political actors, and provision of technical reports—to leverage resource advantages and established connections with policy makers (Baumgartner & Leech, 1998; Cater, 1964; Clawson, Neustadtl, & Scott, 1992; Cobb & Elder, 1983; Harris, 1973; Jones, 1994).

a. Inside strategies are likely to be emphasized when issues are highly technical in nature and require issue expertise in negotiations (Berger, 1999; Walker, 1991; Wilcox, 1998).

4. Business political actors use outside strategies—advertising, public relations approaches, grassroots campaigns, coalitions—to expand the scope of conflict when they are on the defensive, or to react to other actors or events that have expanded the scope of issue conflict (Berger, 2001; Jones, 1994; Schattschneider, 1960; Walker, 1991; Wilcox, 1998). Firms with special expertise in such areas

are often hired to provide these strategic and tactical services.

5. Economic producers use collective strategies (coalitions) when policy issues are highly salient and conflictual (Grefe & Linsky, 1995; Hojnacki, 1997; Hula, 1999; Jacobs, 1999; Levitan & Cooper, 1984; Mucciaroni, 1995; Plotke, 1992), or to present the appearance of greater diversity and disguise core member identities (Hula, 1999; Megalli & Friedman, 1991).

6. Economic producers employ strategies of internal organizational change— adopting proposed requirements, changing internal structures or practices— rather than attempt policy influence when they seek to balance societal and organizational needs, political costs are too high, or the cause appears lost (Buchholz, 1992; Heath, 1997; Renfro, 1993; Sanders, 1998).

7. A strategy of early involvement with policy issues provides advantages to economic producers and other political actors (Buchholz, 1988; Ewing, 1990; Hainsworth, 1990; Heath, 1997; Sanders, 1998; Walker, 1977).

a. Economic actors may negotiate mutually acceptable solutions with competing actors or critics before the scope of conflict expands if they engage early in the issue cycle (Gaunt & Ollenburger, 1995; Greening, 1991; Pires, 1988; Polsby, 1984; Renfro, 1993; Sanders, 1998).

b. Early involvement increases opportunities to influence issue definitions and images (Cobb & Elder, 1983; Rochefort & Cobb, 1994; Sanders, 1998; Stone, 1989) or media-public-policy agendas (Cobb & Elder, 1981; Jones, 1994; Riker, 1993).

Tactics Propositions

8. Economic producers use diverse communication tactics, often in combination, to try to achieve multiple influence goals, for instance, advance or block agenda issues, co-opt opponents, frame issue images and definitions, increase issue salience in media coverage, shape public(s) opinion(s), amend bill language, and affect policy maker votes (Gandy, 1982, 1992; Heinz, Laumann, Nelson, & Salisbury, 1993; Jones & Chase, 1979; Linsky, 1986; Ryan et al., 1987; Schlozman & Tierney, 1986; Van Leuven & Slater, 1991). Communication tactics and approaches are used at many sites in the policy arena and in the larger public arena.

9. Choice of tactics is often based on issue salience, scope of issue conflict, stage of issue life-cycle, and issue type (Cobb & Elder, 1983; Lowi, 1964; Ryan et al., 1987; Schattschneider, 1960; Suarez, 1998; Van Leuven & Slater, 1991; Walker, 1983).

a. When issues are first emerging or are not salient on media and public agendas, economic actors use inside approaches with policy makers, for instance, personal lobbying, meetings with opponents, and issue communication (annual reports, newsletters) with constituents (Hainsworth, 1990; Ryan et al., 1987; Sanders, 1998). Common goals of inside tactics are to resolve issues early or to favorably define (or eliminate) proposed agenda items.

b. If issues are not resolved early, and if issue salience increases and scope of conflict expands, business actors are likely to employ outside tactics such as issue ads, public relations activities, and grassroots campaigns, in addition to their existing inside tactics (Berger, 1999; Buchholz, 1988; Chase, 1984; Ryan et al., 1987; Van Leuven & Slater, 1991). Outside tactics are often used to mobilize supporters, increase issue salience, demonstrate strength of constituency, favorably define and frame problems, and offer alternate solutions.

c. When issues are up for Congressional debate and action, the use of all tactics may intensify, accompanied by committee testimonies and attempts to add amendments or modify bill language (Baumgartner & Leech, 1998; Chase, 1984; Sanders, 1998). The scope of lobbying may be expanded from supporters to opponents and undecideds (Hojnacki & Kimball, 1996). At this point in the policy-making cycle, the goal is to achieve one or more favorable legislative outcomes (passage/nonpassage, amendment, or revised language).

d. If a policy unfavorable to business is enacted, or a favorable one is not passed, economic producers choose whether or not to comply, litigate, or promote a new but related issue to address concerns (Buchholz, 1988; Getz, 1993; Oberman, 1993; Ryan et al., 1987).

10. Lobbying may be the most frequently used communication tactic (Berry, 1977; Herring, 1967/1929; Knoke, 1990; Schlozman & Tierney, 1986; Walker, 1991). However, we know little about the relative proportions of tactics used by economic producers. One study of 186 large companies suggested that lobbying expenditures were ten times as great as PAC and soft money expenditures (Berger, 1999).

11. Economic producers often lobby an issue as individual organizations and through coalitions and business associations (Berger, 1999; Cigler, 1991; McQuaid, 1981; Useem, 1980). Individual businesses may have interests in common with the larger business community on some issues whereas on others their own interests lead them to go it alone.

12. The currency of modern lobbying is information, often on highly technical or complex subjects (Cigler & Loomis, 1986; Petracca, 1992; Stone, 1988). Governmental personnel may not have adequate information to make decisions in some technical areas. Business organizations in these areas contribute their expertise strategically to influence policy.

13. Lobbying may be the most effective communication tactic (Chase, 1984; Crawford, 1939; Gandy, 1982; Grefe, 1981; Harris, 1973; Levitan & Cooper, 1984; Schriftgiesser, 1951; Scott & Hunt, 1965; Sethi, 1982). However, only two studies (Berry, 1977; Milbrath, 1963) have examined the relative effectiveness of lobbying and other tactics at the federal level, and both suggest that personal lobbying is the most productive use of time. Results of quantitative studies of lobbying influence are inconsistent (Baumgartner & Leech, 1998; Smith, 1995).

a. The intensity of lobbying, and who gets lobbied, vary by issue salience and stage of issue life cycle (Hojnacki & Kimball, 1996). Supporters are often lobbied first; as salience increases and scope of conflict expands, lobbying may include opponents and undecideds.

b. Initial lobbying contacts are the most important and influential because they present positions and interpretations (Smith, 1984). Repeat lobbying may not change positions but may help maintain any previously gained influence (Smith, 1993).

c. Lobbying committee members before committee decisions are taken is crucial because committee votes influence floor votes (Fenno, 1973; Wittenberg & Wittenberg, 1994; Wolpe, 1990).

d. Lobbyists don't need to change the minds of policy makers about issues so much as they need to change how policy makers view or interpret issues (Baumgartner & Leech, 1998). Thus, lobbyists attempt to change the terms of issue debate (Baumgartner & Jones, 1993; Jones, 1994), redefine policy issues (Nelson, 1984), or alter the interpretations of issues held by policy makers (Smith, 1984).

14. Lobbying has more influence on policy maker decisions when (Smith, 1995):

a. The policy issue has low visibility and doesn't provoke sharp ideological or party differences (Berger, 1999; Schattschneider, 1960; Schlozman & Tierney, 1986);

b. Lobbyists represent broad coalitions (Fowler & Shaiko, 1987; Rothenberg, 1992);

c. Policy makers believe a lobbyist's issue expertise exceeds their own issue knowledge or expertise (Rothenberg, 1992; Wright, 1990);

d. There is little opposition from other political actors (Fowler & Shaiko, 1987; Schlozman & Tierney, 1986);

e. Interest groups both possess and use comparative resource advantages to carry out lobbying campaigns (Berger, 1999; Smith, 1984);

f. Lobbyists represent groups that have politically active constituents and have offered previous support to policy makers (Smith, 1993);

g. Lobbying is conducted with top-tier officials—committee leaders, presidential insiders—rather than with bureaucrats or staffers (Cigler & Loomis, 1986; Conway, 1986); and

h. Lobbying is carried out by corporate executives rather than hired, professional lobbyists (McQuaid, 1981; Shapiro, 1984; Tierney, 1992; Useem, 1985).

15. PAC contributions buy access to policy makers but not necessarily influence (Alexander, 1985, 1988; Eismeier & Pollock, 1988; Evans, 1986; Hall & Wayman, 1990; Magleby & Nelson, 1990; Morrison, 1986; Sabato, 1985, 1989; Sorauf, 1992).

a. PAC contributions are used to influence both the decisions of policy makers and the election of favored candidates (Cigler & Loomis, 1986; Clawson et al., 1992; Conway, 1986).

16. Economic actors also use PACs to increase organizational visibility, enhance political education of employees, increase capacity for grassroots campaigns, and influence the discussions or activities of committee members apart

from roll-call voting (Conway, 1986; Eismeier & Pollock, 1988; Evans, 1986; Hall & Wayman, 1990; Sorauf, 1992; Wright, 1990).

17. PAC contributions have more influence on roll-call votes when (Smith, 1995):

a. The policy issue has low visibility and doesn't stimulate sharp ideological or party differences (Cigler, 1991; Conway, 1986; Grenzke, 1990; Jones & Keiser, 1987; Malbin, 1984; Neustadtl, 1990; Sabato, 1985, 1989; Sorauf, 1992; Stratmann, 1991; Wright, 1985);

b. There is little opposition from other political actors (Evans, 1986; Godwin, 1988; Jones, 1994; Sabato, 1985, 1989; Schlozman & Tierney, 1986; Stratmann, 1991);

c. Political actors combine PAC contributions with intense lobbying efforts and other communication tactics and forms of business influence (Berger, 1999; Cigler & Loomis, 1986; Clawson et al., 1992; Evans, 1986; Sabato, 1985; Smith, 1995; Wilcox, 1998).

18. Economic producers use nonmonetary assets—issue expertise, professional services, and research data and information sources—to gain access to policy makers (DeGregorio, 1998; Gandy, 1982, 1992; McQuaid, 1981; Petracca, 1992).

19. Economic producers use issue advertising to influence public(s) opinion(s) and legitimize policy positions by naming, describing, and defining issues through rhetorical appeals, metaphors, and symbolic attacks (Crable & Vibbert, 1995; Dionisopoulos, 1986; Edelman, 1971, 1988; Schmertz, 1986; Sethi, 1977).

a. Issue ads strengthen sense of unity among members of the business family and their constituents (Grefe, 1981; Newman, 1982; Sethi, 1977).

b. Issue ads implicitly or explicitly link business values and ideology with public values (Derber, 1998; Domhoff, 1996; Korten, 1995; Schmertz, 1986).

c. Issue ads may be more effective when delivered in print media rather than on television (Heath & Douglas, 1986).

d. Issue ads may lead business organizations to become more responsive to social needs and values (Heath, 1988b).

20. Economic producers testify at public hearings to express positions, define issues and alternatives, and legitimate political credentials (Berger, 1999; Berry, 1977; Jones, Baumgartner, & Talbert, 1993). Congressional representatives in one study suggested that testimony at committee hearings was the most effective channel of political communication for interest groups (Scott & Hunt, 1965).

Outcome Propositions

Economic producers may have more political influence on public policy formation and achieve more favorable legislative results when:

21. The objective is to delay or defeat a policy proposal or agenda item rather than to introduce or gain acceptance of one (Cobb & Elder, 1983; Kingdon, 1984; Petracca, 1992; Sanders, 1998; Schlozman & Tierney, 1986; Tierney, 1992).

22. The objective is to change or introduce parts of a bill rather than the entire proposal (Milbrath, 1963; Schlozman & Tierney, 1986; Tierney, 1992).

23. Bills or policy issues up for action are highly technical in nature and have low salience rather than emotional in nature and highly salient (Conway, 1986; Dickie, 1984; Evans, 1986; Jones, 1994; Jones et al., 1993; Schlozman & Tierney, 1986; Sharp, 1994).

24. Bills or policy issues up for action are characterized by low levels of political partisanship and ideology (Kingdon, 1984; Petracca, 1992; Schattschneider, 1960).

25. Economic resources are available and used effectively over time (Adams, 1973; Berry, 1989; Clawson et al., 1992; Demaris, 1974; Derber, 1998; Domhoff, 1996; Harris, 1973; Jones, 1994; Knoke, 1986; Majone, 1989; Smith, 1984; Tierney, 1992; Vogel, 1996).

26. There are few competing political actors (Evans, 1986; Jones, 1994; Knoke, 1990; Mucciaroni, 1995; Smith, 1995; Tierney, 1992; Walker, 1983).

27. Acting collectively with others through coalitions or alliances (Birnbaum, 1992; Clawson et al., 1992; Grefe & Linsky, 1995; Hula, 1999; Laumann & Knoke, 1987; Levitan & Cooper, 1984; Mucciaroni, 1995; Sanders, 1998). Conversely, influence may be less when businesses are divided and compete with each other (Bauer et al, 1963; Berry, 1989; Evans, 1995; Kingdon, 1984; Mitchell, 1997; Useem, 1984; Vogel, 1996).

28. Issues are located or addressed in "favorable" policy arenas or venues (Baumgartner, 1989; Baumgartner & Jones, 1991, 1993; Kingdon, 1984; Schneider & Teske, 1992; Wilcox, 1998). One strategy for political actors is to "shop" for favorable policy venues for consideration of policy issues or claims (Baumgartner & Jones, 1991, 1993).

29. "Positive" policy alternatives are offered, backed up by research and data, rather than ideological or emotional arguments (Ewing, 1990; Herring, 1967/1929; Korten, 1995; Levitan & Cooper, 1984; McQuaid, 1981; Plotke, 1992; Sethi, 1977; Wilcox, 1998).

30. Advocated policy positions or issues are linked to public interests or the policy maker's constituents (Brenner, 1979; Buchholz, 1988; Cheney & Vibbert, 1987; Sethi, 1987; Smith, M., 1997; Smith, R. 1993; Stone, 1989; Vogel, 1996).

31. Issue definitions and images, policy alternatives, and key terms used in public policy debates are effectively framed (Cheney & Vibbert, 1987; Edelman, 1971, 1988; Jones, 1994; Jones et al., 1993; Mucciaroni, 1995; Riker, 1993; Ryan 1991; Stone, 1989; Vogel, 1996).

32. Information subsidies or information sources used in public policy decision making reflect or convey capitalist ideologies (Gandy, 1982, 1992; Petracca, 1992; Stone, 1988). Such subsidies or sources (e.g., think tanks) generally help define policy issues, alternatives, and solutions in ways consistent with the prevailing capitalist ideology (Gandy, 1982).

33. The symbolic context in which influence resides—prevailing ideologies, symbols, rituals, ceremonies—privileges the issue interpretations and meaning frames advanced by business organizations (Barnes, 1988; Benford & Snow,

2000; Cobb & Elder, 1983; Ryan, 1991). Barnes (1988) contends that the ability to exert power (and influence, in his usage) presumes the right to exert power, which grows out of the existing distribution or pattern of power. This pattern is constituted in part by prevailing symbols, symbolic displays, rituals, and ideologies. Though the pattern of power is constantly in flux, at any given time it privileges certain political actors with greater influence.

34. Defect conditions for policy makers are reduced or eliminated (Mitchell, 1997; Smith, 1993; Tierney, 1992). Defect conditions refer to "relative weak spots in the relationship between the endorsing group and the policy maker" (Smith, 1993, p. 185). If defection conditions are present, it's easier for a policy maker to oppose the position of an economic producer. But if the producer (a) makes contributions to the policy maker's campaign, (b) represents a large number of constituents, and (c) actively communicates its position through lobbying and grassroots campaigns, it's difficult for the policy maker to publicly oppose the organization's position.

35. Institutional mechanisms are favorably affected or changed (Bachrach & Baratz, 1962, 1970; Cobb & Elder, 1981, 1983; Cowles, 1994; Kingdon, 1984; Majone, 1989; Mucciaroni, 1995; Riker, 1986; Schneider & Teske, 1992; Truman, 1968). These include changes or alterations in decision-making processes or procedures, committee compositions, parties in power, and information sources used by policy makers in decisions.

36. The economic producer or producer association is a large-scale enterprise rather than a small business firm or association (Derber, 1998; Dickie, 1984; Harris, 1973; Korten, 1995; Levitan & Cooper, 1984; Ryan et al., 1987; Schriftgiesser, 1951; Useem, 1980, 1984).

    a. However, rate of growth and the relative "success" or importance of a business firm or producer group may be more influential than size (Braam, 1981).

    b. National prominence or reputation of an economic producer or producer group may give it more influence, or at least more impressive political credentials (Schlozman & Tierney, 1986; Scott & Hunt, 1965; Truman, 1968; Useem, 1980; Wilcox, 1998).

In concluding this section, we note that the strategies and tactics identified above are not exclusive to economic producers. Many interest groups use similar techniques of influence (Schlozman & Tierney, 1986), and business may have borrowed certain techniques, for instance, grassroots campaigns, coalitions, and staged events, from consumer activists (Blyskal & Blyskal, 1985; Grefe & Linsky, 1985; Moore, 1980; Sanders, 1998; Wilson, 1986).

Economic producers, however, possess and probably use more political resources, on more political fronts, for longer periods of time, than other advocacy groups. The issue is not whether economic producers influence public policy: They do. Rather, what is needed is to document the extent and nature of this influence, and the factors that affect the forms and levels of such influence, so as to construct more robust theories of economic influence on public policy. In the next section we suggest a research agenda to move us in this direction.

## SUGGESTIONS FOR A COMMUNICATION RESEARCH AGENDA

Our review has demonstrated that theories and claims about the role and influence of business organizations in policy formation are richer than available evidence. Though the list of propositions captures some things we think we know about relationships between economic power and political influence, our understanding remains tentative rather than definitive (Smith, 1995). In this regard, future research opportunities appear to be many, varied, and significant.

Some of these opportunities were identified in the literature review. For example, political science research has concentrated on the votes of legislators and excluded other important interactions among political groups, bureaucrats, and lobbyists. More research on these relationships is needed to complement studies of legislators. A better understanding of policy makers' attitudes toward advocacy groups, and their perceptions of the relative effectiveness of various kinds of influence attempts, would be enlightening, though access to policy makers would be difficult. Certainly, we will need to widen the scope of analysis to include judicial and executive branches of government, especially with the policy-making orientation of the bureaucracy. State and local government interaction with business organizations also remains an understudied area with significant theoretical and practical value.

To advance our understanding of relationships between economic power and political influence from a communication perspective, however, we propose a research framework in the form of a business model of political influence (Figure 1). This model facilitates research efforts in at least three ways. First, the model focuses on business political actors but embeds them within a complex environment of competing actors, agendas, and influence attempts. Second, the model highlights communicative aspects of policy making, including issue framing and a variety of communication channels. Third, the model suggests that influence goals and techniques are multiple and diverse, which implicates the kind of multifaceted influence construct that we believe is essential to better understanding who influences what, and how, in the policy process. We examine each of these three aspects in turn and suggest possible research projects for each.

### Focus on Business Groups

Though the literature regarding federal policy making in this country is vast, relatively few studies have examined business political actors, often focusing instead on policy makers, social movement groups, or membership associations. Quite simply, to understand the roles and influences of business groups in the policy process, we must study what these groups actually do, the issues they select for attention, and the strategies and tactics they use to attempt influence.

Various researchers have noted the difficulties in gaining access to business leaders and to the communication approaches and resources business groups use in the policy arena (Sanders, 1998; Vogel, 1996). Perhaps as a result, most empir-

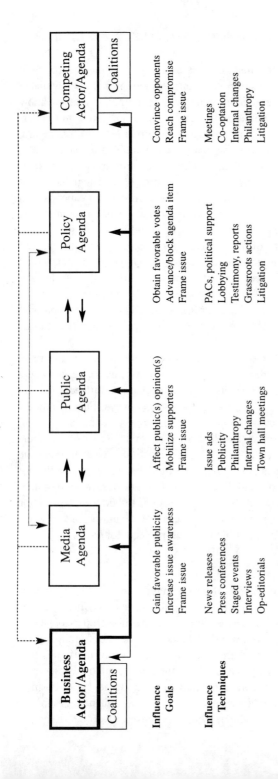

**Figure 1.** This business model of political influence highlights the multiple influence goals that economic producers may seek to achieve in the public policy process and some of the diverse communication approaches and techniques they employ. Other political actors and agendas push back on business actors and each other, creating dynamic and complex interactions at multiple sites in the policy arena and in the larger public arena. The struggle to define and frame policy issues is critical throughout the policy process.

ical studies have focused on aspects of policy activity that are most readily available—PAC contributions and lobbying expenditures. As we have seen, however, business groups attempt public policy influence through many channels and approaches, including issue advertising, public relations actions, grassroots initiatives, and other techniques identified in the model. The selection, use, and bundling of multiple communication channels by business groups to address given issues require further research.

Fortunately, other data sources are increasingly available. For example, *PR NewsWire* is a source for obtaining organizational news releases. Issue advertising expenditures are available in various advertising publications. A number of federal policy and bill-tracking data banks provide lists of hearing participants and testimony transcripts. Business annual reports often document philanthropic contributions and activities, and some companies detail their political activities in these reports, special brochures, or organizational websites. In short, we are increasingly able to document and "measure" a number of communication channels or "inputs" into the policy process. The development of statistical models to examine relationships between such channels and various types of policy outcomes or developments will advance our understanding.

## The Importance of Framing

Our review highlighted three interrelated communication processes that bear on policy formation, and we have argued that greater research attention must be devoted to communicative aspects of policy making. Here again, few studies have examined how business political actors identify agenda issues, go about framing issues and constructing issue images, or strategically manage their involvement in the policy process. Agenda-setting studies have been more concerned with relationships between media and public agendas, the framing literature has focused on social movement groups, and the IM literature is largely descriptive and prescriptive.

The construction or framing of issues and issue images by business political actors is a crucial area of research opportunity. Our model suggests that issue framing may be a recurring influence goal across agendas and a virtual constant in rhetorical contest with competing political actors. If so, many research questions need to be explored. How, for example, do issue definitions and images evolve through issue life cycles? Which political actors are involved, and how do they construct issue images? How do political actors adjust and manipulate meaning frames to compete successfully with each other? What particular frames are used? Are some types of frames particularly compelling and enduring in policy debates? Does existing culture privilege business frames, and if so, how and to what extent?

To address such questions, we suggest the development of "framing histories," which would carefully trace the evolution of issue definitions and meaning frames. Source documents for framing histories include the internal documents of advocacy groups, public hearing and floor debate transcripts, committee reports, mass media coverage, speech texts, press releases and press kits, issue advertisements, organizational annual reports and newsletters, amendments and bills, and so forth. Framing histories may help us to understand why business groups or other political actors sometimes are and other times are not successful in influencing the policy process. They could potentially take us to the heart of the social construction of public policy.

The Concept of Influence

Finally, the model depicts multiple influence goals and techniques, and we believe it essential to begin to develop a multifaceted concept of influence in policy studies. Dependence on voting records as an indicator of the influence of business or other groups is just not adequate for what is a complex and messy policy world. Jones (1994) argued that "black box" approaches to estimating influence are misleading. That is, using statistics to determine relationships between *inputs* into the policy process (often PAC contributions and numbers of constituents) and policy *outputs* or outcomes (usually roll-call votes) inherently excludes important process variables that may ultimately determine policy outcomes.

In addition, researchers have traditionally relied on an overly narrow set of outcomes for assessing influence, ignoring the purposeful neglect of bills till they simply "die" in committee or are dismembered by amendment. Inputs, too, have been narrowly defined. Prepolitical processes such as agenda-setting and framing of issues may well be more effective for business actors than any influence attempts after Congress has taken up a social issue.

We have identified a number of types of influences in this review—defining and framing issues, advancing or blocking agenda issues, shaping public perceptions of issues, increasing issue salience in media coverage, and stimulating grassroots involvement. More broadly, existing culture and symbolic context privilege the influence attempts of some political actors over others. Clearly, influence comes in many forms, and successful influence also may be defined in many ways, ranging from the simple act of participating in policy discussion, to organizing a coalition to advocate a policy position, to modifying the language of a bill, to changing a policy-maker's opinion or vote (Schlozman & Tierney, 1986).

In our view, political influence occurs directly and indirectly, in many sites in the policy arena and in the larger social context, at many different time points. Influence attempts by any political actor are part of a dynamic environment of competing influences that, in the end, help shape policy outcomes. Thus, we define political influence as the ability to affect the perceptions, attitudes, beliefs, opinions, or behaviors (decision making) of others, or the amount or type of issue information held by others.

More of these influences must be identified, abstracted, and studied. It seems likely that certain types of influence may have greater weight than others or may be more effective for certain types of issues or at various issue stages, as the literature suggests. Analyzing multiple forms of influence will increase our understanding of the relative influences of economic producers and other political actors in the legislative arena. One research approach in this regard is to carry out a survival analysis of bills introduced in Congress. Most bills will end in death, but the length of life and the timing of death may be attributable to a number of influences, including business strategies and tactics. Another approach is to use event analysis to document the influence attempts of competing political actors, along with agenda developments and real-world events, during the life cycles of various kinds of policy issues (Berger, 1999).

From a communication perspective, politics and policy making are language struggles, or arguments over ideas, issues, and interpretations (Stone, 1988, 1989). We believe studies that examine policy making as a complex communication process offer great hope for better understanding the roles and influences of economic producers and other political actors. A preoccupation with roll-call votes underestimates the important forms of power and influence exercised in the formation of the social agenda, as well as the identification and definition of social problems, that surround and constrain the policy process.

Who does what and who gets what in the policy process, and how they do it and get it, are central issues in understanding our system of government. The strategies and tactics used by political actors must be identified, and multiple forms of influence must be clearly outlined and researched. This chapter constitutes a step in that direction. We have identified what we think we know about the roles and influences of business organizations in public policy formation, as well as some areas that require further exploration. Clearly, there is a great deal more to accomplish.

## REFERENCES

Adams, W. (1973). The antitrust alternative. In R. Nader & M. J. Green (Eds.), *Corporate power in America* (pp. 130–147). New York: Grossman.

Adkins, L. (1978, June). How good are advocacy ads? *Dun's Review, 111*, 76–77.

Alexander, H. E. (1985, January/February). Political parties and the dollar. *Society, 22*, 49–58.

Alexander, H. E. (1988). Soliciting support through political action committees. In R. L Heath (Ed.), *Strategic issues management* (pp. 258–276). San Francisco: Jossey-Bass.

Altheide, D. L. (1976). *Creating reality: How TV news distorts events.* Beverly Hills, CA: Sage.

Althusser, L. (1971). *Lenin and philosophy, and other essays.* London: New Left Books.

Arnold, R. D. (1982). Overtilled and undertilled fields in American politics. *Political Science Quarterly, 97*, 91–103.

Arrington, C., Jr., & Sawaya, R. N. (1984). Managing public affairs: Issues management in an uncertain environment. *California Management Review, 26*, 148–160.

Bachrach, P., & Baratz, M. S. (1962). Two faces of power. *American Political Science Review, 56*, 947–952.

Bachrach, P., & Baratz, M. S. (1970). *Power and poverty: Theory and practice.* New York: Oxford University Press.

Barnes, B. (1988). *The nature of power.* Chicago: University of Illinois Press.

Bartlett, R. (1973). *Economic foundations of political power.* New York: Free Press.

Bauer, R., de Sola Pool, I., & Dexter, L. (1963). *American business and public policy.* New York: Atherton Press.

Baumgartner, F. R. (1989). Strategies of political leadership in diverse settings. In. B. D. Jones (Ed.), *Leadership in politics* (pp. 114–134). Lawrence: University Press of Kansas.

Baumgartner, F. R., & Jones, B. D. (1991). Agenda dynamics and policy subsystems. *Journal of Politics, 53*(4), 1044–1074.

Baumgartner, F. R., & Jones, B. D. (1993). *Agendas and instability in American politics.* Chicago: University of Chicago Press.

Baumgartner, F. R., & Leech, B. L. (1998). *Basic interests: The importance of groups in politics and political science.* Princeton, NJ: Princeton University Press.

Beard, C. A. (1913). *An economic interpretation of the Constitution.* New York: Macmillan.

Bell, D. (1976). *The coming of post-industrial society.* New York: Basic Books.

Benford, R. D., & Snow, D. A. (2000). Framing processes and social movements: An overview and assessment. In K. S. Cook & J. Hagan (Eds.), *Annual review of sociology, 26* (pp. 611–639). Palo Alto, CA: Annual Reviews.

Bennett, W. L. (1980). Myth, ritual, and political control. *Journal of Communication, 30*(4), 166–179.

Bentley, A. F. (1935/1908). *The process of government.* Evanston, IL: Principia Press.

Berger, B. K. (1999). *Locating the corporate agenda in the agenda-setting process: A study of corporate influence on public policy.* Unpublished doctoral dissertation. University of Kentucky, Lexington.

Berger, B. K. (2001). Private issues and public policy: Locating the corporate agenda in agenda-setting theory. *Journal of Public Relations Research, 13*(2), 91–126.

Berkowitz, D. (1987). TV news sources and news channels: A study in agenda building. *Journalism Quarterly, 64*, 508–513.

Berkowitz, D. (1992). Who sets the media agenda? The ability of policy makers to determine news decisions. In J. D. Kennamer (Ed.), *Public opinion, the press, and public policy* (pp. 81–102). Westport, CT: Praeger.

Berkowitz, D., & Adams, D. B. (1990). Information subsidy and agenda-building in local television news. *Journalism Quarterly, 67*, 723–731.

Berry, J. M. (1977). *Lobbying for the people.* Princeton, NJ: Princeton University Press.

Berry, J. M. (1989). *The interest group society* (2nd ed.). Glenview, IL: Scott, Foresman/Little, Brown.

Birnbaum, J. H. (1992). *The lobbyists: How influence peddlers get their way in Washington.* New York: Random House.

Bliss, T. J. (1996). Leveling the playing field: How citizen advocacy groups influence corporate behavior. (Doctoral dissertation, Fielding Institute, 1996). *Dissertation Abstracts International, 57,* 09A.

Blyskal, J., & Blyskal, M. (1985). *PR: How the public relations industry writes the news.* New York: William Morrow.

Braam, G. P. A. (1981). *Influence of business firms on the government.* New York: Mouton .

Brenner, S. N. (1979, Nov./Dec.). Business and politics—an update. *Harvard Business Review, 57*(6), 149–163.

Brosius, H., & Kepplinger, H. (1995). Killer and victim issues: Issue competition in the agenda-setting process of German television. *International Journal of Public Opinion Research, 7*, N3, 211–231.

Browne, W. P. (1988). *Private interests, public policy, and American agriculture.* Lawrence: University of Kansas Press.

Browne, W. P. (1990). Organized interests and their issue niches: A search for pluralism in a policy domain. *Journal of Politics, 52*(2), 477–509.

Buchholz, R. A. (1988). Adjusting corporations to the realities of public interests and policies. In R. L. Heath and Associates (Eds.), *Strategic issues management: How organizations influence and respond to public interests and policies* (pp. 50–72). San Francisco: Jossey-Bass.

Buchholz, R. A. (1992). *Business environment and public policy: Implications for management and strategy.* Englewood Cliffs, NJ: Prentice Hall.

Cameron, G. T., Sallot, L. M., & Curtin, P. A. (1997). Public relations and the production of news: A critical review and theoretical framework. In B. R. Burleson (Ed.), *Communication yearbook 20* (pp. 111–155). Thousand Oaks, CA: Sage.

Cater, D. (1964). *Power in Washington*. New York: Random House.

Chase, W. H. (1984). *Issue management: Origins of the future*. Stamford, CT: Issue Action Publications.

Cheney, G., & Vibbert, S. L. (1987). Corporate discourse: Public relations and issue management. In F. M. Jablin, L. L. Putnam, K. H. Roberts, & L. W. Porter (Eds.), *Handbook of organizational communication* (pp. 165–194). Newbury Park, CA: Sage.

Cigler, A. J. (1991). Interest groups: A subfield in search of an identity. In W. Crotty (Ed.), *Political science: Looking to the future* (pp. 99–136). Evanston, IL: Northwestern University Press.

Cigler, A. J., & Loomis, B. A. (Eds.). (1986). *Interest group politics* (2nd ed.). Washington, DC: CQ Press.

Clawson, D., Neustadtl, A., & Scott, D. (1992). *Money talks: Corporate PACs and political influence*. New York: Basic Books.

Cobb, R. W., & Elder, C. D. (1981). Communication and public policy. In D. D. Nimmo & K. R. Sanders (Eds.), *Handbook of political communication* (pp. 391–416). Beverly Hills, CA: Sage.

Cobb, R. W., & Elder, C. D. (1983). *Participation in American politics: The dynamics of agenda-building* (2nd ed.). Baltimore, MD: Johns Hopkins University Press.

Coe, B. J. (1983). The effectiveness challenge in issue advertising campaigns. *Journal of Advertising, 12*(4), 27–35.

Cohen, B. C. (1963). *The press and foreign policy*. Princeton, NJ: Princeton University Press.

Conway, M. M. (1986). PACs and Congressional elections in the 1980s. In A. J. Cigler, & B. A. Loomis (Eds.), *Interest group politics* (pp. 70–90 ). Washington, DC: CQ Press.

Cowles, M. G. (1994). The politics of big business in the European community: Setting the agenda for a new Europe. (Doctoral dissertation, American University, 1994). *Dissertation Abstracts International, 56,* 02A.

Crable, R. E., & Vibbert, S. L. (1985, Summer). Managing issues and influencing public policy. *Public Relations Review, 11*(2), 3–16.

Crable, R. E., & Vibbert, S. L. (1995). Mobil's epideictic advocacy: "Observations" of Prometheus bound. In W. N. Elwood (Ed.), *Public relations inquiry as rhetorical criticism* (pp. 27–46). Westport, CT: Praeger.

Crawford, K. G. (1939). *The pressure boys: The inside story of lobbying in America*. New York: Julian Messner.

Curtin, P. A. (1999). Reevaluating public relations information subsidies: Market-driven journalism and agenda-building theory and practice. *Journal of Public Relations Research, 11*(1), 53–90.

Cutlip, S. M. (1962, May 26). Third of newspapers' content PR inspired. *Editor & Publisher*, p. 68.

Dahl, R. A. (1961). *Who governs?* New Haven, CT: Yale University Press.

Dahl, R. A. (1967). *Pluralist democracy in the United States*. Chicago: Rand McNally.

Danielian, L. (1992). Interest groups in the news. In J. D. Kennamer (Ed.), *Public opinion, the press, and public policy* (pp. 63–80). Westport CT: Praeger.

Davis, S. (1995). The role of communication and symbolism in interest group competition: The case of the Siskiyou National Forest, 1983–1992. *Political Communication, 12,* 27–42.

Dearing, J. W., & Rogers, E. M. (1996). *Agenda-setting*. Thousand Oaks, CA: Sage.

DeGregorio, C. (1998). Assets and access: Linking lobbyists and lawmakers in Congress. In P. S. Herrnson, R. G. Shaiko, & C. Wilcox (Eds.), *The interest group connection* (pp. 137–153). Chatham, NJ: Chatham House.

Demaris, O. (1974). *Dirty business: The corporate-political-money-power game*. New York: Harper's Magazine Press.

Derber, C. (1998). *Corporation nation: How corporations are taking over our lives and what we can do about it*. New York: St. Martin's Press.

Dickie, R. B. (1984). Influence of public affairs offices on corporate planning and of corporations on government policy. *Strategic Management Journal, 5,*15–34.

Dionisopoulos, G. N. (1986). Corporate advocacy advertising as political communication. In L. L. Kaid, D. Nimmo, & K. R. Sanders (Eds.), *New perspectives on political advertising* (pp. 82–106). Carbondale: Southern Illinois University Press.

Domhoff, G. W. (1979). *The powers that be.* New York: Random House.

Domhoff, G. W. (1996). *State autonomy or class dominance?* New York: de Gruyter.

Duhe, S. F. (1993). Monsanto and the media: The news process regarding biotechnology (Doctoral dissertation, University of Missouri, Columbia, 1993). *Dissertation Abstracts International, 54,* 09A.

Dutton, J. E. (1993, May). Interpretations on automatic: A different view of strategic issue diagnosis. *Journal of Management Studies, 30*(3), 339–357.

Dutton, J. E., & Jackson, S. E. (1987). Categorizing strategic issues: Links to organizational action. *Academy of Management Review, 12*(1), 76–90.

Dutton, J. E., & Ottensmeyer, E. (1987). Strategic issue management systems: Forms, functions, and contexts. *Academy of Management Review, 12*(2), 355–365.

Dye, T. R. (1986). *Who's running America?* (4th ed.). Englewood Cliffs, NJ: Prentice-Hall.

Edelman, M. (1971). *Politics as symbolic action.* New York: Academic Press.

Edelman, M. (1988). *Constructing the political spectacle.* Chicago: University of Chicago Press.

Edelman, M. (1993). Contestable categories and public opinion. *Political Communication, 10,* 231–242.

Eismeier, T. J., & Pollock, P. H. (1988). *Business, money, and the rise of corporate PACs in American elections.* Westport, CT: Quorum Books.

Ellul, J. (1980). *The technological system.* New York: Continuum.

Elmendorf, F. M. (1988). Generating grassroots campaigns and public involvement. In R. L. Heath (Ed.), *Strategic issues management* (pp. 306–320). San Francisco: Jossey-Bass.

Entman, R. M. (1993). Framing: Toward clarification of a fractured paradigm. *Journal of Communication, 43*(4), 51–58.

Entman, R. M., & Rojecki, A. (1993). Freezing out the public: Elite and media framing of the U.S. anti-nuclear movement. *Political Communication, 10,* 155–173.

Epstein, E. M. (1969). *The corporation in American politics.* Englewood Cliffs, NJ: Prentice Hall.

Evans, D. M. (1986). PAC contributions and roll-call voting: Conditional power. In A. J. Cigler, & B. A. Loomis (Eds.), *Interest group politics* (pp. 114–132 ). Washington, DC: CQ Press.

Evans, D. M. (1995). Before the roll call: Interest group lobbying and public policy outcomes in House committees. *Political Research Quarterly, 49,* 287–304.

Evans, P. B., Rueschemeyer, D., & Skocpol, T. (1985). On the road toward a more adequate understanding of the state. In P. B. Evans, D. Rueschemeyer, and T. Skocpol (Eds.), *Bringing the state back in* (pp. 347–366). New York: Cambridge University Press.

Ewing, R. P. (1982). Advocacy advertising: The voice of business in public policy debate. *Public Affairs Review, 3,* 23–29

Ewing, R. P. (1987). *Managing the new bottom line: Issues management for senior executives.* Homewood, IL: Dow Jones-Irwin.

Ewing, R. P. (1990, Spring). Moving from micro to macro issues management. *Public Relations Review, 16*(1), 19–24.

Fenno, R. F. (1973). *Congressmen in committees.* Boston: Little, Brown

Fox, K. F. (1986). The measurement of issue/advocacy advertising effects. *Current Issues and Research in Advertising, 9,* 61–92.

Fowler, L. L., & Shaiko, R. G. (1987). The grass roots connection: Environmental activists and Senate roll calls. *American Journal of Political Science, 31*(2), 484–510.

Frendreis, J. P., & Waterman, R. W. (1985). PAC contributions and legislative behavior: Senate voting on trucking deregulation. *Social Science Quarterly, 66,* 401–412.

Galambos, L. (1975). *The public image of big business in America, 1880–1940.* Baltimore, MD: Johns Hopkins University Press.

Galambos, L, & Pratt, J. (1988). *The rise of the corporate commonwealth.* New York: Basic Books.

Gandy, O. H., Jr. (1982). *Beyond agenda setting: Information subsidies and public policy*. Norwood, NJ: Ablex.

Gandy, O. H., Jr. (1992). Public relations and public policy: The structuration of dominance in the information age. In E. L. Toth & R. L. Heath (Eds.), *Rhetorical and critical approaches to public relations* (pp. 131–164). Hillsdale, NJ: Erlbaum.

Gans, H. J. (1979). *Deciding what's news*. New York: Random House-Vintage Books.

Garbrah-Aidoo, E. R. (1995). Issue type and the agenda-setting process (Doctoral dissertation, University of Houston, 1995). *Dissertation Abstracts International, 56*, 05A.

Gaunt, P., & Ollenburger, J. (1995). Issues management revisited: A tool that deserves another look. *Public Relations Review, 21*(3), 199–210.

Getz, K. A. (1993). Selecting corporate political tactics. In B. M. Mitnick (Ed.), *Corporate political agency: The construction of competition in public affairs* (pp. 242–273). Newbury Park, CA: Sage.

Getz, K. A. (1997, March). Research in corporate political action. *Business & Society, 36*(1): 32–72.

Gitlin, T. (1980). *The whole world is watching*. Berkeley, CA: University of California Press.

Godwin, R. K. (1988). *One billion dollars of influence: The direct marketing of politics*. Chatham, NJ: Chatham House.

Godwin, R. K. (1992). Money, technology, and political interests: The direct marketing of politics. In M. P. Petracca (Ed.), *The politics of interests* (pp. 308–325). Boulder, CO: Westview Press.

Greening, D. W. (1991). *Organizing for public issues: Environmental and organizational predictors of structure and process*. Unpublished doctoral dissertation, Pennsylvania State University, University Park.

Grefe, E. A. (1981). *Fighting to win: Business political power*. New York: Harcourt Brace Jovanovich.

Grefe, E. A., & Linsky, M. (1995). *The new corporate activism: Harnessing the power of grassroots tactics for your organization*. New York: McGraw-Hill.

Grenzke, J. M. (1990). Money and Congressional behavior. In M. L. Nugent & J. R. Johannes (Eds.), *Money, elections, and democracy*. Boulder, CO: Westview Press.

Grunig, J. E. (1983). Washington reporter publics of corporate public affairs programs. *Journalism Quarterly, 60*, 603–614.

Hainsworth, R. E. (1990). The distribution of advantages and disadvantages. *Public Relations Review, 16*(1), 33–39.

Hainsworth, B. E., & Meng, M. (1988). How corporations define issue management. *Public Relations Review, 14*(4), 18–30.

Hall, R. L., & Wayman, F. W. (1990). Buying time: Moneyed interests and the mobilization of bias in Congressional committees. *American Political Science Review, 84*, 797–820.

Hall, S. (1979). Culture, the media and the "ideological effect." In J. Curran, M. Gurevitch, & J. Woollacott (Eds.), *Mass communication and society* (pp. 315–348). Beverly Hills, CA: Sage.

Hall, S. (1984). The rediscovery of "ideology": Return of the repressed in media studies. In M. Gurevitch, T. Bennett, J. Curran, & J. Woollacott (Eds.), *Culture, society and the media* (pp. 56–90). New York: Methuen.

Hallin, D. C. (1985). The American news media: A critical theory perspective. In J. Forester (Ed.), *Critical theory and public life* (pp. 121–146). Cambridge, MA: MIT Press.

Harris, F. R. (1973). The politics of corporate power. In R. Nader and M. J. Green (Eds.), *Corporate power in America* (pp. 25–41). New York: Grossman.

Heath, R. L. (Ed.). (1988a). *Strategic issues management: How organizations influence and respond to public interests and policies*. San Francisco: Jossey-Bass.

Heath, R. L. (1988b). The rhetoric of issue advertising: A rationale, a case study, a critical perspective—and more. *Central States Speech Journal, 39*, 99–109.

Heath, R. L. (1997). *Strategic issues management: Organizations and public policy challenges*. Thousand Oaks, CA: Sage.

Heath, R. L., & Cousino, K. R. (1990). Issues management: End of first decade progress report. *Public Relations Review, 16*(1), 6–18.

Heath, R., & Douglas, W. (1986). Issues advertising and its effect on public opinion recall. *Public Relations Review, 12*(2), 47–56.

Heath, R. L., & Nelson, R. A. (1986). *Issues management: Corporate public policy making in an information society.* Beverly Hills, CA: Sage.

Heclo, H. (1978). Issue networks and the executive establishment. In. A. King (Ed.), *The new American political system* (pp. 87–124). Washington, DC: American Enterprise Institute.

Heinz, J. P., Laumann, E. O., Nelson, R. L., & Salisbury, R. H. (1993). *The hollow core: Private interests in national policy making.* Cambridge, MA: Harvard University Press.

Herbst, S. (1993). *Numbered voices: How opinion polling has shaped* American politics. Chicago: University of Chicago Press.

Herman, E. (1996). The propaganda model revisited. *Monthly Review, 48,* 115–129.

Herman, E. S., & Chomsky, N. (1988). *Manufacturing consent: The political economy of the mass media.* New York: Pantheon Books.

Herring, P. (1967/1929). *Group representation before Congress.* New York: Russell & Russell.

Hertog, J. K., & McLeod, D. M. (1995). Anarchists wreak havoc in downtown Minneapolis: A multi-level study of media coverage of radical protest. *Journalism and Mass Communication Monographs (Vol. 151).* Columbia, SC: Association for Education in Journalism and Mass Communication.

Hertog, J. K., & McLeod, D. M. (2001). A multiperspectival approach to framing analysis: A field guide. In S. D. Reese, O. H. Gandy, & A. E. Grant (Eds.), *Framing public life: Perspectives on media and our understanding of the social world* (pp. 139–161). Mahwah, NJ: Erlbaum.

Hilgartner, S., & Bosk, C. L. (1988). The rise and fall of social problems: A public arenas model. *American Journal of Sociology, 94,* 53–78.

Hojnacki, M., (1997, January). Interest groups' decisions to join alliances or work alone. *American Journal of Political Science, 41*(1), 61–87.

Hojnacki, M., & Kimball, D. (1996). *Organized interests and the decision of whom to lobby in Congress.* Paper presented at the annual conference of the American Political Science Association, San Francisco.

Hula, K. W. (1999). *Lobbying together: Interest group coalitions in legislative politics.* Washington, DC: Georgetown University Press.

Jacobs, D. C. D. (1999). *Business lobbies and the power structure in America.* Westport, CT: Praeger.

Jones, B. D., Baumgartner, F. R., & Talbert, J. C. (1993). The destruction of issue monopolies in Congress. *American Political Science Review, 87*(3), 657–671.

Jones, B. D. (1994). *Reconceiving decision-making in democratic politics.* Chicago: University of Chicago Press.

Jones, B. L., & Chase, W. H. (1979). Managing public policy issues. *Public Relations Review, 5*(2), 3–23.

Jones, W., Jr., & Keiser, K. R. (1987). Issue visibility and the effects of PAC money. *Social Science Quarterly, 68,* 170–176.

Kasser, S. J., & Truax, G. (1988). Integrating issues management and corporate communications. In R. L. Heath (Ed.), *Strategic issues management* (pp. 155–167). San Francisco: Jossey-Bass.

Kingdon, J. W. (1984). *Agendas, alternatives, and public policies.* Glenview, NY: Scott, Foresman .

Knoke, D. (1990). *Organizing for collective action: the political economies of associations.* Hawthorne, NY: de Gruyter.

Kolko, G. (1962). *Wealth and power in America.* New York: Praeger.

Korten, D. C. (1995). *When corporations rule the world.* West Hartford, CT: Kumarian Press.

Kosicki, G. M. (1993). Problems and opportunities in agenda-setting research. *Journal of Communication, 43*(2), 100–127.

Latham, E. (1952). *The group basis of politics.* Ithaca, NY: Cornell University Press.

Laumann, E. O., & Knoke, D. (1987). *The organizational state.* Madison: University of Wisconsin Press.

Lemert, J. B. (1981). *Does mass communication change public opinion after all? A new approach to effects analysis.* Chicago: Nelson-Hall.

Lemert, J. B. (1992). Effective public opinion. In J. D. Kennamer (Ed.), *Public opinion, the press, and public policy* (pp. 41–62). Westport, CT: Praeger.

Levitan, S. A., & Cooper, M. R. 1984). *Business lobbies: The public good & the bottom line.* Baltimore, MD: Johns Hopkins University Press.

Linsky, M. (1986). *Impact: How the press affects federal policy making.* New York: W. W. Norton.

Lowi, T. J. (1964). American business and public policy: Case studies and political theory. *World Politics, 16,* 677–715.

Lowi, T. J. (1969). *The end of liberalism: Ideology, policy, and the crisis of public authority.* New York: W. W. Norton.

Lusterman, S. (1987). *The organization and staffing of corporate public affairs.* New York: Conference Board.

Magleby, D. B., & Nelson, C. J. (1990). *The money chase: Congressional campaign finance reform.* Washington, DC: Brookings Institution.

Majone, G. (1989). *Evidence, argument, and persuasion in the policy process.* New Haven, CT: Yale University Press.

Malbin, M. J. (Ed.). (1984). *Money and politics in the United States.* Chatham, NJ: Chatham House.

McCombs, M. E., & Shaw, D. L. (1972). The agenda-setting function of mass media. *Public Opinion Quarterly, 36*(2), 176–187.

McConnell, G. (1966). *Private power and American democracy.* New York: Knopf.

McFarland, A. S. (1969). *Power and leadership in pluralist systems.* Stanford, CA: Stanford University Press.

McFarland, A. S. (1976). *Public interest lobbies: Decision making on energy.* Washington, DC: American Enterprise Institute.

McFarland, A. S. (1984). *Common cause.* Chatham, NJ: Chatham House Press.

McFarland, A. S. (1992). Interest groups and the policy making process: Sources of countervailing power in America. In M. P. Petracca (Ed.), *The politics of interests* (pp. 60–79). Boulder, CO: Westview Press.

McLeod, D. M., & Hertog, J. K. (1999). Social control, social change and the mass media's role in the regulation of protest groups. In D. Demers & K. Viswanath (Eds.), *Mass media, social control, and social change* (pp. 305–330). Ames: Iowa State University Press.

McQuaid, K. (1981). The roundtable: Getting results in Washington. *Harvard Business Review, 59*(3), 115–122.

Megalli, M., & Friedman (1991). *Masks of deception: Corporate front groups in America.* Washington, DC: Essential Information.

Megwa, E. R., & Brenner, D. J. (1988). Toward a paradigm of media agenda-setting effect: Agenda-setting as a process. *Howard Journal of Communications, 1*(1), 39–56.

Milbrath, L. (1963). *The Washington lobbyists.* Chicago: Rand McNally.

Miliband, R. (1969). *The state in capitalist society.* New York: Basic Books.

Mills, C. W. (1956). *The power elite.* New York: Oxford University Press.

Mitchell, N. J. (1997). *The conspicuous corporation.* Ann Arbor: University of Michigan Press.

Mizruchi, M. S. (1992). *The structure of corporate political actions.* Cambridge, MA: Harvard University Press.

Moore, D. G. (1980). *Politics and the corporate chief executive* (Research Report No. 777). New York: Conference Board.

Morrison, C. (1986). *Managing corporate political action committees* (Research Report No. 880). New York: Conference Board.

Morton, L. P. (1986). How newspapers choose the releases they use. *Public Relations Review, 12,* 22–27.

Mucciaroni, G. (1995). *Reversals of fortune: Public policy and private interests.* Washington, DC: The Brookings Institution.

Nelson, B. J. (1984). *Making an issue of child abuse.* Chicago: University of Chicago Press.

Neustadtl, A. (1990). Interest-group PACsmanship: An analysis of campaign contributions, issue visibility, and legislative impact. *Social Forces, 69,* 549–564.

Newman, L. N. (1982). Delivering the message. In J. S. Nagelschmidt (Ed.), *The public affairs handbook* (pp. 223–242). Washington, DC: AMACOM.

Nimmo, D. D., & Sanders, K. R. (Eds.). (1981). *Handbook of political communication*. Beverly Hills, CA: Sage.

Oberman, W. D. (1993). Strategy and tactic choice in an institutional resource context. In B. M. Mitnick (Ed.), *Corporate political agency: The construction of competition in public affairs* (pp. 213–241). Newbury Park, CA: Sage.

Olson, M. (1965). *The logic of collective action*. Cambridge, MA: Harvard University Press.

O'Toole, J. E. (1975). Advocacy advertising shows the flag. *Public Relations Journal, 31*(11), 14–16.

Page, B. I. (1996). *Who deliberates? Mass media in modern democracy*. Chicago: University of Chicago Press.

Page, B. I., & Shapiro, R. Y. (1983, March). Effects of public opinion on policy. *American Political Science Review, 77*(1), 175–190.

Pan, Z., & Kosicki, G. M. (1993). Framing analysis: An approach to news discourse. *Political Communication, 10*, 55–75.

Parsons, T. (1967). *The structure of social action* (2nd ed.). Glencoe, IL: Free Press.

Petracca, M. P. (Ed.). (1992). *The politics of interests*. Boulder, CO: Westview Press.

Pires, M. A. (1988). Building coalitions with external constituencies. In R. L. Heath (Ed.), *Strategic issues management* (pp. 185–198). San Francisco: Jossey-Bass.

Plotke, D. (1992). The political mobilization of business. In M. P. Petracca (Ed.), *The politics of interests* (pp. 175–198). Boulder, CO: Westview Press.

Polsby, N. W. (1984). *Political innovation in America*. New Haven, CT: Yale University Press.

Poulantzas, N. (1973). *Political power and social classes* (T. O'Hagan, Trans.). Princeton, NJ: Princeton University Press.

Preston, L. E., & Post, J. E. (1975). *Private management and public policy: The principle of public responsibility*. Englewood Cliffs, NJ: Prentice Hall.

Pritchard, D. (1992). The news media and public policy agendas. In J. D. Kennamer (Ed.), *Public opinion, the press, and public policy* (pp. 103–112). Westport, CT: Praeger.

Protess, D. L., & McCombs, M. (Eds.). (1991). *Agenda setting: Readings on media, public opinion, and policy making*. Hillsdale, NJ: Erlbaum.

Reese, S. D. (2001). Prologue—Framing public life: A bridging model for media research. In S. D. Reese, O. H. J. Gandy, & A. E. Grant (Eds.), *Framing public life: Perspectives on media and our understanding of the social world* (pp. 7–31). Mahwah, NJ: Erlbaum.

Renfro, W. L. (1993). *Issues management in strategic planning*. Westport, CT: Quorum Books.

Riker, W. H. (1986). *The art of political manipulation*. New Haven, CT: Yale University Press.

Riker, W. H. (1993). *Agenda formation*. Ann Arbor: University of Michigan Press.

Rochefort, D. A., & Cobb, R. W. (1994). *The politics of problem definition*. Lawrence: University Press of Kansas.

Rogers, E. M., & Dearing, J. W. (1988). Agenda-setting research: Where has it been, where is it going? In J. A. Anderson (Ed.), *Communication yearbook 11* (pp. 555–594). Newbury Park, CA: Sage.

Rothenberg, L. S. (1992). *Linking citizens to government: Interest group politics at Common Cause*. New York: Cambridge University Press.

Ryan, C. (1991). *Prime time activism: Media strategies for grassroots organizing*. Boston: South End Press.

Ryan, M. H., Swanson, C. L., & Buchholz, R. A. (1987). *Corporate strategy, public policy and the Fortune 500*. New York: Basil Blackwell.

Sabato, L. J. (1985). *PAC Power: Inside the world of political action committees*. New York: W. W. Norton.

Sabato, L. J. (1989). *Paying for elections: The campaign finance thicket*. New York: Priority Press.

Salamon, L. M., & Siegfried, J. J. (1977). Economic power and political influence: The impact of industry structure on public policy. *American Political Science Review, 71*(4), 1026–1043.

Salisbury, R. H. (1984). Interest representation: The dominance of institutions. *American Political*

*Science Review, 78*(1), 64–76.

Salisbury, R. H. (1994). Interest structures and policy domains: A focus for research. In W. Crotty, M. A. Schwartz, & J. C. Green (Eds.), *Representing interests and interest group representation* (pp. 12–20). Lanham, MD: University Press of America.

Salmon, C. T., Reid, L. N., Pokrywczynski, J., & Willet, R. W. (1985). The effectiveness of advocacy advertising relative to news coverage. *Communication Research, 12*(4), 546–567.

Sanders, D. L. (1998). *Issues management and the participation of large corporations in the public policy process.* Unpublished doctoral dissertation, Claremont University, Claremont, CA.

Schattschneider, E. E. (1935). *Politics, pressures and the tariff.* New York: Prentice Hall.

Schattschneider, E. E. (1960). *The semisovereign people: A realist's view of democracy in America.* New York: Holt, Rinehart & Winston.

Schlozman, K. L., & Tierney, J. T. (1986). *Organized interests and American democracy.* New York: Harper & Row.

Schmertz, H. (1986). *Good-bye to the low profile: The art of creative confrontation.* Boston: Little, Brown.

Schneider, M., & Teske, P. (1992). Toward a theory of political entrepreneur: Evidence from local government. *American Political Science Review, 86*(3), 737–747.

Schriftgiesser, K. (1951). *The lobbyists: The art and business of influencing lawmakers.* Boston: Little, Brown.

Scott, A. M., & Hunt, M. A. (1965). *Congress and lobbies.* Chapel Hill, NC: University of North Carolina Press.

Sethi, S. P. (1976). Dangers of advocacy advertising. *Public Relations Journal, 32*(11), 42, 46–47.

Sethi, S. P. (1977). *Advocacy advertising and large corporations: Social conflict, big business image, the news media, and public policy.* Lexington, MA: Lexington Books.

Sethi, S. P. (1982). Corporate political activism. *California Management Review, 24*(3), 32–42.

Sethi, S. P. (1987). *Handbook of advocacy advertising: Concepts, strategies and applications.* Cambridge, MA: Ballinger.

Shapiro, I. S. (1984). *America's third revolution: Public interest and the private role.* New York: Harper & Row.

Sharp, E. B. (1994). The dynamics of issue expansion: Cases from disability rights and fetal research controversy. *Journal of Politics, 56,* 919–939.

Shepsle, K. A., & Weingast, B. R. (1987). The institutional foundations of committee power. *American Political Science Review, 81*(1), 85–104.

Silk, L., & Vogel, D. (1976). *Ethics and profits: The crisis of confidence in American business.* New York: Simon & Schuster.

Skocpol, T. (1988). *The politics of social policy in the United States.* Princeton, NJ: Princeton University Press.

Skocpol, T. (1992). State formation and social policy in the United States. *American Behavioral Scientist, 35*(4), 559–584.

Skocpol, T., & Amenta, E. (1986). States and social policies. *Annual Review of Sociology, 12,* 131–157.

Small, A., & Vincent, G. (1894). *An introduction to society.* New York: American Books.

Smith, M. A. (1997). *The paradox of unity: Business and democracy in America.* Unpublished doctoral dissertation, University of Minnesota, Minneapolis.

Smith, R. A. (1984). Advocacy, interpretation and influence in the U. S. Congress. *American Political Science Review, 78,* 44–63.

Smith, R. A. (1993). Agreement, defection, and interest-group influence in the U.S. Congress. In W. H. Riker (Ed.), *Agenda formation* (pp. 183–207). Ann Arbor: University of Michigan Press.

Smith, R. A. (1995). Interest group influence in the U.S. Congress. *Legislative Studies Quarterly, 20,* 89–139.

Sorauf, F. J. (1992). *Inside campaign finance: Myths and realities.* New Haven, CT: Yale University Press.

Stone, D. A. (1988). *Policy paradox and political reason.* New York: HarperCollins.

Stone, D. A. (1989). Causal stories and the formation of policy agendas. *Political Science Quarterly, 104*(2), 281–300.

Stratmann, T. (1991). What do campaign contributions buy? Deciphering causal effects of money and votes. *Southern Economic Journal, 57,* 606–620.

Suarez, S. L. (1998). Lessons learned: Explaining the political behavior of business. *Polity, 31,* 161–186.

Tierney, J. T. (1992). Organized interests and the nation's capitol. In M. P. Petracca (Ed.), *The politics of interests* (pp. 201–220). Boulder, CO: Westview Press.

Triandafyllidou, A., & Fotiou, A. (1998). Sustainability and modernity in the European Union: A frame theory approach to policy-making. *Sociological Research Online, 3*(1). [Online]. Available: http://www.socresonline.org.uk/3/1/2.html.

Truman, D. B. (1951). *The governmental process.* New York: Knopf.

Truman, D. B. (1968). Groups and society. In N. R. Luttbeg (Ed.), *Public opinion and public policy: Models of political linkage* (pp. 120–138). Homewood, IL: Dorsey Press.

Tuchman, G. (1978). *Making news: A study in the construction of reality.* New York: Free Press.

Useem, M. (1980). Which business leaders help govern? In G. W. Domhoff (Ed.), *Power structure research* (pp. 199–226). Beverly Hills, CA: Sage.

Useem, M. (1984). *The inner circle.* New York: Oxford University Press.

Useem, M. (1985, May-June). Beyond the corporation: Who represents business to the government and public? *Business Horizons, 28*(3), 21–26.

Van Leuven, J. K., & Slater, M. D. (1991). How publics, public relations, and the media shape the public opinion process. In L. A. Grunig & J. E. Grunig (Eds.), *Public relations research annual, vol. 3.* (pp. 165–178). Hillsdale, NJ: Erlbaum.

Verba, S., Schlozman, K. L., & Brady, H. E. (1995). *Voice and equality: Civic voluntarism in American politics.* Cambridge, MA: Harvard University Press.

Vogel, D. (1996). *Kindred strangers: The uneasy relationship between politics and business in America.* Princeton, NJ: Princeton University Press.

Walker, J. L. (1974). Performance gaps, policy research, and political entrepreneurs. *Policy Studies Journal, 3,* 112–116.

Walker, J. L. (1977). Setting the agenda in the U.S. Senate: A theory of problem selection. *British Journal of Political Science, 7,* 433–445.

Walker, J. L., Jr. (1983). The origins and maintenance of interest groups in America. *American Political Science Review, 77,* 390–406.

Walker, J. L., Jr. (1991). *Mobilizing interest groups in America.* Ann Arbor: University of Michigan Press.

Waltzer, H. (1988). Corporate advocacy advertising and political influence. *Public Relations Review, 14*(1), 41–56.

Wiebe, R. H. (1995). *Self-rule: A cultural history of American democracy.* Chicago: University of Chicago Press.

Wilcox, C. (1998). The dynamics of lobbying the Hill. In P. S. Herrnson, R. G. Shaiko, & C. Wilcox (Eds.), *The interest group connection* (pp. 89–99). Chatham, NJ: Chatham House.

Wilson, G. (1986). American business and politics. In A. J. Cigler & B. A. Loomis (Eds.), *Interest group politics* (pp. 221–235 ). Washington, DC: CQ Press.

Wittenberg, E., & Wittenberg, E. (1994). *How to win in Washington* (2nd ed.). Cambridge, UK: Basil Blackwell.

Wolpe, B. C. (1990). *Lobbying Congress: How the system works.* Washington, DC: CQ Press.

Wright, J. R. (1985). PACs, contributions, and roll calls: An organizational perspective. *American Political Science Review, 79,* 400–414.

Wright, J. R. (1990). Contributions, lobbying and committee voting in the U.S. House of Representatives. *American Political Science Review, 84,* 417–438.

# CHAPTER CONTENTS

• The Dimensions of Emotional Intelligence   206

• The Self-Experienced/Expressed Dimension   209
   *Managing Experienced Emotions*   *209*
   *Managing Expressed Emotions*   *210*
   *The Interaction of Experienced and Expressed Emotions*   *210*
   *Studying the Self-Experienced/Expressed Dimension*   *213*

• The Other-Experienced/Expressed Dimension   213
   *Reading and Managing Others' Experienced Emotions*   *213*
   *Managing Others' Expressed Emotions*   *216*
   *The Interaction of Reading/Managing Others' Experienced*   *218*
   *Emotions and Managing Others' Expressed Emotions*

• Exploring the Moral Dimension of Emotional Intelligence   219
   *Constructive Emotional Intelligence*   *219*
   *Destructive Emotional Intelligence*   *221*

• Emotional Intelligence in Context   222

• Discussion   224
   *Future Research*   *225*

• References   226

# 6 Emotional Intelligence as Organizational Communication: An Examination of the Construct

DEBBIE S. DOUGHERTY
*University of Missouri-Columbia*

KATHLEEN J. KRONE
*University of Nebraska-Lincoln*

A large volume of research on emotions in organizations has been produced in the last number of years. This important body of literature has one major limitation: There is no recognized framework from which the literature can be viewed in a holistic manner. This article creates such a framework by reconceptualizing emotional intelligence using a communication orientation. To accomplish this task, we discuss the strengths and limitations of current conceptualizations of emotional intelligence, propose a new model of emotional intelligence, and then place the current literature on emotions in organizations within that model. In this way, both the constructive and destructive possibilities of emotional intelligence are explored.

R ecently, a number of popular culture books have been written about emotional intelligence in general (Goleman, 1995), and about emotional intelligence at work more specifically (Goleman, 1998b; Weisinger, 1998). These publications have assigned emotional intelligence an almost mythical quality in terms of its ability to solve organizational problems. Both Weisinger and Goleman (1998b) claim that their works are based on hundreds of studies supporting the importance of emotional intelligence in organizations. Despite these claims, very few peer reviewed studies have examined emotional intelligence in general, and even fewer have examined the role of emotional intelligence in organizations. Both authors further claim that communication is the key to emotional intelligence. Unfortunately, neither author reviews communication literature, in part because communication scholars have yet to examine emotional

---

Correspondence: Debbie S. Dougherty, University of Missouri-Columbia, Department of Speech Communication, 115 Switzler Hall, Columbia, MO 65201; email: doughertyd@missouri.edu.

*Communication Yearbook 26*, pp. 202–229

intelligence. Consequently, these works provide overly optimistic examinations of vaguely conceptualized constructs, potentially leading to the damaging commodification of emotional intelligence (Fineman, 2000a). Given the extensive and unique body of literature on emotions in organizations, it is likely that emotional intelligence is uniquely enacted in organizational settings (Abraham, 2000). However, current conceptualizations of emotional intelligence provide little insight into emotional intelligence in general and its enactment in organizations more specifically.

Several problems emerge from the present treatment of emotional intelligence. First, the construct lacks distinction from other constructs such as social intelligence (Davies, Stankov, & Roberts, 1998). This is true in both popular press and scholarly works. For example, Goleman (1998a, 1998b) claims that important components of emotional intelligence are constructs such as trustworthiness, conscientiousness, and self-confidence. Unquestionably these characteristics will improve chances for success in organizations. They may also be a form of social intelligence. However, it is difficult to argue that these constructs are emotional in nature. For example, an individual who is highly emotionally intelligent may give the appearance of trustworthiness, but may not necessarily be trustworthy. Weisinger's (1998) recommendations for becoming more emotionally intelligent similarly lack distinction from advice offered in standard counseling practices. Because counseling guidelines were developed to manage relationships, they may or may not help a person become more emotionally intelligent. Peer reviewed studies have also acknowledged the lack of distinction separating emotional intelligence from other forms of social success. For example, Mehrabian (2000) states that "emotional intelligence has been used as an overarching construct to describe individual differences associated with life success" (p. 134). Because emotional intelligence is indistinguishable from other constructs, it loses its importance as a tool researchers can use to understand organizations. It also becomes an ineffective practical tool for managers attempting to improve their organizations.

A primary reason for the failure to distinguish between emotional intelligence and other constructs is the psychological orientation of current discussions about emotional intelligence. Given the complex interactional nature of emotional intelligence (Abraham 1999, 2000; Mayer & Salovey, 1993), a psychological approach may contribute to a discussion of emotional intelligence, but it would necessarily be inadequate for a more complex understanding of the construct. An attempt has been made by psychologists to distinguish between emotional intelligence and other forms of intelligence. The most frequently used conceptualization contends that emotional intelligence is comprised of "recognizing emotion, reasoning both with emotion and emotion-related information, and processing emotional information as a part of general problem-solving" (Mayer & Geher, 1996, p. 90). With the possible exception of recognizing emotion, these components of emotional intelligence are psychological in nature. This is not surprising given that most of the researchers currently examining emotional intelligence are psychologists.

Unfortunately, conceptualizing emotional intelligence from a psychological perspective has been ineffective in distinguishing it from other forms of intelligence and from personality traits (Davies, Stankov, & Roberts, 1998).

One viable reason for researchers' failure to distinguish emotional intelligence from other concepts may be its paucity within the field of communication. Both popular culture and scholarly writings suggest that there is an unmistakable interactional component to emotional intelligence that places it firmly within the field of communication (Goleman, 1995, 1998a, 1998b; Mayer & Salovey, 1993; Weisinger, 1998). Despite the recognition of the importance of communication, research and literature reviews have been from a psychological orientation (see for exception Abraham 1999, 2000). Whereas it is the focus on emotions that distinguish emotional intelligence from other forms of social intelligence (Salovey & Mayer, 1990), it is the interactional nature of emotional intelligence that most clearly distinguishes it from general intelligence. Intelligence quotient (IQ) is primarily cognitive, whereas emotional intelligence is primarily interactive and manifests itself in a person's communication related behavior (Oatley & Jenkins, 1992). Emotional intelligence is manifested and can be measured only within communication.

A final problem with the present treatment of emotional intelligence, both by researchers and popular culture authors, is the focus on the potential positive aspects of emotional intelligence. Interestingly, scholars seem to assume a correlation between personal/organizational success and moral character. In fact, "the moral and value territory on which emotional intelligence treads is, typically, unquestioned" (Fineman, 2000a). Although there is some minimal acknowledgement of possible negative uses of emotional intelligence (Abraham, 1999), most work focuses on the constructive possibilities of emotional intelligence, particularly as they relate to the potential for individual and organizational success. For example, scholars have linked emotional intelligence to success (Mehrabian, 2000), limiting emotional dissonance (Abraham, 2000), organizational success (Abraham, 1999), midlife resilience (Vaillant & Davis, 2000), and adaptive goal orientation and life satisfaction (Martinez-Pons, 1997). Not only do scholars suggest that emotional intelligence leads to personal success, but they also assume that emotionally intelligent people are generally more pleasant and kinder individuals: "The emotionally intelligent person is often a pleasure to be around and leaves others feeling better. The emotionally intelligent person, however, does not mindlessly seek pleasure, but rather attends to emotion in the path toward growth" (Salovey & Mayer, 1990, p. 201). As with general intelligence, however, individuals who are high in emotional intelligence may lack strong moral or ethical character. Furthermore, the institutionalized, product-oriented nature of Western organizations provides a strong incentive for emotional intelligence related abuse and appropriation (Fineman, 2000a, p. 108). By focusing only on the positive effects of emotional intelligence, researchers fail to question the way the term "emotional intelligence" may be used in organizations to rationalize and reify emotion centered control. Consequently, by failing to examine the potential negative consequences of emotional intelligence, scholars are allowing for the unquestioned appropriation of an academic construct by practitioners whose objectives may be inconsistent with the construct. Because people rely on organizations for financial, esteem, and affiliative purposes (Flam, 1993), it becomes difficult to escape emotional intelligence related abuse. It is important to provide an understanding of both emotional intelligence related constructive and destructive possibilities.

The present article attempts to address these problems by providing a communication orientation to emotional intelligence with six distinct but interrelated emotional intelligence constructs as they relate to organizational communication. These components are best understood within a three dimensional framework of self/other, experienced/expressed emotions, and a moral dimension. This framework serves two functions: First it provides a means of understanding the current emotions in organizations literature and second by providing a starting point for organizational communication research specifically designed to explore emotional intelligence. Although the components of emotional intelligence are discussed separately in an attempt to provide clarity, it is important to note that they are part of an interrelated and ongoing process. We will now examine the dimensions of emotional intelligence followed by a discussion of the constructs.

## THE DIMENSIONS OF EMOTIONAL INTELLIGENCE

Historically, research has focused on general intelligence, better known as intelligence quotient (IQ). Traditionally, IQ has been viewed as purely cognitive. However, cognitive ability tests have been inadequate predictors of success in organizations (Wagner, 1994), particularly leadership performance (Fiedler & Link, 1994). Most people can relate to these conclusions. Stories of bosses or coworkers who are intellectually brilliant but emotionally underdeveloped are commonplace. Consequently, there is an increasing acceptance that intelligence is located within "interaction between the organism, the task the organism confronts, and the situation in which the task is confronted" (Snow, 1994, p. 3). In other words, there is an interface between the cognitive components of intelligence and the social context. Although the cognitive processes of intelligence have been examined, the social components, or intelligences, are just now being explored.

According to Mayer and Geher (1996), general intelligence, better known as intelligence quotient, only indicates a person's intellectual ability, but does not provide information about the "specific intelligences that comprise it" (p. 89). Although general intelligence is highly correlated with other forms of intelligence, they are conceptually distinct (Mayer & Geher, 1996). The idea of social intelligence is not new. The term was originally coined in the 1920s (Mayer & Salovey, 1993). Because social intelligence was difficult to measure, it was later declared useless by intelligence researchers. Recent research has attempted to clarify social intelligence with constructs such as intrapersonal and interpersonal intelligence (Gardner, 1983).

According to the originators of the term, emotional intelligence is a specific form of social intelligence. Salovey and Mayer (1990), define emotional intelligence as "a type of social intelligence that involves the ability to monitor one's own and others' emotions, to discriminate among them, and to use the information to guide one's thinking and actions" (p. 189). Although definitions of social intelligence vary widely, they all agree that some human interface is necessary for the enactment of social intelligence (for review see Solovey & Mayer, 1990). Whereas social intelligence has been historically difficult to test, emotional intelligence can be distinguished from other forms of social intelligence "as involving the manipulation of emotions and emotional content" (Mayer & Salovey, 1993, p. 436). Because of its specificity, emotional intelligence may have better discriminant validity than other social intelligences. For this reason, emotional intelligence has the potential to be examined in a systematic manner.

Given the previous discussion, it is clear that emotional intelligence is a social construct. Further, emotions are both experienced and expressed, suggesting a communication orientation. As discussed previously, emotional intelligence is manifested and can be measured only through communication (Oatley & Jenkins, 1992). Consequently, emotional intelligence can be placed along two intersecting dimensions: self/other and experienced/expressed emotions (see Figure 1). A third dimension also becomes apparent when issues of ethics, morality, and personal success are viewed as being at the heart of emotional intelligence related behaviors in organizations. A morality dimension is found at the intersection of the first two dimensions (see Figure 1). Along that dimension lies the constructive/destructive components of emotional intelligence.

Communication scholars have noted that it is important to look beyond simple dichotomies to avoid the oversimplification of emotional experiences in organizations (Tracy, 2000; Waldron, 1994). Importantly, although the three dimensions of emotional intelligence intersect to create six emotional intelligence constructs, those intersections would best be understood as fuzzy lines instead of points of absolute difference between the components. The lines are permeable and interconnected. The permeability of the dimensions recognizes the highly complex nature of both emotional intelligence and communication in general. The interconnections between the components will be discussed more thoroughly in later sections.

The self/other dimension recognizes the interactional nature of emotional intelligence. This focus on interaction centralizes the social implications of emotional intelligence while moving emotional intelligence further away from a psychological orientation. The experienced/expressed dimension moves emotional intelligence firmly into a communication orientation. Not only is communication used to express/suppress self-emotions and influence the emotions others experience, the expression of emotion is communication. As a result, emotional intelligence can be observed and understood from different levels of communication

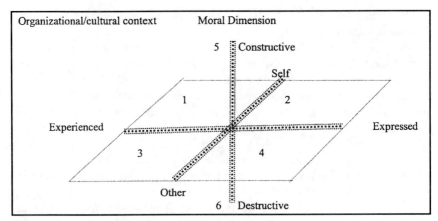

1. Managing self-experienced emotions
2. Managing self-expressed emotions
3. Reading and managing others' experienced emotions
4. Managing others' expressed emotions
5. Constructive emotional intelligence
6. Destructive emotional intelligence

**Figure 1.** Three dimensions and six constructs of emotional intelligence.

analysis. The morality dimension cuts through the heart of the other two dimensions, recognizing that emotional intelligence can be used in both ethical and unethical ways.

Recognizing the significance of the context within which emotions are enacted is one more means of avoiding viewing this model as a set of simple dichotomies. It is likely that emotional intelligence is highly dependent on the context in which it is enacted. The literature suggests that unique emotional issues are present in organizations. Consequently, the organization, organizational culture, and other contextual norms and processes—such as power and history—provide the contextual boundaries for this emotional intelligence model. The context surrounding the enactment of emotional intelligence can be understood as both general to all organizations and as unique to a given organization.

Based on Davies et al.'s (1998) conceptualization and on a reading of other relevant literature (Abraham, 1999; Salovey & Mayer, 1990) emotional intelligence can be divided into six distinct but interrelated constructs that can be placed along the three, previously mentioned, dimensions of emotional intelligence: managing self-experienced emotions, managing self-expressed emotions, reading/managing others' experienced emotions, managing others' expressed emotions, constructive emotional intelligence, and destructive emotional intelligence.

Although little peer-reviewed research has examined emotional intelligence in organizations, there has been an increasing examination of emotionality in organizations. This body of work provides clues to the functioning of emotional intelligence in organizations. Each construct will be discussed as it relates to the literature exploring emotions in organizations.

## THE SELF-EXPERIENCED/EXPRESSED DIMENSION

Research provides the greatest insight into the self component of the experienced/expressed dimension of emotional intelligence. Although the two primary constructs can be examined separately, it is also important to remember that the lines separating the constructs are fuzzy, not absolute. As a result, it is also important to examine the constructs in relationship to each other. Consequently, in this section managing experienced emotions and managing expressed emotions will be considered followed by a discussion of the interaction between experienced and expressed emotions. The section will conclude by exploring research issues for this dimension.

Managing Experienced Emotions

Not surprisingly, given the psychological bent of emotional intelligence scholars, managing experienced emotions has received the greatest attention in the emotional intelligence literature. This component may also appear more often because it is the easiest to assess through simple self-response questionnaires. The problem with these studies is that they do not examine the relationship of communication to managing felt emotions. In organizations, individuals have a number of tactics they can utilize when managing their emotions. For example, when the first author becomes bored with her work, she checks her mail and chats with the secretary. This lifts the boredom sufficiently to return to a sometimes tedious task.

Some research indicates that, while at work, individuals remember experiencing more negative than positive emotions (Lee & Jablin, 1995). For example, Waldron and Krone (1991) found that negative emotions were rated as more common and as more intense than positive emotions. Furthermore, negative emotions tend to be more significant to organizational members than positive emotions. Other research, however, discovered no difference between the experience of positive and negative emotions at work (Fiebig & Kramer, 1998). Kitayama (1996) found that people focus more on negative emotions than positive emotions, especially when they are concentrating on a heavy (difficult) task. One means emotionally intelligent individuals can deliberately use when managing the emotions they experience is by reframing the context. People may experience less anger, or may even experience different emotions, if they reframe the context (Goleman, 1995). A similar construct is cognitive appraisal (Lazarus, 1991) in which the way a person thinks about a situation determines the resulting emotion (Hochschild, 1983; Tracy & Tracy, 1998). Similarly, constructivism (Delia, O'Keefe, & O'Keefe, 1982) suggests that each individual thinks about a situation differently depending on their personal constructs and their cognitive complexity. Reframing differs from these two perspectives in that it is a deliberate act in which the context of an event is shifted in order to create an understanding of another person's perspective (Goleman, 1995), or an altogether different context may be applied to an event. For example, airline attendants are encouraged to think of their unruly passengers as family members (Hochschild, 1983), and 911 operators are encouraged to treat callers as if they were a member of their own family (Tracy & Tracy, 1998). Individuals reframe the emotions they feel through communication strategies (Tracy & Tracy, 1998). Furthermore, the emotive effort expended on managing experienced emotions depends on the perceived nature of the communicative relationship between service workers and customers (Kruml & Geddes, 2000). It is likely that there are other means of managing the emotions we feel, although these forms have not yet been identified in the literature.

Managing Expressed Emotions

It is important for individuals to understand appropriate emotional displays within a given social context. Our ability to manage our emotions is a reflection of this need. The greater our ability to feel and express appropriate emotions, the greater our emotional intelligence. Managing expressed emotions manifests itself in both the expression and suppression of emotions (Tracy & Tracy, 1998). Research indicates that employees are more likely to suppress negative than positive emotions (Fiebig & Kramer, 1998; Lee & Jablin, 1995; Waldron & Krone; 1991). Although subordinates are more likely to suppress negative emotions with a boss, they are more likely to discuss among themselves a negatively valenced incident than a positively valenced incident (Sias & Jablin, 1995). Therefore, although individuals manage negative emotions more closely, they do find an outlet for those emotions at a later time. Interestingly, communication research suggests that 911 operators' often suppress all experienced emotions, striving instead for a neutral expression of emotions when interacting with callers (Shuler & Sypher, 2000).

Although each of these studies presents interesting findings, most communication scholars understand organizations in general and emotions in organizations more specifically in complex ways. Consequently, the bulk of the communication research (including much discussed in the previous two sections) focuses on the interaction between experienced and expressed emotions.

The Interaction of Experienced and Expressed Emotions

Although managing experienced emotions and managing expressed emotions can be separated for the sake of discussion, the greatest insight is obtained by examining them in relationship to each other. Experienced emotions clearly influence expressed emotions. The intertwining of experienced and expressed emotions is best understood through the notions of emotion work, emotional labor, and bounded emotionality in organizations. Interestingly, each of these constructs were either created by or heavily pursued by communication scholars, possibly because these lines of research are less dichotomous than the pursuit of either experienced or expressed emotions as individual research agendas. Furthermore, because of their interactive and communicative nature (Shuler & Sypher, 2000), these areas of research are appropriately examined from a communication orientation.

*Emotion work.* Emotion work is defined as managing the emotions we choose to experience and express in order to function better at work (Tolich, 1993). According to Waldron (1994), there are three types of rules that guide emotion work: constitutive rules, regulative rules, and heuristic rules. The ability to adhere to these rules is most likely strongly related to emotional intelligence. Each of these rules will be discussed. Constitutive rules are social constructions that determine what will count as an emotion. For example, some authors suggest that social constructions tend to emphasize feminine emotions while de-emphasizing masculine emotions (Hearn, 1993), despite the fact that masculine emotions (and men's control over those emotions) are prevalent in organizations with potentially dangerous outcomes (Messerschmidt, 1996). Given the emphasis on feminine emotions, it is interesting that men tend to rate themselves as more emotionally intelligent than women rate themselves (Petrides & Furnham, 2000). Consequently, whereas social constructions privilege feminine emotions, social constructions of reality construct men as more capable of managing those emotions than women. This is consistent with previous research on emotions in organizations (Hochschild, 1983).

Regulative rules determine the appropriate means of displaying and interpreting emotional experiences. The previously discussed suppression of the expression of negative emotions is reflective of organizational regulative rules. Finally, heuristic rules are individualized displays of emotions. Heuristic rules help individuals adapt to the idiosyncrasies of their work experience (Waldron, 1994). Although individualized, heuristic rules are "still designed to further individual or organizational objectives" (Waldron, 1994, p. 405). Whereas constitutive and regulative rules create generalized standards for the experience and expression of emotions, heuristic rules acknowledge that individuals adhere to those standards in unique ways. Tolich (1993) found that when given the opportunity to display a more autonomous set of pleasant emotions, check-out clerks at a grocery store were able to create a loyal customer following. It is likely that emotionally intelligent individuals will best understand and work within these three rules.

*Emotional labor.* A second concept that provides an understanding of the interaction between experienced and expressed emotions is emotional labor (Hochschild, 1983). Emotional labor is similar to emotion work in that it is a means of achieving an end in organizations. However, emotion work is controlled by the individual whereas emotional labor is controlled by the organization. Emotional labor is an important "communication accomplishment. It is in and through interaction that we express, repress, or manufacture emotion, in our workplaces and elsewhere" (Shuler & Sypher, 2000, p. 51). Putnam and Mumby (1993) explain that emotions are treated as a commodity in emotional labor, no longer belonging to the individual but to the organization for manipulation and display. Research on emotional labor focuses on how individuals express organizationally prescribed emotions (Ashforth & Humphrey, 1993; Hochschild, 1983; Sutton & Rafaeli, 1988).

Of central importance to the study of emotional labor is emotional dissonance, or the gap between experienced and expressed emotions (Abraham, 2000; Hochschild, 1983; Rafaeli & Sutton, 1987). Scholars have identified three means organizational members use to cope with the gap between managing experienced emotions and managing expressed emotions. Employees may internalize prescribed emotions through deep acting—an emotional display that requires the actor to believe the emotions being expressed (Ashforth & Humphrey, 1993; Hochschild, 1983). Research indicates that deep acting can lead to a sense of self-estrangement, a state with catastrophic psychological consequences (Hochschild, 1983). Employees may adapt to emotional dissonance through surface acting—an emotional display that is not intended to communicate sincerity—in an attempt to maintain their sense of themselves as separate from their roles (Ashforth & Humphrey, 1993; Hochschild, 1983). Although surface acting does not risk estrangement from self, it does tend to produce an unconvincing performance. Consequently, surface acting may lead to professional failure (Hochschild, 1983). Finally, employees can adapt to emotional dissonance through a spontaneous and genuine expression of emotion (Ashforth & Humphrey, 1993). Whereas this form of expression is the most genuine and the healthiest, it does not seem to be widely encouraged. Each of these means of managing the gap between experienced and expressed emotions could provide insight into emotional intelligence.

*Bounded emotionality.* Bounded emotionality was originally created as a response to March and Simon's bounded rationality in organizations (Mumby & Putnam, 1992). Although there are many bounded emotionality parallels to bounded rationality, they are by no means mutually exclusive (Mumby & Putnam, 1992). Briefly, bounded emotionality involves an "alternative mode of organizing in which nurturance, caring, community, supportiveness, and interrelatedness are fused with individual responsibility to shape organizational experiences" (Mumby & Putnam, 1992, p. 474). Research examining bounded emotionality has begun to emerge in the literature. Best known is a study by Martin, Knopoff, and Beckman (1998) examining bounded emotionality at The Body Shop. These authors conclude that although bounded emotionality does exist, it is in some ways self-defeating, creating norms that prevent the spontaneous expression of emotion. Furthermore, they conclude that although bounded emotionality may be liberating for some, it could also be a dangerous and highly invasive control mechanism.

## Studying the Self-Experienced/Expressed Dimension

The relationship between the self-experience of emotion and the self-expression of emotion is so strong that they are typically examined as one construct: self-emotion management (e.g., Cook, Greenberg, & Kusche, 1994; Davies et al., 1998). For this reason the discussion of the two components' direct link to emotional intelligence is combined.

The ability to control both experienced emotions and expressed emotions is an important element of emotional intelligence in organizations. Previous research has treated self-emotion management as an outcome and as situated outside a context. In a review of emotional intelligence literature, only the EQ test, out of six scales, provided any contextual information (see Davies et al., 1998). The EQ test, however, provides limited context and limits responses to simplistic multiple choice answers. None of the scales were designed to study how individuals manage their own emotions. Consequently, a limited understanding of decontextualized outcomes of self-emotion management has been generated. In order to study self-emotion management, communication scholars must (a) conceptualize it as both a process and an outcome of emotional intelligence, and (b) factor in contextual issues that provide a framework for self-emotion management.

## THE OTHER-EXPERIENCED/EXPRESSED DIMENSION

Not only is emotional intelligence related to the management of self-emotion, but emotionally intelligent individuals are also able to observe and manage other's emotions. In this section, reading and managing others' experienced emotions will be discussed. Managing others' expressed emotions will then be explored followed by an examination of the interaction of the constructs.

## Reading and Managing Others' Experienced Emotions

Reading and managing others' experienced emotions contains two separate processes that must be considered when examining emotional intelligence: reading emotions and managing experienced emotions. Although these components are part of the same process, they can be distinguished from each other. Reading emotions at its most simple level means identifying the emotions being experienced and displayed by others. At its most complex, reading emotions involves recognizing and understanding the emotions experienced by others. Managing emotions means shaping others experiences of a set of given emotions. Although reading emotions and managing experienced emotions can interact, interaction is not a necessary condition. For example, an individual can read others' emotions without being able or willing to manage the emotions. Furthermore, it is possible to manage others' emotions without first identifying the emotions being experienced. However, it seems that highly emotionally intelligent individuals would be more likely to simultaneously read and manage others' emotions. Both reading emotions and managing others' emotions will be discussed.

*Reading emotion.* Reading others' emotions is an important element of emotional intelligence with wide ranging social implications: "We assume that we can correctly identify emotions in ourselves and others. We use emotion terms widely in almost every kind of discourse, with the exception of the scientific and technical. A priori, then, emotions have functions in most of what is written and spoken" (Oatley & Jenkins, 1992, p. 77). Clearly the ability to recognize and understand emotions is an important component of social interaction. At its base, reading emotions is the ability to identify others' emotions. Three emotional intelligence studies have examined individuals' ability to properly assign emotions to another person (Davies et al., 1998; Mayer, DiPaolo, & Salovey, 1990; Mayer & Geher, 1996). Mayer and Geher discovered that individuals who are better able to read others' emotions have higher self-reported SAT scores. Furthermore, Cook, Greenberg, and Kusche, (1994) found that the ability to understand emotions in self and other was negatively associated with behavioral problems in school-age children. Despite the obvious importance of reading emotions, little research has examined the role of reading others' emotions in interactions between managers and subordinates. In this section the process of identifying emotions will be examined followed by a discussion of upward and downward emotion management in organizations.

It is first important to discuss how emotions are identified. The assumption that empathy is the foundation of identifying emotions can be found in both scholarly writings (Abraham, 1999; Salovey & Mayer, 1990) and the popular press (Goleman, 1995). Initially these authors' assessment makes intuitive sense. Individuals can identify others' emotions because they know how they would feel in a given situation. Although some research supports a link between reading emotions and empathy (Mayer et al., 1990), the ability to identify others' emotions is more sophisticated than suggested. In order to empathize it is necessary to understand the context in which emotions are expressed. However, others' pure emotions can be identified, even if the context is not understood. Ekman and Friesen (1975) identified six universal emotions and appropriate expression of those emotions. Most individuals can identify the six universal emotions merely by looking at pictures. of people expressing those emotions. In other words, context becomes less relevant when identifying others' basic emotions. Davies et al. (1998) quantitative analysis provides support for the argument that there is little to no correlation between empathy and the ability to read other's emotions. Whereas empathy is not necessarily involved in identifying emotions, it is probably an essential component of understanding emotions. Understanding occurs at a deeper level than merely identifying emotions. Understanding suggests a communicative connection between people that is best achieved through interaction. Empathy is likely to help people appreciate the emotions experienced by others beyond being able to label others' emotions.

Not only is it important to understand how emotions are identified, but it is also important to understand organizational contexts in which emotions are identified. Upward emotion reading will now be discussed. It seems likely that the less power individuals have, the more carefully they must manage their own emotions and read their managers' emotions (Hochschild, 1983). Although this makes intuitive sense, only one study was identified that examined, albeit indirectly, the role of upward emotion reading in organizations. Day and Crain (1992) found that nonleaders rated their relationship more positively with leaders who scored high on positive affect tests. This finding suggests that subordinates are highly cognizant of their mangers' emotions. Although not directly related to emotions, the upward influence literature (Deluga & Perry, 1991; Krone, 1992, 1994; Wayne & Ferris, 1990) and the impression management literature (Wayne & Liden, 1995) indicate that successful nonleaders are highly aware of their manager's behaviors and responses. Emotional intelligence research in organizations would explicitly examine the process individuals use to read managers' emotions. It is also important to understand the link between accurate upward reading and success in an organizational context.

Not only is it important for employees to read managers' emotions, but it is equally important for managers to be able to read employee emotion. Surprisingly, even less has been written about downward emotion reading than upward emotion reading. As previously stated, one explanation may be our assumption that employee emotions are unimportant and irrelevant to organizations. Hochschild (1983) calls this concept the doctrine of feelings and suggests that lower status individuals' emotions are considered to be more inconsequential than higher status individuals. Some research does provide clues to the role of downward emotion reading in organizations. Wayne and Liden (1995) concluded that managers gave higher performance ratings to employees they liked, indicating that managers attend to and respond favorably to positive emotional expression. Day and Crain (1992) concluded that leaders perceive a higher quality of relationship with members when the member demonstrated a high ability and low negative affect. In other words, managers were more favorably disposed to members who were emotionally neutral in terms of negative emotions. Emotional intelligence research should examine both the process managers use to read members' emotions and the outcome of effective emotion reading.

*Managing others' experienced emotions.* The ability to regulate emotions in others is an important component of emotional intelligence (Salovey & Mayer, 1990). Whereas scholars of emotional intelligence do not tend to clearly distinguish between managing experienced emotions and managing expressed emotions, researchers exploring emotions in organizations make a clear distinction between felt and displayed emotions (e.g., Hochschild, 1983).

Although managing others' experienced emotions seems complex, research has discovered that it is actually relatively easy to produce positive affect in others (Isen & Baron, 1991). Isen and Baron suggest that minor incidents, such as finding a dime in a public telephone, have been known to create mild positive feelings. The obvious question then is if positive affect or emotions are so easy to produce, why as previously stated, do some people have such difficulty remembering positive emotional experiences in organizations? One possible answer is that organizational members are not using their emotional intelligence to effectively manage others' felt emotions.

Managing Others' Expressed Emotions

A fourth component of emotional intelligence is the management of others' expressed emotions. Given the multiple functions organizations play in employees' lives, managing others' emotions is far more complex than it would initially seem. For example, in terms of productivity, helping others' achieve a high positive affect may both improve and harm organizational productivity (Isen & Baron, 1991). On the other hand, from a humanistic standpoint, it is important that employees be encouraged to experience joy, satisfaction, and general feelings of good will. Managing others' expressed emotions so as to achieve multiple goals is a highly complex process requiring high levels of emotional intelligence. Interestingly, although managing others' expressed emotions is an important aspect of emotional intelligence, very little has been written about it within the emotional intelligence literature. Although scholars allude to its importance, they fail to discuss how it might operate (e.g., Abraham, 1999; Mayer & Salovey, 1993). Research on emotionality in organizations has been far more vocal about managing others' expressed emotions. This body of research focuses either on managerial control over employee emotional expression, or on cultural control over employee emotional expression. Each of these issues will be discussed.

*Managerial control.* According to Waldron (1994) "worker emotion has been prominent in the theory and practice of management, but it has been viewed primarily as a kind of undeveloped management resource, ideally developed and controlled by adjustments in work practices or management exhortation" (p. 389). Not only is this true for emotions in general, but is particularly emphasized with emotional intelligence in organizations (Fineman, 2000a). Managerial control over expressed emotions can be identified in the emotional labor literature. Managers can work in many different ways to encourage employees to display the appropriate, commodified, emotional expressions. For example, employees are encouraged to display commodified emotions by rewriting training manuals, incentives, and training for specific emotional displays (Sutton & Rafaeli, 1988), and through training and socialization (Hochschild, 1983). Both of these studies concluded, however, that the pace of work dictated the depth of employee emotion management, regardless of the training and socialization mechanisms used to produce deep acting. These findings would suggest that highly regulated means of managing members' emotions, isolated from the demands of the work, are ineffective.

Tolich's (1993) findings provide insight into effective management of employees emotions. He would describe the emotional labor required by Sutton and Rafaeli's organization as highly regulative and therefore as potentially leading to emotional dissonance. Tolich found that autonomous displays of pleasant emotions were more likely to obtain customer loyalty than were regulated emotional displays. With autonomous emotions, management specifies that employees must display a generally positive affect. However, the display of the positive emotions is entrusted to the employees. When the emotion management is autonomous, employees gain a sense of commitment from the enacted emotion. Autonomous emotion management needs further exploration, not only in terms of its effectiveness in achieving customer loyalty, but also as a means of achieving employee loyalty while creating a sense of fun.

Sutton's (1991) work in a bill collection agency provides another form of managerial emotion management. Managers encouraged appropriate emotional display through rewards and punishments. Three coping mechanisms were used by employees to meet managerial demands for emotional displays. Cognitive appraisals were used to change the nature of the way collectors thought about their relationships with debtors. This concept is similar to Goleman's (1995) reframing in which individuals could successfully choose their emotions by reframing the context. Displacement of aggression was used to express emotions in such a way that the debtor did not know emotions were being expressed. Joking was the third coping mechanism. Collectors would joke with one another about their customers. Each of these coping mechanisms was actively encouraged by management. Sutton indicated that managers were highly effective in managing employee emotional expression

Clearly there is emotional intelligence involved in managing emotional labor. However, there is little heart involved in managing others emotions without concern for subordinates humanity and sense of self (Fineman, 1993). Researchers must begin to examine how managers can manage others' emotions without appropriating those emotions for commodified organizational ends (see Fineman, 2000a). Putnam and Mumby (1993) suggest that managers should manage felt emotions where employees are encouraged to express their emotions in a positive and effective manner instead of hiding and dismissing those emotions. Because emotional intelligence can be learned over time, felt emotions is a viable alternative to emotional labor.

*Cultural control.* In addition to managerial control of emotions, researchers have discussed cultural control of employee emotions. The idea that culture can be used to manage employee emotions suggests a form of organizational, as opposed to individual, emotion management (Weisinger, 1998). Instead of understanding emotional intelligence from an individual perspective, a cultural approach suggests that emotional intelligence is a product of ongoing organizing processes. Van Maanen and Kunda, (1989) claim that any attempt to manipulate organizational culture is also an attempt to manage emotions. They identified organizational rituals as an important means of influencing how members feel and think. For example "Disneyland, by design, bestows identity by systematically putting newcomers through a process carefully set up to strip away the job relevance of other sources of identity and learned response and replace them with others of organizational relevance. It works" (p. 69). Isen and Baron (1991) argue that the shared system of beliefs, attitudes and values derived from organizational culture can influence positive affect in organizations. For example, by encouraging a culture in which care and compassion are the norm, an ecology of compassion can be created (Frost, Dutton, Worline, & Wilson, 2000).

Organizational management of member emotion may provide an interesting approach to emotional intelligence. Instead of viewing emotional intelligence as an individual construct, it would be conceptualized as a contextual construct occurring at the individual, dyadic, group, and organizational levels. The unit of analysis would vary from individuals in organizations to the organization as a whole. Whereas this type of approach would not be possible from a psychological orientation to emotional intelligence, it is possible when viewing emotional intelligence as communication. A psychological orientation views emotional intelligence as a purely individual and cognitive function. A communication orientation would view emotional intelligence as an array of transactions in which individuals influence each other, creating a system of norms and organizational level behaviors. Hence, a culture level approach to emotional intelligence is possible.

## The Interaction of Reading/Managing Others' Experienced Emotions and Managing Others' Expressed Emotions

Although reading and managing others' experienced emotions can be discussed separately from managing other's expressed emotions, these issues are best understood in relationship to each other. The line separating the two constructs is a fuzzy line, creating some important overlap and interactions.

Successful reading of others' emotions is an important organizational issue. Unfortunately, research has oversimplified reading emotions. It has been conceptualized as a unidirectional, outcome oriented, decontextualized construct. For example, Mayer et al. (1990) asked participants to identify emotional expressions in six photographs, identify emotions within abstract designs, and within different colors. In a recent examination of the efficacy of emotional intelligence, the same measurement was used (Davies et al., 1998). This measurement fails to acknowledge that others' ongoing and shifting behaviors influence reading emotions. Furthermore, although context is not required for reading pure emotions, these authors fail to acknowledge that the context can provide important clues to the accurate reading of emotions. This simplification of reading emotions may explain why researchers have been unsuccessful in its measurement (see Davies et al., 1998).

It is possible to better understand emotional intelligence by treating reading and managing others' experienced emotions, and managing others expressed emotions as part of a transactional process. By conceptualizing reading and managing emotions as transactional, communication scholars can conceptualize the constructs as a complex process that shifts within changing contexts. For example, we have discussed how subordinates read managers' emotions, and how managers read subordinates' emotions. However, managers and subordinates must read and react to each others' emotional expressions in a simultaneous and ongoing manner. The adjustment of emotional expression based on simultaneous and ongoing upward and downward reading of emotions and managing of self and other emotions represents a realistic, but complex vision of emotional intelligence. Understanding the transaction of emotional intelligence between leaders and nonleaders would provide a fascinating and important contribution to organizational communication research.

## EXPLORING THE MORAL DIMENSION
## OF EMOTIONAL INTELLIGENCE

To this point, both scholarly and popular press works have been based on the assumption that moral character and personal success are synonymous. In other words, these authors assume that what is good for the individual is also moral (Fineman, 2000a). Recognizing a moral dimension to emotional intelligence allows for the understanding that emotional intelligence can be used in both ethical and unethical ways and that individuals who are emotionally intelligent have a varying range of moral intentions. In this section, the possible effects of emotional intelligence will be explored, both in terms of the constructive and destructive possibilities.

### Constructive Emotional Intelligence

It seems clear that learning to read and manage our own emotions and those of others could enhance individual and organizational success. It is, in fact, the constructive possibilities surrounding emotional intelligence that have been emphasized in both the popular press and scholarly works (see for example Abraham, 1999, 2000; Martinez-Pons, 1997; Mehrabian, 2000; Vaillant, & Davis, 2000). From a communication perspective, when used by an ethical person, emotional intelligence has the potential to create a sense of community through the positive expression of emotions and the honest discussion of "outlaw emotions" (Jaggar, 1989, p. 160). Furthermore, emotional intelligence can become a positive force in decision-making processes and in organizational change. Each of these issues will be discussed.

A true community is not characterized by an unnatural peace and is not created through managerial manipulation. Instead, community—as it is used here—is carefully cultivated by its members. Communities recognize and value outlaw emotions as necessary for humane organizational change. Used by an ethical person, emotional intelligence can cultivate a sense of community in at least two important ways. First, emotional intelligence can cultivate a sense of community by legitimizing the expression of authentic "work feelings" (Putnam & Mumby, 1993). Traditionally, emotions in organizations have been viewed as a managerial tool. Consequently, displays of emotions have been carefully orchestrated by management, creating an empty facade that customers will presumably find pleasant. Putnam and Mumby contend that instead of mandating a particular display of emotions that may create estrangement from felt emotions, managers should encourage the expression of honest emotions in ways that will create human bonds between employees, coworkers, and customers. For example, organizations can create an "ecology of compassion" in which the culture of an organization encourages expressions of compassion (Frost, Dutton, Worline, & Wilson, 2000, p. 25). In this way both the individual and the organization benefit from emotional expressions. Emotionally intelligent employees are more likely to be able to express emotions in constructive ways that can contribute to the building of a sense of community within the organization.

Emotionally intelligent individuals may also build a sense of community by effectively expressing, reading, and managing "outlaw emotions," or the emotional responses of "subordinated individuals who pay a disproportionately high price for maintaining the status quo" (Jaggar, 1989, p. 160). Typically the status quo in organizations is most harmful to marginalized groups such as women, people of color, people with disabilities, and older workers. Traditionally, when these groups publicly express their distress at the injustice they face within organizations, their behavior is interpreted as uncooperative or otherwise difficult. Emotionally intelligent individuals may be able to utilize the expression of these outlaw emotions for the thoughtful reconsideration of the status quo. For example, when an individual refuses to laugh at sexist or racist jokes and expresses displeasure with the joke teller, emotionally intelligent individuals may use this occasion to cause others to reconsider exclusionary humor and its impact on nondominant group members. In this way communicating with high levels of emotional intelligence can create a sense of community that values and respects differences among organizational members.

Not only does emotional intelligence have the ability to develop an inclusive sense of community among organizational members, but high levels of emotional intelligence could also legitimize the expression of emotion in organizational decision making. Traditionally, emotions have been separated from the decision-making process (Howard, 1993, p. 613). This false separation of emotion from the decision making process may be responsible for disastrous decisions made in an organizational setting. For example, a stronger expression and reading of fear concerning the risks of launching the space shuttle Challenger might have helped avert a terrible tragedy (Messerschmidt, 1996). Through the creation of an inclusive sense of organizational community and through accepting the emotional processes involved in organizational decision making, emotional intelligence can become a triggering force in organizational change.

## Destructive Emotional Intelligence

It is politically innocent to believe that learning to read and manage our own emotions and those of others can only be used to enhance individual and organizational well-being. Unfortunately, this is how emotional intelligence has been constructed in the popular press (e.g., Goleman, 1998b). For example, after the killings at Columbine High School, the first author watched a news broadcast advocating the teaching of emotional intelligence in school. The report failed to acknowledge that the killers may have been pushed to the social fringes by emotionally intelligent bullies. Teaching bullies to be more emotionally intelligent may have increased their effectiveness at ostracizing and marginalizing less emotionally intelligent others. In other words, teaching emotional intelligence without acknowledging its darker implications may increase the ability of unethical individuals to commit acts of evil. Like any other form of intelligence, emotional intelligence can be used to serve good and bad ends. An unscrupulous or nonreflective use of emotional intelligence can have negative consequences for individuals and organizations alike. Two destructive uses of emotional intelligence would be emotional labor and the maintenance of an unjust status quo.

When emotional intelligence is totally appropriated by the organization, it can become emotional labor of the sort that leads to stress, burnout, and self-estrangement (Hochschild, 1983). For example, as previously mentioned, manipulating members to deep act commodified emotions may cause members to because estranged from their real emotions. Hochschild (1983) found that some women were unable to engage in a normal sexual relationship because of this estrangement from self. Krumel and Geddes (2000) confirmed the existence of emotional dissonance as a consequence of emotional labor across service organizations. The real pain, however, may come from the totalizing and participatory nature of emotion labor within which identities are created and forfeited (Tracy, 2000). When emotional control becomes diffused and pervasive, self-participation in that process becomes difficult to avoid and painful to participate in (Tracy, 2000).

Emotional intelligence also can be used by self-serving individuals to manipulate others in ways that maintain an unjust status quo (Harlos & Pinder, 2000). Although they may be few in number, individuals can become adept at reading and managing their own and others' emotions in ways that allow them to maintain senseless or harmful positions of dominance (Hearn, 1993). For instance, studies of domestic violence have identified among men who batter women a personality that grows inwardly calm and more controlled while appearing to go into an uncontrollable rage (Jacobson & Gottman, 1998). The ability to appear threatening and out-of-control while remaining inwardly calm is an effective way to terrorize others into submission. Although individuals in work settings may not use their emotional intelligence to terrorize, it is not difficult to imagine that they could use it to control and quiet opposing voices. In fact, acts of domination themselves tend to be highly emotional (Fineman, 2000b; Hearn, 1993).

It also is not difficult to imagine a highly controlled and hostile response to emotionally intelligent attempts to challenge sexist or racist practices at work. Not only is it possible for unscrupulous individuals to use emotional intelligence to help maintain an unjust status quo, but emotional intelligence can also be appropriated at the organizational level to terrorize, manipulate, and control employees. By co-opting the term "emotional intelligence," it is possible for managers to reinforce the rationalization of organizational emotions. Already emotional intelligence tests are being given to employees with the understanding that those who fail may be excluded from promotions or may be subject to intensive emotion training that indoctrinates a single form of emotional expression (Fineman, 2000a). In this way emotional intelligence can be used as an ideological construct that hegemonically reinforces the very structures it seems to oppose.

Emotionally intelligent individuals have a choice between using their abilities for acts of good and acts of evil. One interesting question is how a choice is made. A simple response would be that ethical people make ethical emotional intelligence related decisions. However, people are not all good or bad, ethical or unethical. Each individual contains within them a simultaneous coexistence of good and bad, right and wrong. Consequently, "emotion marks and expresses moral outrage and gives force to the relational obligations. Listening carefully to the emotional pulse of an organization should give researchers and members clues to its ethical health" (Waldron, 2000, p. 79). Future research should examine how the emotional intelligence dialectic between good and bad is understood and managed by organizational members. A place to begin such research would be through understanding emotional intelligence as a complex, interactive process. Rather than constructing emotional intelligence as either guaranteeing or destroying social harmony, emotional intelligence may be better understood as one more inner and interactive resource that individuals and organizations bring with them to the struggle for interpretive control in politicized work settings.

## EMOTIONAL INTELLIGENCE IN CONTEXT

Although contextual issues related to emotional intelligence have been discussed indirectly throughout this paper, it is also important to consider context in a more direct manner. Emotional intelligence is shaped and understood through the context in which it is enacted. Clearly different contexts demand different emotional expression and experiences. There are numerous ways in which context can be explored. For example, context may be dependent on the unique organizational culture (Van Maanen & Kunda, 1989), by the demands of a profession (Pierce, 1996), or by the larger cultural setting within which an organization is set (Krone, Chen, Sloan, & Gallant, 1997; Krone & Morgan, 2000). Furthermore, context may be historical, power related, or normative (Tracy, 2000). As a result of the complexity of organizational context, emotional intelligence can be studied in terms of its unique enactment within an organization or as it is enacted across organizations. Culture will be discussed to illustrate the potential of context in the scholarly examination of emotional intelligent.

Many cultural pressures influence the enactment of emotional intelligence in organizations. At the level of the organization, the unique culture influences how emotions are enacted (Van Maanen & Kunda, 1989), in part through the construction and reconstruction of organization level emotion rules (Waldron, 1994). Whereas some rules can be found across organizations, other rules such as heuristic rules, are unique to the demands of an organizational culture. Disney provides an excellent example of how organizational culture influences emotional experience (Van Maanen & Kunda, 1989).

Not only does the organizational culture influence emotional expression, but the demands of a profession or occupation also influence emotional expression. For example, litigators (especially men) tend to use intimidation and strategic friendliness emotional labor strategies in order to be successful in their profession (Pierce, 1996) and the cruise ship industry demands that employees be constantly on stage (Tracy, 2000). Finally, the broader culture within which the organization is set also influences emotional experiences. For example, whereas Western organizations tend to dichotomize the expression of emotions from rationality, Chinese workers view emotions as inextricably intertwined with rationality (Krone et al., 1997). Consequently, Chinese managers provide more holistic metaphors of emotional experiences than Western managers (Krone & Morgan, 2000). As a result of their tendency to integrate emotional experiences, Chinese managers may display high levels of emotional intelligence (Krone et al., 1997). The cultural implications of emotion rules can best be understood in multinational organizations within which multiple cultures operate. For example, whereas Japanese men often touch other men at work to show care and cohesion, men from the United States tend to interpret this behavior as threatening their masculinity (Hamada, 1996). When cultural issues such as race and gender intersect, an even more complex vision of context can be created. For example, African American women and European American women express conflict both similarly and differently. Although both African American women and European American women tended to report a desire to reduce conflict, African American women reduced conflict by confronting it and European American women reduced conflict by avoiding it (Shuter & Turner, 1997). Clearly context at the level of culture has multiple levels and layers of potential analysis. Depending on which cultural arena one explores, it is possible to conduct interesting analysis of emotional intelligence at the individual, organizational, and cross-organization levels.

## DISCUSSION

Although the dimensions of emotional intelligence have been discussed as if they were separate and distinct, a much more complex understanding of emotional intelligence is created when the dimensions are viewed as comprised of fuzzy instead of absolute lines. Because the lines are fuzzy, components of emotional intelligence can be understood as interactive and complex. In other words, there are a complex and fluid set of connections between the components. Whereas researchers may choose to examine the components of emotional intelligence separately in an attempt to provide depth in their exploration, it is important to emphasize the relationship between the components. Furthermore, it is imperative that emotional intelligence be understood as a process, and not merely as an outcome. Conceptualizing emotional intelligence as an outcome would not only oversimplify a complex issue, but would distort our understanding of emotional intelligence as communication.

As apparent in the literature reviewed in this article, much of our understanding of emotional intelligence comes from integrating literature on emotions in organizations. The question becomes, should we study emotional intelligence as a distinct theoretical framework? Or should researchers continue to study the components of emotional intelligence within other theoretical frameworks? There are strong arguments for both positions. Those who would argue against the study of emotional intelligence could legitimately claim that the use of the term "intelligence" suggests that the only way to legitimize emotions in organizations is to use an intelligence metaphor. This may appropriate and subordinate emotions to rationalized ends. This appropriation can be seen occurring in the popular use of the construct by both consultants and practitioners (Fineman, 2000a). On the other hand, the term "intelligence" may elevate the importance of emotions in organizations, creating a discourse in organizations that could lead to a greater acceptance of real emotions within organizations. Furthermore, emotional intelligence, as discussed in this paper, provides a framework that can be used to draw together multiple literatures examining affect and emotions in organizations. This framework can be used, then, to provide a clearer understanding of the role of emotions in organizations. Although we believe that emotional intelligence should be used as a framework to clarify our understanding of emotions in organizations, we urge a sensitivity to the destructive possibilities of emotional intelligence. Instead of relinquishing the term, scholars should continue to explore the concept while questioning the current use of emotional intelligence for commodified ends.

Emotional intelligence can be divided into six distinct but related elements. Managing self-experienced emotions is defined as the ability to identify and reframe the emotions we experience. Closely related to managing experienced emotions is managing self-expressed emotions. Managing self-expressed emotions occurs through both the expression and suppression of emotions.

Reading/managing others' experienced emotions is the identification and management of others' emotions. Managing others' expressed emotions has the most obvious connection to existing organizational communication research. The literature on emotionality in organizations indicates two means of emotion management in organizations: managerial behavior and cultural manipulation. Depending on the type of management tactics, emotion management may be ineffective (Sutton & Rafaeli, 1988) or successful (Sutton, 1991). Cultural management can be devastatingly effective, at least in part because it is expected and accepted within general organizing processes. Emotional intelligence is usually framed in terms of its constructive potential. However, there is also potential for unethical manipulation, suggesting a destructive side to emotional intelligence. Researchers need to examine all of the possible outcomes of emotional intelligence, and not just the positive aspects discussed by popular media sources. This means examining both the constructive and destructive possibilities of emotional intelligence

## Future Research

It is important for researchers to provide a balanced examination of emotional intelligence. Organizational researchers' inclination may be to focus on emotion management of others because of its obvious link to traditional top-down managerial control over workers. However, organizations are equally likely to be affected by the self-emotion management of workers and managers as well as the ability of managers and workers to read each others' emotions. An ideal examination of emotional intelligence would include all four aspects of emotional intelligence in research through either an interpretative analysis of themes, a quantitative analysis of main and interaction effects, or a creative combination of interpretive and quantitative research.

Because of the lack of research on emotional intelligence in the communication literature, the area is wide open for scholars to explore. A number of interesting questions and research projects present themselves. One interesting question involves the expression of emotional intelligence across cultures. It is important to understand both cultural differences and points of intersection that can create a dialogue between cultural groups within organizations. Consequently, understanding emotional intelligence across cultures would help inform culture-related issues in organizations.

Emotional intelligence in organizations offers a rich arena for organizational communication research. It is important to fully explore each of the three dimensions of emotional intelligence, both separately and in interaction with each other, using both interpretive and quantitative methods. Interpretive scholars should explore the meaning of emotional intelligence in organizations in order to generate a richer understanding of the construct. For example, how do people perceive themselves and others using emotional intelligence in organizations? How do organizational members choose between constructive and destructive emotional intelligence? What are the extent of the constructive and destructive uses of emotional intelligence? These questions seem best understood through interviews, observations, group discussions, and other forms of creative interpretive research.

Quantitative scholars can also advance our understanding of emotional intelligence in organizations in creative ways. Each of the emotional intelligence constructs should be explored in terms of what makes a person emotionally intelligent and how to identify emotionally intelligent people. Furthermore, it is important to understand if emotional intelligence is situational, trait like, or a combination of both. Traditional paper and pencil measures of self-perceived behavior is inadequate to test an interactive construct such as emotional intelligence. Instead, creative measures are required. For example, self-emotion management may be tested, in part, by asking individuals to list the emotions they have experienced. The ratio of positive to negative emotions listed, the total number of emotions listed, and the varying degrees to which individuals remember experiencing emotions may all indicate emotional intelligence. For example, does a person list both joy and anger? Does the individual identify experiencing varying degrees of anger such as annoyed, irritated, miffed, and so forth? Although listing emotions may not identify all of the emotions ever experienced by a given person, it may provide an understanding of the emotional repertoire available to a person at any given point in time. It is then possible to explore strategies for expressing emotions and identifying strategies that are perceived as most appropriate by others. Other creative research projects may use computer animation to determine the ability of participants to read complex emotional expressions.

We have attempted to provide a starting point from which research on emotional intelligence can proceed. Because of its communicative nature, emotional intelligence deserves adoption and extensive study by organizational communication researchers. Although emotional intelligence was popularized in the popular culture by Goleman's (1995) book, emotional intelligence was initially recognized by scholars and remains an important academic construct. If communication scholars fail to take the lead in researching emotional intelligence, we will also fail to influence the conceptualization of a construct that may prove to have far-reaching organizational and social implications.

## REFERENCES

Abraham, R. (1999). Emotional intelligence in organizations: A conceptualization. *Genetic, Social, and General Psychology Monographs, 125,* 209–224.

Abraham, R. (2000). The role of job control as a moderator of emotional dissonance and emotional intelligence—outcome relationships. *Journal of Psychology, 134,* 169–184.

Ashforth, B. E., & Humphrey, R. H. (1993). Emotional labor in service roles: The influence of identity. *Academy of Management Review, 18,* 88–115.

Cook, E. T., Greenberg, M. T., & Kusche, C. A. (1994). The relations between emotional understanding, intellectual functioning, and disruptive behavior problems in elementary-school-aged children. *Journal of Abnormal Child Psychology, 22,* 205–219.

Davies, M., Stankov, L., & Roberts, R. D. (1998). Emotional intelligence: In search of an elusive construct. *Journal of Personality and Social Psychology, 75,* 989–1015.

Delia, J. G., O'Keefe, B. J., & O'Keefe, D. J. (1982). The constructivist approach to communication. In F. E. X. Dance (Ed.), *Human communication theory: Comparative essays* (pp. 147–191). New York: Harper & Row.

Deluga, R. J., & Perry, J. T. (1991). The relationship of subordinate upward influencing behavior, satisfaction and perceived superior effectiveness with leader-member exchanges. *Journal of Occupational Psychology, 64,* 239–252.

Day, D. V., & Crain, E. C. (1992). The role of affect and ability in initial exchange quality perceptions. *Group and Organization Management, 17,* 380–397.

Ekman, P., & Friesen, W. V. (1975). *Unmasking the face.* Englewood Cliffs, NJ: Prentice Hall.

Fiebig, G. V., & Kramer, M. W. (1998). A framework for the study of emotions in organizational contexts. *Management Communication Quarterly, 11,* 536–572.

Fiedler, F. E., & Link, T. G. (1994). Leader intelligence to knowledge construction: A sociogenetic process approach. In R. J. Sternberg & R. K. Wagner (Eds.), *Mind in context: Interactionist perspectives on human intelligence* (pp. 152–167). Cambridge, UK: Cambridge University Press.

Fineman, S. (1993). Organizations as emotional arenas. In S. Fineman (Ed.), *Emotion in organizations* (pp. 9–35). Newbury Park, CA: Sage.

Fineman, S. (2000a). Commodifying the emotionally intelligent. In S. Fineman (Ed.), *Emotion in organizations.* (2nd ed., pp. 101–114). London: Sage.

Fineman, S. (2000b). Emotional arenas revisited. In S. Fineman (Ed.), *Emotion in organizations.* (2nd ed., pp. 1–24). London: Sage.

Flam, H. (1993). Fear, loyalty and greedy organizations. In S. Fineman (Ed.), *Emotion in organizations* (pp. 58–75). Newbury Park, CA: Sage.

Frost, P. J., Dutton, J. E., Worline, M. C., & Wilson, A. (2000). Narratives of compassion in organizations. In S. Fineman (Ed.), *Emotion in organizations.* (2nd ed., pp. 25–45). London: Sage.

Gardner, H. (1983). *Frames of mind.* New York: Basic Books.

Goleman, D. (1995). *Emotional intelligence.* New York: Bantam Books.

Goleman, D. (1998a). What makes a leader. *Harvard Business Review, 76*(6) 92–102.

Goleman, D. (1998b). *Working with emotional intelligence.* New York: Bantam Books.

Hamada, T. (1996). Unwrapping Euro-American masculinity in a Japanese multinational corporation. In C. Cheng (Ed.), *Masculinities in organizations* (pp. 160–176). Thousand Oaks, CA: Sage.

Harlos, K. P., & Pinder, C. C. (2000). Emotion and injustice in the workplace. In S. Fineman (Ed.), *Emotion in organizations.* (2nd ed.; pp. 255–276). London: Sage.

Hearn, J. (1993). Emotive subjects: Organizational men, organizational masculinities and the (de)construction of "emotions." In S. Fineman (Ed.), *Emotion in organizations* (pp. 142–166). Newbury Park, CA: Sage.

Hochschild, A. R. (1983). *The managed heart: Commercialization of human feeling.* Berkeley: University of California Press.

Howard, N. (1993). The role of emotions in multi-organizational decision-making. *Journal of Operational Research Society, 44,* 613–623.

Isen, A. M., & Baron, R. A. (1991). Positive affect as a factor in organizational behavior. In L. L. Cummings & B. M. Staw (Eds.), *Research in organizational behavior 13* (pp. 1–53). Greenwich, CT: Jai Press.

Jacobson, N. S., & Gottman, J. M. (1998). *When men batter women: New insights into ending abusive relationships.* New York: Simon & Schuster.

Jaggar, A. M. (1989). Love and knowledge: Emotion in feminist epistemology. In A. M. Jaggar & S. R. Bordo (Eds.), *Gender/body/knowledge* (pp. 145–171). New Brunswick, NJ: Rutgers University Press.

Kitayama, S. (1996). Remembrance of emotional speech: Improvement and impairment of incidental verbal memory by emotional voice. *Journal of Experimental Social Psychology, 32,* 289–308.

Krone, K. J. (1992). A comparison of organizational, structural, and relationship effects on subordinates' upward influence choices. *Communication Quarterly, 40,* 1–15.

Krone, K. J. (1994). Structuring constraints on perceptions of upward influence and supervisory relationships. *Southern Communication Journal, 59*, 215–226.

Krone, K. J., Chen, L., Sloan, D. K., & Gallant, L. M. (1997). Managerial emotionality in Chinese factories. *Management Communication Quarterly, 11*, 6–50.

Krone, K. J., & Morgan, J. M. (2000). Emotion metaphors in management: The Chinese experience. In S. Fineman (Ed.), *Emotion in organizations* (2nd ed., pp. 83–100). London: Sage.

Kruml, S. M. & Geddes, K. (2000). Exploring the dimensions of emotional labor: The heart of Hochschild's work. *Management Communication Quarterly, 14*, 8–49.

Lazarus, R. S. (1991). Cognition and motivation in emotion. *American Psychologist, 46*, 352–367.

Lee, J., & Jablin, F. M. (1995). Maintenance communication in superior-subordinate work relationships. *Human Communication Research, 22*, 220–257.

Martin, J., Knopoff, K., & Beckman, C. (1998). An alternative to bureaucratic impersonality and emotional labor: Bounded emotionality at The Body Shop. *Administrative Science Quarterly, 43*, 429–469.

Martinez-Pons, M. (1997). The relation of emotional intelligence with selected areas of personal functioning. *Imagination, Cognition and Personality, 17*, 3–13.

Mayer, J. D., DiPaolo, M., & Salovey, P. (1990). Perceiving the affective content in ambiguous stimuli: A component of emotional intelligence. *Journal of Personality Assessment, 54*, 772–781.

Mayer, J. D., & Geher, G. (1996). Emotional intelligence and the identification of emotion. *Intelligence, 22*, 89–113.

Mayer, J. D., & Salovey, P. (1993). The intelligence of emotional intelligence. *Intelligence, 17*, 433–442.

Mehrabian, A. (2000). Beyond IQ: Broad-based measurement of individual success potential or "emotional intelligence." *Genetic, Social, and General Psychology Monographs, 126*, 133–239.

Messerschmidt, J. W. (1996). Managing to kill: Masculinities and the space shuttle Challenger explosion. In C. Cheng (Ed.), *Masculinities in organizations* (pp. 29–53). Thousand Oaks, CA: Sage.

Mumby, D. K, & Putnam, L. L. (1992). The politics of emotion: A feminist reading of bounded rationality. *Academy of Management Review, 17*, 465–486.

Oatley, K., & Jenkins, J. M. (1992). Human emotions: Function and dysfunction. *Annual Review of Psychology, 43*, 55–85.

Petrides, K. V,. & Furnham, A. (2000). Gender differences in measured and self-estimated trait emotional intelligence. *Sex Roles, 42*, 449–461.

Pierce, J., (1996). Rambo litigators: Emotional labor in a male-dominated occupation. In C. Cheng (Ed.), *Masculinities in organizations* (pp. 1–28). Thousand Oaks, CA: Sage.

Putnam, L. L., & Mumby, D. K. (1993). Organizations, emotion and the myth of rationality. In S. Fineman (Ed.), *Emotion in organizations* (pp. 36–57). Newbury Park, CA: Sage.

Rafaeli, A., & Sutton, R. I. (1987). Expression of emotion as part of the work role. *Academy of Management Review, 12*, 23–37.

Salovey, P., & Mayer, J. D. (1990) Emotional intelligence. *Imagination, Cognition and Personality, 9*, 185–211.

Shuler, S., & Sypher, B. D. (2000). Seeking emotional labor: When managing the heart enhances the work experience. *Management Communication Quarterly, 14*, 50–89.

Shuter, R., & Turner, L. (1997). African American and European American women in the workplace: Perceptions of conflict communication. *Management Communication Quarterly, 11*, 74–96.

Sias, P. M., & Jablin, F. M. (1995) Differential superior-subordinate relations, perceptions of fairness, and coworker communication. *Human Communication Research, 22*, 5–38.

Snow, R. E. (1994). Abilities in academic tasks. In R. J. Sternberg & R. K. Wagner (Eds.). *Mind in context: Interactionist perspectives on human intelligence* (pp. 3–37). Cambridge, UK: Cambridge University Press.

Sutton, R. I. (1991). Maintaining norms about expressed emotion: The case of bill collectors. *Administrative Science Quarterly, 36*, 245–268.

Sutton, R. I., & Rafaeli, A. (1988). Untangling the relationship between displayed emotions and orga-nizational sales: The case of convenience stores. *Academy of Management Journal, 31,* 461–487.

Tolich, M. B. (1993). *Riding the waves of culture: Understanding diversity in global business.* Chicago: Irwin.

Tracy, S. J. (2000). Becoming a character for commerce: Emotion labor, self-subordination, and dis-cursive construction of identity in a total institution. *Management Communication Quarterly, 14,* 90–128.

Tracy, S. J., & Tracy, K. (1998). Emotion labor at 911: A case study and theoretical critique. *Applied Communication Research, 26,* 390–411.

Vaillant, G. E., & Davis, J. T. (2000). Social/emotional intelligence and midlife resilience in school-boys with low tested intelligence. *American Journal of Orthopsychiatry, 70,* 215–222.

Van Maanen, J., & Kunda, G. (1989). "Real feelings": Emotional expression and organizational cul-ture. In B. M. Staw & L. L. Cummings (Eds.), *Research in organizational behavior* (Vol. 11, pp. 43–103). Greenwich, CT: JAI Press.

Wagner, R. K. (1994). Context counts: The case of cognitive-ability testing for job selection. In R. J. Sternberg & R. K. Wagner (Eds.), *Mind in context: Interactionist perspectives on human intelli-gence* (pp. 133–151). Cambridge, UK: Cambridge University Press.

Waldron, V. R. (1994). Once more, with feeling: Reconsidering the role of emotion in work. In S. A. Deetz (Ed.), *Communication yearbook 17* (pp. 388–416). Thousand Oaks, CA: Sage.

Waldron, V. R. (2000). Relational experiences and emotion at work. In S. Fineman (Ed.), *Emotion in organizations* (2nd ed., pp. 64–82). London: Sage.

Waldron, V. R., & Krone, K. J. (1991). The experience and expression of emotion in the workplace: A study of a corrections organization. *Management Communication Quarterly, 4,* 287–309.

Wayne, S. J., & Ferris, G. R. (1990). Influence tactics, affect, and exchange quality in supervisor-sub-ordinate interactions: A laboratory experiment and field study. *Journal of Applied Psychology, 75,* 487–499.

Wayne, S. J., & Liden, R. C. (1995). Effects of impression management on performance ratings: A longitudinal study. *Academy of Management Journal, 38,* 232–260.

Weisinger, H. (1998). *Emotional intelligence at work.* San Francisco: Jossey-Bass.

# CHAPTER CONTENTS

• Professionalism                                             232
    *Codes of Ethics*                     233
    *Body of Knowledge*                   236
    *Accreditation and Licensing*         238
    *Autonomy*                            239
    *Public Service*                      241
    *Power Approach*                      241
    *Summary of Implications*             242

• Social Responsibility                                       243
    *Social Responsibility and the Press*          244
    *Corporate Social Responsibility*              247
    *Social Responsibility and Public Relations*   251
    *Summary of Implications*                      253

• Implications for Ethical Decision Making in Public Relations   254

• Conclusions and Implications                                256

• References                                                  259

# 7 Professionalism and Social Responsibility: Foundations of Public Relations Ethics

LOIS A. BOYNTON
*University of North Carolina at Chapel Hill*

The primary foundations of public relations ethics literature focus on professionalism and social responsibility. This manuscript traces the roots of the two concepts. The discussion of professionalism includes its trait-related definitions as well as the emerging power-based approach to understanding professions. The roots of public relations' emphasis on social responsibility can be traced through both journalism and business/organizational communication disciplines. In the last few decades, public relations has contributed its own concepts for socially responsible practices—issues management and values advocacy. Theoretical foundations of deontology and teleology contribute to the understanding of how professionalism and social responsibility contribute to ethical decision making among public relations practitioners. A combination of duty-based and utilitarian foci may help practitioners balance their multifaceted loyalties to their organizations, profession, society, and themselves.

Most public relations practitioners, at some point in their careers, will face decisions that involve ethical consequences. Some encompass personal clashes with management policies or organizational norms; others address differences in an organization's interests and those of its publics. Some situations are fraught with poor judgments and others reflect sound reasoning. Although many decisions may not be as fateful as those surrounding the Exxon Valdez oil spill or the Johnson & Johnston Tylenol tampering incident (Center & Jackson, 1995), there are decisions to be made, rules and norms to be considered, and consequences to live with.

The dominant frames of reference for the discussion of public relations ethics are professionalism and social responsibility, two concepts that form the foundation to educate practitioners, discuss professional dilemmas, and legitimize the practices and ethical nature of public relations. Although status often takes prece-

---

Correspondence: Lois A. Boynton, School of Journalism and Mass Communication, University of North Carolina at Chapel Hill, 397 Carroll Hall, CB# 3365, Chapel Hill, NC 27599-3365; email: lboynton@email.unc.edu

*Communication Yearbook 26*, pp. 230–265

dence in the literature, social responsibilities also are encouraged. However, both concepts are complex, and scholars often disagree on even the most basic issues. For example, whether public relations is, in fact, a profession has been bantered about by practitioners, scholars, and the discipline's critics for more than a half century. Further, social responsibility has been discussed independently as well as a subset or goal of professionalism. Although rooted in both corporate and journalism ethics, social responsibility's common backgrounds are not typically discussed in tandem.

The purpose of this manuscript is to provide a detailed discussion of the two primary underpinnings of public relations ethics—professionalism and social responsibility. The analysis draws not only from public relations literature, but also scholarly work within organizational communication, journalism, professional ethics, business ethics, and philosophy. The discussion begins with the roots and complexities of professionalism.

## PROFESSIONALISM

Public relations traditionally has drawn on the concept of professionalism to show a responsible commitment to society and to reinforce a credible image. Practitioners wrestle with the implications of professionalism as a means of gaining legitimacy, offering public service, and standardizing ethical ideals. But whether public relations is a profession or merely incorporates some professional characteristics has been argued extensively in academic and trade literature (Baker, 1993; Bissland & Rentner, 1989; Bivins, 1993; Decker, 1963; Jackson, 1988; Moss, 1950; Nelson, 1994b; Shoemaker & Reese, 1996; Wright, 1993; Wu, Weaver, & Johnson, 1996). Ironically, the most recognized proponent of public relations—Edward Bernays—did not consider his occupation to be a profession, but rather a vocation because of its focus on economic gain over public service (Baker, 1993). Others have deemed public relations a semiprofession because it does not meet all of the characteristics associated with a profession, including specialized skills, occupational autonomy, and self-regulation (Bissland & Rentner, 1989; Etzioni, 1969). In order to determine professional aspects of the field, it is important to define the concept. Unfortunately, this is no easy task; a single definition has not emerged (Bayles, 1988).

Historically, the criteria of a profession required knowledge mastery and public declaration of a commitment to high standards (Barker, 1992). By the 1800s, an individual's character was an important demonstration of professionalism to engender public approval and acceptance as a profession. The Industrial Revolution ushered in the expansion of the concept beyond doctors, lawyers, and ministers, and by the 1900s, knowledge and skill surpassed reputation and public standing as vital characteristics of professionals. McDowell (1991) and Reeck (1982) contend that both the mastery of skills and character traits are essential elements of today's professions because they combine an internal commitment to extensive training and external commitment to service to others.

Today, the term most often is defined by specific attributes. These features typically include: (a) specialized knowledge based on extensive training, accreditation, or licensing; (b) a greater sense of public service than self-serving interests, reflecting a high level of responsibility toward clients, peers, and society; (c) autonomy to practice specialized skills independently; and (d) self-control and self-regulation, typically signified by a voluntary commitment to codes of ethical standards (Barber, 1988; Bayles, 1988; Hughes, 1988; Labacqz, 1985; Millerson, 1964; Page, 1975; Sallot, Cameron, & Lariscy, 1997).

Other characteristics include wide societal recognition, organization through associations, loyalty to colleagues, and job commitment (Kultgen, 1988). Both Barber (1988) and Kultgen (1988) have argued that there are different levels of professionalism, depending on the extent to which these attributes apply. For example, lawyers and doctors are at a higher level of professional development than social workers or communication practitioners, reflecting differences in autonomy and public service issues.

Standards of professionalism set by public relations practitioners mirror those of other professions: an established curriculum, broad autonomy, a self-governed organization able to reprimand members, and an established code of ethics (Nelson, 1994b; Wright, 1981; Wylie, 1994). Bissland and Rentner (1989) argued that public relations has acquired some of the attributes of a profession with established codes, a body of knowledge, and accreditation systems. Sallot, Cameron, and Lariscy (1997) found that practitioners they surveyed generally agreed that public relations has established norms and ethics codes, an accreditation process, and skills specific to the vocation; however, the field still lacked business and organization status as well as standards for licensing. The following sections further explain the key components of professionalism, particularly regarding how they are applied in the public relations profession, beginning with ethics codes.

Codes of Ethics

A consistent element throughout these definitions of professionalism is the existence of ethical norms. Reeck (1982) contended "[E]thical choice is a built-in feature of professional work. Without ethics no one can be professional in the full meaning of the term" (p. 18). These norms usually are standardized into ethics codes, established standards to guide behavior of professionals (Harris, 1994; Jackson, 1994; Olson, 1999).

Harris (1994) explained that ethics codes were considered more essential as professions became more complex and society intensified its scrutiny of professional behavior. "It is not that people generally acted unprofessionally before there were codes; what we get is a codification of existing good practice" (p. 109). Codes evolve as problems and new professional and societal issues arise

(Donaldson, 1989; Harris, 1994; Seib & Fitzpatrick, 1995). In fact, Hayry and Hayry (1994) argued that those professions that decline to change with the times often face substantial pressure from society and perhaps legal regulation. Designed to steer professionals through daily decision-making, codes can identify ethical expectations for novices and deter government intervention (Bovet, 1993; Jurgensen & Lukaszewski, 1988; Sieb & Fitzpatrick, 1995; Wright, 1993).

Additionally, codes need to be evaluated periodically to ensure they remain applicable to a profession. Hayry and Hayry (1994) explained, "Since human interests, preferences, values and desires are subject to alterations, and since the development of professional practices and skills frequently enables professionals to meet an expanding sphere of needs, justifiable ethics codes must be open to change" (p. 143). An essential element of ethics code evolution and change is dialogue, particularly within the profession and, in some cases, with the publics and communities affected by the profession (Harris, 1994; Jackson, 1994). According to Jackson (1994), dialogue is needed "not just with a view to regular revisions of a code's wording, but to sustain a genuinely shared understanding of a code's meaning" (p. 122).

Bayles (1988) argued that professions prefer developing and enforcing their own standards because of the specialized issues they claim to face. Those outside the profession are not trained to make judgments on these issues. Although some critics have insisted that ethics codes can be static generalizations (Anderson, 1996), Kultgen (1988) argued that professionals should "view ethical codes as hypotheses for critical debate, not final dogmas" (p. 420). Jackson (1994) explained that dialogue is essential to understand how different practitioners within the same profession may interpret a code. As a result, "open disagreement is less damaging to a profession than hidden unacknowledged variations in interpretation" (p. 119) that ultimately may create confusion or damage reputations. Meyer (1987) drew similar conclusions for the communication profession, noting, "Because of the ambiguities in codes, it may be that their main benefit is in the process rather than the final product" (p. 20). Former *Public Relations Journal* Editor Michael Winkleman (1987) concurred, stating, "One of the chief benefits of creating a code is the process of putting it together, of thinking it through" (p. 32).

Public relations practitioners generally support an interaction and discussion approach to ethics as a means of elucidating norms and values to both practitioners and the public (Bivins, 1993). The difficulty that some critics have noted is the ineffectiveness of the professional socialization process to share ethical norms. Shamir, Reed, and Connell (1990) argued that professionalism in public relations has not been powerful enough to override personal ethics norms. Hence, clarifying values is essential for a practitioner to effectively address ethical dilemmas as they arise (Grunig, 2000; Parsons, 1993; Pratt, 1991). Grunig (2000) stressed the importance of solidifying public relations' professional values for the discipline and its practitioners to be accepted as valuable contributors to society. Today's practitioners also are called upon to counsel clients and employers about ethically sound behaviors. However, the dialogue at that point focuses on implementation rather than development of ethical standards (Kruckeberg, 1992).

The public relations profession at least appears to promote the concept of change through discussion, as evident by the regular updates of the Public Relations Society of America (PRSA) code of ethics, a product of some dialogue. Representative committees have drafted public relations standards, and legal counsel and membership input have been sought as the PRSA code evolved through the years. Stepping outside its own circle of influence, PRSA has solicited input from other professions, including law, accounting, and engineering, and has responded to concerns raised by regulatory organizations including the Securities and Exchange Commission and the Federal Trade Commission (Carey, 1957; Decker, 1963; Jackson, 1988; Lee, 1951).

Whether PRSA fulfilled the dialogue criterion is questionable, since the lion's share of articles in its official publication only mentioned the existence of a code of standards. Public Relations Journal, the official publication of PRSA, included about 400 articles on ethics throughout its more than 50 years, but most lack depth of discussion. The vast majority of articles, 80%, merely mentioned the existence of the association ethics code, and very little discussion on ethical foundations or decision-making appeared in its pages (Boynton, 1999). PRSA executives attempted to generate interest and dialogue about ethical issues, and *Public Relations Journal* published an ethics column in the 1980s (Cooper, 1984; McCammond, 1983, 1987). However, there remained a discomfort by members to publicly discuss what can—and does—go wrong in public relations (Jurgensen & Lukaszewski, 1988).

Despite efforts to formalize ethical norms in public relations, critics have pointed to a number of shortfalls. Because it is difficult to define the field of public relations and what constitutes ethical behavior, the codes can be ambiguous, lacking in substance, inconsistently applied, and generally difficult to enforce (Kruckeberg, 1993; L'Etang, 1996; Olasky, 1985; Sieb & Fitzpatrick, 1995). Wright (1993) asserted that ethics codes "are only as good as those who subscribe to them, and don't reward people for their ethical behavior" (p. 14).

Professional associations or individual companies typically develop codes of ethics, thereby limiting enforcement to members or employees who constitute only a fraction of those involved in public relations. That is, for example, only members of PRSA must ascribe to its code of ethics. As only about one tenth of public relations practitioners are members of professional associations such as PRSA and International Association of Business Communicators (Sieb & Fitzpatrick, 1995), code clout is seriously limited. Additionally, very few practitioners have been disciplined in the code's 50-year history. To avoid punishment, a practitioner may merely resign association membership (Budd, 1991; Pratt, 1991; Wright, 1993).

Although some PRSA members favored publishing ethics violations as part of the enforcement process, the association has protected the privacy of violators and has not publicly announced the results of its investigations (Pratt, 1991). Pratt argued that improved enforcement would not only reinforce ethical behavior among practitioners but also demonstrate the profession's commitment to self-governance and high ethical standards. Problems are promulgated because code stipulations can conflict, particularly on the broadest scale, such as conflict between serving client and public interests (Bivins, 1993; Iggers, 1998; Meyer, 1987; Schmuhl, 1984).

Public relations codes are not the only ones facing criticism. Professional ethics critics have lodged complaints in general that ethics codes are self-serving, designed to protect professional status, and can be inflexible, vague, or unenforceable. Interpretation of code provisions can vary from professional to professional, which also may create inconsistent practices (Harris, 1994; Jackson, 1994; Labacqz, 1985).

Although public relations codes are considered flawed, the continued growth in the number of organizations with formalized codes may validate the practice of codifying certain standards, particularly as they reflect the responsibilities that practitioners have toward the public. Rather than merely being a laundry list of proper etiquette or injunctions against poor behavior, codes should address professional character, argued Labacqz (1985). "Codes may be couched in actional language ('do this,' 'avoid that'), but their meaning emerges only when we look behind these specifics to a sense of the overall picture of the type of person who is to embody those actions" (p. 71). Although the ethics code is a common element in defining the attributes of professionalism, other factors also typify professional behavior. These factors include an established body of research knowledge, accreditation or licensing of professionals, autonomy to practice specialized skills, and a public service priority. Each one will be addressed in the next section, beginning with the commitment to training.

Body of Knowledge

The codification of ethics is perhaps the most often cited characteristic of professions; however, other facets must be included as well. Professionals in general are committed to extensive initial and ongoing training to master and maintain specialized skills based on a body of knowledge, a recognized collection of research specific to the discipline (Airaksinen, 1994; Chadwick, 1994; Fulford, 1994; Laczniak & Murphy, 1993; Labacqz, 1985; Sieb & Fitzpatrick, 1995). The medical community educates future doctors, nurses, and physician assistants not only in basic sciences and medical techniques but also regarding legal issues and patient relations, for example. Attorneys have had extensive education in federal, state, and local laws; courtroom practices; and public speaking (Fulford, 1994; Marston, 1968).

Proper ethical conduct also is part and parcel of valid professional training, according to Labacqz (1985). Novices typically learn about expectations and ideals from other professionals who serve as role models. Although this socialization process can reinforce positive behaviors, it also can bolster negative conduct or discourage exploration of values and practices. As a result, most professions require continuing education and, in some instances, licensing to ensure practitioners not only improve skills but also understand the ethical dimensions of their activities.

Public relations is considered a rather new profession, and training and education specific to the discipline began nearly 80 years ago. The first public relations undergraduate course was offered in 1923 at New York University; today more than 200 colleges and universities offer public relations classes (Cutlip, Center, & Broom, 2000). A graduate program was introduced in 1947 at Boston University, and around a dozen colleges provided undergraduate public relations programs in the 1950s. By 1981, 51 schools provided graduate-level public relations programs (Hesse, 1984). According to the 1999 study by the Commission on Public Relations Education (1999), about 70 master's programs are now in operation.

The public relations curriculum has seen changes through the decades, particularly as technology evolved and new communication venues became available. However, there has been consistent agreement since the early years that public relations training should include not only specific communication skills such as writing and public speaking, but also broad education in other disciplines including social sciences, foreign languages, business foundations, and philosophy. Practical experience through internships and apprenticeships also has received support by educators and advisers (Sallot, Cameron, & Lariscy, 1997; Fenton, 1977; Commission on Public Relations Education, 1999; Wylie, 1983). As communication became more widely recognized for its theoretical contributions (Lowery & DeFleur, 1995), educators also recommended courses in theory and research methods.

Despite some documented lapses in scrupulous behavior, training in proper ethical practices has been considered vital (Harrison, 1990; Pratt, 1991; Sallot, Cameron, & Lariscy, 1997). The initial professional training is considered crucial to establish theoretical and ethical foundations and develop specialized skills. Credence also has been given to continuing education to ensure public relations professionals improve abilities and address emerging issues surrounding technologies and practices (Marston, 1968; Paluszek, 1988). Training is provided through for-profit companies as well as colleges and universities, with a growing interest in distance learning (Commission on Public Relations Education, 1999; Nages & Truitt, 1987). In 1981, the Public Relations Society of America was permitted to grant continuing education units to those who completed professional development training (Jackson, 1988).

Additionally, public relations scholars and practitioners emphasize research and critical examination of the profession. Annotated bibliographies of public relations-related literature have been published since 1957 when the Foundation for Public Relations Research and Education issued its first edition, compiled by researcher Scott M. Cutlip. Scholarly journals devoted specifically to public relations emerged in the mid-1970s (Cutlip, Center, & Broom, 2000). By 1978, there were 20,000 titles listed in six editions of the bibliographic publication (Walker, 1978). However, Wylie (1983) expressed concern that public relations did not have a definitive body of knowledge. Three years later the Public Relations Society of America formed a committee to identify relevant literature, and the first Body of Knowledge outline was issued in 1988 (Cutlip, Center, & Broom, 2000; Jackson, 1988).

Despite this advancement, professional ethicists express concern about late-developing knowledge bases. Barber (1988) pointed out that emerging professions tend to pour their energies into developing an ethics code first, before other important aspects of professionalism—such as an established body of knowledge—are fully developed. "Unfortunately, because the knowledge on which their occupational performance is based is not highly developed, the codes they construct are full of vague generalities, and therefore hard for the individual practitioner to apply in concrete cases," he said (p. 38). This appears to be the case at least for PRSA, which introduced its ethics code in 1950 (Calver, 1951), seven years before the first public relations bibliography was issued and 38 years before its body of knowledge was officially established.

## Accreditation and Licensing

Closely tied to basic and continuing education is the practice of accrediting public relations professionals. Both Public Relations Society of America and International Association of Business Communicators, the two leading national public relations organizations, offer accreditation programs for their respective members who have at least five years of professional experience.

PRSA was the first national public relations organization to accredit its members, beginning in 1964. PRSA provides Accredited in Public Relations (APR) credentials, and IABC offers Accredited Business Communicator (ABC) certification for members who successfully complete written and oral exams. In 1998, PRSA began facilitating a Universal Accreditation Program, which cojoined the programs of eight public relations organizations. IABC continued its separate accreditation designation (IABC, 1999; Jackson, 1988; PRSA, 1999; Wright, 1981). The associations created the professional development designation to recognize practitioner abilities and improve the profession's reputation, although the latter benefit gains considerably more attention than the former (Wright, 1981).

Public relations accreditation has received mixed reviews. According to a national survey conducted several years ago, members of associations ranked accreditation more important than non-members did, but neither group gave it significant credence (Gilsdorf & Vawter, 1983; Pratt, 1991). Noted public relations ethics researcher Cornelius B. Pratt (1991) attributed this lukewarm reception to practitioner skepticism about the perceived value of association certification. This point is reflected in the fact that only a small percentage of members have obtained accreditation status (Cutlip, Center, & Broom, 2000; Forbes, 1986; Wright, 1981). However, researcher Donald K. Wright (1981) found that those practitioners who achieved accreditation tended to report more professional attributes, including high ethical standards.

Because voluntary accreditation lacks widespread support among public relations practitioners, it is not surprising that licensing has not been instituted. Although common among professions such as law and medicine, licensing is not required among many professional occupations, including journalism and public relations. A few practitioners have argued in favor of licensing as a means of solidifying what constitutes public relations, enforcing ethics codes, and improving the public's perception of the practice (Forbes, 1986; Wylie, 1983).

Although licensing received regular endorsement by the notable Edward Bernays (1983, 1986, 1992), the concept was widely perceived by public relations critics as, at minimum, impractical, and at most, a violation of the First Amendment (Lesly, 1986; Paluszek, 1988). If public relations has a role in contributing to the marketplace of ideas and free expression, licensing would infer competency requirements to communicate. Only state licensing would be permitted, but critics noted that state regulation would stifle public relations professionals' ability to practice their trade nationally and internationally (Cutlip, Center, & Broom, 2000; Lesly, 1986). Legislators surveyed by professor Bill Baxter (1986) said licensing should be enacted only if a profession could cause harm to society, a concern they said did not apply to public relations. Other legislators stated government intervention could restrict competition. Individual practitioners, not regulators, must govern appropriate behavior, opponents stated (Sieb & Fitzpatrick, 1995; Wright, 1993).

Autonomy

Another challenge facing the profession is the level of autonomy accessible to public relations practitioners. This concept involves not only on-the-job independence as Bissland and Rentner (1989) determined, but also the use of peer- and self-monitored controls such as ethics codes to guide appropriate behavior (Friedson, 1970; Jackson, 1988). Kultgen (1988) contended that high-level professions including law and medicine have greater ability to practice independently than lower-level ones. Bivins (1989a) argued that autonomy infers a certain level of objectivity when solving problems. In public relations, this facet involves practitioner ability to examine both the organization's and its publics' views and provide an unclouded recommendation.

However, public relations practitioners who serve as organization advocates may discover that loyalty to the organization is valued over objectivity (Bovet, 1993; Marston, 1968; Sharpe, 1986). Hence, autonomy can become a double-edged sword—public relations professionals who are at a high enough level in their organizations to provide objective advice may be expected to support the position of the organization's dominant coalition of managers (Parsons, 1993; Theus, 1995). Dominant coalition is a term coined by Cyert and March (1992) and applied to public relations by scholar James E. Grunig to describe the controlling group within an organization that sets organizational strategy and goals (Dozier, Grunig, & Grunig, 1995; Grunig, 1989).

Further, the individual's role or function may affect the extent of professionalism. That is, those who serve in lower organizational ranks and lack autonomy or general decision-making authority may not face the quantity or quality of ethical problems that those in supervisory or management roles do. Public relations roles have been defined in a number of ways in the last 20 years. Public relations researchers Glen Broom and George Smith (1979) categorized public relations practitioners into four categories in descending order of autonomy. The expert prescriber holds the greatest autonomy in an organization, taking charge of the public relations research and evaluation, and development and implementation of plans. The communications facilitator mediates the organization-publics relationship to ensure an effective dialog exists. The problem-solving process facilitator works primarily within the organization and collaborates with managers to maximize communication. Finally, the communication technician implements public relations plans and generally does not serve in managerial roles. Broom and Dozier (1986) determined through a noted longitudinal study that, although practitioners could employ all four roles, one role would dominate in their practice.

Several years later, Dozier (1992) narrowed the selection to two roles: the technician who performs assigned tasks and the manager who consults with executives, plans, and directs strategies. In the last several years, however, Leichty and Springston (1996) contested the technician-manager dichotomy, arguing that many practitioners perform both functions in tandem. They proposed four categories that defined roles within the context of stakeholder activity. "Internals" practice public relations at an organizational level, "traditional managers" work with a variety of stakeholders as part of the dominant coalition, "externals" address issues affecting those outside the organization, and "generalists" have a hybrid role. These researchers determined that public relations practitioners often assumed both technician and managerial roles in their jobs, some to a greater degree than others.

Early public relations researcher Albert Sullivan (1965) contended that public relations technician values involve creativity, productivity, and strategy, but did not particularly include ethical responsibilities (Grunig, 2000; Pearson, 1989a). Challenging this argument was researcher Thomas Schick (1996) who posited that technician activities not only involve ethical issues, but that these workers have autonomy to perform their tasks in an ethical or unethical manner. By working within a professional context, technicians are subject to the profession's guidelines; they are not absolved of responsibility because they have limited power or autonomy. This argument may provide a more accurate picture of public relations roles in light of business structural changes; that is, downsizing and corporate rightsizing might force ethical decision making to lower levels (Paradice & Dejoie, 1991; Schick, 1996).

## Public Service

As noted previously, autonomy has been tied to an interest in serving public needs. Professionals emphasize public service over self in the course of providing an indispensable service (Bissland & Rentner, 1989; Bivins, 1993; Bottery, 1995; Loevinger, 1996; Millerson, 1964; Smith, 1994). Public relations practitioners often serve as an organization's social conscience, Sieb and Fitzpatrick (1995) said, and executive Robert L. Dilenscheider (1999) recently called upon his peers to encourage their business owners and clients to "assume[e] greater responsibility for the lives their businesses affect" (p. 16). According to Sieb and Fitzpatrick (1995), a dual role exists, in which practitioners serve as "intermediaries between organizations and their publics in a role that requires adherence to public service and social responsibility" (p. 47; see also Kruckeberg, 1992; L'Etang, 1996).

Yet, despite an altruistic goal, critics have argued that public relations practitioners are inclined toward economic, not public service, ends (Ranney, 1977). Public relations professionals typically are responsible for improving and enhancing an organization's image and the trust the public has in it (Sieb & Fitzpatrick, 1995; Judd, 1989). As a result, society may not be the primary benefactor. There is an undercurrent of a self- or organization-centered goal to heighten credibility and advance professional status (Kruckeberg, 1992). This narrow focus of professionalism has led critics to seek alternative definitions of professionalism that do not rely so staunchly on traits or characteristics. One such alternative is the power approach.

## Power Approach

The long-standing approach to define professionalism through traits—adherence to codes, ascription to a body of knowledge, achievement of accreditation or licensing, establishment of autonomy, and aspiration to public service—has been challenged in recent years as outmoded (Grunig, 2000; Pieczka & L'Etang, 2001). Instead of focusing on organizational functions and roles, these authors have proposed examining professions regarding a "power approach" (Pieczka & L'Etang, 2001, p. 225) that defines the relationship of the practitioner and client within the larger society. Researchers and professionals have relied too heavily on an introverted and insulated look at public relations professionalism on personal and organizational levels to the exclusion of examining the social context, critics argue. Ultimately, the power ascribed to public relations is based on sociopolitical factors that may vary from one culture to another.

Ethicist Eric Mount, Jr. (1990) posited that professional ethics must include the contexts of behaviors; that is, the institutions in which individuals function and the meanings that surround those institutions. Professionals gain autonomy and privileges to practice specialized skills they provide society. Professions rely on established standards, usually formalized as ethics codes, to provide a checks-and-balance measure of occupational obligations and power. Ethics codes solidify certain ideals and expectations with which practitioners must comply to maintain their privileged status (Reamer, 1995; Welfel & Lipsitz, 1984).

The importance of the power argument can be seen in traditional, trait-based discussions of public relations. Ethicists argue that codes of ethics evolve based on social changes. That is, ethics are fundamentally values in action and, as a result, tend to change as society changes (Levy, 1972, 1973). For example, the Public Relations Society of America added code provisions addressing diversity as women and minorities gained status within the profession and societal regulations required equal job access (Boynton, 1999). Such changes reflect the function of public relations within the larger social context. The codes themselves, however, reinforce peer- and self-monitoring controls, issues that Grunig (2000) and Pieczka and L'Etang (2001) argue may limit the ultimate scope of professionalism in public relations.

## Summary of Implications

Professionalism in public relations has ostensibly been defined by specific traits—self-regulation through voluntary commitment to codes of ethical standards, specialized knowledge based on extensive training or licensing, autonomy to practice specialized skills independently, and a greater sense of public service than self-serving interests. Definitions that rely so strongly on traits point to some shortcomings in the consideration of public relations as a true profession.

First, professional associations such as PRSA and IABC develop and update public relations ethics codes. As a result, only association members are required to ascribe to these ethical standards. Profession-wide adherence to standardized ethics codes is thereby unenforceable and unachievable. Second, although public relations professionals have established a body of knowledge, critics have noted that emerging and semiprofessions tend to focus on ethics code development before the knowledge foundation is established. Instead, critics argue, the knowledge base should provide the solid foundation upon which ethics codes emerge. Without an emphasis on knowledge foundations before code development, the result may be trivialized codes or an incomplete or unstructured body of knowledge.

Third, accreditation and licensing, which allow practitioners to "profess" their knowledge and commitment to ethical standards, have not received significant support among public relations practitioners. Only a fraction of practitioners have been accredited through associations, and the designation remains optional. The lack of accreditation credibility within the profession precludes its perceived value externally. Fourth, the degree to which public relations practitioners are autonomous in their practice of ethical public relations has been argued in the literature. Those who work in lower levels and lack autonomy and decision-making authority may not face the magnitude of ethical problems that those above them do. Further, practitioners who work within an organization's dominant coalition may have greater decision-making authority, but a large number of practitioners do not make organization-level decisions. Finally, public relations practitioners have an altruistic goal to serve the public interest. Critics argue, however, that self- or organization-centered goals result in an emphasis on economic, not public service, gains.

The trend away from a larger social context may have affected the recognition of public relations as a full profession. More recent research, however, may direct the public relations profession beyond its insulated focus on personal and organizational goals. Instead, a power approach may more accurately define the relationship of the practitioner and client within the larger society. One avenue that may help public relations refocus on the societal context is the concept of social responsibility. The roots and implications of social responsibility theory are discussed in the following section.

## SOCIAL RESPONSIBILITY

Social responsibility, according to Wright (1976), is a value that specifies that every institution—from family to firm—is responsible for its members' conduct and can be held accountable for its actions. In addition to this public interest perspective, social responsibility is considered an ideal means of enhancing the professional credibility and decision-making clout of public relations practitioners (Judd, 1989; L'Etang, 1993; Wright, 1976). Hence, the concept is not solely one of selfless service, but also used for self-interest gains.

A contingent of well-known scholars including L'Etang (1993), Heath and Ryan (1989), Martinson (1994), Peterson (1966, 1974), Judd (1989), and Wright (1976) have examined the pros and cons of corporate and media social responsibility. There is an intriguing distinction made in the literature between the development of corporate social responsibility and social responsibility of the press. Although the press concept of social responsibility and the corporate concept of social responsibility have numerous similarities including common developmental timetables, discussions generally have remained distinct, even in the public relations literature where the two disciplines are likely to overlap.

Shades of social responsibility concerns emerged at the turn of the century as both businesses (and their publicists) and the press were spurned for public disinterest and sensational claims (Bernays, 1984; Goldman, 1984; Gross, 1966). The issue re-emerged in the decade following World War II when the press was admonished and advised by a group of academic media critics, and public relations practitioners and their business clients were challenged by consumer advocates (Abel, 1984; Ewen, 1996; L'Etang, 1996; Peterson, 1966). Likewise, activities surrounding the Civil Rights Movement and Watergate fueled a social responsibility surge well into the 1980s. Concepts of social responsibility honed by media and corporate/organizational critics and scholars contributed to the public relations profession's application of social responsibility ideals.

By the 1980s, public relations had unique social responsibility concepts and practices in its own right, including issues management and values advocacy (Bostdorff & Vibbert, 1994; Cheney & Vibbert, 1987; Heath, 1980, 1990). Dedication to social responsibility has been a cornerstone of public relations, evident by its incorporation in the profession's first code of standards issued by Ivy Ledbetter Lee in 1906 (Ewen, 1996), and each iteration of the Public Relations Society of America code since 1950 (Boynton, 2000).

In public relations, social responsibility often is positioned within the context of the Social Responsibility Theory of the Press (Peterson, 1966, 1974; Wright, 1976), perhaps due to the profession's journalistic roots and relationships. However, public relations involves not only mediated communication but also interpersonal communication (Bostdorff & Vibbert, 1994; Cheney & Vibbert, 1987). As a result, it is important to assess other perspectives to better understand public relations beyond media relations, including issues management, values advocacy, and enlightened self-interest (Bostdorff & Vibbert, 1994; Cheney & Vibbert, 1987; Heath, 1990; Heath & Ryan, 1989; L'Etang, 1993; Martinson, 1994). This discussion first explores the social responsibility theory of the press and its application to public relations.

Social Responsibility and the Press

The social responsibility press theory is based on the notion that with the power of freedom comes responsibility to the public interest. First Amendment press freedoms ensure few checks are placed on the media, particularly in comparison to for-profit businesses and nonprofit organizations. Such freedoms engender power that should be employed responsibly, media critics argued (Peterson, 1966). What that responsibility entails and who decides which public interests to serve, however, are not always clear.

Iggers (1998) indicated responsibility refers to providing people with the information necessary to participate in a democratic society. Other scholars identified concepts that were later codified, including truth, accuracy, fairness, honesty, avoiding conflicts of interest, and minimizing harm (Donaldson, 1989; L'Etang, 1996; Meyer, 1987; Siebert, 1974). Likewise, the term "public interest" is elusive in nature. It has been defined broadly as all sides of an issue and linked strongly to free speech tenets and libertarian ideals of robust debate in the marketplace of ideas (Abel, 1984; Donaldson, 1989). Specifically, the United States Supreme Court stated that public interest "encompasses the presentation of vigorous debate or controversial issues of importance and concern to the public" (Red Lion, 1969). Beyond a democracy context, the term remains relatively obscure. However, a glimpse into the philosophical and historical context may shed light on the intention of these terms.

The social responsibility concept, which gained strength around the turn of the twentieth century, made inroads with a change in philosophy regarding the capabilities of humankind. During the Age of Enlightenment of the seventeenth and eighteenth centuries, man was deemed rational and eminently qualified to sift for and find the truth (Mill, 1956; Milton, 1992; Peterson, 1974). With this libertarian philosophy, humans merely needed to apply their innate reason to distinguish truth from falsehood. Peterson (1966) noted, "By feeding his free mind from the open marketplace of ideas, man can discover the all-embracing truths which unify the universe and everything in it" (p. 37).

However, a shift in philosophical thinking occurred during the Industrial Revolution. As philosophers moved from a libertarian approach to one of social responsibility, they unveiled a potentially flawed humanity, neither purely rational nor incorruptible, and hence in need of protection. Although social responsibility theory did not discount the human ability to reason, humans were viewed "not so much irrational as lethargic" (Peterson, 1974, p. 100), and therefore easily manipulated. The press was chastised for snowballing sensationalism, half-truths and blatant falsehoods, and for generally disregarding the responsibilities of press freedoms (Peterson, 1974).

The media up until this point had espoused a libertarian philosophy of freedom from interference in the quest for truth. Press duties entailed informing the public, safeguarding liberty by watching government, serving the economic system through advertising, entertaining, and being self-sufficient. Peterson (1974) noted, "Freedom of the press, as originally conceived, was essentially a negative freedom which implied no standards of performance or responsibility" (p. 100). In the nineteenth century, however, editors and publishers began to link freedom and responsibility. The media, as the more "alert elements of the community," (p. 100) had to safeguard the citizenry.

Peterson (1966, 1974) contended that the social responsibility concept began with a libertarian foundation and added a media obligation dimension. The media's newfound obligation may have been predicated on the need to respond to growing criticism of its dubious practices. Despite libertarian roots of sorts, social responsibility press theory created something of a radical shift because libertarianism established neither a public right to know nor a moral obligation of the press. Perhaps publishers found an ally in a notion that permitted an expansion of power through public duty; perhaps it was merely a defensive measure to counter criticism and avoid outside interference.

This interest in journalistic responsibility and accountability gelled in the 1920s when the first industry-wide ethics code appeared, drafted by the American Society of Newspaper Editors. Schmuhl (1984), Peterson (1966), and Gross (1966) also noted the importance of the Report by the Commission on Freedom of the Press in 1947 and credited it with revitalizing an interest in media ethics and social responsibilities. The first volume of the report, supported by grants from Time, Inc., and Encyclopedia Britannica, Inc., and printed in March 1947, was written by a 13-member panel led by then University of Chicago Chancellor Robert Hutchins. Despite partial media sponsorship, the Commission drew members mostly from academia (Abel, 1984; Leigh, 1947).

Although the initial response by the media was "visceral hostility," (Schmuhl, 1984, p. 4–5) the so-called Hutchins Commission report may have gained credibility after the initial sting waned. An underlying potential for government intervention simmered throughout the report, despite insistence by its authors that "[t]he principle aim . . . is not to recommend more governmental action but to clarify the role of government in relation to mass communication" (Leigh, 1947, p. 81). The Commission recommended that the media, with their growing power and pervasiveness in society, could voluntarily accept responsibility for the quality and diversity of information it distributed to the American public.

But a veiled threat of governmental authority was apparent: "The Commission hopes that the press itself will recognize its public responsibility and obviate governmental action to enforce it" (p. 91). The original social responsibility concept does not infer government intervention; however, this element became visible in the Commission report and subsequent literature. Drechsel (1992), for example, noted that a key premise of the social responsibility theory is that "government intervention may be necessary if the press fails in significant ways to uphold its moral obligations" (p. 19).

The Commission report cited five duties of the press including accurate and accessible reports, and a forum for idea exchange that reflected society's diversity and goals (Leigh, 1947). First, the Commission called for a "truthful, comprehensive, and intelligent account of the day's events in a context which gives them meaning" (p. 21). Considered a "stalwart media principle," (Abel, 1984, p. 41) this stipulation addressed accuracy and dissemination of not only the facts but also the truth about the facts, and delineated fact from opinion (Leigh, 1947; Peterson, 1966). The second standard called upon the media to provide "a forum for the exchange of comment and criticism" (Leigh, 1947, p. 23). This criterion addressed the dissemination of all significant views, even if those views were unpopular or in conflict with those of the press (Abel, 1984; Leigh, 1947; Peterson, 1974).

The third Commission standard said the media should present "a representative picture of the constituent groups in the society" (Leigh, 1947, p. 26). This measure considered diversity of coverage, accurate portrayal of all social groups, and avoidance of stereotypes (Abel, 1984, Leigh, 1947). The fourth Commission standard required "the presentation and clarification of the goals and values of the society" (Leigh, 1947, p. 27). Peterson (1966, 1974) stressed that this provision required the media to respect accepted societal values and traditions, and to allow comment and clarification of values via such venues as editorial pages.

Lastly, the Hutchins Commission indicated the media should provide "full access to the day's intelligence" (Leigh, 1947, p. 28). This standard traditionally meant that the media should serve as an agent to the public in "breaking down barriers to the free flow of news" (Peterson, 1966, p. 43) and ensure the public has access to information necessary to make informed democratic decisions. The concept of the public's right to know was born from the Hutchins Commission, according to the literature. Some authors have indicated that this standard may also refer to the public's access to the media (Abel, 1984); however, most media authors contend this referred solely to the media's access to information for the public. Access to the media may be best addressed through the Commission's second standard—addressing comment and criticism (Leigh, 1947). The media accepted the first duty as its own; the remaining four, however, were often considered tantamount to press freedom interference (Peterson, 1966).

Christians (1986) credited the Commission with establishing social responsibility theory of the press as a valid mass media ethic. However, researchers have indicated many of the concepts espoused in the Hutchins report already were circulating through the media world. Still, the Commission's conclusions were not met with much enthusiasm (Gordon & Kittross, 1999; Peterson, 1966). Regardless of the underwhelming response at the time the report was issued, examples of all five of the Hutchins Commission standards exist in today's journalism and public relations ethics codes. Despite complaints and research reports that the media were unwilling to accept the bulk of the Commission's findings, it appears that, over time, the standards of social responsibility voiced by the Commission became part of today's media and public relations ethical tenets (Boynton, 2000).

Interest in press ethics codes surged again more than 20 years after the Commission report during periods of social upheaval surrounding the Civil Rights Movement, Vietnam War, and Watergate. A flurry of code updates by the broadcast industry in the 1960s and print journalism in the 1970s reflected both the public's sharp scrutiny and the media's renewed interest in accountability (Schmuhl, 1984). Print media associations considered adding teeth to their ethics codes through member sanctions but did not follow through (Meyer, 1987).

Social responsibility has implications for all communicators because of the appeal of serving the public interest. In addition to its press roots, social responsibility often is addressed within the context of business activity. Additionally, this concept had a significant impact on the public relations profession. The following section examines corporate social responsibility and the influence on public relations.

## Corporate Social Responsibility

Corporate magnate William Vanderbilt often is credited (although he denied it) with uttering the infamous phrase, "the public be damned," (Tedlow, 1979, p. 5) reinforcing the pervading nineteenth century notion that businesses acted on self-interest alone without concern for the good of society. By the turn of the century, the general public protested what it considered to be irresponsible behavior, and the American government ushered in regulations to force businesses to modify their self-centered practices. Despite advances through most of the twentieth century, an undercurrent of self-interest remained and public skepticism ebbed and flowed (Cheney & Vibbert, 1987; L'Etang, 1996).

In more recent decades, critics including Nobel Prize winner Milton Friedman (1994) and public relations executive Henry G. Manne (1970) echoed nineteenth century sentiments and reinforced libertarian notions. Friedman (1994) considered social responsibility to be socialistic, subversive, and incompatible with democracy; Manne (1970) regarded it as part of an "anti-free-enterprise campaign" that long plagued America.

In a capitalistic, market-driven society, the sole responsibility of corporations is to make legally profitable use of investor finances, and corporate executives are stewards of those investments. To spend company funds on social needs not approved by stockholders would be a form of taxation and ultimately a "suicidal impulse," stated Friedman (1994, p. 141). Individuals may spend their personal funds as they see fit, and independent business owners may invest in community goodwill, but they should not lose sight of the self-serving motives. "This may gain them kudos in the short run," he said, "but it helps to strengthen the already too prevalent view that the pursuit of profits is wicked and immoral and must be curbed and controlled by external forces" (p. 141).

Part of the difficulty may stem from what some authors say is an erroneous dichotomy. Social responsibility and profitability are not opposites (Aupperle, Carroll, & Hatfield, 1985), although this misconception of economics and ethics as antonyms has been propagated in research (Glover, Bumpus, Logan, & Ciesla, 1997; Hegarty, 1995; Hegarty & Sims, 1978). Economic ends are not wholly unethical ends. Instead, profit is a factor to consider in business accountability. If a company ceased to make money or went bankrupt, it no longer would be a responsible community participant (Heath, 1990; L'Etang, 1993). However, the self-interest perception magnified by Friedman (1994) and Manne (1970) still plagued many corporations as the public began to demand more of companies than their financial duties (Heath, 1990; L'Etang, 1993). No longer was it appropriate for an organization to assume that self-service would suffice. The public expected corporations to be responsible to the public interest and often discussed the ways corporations could be more responsible (Hagel, 1965).

In recent decades, nonprofit organizations have faced scrutiny similar to that of their for-profit counterparts. Despite the general perception that nonprofits have social responsibility objectives (Bowen, Nygren, Turner, & Duffy, 1994; Salamon, 1992), the motives of these service organizations were examined closely by fiscally wiser, more skeptical donors in the last two decades (Gergen, 1992; McLaughlin, 1995). Charity scandals, including fraud by the PTL Network televangelist Jim Bakker and financial misdeeds by former United Way of America President William Aramony (Scala, 1992), led donors and potential contributors to demand more information from charity organizations about how donations are used.

Nonprofit organizations became more responsible to donors and more keenly aware that they could not expect automatic support without accountability. Self-policing groups urged charities to maintain high levels of fiscal and administrative responsibility following the fallout of the Bakker scandal in the late 1980s

(McLaughlin, 1995; Olcott, 1992; Scala, 1992). Many nonprofit organizations did not balk. After all, the introspective, self-examination approach was much preferred over government intrusion, which could stifle the independent nature of nonprofits and perhaps contribute further to loss of public confidence (Magnusson, 1995; O'Connell, 1994). Discovering the hard way that there are costs associated with gaining public trust, many nonprofits re-examined problems and adopted proactive strategies. Research and priority setting were presented as valuable tools for building images and continuing growth, and led nonprofits into territory once occupied only by their for-profit counterparts (Himes, 1995; McLaughlin, 1995; Nunns, 1996; Skolnik, 1993).

Because social responsibility involves a number of different functions—communication, strategic planning, audience monitoring, and acting responsibly—typically it is addressed by more than one department of an organization, including public relations, legal, financial, and executive groups. The combination of perspectives is essential to ensure that the corporation accurately understands the values and needs of its constituents at any given time (Heath, 1990; L'Etang, 1993). L'Etang (1996) noted that social responsibility quite often has been a reactive measure when an organization responds to a concern or crisis. However, she stressed the importance of being proactive as well, anticipating needs before they reach crisis stage. It not only is important to take responsibility when something bad happens but to be accountable to the organization, its employees, and actions before problems arise. Similarly, Heath (1990) explained that social responsibility should include ongoing monitoring of situations and stakeholders so organizations may keep abreast of pervading views and potential problems.

Cheney and Vibbert (1987) noted that social responsibility involves both internal publics, most notably, employees; and external constituents, including customers, suppliers, community, and other stakeholders affected by a corporation's actions. According to Cheney (1995), responsibilities are owed to both internal and external publics, and addressing one without the other is incomplete and perhaps inappropriate.

An organization's success or failure could have tremendous effects on the employees. In times of prosperity, employees are able to keep their jobs and perhaps receive raises and promotions. In times of crisis, employees may lose not only salary but also a voice in and for the organization. Cheney (1995) argued that it is important to include internal publics when developing socially responsible policies and actions. He defined workplace democracy as organizational governance that balances employee views with organizational objectives and encourages employee participation in company decision making. These voices, however, often are muted by hierarchical organization structures.

Over the past several decades, many companies, including AT&T and Xerox, have attempted to democratize the workplace, or at least incorporate some democratic approaches to conducting business, which enabled employees to participate in decision making. This strategy has been implemented with varying degrees of success through Total Quality Management (TQM) and other empowerment programs that allow employees to take additional responsibilities (Deming, 1994; Kirkman & Rosen, 1999; Potterfield, 1999; Staiti, 1997; White & Wolf, 1995). Unfortunately, democratization can be difficult to employ, particularly in capitalistic and noncollectivist societies like the United States. First attempts at TQM failed in the 1950s because the concept was connected with Marxism (Cheney, 1995; White & Wolf, 1995). TQM programs can be stymied by well-entrenched practices that do not fit participatory structures. Problems can result from consensus toward majority interests that may devalue or overshadow minority views. Further, peer-monitoring processes might disintegrate because of paranoia. Although on an equal employment footing, peer monitors hold additional power over those they evaluate (Cheney, 1995).

However, these approaches have several advantages; interestingly, the greatest benefactor is the corporation. TQM and empowerment strategies are designed to improve worker productivity, product quality, and customer satisfaction, as well as enhance employee autonomy and job satisfaction (Herrenkohl, Judson, & Hefner, 1999; Mahoney & Thor, 1994; Thiagarajan & Parker, 1999; Weiss, 2000). Employees also are potential image builders for an organization, representing the company to the community. In fact, many advocacy messages have targeted employees first to create a sound internal foundation. General Motors and the U.S. Forest Service have employed this strategy, for example (Cheney & Vibbert, 1987).

Although literature dealing with corporate social responsibility referred to internal publics, media social responsibility excludes employees from its focus. In mass communication literature, social responsibility is presented most consistently as an external concept; that is, how journalists relate to readers, sources, and communities (Gross, 1966; Lloyd, 1991; Peterson, 1974). Journalism ethics codes and the Hutchins Commission report that serve as the basis for press social responsibility do not address internal, employee issues. Perhaps internal interests are more accurately addressed through Breed's social control in the newsroom theory, introduced in the 1950s. Breed (1955) posited that journalistic norms of reporter behavior and rewards are shared and reinforced among newsroom personnel. Novice journalists learn what stories are most likely to be used and what behaviors are considered responsible from experienced reporters and through editor expectations (Bordon, 1997; Breed, 1955).

Once an internal foundation is laid, it is important to consider responsibilities owed to external publics. The organization should keep an accurate pulse on public beliefs and values in order to understand and interpret support and dissention. The company's action might have short-term and long-term effects on its publics. For example, the community in which a company is located could be affected by business actions. A company's successes and failures influence its community's economic base, and its environmental practices can affect the health and welfare of the citizens (Cheney & Vibbert, 1987; Heath, 1990; Wright, 1976).

Although the needs of external and internal audiences may occasionally conflict, it is important to assess the breadth of views and make decisions based on balancing universal principles, contend Cheney and Vibbert (1987). The views of all publics are valuable; however, researchers have generally conceded that publics have not contributed substantially to decisions made regarding a company's social responsibility actions. Hence, if employees contribute minimally and external publics are not well consulted, it appears that these decisions are made by a very small faction—management (Cheney, 1995). This may explain why L'Etang (1996) said that the level of socially responsible behavior might be based on how well the organization's management understands the social responsibility concept.

One source of alternative thinking may come from the public relations profession. Public relations practitioners have played an important role in corporate social responsibility. In fact, public relations may have been spawned from the lack of corporate and media responsibility around the turn of the century. Since then, the profession has reacted with communication and business advancements in crucial times of social change, such as wars and periods of economic turmoil (Cheney & Vibbert, 1987). Often considered the social conscience of an organization (Judd, 1989; Sieb & Fitzpatrick, 1995), trained public relations practitioners have skills in communication, rhetoric, promoting mutual understanding, and encouraging dialogue between an organization and its publics. Definitions of public relations often include managing relationships toward conflict resolution and mutual understanding, the cornerstone of social responsibility (Cutlip, Center, & Broom, 2000; Grunig, 2000).

## Social Responsibility and Public Relations

In public relations literature, social responsibility is referred to as an organization's positive contributions to a community (monetary or otherwise), avoidance of harm to the community, or a combination of both. Esrock and Leichty (1998) were quick to point out, however, that a counter-flurry of good deeds following a harmful act is neither effective nor responsible. Heath and Ryan (1989) identified three categories of social responsibility in public relations: (a) moral rectitude, a problem-solving function; (b) image building, a self-congratulatory function; and (c) consultation, a research-based function to keep a pulse on an organization's publics.

The first two categories reflect enlightened self-interest, which is based on the premise that good acts constitute good and ethical behavior (Boatright, 2000). Very often this approach is viewed within the context of philanthropy. A goodwill gesture has a certain self-preservation flavor to it, something Wright (1976) and L'Etang (1996) said is insufficient for today's responsible corporation. Philanthropic gestures are merely a means to an end—profitability—and not ends in themselves. The latter of Heath and Ryan's (1989) categories, also identified since the 1970s as issues management, may provide the alternative perspective necessary to escape the entrenched perspective of what constitutes socially responsible public relations practices.

Issues management is a systematic process to examine and act on public policy that may affect the organization and its publics (Heath, 1990). It involves: (a) communicating, which includes informing stakeholders, changing perceptions, and fostering understanding and reconciliation; (b) monitoring to acquire accurate and timely information about the environment; (c) achieving responsibility by working with changes in ethical climates; and (d) strategic planning to determine how changes in public policies may create business opportunities. Ideally, Grunig (2000) argued, issues management should be a two-way symmetrical approach to reinforce mutual understanding and conflict resolution.

Researchers and practitioners stress that organizations should consider stakeholder views, identify the effects of their actions on stakeholders, and work toward mutual understanding. Stakeholder ethics emphasizes an organization's obligations to both internal and external publics, realizing that these interests may conflict. Ethical action involves respecting rights of others without compromising ethical principles. L'Etang (1996) argued that universal principles such as equality and justice should be applied because they are ethically sound, not because they might enhance the organization's image. Organizations should monitor their environments and identify publics and their interests to determine the courses of action that will respect all stakeholder rights (Heath & Ryan, 1989; L'Etang, 1996).

Although the authors conceded that this might be a lofty goal, they considered it feasible for a corporation to re-invent itself in ethically healthy ways. Strategies can be developed based on the level of cooperation or threat perceived from the stakeholder. For example, highly supportive stakeholders could be nurtured, and moderate supporters could be involved in appropriate issues to increase support. Organization positions should be defended against nonsupporters, although cultivating a more positive relationship also should be pursued. Stakeholders with little cooperation or threat should be monitored for possible problems or opportunities (Abzug & Webb, 1999; Savage, Nix, Whitehead, & Blair, 1991). Unfortunately, monitoring might create difficulties for public relations practitioners who are not always included in an organization's strategic planning or ethical decision-making processes (Heath, 1990; Judd, 1989).

Bostdorff and Vibbert (1994) addressed a related concept, values advocacy, which focuses on building images, countering criticism, and presenting messages that can be factors in later public debate. Although values advocacy appears to be less symmetrical than the concepts of mutual understanding, it involves two-way communication using what Aristotle referred to as epideictic, or ceremonial, rhetoric that is not considered argumentative or partisan in nature. Epideictic rhetoric focuses on consensual or universally approved values such as freedom, independence, and the ability to make one's own decisions.

Once these themes are well established—and aligned as part of a company's values structure—they can be reinforced in the public policy arena when required. For example, when Phillips Petroleum faced economic difficulties in the 1970s during the oil crisis, the company perceived having three choices—continue its current product advertising, remove advertising altogether until the crisis passed, or alter its messages to focus on valued ideals instead of product. It was most effective for the long-term, executives decided, to develop a values advocacy campaign that focused on the company's human-interest deeds, including developing products used in lifesaving medical equipment and shatterproof highway guards. The company's own evaluation indicated these public-focused messages helped repair not only the company's image but also the petroleum industry's stature following the crisis (Bostdorff & Vibbert, 1994; Cheney & Vibbert, 1987).

Other organizations have used epideictic rhetoric as a segue to the political arena. For example, Planned Parenthood challenged pro-life groups' charges of immorality by positioning its activities as morally sound; the universal principle was freedom of choice. They counted on public agreement that not only is the ability to choose desirable, but that any organization that tries to deny legal choice is itself immoral (Bostdorff, 1992).

In these and other examples, it appears that an organization's motivation may play a pivotal role in deciding whether the actions are socially responsible (Bostdorff & Vibbert, 1994; Condit & Condit, 1992; Porter, 1992). For example, did Phillips Petroleum issue advocacy messages because they were morally sound and helpful to the community? Or was the strategy an attempt to link the company with universally appealing ideals to regain community favor in the event of a lengthy oil crisis? Nelson (1994a) noted that advocacy messages could be considered propagandistic and deceptive. He recommended that public relations practitioners look to higher ethical principles when employing rhetoric. L'Etang (1993) noted that some people act morally in general, and others may consider what is right within the context of their wants at the time. Examining the company's motivation may reveal whether the messages involve enlightened self-interest or conflict resolution and mutual understanding.

## Summary of Implications

With its roots in journalism, public relations has drawn on the social responsibility of the press to understand its public service duties. The power derived from professional status requires journalists—and public relations practitioners—to acknowledge their responsibilities to public interests. This press theory, solidified through the Hutchins Commission Report of 1947, is visible in public relations ethics code provisions that encourage practitioners to balance personal and organizational interests with those of the public at large.

Public relations is more than media relations, however, and aspects of corporate social responsibility theory may also contribute to the understanding of the public relations professions' responsibilities to society. Organizational self-service has been discouraged through the decades. Beyond even an enlightened self-interest approach, corporations are encouraged to understand and anticipate the needs of their constituents. Because of this breadth of public relations scope, it would be useful for researchers to acknowledge both its journalistic and business/organizational communication roots.

The public relations profession also has contributed its own concepts for socially responsible practices. Issues management and values advocacy are two research-based functions that encourage practitioners to monitor, understand and build consensus with their publics. These approaches typically reflect two-way symmetrical communication, which has been identified as the most ethical means of practicing public relations (Grunig, 1989).

How do these concepts affect ethical decision making in public relations? With the two concepts of professionalism and social responsibility identified, it is important to discuss how these foundations may be involved in the ethical decision-making process of public relations. The following section identifies the theoretical roots—namely deontology and teleology—that affect how these concepts are applied in decision making.

## IMPLICATIONS FOR ETHICAL DECISION MAKING IN PUBLIC RELATIONS

Ethical theory presents public relations practitioners with useful principles for decision making. Bowen (2000) argued that ethical public relations is duty based, which reflects the deontological approach to ethics. Additionally, L'Etang (1992) presented evidence that deontological, or Kantian, ethics provide the most suitable foundation for the development of ethics codes—a characteristic of professionalism.

According to deontology, certain normative principles or rules must be obeyed at all cost, regardless of circumstances (Bowen, 2000; Laczniak & Murphy, 1993; McElreath, 1997). Nineteenth century philosopher Immanuel Kant indicated categorical imperatives must be strictly adhered to; what is morally correct for one is morally correct for all people. He defined two categories of moral directives that all persons should agree on. Strict duties identify wrong actions such as causing harm or lying, and meritorious duties define valuable actions such as providing assistance and expressing gratitude. In professionalism, for example, acting responsible toward public interests is an important obligation; certain duties ought to be observed. Harris (1994) found many professions word ethics codes as categorical imperatives. Bowen (2000) argued that duty is one of three imperatives of ethical public relations. Intention and dignity and respect for others complete her ethical consideration triangle.

Rules-based decision making is not without its flaws, however. First, the principles do not provide direction for instances in which two values conflict (Black,

Steele, & Barney, 1995). In public relations, for example, practitioners have obligations to protect an organization's confidential information as well as duties to keep its publics adequately informed. Second, different disciplines may honor different obligations (Denise, Peterfreund, & White, 1996). For example, whereas journalists define objectivity as a primary duty, public relations practitioners advocate for their organization or build consensus between the organization and its publics (McBride, 1989). Obligations might further be complicated by societal differences (L'Etang, 2001), and cultural diversity may make it difficult to identify universal imperatives, according to Laczniak and Murphy (1993).

Third, certain rules may restrict or lead individuals to misplace emphasis. For example, psychologists have an obligation to maintain client confidences. But, if the individual being counseled threatens to harm someone, must the psychologist maintain the confidence or make an exception to protect a life? A conflict between following rules and considering circumstances and contexts creates a dilemma. According to Labacqz (1985), "The situational challenge puts all rules in jeopardy: rules are clearly tenuous if everything hinges on the good or bad results that can be brought about in any situation. And yet . . . most of us are not altogether comfortable with the suggestion that we should break the rule *any time* we think that we could do more good than harm by doing so" (p. 20–21).

Normatively then, professionalism and social responsibility are duty driven. Public relations researchers (Bowen, 2000; L'Etang, 1992) have argued that the profession is guided by standards that ensure personal and organizational interests are balanced with societal interests. In reality, however, it appears that the desire for professional status often clouds the duty to society. It may be viable, as a result, to balance the deontological ethic with teleological perspectives to ensure a greater societal good emerges.

When applying teleology, individuals emphasize consequences; that is, the ends justify the means, and ethical actions result in the greatest good (Sieb & Fitzpatrick, 1995). Restricted teleology calculates consequences only for a particular person or group. Universal teleology, known as utilitarianism, addresses society as a whole, and should be considered the more viable of the two teleological approaches for public relations. That is, the most ethical action leads to good results for a greater number of people and produces greater good than other alternatives, according to nineteenth century philosopher John Stuart Mill (1956, 1979). Hence, both the quality and quantity of good should be assessed before decisions are made. Cost-benefit analyses of various consequences help determine the proper course of action in various situations.

Contemporary philosopher Jurgen Habermas (1984) also supported consideration of all views and consequences to reach the most valuable conclusion to a problem. His discourse theory points to the essential role of symmetrical communication to ensure ethical outcomes result. Pearson (1989a, 1989b) argued the need to consider multiple viewpoints through dialogue, which he based on Habermas' discourse ethic and Grunig's two-way symmetrical communication.

Critics, however, argue that identifying all potential consequences is exceedingly difficult, time consuming, and unrealistic. Individuals may overlook unanticipated consequences or slight minority interests in favor of majority well-being (Black, Steele, & Barney, 1995). Although utilitarianism should consider all players equally, decision makers may not be so egalitarian, Spicer (1997) argued. He explained that the business world overlooks some stakeholder positions because decision makers may focus on corporate allegiance or profitability.

Despite its shortcomings, the utilitarian perspective complements the duty-bound perspective. A consensus-building approach to public relations based on utilitarianism may help a societal focus re-emerge in balance with personal and organizational needs. A societal focus, then, helps public relations practitioners meet social responsibility duties, which contributes ultimately to professional status. Hence the balance of duty and utility provide a strong theoretical foundation for ethical public relations.

## CONCLUSIONS AND IMPLICATIONS

What becomes clear through this discussion of social responsibility and professionalism is that there are numerous factors creating ethical tensions for public relations practitioners. For example, individual beliefs might clash with organizational objectives, or professional goals might incite societal objections. The public relations practitioner faces the daunting task of juggling the competing loyalties of a vast array of stakeholders to arrive at ethically sound solutions.

Several important concepts feed into the understanding of public relations ethics. The primary emphasis—or context—for ethics in academic, educational, and trade literature is on professionalism and social responsibility, which combine internal commitment to extensive training and external commitment to service to others. Social responsibility is considered both an element and an outcome of professionalism, which points to the potential duality of these concepts. That is, socially responsible behavior is both a professional attribute and a valued course of action for public relations practitioners. A dual approach to the discussion of these ethical foundations may be furthered by Giddens' (1984) structuration theory, which proposes that concepts may be both interdependent and distinct.

Why the focus on professionalism and social responsibility? Perhaps because that is where the element of control lies. That is, a profession attempts to muster its power from its peers. Although this approach has been only marginally successful—evident by the small percentage of practitioners who belong to professional associations such as the Public Relations Society of America—it is a natural power base. The profession defines certain values and attributes to which its members must ascribe. Individuals who value these attributes conform to the standards of the profession and encourage their organizations to assume these standards in a socially responsible fashion.

Despite the propensity of public relations researchers to focus on professionalism and social responsibility, these concepts are but two considerations that practitioners should take in decision making, according to emerging ethical decision-making theory. Principles of deontology and teleology provide foundations for understanding the ethical decision-making process, and internal and external factors also may influence what directives individuals employ.

As some critics have complained, however, public relations textbooks and much of the extant literature focus on professional characteristics instead of establishing theoretical and philosophical foundations for individual moral reasoning and recognizing the influence of organizational norms and cultural values on ethical decision making (Bivins, 1989b; L'Etang, 1996). An exception is McElreath's (1997) public relations textbook, which focuses specifically on creating ethically sound public relations campaigns. Since decision makers should make informed judgments, this limited scope may impair even the most promising public relations practitioner.

Despite the increased interest and attention on public relations ethics in general, several problems and gaps are exposed in researching, teaching, and implementing public relations ethics. Three primary areas of concern emerge—a gap between normative proposals and the reality of practice, the motivation of ethical study in public relations, and a lack of focus on the decision-making processes of public relations practitioners.

First, difficulties lie in bridging normative theory with realistic situations faced by practitioners. From a theoretical perspective, Grunig (2000), Grunig and Hunt (1984), and others, have long espoused an excellence model of public relations that they argue is the most ethical practice. These researchers determined that a two-way symmetrical model of public relations that balances interests of both the organization and its publics is practiced in the field, although admittedly sparingly.

However, critics complain that the excellence model does not adequately address the external influences that practitioners face. They contend that it is unrealistic to assume that a personal commitment to negotiation and bargaining by public relations practitioners ensures the ability to employ those principles within organizations (L'Etang, 1996). Public relations practitioners must juggle issues on numerous levels with many stakeholders (professional peers, organization, community, society, etc.), and many do not feel that they have a substantive role in the organization's decision-making processes (Fitzpatrick, 1996). Even Grunig has admitted that executive management must favor collaboration and two-way symmetry for it to be implemented by and within an organization (Grunig, 2000).

Second, despite the attempt to emphasize professional duty, the root interest in public relations professional ethics may reflect more of a self-serving goal than a public interest goal (Hunt & Tirpok, 1993). Extant literature reflects this focus. For example, Bissland and Rentner (1989) defined professionalism as "a means by which an occupation gains status, power, and often, material rewards in society; being a professional isn't merely prestigious, it also is highly advantageous" (p. 92). L'Etang (1996) contended that the appeal of public relations ethics "can thus be seen as instrumental in its own status" (p. 95). That is, practitioners have exemplified moral conduct more for validation as professionals and less for the good provided to society. This profession-centered motivation of many practitioners may affect not only public relations' perception, but also how its practitioners operate when faced with ethical challenges.

Third, researchers give little attention to effective decision-making processes in ethical public relations. Instead, they focus on ethics tools such as codes of professional standards (Kruckeberg, 1992; Sieb & Fitzpatrick, 1995). Although ethics codes provide rules to guide behavior, they neither solve ethical problems nor make practitioners more ethical (Budd, 1991). McElreath (1997) came closest to examining the big picture with modified journalism and marketing decision-making models that incorporate internal and external influences on the personal, organizational, professional, and societal levels, using the language of the public relations profession. His primary focus remains on professionalism, however.

A number of disciplines examine ethical decision making, including business management, administration, marketing, finance, accounting, public administration, social work, health professions, and, to a lesser degree, communication. These studies fall into two general categories. First, influential factors models describe agents contributing to an individual's decision-making prowess, including personal characteristics such as gender, education, and level of moral development; organizational environment; and cultural norms (e.g., Bordon, 1997; Larimer, 1997; Vasquez & Taylor, 1999; Vitell, Nwachukwu, & Barnes, 1993). Second, how-to models describe the processes used by individuals when making decisions. These processes may be normative or reality based; that is, some models explain how professionals ought to make decisions and others explicate how people have made ethical decisions (e.g., Brousseau, 1995; Hill, Glaser, & Harden, 1998; McDonald, 1999). Most of the models are in developmental and proposal stages; few have been tested empirically.

This broad focus does not rule out the applicability of existing models as frameworks for public relations practitioners. In fact, the public relations profession may draw successfully from related disciplines. Some public relations researchers focus on journalism for ethics discussions, because of the long-standing relationship between the two disciplines. Many of today's public relations practitioners have roots in journalism, either as journalism school graduates or through previous careers as reporters (Wright, 1976). Additionally, practitioners work in for-profit and nonprofit organizations and may use the processes and procedures of the businesses and disciplines in which they are involved.

Additional research may determine what decision-making characteristics are specific to the public relations field. What factors influence the public relations practitioner's decisions and actions, including individual characteristics, organizational norms, professional standards, social and cultural elements? Are certain characteristics more influential than others? For example, what role does the public relations profession itself play in influencing decision making in relation to cultural and organizational factors? Should professionalism remain the focal point or should a richer context be employed? Understanding how practitioners make decisions may help address the first two concerns as well; the gap in theory and practice, and the motivations of ethical study. That is, decision-making behavior may shed light on how public relations practitioners perceive ethics and ethical behavior as a distinct function of the discipline.

## REFERENCES

Abel, E. (1984). Hutchins revisited: Thirty-five years of social responsibility theory. In R. Schmuhl, (Ed.), *The responsibility of journalism* (pp. 39–48). Notre Dame, IN: University of Notre Dame Press.

Abzug, R., & Webb, N. J. (1999). Relationships between nonprofit and for-profit organizations: A stakeholder perspective. *Nonprofit and Voluntary Sector Quarterly, 28*(4), 416–431.

Airaksinen, T. (1994). Service and science in professional life. In R. F. Chadwick (Ed.), *Ethics and the professions* (pp. 1–13). Brookfield, VT: Avebury.

Anderson, A. (1996). *Ethics for fundraisers.* Bloomington: Indiana University Press.

Aupperle, K. E., Carroll, A. P., & Hatfield, J. D. (1985). An empirical examination of the relationship between corporate social responsibility and profitability. *Academy of Management Journal, 28*(2), 446–463.

Baker, L. W. (1993). *The credibility factor: Putting ethics to work in public relations.* Homewood, IL: Business One Irwin.

Barber, B. (1988). Professions and emerging professions. In J. C. Callahan (Ed.), *Ethical issues in professional life* (pp. 35–39). New York: Oxford University Press.

Barker, S. F. (1992). What is a profession? *Professional Ethics, 1*(1 & 2), 73–99.

Baxter, B. L. (1986). Lawmakers' views on licensing in public relations. *Public Relations Review, 12*(4), 12–15.

Bayles, M. D. (1988). The professions. In J. C. Callahan (Ed.), *Ethical issues in professional life* (pp. 27–30). New York: Oxford University Press.

Bernays, E. L. (1983). The case for licensing PR practitioners. *Public Relations Quarterly, 28*, 32.

Bernays, E. L. (1984). Father of PR analyzes its history. *Communication World, 6*, 38–39.

Bernays, E. L. (1986). *The later years: Public relations insights 1956–1986.* Rhinebeck, NY: H&M Publishers.

Bernays, E. L. (1992). Securing the future of public relations. *PR Update, 2*(1), 8–9.

Bissland, J. H., & Rentner, T. L. (1989). Education's role in professionalizing public relations: A progress report. *Journal of Mass Media Ethics, 4*(1), 92–105.

Bivins, T. H. (1989a). Ethical implications of the relationship of purpose to role and function in public relations. *Journal of Business Ethics, 8*, 65–73.

Bivins, T. H. (1989b). Are public relations texts covering ethics adequately? *Journal of Mass Media Ethics, 4*(1), 39–52.

Bivins, T. H. (1993). Public relations, professionalism and the public interest. *Journal of Business Ethics, 12*, 117–126.

Black, J., Steele, B., & Barney, R. (1995). *Doing ethics in journalism: A handbook with case studies* (2nd ed.). Boston: Allyn & Bacon.

Boatright, J. R. (2000). *Ethics and the conduct of business* (3rd ed.). Upper Saddle River, NJ: Prentice Hall.

Bordon, S. L. (1997). Choice processes in a newspaper ethics case. *Communication Monographs, 64*(1), 65–81.

Bostdorff, D. M. (1992). "The decision is yours" campaign: Planned Parenthood's characteristic argument of moral virtue. In E. L. Toth & R. L. Heath (Eds.), *Rhetorical and critical approaches to public relations* (pp. 301–313). Hillsdale, NJ: Erlbaum.

Bostdorff, D. M., & Vibbert, S. L. (1994). Values advocacy: Enhancing organizational images, deflecting public criticism, and grounding future arguments. *Public Relations Review, 20*(2), 141–158.

Bottery, M. (1995). Towards a concept of the ethical professional. *Professional Ethics, 4*(1), 23–48.

Bovet, S. F. (1993, November). The burning question of ethics: The profession fights for better business practices. *Public Relations Journal, 49*(11), 24–25, 29.

Bowen, S. A. (2000). A theory of ethical issues management: Contributions of Kantian deontology to public relations' ethics and decision-making. (Doctoral dissertation, University of Maryland, 2000). *Dissertation Abstracts International 61*(08A), 2970.

Bowen, W. G., Nygren, T. I., Turner, S. E., & Duffy, E. A. (1994) *The charitable nonprofits: An analysis of institutional dynamics and characteristics.* San Francisco: Jossey-Bass.

Boynton, L. A. (1999, September). *Codes of silence: The quiet evolution of the PRSA code of ethics as documented in Public Relations Journal 1945–1990.* Unpublished manuscript.

Boynton, L. A. (2000, March). *Professional and socially responsible communicators: An analysis of ethics codes of public relations and journalism associations.* A paper presented to the Southeast Regional Colloquium of the Association for Education in Journalism and Mass Communication, Chapel Hill, NC.

Breed, W. (1955). Social control in the newsroom: A functional analysis. *Social Forces, 33*(4), 326–335.

Broom, G. M., & Dozier, D. M. (1986). Advancement for public relations role models. *Public Relations Review, 12*(1), 37–56.

Broom, G. M., & Smith, G. D. (1979). Testing the practitioner's impact on clients. *Public Relations Review, 5*(4), 47–59.

Brousseau, P. L. (1995). Ethical dilemmas: Right vs. right. *Spectrum, 68*(1), 16–22.

Budd, J. F., Jr. (1991). *Ethical dilemmas in public relations.* Gold Paper, No. 8. Bourenmouth, UK: Roman Press.

Calver, H. N. (1951, February). Now that we have a code. *Public Relations Journal, 7*(2), 3–4, 17.

Carey, J. L. (1957, March). Professional ethics are a helpful tool. *Public Relations Journal, 13*(3), 7, 14, 18.

Center, A. H., & Jackson, P. (1995). *Public relations practices: Managerial case studies and problems* (5th ed.). Englewood Cliffs, NJ: Prentice Hall.

Chadwick, R. F. (Ed.). (1994). *Ethics and professions.* Brookfield, VT: Avebury.

Cheney, G. (1995). Democracy in the workplace: Theory and practice from the perspective of communication. *Journal of Applied Communication Research, 23,* 167–200.

Cheney, G., & Vibbert, S. L. (1987). Corporate discourse: Public relations and issues management. In F. M. Jablin, L. L. Putnam, K. H. Roberts, & L. W. Porter (Eds.), *Handbook of organizational communication—An interdisciplinary perspective* (pp. 165–194). Newbury Park, CA: Sage.

Christians, C. (1986). Reporting and the oppressed. In D. Elliott (Ed.), *Responsible journalism* (pp. 109–130). Beverly Hills, CA: Sage.

Commission on Public Relations Education. (1999). *Public relations education for the 21st century: A port of entry.* New York: Commission on Public Relations Education.

Condit, C. M., & Condit, D. M. (1992). Smoking or health: Incremental erosion as a public interest group strategy. In E. L. Toth, & R. L. Heath (Eds.), *Rhetorical and critical approaches to public relations* (pp. 241–256). Hillsdale, NJ: Erlbaum.

Cooper, M. W. (1984, January). Exclusive interview with Barbara W. Hunter, PRSA's 1984 president. *Public Relations Journal, 40*(1), 10–11.

Cutlip, S. M., Center, A. H., & Broom, G. H. (2000). *Effective public relations* (8th ed.) Upper Saddle River, NJ: Prentice-Hall.

Cyert, R. M., & March, J.G. (1992). *A behavioral theory of the firm* (2nd ed.) Cambridge, MA: Blackwell Business.

Decker, F. K. (1963, April). The path toward professionalism: PRSA's code and how it operates. *Public Relations Journal, 19*(4), 7–8, 10.

Deming, W. E. (1994). *The best of Deming.* (Collected by Ron McCoy). Knoxville, TN: SPC.

Denise, T. C., Peterfreund, S. P., & White, N. P. (1996). *Great traditions in ethics* (8th ed.). Belmont, CA: Wadsworth.

Dilenschneider, R. L. (1999, Spring). Public relations for the new millennium: Back to social responsibility. *Public Relations Strategist, 5*(1), 12–16.

Donaldson, J. (1989). *Key issues in business ethics.* San Diego: Academic Press.

Dozier, D. M.(1992). The organizational roles of communications and public relations practitioners. In J. E. Grunig (Ed.), *Excellence in public relations and communication management* (pp. 327–356). Hillsdale, NJ: Erlbaum.

Dozier, D. M., Grunig, L. A., & Grunig, J. E. (1995). *Manager's guide to excellence in public relations and communication management.* Mahwah, NJ: Erlbaum.

Drechsel, R. E. (1992). Media ethics and media law: The transformation of moral obligation into legal principles. *Notre Dame Journal of Law, Ethics and Public Policy, 5*, 5–32.

Esrock, S. L., & Leichty, G. B. (1998). Social responsibility and corporate web pages: Self-presentation or agenda-setting? *Public Relations Review, 24*(3), 305–319.

Etzioni, A. (1969). *The semi-professions and their organization.* New York: Free Press.

Ewen, S. (1996). *PR! A social history of spin.* New York: BasicBooks.

Fenton, M. (1977, August). More on professionalism. *Public Relations Journal, 33*(8), 16.

Fitzpatrick, K. R. (1996). The role of public relations in the institutionalization of ethics. *Public Relations Review, 22*(3), 249–258.

Forbes, P. S. (1986). Why licensing is an opportunity for public relations. *Public Relations Review, 12*(4), 9–11.

Friedman, M. (1994). The social responsibility of business is to increase its profits. In W. A. Wines & S. Adverson (Eds.), *Readings in business ethics and social responsibility* (pp. 137–141). Dubuque, IA: Kendall/Hunt.

Friedson, E. (1970). *Professional dominance.* New York: Atherton.

Fulford, K. W. M. (1994). Medical education: Knowledge and know-how. In R. F. Chadwick (Ed.), *Ethics and the professions* (pp. 14-26). Brookfield, VT: Ashgate.

Gergen, D. R. (1992, April 20). Reforming welfare at the very top. *U.S. News & World Report, 112*(15), 43.

Giddens, A. (1984). *The constitution of society: Outline of the theory of structuration.* Berkeley: University of California Press.

Gilsdorf, J. W., & Vawter, L. K. (1983). Public relations professionals rate their associations. *Public Relations Review, 9*, 26–40.

Glover, S. H., Bumpus, M. A., Logan, J. E., & Ciesla, J. R. (1997). Re-examining the influence of individual values on ethical decision making. *Journal of Business Ethics, 16*, 1319–1329.

Goldman, E. F. (1984). *Two-way street: The emergence of PR counsel.* Boston: Bellman.

Gordon, A. D., & Kittross, J. M. (1999). *Controversies in media ethics* (2nd ed.). New York: Longman.

Gross, G., (Ed.). (1966). *The responsibility of the press.* New York: Fleet.

Grunig, J. E. (1989). Symmetrical presuppositions as a framework for public relations theory. In C. H. Botan, & V. Hazelton Jr. (Eds.), *Public relations theory* (pp. 17–44). Hillsdale, NJ: Erlbaum.

Grunig, J. E. (2000). Collectivism, collaboration, and societal corporatism as core professional values in public relations. *Journal of Public Relations Research, 12*(1), 23–48.

Grunig, J. E., & Hunt, T. (1984). *Managing public relations.* New York: Holt, Reinhart, & Winston.

Habermas, J. (1984). *The theory of communicative action.* (T. McCarthy, Trans.). Boston: Beacon Press.

Hagel, R. C. (1965, August). The social consequences of public relations. *Public Relations Journal, 21*(8), 27.

Harris, N. G. E. (1994). Professional codes and Kantian duties. In R. F. Chadwick (Ed.), *Ethics and the professions* (pp. 104–115). Brookfield, VT: Ashgate.

Harrison, S. L. (1990). Pedagogical ethics for public relations and advertising. *Journal of Mass Media Ethics, 5*(4), 256–262.

Hayry, H., & Hayry, M. (1994). The nature and role of professional codes in modern society. In R. F. Chadwick (Ed.), *Ethics and the professions* (pp. 136–144). Brookfield, VT: Ashgate.

Heath, R. L. (1980). Corporate advocacy: An application of speech communication perspectives and skills—and more. *Communication Education, 29,* 370–377.

Heath, R. L. (1990). Corporate issues management: Theoretical underpinnings and research foundations. In J. E. Grunig & L. A. Grunig (Eds.), *Public relations research annual 2* (pp. 29–65) Hillsdale, NJ: Erlbaum.

Heath, R. L., & Ryan, M. (1989). Public relations' role in defining corporate social responsibility. *Journal of Mass Media Ethics, 4*(1), 21–38.

Hegarty, W. H. (1995). Effects of group norms and learning on unethical decision behavior. *Psychological Reports, 76,* 593–594.

Hegarty, W. H., & Sims, H. P., Jr. (1978). Some determinants of unethical decision behavior. *Journal of Applied Psychology, 63,* 451–457.

Herrenkohl, R. C., Judson, G. T., & Heffner, J. A. (1999). Defining and measuring employee empowerment. *Journal of Applied Behavioral Science, 35*(3), 373–389.

Hesse, M. B. (1984, March). Blueprint for graduate study: From idealism to reality. *Public Relations Journal, 40*(3), 22.

Hill, M., Glaser, K., & Harden, J. (1998). A feminist model for ethical decision making. *Women & Therapy, 21*(3), 101–121.

Himes, D. P. (1995, August). How to keep your donors. *Fund Raising Management, 26*(6), 34.

Hughes, E. C. (1988). Professions. In J. C. Callahan (Ed.), *Ethical issues in professional life* (pp. 31–35) New York: Oxford University Press.

Hunt, T., & Tirpok, A. (1993). Universal ethics code: An idea whose time has come. *Public Relations Review, 19*(1), 1–11.

Iggers, J. (1998). *Good news, bad news—Journalism ethics and the public interest.* Boulder, CO: Westview Press.

International Association of Business Communicators. (1999) *Becoming an accredited business communicator.* [Online]. Available: http://www.iabc.com/about/accredit/abc.htm.

Jackson, J. (1994). Common codes: Divergent practices. In R. F. Chadwick (Ed.), *Ethics and the professions* (pp. 116–125). Brookfield, VT: Ashgate.

Jackson, P. (1988, October). Demonstrating professionalism. *Public Relations Journal, 44*(10), 27–29.

Judd, L. R. (1989). Credibility, public relations and social responsibility. *Public Relations Review, 15*(2), 34–40.

Jurgensen, J. H., & Lukaszewski, J. E. (1988, March). Ethics: Content before conduct. *Public Relations Journal, 44*(3), 48, 47.

Kirkman, B. L., & Rosen, B. (1999). Beyond self-management: Antecedents and consequences of team empowerment. *Academy of Management Journal, 42*(1), 58–74.

Kruckeberg, D. (1992). Ethical decision-making in public relations. *International Public Relations Review 15*(4), 27–37.

Kruckeberg, D. (1993). Universal ethics code: Both possible and feasible. *Public Relations Review, 19*(1), 21–31.

Kultgen, J. (1988). The ideological use of professional codes. In J. C. Callahan (Ed.), *Ethical issues in professional life* (pp. 411–421). New York: Oxford University Press.

Labacqz, K. (1985). *Professional ethics: Power and paradox.* Nashville, TN: Abingdon Press.

Laczniak, G. R., & Murphy, P. E. (1993). *Ethical marketing decisions: The higher road.* Boston: Allyn & Bacon.

Larimer, L. V. (1997). How employees decide which way to go. *Workforce, 76*(12), 109–111.

Lee, B. W. (1951, December 20). Code enforcement machinery adopted. *Public Relations Journal,* 7(12), 28–29.

Leigh, R. D. (Ed.). (1947). *A free and responsible press: A general report on mass communication: Newspapers, radio, motion pictures, magazines, and books.* Chicago: University of Chicago Press.

Leichty, G., & Springston, J. (1996). Elaborating public relations roles. *Journalism and Mass Communication Quarterly 73*(2), 473–474.

Lesly, P. (1986). Why licensing won't work for public relations. *Public Relations Review, 12*(4), 5.

L'Etang, J. (1993). Public relations and corporate social responsibility: Some issues arising. *Journal of Business Ethics, 13,* 111–123.

L'Etang, J. (1996). Corporate responsibility and public relations ethics. In J. L'Etang, & M. Pieczka (Eds.), *Critical perspectives in public relations* (pp. 82–105). Boston: International Thomson Business Press.

Levy, C. S. (1972). The context of social work ethics. *Social Work, 17,* 95–101.

Levy, C. S. (1973). The value base of social work. *Journal of Education for Social Work, 9,* 34–42.

Lloyd, S. (1991). A criticism of social responsibility theory: An ethical perspective. *Journal of Mass Media Ethics, 6*(4), 199–209.

Loevinger, L. (1996). Enforcing ethical standards of professional associations. *Professional Ethics, 5*(1 & 2), 157–166.

Lowery, S. A., & DeFleur, M. L. (1995). *Milestones in mass communication research* (3rd ed.). White Plains, NY: Longman.

Magnusson, P. (1995, July 3). It's open season on nonprofits. *Business Week, 3431,* 31.

Mahoney, F. X., & Thor, C. G. (1994). *The TQM trilogy: Using ISO 9000, the Deming prize and the Baldrige award to establish a system for total quality management.* New York: American Management Association.

Manne, H. G. (1970, December). The myth of corporate responsibility. *Public Relations Journal, 26*(12), 6–8.

Marston, J. (1968, July). Hallmarks of a profession. *Public Relations Journal, 24*(7), 8–10.

Martinson, D. L. (1994). Enlightened self-interest fails as an ethical baseline in public relations. *Journal of Mass Media Ethics, 9*(2), 100–108.

McBride, G. (1989). Ethical thought in public relations history: Seeking a relevant perspective. *Journal of Mass Media Ethics 4*(1), 5–20.

McCammond, D. B. (1983, November). A matter of ethics. *Public Relations Journal, 39*(11), 46-47.

McCammond, D. B. (1987, January). Take-home quiz. *Public Relations Journal, 43*(1), 7.

McDonald, M. (1999). *A framework for ethical decision-making.* [Online]. Available: http://www.ethics.ubc.ca/mcdonald/decisions.html.

McDowell, B. (1991). *Ethical conduct and the professional's dilemma: Choosing between service and success.* New York: Quorum Books.

McElreath, M. P. (1997). *Managing systematic and ethical public relations campaigns* (2nd ed.). Boston: McGraw Hill.

McLaughlin, T. (1995, August). Lessons from United Way. *Association Management, 47*(8), 25.

Meyer, P. (1987). *Ethical journalism* (2nd ed.). New York: Longman.

Mill, J. S. (1956). *On liberty.* Currin V. Shields (Ed.). Upper Saddle River, NJ: Prentice Hall.

Mill, J. S. (1979). *Utilitarianism.* Indianapolis, IN: Hackett.

Millerson, G. (1964). *The qualifying associations.* London: Routledge & Kegan Paul.

Milton, J. (1992). *Areopagitica: Freedom of the press.* Santa Barbara, CA: Bandanna Books.

Moss, E. K. (1950, October). Is public relations a profession? *Public Relations Journal, 6*(9), 7–8, 10.

Mount, Eric. Jr. (1990). *Professional ethics in context: Institutions, images, and empathy.* Louisville, KY: Westminster/John Knox Press.

Nages, N. R., & Truitt, R. H. (1987). *Strategic public relations counseling: Models from the Counselors Academy.* New York: Longman.

Nelson, R. (1994a). Issues communication and advocacy: Contemporary ethical challenges. *Public

Relations Review, 20(3), 225–231.

Nelson, R. (1994b) The professional dilemma. Public Relations Update, 1.

Nunns, S. (1996, September). Exemption extinction? What happens when a public good is subject to a free market? American Theatre, 13(7), 63–65.

O'Connell, B. (1994, March). The future looks good—for those who invest in it. Fund Raising Management, 24(1), 41.

Olasky, M. (1985). Ministers or panderers: Issues raised by the Public Relations Society Code of Standards. Journal of Mass Media Ethics, 1(1), 43–49.

Olcott, W. (1992, April). Two different worlds. Fund Raising Management, 24(2), 6.

Olson, A. T. (1999). Authoring a code: Observations on process and organization. [Online]. Available: http://csep.iit.edu/codes/coe/Writing_A_Code.html.

Page, B. B. (1975). Who owns the professions? Hastings Center Report, 5(5), 7–8.

Paluszek, J. (1988, October). The time has come. Public Relations Journal, 44(10), 30–31.

Paradice, D. B., & Dejoie, R. M. (1991). The ethical decision-making processes of information system workers. Journal of Business Ethics, 10, 1–12.

Parsons, P. H. (1993). Framework for analysis of conflicting loyalties. Public Relations Review, 19(1), 49–57.

Pearson, R. (1989a). Albert J. Sullivan's theory of public relations ethics. Public Relations Review, 15(2), 52–62.

Pearson, R. (1989b). A theory of public relations ethics. (Doctoral dissertation, Ohio University, 1989). Dissertation Abstracts International, 50(12A), 4096.

Peterson, T. (1966). Social responsibility—Theory and practice. In G. Gross (Ed.), The responsibility of the press (pp. 33–49). New York: Fleet.

Peterson, T. (1974). Social responsibility theory of the press. In F. S. Siebert, T. Peterson, & W. Schramm, (Eds.), Four theories of the press (pp. 73–103). Urbana: University of Illinois Press.

Pieczka, M., & L'Etang, J. (2001). Public relations and the question of professionalism. In R. L. Heath (Ed.), Handbook of public relations (pp. 223–235). Thousand Oaks, CA: Sage.

Porter, W. M. (1992). The environment of the oil company: A semiotic analysis of Chevron's "People Do" commercials. In E. L. Toth & R. L. Heath (Eds.), Rhetorical and critical approaches to public relations (pp. 187–204). Hillsdale, NJ: Erlbaum.

Potterfield, T. A. (1999). The business of employee empowerment: Democracy and ideology in the workplace. Westport, CT: Quorum.

Pratt, C. B. (1991). Public relations: The empirical research on public relations. Journal of Business Ethics, 10, 229–236.

Public Relations Society of America. (1999) Universal accreditation program. [Online]. Available: http://www.prsa.org/accred.html.

Ranney, M. (1977, June). Save us from professionalism. Public Relations Journal, 33(6), 27–28.

Reamer, F. G. (1995). Social work values and ethics. New York: Columbia University Press.

Red Lion Broadcasting Co., Inc. v. FCC (1969). 395 U.S. 367.

Reeck, D. (1982). Ethics for the professions: A Christian perspective. Minneapolis, MN: Augsburg.

Salamon, L. M. (1992). America's nonprofit sector: A primer. New York: Foundation Center.

Sallot, L. M., Cameron, G. T., & Lariscy, R. A. W. (1997). Professional standards in public relations: A survey of educators. Public Relations Review, 23(3), 197–216.

Savage, G. T., Nix, T. W., Whitehead, C. J., & Blair, J. D. (1991). Strategies for assessing and managing organizational stakeholders. Academy of Management Executive, 5, 61–75.

Scala, R. P. (1992, April). Aramony quits United Way. Fund Raising Management, 24(2), 9–10.

Schick, T. A. (1996). Technician ethics in public relations. Public Relations Quarterly, 41(1), 30–35.

Schmuhl, R. (1984). Introduction: The road to responsibility. In R. Schmuhl (Ed.), The responsibilities of journalism (pp. 1–18). Notre Dame, IN: University of Notre Dame Press.

Shamir, J., Reed, B. S., & Connell, S. (1990). Individual differences in ethical values of public relations practitioners. Journalism Quarterly, 67(4), 956–963.

Sharpe, M. L. (1986). Recognition comes from consistently high standards. Public Relations Review,

17–26.

Shoemaker, P. J., & Reese, S. D. (1996). *Mediating the message: Theories of influences on mass media content.* White Plains, NY: Longman.

Sieb, P., & Fitzpatrick, K. (1995). *Public relations ethics.* Fort Worth, TX: Harcourt Brace.

Siebert, F. S. (1974). The libertarian theory of the press. In F. S. Siebert, T. Peterson, & W. Schramm (Eds.), *Four theories of the press* (pp. 39–71). Urbana: University of Illinois Press.

Skolnik, R. (1993, September). Rebuilding trust: Nonprofits act to boost reputations. *Public Relations Journal, 49*(9), 29.

Smith, J. (1994). Strong separatism in professional ethics. *Professional Ethics, 3*(3 & 4), 117–140.

Spicer, C. (1997). *Organizational public relations: A political perspective.* Mahwah, NJ: Erlbaum.

Staiti, C. (1997, March 10). Xerox Corp.: A worldwide system delivers service that's anything but carbon-copy. *Computerworld, 31*(10), S12.

Sullivan, A. J. (1965). Values of public relations. In O. Lerbinger, & A. J. Sullivan (Eds.), *Information, influence & communication: A reader in public relations* (pp. 412–439). New York: Basic Books.

Tedlow, R. S. (1979). *Keeping the corporate image: Public relations and business: 1900–1950.* Greenwich, CT: JAI Press.

Theus, K. T. (1995, May). *To whom is moral duty owed? Obligation, blame and publics.* Paper presented to the Public Relations Division of the International Communication Association, Albuquerque, NM.

Thiagarajan, S., & Parker, G. (1999). *Teamwork and teamplay: Games and activities for building and training teams.* San Francisco: Jossey-Bass/Pheiffer.

Vasquez, G. M., & Taylor, M. (1999). What cultural values influence American public relations practitioners? *Public Relations Review, 25*(4), 433–449.

Vitell, S. J., Nwachukwu, S. L., & Barnes, J. H. (1993). The effects of culture on ethical decision-making: An application of Hofstede's typology. *Journal of Business Ethics, 12,* 753–760.

Walker, A. (1978, July). Reading one's way to professionalism. *Public Relations Journal, 34*(7), 42.

Weiss, A. (2000). *Good isn't good enough: Nine challenges for companies that choose to be great.* New York: Amacom.

Welfel, E. R., & Lipsitz, N. E. (1984). The ethical behavior of professional psychologists: A critical analysis of the research. *Counseling Psychologist, 12*(3), 31–42.

White, O. F., & Wolf, J. F. (1995, November). Is this ice cream American? *Administration & Society, 27*(3), 307–321.

Winkleman, M. (1987, October). Soul searching. *Public Relations Journal, 39*(10), 28–31.

Wright, D. K. (1976). Social responsibility in public relations: A multi-step theory. *Public Relations Review, 2*(3), 24–36.

Wright, D. K. (1981). Accreditation's effects on professionalism. *Public Relations Review, 7*(1), 48–61.

Wright, D. K. (1993). Enforcement dilemma: Voluntary nature of public relations codes. *Public Relations Review, 19*(1), 13–20.

Wu, W., Weaver, D., & Johnson, O. V. (1996). Professional roles in Russian and U.S. journalists: A comparative study. *Journalism and Mass Communication Quarterly, 73*(3), 534–548.

Wylie, F. (1983, January). Urgent needs and primary challenges. *Public Relations Journal, 39*(1), 29.

Wylie, F. (1994). Commentary: Public relations is not yet a profession. *Public Relations Review, 20,* 1–3.

# CHAPTER CONTENTS

• What is *Kuuki*?                                                        269
    *Hegemony*                                        272
    *Spiral of Silence*                               272
    *Agenda Setting*                                  273
    *Enforcement of Social Norms*                     273
    *Spiral of Cynicism*                              273
    *Social Psychological Theories on Conformity, Contagion,*   273
    *or Mass Hysteria*
    *Other Theories on Mass Media Influence*          274

• The *Kuuki* Phenomena in Modern History                                274
    *Jingoism as* Kuuki                               274
    *Antiwar* Kuuki                                   278
    Kuuki *for Justice*                               283

• Measurement of *Kuuki*                                                 285
    *Magnitudes and Trends of Opinions*               286
    *Intensity of Opinions*                           288
    *The Tripolar* Kuuki *Model*                      290

• Summary and Conclusions                                                291

• Note                                                                   294

• References                                                             294

# 8 Climate of Opinion, *Kuuki*, and Democracy

ITO YOUICHI
*Keio University at Shonan Fujisawa*

This article deals with the "climate of opinion" not only among the general public but also within the mass media and government sectors. It discusses how the climate of opinions in different sectors influence each other and political decision making as a final outcome. *Kuuki* refers to a Japanese as well as a Chinese and Korean concept meaning a climate of opinion with strong political and social pressure requiring compliance. Many historical examples of *kuuki* pressures such as anti-Semitism, jingoism, anti-Communism, and antiwar movements are introduced and analyzed. The article also deals with how climate of opinions or *kuuki* within and across different sectors can be estimated quantitatively. It discusses the conditions under which *kuuki* emerges and functions politically. It sheds new light on the mechanisms of social and political pressures and decision making, especially on the macro or societal level.

*I see you stand like greyhounds in the slips, / Straining upon the start. The game's afoot:*
*Follow your spirit, and upon this charge / Cry 'God for Harry, England, and Saint George!'*
William Shakespeare, *Henry V* (Act 3, Scene 1)

On September 14, 2001, the U.S. Congress approved a resolution requested by President Bush to use the U.S. Armed Forces in response to the terrorist attack on the World Trade Center Buildings in New York. In the Congress, one member, Barbara Lee (D-Cal.), voted against the bill. According to Reuters, since the night of that day, many faxes and telephone calls of protests

Author's note: The Japanese, Chinese, and Korean names in this article are described in their traditional order, the family name first followed by the given name. Earlier drafts of this article were presented at the ICA conference in Jerusalem, Israel, July 20-24, 1998; the International Political Science Association Workshop in Quebec, Canada, August 30, 1999; and the 35th Anniversary Conference at the School of Journalism and Communication, The Chinese University of Hong Kong, July 24-26, 2000. I thank participants of these conferences for their helpful comments. I am indebted to Anne Cooper-Chen of Ohio University, Joseph Cappella of the University of Pennsylvania, David Weaver of Indiana University, and Desmond Patrick of AskWrite International for valuable comments on earlier drafts.

Correspondence: Ito Youichi, 253-0054 Chigasaki-shi, Higashikaigan Minami 2-7-17, Japan; email: ito3045@sfc.keio.ac.jp (UNIX) or 0512087601@jcom.home.ne.jp.

and harassment began to reach Congresswoman Lee's office and residence. Accordingly, the police offered her 24-hour, round-the-clock protection ("Hansen," 2001).

On October 16, 2001, the city council of Berkeley, California, passed a resolution condemning the bombing of Afghanistan by the U.S. military as well as the original act of terrorism itself. Five members of the council supported the resolution and four opposed it. When this news was reported by *The Wall Street Journal,* telephone calls and faxes condemning the resolution deluged the Berkeley City Council ("Kuubaku," 2001).

In fact, phenomena of this kind have existed since ancient times. In 415 B.C. Athens, two generals, Nicias and Alcibiades argued whether or not Athens should send troops to Sicily. Alcibiades, who repeatedly emphasized the superiority of Athenians over "weak" Sicilians, won the popular vote and Athens decided, in 415 B.C., to send an expeditionary force to attack Syracuse in Sicily. The war dragged on for three years until the end of 413 B.C. and by that time Athens was completely defeated. According to Thucydides [460 B.C.-400 B.C.], the great Greek historian who joined this expedition and wrote about it, supporters of Nicias, who had at the beginning foreseen the dangers and so were opposed to the expedition, could not help but keep silent for fear of being accused by the majority of antipatriotism (quoted in Sudo, 2001, p. 35).

These social, political, and psychological pressures demanding compliance to a certain specific opinion, policy, or group decision and usually accompanied by threats and social sanction, are called *kuuki* in Japanese. As will be elaborated on in the next section, similar concepts have existed all over the world since ancient times. However, as this word began to be used as an academic or quasi-academic term first in Japan, let us see how the concept evolved.

Immediately before the Russo-Japanese War [1904–05], Japanese newspapers were divided into two groups: prowar and antiwar. As tension mounted and the war broke out, prowar newspapers expanded circulation whereas that of the antiwar newspapers declined. Not only that, but also one of the major antiwar newspapers, *Kokumin Shimbun,* was attacked by angry mobs, set on fire, and eventually went bankrupt. Another major antiwar newspaper, *Yorozu Choho,* changed its editorial policy during the war and switched to the prowar side. Before the war, *Yorozu Choho* was well known for antigovernment and anti-elite reporting. It was especially well known for breaking news concerning the scandalous behavior of politicians.

When this newspaper switched its editorial policy at the time of the Russo-Japanese War, Kuroiwa Ruiko, the president and chief editor of this newspaper, said: "Newspapers should be antigovernment during peacetime, and chauvinistic during wartime."

When the Manchurian Incident broke out in 1931, Japanese newspaper managers, who were fighting "circulation wars" similar to that between Pulitzer and Hearst in the United States, recalled Kuroiwa's remark. As a result, almost all major Japanese newspapers carried chauvinistic and jingoistic articles. They not only supported the military but also criticized "weak" civilian government leaders. As a result, within the Japanese government, moderate statesmen were gradually replaced by hawkish expansionists and the government was finally taken over by the military.

In 1977, a social critic, Yamamoto Shichihei published a famous book entitled *A Study of* Kuuki (in Japanese) in which he argued that *kuuki* was more responsible for Japan's history from 1930 through 1945 than anybody or anything else (Yamamoto, 1977).

## WHAT IS *KUUKI*?

The strict literal translation of *kuuki* is "air" in English. Functionally, however, the closest English equivalent for it is said to be "climate of opinion." In the fifth edition of *Dictionary of Media & Communication Studies, kuuki* is simply introduced as "a climate of opinion requiring compliance" (Watson & Hill, 2000, pp. 165–166).

According to Noelle-Neumann (1984, p. 78), the term "climate of opinion" was coined and first used by the English philosopher Joseph Glanvill [1636–80]. He used it in the meaning similar to public opinions (plural) or people's opinions. Criticizing "dogmatists" he wrote that those who respect *"Climates of Opinions* are more cautious in their resolves, and more sparing to determine" (quoted in Noelle-Neumann, 1984, p. 78).

Nowadays, "climate of opinion" refers to distribution patterns of public opinions rather than the opinions themselves. I have checked the indexes of many English language books on public opinion, but it appears in few books. Except for the "spiral of silence" theory, climate of opinion seems to be considered as a somewhat general, obscure, and weak framework in which political leaders are expected to make decisions (see, for example, Hellmann, 1969). According to these books, the climate of opinion may or may not influence each individual's attitudes and opinions or a political leader's decisions. On the other hand, the Japanese concept of *kuuki* connotes a far stronger political, social, and psychological pressure.

The ancient Chinese thought that there existed some substance or energy that moves or drifts back and forth across the border between the inside and outside of individuals and determines or restricts their thoughts and behavior. They called it *qi*, or *ki* in Japanese and Korean, or "spirit" in English.

The word *kuuki* is related to *reiki*. According to *The New Oxford Dictionary of English* (1998), *reiki* is "a healing technique based on the principle that the therapist can channel energy into the patient by means of touch to activate the natural healing processes of the patient's body and restore physical and emotional well-being. - ORIGIN Japanese, literally 'universal life energy.'"

Note that *reiki* and *kuuki* both have *ki* or "spirit" at the end. Whereas *reiki* energizes individuals "to restore physical and emotional well-being," the situation to which *kuuki* leads individuals and indeed the whole of society can be dangerous, as will be discussed later.

The modern Chinese still seem to believe in this concept. The late Deng Xiao Ping said in his speech on June 9, 1989, five days after the Tiananmen Square Incident: "This storm would come anyway, soon or later. It is determined by the major international climate *(da qi hou)* and the minor climate *(xiao qi hou)* from inside China itself, which can not be changed by the will of the people" ("Saiko," 2001, p. 5). The "major international climate *(da qi hou)*" referred to the collapse of the former Soviet bloc and the spread of liberalization and democratization in Eastern Europe. The "minor climate *(xiao qi hou)* from inside China" referred to the inclination toward liberalization and democratization promoted by reformist leaders such as Zhao Zi Yang and Hu Yao Bang, who were supported by intellectuals and students.

The *qi hou* mentioned by Deng may not be exactly the same as *kuuki* in Japanese, but it is similar to it in the sense that it is considered to affect collective decision making. It is very powerful because the pressure comes from both outside and inside, that is, the combination of a demand for compliance to some specific policy from outside and a willingness or motivation to comply with it from inside.

Koreans also share this attitude. Lee O. Young, a former Minister of Culture in Korea, and now a Professor at Iwa Women's College in Seoul, stated in an interview with a Japanese journalist that in present-day Korea "anti-Japanism" is the kind of "*kuuki* that nobody could resist" ("Kankoku," 1999, p. 5). To proclaim or admit that he or she is a Japanophile spells social suicide for a Korean political or intellectual leader. Professor Lee stated, in the same interview, that because he is a Japanologist, he is continually being suspected by the Korean people of being a Japanophile, which made it particularly difficult for him, as Minister of Culture, to promote the liberalization of Japanese popular culture.

In other words, Lee's cultural policy was shaped by pressure from outside, such as the threat of possible protests and criticism, as well as his own internal pressure: his willingness to comply with, and his wish not to offend, the Korean public. Of course, anybody can be faced with this dilemma, but Mr. Lee was particularly sensitive to it because he is a Japanologist.

Although Lee mentioned *kuuki* in Japanese in this interview, this is a borderline case because "anti-Japanism" sounds more like a matter of attitudes than a specific opinion, policy, or decision. However, since he used the term in relation to the liberalization of Japanese popular culture, the use of *kuuki* may be appropriate. However, "anti-Japanism" in general should be referred to as *fun'iki* or "atmosphere," which is less specific and more obscure than *kuuki*.

If I wrote that a *qi, ki,* or "spirit" moves back and forth between the inside and outside of individuals and affects their attitudes and opinions, I would probably be regarded as unscientific or "animistic." However, the theories of "spiral of silence" or "spiral of cynicism" make similar arguments. The "spiral process" in these theories refers to interactions between social phenomena and individual motivation or attitudes.

In the case of the spiral of silence theory, sanction as a social pressure and an individual's fear of isolation reinforce each other (Noelle-Neumann, 1984). In the case of the spiral of cynicism theory, cynicism is transmitted from the mass media to individuals as well as among individuals by passing "memes" or (cultural) "genes" (Cappella, 2001). A concept like "meme," which was coined by the famous biologist Richard Dawkins (1989) and derived from the Greek *mimesis* meaning "to imitate," sounds as mysterious and "animistic" as *qi* or *ki* (see Susan Blackmore's *The Meme Machine,* 1999, for the social implications of "memes").

As for the interaction between social phenomena and individual motivation, there exist many examples that are more similar. Racism as a social phenomenon interacts with people's innate desire for superiority or self-esteem. Jingoism as a foreign policy interacts with human, especially male, aggressiveness or "struggle instinct." Thus, when certain conditions are met, some spiral process or interaction between social phenomena and people's innate motivation, belief, or inclinations can produce a monster that people find difficult to resist. *Kuuki* is a social construct and exists outside the individual. However, it includes *ki* or "spirit," the implication of which is the existence of an interaction between *kuuki* and the *ki* or "spirit" inside individuals.

Elisabeth Noelle-Neumann was very interested in the notion of *kuuki* and mentioned it in the preface to the Japanese translation of *The Spiral of Silence* (Noelle-Neumann, 2000, p. vii). Furthermore, she asked me in person many questions about *kuuki*. She said: "the closest German word for it would be Zeitgeist, which translates into English as 'the spirit of the times'" (Noelle-Neumann, 1984, p. 137). In fact, the German concept of zeitgeist seems more akin to *kuuki* than "climate of opinion" in the sense that it implies strong social pressure. For example, Noelle-Neumann quotes from Goethe as follows:

If one side now especially stands forth, seizes possession of the crowd, and unfolds itself to the degree that those who are opposed must pull back into a corner and, for that moment at least, conceal themselves in silence, then one calls this predominance the spirit of the times *(Zeitgeist)* and indeed, for a period, it will have its way. (Quoted in Noelle-Neumann, 1984, p. 137)

Note also that *geist* is the equivalent of *ki, qi,* or "spirit," and therefore, zeitgeist, like *kuuki,* implies that it interacts with the *geist* inside individuals.

According to Yamamoto (1977, p. 58), the ancient Greeks and Jews were already aware of the danger of group decisions made under the influence of the "spirit" (or when the "spirit" is working). Thus, they, and especially the Jews, because of their strong faith in their sole, omnipotent god, established a tradition

of avoiding group decisions made under the influence of "spirit," which liberat-
ed decision makers and group members from making hasty decisions under the
influence of this compelling "spirit." Technically, it means tolerance toward dissent, thorough discussion, and the avoidance of an easy consensus.

There is no such tradition in Japan. On the contrary, the Japanese tend to give
priority to consensus and avoid discussions that may delay a consensus.
Therefore, Yamamoto (1977) argued that *kuuki* is a dangerous phenomenon,
especially for Japan. *Kuuki*, or *ki* has a somewhat "animistic" connotation. When
it comes to something "animistic," wrote Yamamoto (p. 60), rational people
"would immediately dismiss it as ridiculous and barbaric and decide that the best
policy is to ignore it." That is what Japanese leaders in the early Meiji period
(late nineteenth century) did in regard to modernization and enlightenment. Even
if they ignored it: "what existed continued to exist anyway and dominated the
Japanese people leading us to the edge of self-destruction." Thus, "all the important policy decisions since the Sino-Japanese War [1894–95] through the Pacific
War [1941–45] were made under the strong influence of *kuuki*. Therefore, it is
necessary for us to study it instead of ignoring it" (p. 61).

I have talked about this concept often outside Japan and received many questions regarding the difference between *kuuki* and similar concepts and ideas. Let
me briefly answer these questions.

Hegemony

Gramsci's hegemony is similar to *kuuki* in the sense that they both control
people by coercion (including potential or predictable coercion) from outside and
willingness or motivation (including those indoctrinated through socialization)
from inside. However, whereas hegemony is assumed to function always for the
benefit of the power elite or the capitalist class, there is no such assumption in
the concept of *kuuki*. It is true that *kuuki* has functioned many times in history for
the benefit of the power elite and the capitalist class. At the same time, however,
it intimidated the Japanese Emperor, drove the President of the United States to
resign in disgrace, and ousted numerous prime ministers from office in many
capitalist democracies. In addition, if hegemony refers to a general framework,
thought pattern, or attitude, it is different from *kuuki*. *Kuuki* has to be related to
some specific opinion, policy, or decision.

Spiral of Silence

As already mentioned, the spiral of silence and *kuuki* are also similar. The spiral of silence theory apparently assumes pressure from outside as well as from
inside individuals. If *kuuki* was always produced and sustained by the mass
media only, these two concepts might be almost identical. However, *kuuki* can
emerge from the general public or the power elite and intimidate journalists, too.
In the spiral of silence theory there is an assumption that mass media transform
a minority opinion into a majority opinion. There is no such assumption in the

*kuuki* theory. It just deals with the function or impact of *kuuki* on policy decisions, mass media contents, and public opinion, regardless of where it originates or how it was produced.

## Agenda Setting

The agenda-setting theory focuses on agenda whereas the *kuuki* theory focuses on the nature, attributes, or directions of the content. In this sense, they are different. In addition, as long as mass media contents maintain variety or heterogeneity, their effects on policy making are not predictable even if they do have a strong influence on individual attitudes and behavior. In other words, as long as mass media contents remain heterogeneous, it is unlikely that *kuuki* is created as a result of the agenda-setting function of mass media.

In recent developments of this theory, however, some researchers point out the "inter-media consonance" regarding agenda (Mathes & Pfetsch, 1991; Noelle-Neumann & Mathes, 1987). When the subject matter is critically important for the society, mass media contents become monolithic as far as the agenda is concerned. Even if the agenda does becomes monolithic, if the attributes or directions of contents are varied, kuuki would not be produced. However, if the agenda happens to pertain to social norms, morals, or ethics, the agenda determines the direction of the content. For example, any scandal automatically determines the direction of the content, which is criticisms of the people involved. In this rather roundabout way, *kuuki* can be created by the agenda-setting function of mass media.

## Enforcement of Social Norms

When the mass media report violation of social norms, morals, and ethics not to speak of laws, it is likely that *kuuki* demanding punishment is produced and the people involved cannot help but cope with it (Berelson, 1963). In fact, many political leaders have had to resign for this reason. As mentioned before, however, *kuuki* is not always created by the mass media. It can be created by political leaders and can intimidate journalists.

## Spiral of Cynicism

As mentioned before, the "spiral process" resembles the *kuuki* process. However, cynicism seems to be a matter of attitudes rather than specific opinion, policy, or decision. Also, *kuuki* motivates or energizes people to act or speak out whereas cynicism seems to deprive people of motivation or energy. If the oxymoron "spirit of cynicism" is self-contradictory, so is the *kuuki* of cynicism.

## Social Psychological Theories on Conformity, Contagion, or Mass Hysteria

*Kuuki* and these theories are similar in the sense that they both deal with the social influence on individuals and the interactions between society and individuals. However, *kuuki* is recognized by people as an obvious pressure and not by any means a contagion of which people may not be aware. Also, the *kuuki* phenomena is a matter of specific opinion, policy or decision and has little to do with more general behavioral patterns such as fashion, mood, or fad. It is different from mere atmosphere or an intellectual trend, which lack pressure for compliance.

*Kuuki* may overlap with mass hysteria in some extreme cases, but in most cases *kuuki* is less irrational or emotional because it has to do with specific opinion, policy, or decision. For example, jingoism or antiwar movements can be *kuuki* but they would not be called mass hysteria. Also, *kuuki* is recognized as pressure but mass hysteria is a matter of general irrational contagion.

### Other Theories on Mass Media Influence

There are many other theories on mass media influence including "framing," which has become popular recently. However, as long as mass media contents are assumed to be completely diversified in terms of both agenda and political inclinations *kuuki* cannot be created on the societal level as a mass media source of influence.

Yamamoto, as a social critic, used the *kuuki* concept in order to criticize the Japanese political culture. Therefore, he did not discuss any specific case examples in other countries except for ancient Greece and ancient Israel. However, the *kuuki* phenomena are probably far more ubiquitous and universal in modern times than Yamamoto thought.

## THE *KUUKI* PHENOMENA IN MODERN HISTORY

### Jingoism as *Kuuki*

*The Spanish-American War (United States).* Although there existed complicated political and economic reasons behind this war when it erupted in 1898, the direct cause of the war was the sinking of the American battleship Maine in Havana harbor by an explosion that caused the death of 260 members of the crew. Let us look at some further explanations in the *Encyclopedia Americana.*

> The destruction of the battleship, on the night of Feb. 15, 1889, was attributed by the American press to a Spanish bomb. Actually, the cause of the sinking, whether due to an internal or external explosion, has never been proved. In any case the indignation in the United States caused by the sinking raised *the war spirit to the boiling point* [italics added]. (*Encyclopedia Americana, 1964,* 360w)

The "war spirit" at the "boiling point" obviously indicates the existence of *kuuki*. Spain "was in no condition militarily or economically to fight the United States," and consequently the Spanish government "employed every means to prevent the outbreak of war." The Spanish government informed the American ambassador in Madrid "that the Spanish government was making all the concessions that public opinion would tolerate." However, President McKinley, on his side, was "*under tremendous pressure from public opinion to embark on a war to liberate the Cubans from 'Spanish tyranny' and avenge the Maine* [italics added]" (*Encyclopedia Americana, 1964,* 360w).

Thus, on April 25, 1898, the American Congress declared the existence of a state of war. Note that President McKinley "was under tremendous pressure from public opinion." It is also well-known that at that time the major newspaper syndicate led by William R. Hearst [1863–1951] and the other syndicate led by Joseph Pulitzer [1847–1911] were fighting a fierce "circulation war." When a *Journal*'s correspondent sent a telegram from Havana stating that everything was quiet there, William Hearst sent a telegram back to him stating: "You furnish the pictures. I'll furnish the war." This is a well-known fact and is dramatized in Orson Wells' movie satirizing Hearst, "Citizen Kane." It is now widely accepted that Hearst's "sensational methods helped transform the Cuban insurrection of 1895 into the Spanish-American War of 1898" (*Encyclopedia Americana, 1964,* p. 36).

Frederick (1993) also states the following:

> When Cuba began a bloody revolt against its Spanish colonial rulers, American expansionists called on President William McKinley to intervene and take Cuba. McKinley heisted, but public opinion was inflamed by the sensational coverage in the two newspapers. When a Spanish general herded Cuban farmers into squalid concentration campus and many civilians died, Hearst's Journal dubbed the general the "butcher" of Havana and editorialized for intervention and annexation of Cuba. In 1898 Hearst even published a purloined private letter in which the Spanish ambassador in Washington sharply criticized President McKinley. Then the American battleship Maine mysteriously exploded in the Havana harbor. McKinley could no longer resist the surging pressure for intervention, and Congress passed a declaration of war. (p. 221)

However, it would be incorrect to think that the war was caused by American "yellow journalism" only. As will be demonstrated in the Japanese case in the next section, jingoistic *kuuki* cannot be created by the mass media only. The general public is needed as an indispensable partner for it to occur.

The Spanish-American War of 1898 was a typical war caused by *kuuki*. Although Yamamoto (1977) did not say so exactly, what he meant was that the wars Japan fought during the period between 1930 and 1945 were this type of war.

*The Manchurian Incident [1931], the Sino-Japanese War [1940–45], and the Pacific War [1941–45; Japan].* It was briefly described at the beginning of this article how the experiences of Japanese journalists at the time of the Russo-Japanese War [1904–05] affected their reporting and editorial policies years later at the time of the Manchurian Incident [1931] and onward through to the end of the Second World War. That part of modern Japanese history was one of the major motivations leading Yamamoto Shichihei to write *A Study of* Kuuki. Let us examine a little more in detail the *kuuki* process from the Manchurian Incident [1931] through to the end of the Second World War [1945].

In Japan, in the 1930s and 40s, there was no political party equivalent to the Nazis or the Fascists or a leader equivalent to Hitler or Mussolini. Westerners and the Chinese have accused Emperor Hirohito and Prime Minister Tojo Hideki as being the equivalents of Hitler and Mussolini. They were certainly responsible in the sense that they could not control the military properly, but Emperor Hirohito was by no means like the German Kaiser Wilhelm II, and Tojo was by no means like Hitler or Mussolini.

The German Kaiser Wilhelm II talked much about politics, leaving several infamous inflammatory remarks such as the "yellow peril" to poison the minds of future generations. In contrast, Emperor Hirohito published three scholarly books during his lifetime. The subjects dealt with in these three books pertain to shellfish, marine bacteria, and other marine life forms. It was said that he was happiest when he was observing marine bacteria through a microscope in his research laboratory. He left very little, for a head of state, in the way of political statements or written political commentary.

Tojo was merely a competent military bureaucrat before he became Prime Minister in 1941. He was a man more like Dwight Eisenhower or Douglas MacArthur than Hitler or Mussolini. The *Encyclopedia Americana* (index) introduces Tojo as just a "Japanese army officer" whereas it introduces Hitler as "a German dictator" and Mussolini as "an Italian dictator." Tojo became the Prime Minister on October 17, 1941, only 6 weeks before the attack on Pearl Harbor, and when the island of Saipan was captured by the U.S. Forces in August 1944, one year before Japan's surrender, he apologized to the National Diet, resigned as prime minister, and completely retired from politics. Although Tojo may have pursued power, there was no scandal attached to his name regarding money or sex. He led an average and commonplace family life and apparently never had any flamboyant love affairs as those enjoyed by Hitler and Mussolini. His personal life was probably more unblemished than either Eisenhower or Roosevelt, who both proved to have had feet of clay where extramarital affairs are concerned. Tojo lived in an ordinary middle-class house and his way of life was unpretentious, if not humble. If Emperor Hirohito and Prime Minister Tojo were such seemingly innocuous personalities who was to blame for Japan's history from 1930 through 1945?

Hata Seiryu, a former editor-in-chief of the *Asahi Shimbun,* answered this question in a long column written in 1987 immediately before his retirement. According to him, the most responsible was the (military) government and then the newspapers. This statement is persuasive considering that Hata was the editor-in-chief of the most prestigious national newspaper in Japan, worked as a leading journalist before the Second World War, and had reached this conclusion by the time of his retirement. Reflecting on his entire journalistic career and especially the hectic 15 years from 1930 through 1945, he testified as follows:

> Newspapers at that time did not necessarily try to flatter those in power. Rather, they wrote to please readers. I may sound evasive, but *there certainly existed some kind of mechanism that aggravated the situation through subtle interactions [between newspapers and the public].* Readers were waiting for articles reporting the exploits of the victorious Imperial Forces. Newspapers indulged themselves in a competition to appear more patriotic and to see who could print the most articles urging and exalting victory. Newspaper companies cooperated through the dispatch of comfort or entertainment groups, calls for patriotic songs, campaigns for contributions to build more airplanes, and various other ways. The heavy responsibility that the newspapers bear is second only to that of the government. However, I disagree with the claim that "the general masses were victims." Newspapers form public opinions, but public opinion also influences newspapers. The general masses are not like horses that can be tamed and trained to do their masters' bidding [italics added]. ("Senso," 1987, p. 4)

Hata's personal and intuitive realization is in fact supported by abundant academic literature. Kakegawa (1972), Ikei (1981, 1988), and Tsukamoto (1986) content analyzed prewar Japanese newspapers and severely criticized prewar Japanese journalism: Also see commentaries and memoirs by journalists such as Chamoto (1984), Ishida (1995), Maesaka (1989, 1991), and Suzuki (1995).

Ikei (1981, 1988) emphasized that it was only after 1937, or 1934 at the earliest, that government control of journalism became tight. In the book provocatively entitle, *Newspapers Ruined Japan: Agitations Toward the Pacific War* (in Japanese), Ishida (1995, pp. 21–22) states that Japanese newspapers enjoyed the freedom of expression until 1936 or late 1932 at the earliest. Maesaka (1991, pp. 202–204) also argues that newspapers could have criticized the military if they wished at least until around 1936, and if all major newspapers had done so at that time, Japanese national policies would have certainly been affected. As mentioned already, at the time of the Russo-Japanese War [1904–05], newspapers had the freedom to publish antiwar editorials if they wished. It is said that Japan's democracy before the Second World War reached its peak during the Taisho period [1912–26], which is called the "Taisho Democracy."

In spite of that, major Japanese newspapers in the early 1930s were so concerned with the growth of circulation and profits, they did not seem to notice what they were doing to themselves. By carrying jingoistic articles to expand their circulations, they were helping the military replace civilian leaders and take over the government. When they finally woke up to what was going on, it was

too late. Their freedom of expression had been curtailed by the military government. "[Japanese] journalists should never forget that it was the lack of mission
consciousness, courage, and international sensitivity in journalism that brought
the collapse of the nation" (Maesaka, 1991, p. 204).

"Some kind of mechanism that aggravated the situation through subtle interactions [between newspapers and the public]" mentioned in Hata's memoirs,
quoted above, describes what is now called the *kuuki* process. By provoking and
promoting the "war spirit," Japanese newspapers in the 1930s created a jingoistic *kuuki*, which throttled their own necks. As Tsukamoto (1986) wrote:

> Newspapers uncritically flattered the military's coercive logic for invasion and indulged
> themselves to excessive compliance at the time of the Manchurian Incident. This very fact
> facilitated the suppression of speech and the press by the expanding military, which eventu-
> ally brought the situation in which journalism had to surrender. (p. 163)

As discussed in the next section, however, individuals can have an "antiwar
spirit" as well as a "war spirit." By the end of the 1930s the number of Japanese
casualties in China had climbed to a considerable level. As a natural result, the
number of people who were wearying of the endless war in China was increasing. If Japanese newspapers had maintained the degree of freedom that they used
to enjoy during the Taisho Democracy period (1912–26) and had encouraged and
promoted an "antiwar spirit" growing in the masses, an antiwar *kuuki* might have
been created. Then, a powerful civilian prime minister might have emerged and
proclaimed a withdrawal from China. Consequently, there would have been no
war with the United States and the United Kingdom.

Such an antiwar *kuuki* process emerged and functioned in France in the 1960s
(withdrawal from Indochina and Algeria) and in the United States in the 1970s
(withdrawal from Vietnam). Unfortunately, however, this did not happen in
Japan because of the immaturity of its democracy, the military bureaucrats'
resistance against admitting failure, and the complexities of international politics
at that time such as the military alliances with Germany and Italy and the fear of
the international communist movement and its sponsor the Soviet Union.

### Antiwar *Kuuki*

*The Gulf War (Japan).* The so-called "Gulf Crisis" broke out with the Iraqi
invasion of Kuwait on August 2, 1990. Considering Japan's heavy dependence
on Middle Eastern oil, its economic profits from that area from trade, and Japan's
economic and military capabilities, it was inconceivable that Japan could remain
removed from the crisis and avoid involvement. On August 14, President Bush
of the United States telephoned Premier Kaifu asking for Japan's contribution to
the solution of the crisis. The government had already determined that Japan
would make economic contributions, but the question was: What else should and
could be done?

Thus, Premier Kaifu announced on August 29, 1990, his intention to sponsor a new law tentatively entitled the United Nations Peace Cooperation (UNPC) Law to permit the government to dispatch the military to troubled areas. Japanese cabinets have traditionally taken the view that the activities of the Japanese Self-Defense Force is limited to pure self-defense against direct attack and any participation in UN Forces is not allowed in light of the new postwar Constitution.[1]

On September 26, 1990, Premier Kaifu proposed an outline of the UNPC Law to the ruling party (the Liberal Democratic Party) leaders and obtained their approval. It was made clear that the purpose of this law was to assist the United Nations' peace-keeping activities such as transportation, communication, supply, medical and public health, surveillance, and so forth, and the Self-Defense Force would not be engaged in any coercion by force or use of force.

As soon as Premier Kaifu expressed his intention to enact the UNPC Bill on August 29, a vociferous section of the Japanese public strongly reacted against it. They were of the older generations rather than the younger and proved to be mostly women. The Second World War was and is a great "trauma" for the Japanese, especially the older generation. The idea of being involved in a war outside Japan reminded them of their miserable experiences in the past, and they sent hundreds of thousands of letters to newspapers describing their devastating experiences.

Not many of those letters seriously discussed the situation in the Middle East. Their typical logic was that they had had terrible experiences during the Second World War so they didn't want their children and grandchildren to have the same experiences. The idea of sending noncombat troops to the Middle East under the control of the United Nations had little to do with their experiences in Manchuria during the Second World War. For those who had had really miserable experiences in the past, however, such "small differences" did not matter. The idea of being involved in a war outside Japan horrified them.

According to a public opinion survey conducted by the Prime Minister's Office in 1989, before the Gulf Crisis, 47% of respondents opposed any "participation in" the UN Force by Japan's Self-Defense Force. After the outbreak of the Gulf Crisis, however, the percentage of objections increased to 53% in the *Yomiuri* newspaper survey and 58% in the *Asahi* newspaper survey. The possible outbreak of a war may have made the public more serious and negative, and the reactions of the older generation mentioned above may have affected the outlook of the younger generation.

The declining support rate in the cabinet also indicated the unpopularity of the UNPC Bill. According to monthly surveys conducted by the *Yomiuri*, supporters of the Kaifu Cabinet's policy accounted for 60% in July and 63% in August, but the figure plummeted through September and October and reached 48% in November. Public support of the ruling party (LDP) decreased similarly during this period. Correspondingly, the percentage of nonsupporters increased from 23% in July to 36% in November.

The Japanese mass media were divided into two groups: those who supported the UNPC Bill and those who opposed it. Prominent members of the mass

media in the former group were the *Asahi Shimbun, the Mainichi Shimbun,* and
the television networks affiliated with them; some in the latter group were the
*Yomiuri Shimbun,* the *Sankei Shimbun,* and their affiliated TV networks. Let us
examine how the *Asahi,* who opposed the bill, and the *Yomiuri,* who supported
it, functioned during the two months when Prime Minister Kaifu and the other
Japanese government leaders were trying to pass the bill.

The opposition against the bill by the *Asahi* and others was not too strong in
the beginning. There was little difference between the *Asahi* and the *Yomiuri*
before the middle of October except for some editorials. In the middle of
October, however, it became clear that the public's resistance against the bill was
quite strong and some ruling party leaders became cautious. Then, the *Asahi*
became bolder.

Its headlines became more sensational and defiant and the contents often
became sentimental. Certain symbols and slogans that remind the Japanese of the
Second World War increased in *Asahi* articles. For example, an article introduc-
ing the uneasiness and complaints of SDF soldiers was headlined "Mother Says
Don't Go, But If It Is An Order . . ." ("Jieikan no honne [1]," 1990, p. 31). An
*Asahi* article quoted one soldier's opinion that Japanese troops would be used as
shields for U.S. troops ("Jieikan no honne [2]," 1990, p. 30).

The *Asahi* carried an interview with a popular comedian, Nishikawa Kiyoshi,
who had become a Diet member, and his American wife Helen. In the article,
Nishikawa said: "In my childhood, my Mother always told me that an atomic
bomb could have been dropped on Kohchi (his home town)." His wife Helen
added: "As a mother of three children, I cannot let Japan get involved in a war
again" ("Jieitai no haken," 1990, p. 14).

Claims of opposition parties screamed from *Asahi*'s headlines, "*haken* (a
generic term to mean dispatch)" was replaced by "*hahei* (military expedition, or
sending military troops to attack)," and specially enlarged columns for letters to
the editor carried many stories of the miserable experiences suffered during the
Second World War. As a result, the *Asahi* and some other members of the mass
media (including *Terebi Asahi,* a major television network affiliated with the
*Asahi Shimbun*) became the rallying point for a campaign against the bill. It is
certain that this campaign incited the general public's "antiwar spirit" and created an antiwar *kuuki.*

The *Yomiuri,* which supported the UNPC Bill, criticized such *kuuki* in Japan
at that time as follows:

> Some opposition parties, including the [Japanese] Socialist Party, cry sensational slogans
> such as "Don't Send Our Boys to the Battle Fields" or "Don't Take Up the Gun, Boys". They
> intentionally mix "*haken* [a generic term to mean dispatch]" and "*hahei* [military expedition]"
> and propagandize as if Japan was waging a war.

Not only opposition parties but also the television news broadcasts are responsible for reinforcing this war image. They show films of SDF soldiers and tanks on maneuvers in the background as they report the news. ("Kyoryoku hoan," 1990, p. 3)

As a result of the interaction between some of the mass media and the general
public, the antiwar or anti-UNPC Bill *kuuki* became so powerful that Prime
Minister Kaifu deemed it impossible or politically too risky to promote it further.
So, he decided to give up and announced on November 5 that he was dropping the
bill, to the great disappointment of the governments of the Western military bloc.
What should be noted in this case is that the Japanese mass media were divided (as in the case of the Russo-Japanese War) into the pro-UNPC Bill side and
the anti-UNPC Bill side. Only the anti-UNPC side joined the *kuuki* process and
succeeded in making the Prime Minister give up the enactment of the bill. In
other words, the mass media that were in the *kuuki* process had influence on the
policy decision but those who were out of it had no influence.

*The Vietnam War (United States).* When American involvement in Vietnam
began is not clear. Maybe it depends on the definition of "involvement." "It
appears that the public really did not become widely aware of that involvement
until the 1964 election and that many were largely unaware until the increase of
troop buildups in late 1965" (Monroe, 1975, p. 200). According to Page and
Brody (1975):

At the outset of 1968, nearly 500,000 American troops were in Vietnam; at least 20 billion
dollars per year were being spent on the war; and each week about 100 Americans—and
countless Vietnamese—were being killed. The war had a direct impact upon the lives of ser-
vicemen, their families, and friends. It affected many others indirectly, through rampant infla-
tion and curtailment of domestic governmental spending.

Most Americans were thoroughly sick of the war. By late March, 1968, nearly two-thirds of
the people disapproved of the way President Johnson was handling Vietnam, and a plurality
thought it had been a mistake to send U.S. troops to fight there. Dissent was loud on university campuses, in the U.S. Senate and even on Wall Street. (p. 446)

Although the war officially ended in January 1973, in reality it did not end
until April 1975 when U.S. troops completely withdrew from Indochina. Apart
from whether the United States was "defeated" or not, at least the United States did
not win the victory and could not achieve its initial goals. What were the reasons?
One of the obvious reasons was public opinion. As early as 1968, many public
opinion surveys indicated that those who thought that American involvement in
Vietnam was a mistake exceeded those who did not agreed with it, as indicated in

the above quotation. In the 1960s the Vietnam War was the most frequently covered subject in American news magazines and the most important issue recognized by respondents in public opinion surveys (Funkhouser, 1991). Naturally, therefore, it was the most important issue of elections in the late 1960s and early 1970s. Political leaders including presidential candidates had to make their positions clear regarding the Vietnam War.

According to Monroe (1975, p. 208), there were two kinds of people who opposed the war; "those who were opposed for moral reasons and those who might be best called the 'war weary.'" The first group "represented only a tiny fraction of the American public at any given time and was perhaps a tenth as large as the remaining groups of nonsupporters."

Did anti-Vietnam War movements in the United States and elsewhere contribute to the end of the war? Monroe (1975) says definitely not:

> It can probably not be proved, but there is certainly reason to suspect that the net effect of several years of active protest against the war was probably to retard the development of opposition to it in public opinion. In short, the occurrence of vocal and sometimes violent dissent on the war presented a clear and present reference point for many people for whom the issue would have otherwise remained a vague one, and reactions to that reference point were so negative as to offer an additional psychological basis for supporting the war. (p. 208)

> At the elementary level of appraising public opinion, it is clear that most of the popular stereotypes about opinions on the war were simply not correct. The presidential assertion of the existence of a "silent majority" that always gave its support to administration policy was undoubtedly an overstatement with political motivations, but it did give a more accurate view of the situation than would reliance on casual observation of vocal dissent. . . . To blindly and indiscriminately attack an individual's most deeply held values for the purpose of changing one of his [or her] opinions is likely to be quite counterproductive. (p. 216)

As Monroe's book was published in 1975, there still remains the aftermath of the "crush of opinions" among Americans. However, I do not agree with Monroe's view. Like it or not, "vocal and sometimes violent dissent" in my view did have an effect. If loud vocal dissent was completely isolated, it would not, but in a situation where the opposition out-numbered supporters, opposition was expanding and support was shrinking, it must have had a considerable effect on policy decisions.

As has already been shown by several examples in history, even heads of states could not resist *kuuki*. *Kuuki* is not only a matter of a pattern of opinion distribution but also, as to be elaborated later, a question of the intensity of the opinion. The intensity comes from some "spirit" inherent in individuals. Some spirits are evil, egoistic, and destructive, but some others are noble, altruistic, and constructive. Humans have many contradictory spirits such as the "war spirit" and "antiwar spirit," "parochialism," and "internationalism," a "spirit of justice" and a "criminal spirit," a "democratic spirit" and an "authoritarian spirit," a "capitalistic spirit" and a "socialistic spirit," and so on. Monroe accuses vocal dissent for attacking "an individual's most deeply held values." What he meant by values may be those such as democracy, freedom, the free market system, and so on. However, the "antiwar spirit" or pacifism can also be somebody else's most deeply held value.

Therefore, what kind of *kuuki* develops as a social construct depends on which spirit or basic value in each individual is provoked and incited by the mass media. Actually, this is the lesson that political and military leaders learned from the Vietnam War. Subsequently, in the wars following Vietnam such as the Falkland's and the Gulf War, military authorities carefully censored and controlled mass media contents so that they would not provoke and incite an "antiwar spirit" in individual viewers and readers so that an antiwar *kuuki* could not be created (see Watson & Hill, 2000 for the Falkland War; and Bennette & Paletz, 1994, Greenberg & Gantz, 1993, Paletz, 1999, for the Gulf War).

## *Kuuki* for Justice

Perloff (1998) summarizes the long and complicated Watergate scandal in the United States as follows:

> Over the course of the summer and fall of 1972, *The Washing Post* doggedly followed the story of the break-in at the Democratic National Committee Headquarters at the Watergate Hotel. *The Post's* Bob Woodward and Carl Berstein, through hard-hitting and painstaking reporting, were able to connect the Watergate burglary to the Nixon White House, were able to show that Nixon campaign funds had been involved in the break-in, and were able to document that political sabotage had played an integral role in the Nixon reelection campaign. What followed is now history: the trial of the Watergate burglars, astonishing revelations of a White House cover-up, televised coverage of Senate committee hearings, disclosure that Nixon employed a secret tape recording system in the Oval Office, the House Judiciary Committee's vote on three articles of impeachment, and Nixon's resignation on August 9, 1974. (p. 227)

Why did President Nixon have to resign in disgrace? Was that simply because two young reporters wrote about the five burglars who broke into the Democratic National Committee Headquarters? Perloff (1998) answers this question as follows:

> Without taking anything away from Woodward and Bernstein, who demonstrated great courage and tenacity, the fact is that *The Post* did not bring the president down. It started the ball rolling, to be sure, its reports a necessary condition for the emergence of Watergate as an issue on the national stage, but not a sufficient one. To adequately explain how events transpired in the Watergate scandal, we need to consider not just *The Post's* reports, but the larger political context in which the media work. (p. 227)

Let us see how American political scientists and political communication experts have explained the "larger political context" that is called in this article the *kuuki* process. According to Davis (1990):

> The Langs (1983) provide an extensive analysis of the Watergate crisis that draws on both narrative theory and social construction of reality. They argue that Watergate failed to become an issue in the 1972 campaign because of the narrative structure used to present it to the public. They point out that even though there was more than adequate coverage of Watergate in the press, almost all of it framed Watergate as a partisan issue. McGovern's assertions about Watergate were "balanced" by White House denials. Perhaps as a consequence, poll results showed that very few Americans knew much about Watergate and those who did tended to be McGovern supporters. Most people didn't bother to learn about something that was so clearly framed as just another election year brouhaha. (p. 171)

This stage in the Watergate incident can be described for the benefit of this article's approach as that time in 1972 just preceding the moment when the people's "spirit of justice" was aroused. Therefore, the *kuuki* process had not yet started.

> The Langs point out that Watergate didn't begin to gain broad public attention or interest until Judge Sirica was presented by the media as a credible and presumably objective spokesperson for the "cover-up scenario." Subsequently, the press abandoned its practice of balancing Watergate stories and printed news that was more or less exclusively supportive of the cover-up narrative. Even with this imbalance in coverage, many political independents and Nixon Democrats remained convinced of Nixon's innocence until the independent prosecutor was fired during the Saturday Night Massacre. Nixon's "third rate burglary" narrative failed to survive the firestorm of media coverage that followed this event. Only committed Republicans retained their faith. (Davis, 1990, p. 171)

The American people's "spirit of justice" gradually became stirred up during the time of the hearings held by Judge Sirica, the series of "cover-ups," and the dismissal of the independent prosecutor by President Nixon (the Saturday Night Massacre).

According to McCombs, Einsiedel, and Weaver (1991):

> The process had three elements: First, certain events were highlighted, drawing people's attention and creating discussion. Second, the media framed events in some contexts. What did the events mean? Was there any reason for concern? Third, the media linked the specific events of Watergate to more general political symbols. (p. 72)

The "more general political symbols" mentioned here have to do with the "spirit of justice" inherent in each American citizen. The same is true with Richard

Perloff's following explanation:

> In sum, the media helped to build consensus around the Watergate issue. They did so not by directly persuading the public to change its attitudes toward impeachment. Rather, they influenced the process on a number of levels. Highlighting some events rather than others, framing issues through the use of language and metaphors, linking the news to familiar political symbols, connecting the public to political elites through opinion polls, and calling on time-honored political values that forced political actors to consider the larger implications of their actions. (Perloff, 1998, p. 230)

The "more familiar political symbols" mentioned here are the same as the "more general political symbols" mentioned by McCombs, Einsiedel, and Weaver (1991); "time-honored political values," and "the larger implications of their actions" all can be explained in terms of the "spirit of justice" shared by mature citizens in all democratic societies and *kuuki* as a social construct with tremendous pressure for compliance

In addition, after reviewing the Watergate case, Molotch, Protess, and Gordon (1987) concluded as follows:

> The critical issue is not so much the technical and substantive nature of a given message (although such things do matter), but how that message relates or fails to relate to the practical purposes—at that point—of actors in a number of other significant realms. Media "effects" on policy (as on anything else) come from the capacity of journalists to play a role (delimited, but omnipresent) in this larger ecology of individual and institutional practices. (p. 46)

This conclusion is basically the same as the conclusion of my article entitled "Mass Media's Influence on Government Decision Making" (Ito, 1996a), which analyzed the Japanese prime minister's decision to withdraw the bill to dispatch Japanese troops to the Persian Gulf area at the time of the Gulf War. The conclusion of that article was as follows:

> The mass media that were a part of the "dominant kuuki" or the mainstream opinion created in the triadic relationship among the three major elements of collective decision making—the masses, mass media, and government—had influence, but those that were not a part of it had no influence on the Prime Minister's decision to withdraw the bill. (p. 51)

## MEASUREMENT OF *KUUKI*

Yamamoto Shichihei's *A Study of* Kuuki (1977) has been recognized by many Japanese journalists and political and social critics as a post-Second World War masterpiece in the field of political and social commentary. Since its publication, the term *kuuki* has often been used in journalism and opinion magazines. However, it is not yet used by academicians as part of their jargon. The following three reasons are conceivable for this.

1. Yamamoto suggested this concept in order to explain and criticize political and social phenomena peculiar to Japan. Although Yamamoto wrote that the mechanism was recognized by ancient peoples in West Asia (his specialty), he never tried to apply this concept to similar phenomena in modern times in countries other than Japan. Therefore, academicians have thought that this concept lacked international universality, or applicability outside Japan.

2. Because Yamamoto was a social critic and not a social scientist, he never tried to measure or quantify *kuuki*.

3. Yamamoto was an outspoken anti-Marxist or antileftist social critic; therefore, his theories and concepts have never been used by Marxist or critical leftist scholars.

As for the ubiquity of the *kuuki* phenomena in countries other than Japan, enough examples have already been introduced in previous sections. It is true that Yamamoto used this concept to criticize many political and social movements by leftist groups. It is because he thought that leftist values including, the "antiwar spirit" as seen in the withdrawal of the United Nations Peace Cooperation Bill discussed in the previous section, became too widespread among the Japanese general public. However, as repeatedly mentioned, he criticized the Japanese jingoism before the Second World War using the *kuuki* concept. Therefore, the *kuuki* concept is by nature neither rightist nor leftist. It is a neutral concept that can be applied to prowar and antiwar movements. The rest of this section is devoted to the second problem, the operationalization or quantification of *kuuki*.

### Magnitudes and Trends of Opinions

*Public opinion survey data.* One of the best indicators of *kuuki* is obviously public opinion survey data. However, a single snapshot survey result is not sufficient. In order for some climate of opinion to be felt as *kuuki* or as pressure, the number of the supporters of the opinion need to be increasing. If they are decreasing, nobody would feel any pressure. Therefore, the data needs to be longitudinal trend data.

If reliable public opinion survey results indicate that the high percentage of respondents support or agree with some specific opinion, and the supporters of the opinion keep increasing, it is very likely that there exists *kuuki* in that society regarding that subject (although the nature of the subject is important, as will be elaborated later).

There exist many arguments insisting that public opinion surveys are not necessarily reliable. This is true when the percentages of neutral and ambiguous responses, such as "I don't know," "no opinion," or "it depends," are high. However, when the answers are clear and the result is overwhelming, with a very small percentages of neutral or ambiguous answers, the result may be considered highly reliable.

Monroe's (1975, p. 201) Figure 11.1 indicates the longitudinal trends of the anti-Vietnam War opinions in the United States from 1965 through 1973. It also indicates the change of *kuuki* from prowar to antiwar. If figures such as this were always easily available, it would be a snap to conduct scientific research on the political functions of *kuuki*. Actually, however, it is extremely difficult to secure data on a specific public opinion over a long period of time.

When the responses to the same question over a long period of time were not available, questions similar to each other were collected and the responses were "abstracted" to the level of "positive" versus "negative," "yes" versus "no," or "favorable" versus "unfavorable." Strouse's (1975, p. 156) Table 5-3 is an example. When the question or answer categories are not identical, however, it is very difficult to construct persuasive trend data. It is probably for this reason that Strouse uses a table instead of a figure.

*Content analysis.* Suppose there exists a collection of several different kinds of mass media, which as a whole accurately reflect public opinion, then public opinion could be measured through the systematic content analysis of such a collection of mass media. If public opinion can be measured by content analysis of mass media, longitudinal trend data could be obtained more easily than by conducting public opinion surveys.

However, a difficult problem involved with this method is to separate public opinion from the opinions the mass media themselves and others that cannot be included in the public opinion category. Thus, we classified each article of several different newspapers (taking political balance into account) with a view of those whose opinion it represented. It may represent the opinion of the prime minister, a government official, a ruling party member, an opposition party member, a newspaper editor, a journalist, a social critic, an expert on that particular issue, a general reader, a foreign government, a labor union, a corporate executives' union, and so on.

Then we determined which categories of opinions constitute (a) public opinion, (b) indigenous mass media opinion different from the mere reporting of somebody else's opinion, (c) government opinions such as those of the prime minister, cabinet members, and government bureaucrats, and (d) none of the above, such as the opinions of foreign governments.

What constitutes public opinion or government opinion is likely to depend on the political system of the country as well as the nature of the issue. Under the parliamentary cabinet system, for example, opinions of ruling party members should be divided into public opinion and government opinion. We classified ruling party members into those who are considered to be a part of the administration (judging from their positions) and those who are judged to be outside the administration. An opinion of the former was classified into the government opinion category and that of the latter into the public opinion category. Opinions of opposition party members, social critics, general readers, labor unions, corporate executives, and naturally, public opinion survey results as well as public demonstrations were classified into the public opinion category.

Figure 1 is a simplified image graph indicating the change of public opinion regarding the United Nations Peace Cooperation Bill in Japan in 1990, which is based on the content analysis of mass media. Figure 1 is shown as an image graph without exact quantitative values chiefly because the details of measuring techniques are to be discussed in a separate paper.

As is obvious from the method described above, the longitudinal trends of opinions in the government sector and those of the mass media themselves become available as by-products. Figures 2 and 3 indicate simplified image graphs indicating the changes of opinions in the government sector and mass media. By comparing Figures 1, 2, and 3, we can conclude that in the case of the United Nations Peace Cooperation Bill, public opinion was strongly negative and against it from the beginning. The mass media at first were divided and ambivalent. However, being influenced by public opinion, the mass media as a whole gradually became more negative. The prevailing opinion in the government sector as defined above naturally and consistently supported the bill. However, even they were influenced by public opinion and the mass media and the number of positive opinions slightly decreased while the number of negative opinions increased, even in the government sector.

Because Figures 1, 2, and 3 are based on the same content analysis, they may be integrated into one figure. Figure 4 indicates the result, which shows the longitudinal trends of the climate of opinion across the three sectors: public opinion, mass media, and government.

## Intensity of Opinions

The degree of influence of *kuuki* is determined by not only the magnitude and the longitudinal trend of the opinion but also by the degree of intensity. The intensity of opinion depends on the nature of the issue. If the issue has to do with some "spirit," basic values, fundamental social norms, national or personal identity, prejudice, hatred and other deeply held beliefs by individuals, the intensity of opinion tends to be strong. Clamorous outbursts, violent actions, legal suits, and other actions to which people would not normally dare to resort indicate that the opinion is closely related to those deeply held "spirits," values, norms, prejudices, hatreds, and so on. The degree of intensity is very difficult to measure quantitatively. It needs to be described qualitatively and be "understood" by readers.

For example, President Nixon resigned not only because he lost public support. The "qualitative" side of that case also needs to be taken into account. President Nixon's numerous misdeeds and wrongdoings against public morals and social norms were laid bare by the mass media reports. It must have been a tremendous shame and humiliation for him. He was faced with impeachment

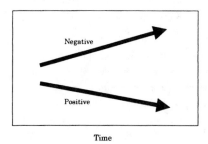

**Figure 1.** Change of Public Opinion Based on the Content Analysis of Mass Media

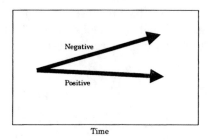

**Figure 2.** Change of Mass Media Opinions

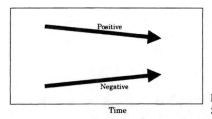

**Figure 3.** Change of Opinions in the Government Sector

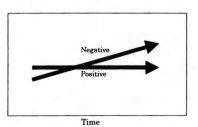

**Figure 4.** Change of Opinions *Across* the Three Sectors

before the Senate, another unbearable shame. Furthermore, the Republican Party was losing many elections because of him. According to Strouse (1975):

> Of the four elections, only one Republican won. All the districts were considered safe Republican districts and at least one district had not had a Democrat represent it in Congress for over fifty years. In one Michigan district, former President Nixon himself campaigned (the Republican lost). These losses prompted several senior Republicans in both the House and Senate to call for the president to resign for the good of the country and the Republican party. (pp. 158–159)

Although this is a rationalistic factor, it should also be included in the intensity of *kuuki*. The same is true with the case of the United Nations Peace Cooperation Bill in Japan. Ruling party members worried that if the Prime Minister further pursued the enactment of that unpopular bill, they might lose their elections. That was a rational judgment, but contributed to the intensity of *kuuki* together with many other irrational elements.

### The Tripolar *Kuuki* Model

One of the major characteristics of modern democracy is the polarization or division of power. Therefore, political decision making in modern democracies is made as a result of interactions among many "poles" or sectors of political power. In highly developed pluralistic democracies, the government can be considered as just one of such poles or sectors although it is where the final decision is made. Among those many poles or sectors that influence political or societal decisions, government, mass media, and the public are probably the most fundamental. For this reason, a "tripolar" model for political and social decision making is suggested in this section.

When there exists a high degree of intermedia as well as intersector consonance regarding some specific opinion or policy, it is very likely that it exerts strong political or social pressure. Especially when the following five conditions are met; then it is called *kuuki* and can have a particularly strong influence.

1. The majority opinion accounts for the majority in more than two of the three sectors: government, mass media, and the public.

2. The majority opinion accounts for the majority across the three sectors.

3. The majority opinion increases over time.

4. The intensity of the majority opinion is escalating.

5. The subject matter tends to stir up the "spirits" inherent in individuals such as basic values, norms, prejudices, antagonism, and loyalty to the collective or patriotism.

When these conditions are met and *kuuki* is created, it functions as a strong political or social pressure, resulting in the minority side becoming ever more silent and acquiescent and changing or modifying its opinion or policy, or its members resigning from their positions. This is the "tripolar *kuuki* model" suggested in my previous articles (Ito, 1993a, 1993b, 1993c, 1996a, 1996b).

Thorough empirical research of the actual cases discussed in this article, such as the Spanish-American War, the Vietnam War, and President Nixon's resignation, should indicate that most of these five conditions were met at the moment when some critical decision was made. Take President Nixon's resignation for example. After reviewing the case, Molotch, Protess, and Gordon (1987) write as follows:

> We therefore disagree with those who would assign "credit" for the Nixon exposure to the media, just as we would disagree with those who would assign it to the Congress. Nor should the credit go, in some acontexual, additive sense to both of these sectors. Instead, the Watergate "correction" was the result of the ways in which news of the Nixon scandals fit the goals and strategic needs of important media and policy actors. They are a part of an evolving "ecology of games" (Long, 1958), part of a "dance" (Gitlin, 1980; Molotch, 1979) in which actors have, by virtue of their differential skills and status positions, varying access to participate. Because they so continuously anticipate each other's moves, their activities are, as a matter of course, mutually constituted. (p. 45)

What was "mutually constituted" as a result of the interactions between mass media and the Congress (a part of public opinion in our definition) is nothing but *kuuki* in our context. According to our content analysis method for the measurement of *kuuki* described in the previous section, statements, actions, and decisions by members of Congress would be classified in the public opinion category because they are expected to and actually do represent public opinions that change from time to time responding to the situation. Public opinion does not refer to public opinion survey results only. If statements, actions, and decisions by members of Congress (except those who are formally incorporated in the administration) were understood as public opinion, the "tripolar *kuuki* model" mentioned above would become easier to understand. Furthermore, if public opinion at that time was understood as the activation of the American nation's "spirit of justice," it would be easier to understand why that particular kuuki was so powerful it drove the President of the United States to resign in disgrace.

## SUMMARY AND CONCLUSIONS

*Kuuki* is similar to the "climate opinion," "zeitgeist" (German), or "hegemony" (Gramsci, 1971) but slightly different from all of them as discussed at the beginning of this article. A Japanese social critic, Yamamoto Shichihei used this concept in order to analyze and explain modern Japanese history and to criticize Japanese political culture. He apparently thought that the *kuuki* phenomena were very "Japanese." However, one of the points of this article is that, as seen in many examples outside Japan, the *kuuki* phenomena are more universal and ubiquitous than Yamamoto had thought.

In order to make this concept academically useful, special efforts have been made to operationalize or quantify the *kuuki* phenomena. Questionnaire survey results, content analyses, or the combination of the two are conceivable. Since the data on longitudinal changes are indispensable, content analyses may be more useful than questionnaire surveys.

American mass communication research has traditionally been rather weak in macro analyses. As long as mass media remain diverse and heterogeneous, changes of individual attitudes or behavior do not necessarily lead to political or social changes. In order to study mass media influence on the macro level, more research is necessary on consonance or congruity among different mass media and different sectors for decisions or changes on the macro level. The mass media that are in the *kuuki* process are likely to have influence on decisions and changes on the macro level but those who are out of it may have no influence.

As a synthesis of the quantification of the *kuuki* phenomena, the "tri-polar *kuuki* model" was suggested. Simply speaking, when the majority opinion across the three basic sectors of political power, that is, government, mass media, and the general public, meets several criteria specified in the previous section, it can be called kuuki and can exert very powerful pressure for compliance. In some cases, it was so powerful that even presidents of the United States and the Japanese emperor had to bend to it.

As shown in the case of jingoism, *kuuki* can be undemocratic and destructive. Whereas Yamamoto's writings only argued this aspect, this article has hoped to shed light on other aspects of *kuuki* that can be democratic and constructive, as in the cases of the Vietnam War and President Nixon's resignation. In some cases, it is difficult to determine whether it was democratic or undemocratic, constructive or destructive. For example, *kuuki* among the Japanese public at the time of the Gulf War stopped the Japanese government's attempt to dispatch the military to the Persian Gulf area. Whether this was good or bad cannot be easily determined. The most dangerous case is when *kuuki* is taken advantage of by undemocratic groups or selfish and intolerant political leaders. Even if the situation is not as bad as this, *kuuki* can make people's viewpoint narrower and limit their policy options.

Japanese society has traditionally been extremely consensus oriented. The "consensus" refers to the state of no objectors. Japan has been extreme in the sense that discussions were often discouraged or even restricted because they could become obstacles to consensus building. Under the Japanese constitution before the Second World War, the prime minister who failed to build a consensus in the cabinet on important issues had to apologize and resign, which led to "rule by *kuuki*" in Japan (Yamamoto, 1977). Studies of *kuuki* after the war are making us aware of the danger of this tradition. As mentioned already, partly because Yamamoto was an expert on West Asia, he found a hint of a solution in West Asian cultures, especially the Jewish tradition. That is respect of dissent, thorough discussion, and decision by majority rule (assuming the existence of minority opinions) rather than the consensus rule (assuming no objectors). This Jewish tradition may be incorporated in modern Western political culture.

Via different routes, different traditions, and different kinds of experiences, the peoples of the world are reaching similar conclusions: the importance of tolerance of dissent, freedom of expression, and thorough debate before a final decision is reached.

*Postscript: The effects of the destruction of the stone Buddha statutes of Bamian by the Taliban on the current political situation in Japan*

As already mentioned, at the time of the Gulf War, antiwar *kuuki* among the Japanese masses prevented the Japanese government's attempt to dispatch the Japanese military to the Persian Gulf area. This year, however, a special law similar to the United Nations Peace Cooperation Law of 12 years ago passed the National Diet with little resistance and Japanese navy vessels are now (early November 2001) heading for the Indian Ocean. Their mission includes unlimited free fuel supply to American navy vessels in the Indian Ocean ("Tai tero," 2001, p. 2.). Ground troops (mostly noncombat troops for transportation, medical care, and communication) and air cargo units are to follow. The antiwar *kuuki*, so strong at the time of the Gulf War, did not materialize this time. There are several reasons for this.

One of them is that 24 Japanese bank executives and officers were killed at the World Trade Center in New York. The second reason was that the international community was quite cold to or critical of Japan for not having participated in the Gulf War even though Japan contributed 13 billion dollars (Germany 5.5 and South Korea 0.3 billion dollars) to the cost of the multinational force. After the war, the Kuwaiti government thanked 20 some countries for their help to Kuwait through advertisements published in the major international newspapers including *The New York Times*. They, however, "forgot" to include Japan in this list of countries.

The third reason, which may be overlooked by non-Buddhists, is the destruction of the big stone Buddha statutes of Bamian by the Taliban. As an example, while the bill to send the Japanese military to the Pakistan-Afghanistan area was being discussed in the National Diet, Tanaka Hidemichi, a professor at Tohoku University, wrote in a national newspaper the following:

> The smoke from the World Trade Center in New York immediately intermingled in me with the smoke from the stone Buddha statutes of Bamian. I was outraged, and thought that this terroristic killing of thousands of people was an act against civilization and culture, just as was the destruction of the statues; this treasure of cultural heritage produced more than one thousand years ago. ("Kyudan subeki," 2001)

Even Higuchi Keiko, a leftist feminist social critic and outspoken supporter of the Japan Socialist Democratic Party, who would normally support an antiwar movement, expressed anger against the Taliban "as a faithful Buddhist" (according to her) in television programs. In a news program telecast on November 4, NTV (Channel 4) showed a group of huge Buddhist ruins in Uzbekistan near the border with Afghanistan, in which the video scene of the blowing up of the Buddha statutes of Bamian by the Taliban was repeatedly shown in the background. At the end of the program, the newscaster commented that these parts of the Buddhist cultural heritage in Uzbekistan, near the border with Afghanistan, would also be endangered if the area were to be occupied by the Taliban.

The destruction of the stone Buddha statutes of Bamian certainly hurt the feelings or "spirit" of most Japanese people. Apart from how large the faithful Buddhist population in present-day Japan is, Buddhism accounts for a large part of Japanese history, culture, and national identity. This act thus "deflated" and weakened the "antiwar spirit" in most Japanese citizens.

## NOTE

1. The dispatch of Japan's military troops to troubled areas has been a delicate issue since the Korean War that began in 1950. Because of bitter experiences before and during the Second World War, Japan soon afterwards completely rewrote its prewar constitution and enacted, in November 1946, a highly idealistic constitution, under the guidance of the American occupation authority. For example, Article 9 of the present Japanese Constitution proclaims:

> Aspiring sincerely to an international peace based on justice and order, the Japanese people forever renounce war as a sovereign right of the nation and the threat or use of force as a means of settling international disputes.

> In order to accomplish the aim of the preceding paragraph, land, sea, and air forces, as well as other war potential, will never be maintained. The right of belligerency of the state will not be recognized.

## REFERENCES

Bennett W. L., & Paletz, D. (Eds.). (1994). *Taken by storm: The media, public opinion, and U.S. Foreign policy in the Gulf War.* Chicago: University of Chicago Press.

Berelson, B. (1963). Communications and public opinion. In W. Schramm (Ed.), *Mass communications* (pp. 527–543). Urbana: University of Illinois Press.

Blackmore, S. (1999). *The meme machine.* Oxford, UK: Oxford University Press.

Cappella, J. N. (2001, October). *Political cynicism in the United States: Effects realized through new and old communication media.* Paper delivered at the international symposium commemorating the 50th anniversary of the Japan Society for Studies in Journalism and Mass Communication,

Tokyo, Japan.

Chamoto, S. (1984). *Senso to jahnarizumu* [War and journalism]. Tokyo: Sanichi Shobo.

Davis, D. K. (1990). New and politics. In D. L. Swanson & D. Nimmo (Eds.), *New directions in political communication* (pp. 147–184). Newbury Park, CA: Sage.

Dawkins, R. (1989). *The selfish gene* (rev. ed.). New York: Oxford University Press.

*The Encyclopedia Americana.* (1964).

Frederick, H. H. (1993). *Global communication and international relations.* Belmont, CA: Wadsworth.

Funkhouser, G. R. (1991). The issues of the sixties: An exploratory study in the dynamics of public opinion. In D. L. Protess & M. McCombs (Eds.), *Agenda setting: Readings on media, public opinion, and policymaking.* Hillsdale, NJ: Erlbaum.

Gitlin, T. (1980). *The whole world is watching: Media in the making and unmaking of the new left.* Berkeley: University of California Press.

Gramsci, A. (1971). *Selections from the prison notebooks.* New York: International.

Greenberg, B. S., & Gantz, W. (Eds.). (1993). *Desert storm and the mass media.* Cresskill, NJ: Hampton.

Hansen no kain giin wo keigo [Anti-war Congresswoman is protected]. (2001, September 18). *Sankei Shimbun*, p. 3.

Hellmann, D. C. (1969). *Japanese foreign policy and domestic politics.* Los Angeles, CA: University of California Press.

Ikei M. (1981). 1930-*nendai no masumedia: Manshu jihen eno taio o chuhshin to shite* [Mass media in the 1930s: Focussing on their reports on the Manchurian Incident]. In K. Miwa (Ed.), *Saiko: Taiheiyo senso zenya* (pp. 142–194). Tokyo: Sohseiki.

Ikei M. (1988). *Nitchu senso to Nihon no masumedia no taiou* [The Sino-Japanese War and the Japanese mass media]. *Keio Gijuku Daigaku Hogaku Kenkyu, 61*(1), 41–65.

Ishida, O. (1995). *Shimbun ga Nihon wo dame ni shita: Taiheiyo senso sendo no kohzu* [Newspapers ruined Japan: Agitation supporting the Pacific War]. Tokyo: Gendai Shorin.

Ito, Y. (1993a). Mass communication theories in Japan and the United States. In W. Gudykunst (Ed.), *Communication in Japan and the United States* (pp. 249–287). Albany: State University of New York Press.

Ito, Y. (1993b). The future of political communication research: A Japanese perspective. *Journal of Communication, 43*(4), 69–79.

Ito, Y. (1993c). New directions in communication research from a Japanese perspective. In P. Gaunt (Ed.), *Beyond agendas: New directions in communication research.* Westport, CT: Greenwood.

Ito, Y. (1996a). Mass media's influence on government decision making. In D. L. Paletz (Ed.), *Political communication in action: States, institutions, movements, audiences* (pp. 37–52). Cresskill, NJ: Hampton.

Ito, Y. (1996b). Masses and mass media influence on government decision-making. In D. L. Paletz (Ed.), *Political communication research* (pp. 63–89). Norwood, NJ: Ablex.

Jieitai no haken wa mitome raremahen [The dispatch of the Self Defense Force should not be approved]. (1990, October 16). *Asahi Shimbun*, p. 14.

Jieikan no honne (1): Kaigai hahei wo tou [Soldiers' true opinions: Questioning overseas military expedition]. (1990, October 24). *Asahi Shimbun*, p. 31.

Jieikan no honne (2): Kaigai hahei wo tou [Soldiers' true opinions: Questioning overseas military expedition]. (1990, October 25). *Asahi Shimbun*, p. 30.

Kakegawa, T. (1972). *Masu media no tohsei to taibei roncho* [Control of mass media and editorials on the United States]. In Hosoya, C., Saito M., Imai, S. & Royama, M. (Eds.), *Nichibei kankei-shi 4: Kaisen ni itaru 10 nen (1931-1941)* (pp. 3–80). Tokyo: Tokyo Daigaku Shuppankai.

Kankoku no nihon bunka kaiho [Liberalization of Japanese culture in Korea]. (1999, January 5). *Sankei Shimbun*, p. 5.

Kuubaku Hinan no Ketsugi: Bahkuri shigikai [Berkeley city council passes a resolution of condemnation against the bombing]. (2001, October 18). *Asahi Shimbun*, p. 38.

Kyoryoku hoan no genten wo miushinauna [The original point of the "Cooperation Law" should not be lost]. (1990, November 1). *Yomiuri Shimbun*, p. 3.

Kyudan subeki bunka hakai [Destruction of culture to be accused of]. (2001, October 27). *Sankei Shimbun*, p. 3.

Lang, G. E., & Lang, K. (1983). *The battle for public opinion: The president, the press, and the polls during Watergate*. New York: Columbia University Press.

Long, N. E. (1958). The local community as an ecology of games. *American Journal of Sociology, 64*, 251–261.

Maesaka, T. (1989). *Senso to shimbun, 1926–1935: Hei wa kyoki nari* [War and the press, 1926–1935: A soldier is a weapon]. Tokyo: Shakai Shiso-sha.

Maesaka, T. (1991). *Senso to shimbun, 1936–1945: Genron shishite kuni tsuini horobu* [War and the press, 1936–1945: The newspaper perished and the country collapsed at last]. Tokyo: Shakai Shiso-sha

Mathes, R., & Pfetsch, B. (1991). The role of the alternative press in the agenda-building process: Spill-over effects and media opinion leadership. *European Journal of Communication, 6*, 33–62.

McCombs, M., Einsiedel, E., & Weaver, D. (1991). *Contemporary public opinion: Issues and the news*. Hillsdale, NJ: Erlbaum.

Molotch, H. L. (1979). Media and movements. In M. Zaid & J. D. McCarthy (Eds.), *The dynamics of social movement* (pp. 71–93). Cambridge, MA: Winthrop.

Molotch, H. L., Protess, D. L. & Gordon, M. T. (1987). The media-policy connection: Ecologies of news. In D. Paletz (Ed.), *Political communication research: Approaches, studies, assessments*. Norwood, NJ: Ablex.

Monroe, A. D. (1975). *Public opinion in America*. New York: Dodd, Mead & Company.

*The New Oxford Dictionary of English*. (1998).

Noelle-Neumann E. (1984). *The spiral of silence: Public opinion—Our social skin*. Chicago: University of Chicago Press.

Noelle-Neumann, E. (2000). *Chimmoku no rasen riron* (Japanese translation of Noelle-Neumann, 1984). (K. Ikeda & T. Anno, Trans.). Tokyo: Burehn Shuppan.

Noelle-Neumann, E. & Mathes, R. (1987). The "event as event" and the "event as news": The significance of "consonance" for media effects research. *European Journal of Communication, 2*, 391–414.

Page, B. I. & Brody, R. A. (1975). Policy voting and the electoral process: The Vietnam War issue. In S. Welch & J. Comer (Eds.), *Public opinion: Its formation, measurement, and impact* (pp. 444–469). Palo Alto, CA: Mayfield.

Paletz, D. L. (1999). *The media in American politics: Contents and consequences*. New York: Longman.

Perloff, R. M. (1998). *Political communication: Policies, press, and public in America*. Mahwah, NJ: Erlbaum.

Saiko: Tenanmon jiken [Reconsidering the Tiananmen Square Incident]. (2001, June 10). *Sankei Shimbun*, p. 5.

Senso to shimbun [War and the press]. (1987, August 29). *Asahi Shimbun*, p. 4.

Strouse, J. C. (1975). *The mass media, public opinion, and public policy Analysis: Linkage explorations*. Columbus, OH: Charles E. Merrill.

Sudo, Y. (2001). *Shichiriato no kagayakeru girisha toshi, shurakuhsai* [Syracuse, the brilliant Greek city in Sicily]. *FUJITSU Hisho, 43*, 32–35.

Suzuki, K. (1995). *Senso to shimbun* [War and the press]. Tokyo: Mainichi Shimbun-sha.

Tai tero kyodo no seiko wo [May the collaborative actions against terrorism succeed]. (2001, November 25). *Sankei Shimbun*, Editorial, p. 2.

Tsukamoto, M. (1986). *Jitsuroku: Sinryaku senso to shimbun* [Document: Aggressive war and the press]. Tokyo: Shin Nihon Shuppan.

Watson, J., & Hill, A. (2000). *Dictionary of media & communication studies*. London: Arnold.

Yamamoto, S. (1977). *Kuuki no kenkyu* (A study of *kuuki*). Tokyo: Bungei Shunju-sha.

# CHAPTER CONTENTS

• The Problem     299
*The Focus*     *300*
*Conceptual Grounding*     *301*

• Classical Liberalism and Identity Polemics     302
*Assimilationism*     *303*
*Pluralism*     *304*
*Integrationism*     *305*
*Separatism*     *306*
*An Ideological Circle*     *308*

• Ideological Messages in Academic Conceptions     309
*Assimilationism-Integrationism*     *310*
*Pluralism-Integrationism*     *312*
*Pluralism-Separatism*     *315*

• Discussion     317
*Identity Polemics in the Academe*     *318*
*Social Engagement and Social Responsibility*     *319*

• References     321

# 9 Unum vs. Pluribus: Ideology and Differing Academic Conceptions of Ethnic Identity

YOUNG YUN KIM
*University of Oklahoma*

This essay addresses the blurring boundaries in the American academe between scientific inquiry on the one hand, and politics and other forms of practice on the other. It examines the politicization of interethnic and intercultural research across social science disciplines, with a special focus on various ways ethnic identity is conceived. Differing identity conceptions are examined in relation to the founding ideology of classical liberalism embodied in the traditional perspective on ethnic identity, "assimilationism," as well as to its more recent varieties, "pluralism," "integrationism," and "separatism." The analysis shows how, in varying degrees, each of these four ideological positions is implied or explicitly communicated in academic conceptions of ethnic identity. The analysis further reveals a trend in social research paralleling the societal trend toward pluralism, a trend that has significantly been intensified and pushed toward separatism by the advocacy of "critical" researchers who are dedicated to "emancipatory" goals for interethnic and intercultural relations. The essay ends with a call for rigorous self-reflection and cross-examination of the long-term implications of ideological messages flowing from the differing knowledge claims on the nature of ethnic identity and its place within and between societies.

## THE PROBLEM

The twentieth-century United States ended much as it began—with record levels of immigration. Where the two eras sharply diverge is in the civic cultures that greeted these newcomers. Italians and Russian-Jewish children arriving in the early 1900s soon found themselves waving the flag in classrooms explicitly devoted to their "Americanization." By contrast, Chinese, Salvadoran, and Pakistani children arrivi ng today may wind up in schools intent on teaching them what it means to be, well, Chinese, Salvadoran, and Pakistani.

Correspondence: Young Yun Kim, Department of Communication, University of Oklahoma, Norman, OK 73019; email: youngkim@ou.edu

*Communication Yearbook 26*, pp.298–325

This change reflects a fundamental ideological shift in the century from the relatively simple civic consensus to one that emphasizes "ethnic identity" side by side, if not in place of, the larger identity of American citizenry. The shift toward pluralism in the American ideological milieu has galvanized some Americans into what is referred to as "identity politics," "politics of difference," or "politics of recognition" (cf. Taylor, 1992; Woodward, 1997). Often lost in the highly charged identity polemics are the main ideals of *E Pluribus Unum*, an American dictum that envisions people with different roots co-existing, learning from each other, and looking across and beyond the frontiers of group differences without prejudice or illusion in the interest of a dynamic and cohesive society. The current polemics seem to deny the fact that some of the most interesting things in American history have happened, in fact, at the interface of various ethnic roots. Essayist Russell Baker (1994) laments this situation in an essay entitled "Gone with the Unum":

> I have always been an "E Pluribus Unum" person myself, but the future does not look bright for an "E Pluribus Unum" America. The melting pot in which the Pluribus were to be combined into the Unum was not the success its advertisers had promised. . . . What is new these days is the passion with which we now pursue our tribal identities. . . . O, Unum, what misery we courted when we forsook thee for Pluribus. (p. A15)

## The Focus

College campuses today lead the larger society in identity polemics. More than any other segment of the society, it is college campuses where "diversity" or "multiculturalism" is a cause celebre and often a point of contention and unrest. Students are defined more by differences than by similarities. The larger and more selective the college, the greater the number of advocacy groups focused on particular student populations, with each campus activity appealing to smaller pockets of students. Arthur Levine (2000), president of Teachers College, Columbia University, describes a Korean student who, when asked to describe himself, said "he never thought about the fact that he was Asian until he came to college. In his freshman year, he thought being Asian was the most important aspect of his being. By his junior year, being Korean became his primary self-descriptor" (p. 17).

The politicized diversity is mirrored in the salience of pluralistic conceptions of ethnic identity in contemporary social research. This essay presents an initial examination of various theoretical ideas and models addressing issues of ethnic identity. The task is to glean ideological messages, implied or explicitly argued, emanating from many different academic conceptions. In so doing, the author seeks to gain a better understanding of how, and why, researchers converge or diverge in their descriptions and explanations with respect to the nature of ethnic identity and its place in multiethnic communities, both in domestic and international contexts. Efforts are made to review a broad range of academic writings representing different disciplinary and methodological perspectives. To maximize comprehensiveness of this overview necessarily limits its thoroughness. This limitation is compensated by a closer examination of a handful of theories reflecting varied ideological views.

The impetus for this inquiry comes from the increasingly visible divergence among social researchers in basic notions about the place of ideology in academic investigation. On the one hand, the social scientific principle of value-neutrality continues to serve as an intellectual anchor for "disciplinary" researchers. Social scientists, including conventional phenomenological-interpretive researchers, continue to strive to put aside a specific political agenda in the process of academic investigation. The common goal is to contribute to knowledge in a particular discipline, with development of knowledge being given priority. Although research is seen as ultimately making a contribution to practice, that contribution is not to drive the conduct of research as an immediate or specific goal. The disciplinary research aim is the production of general purpose knowledge, which is valued as much for its own sake as for any instrumental value it has. Increasingly, however, the disciplinary model and its value-neutral stance has been replaced by the model of "social engineering," "social engagement" or "social activism." The shift in emphasis from theory to practice has been fueled by nontraditional critical scholars, who mount vigorous arguments to gear research directly to "emancipatory" political goals of eliminating "White racism" at home and countering Western/American "imperialism" abroad. (Billig et al., 1988; Diesing, 1991; Graff, 1992; Hammersley, 1995; Thornton, 1996). Indeed, pressure is felt by many traditional researchers who find the field too political, so much so that a given theory, along with the credibility of the theorist, appears to be dismissed by some based on the implied question, "Whose side are you on?" (Ward, 1993).

Conceptual Grounding

To accommodate a wide range of different conceptual and methodological approaches, *ethnic identity* is defined broadly to represent other similar terms such as "cultural," "subcultural," "national," "ethnolinguistic," and "racial" identity. Ethnic identity designates both a sociological or demographic classification, as well as an individual's psychological identification with a particular ethnic group. The psychological and sociological meanings of ethnic identity are regarded as two inseparable correlates of the same phenomenon. Likewise, the term *ideology* is used broadly as a multidimensional concept (Van Dijk, 1998). On the one hand, ideology refers to a social phenomenon, "a latent consciousness or philosophy" largely shared by people within a society as "a society's way of life" or "what passes for common sense within a society" (Billig, 1991, pp. 27–29). As well, ideology is used to mean the intellectual beliefs of thinking individuals that are stimulated, substantiated, and constrained by the shared beliefs of the society at large. Here, individuals are regarded as formulating and expressing their opinions by invoking socially shared beliefs as their own. Even in making remarks that are self-serving or internally contradictory, individuals are assumed to consider their argument reasonable or even persuasive in the eyes of a rational audience.

In examining ideological messages implied or advocated in academic conceptions of ethnic identity, the author utilizes the four distinct but interconnected positions on ethnic identity and interethnic relations: (a) assimilationism, (b) pluralism, (c) integrationism, and (d) separatism. The author identified these ideological variations in an earlier qualitative-interpretive analysis (Kim, 1999), which utilized different sorts of data including the messages of political and civic leaders, activists, academicians, and ordinary citizens who directly or indirectly participated in public debates on issues of ethnicity and race. Some of the messages were naturally occurring and others in the form of personal reflections and testimonials. All messages were available in public sources such as books written for general public consumption, newspapers and news magazines, and radio programs. The four ideological views, described below, represent the diverse and often divergent opinions voiced in contemporary American society, criss-crossing many conventional social categories such as ethnicity, race, and political party affiliation.

## CLASSICAL LIBERALISM AND IDENTITY POLEMICS

The United States is widely regarded as a construction organized by "classical liberalism," a political ideology of the Enlightenment tradition rooted in the European and Anglo-American philosophers such as John Locke, Adam Smith, and John Dewey (cf. Rorty, 1998). Enshrined in the Declaration of Independence, the Constitution, and the Bill of Rights, ideals of classical liberalism constitute the core of the American ethos, projecting a vision of American society. Central to this ideology is the mindset of *individualism*, "the social priority of the individual vis-à-vis the State, the established Church, social classes . . . or other social groups" (Abercrombie, 1980, p. 56)—one that celebrates individual achievement, self-reliance, and personal responsibility (Sampson, 1977, p. 769). Individualism recognizes and values the fact that "we are all different," and questions the validity and morality of categorical thought. An important correlative of individualism, thus, is *universalism*, a view of human nature presupposing social categories such as ethnicity that is embodied in such cultural values as equal rights afforded to all individuals as the requisite of a free and democratic society.

The primacy of the individual over the group hinges on the value of equality as it pertains to the premise that a fair society and the basic liberty of the individual can only be attained through a uniform application of all laws and rules applied to all citizens. Equality in this sense means *procedural equality*—in the sense of "being treated fairly" for "fair play"—rooted in a "biopsychological" (or "naturalistic") worldview and the Aristotelian notion of "equity" (or "distributive justice"; cf. Rossides, 1976, pp. 13–14; Tsuda, 1986, pp. 62–63). This view accepts and appreciates the merit-based system of assessment of social rewards and social standing. This system is reflected in the commonly accepted notion that individuals must "earn" and "deserve" social rewards and predicaments, based on what they do and not what they are. Underlying this presumption is a yet more fundamental understanding of individual difference, that is, "there is a natural distribution of human talent, ranging from the few individuals of genius and talent to the defective and delinquent" (Rossides, 1976, p. 9).

Assimilationism

The ideology of classical liberalism is directly expressed in the dictum, *E Pluribus Unum*—the principle behind the American ethos that seeks to transcend a tribal, ancestral, and territorial condition. Even though each person is unique, all humans are endowed with the same set of fundamental rights and responsibilities. Prejudice directed against a particular social group, ethnic or otherwise, is wrong not only because it is irrational but also because its focus on social categories contravenes the intellectual or moral prescription to value the unique qualities of the individual. Essayist Henry Grunwald captured this liberal tradition in a bicentennial essay (Grunwald, 1976): "The U.S. was not born in a tribal conflict, like so many other nations, but in a conflict over principles. Those principles were thought to be universal, which was part of the reason for the unprecedented policy of throwing the new country open to all comers" (p. 35).

The idea of *E Pluribus Unum* underpins *assimilationism*, the traditional organizing principle for a society of many different ethnic heritages. Originally popularized by Jewish immigrant Israel Zangwill's interpretation of it in his 1908 play *The Melting Pot* (cited in Postiglione, 1983, p. 16), assimilationism calls for the conversion of alien or indigenous minority cultures into a mainstream cultural tradition and the accompanying fusion of diverse elements into a coherent system of ideas and practices. Assimilationism advocates the primacy of *individual identity*, the basic constituent of *American identity*. The assimilationist view advocates the universalistic ideal of a "color-blind society" and a similarly universalistic approach to international relations built on common humanity. What is ultimately desirable is the relationship between individuals in which everyone is treated as an individual, a fellow American citizen, and a fellow human being. With respect to immigrants and ethnic minorities, assimilationists expect them to mainstream themselves into the normative institutions and linguistic-cultural practices. Mainstreaming in the context of the United States, of course, would entail a degree of Anglo-conformity (Gordon, 1964, 1981) in public spheres of life, consistent with the old folk wisdom, "When in Rome, do as Romans do." In the realm of private life, assimilationists would expect each individual to make his or her own choices as one's private life is not to be subjected to anyone else's dictates, especially of the government. Such assimilationist ideas are expressed in the following self-reflection of Glenn C. Loury (1993) on his identity as an African-American and as an individual human being:

> The most important challenges and opportunities that confront me derive not from my racial condition, but rather from my human condition. . . . The expression of my individual personality is to be found in the blueprint that I employ to guide this project of construction. The problem of devising such a plan for one's life is a universal problem, which confronts all people, whatever their race, class, or ethnicity. (pp. 7–10)

In this assimilationist vision, the government is responsible for universally applying societal rules to all its citizens irrespective of skin color and religious creed. Immigrants and ethnic minorities, in turn, are expected to be largely responsible for assimilating themselves socially and culturally, so as to become fully functional in the American society. Each person, and each person alone, is seen as ultimately responsible for his or her own achievement of status. Everyone is expected to "play by the rules," while excessive insistence on group-based policies such as prolonged bilingual education is viewed as fundamentally an "un-American" idea that endangers the larger fraternity of all Americans. An excessive claim of group identity over individual identity is deemed unacceptable because it renders itself to what Pico Iyer (1990) calls "state-sponsored favoritism" that mandates ethnic "preferences," "quotas," and even "reverse discrimination." Making employment or admission decisions based on ethnic identity is considered counterproductive as it obscures differential individual merits that must be earned individually.

### Pluralism

Given these ideals, however, Americans are far from being of a same mind about various social issues. In fact, the opposite is true when it comes to interethnic relations. There is a profound dilemma, a contradiction arising from the inevitable gap between the ideals of classical liberalism that has served as the assimilationist view of ethnic identity and the reality of everyday life not measuring up to the ideals. The seed for the contradiction is the awareness that the ideals of individualism, universalism, and procedural equality are not always applied to those of traditionally nondominant group backgrounds. A natural response to such discrepancies has been a movement that challenges the status quo. In this movement, the primacy of individual identity has been challenged by contrary claims of *group identity*. The melting-pot metaphor has been replaced by newer ones such as "mosaic," "quilt," and "salad bowl" that emphasize the distinctiveness of ethnic groups. Underlying this relativistic construction of personhood and society is the world view of *relativism*, which classifies humanity into distinct groups and thus de-emphasizes universalities in human conditions.

In this pluralistic perspective, equality is defined less in terms of fairness of rules as in the assimilationist procedural equality and more in terms of *status equality*, which demands equal results in the interest of "emancipation" of "oppressed" groups and the "pride" and "dignity" of their members. Here, ethnic identity is not only to be recognized and respected, but also to be a source of "entitlement" and a means to combat practices that are deemed unjust. This contrary ideological position rejects the biopsychological explanation of status inequality and the merit-based system of social rewards, and replaces it with a "sociocultural" ("structural" or "institutional") explanation. Ethnic groups are seen as inherently equal in their original states, but their original natures are seen as being distorted and corrupted in the process of interaction with others in society and through the development of sociocultural institutions (language, culture, property, and law) and social stratification among people (Tsuda, 1986, pp. 62–63). The classical liberal constructs of individual identity, universalism, and procedural equality, therefore, are deemed a false ideology in that it serves only the end of legitimizing the capitalist system of "winners" and "losers" in society. Instead, arguments are made for a redistribution of power and resources to overcome inequalities in group status (e.g., Hacker, 1992), and for a greater diversity of the university curriculum by replacing it with one "that would focus on the achievements of marginalized peoples and on the sins of the nation's founders" (Traub, 1998, p. 25).

Molefi Keith Asante offers an eloquent argument against the "old" liberal ideals and a succinct advocacy for the counter-ideals of group identity, relativism, and status equality. In an essay entitled "Racism, Consciousness, and Afrocentricity," Asante (1993) reflects on his experience of growing up in a "racist society" and explains how he came to reject W. E. B. Du Bois' notion of "double consciousness" as a tragic outcome inescapable in the "Eurocentric" society. Asante, thus, advocates "Afrocentricity" as an intellectual model based on which African Americans can claim an equal identity and status as a distinct people:

> The feeling that you are in quicksand is inescapable in the quagmire of a racist society. You think that you can make progress in the interpretation of what's happening now only to discover that every step you take sinks the possibility of escaping. You are a victim despite your best efforts to educate those around you to the obvious intellectual mud stuck in their minds. . . . Even from my young adult years I thought a precondition of my fullness, a necessary and natural part of my maturity, was the commitment to be who I am, to be Afrocentric. . . . Afrocentricity is the active centering of the African in subject place in our historical landscape. This has always been my search; it has been a quest for sanity. (pp. 142–143)

## Integrationism

Straddled between the above-described poles of assimilationism and pluralism is *integrationism*, emphasizing the need to moderate the often tortured reality of identity politics that has become a "sore spot" for many Americans. Integrationist voices search for some kind of reconciliation, a position that sociologist Alan Wolfe (1998) asserts as occupying "the vital center," the "middle" America. They reflect the struggle of mainstream Americans to seek mutual tolerance, accommodation, and balance, as well as ambivalence and contradiction. Integrationists may, for example, support bilingual programs, but only if they are short-lived and not used as a political instrument of power demanded by every group for its own separate slice of the political pie, or they may support multiculturalism but only to the extent that ethnic identity is subsumed under the broader, more universalized American or human identity. They may support affirmative action programs based on group identity, but consider quota systems as unfair, divisive, and ultimately counterproductive. Such an attempt at ideological integration and reconciliation is exemplified in a remark former President Clinton made in 1998: "I believe there is an independent value to having young people learn in an environment where they're with people of many different racial and ethnic backgrounds. And the question is, How can you balance that with our devotion to merit?" (reported in *The New York Times*, July 9, 1998, p. A21). Messages of reconciliation such as these can be traced to the Civil Rights movement led by Martin Luther King, Jr. In this movement, the traditional liberal ideals of individualism, universalism, and procedural equality were upheld in the struggle to eliminate systematic discrimination against African Americans as a group.

Integrationist voices often escape media attention or get lost in the midst of more conspicuous messages of committed ideologues. Yet messages of reconciliation are all around us. In his autobiography, *Walking in the Wind* (1998), John Lewis, a leader of the Civil Rights movement since the 1960s and currently a Democratic Congressman from Georgia, articulates his abiding faith in the "Beloved Community," a vision of what society could become were people of all class and ethnic backgrounds to reach across the barriers that divide them. Richard Rorty, in his book, *Achieving Our Country* (1998), argues for ideological moderation and objects to intransigent "leftists" and "conservatives." In *Someone Else's House* (1998), Tamar Jacoby calls for *realism* that appreciates the real progress between Blacks and Whites that has taken place in American society. Gerald Graff in *Beyond the Culture Wars* (1992) and Alan Ryan in *Liberal Anxieties and Liberal Education* (1998) argue in support of multiculturalism in principle, while insisting on moderating rigid, category-based ideas of cultural diversity in the academe.

Separatism

The full spectrum of American public discourse on interethnic relations further includes the marginal voices of separatism, often characterized as views of extremism. Whereas the aforementioned messages of assimilationism, pluralism, and integrationism commonly adhere to the societal goal of interethnic integration (while disagreeing on specific visions as to how to achieve this goal), extremist messages frequently express a preference for a maximum ingroup-outgroup separation. Often, the rigidity with which cultural identity boundaries are drawn galvanizes Americans into "us against them" posturing. In some cases, the claims of equal and distinct identity tends to manifest itself in tendencies of extreme collective self-glorification and denigration of other groups, and, of course, in varying degrees of violence and terror.

Some of the easily identifiable separatist messages come from those identified with "extreme right" or "extreme left" groups. Among the extreme right in the United States are the Ku Klux Klan, Neo-Nazi, Skinheads, and those of the so-called "Patriot" movements. Members of such groups are known for their commitment to racial purism, the supremacy of the White race, and, in some cases, even arms training and preparation for a race war (The Southern Poverty Law Center, 1998). Essentially same separatist messages come from the extreme "left," such as the New Black Panthers and the Nation of Islam. Internationally, extremist messages come from religious radical groups such as the Taliban in Afghanistan who believe that everything that you do is godly inspired and permitted and legitimized and that you are the owner of absolute truth, so that you can do anything, even the worst deeds of violence. Milder forms of separatism are voiced by those who are unaffiliated with a recognized extremist group. Although not always explicit, separatist views can be easily inferred from the inflammatory rhetorical devices employed to condemn or scapegoat an outgroup or position the ingroup as "victims": minority student protesters chant, "Down with racism, Western culture's got to go" (*The New York Times*, October 25, 1995, pp. A1, B8); a group of Hispanic students occupied a building to demand separate Hispanic housing (*The New York Times*, April 20, 1994, p. B8).

*Thus, the extremes meet.* As much as the separatist messages of the extreme right and the extreme left differ dramatically in respective claims, they converge in rigid ingroup-outgroup distinction, characterization of the ingroup as "victims," full-blown confrontational rhetorical posturing, and fortification of mutually intransigent moral claims. As Billig and associates (1988) observe, "the extreme bigot is free to play consistently and unambiguously in an area which is beyond reality but which taunts reality. There is no need to hedge and qualify statements in order not to pass a seemingly unreasonable judgment" (p. 118). Extreme separatist arguments do not resonate with most Americans. They are usually considered "unreasonable" and are met with messages of rejection of one kind or another. Even though mainstream Americans diverge in their views on the locus of American life, they are largely united in their objection to the separatist vision of the United States and the world in a shared condemnation of categorical, group-based hatred.

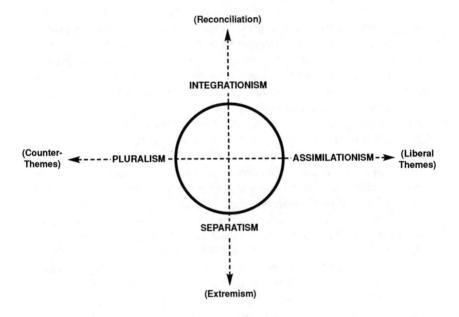

**Figure 1.** Four Views on Ethnic Identity in an Ideological Circle

An Ideological Circle

Together, the above four positions on ethnic identity and interethnic relations form an ideological circle (see Figure 1), in which each position defines, and is defined by, the other. As such, the circle highlights the ideological dilemma that plays out in everyday public discourse in the United States today. The vision and principles embodied in *E Pluribus Unum* continue to be voiced in the form of assimilationism, while being vigorously challenged by the counter-themes of pluralism advocating the primacy of group identity, along with the reconciliatory efforts to promote ideological balance and moderation in integrationism, as well as separatism of the extreme right and the extreme left, closing the circle.

The above analysis demonstrates that the classical liberal ideals continue to occupy the mainstream of American consciousness on interethnic relations in the form of assimilationism and integrationism, even as they are vigorously challenged by voices of pluralism and, to a lesser extent, of extremism. This characterization of the American ideological landscape is consistent with Wolfe's (1998) assessment of "the new middle-class morality" (p. 309). Based on 200 in-depth interviews conducted in Boston, Atlanta, Tulsa, and San Diego metropolitan areas, Wolfe (1998) has found "little support for the notion that middle-class Americans are engaged in bitter cultural conflict with one another" (p. 278). Instead, according to Wolfe, they are "struggling to find ways in which their core beliefs can be reconciled with experiences that seem to contradict them" (p. 281), while insisting on a set of values "capacious enough to be inclusive but demanding enough to uphold standards of personal responsibility" (p. 322). Demonstrating the continuing vitality of assimilationist-integrationist ideals in the United States is the trend of increasing personal relationships across ethnic boundaries. Indeed, 30–70% of Blacks, virtually all Latinos and Filipinos, the majority of American Indians and Native Hawaiians, as well as a significant proportion of White-identified persons are of multiracial-multiethnic origins (Root, 1993, p. 9). Over a period of approximately two decades, the number of interethnic marriages in the United States has escalated from 310,000 to more than 1.1 million, and the incidence of births of mixed-race babies has multiplied 26 times as fast as that of any other group (Smolowe, 1993, pp. 64–65).

Further evidence of continuing assimilationist-integrationist ideological tradition is provided in the results of various public opinion polls. Gallop polls taken over the past 25 years (1972 through 1997) show a dramatic increase in percentage of white Americans who are willing to vote for a Black candidate for president rose (from 35% to 93%) and who approve of marriage between Blacks and Whites (from 25% to 61%) (*USA Today*, August 8, 1997, p. A11). Findings from the public reinforce this trend. In a 1993 Time/CNN poll of over 1,100 Americans, for instance, 96% of the respondents agreed with the assimilationist statement, "It should be the duty of all immigrants to learn English if they plan to stay in this country." In response to the question, "Which comes closest to your view on bilingual education in public schools?" only 11% agreed with the pluralist view that that "children of immigrants should be taught in their native language indefinitely." The other 48% of the respondents who indicated "children of immigrants should be taught in their native language only until they know enough English to join regular classes," and with the remaining 40% who said "all children should be taught in English" (Gray, 1993, p. 70). A more recent survey conducted among a random sample of 1,003 adults in all 50 states finds that 91% regard "being an American" to be "a big part of who I am" and three-quarters of African-Americans polled believe that race plays "not much role" in who they are (Powers, 2000).

## IDEOLOGICAL MESSAGES IN ACADEMIC CONCEPTIONS

Directly or indirectly, social researchers are participants in the ideological polemics of American society. Below, the varying views on issues of ethnic identity gleaned from a wide range of academic writings that address issues of ethnic identity. Against the backdrop of the on-going methodological debate, the following analysis examines the blurring boundaries between scientific inquiry on the one hand, and politics and other forms of practice on the other. The analysis identifies the ideological messages that are implicitly or explicitly communicated in various theoretical conceptions of ethnic identity. A wide range of literature is examined across methodological and disciplinary perspectives. The aim is to develop a broad perspective on specific points of ideological convergence and contention in how academic researchers describe and explain the nature of ethnic identity and its role in interethnic relations within and across societies.

## Assimilationism-Integrationism

Issues of ethnic identity has been extensively addressed in studies of cross-cultural adaptation for the past several decades. Social scientific theories since the 1930s have been predicated on the premise that adaptation of immigrants and other ethnic minorities is an important and desirable goal for the individuals as well as for the society as a whole. This affirmative view of cross-cultural adaptation is consistent with the widely held assimilationist view in the United States that calls for the convergence and fusion of alien or minority cultures into a coherent system of ideas and practices of the society at large (Postiglione, 1983).

Numerous empirical studies document the assimilative trend. (See Kim, 2001, for a thorough review of the literature.) Sociological studies have investigated minority-majority relations in which minority groups are structurally integrated into the political, social, and economic systems of the society at large. Anderson and Saenz (1994), for example, investigated the intermarriage of Mexican Americans with Anglos in the United States and identified opportunity for contact, levels of Spanish language maintenance, and internal status diversity (i.e., a wide range of socioeconomic mobility). The assimilative trend is even more definitively evidenced in cross-generational studies, including Page's (1994) study of the Japanese and their children in Brazil. According to Page, the Japanese first immigrated to Brazil in 1908 as contract workers at coffee plantations and strongly resisted assimilation, and yet the present third-generation Japanese-Brazilians are on the whole fully integrated into Brazilian society, entering into racially mixed marriages as freely as other Brazilians. Lind (1995) documented that the European immigrant groups in the United States began as distinct groups at the beginning of the twentieth century and are now almost completely assimilated. According to Lind, four fifths of Italian-Americans, half of American Jews, one-third of Hispanics, and one-half of Asian-Americans have married outside their officially designated categories since 1950. Lind further reports that the number of children born to Black-White marriages quintupled between 1968 and 1988, and a growing number of mixed-race Americans are now lobbying for their own "multiracial" category.

The assimilative trend is further documented in a study by the American Jewish Committee that shows a significant increase in the members' merging into non-Jewish organizations and a substantial decrease in their Jewish identification (Zweigenhalf, 1979–1980). Masuda, Matsumoto, and Meredith (1970) similarly demonstrates that ethnic identity of Japanese-Americans in the United States gradually has decreased across the generations. Triandis, Kashima, Shimada, and Villareal (1986) and Suro (1998) report that Hispanics who have been in the U.S. for a long time showed diminished Hispanic "cultural scripts" in their judgments and increased social interactions with non-Hispanics. Namazi (1984) likewise observes an assimilative trend among Mexican, Cuban, and Middle Eastern immigrants. In Canada, McCauley (1991) reports decreasing traditional forms of behavior in the French and English Canadian populations of Penetanguishene in southern Ontario. In a study of language maintenance and shift by Morgan (1987), Haitian migrants in the Dominican Republic are reported to have shifted, over time, from their native language, Creole, to the host language, Spanish. Other assimilative patterns such as increasing sense of control and satisfaction among Korean immigrants (Kim, 1976, 1977, 1978a) and Indochinese refugees (Kim, 1978b, 1980, 1989, 1990) have been documented, along with a progressive convergence of the "subjective meaning system" of Puerto Ricans in New York toward that of Anglo Americans (Szalay & Inn, 1988).

Emerging from these and many other empirical findings is the nature of ethnic identity that is, over time, gradually transformed into a new identity. That is, the original ethnic identity is increasingly mainstreamed in the host society. This basic reality of assimilation is further elaborated in this author's theory (Kim, 1988, 1995a, 1995b, 2001), intended as a comprehensive account of immigrant adaptation from an interactive and interdisciplinary perspective. Defining adaptation as a natural process of individuals striving to establish a relatively stable, reciprocal, and functional relationship with the environment, the author explains that adaptation is an activity that is "almost always a compromise, a vector in the internal structure of culture and the external pressure of environment" (Sahlins, 1964, p. 136). In this framework, "assimilation" is defined as a state of the highest degree of "acculturation" of the host cultural elements and "deculturation" of the original cultural habits that is theoretically possible. Assimilation is, thus, an "ideal" state characterized by the maximum possible convergence of strangers' internal conditions to those of the natives.

The theory offers a dynamic and evolving conception of ethnic identity that is not locked into a single category. The ethnic identity of an individual is explained to undergo the gradual transformation toward an increasingly "intercultural identity," a movement from an "ascribed identity" to an "achieved identity." Despite the pivotal importance of the original ethnic identity in the psychosocial functioning of an individual, the acculturative pressures of the host environment stimulate its adaptive alteration in the direction of a higher level of psychic integration. Cumulative experiences of cross-cultural adaptation are explained to bring about an identity that is increasing more "universalized" and "individuated" in self-other orientation, and more flexible and less rigidly bound by group categories. Although validating the assimilationist view of ethnic identity, the theory addresses pluralists' concern for the maintenance of original ethnic identity. It does so by highlighting the fact that intercultural identity development does not come about without "costs." The adaptation process is explained in terms of "stress-adaptation-growth dynamic," a process filled with ambivalence and internal conflict between one's loyalty to the original identity and a necessity to embrace a new one. Yet, according to the theory, it is the stressful experience that "pushes" individuals to restructure their existing internal conditions to regain an internal equilibrium. This functional interrelatedness of stress and adaptation describes the process of organizing and reorganizing oneself, bringing about psychological "growth" at a higher level of self-integration.

The present author disputes the pluralist view that the long-term identity evolution toward assimilation necessarily entails "giving up" or "discarding" the original identity. There is no necessary contradiction between maintaining a positive ethnic identity and developing a more complex intercultural identity. The author further rejects the dichotomous view that individuals have to choose either one or the other, and proposes the concept of *intercultural identity* as a viable self-other orientation that facilitates social integration and discourages unwarranted divisiveness along ethnic lines. Similar theoretical ideas have been offered by others. Adler (1982), employing the concept "multicultural person," describes the new identity as being based "not on 'belongingness' which implies either owning or being owned by a single culture, but on a style of self-consciousness that situates oneself neither totally *a part of* nor totally *apart from* a given culture" (p. 391). Hall (1976) offers the concept "boundary-ambiguity syndromes" (p. 227) to describe the psychological development incorporating new dimensions of perception and experience through intercultural contact and learning. Casmir's (1999) notion of "third-culture building" as a goal for intercultural communicators is also consistent with the conception of intercultural identity.

Pluralism-Integrationism

Assimilationist theoretical conception and research findings, however, has been questioned since the 1970s when the "new ethnicity" movement began, prompted by the Civil Rights movement in the United States. The trend in the academic discourse reflects an increasing emphasis on identity maintenance of ethnic minorities and de-emphasis on integration and assimilation into the mainstream culture. Whereas the theoretical conceptions of ethnic identity discussed in the preceding section highlight the pliable and adaptive nature of ethnic identity, pluralistic conceptions tend to focus on the distinctive and enduring nature of ethnic identity, or lack of adaptive change. Michael Novak, author of *The Rise of the Unmeltable Ethnics* (1971), argues against cultural assimilation and advocates "equal ethnicity for all." He describes the feelings of alienation held by one large ethnic group, Poles, who were drawn to ethnic power movements in the competition for jobs, respect, and attention. In another article, Novak (1973) contends:

There is no such thing as *homo Americanus*. There is no single culture here. We do not, in fact, have a culture at all—at least, not a highly developed one, whose symbols, images, and ideals all of us work out of and constantly mind afresh; such "common culture" as even intellectuals have is more an ideal aspired to than a task accomplished. (p. 18)

Pluralistic messages are also suggested in social scientific conceptions of ethnic identity. Teske and Nelson (1974) argue for a "bi-directional" conception of
the adaptation process, a process that does not require changes in values within
the acculturating group. Likewise, Stonequist (1964) views the adaptation process
as following one of three distinct paths: (a) assimilation into the dominant group;
(b) assimilation into the "subordinate" group; or (c) some form of accommodation
and reconciliation of the two societies. Other studies document a continued structure of ethnic group characteristics from one generation to another. Glazer and
Moynihan (1963) conclude a sociological analysis by stating that ethnicity per-
vades all spheres of life among ethnic minorities: "The point about the melting pot
is that it did not happen" (p. 290). Others (e.g., Greeley, 1974; Parenti, 1967;
Wolfinger, 1965) have found that ethnic minorities in the United States possess
political orientations different from those of mainstream Americans, evidence in
respective voting patterns that persist for many generations.

Pluralistic conception of ethnic identity is further suggested by Berry and
associates (Berry, 1980, 1990; Berry & Sam, 1997), whose "psychological acculturation" model is built on two key questions concerning the subjective identity
orientation: "Are cultural identity and customs of value to be retained?" and "Are
positive relations with the larger society of value and to be sought?" By combining the response types (yes, no) to these two questions, the model generates
"integration" (yes, yes), "assimilation" (no, yes), "separation" (yes, no), and
"marginality" (no, no). A modified version of this model is offered by Bourhis,
Moise, Perreault, and Senecal (1997), replacing "marginality" with "anomie"
and "individualism." In both models, a pluralistic message is implied as ethnic
identity is conceived entirely as a matter of individual choice (acceptance/rejec-
tion) whereas no consideration is given to the practical necessity of adaptive
identity articulated in Kim's (1988, 1995a, 1995b, 2001) theory. A similar pluralistic view is implied in the conception of "assimilation ideology" offered by
Bourhis and associates (1997) as an ideology that "expects immigrants to aban-
don their own cultural and linguistic distinctiveness for the sake of adopting the
culture and values of the dominant group constituting the core of the nation
state." The authors describe the assimilation ideology as being

> likely to emerge in settings where the state apparatus has long been mobilized to serve the
> interest of a particular class or ethnocultural group. Usually, it is the economically and polit-
> ically dominant group that is most successful in *imposing* its own private values and culture
> as the core of the founding *myths* of the nation-state [italics added]. (p.148)

There are other pluralistic social scientific conceptions that incorporate a
degree of the integrationist view. Phinney (1989), for instance, describes "ethnic
identity development" emphasizing the importance for minority adolescents to
achieve a "commitment" to one's ethnic identity. Arguing that not achieving such
a commitment would result in a significant detriment to the individual's psychological and social functioning, Phinney (1989) identifies three stages of ethnic

identity development: (a) the stage of "an unexamined ethnic identity" during which the adolescent remain largely passive in reacting to ethnic images and stereotypes; (b) the stage of "exploration" of what it means to be a member of a specific ethnic group in society, which is equivalent to the identity crisis or moratorium described by Erikson (1969); and (c) the stage of "resolution," in which the adolescent develops "an achieved ethnic identity," and makes "a commitment to a particular way of being a member of [his or her] group" (p. 41). In highlighting minority adolescents' struggle to "finally obtain a secure sense of themselves as ethnic group members," Phinney (1989) also discusses the possibility that, for some adolescents, a secure ethnic identity can take the form of "bicultural identity."

Additional pluralist-integrationist approaches are offered in a variety of multidimensional theories that incorporate psychological factors (including ethnic identity orientation), situational factors, and macro-societal factors to explain interethnic relations. For example, social identity theory (Tajfel, 1978; Tajfel & Turner, 1979, 1986; Turner, 1987) offers a balanced conception of ethnic identity. The theory is built on a pluralistic conception of social identity as "that part of an individual's self-concept which derives from his knowledge of his membership in a social group (or groups) together with the value and emotional significance attached to that membership" (Tajfel, 1978, p. 63). Individuals are postulated as identifying with a group such that a positive self-identity is maintained and that this tendency is often enacted in the form of ingroup loyalty and outgroup discrimination. The theory further explains how social identity plays out in intergroup situations employing a multiple factors, from micro-level psychological and situational factors to macro-level sociologicial factors such as institutional-structural conditions of the society. Within this broad conceptual framework, the theory explains that interactants' behaviors are influenced by the salience of their group membership and the threat that such perception of one's group membership presents to one's social identity.

Comprehensive theories reflecting pluralist-integrationist messages also include communication accommodation theory (Gallois, Giles, Jones, Cargile, & Ota, 1995) and its original rendition speech accommodation theory (Giles, Mulac, Bradac, & Johnson, 1987). Grounded in social identity theory, communication accommodation theory explains different types of intergroup communication behavior ("convergent," "divergent," and "maintenance") based on the psychological factor ("accommodative orientation") of interactants. Also included in this theory are factors of "immediate situation" (e.g., "goals and addressee focus") and of broader "sociohistorical context" (e.g., "history of rivalry or conflict between groups") influencing the interactants' "evaluation [of the encounter] and future intentions." The theory has generated a substantial amount of empirical research, including a recent study by Petronio, Ellemers, Giles, and Gallois (1998) that focuses on the "sociostructural relations between groups" and the individual communicators' "identity choices" contributing to the level of "miscommunication." Similarly, a broad multidimensional theory is presented by this author (Kim, 1997) to explain "associative" and "dissociative" communication behavior of individuals in interethnic encounters. Behaviors closer to the associative end of this continuum are described as increasing the likelihood of mutual understanding, cooperation, and the "coming-together" of the involved persons in a constructive engagement. Conversely, behaviors at the dissociative end are described as contributing to misunderstanding, competition, and the "coming-apart" of the relationship. The theory then links associative-dissociative communication behavior to three layers of contextual factors: (a) communicator factors (including "identity strength" and "identity bias"), (b) situational factors (including "status equality/inequality" and "ethnic homogeneity/heterogeneity), and (c) environmental factors (including "societal ideology" and "history of subjugation").

Social-psychological and communication theories such as these reveal varying degrees of pluralist-integrationist perspective on ethnic identity and its role in interethnic communication and relationship. The theories account for both pluralistic and assimilationistic possibilities of the enactment of ethnic identity in interethnic relations. Ethnic identity is conceived not as a fixed or monolithic social category, but as a more flexible and variable entity that works with other significant factors simultaneously operating in an interethnic encounter. Similar conceptions of identity flexibility are observed in various models of "intercultural communication competence" or "effectiveness." Cupach and Imahori (1993), for example, highlight the ability to "manage" each other's ethnic identity as a key to being a competent intercultural communicator. From an interpretive perspective, Collier and associates (Collier & Bornman, 1999; Collier & Thomas, 1988) emphasize "identity negotiation." A similar identity conception underlies Ting-Toomey's (Ting-Toomey, 1993; Ting-Toomey & Kurogi, 1998) theory in which identity negotiation is placed at the center of "communicative resourcefulness" in intercultural encounters.

## Pluralism-Separatism

Conceptions of ethnic identity implied in many of the phenomenological interpretive analyses are largely pluralistic. Ethnographic researchers describe common life patterns, practices, and symbols that constitute an ethnic identity as a communal phenomenon—a kind of shared tradition linking individual members to a common future. Ethnographic studies often provide a set of essential elements that give a cultural or subcultural community its distinct character. Among such studies are the studies investigating communication patterns of Russian "cultural pragmatics" (Carbaugh, 1993), Greek interpersonal communication patterns (Broome, 1990), and interpersonal communication and relationship patterns in Columbia (Fitch, 1998). Other ethnographic studies describe subcultural communities in the United States, including African-Americans (e.g., Daniel & Smitheran-Donaldson, 1990; Hecht, Collier, & Ribeau, 1993; Kochman, 1986, 1990), Native Americans (e.g., Pratt, 1998; Wieder & Pratt, 1990), and

White Americans (e.g., Martin, Krizek, Nakayama, & Bradford, 1996). The most explicit and unambiguous pluralistic messages are found in critical scholars' writings, with at least some of them connoting a separatist view of ethnic identity and interethnic relations. The critical inquiry is, of course, by no means internally homogeneous, with different conceptions and competing lines of thought variously represented in "poststructuralism," "postmodernism," "postimperialism," " muted group and standpoint theory," "critical pragmatism," and "cultural studies," among others (Hammersley, 1995, p. x). Nevertheless, there are some ontological-political common threads running through all critical conceptions of ethnic identity. One common thread is the primary focus on some form of identity conflict, which is attributed to none other than intergroup status- or power inequality. Critical researchers also are unanimous in their opposition to the traditional normative-representational social research. Critical researchers see the social science tradition as serving to reproduce the status quo of the dominant ideological construct, assimilationism. Young (1998), for example, characterizes the social science research as a "totalizing" science that serves as "the beholders of cultural individualism" of European societies whose work "has led to a theory of politics about individual power" neglecting the "battles of cultural politics" (p. 148). Young argues that social science researchers pay "no attention" to "morally charged politics of marginal voices" (p. 168).

Accordingly, critical researchers tend to put aside, or reject, the long-term assimilative change in immigrants and ethnic minorities articulated in social scientific theories and documented in social scientific research findings. Instead, Collier and Bornman (1999), for example, focus on the "dialectic tensions in group and individual identity orientations" in investigating several historically dominant and nondominant ethnic groups in South Africa. Hedge (1988), based on interviews with 10 Asian Indian women in the United States, characterizes the adaptation experience of these women in light of their "struggle" and "displacement," as they face the "contradictions" between their internal identity and external "world in which hegemonic structures systematically marginalize certain types of difference" (p. 36). A similar opposition to assimilation of "members of marginalized communities" is claimed by Flores (2001). From a "Chicana feminist" perspective, Flores (2001) appears to dismiss assimilation as a "myth." Instead, Flores argues that members of "marginalized communities," including "those of us in academia," produce "oppositional readings of dominant or mainstream texts" as a "strategy of resistance" (p. 27).

In theorizing about the communication patterns of ethnic minorities, Orbe (1998) offers a pluralistic notion of status equality in his "co-cultural theory." Consistent with the emancipatory goal of the critical inquiry, Orbe chooses the word "co-cultural" over other terminologies such as subcultural, subordinate, and minority to signify the notion that "no one culture in our society is inherently superior to other coexisting cultures" (p. 2). Orbe's theory then examines the communication practices of co-cultural group members (who are traditionally "muted" social groups including ethnic minorities, women, gays/lesbians/bisexuals, and those from a lower socio-economic status). Orbe sees their experiences to be "often made invisible by the pervasiveness of the dominant culture" (p. 1). Exploring the complex theoretical relationship between culture, power, and communication, Orbe explicates specific "co-cultural communication strategies"—from "avoiding," "mirroring," "embracing stereotypes," and "censoring self," to "educating others," "bargaining," "attacking," and "sabotaging others." Each of these strategies is explained as having been derived from the "standpoint" of co-cultural group members, who would choose different sets of strategies in accordance with one or more of three "preferred communication outcome" with respect to members of the dominant group: "assimilation," "accommodation," and "separation."

Pluralist-separatist ideological messages are also offered by Tsuda (1986). Tsuda criticizes the Western ideological domination as the genesis of "distorted intercultural communication" around the world. Tsuda argues, in particular, that the dominance of English language embodies the dominance of Western cultural ideology, which imposes an overt restriction on non-Western peoples' freedom of expression and damages their identity. Likewise, Young (1996) presents his criticism of Western "cultural imperialism" by depicting today's global reality as one of power asymmetry between communicators rooted in "oppressive" and "imperialistic" Western cultural-institutional systems. Characterizing his view as a "moderation" or "middle-path between imperial universalism and separatist cultural relativism" (p. 4), Young (1996) offers a vision of "true intercultural communication" in which "there is joint interest, a common interest, so that one is eager to give and the other to take" (p. 183). Young (1996) further argues that it is only when we understand "the process through which cultural exclusion and manipulation of identity of culturally different people is carried out in everyday communication," can we have a clear basis for an "effective politics aimed at changing empirically observable mechanisms for the creation of ideology or the assertion of the reality of one culture over another" (p. 29).

## DISCUSSION

The academic conceptions of ethnic identity examined above reveal a full range of views in the contemporary ideological landscape of American society depicted in Figure 1. Intended or unintended, and implicit or explicit, the conceptions of ethnic identity emerging from the literature represent the four differing but interacting positions in the ideological circle: assimilationism, pluralism, integrationism, and separatism. Of the four positions, most of the social scientific writings emanate assimilationist or integrationist views, while many phenomenological-interpretive writings indicate more pluralistic identity conceptions. Explicit pluralist-separatist arguments are made by critical researchers, some of whose ideas approach what most Americans outside the academic community would see as extreme.

As a researcher grounded in positive science and systems methodology, this author is mindful of possible unintentional misinterpretations and mischaracterizations of the works of phenomenological-interpretive and critical researchers. As such, the following summary and observations are offered as a tentative first step in working toward a more accurate and complete understanding of the ongoing identity polemics in academic writings on ethnic identity and its role in interethnic relations.

Identity Polemics in the Academe

The main research aim for traditional social scientists is to describe and explain a given reality as is, based on a set of generalizable, probability-based theoretical statements (propositions or theorems) explicated in the form, "If A, then B." In this provisional form of prediction, the researcher leaves possible outcomes open to both pluralistic and assimilationistic tendencies. In this normative-representational research tradition, researchers strive to adhere to value neutrality in investigating the phenenomon of adaptive change in ethnic identity in the direction of increasing assimilation in the mainstream society. Social scientific researchers generally view this adaptation process as a desirable goal for the individual's effective functioning in the society, as well as for the integrity of the society itself. Ethnic identity is conceived largely as a dynamic and evolving entity that transforms over time beyond the boundaries of the original ascribed identity. An extensive body of research data provides empirical support for the theorized phenomenon of long-term adaptive change. Although few social scientific conceptions explicitly take a side of either assimilative and pluralistic ideals, they implicitly substantiate, conceptually and empirically, the assimilative vision of *E Pluribus Unum* and of transcending group categories in the interest of peace and peaceful social change.

Some of the social scientific theories project more integrationist ideals of balancing the goal of interethnic harmony that seek to somehow reconcile the pluralistic claims of distinct ethnic identity with the goal of harmonious interethnic relations. More recent social scientific theories offering such integrationist conceptions incorporate some of the pluralistic concerns about ethnic identity maintenance and interethnic power inequality. This author's (Kim, 1988, 1995a, 1995b, 2001) theory, for example, balances "host communication" with "ethnic communication," taking into account the environmental conditions such as "host receptivity," "host conformity pressure," and "ethnic group strength." Other multidimensional theories of intercultural and interethnic communication such as communication accommodation theory (Gallois et al., 1995) include macrostructural factors such as history of intergroup conflict, along with situational and psychological factors such as accommodative or non-accommodative identity orientation. In these theories, ethnic identity is conceived not as a fixed or monolithic social category, but as a more flexible and "variable" psychological orientation that is "negotiated" and "managed" in interethnic situations.

Countering these assimilationist-integrationist conceptions of ethnic identity are the pluralistic conceptions prevalent in traditional ethnographic analyses of ethnic communities. Grounded in a relativistic view of culture and ethnicity, most of the ethnographic descriptions of ethnic identity emphasize the enduring nature of ethnic identity—the shared life patterns, practices, and symbols connoting a common tradition and common future. Highlighted in such communal conceptions of ethnic identity is a pluralistic "us-and-them" orientation that stresses group distinctiveness (rather than similarities) and ethnic identity maintenance (rather than identity flexibility and adaptive change). In most ethnographic writings, these pluralistic messages are implied. Few explicitly advocate either ideological position.

Reaching beyond the ethnographic descriptions are the clearly politicized pluralistic conceptions by critical researchers with a dedicated political interest in seeking emancipatory goals for ethnic minorities. Critical researchers actively oppose assimilationist-integrative conceptions of ethnic identity, as well as the social scientific theories representing the reality of adaptive convergence of ethnic identities over time. The critical researchers' advocacy of pluralistic ideals—.the primacy of distinct ethnic identity and equal group status—is reflected in the common conception of ethnic identity as a largely ascription-based and monolithic entity, coupled with an "us-against-them" posture of separatism. Intended or not, some critical researchers' writings suggest a sense of "ethnic identity at any cost"—an implicit message that gives ethnic identity an absolute moral imperative. This moral presupposition overlooks the potential "dark side" of a rigid, categorical adherence to ethnic identity, that is, the tendencies of collective ingroup glorification and outgroup denigration. The "all-or-none" and "either-or" view glosses over the fact that many people's identities are not locked into a single category but incorporate other identities as well. The tendency of critical researchers to view ethnic identity almost exclusively in terms of power inequality and conflict oversimplifies the complex reality in which macrostructural, situational, and psychological forces all work together simultaneously and interactively.

## Social Engagement and Social Responsibility

The varying types of ideological messages gleaned from the present analysis reveal that all researchers are directly and indirectly engaged in the ongoing identity polemics of the American public at large. By the presupposition of flexible identity, and by the suggested practical implications derived from their theories, even traditional social scientists adhering to value-neutrality find themselves rendering an intellectual and empirical substantiation for assimilative-integrative tendencies of identity transformation. Such is the case even when many social scientific theories offer ideologically balanced, value-neutral conceptions of ethnic identity, in which both assimilative-integrative tendencies with pluralistic-separatist tendencies are explained and predicted. In contrast, the pluralist-separatist conceptions of ethnic identity offered by critical researchers do not seek to depict balanced theoretical accounts of ethnic identity and, instead, focus on the reality of the negative effects arising from domestic and international interethnic interface on ethnic groups of less power and status. Critical researchers appear to be concerned not so much with presenting an accurate and balanced representation of the complex and varied ways ethnic identity plays out in reality, as with forcefully advocating ethnic identity maintenance and equal power relations between ethnic groups.

This methodological-ideological divergence lies at the heart of the on-going identity polemics in the current academic conceptions of ethnic identity. For both traditional and critical researchers, the profound methodological-ideological divergence presents an enormous intellectual chasm that cannot be easily bridged. Efforts have been made by some researchers to either reconcile and merge (e.g., Collier, 1998), or embrace in a dialectic relationship (e.g., Martin & Nakayama, 1999), the oppositional methodological-ideological systems. We have yet to see whether or not the fundamental philosophical differences can be effectively integrated into a viable methodological alternative in which the normative-representational goals of traditional social research and the emancipatory goals of critical research can be reasonably addressed and met. For such a synthesis to be sought, it is essential that all researchers of all methodological-ideological orientations engage in rigorous reflections and cross-examinations, so as to form a clearer understanding of the varied methodological-ideological underpinnings implied or forcefully argued in their own and each other's work. All social researchers need to be cognizant of the profound, long-term ideological consequences their knowledge claims implicate, intended or not, with a greater sense of social responsibility.

With this future need in mind, the present analysis offers an initial assessment of a number of specific points of contention (as well as convergence) among various existing conceptions of ethnic identity. Through this analysis, the author has come to a tentative understanding of the identity polemics in social research as being fundamentally rooted in two very different versions of what an ideal society or an ideal world should be and how ethnic (along with other) differences should be managed. On the one hand, the assimilationist version, traceable to the political philosophy of classical liberalism, is built on the premise of the primacy of individual identity and emphasizes *Unum* or its universalized form of American or human identity—along with the principle of procedural equality to be applied across the board while recognizing unequal status present among individuals in all human groups. On the other hand, the pluralist version of an ideal society (or world) emphasizes *Pluribus* in opposition to the traditional assimilationist ideals by emphasizing the counterthemes of the primacy of group identity and status equality between groups.

In the end, viability of an academic conception of ethnic identity has to be assessed based on the extent to which it serves to help understand the divergent realities of everyday folks outside the academe. Against the backdrop of the largely assimilative-integrative American ideological milieu described earlier in this essay, this author poses some basic questions that may be considered by social researchers seeking to make knowledge claims about ethnic identity. Is rigid adherence to the ethnicity of our youth feasible or desirable? Is ethnic identity in its pure form more a nostalgic notion than a reality? Can the desire for some form of collective uniqueness be satisfied without resulting in divisions and conflicts among groups? At what point do we cross the line from rightful and constructive claims for group identity to disastrous collisions with undue prejudice directed against one another? How can a society of multiple ethnic identities such as the United States support and give confidence to all groups while upholding the communal values and responsibilities that transcend allegiance to each group? Can a society, and indeed the world, achieve this goal despite the increasing trend of disunity and "unbounded and unwholesome pluralism" (Etzioni, 1993, p. 217)? Who can and will help bridge the chasms created by contentious identity politics? Can or should academic inquiry help form "a more perfect union"?

## REFERENCES

Abercrombie, N. (1980). *Class, structure and knowledge.* Oxford, UK: Basil Blackwell.

Adler, P. (1982). Beyond cultural identity: Reflections on cultural and multicultural men. In L. Samovar & R. Porter (Eds.), *Intercultural communication: A reader* (pp. 389–408). Belmont, CA: Wadsworth.

Anderson, R., & Saenz, R. (1994). Structural determinants of Mexican American intermarriage, 1975–1980. *Social Science Quarterly, 75,* 414–430.

Asante, M. (1993). Racism, consciousness, and Afrocentricity. In G. Early (Ed.), *Lure and loathing: Essays on race, identity, and the ambivalence of assimilation* (pp. 127–148). New York: Penguin.

Baker, R. (1994, May 5). Gone with the *Unum. New York Times,* p. A15.

Berry, J. (1980). Acculturation as varieties of adaptation. In A. Padilla (Ed.), *Acculturation: Theory, models and some new findings* (pp. 9–25). Washington, DC: Westview Press.

Berry, J. (1990). Psychology of acculturation: Understanding individuals moving between cultures. In R. Brislin (Ed.), *Applied cross-cultural psychology* (pp. 232–253). Newbury Park, CA: Sage.

Berry, J., & Sam, D. (1997). Acculturation and adaptation. In J. Berry, M. Segall, & C. Kagitcibasi (Eds.), *Handbook of cross-cultural psychology,* (2nd ed., vol. 1 pp. 291–326). Boston: Allyn & Bacon.

Billig, M. (1991). *Ideology and opinions: Studies in rhetorical psychology.* London: Sage.

Billig, M., Condor, S., Edwards, D., Gane, M., Middleton, D., & Radley, A. (1988). *Ideological dilemmas: A social psychology of everyday thinking.* London: Sage.

Bourhis, R., Moise, L., Perreault, S., & Senecal, S. (1997). Toward an interactive acculturation model: A social psychological approach. *International Journal of Psychology, 32*(6), 369–386.

Broome, B. (1990). "Palevome": Foundations of struggle and conflict in Greek interpersonal communication. *Southern Journal of Communication, 55,* 260–275.

Carbaugh, D. (1993). Competence as cultural pragmatics: Reflections on some Soviet and American encounters. In R. Wiseman & J. Koester (Eds.), *Intercultural communication competence* (pp. 168–183). Newbury Park, CA: Sage.

Casmir, F. (1999). Foundations for the study of intercultural communication based on a third-culture building model. *International Journal of Intercultural Relations, 23*(1), 91–116.

Collier, M. (1998). Researching cultural identity: Reconciling interpretive and postcolonial perspectives. In D. Tanno & A. Gonzalez (Eds.), *Communication and identity across cultures* (pp. 122–147). Thousand Oaks, CA: Sage.

Collier, M., & Bornman, E. (1999). Core symbols in South African intercultural friendships. *International Journal of Intercultural Relations, 23*(1), 133–156.

Collier, M., & Thomas, M. (1988). Cultural identity: An interpretive perspective. In Y. Kim & W. Gudykunst (Eds.), *Theories in intercultural communication* (pp. 99–120). Newbury Park, CA: Sage.

Cupach, W., & Imahori, T. (1993). Identity management theory: Communication competence in intercultural episodes and relationships. In R. Wiseman & J. Koester (Eds.), *Intercultural communication competence* (pp. 112–131). Newbury Park, CA: Sage.

Daniel, J., & Smitherman-Donaldson, G. (1990). How I got over: Communication dynamics in the Black community. In D. Carbaugh (Ed.), *Cultural communication and intercultural contact* (pp. 27–40). Hillsdale, NJ: Erlbaum.

Diesing, P. (1991). *How does social science work? Reflections on practice.* Pittsburgh, PA: University of Pittsburgh Press.

Erikson, E. (1969). Growth and crises of the healthy personality. In H. Chiang & A. Maslow (Eds.), *The healthy personality* (pp. 30–34). New York: Van Nostrand Reinhold.

Etzioni, A. (1993). *The spirit of community: Rights, responsibilities, and the Communitarian agenda.* New York: Crown.

Fitch, K. (1998). *Speaking relationally: Culture, communication, and interpersonal connection.* New York: Guilford Press.

Flores, L. (2001). Challenging the myth of assimilation: A Chicana feminist response. M. J. Collier (Ed.), *Constituting cultural difference through discourse* (pp. 26–46). Thousand Oaks, CA: Sage.

Gallois, S., Giles, H., Jones, E., Cargile, A., & Ota, H. (1995). Accommodating intercultural encounters: Elaborations and extensions. In R. Wiseman (Ed.), *Intercultural communication theory* (pp. 115–147). Thousand Oaks, CA: Sage.

Giles, H., Mulac, A., Bradac, J., & Johnson, P. (1987). Speech accommodation theory. In M. McLaughlin (Ed.), *Communication yearbook 10* (pp. 13–48). Newbury Park, CA: Sage.

Glazer, N., & Moynihan, D. (1963). *Beyond the melting pot.* Cambridge, MA: MIT Press.

Gordon, M. (1964). *Assimilation in American life: The role of race, religion, and national origins.* New York: Oxford University Press.

Graff, G. (1992). *Beyond the culture wars: How teaching the conflicts can revitalize American education.* New York: Norton.

Gray, P. (1993, Fall). Teach your children well. *Time,* (special issue, "The new faces of America"), 69–71.

Greeley, A. (1974). *Ethnicity in the United States: A preliminary reconnaissance.* New York: Wiley.

Grunwald, H. (1976, July 5). Loving America. *Time,* 35–36.

Hacker, A. (1992). *Two nations: Black and White, separate, hostile, unequal.* New York: Scribner's.

Hall, E. (1976). *Beyond culture.* New York: Doubleday.

Hammersley, M. (1995). *The politics of social research.* London: Sage.

Hecht, M., Collier, M., & Ribeau, S. (1993). *African American communication: Ethnic identity and cultural interpretation.* Newbury Park, CA: Sage.

Hedge, R. (1998). Swinging the trapeze: The negotiation of identity among Asian Indian immigrant women in the United States. In D. Tanno & A. Gonzalez (Eds.), *Communication and identity across cultures* (pp. 34–55). Thousand Oaks, CA: Sage.

Iyer, P. (1990, September 3). The masks of minority terrorism. *Time,* 86.

Jacoby, T. (1998). *Someone else's house: America's unfinished struggle for integration.* New York: Free Press.

Kim, Y. Y. (1976). *Communication patterns of foreign immigrants in the process of acculturation: A survey among the Korean population in Chicago.* Unpublished doctoral dissertation, Northwestern University, Evanston, IL.

Kim, Y. Y. (1977). Communication patterns of foreign immigrants in the process of acculturation.

*Human Communication Research, 4,* 66–77.

Kim, Y. Y. (1978a). A communication approach to acculturation processes: Korean immigrants in Chicago. *International Journal of Intercultural Relations, 2*(2), 197–224.

Kim, Y. Y. (1978b). Interethnic and intraethnic communication: A study of Korean immigrants in Chicago. In N. Jain (Ed.), *International and intercultural communication annual* (Vol. 4, pp. 53–68). Falls Church, VA: Speech Communication Association.

Kim, Y. Y. (1980). *Indochinese refugees in Illinois: Vols. 1–5.* (Research report submitted to the U.S. Department of Health, Education and Welfare Region V, Grant P: 95–549). Chicago: Travelers Aid Society.

Kim, Y. Y. (1988). *Communication and cross-cultural adaptation: An integrative theory.* Clevedon, Avon, UK: Multilingual Matters.

Kim, Y. Y. (1989). Personal, social, and economic adaptation: The case of 1975–1979 arrivals in Illinois. In D. Haines (Ed.), *Refugees as immigrants: Survey research on Cambodians, Laotians, and Vietnamese in America* (pp. 86–104). Totowa, NJ: Rowman & Littlefield.

Kim, Y. Y. (1990). Communication and adaptation of Asian Pacific refugees in the United States. *Journal of Pacific Rim Communication, 1,*191–207.

Kim, Y. (1995a). Cross-cultural adaptation: An integrative theory. In R. Wiseman (Ed.), *Intercultural communication theory* (pp. 170–193). Newbury Park, CA: Sage.

Kim, Y. (1995b). Identity development: From cultural to intercultural. In H. Mokros (Ed.), *Information and behavior, Vol. 5. Interaction and identity* (pp. 347–369). New Brunswick, NJ: Transaction.

Kim, Y. (1997). The behavior-context interface in interethnic communication. In J. Owen (Ed.), *Context and communication behavior* (pp. 261–291). Reno, NV: Context Press.

Kim, Y. (1999). *Unum* and *pluribus*: Ideological underpinnings of interethnic communication in the United States. *International Journal of Intercultural Relations, 23*(4), 591–611.

Kim, Y. (2001). *Becoming intercultural: An integrative theory of communication and cross-cultural adaptation.* Thousand Oaks, CA: Sage.

Kochman, T. (1986). Black verbal dueling strategies in interethnic communication. In Y. Kim (Ed.), *Interethnic communication* (pp. 136–157). Newbury Park, CA: Sage.

Kochman, T. (1990). Force fields in Black and White communication. In D. Carbaugh (Ed.), *Cultural communication and intercultural contact* (pp. 193–217). Hillsdale, NJ: Erlbaum.

Levine, A. (2000, June 11,). The campus divided, and divided again. *The New York Times,* Op-Ed Sec., p. 17.

Lewis, J. (1998). *Walking with the wind.* New York: Simon & Schuster.

Lind, M. (1995). *The American nation: The new nationalism and the fourth American revolution.* New York: Free Press.

Loury, G. (1993). Free at last? A personal perspective on race and identity in America. In G. Early (Ed.), *Lure and loathing: Essays on race, identity, and the ambivalence of assimilation* (pp. 1–12). New York: Allen Lane/Penguin.

Martin, J., Krizek, R., Nakayama, T., & Bradford, L. (1996). Exploring whiteness: A study of self labels for White Americans. *Communication Quarterly, 44,* 125–144.

Martin, J., & Nakayama, T. (1999). Thinking dialectically about culture and communication. *Communication Theory, 1,* 1–25.

Masuda, M., Matsumoto, G., & Meredith, G. (1970). Ethnic identity in three generations of Japanese Americans. *Journal of Social Psychology, 81*(2), 199–207.

McCauley, T. (1991, June). *Social change in a bi-cultural community: A case study of Penetanguishene.* Paper presented at the annual convention of the Canadian Society for Sociology and Anthropology, Kingston, Ontario.

Morgan, N. (1987). *Language maintenance and shift among Haitians in the Dominican Republic.* Unpublished doctoral dissertation, University of New Mexico, Albuquerque.

Namazi, K. (1984). Assimilation and need assessment among Mexican, Cuban, and Middle Eastern immigrants: A multivariate analysis (Doctoral dissertation, University of Akron, 1984).

Dissertation Abstracts International, 45(03), 949A. (University Microfilms No. DA8414649)

Novak, M. (1971). The rise of the unmeltable ethnics. New York: Macmillan.

Novak, M. (1973 May/June). The new ethnicity. The Humanist, 18–21.

Orbe, M. (1998). Constructing co-cultural theory: An explication of culture, power, and communication. Thousand Oaks, CA: Sage.

Page, J. (1994 January/February). Japanese Brazilian style. Americas, 34–41.

Parenti, M. (1967). Ethnic politics and the persistence of ethnic voting identification. American Political Science Review, 67, 717–726.

Petronio, S., Ellemers, N., Giles, H., & Gallois, C. (1998). (Mis)communicating across boundaries: Interpersonal and intergroup considerations. Communication Research, 25(6), 571–595.

Postiglione, G. (1983). Ethnicity and American social theory: Toward critical pluralism. Lanham, MD: University Press of America.

Powers, R. (2000, May 7). Americans dreaming. The New York Times Magazine (Special Edition), pp. 22, 67–68.

Pratt, S. (1998). Razzing: Ritualizing uses of humor as a form of identification among American Indians. In D. Tanno & A. Gonzalez (Eds.), Communication and identity across cultures (pp. 56–79). Thousand Oaks, CA: Sage.

Root, M. (1992). Within, between, and beyond race. In M. Root (Ed.), Racially mixed people in America (pp. 1–11). Newbury Park, CA: Sage.

Rorty, R. (1998). Achieving our country: Leftist thought in twentieth-century America. Cambridge, MA: Harvard University Press.

Rossides, D. (1976). The American class system: An introduction to social stratification. Washington, DC: University Press of America.

Ryan, A. (1998). Liberal anxieties and liberal education. New York: Hill & Wang.

Sampson, E. (1977). Psychology and the American ideal. Journal of Personality and Social Psychology, 35, 767–782.

Sahlins, M. (1964). Culture and environment: The study of cultural ecology. In S. Tax (Ed.), Horizons of anthropology (pp. 132–147). Chicago: Aldine.

Smolowe, J. (1993, Fall). Intermarried . . . with children: The new face of America [Special issue]. Time, 64–65.

Southern Poverty Law Center (1998, Spring). Intelligence Report, 90.

Stonequist, E. (1964). The marginal man: A study in personality and culture conflict. In E. Burgess & D. Bogue (Eds.), Contributions to urban sociology (pp. 327–345). Chicago: University of Chicago Press.

Suro, R. (1998). Strangers among us: How Latino immigration is transforming America. New York: Knopf.

Szalay, L., & Inn, A. (1988). Cross-cultural adaptation and diversity: Hispanic Americans. In Y. Y. Kim & W. Gudykunst (Eds.), Cross-cultural adaptation: Current approaches (pp. 212–232). Newbury Park, CA: Sage.

Tajfel, H. (1978). Social identity and intergroup behavior. Social Science Information, 13, 65–93.

Tajfel, H. (Ed.). (1978). Differentiation between social groups. London: Academic Press.

Tajfel, H., & Turner, J. (1979). An integrative theory of intergroup conflict. In W. Austin & S. Worchel (Eds.), The social psychology of intergroup relations (pp. 33–47). Monterey, CA: Brooks/Cole.

Tajfel, H., & Turner, J. (1986). The social identity theory of intergroup behavior. In S. Worchel & W. Austin (Eds.), Psychology of intergroup relations (2nd ed.; pp. 7–24). Chicago: Nelson-Hall.

Taylor, C. (1992). Multiculturalism and the politics of recognition. Princeton, NJ: Princeton University Press.

Teske, R., & Nelson, B. (1974). Acculturation and assimilation: A clarification. American Anthropologist, 1, 351–367.

Thornton, M. (1996). Hidden agendas, identity theories, and multiracial people. In M. Root (Ed.), The multiracial experience: Racial borders as the new frontiers (pp. 101–120). Thousand Oaks, CA: Sage.

Ting-Toomey, S. (1993). Communicative resourcefulness: An identity negotiation perspective. In R. Wiseman & J. Koester (Eds.), *Intercultural communication competence* (pp. 72–111). Newbury Park, CA: Sage.

Ting-Toomey, S., & Kurogi, A. (1998). Facework competence in intercultural conflict: An updated face-negotiation theory. *International Journal of Intercultural Relations, 22*(2), 187–225.

Traub, J. (1998, June 28). Nathan Glazer changes his mind, again. *New York Times Magazine,* 22–25.

Triandis, H., Kashima, Y., Shimada, E., & Villareal, M. (1986). Acculturation indices as a means of confirming cultural differences. *International Journal of Psychology, 21,* 43–70.

Tsuda, Y. (1986). *Language inequality and distortion in intercultural communication: A critical theory approach.* Amsterdam: John Benjamins.

Turner, J. (1987). *Rediscovering the social group.* Oxford, UK: Basil Blackwell.

Van Dijk, T. (1998). *Ideology: A multidisciplinary approach.* Thousand Oaks, CA: Sage.

Ward, A. (1993). Which side are you on? *Amerasia Journal, 19*(2), 109–112.

Wieder, L., & Pratt, S. (1990). On being a recognizable Indian among Indians. In D. Carbaugh (Ed.), *Cultural communication and intercultural contact* (pp. 45–64). Hillsdale, NJ: Erlbaum.

Wolfe, A. (1998). *One nation, after all.* New York: Viking.

Wolfinger, R. (1965). The development and persistence of ethnic voting. *American Political Science Review, 59,* 896–908.

Woodward, K. (Ed.). (1997). *Identity and difference.* Thousand Oaks, CA: Sage.

Young, R. (1996) *Intercultural communication: Pragmatics, genealogy, deconstruction.* Philadelphia: Multilingual Matters.

Zweigenhalf, R. (1979–1980). American Jews: In or out of the upper class? *Insurgent Sociologist, 9,* 24–37.

# CHAPTER CONTENTS

- Patient-Physician Communication:                                    330
  Overview and Managed Care Context
  *Patient-Physician Communication and Outcomes*                      *330*
  *Patterns of Patient-Physician Communication*                       *331*
  *Managed Care and Patient-Physician Communication*                  *333*

- Telemedicine and Patient-Physician Communication                    335
  *Definitions*                                                       *335*
  *Patient-Physician Communication Via Telemedicine*                  *336*
  *Benefits of Telemedicine*                                          *339*
  *Attitudinal Barriers to Telemedicine*                              *340*
  *Patient-Physician Trust*                                           *341*

- Patient-Physician Communication Via Electronic Mail                 342
  *Email and the Patient-Physician Relationship*                      *343*
  *Guidelines for Email Use*                                          *344*
  *Patient Perspectives on Email*                                     *345*
  *Patients' Privacy Concerns*                                        *346*
  *Physician Perspectives on Email*                                   *347*
  *Physicians' Privacy Concerns*                                      *348*

- The Internet and Patient-Physician Communication                    349
  *Patient Internet Use*                                              *350*
  *Sources of Physician Resistance to Patient Internet Use*           *351*
  *Patient-Physician Negotiation of Internet Information*             *354*
  *The Internet and the Future of Patient-Physician Communication*    *356*

- Directions for Future Research                                      357

- References                                                          359

# 10 Telehealth, Managed Care, and Patient-Physician Communication: Twenty-first Century Interface

RUTH M. GUZLEY
*California State University, Chico*

NORAH E. DUNBAR
*California State University, Long Beach*

STEPHANIE A. HAMEL
*The University of Texas, Austin*

The patient-physician relationship has undergone significant recent transformation as a societal shift toward patient autonomy occurred, and as health care moved toward the managed care model. Not yet settled into their new roles, physicians and patients alike now face another wave of change in their relationship associated with integration of technological systems in the medical field to promote and protect health. This integration is referred to as telehealth. In this chapter, we examine what is known about the effects of the managed care model and telehealth as intertwined-change forces that are influencing patient-physician communication. Specifically, three aspects of telehealth are reviewed: telemedicine, email, and the Internet. Although telemedicine is not a new technology, empirical research examining its effects on patient-physician communication is limited. Similarly, email is increasingly being used by physicians in lieu of face-to-face interactions to diagnose and manage the treatment of patients; however, little research addresses its effectiveness with regard to communication between physicians and patients. Finally, the Internet has opened the floodgates of health information to the public, bringing with it myriad concerns about the credibility, quantity, and understandability of such information. How this information is processed within the patient-physician relationship remains unclear. To close, we offer conclusions and directions for future research in this area.

T he revered patient-physician relationship is currently undergoing significant change both internally and externally (Darkins & Cary, 2000). From the inside, the relationship has been affected by a broad movement toward

Correspondence: Ruth M. Guzley, Department of Communication Arts & Sciences, California State University, Chico, CA 95929-0502; email: rguzley@csuchico.edu

*Communication Yearbook 26*, pp. 326–364

greater patient autonomy and involvement in health care decisions. The need for this shift has been acknowledged by health communication researchers (Sharf & Street, 1997) who have even questioned whether the term "patient" is an acceptable one given the shift in patient role from passive to active (Sharf, 1988). In addition, Sharf addresses the need for patient education in communication skills to aid in this role adjustment.

Coinciding with increased patient desire for a more participative role in their health care decisions, and in response to dissatisfaction with the traditional paternalistic model of interacting with patients, some physicians have championed the adoption of a "patient-centered" approach to medical care. Although Roter (2000) recently called attention to the fact that the term "relationship-centered" may be a more accurate reflection of the reciprocal nature of the patient-physician relationship, both terms, it appears, are intended to reflect a patient-physician relationship that is grounded in mutuality and that fit the characteristics explicitly tied to patient-centered care (PCC) as described above. PCC represents a drastic departure from the clinical approach that concentrated on the illness rather than the patient's experience of the illness. In its most basic form PCC is grounded in recognition of the patient as the center of concern. Lambert et al. (1997) argue that patient-centered care "requires that patient needs, preferences, and beliefs be respected at all times" (p. 27). In PCC patients are encouraged to be active and informed partners in their health care, participating in decision making with their physician (Krupat et al., 2000). Evidence to date shows impressive health-related outcomes associated with physicians' use of the patient-centered approach as well as increased patient satisfaction (Smith et al., 2000). Effective communication is considered central to PCC (Bensing, Verhaak, van Dulmen, & Visser, 2000).

External forces have also been at work in reshaping the patient-physician relationship, notably the growth of managed care as a health care delivery system (Darkins & Cary, 2000). Mechanic and Schlesinger (1996) offer a broad definition of managed care as "organizational arrangements that seek to alter treatment practices so that care of acceptable quality can be provided at lower cost…[more specifically] managed care refers to organizational structures and strategies designed to constrain expenditures" (p. 1694).

Managed care has received considerable attention by both academicians and the popular press. In this structure, the roles of physicians and patients, and subsequently how they communicate with one another, have been effected significantly. Although managed care includes nonphysician health care providers who interact with patients (e.g., nurse practitioners, physician assistants) as well as primary care physicians, physicians' relationships with patients remain central in empirical study for reasons articulated well by Emanuel and Dubler (1995): They outnumber nonphysician providers, the majority of Americans receive their health care from physicians as opposed to nonphysician providers, and the extensive body of research on patient-physician interactions has given us time to reflect on the relationship and provides a good foundation from which to make educated projections.

Running parallel to managed care as an external change force but largely undocumented by health communication researchers, another significant but more subtle influence on the patient-physician communication has been growing steadily—the influence of communication technology (Orvell, Rockefeller, Price, Reynolds, & Kassirer,1995). The increasing coverage of health topics by the media, the popularization of Internet health sites, increasing use of email by physicians, and new technologies used in health care settings have created both challenges and opportunities for communication between patients and physicians.

In general, the communication functions of technology in health care can be located under the umbrella of "telehealth." Telehealth is defined as "the integration of telecommunications systems into the practice of protecting and promoting health" (Darkins & Cary, 2000, p. 2). Within the current social context of growing interest in full patient participation in health care decisions, telehealth offers a comprehensive approach to health care with significant opportunities. Darkins and Cary (2000) address the importance of telehealth to the patient-physician relationship in this way:

> Patients are realizing that there are risks as well as benefits to treatment and so demand more involvement in making any treatment decision of which they will bear the ultimate consequences. Telehealth offers an ideal tool to promote this sharing of information and help in managing patients with chronic diseases, especially in primary care. In doing this telehealth changes aspects of the conventionally accepted roles of both patient and physician in the doctor-patient relationship. (p. 47)

Currently, both physicians and patients are stuck in uneasy roles that came about as patients sought more autonomy in medical decisions and as health care delivery moved predominantly to the managed care model. While some patients are pushing to have more and more information about their health conditions and treatment, as well as greater say in health care decisions that effect them, other patients are resistant to move into the "informed patient" mode and cling to the traditional paternalistic patient-physician model. Elderly patients provide one example of the latter group (Beisecker, 1988). Physicians, on the other hand, are having their own identity crisis. After a long history of professional autonomy and relative control over the patient-physician relationship, they find themselves as "double agents"—forced to adopt cost control procedures characteristic of managed care organizations, which limit available time to spend with patients (among other things), while still bound to the patient by their long-standing fiduciary role. This switch has been particularly difficult for those physicians who have sought to practice patient-centered care.

As yet, little research addresses these dual change forces on patient-physician communication. The purpose of this chapter is to initiate a step in that direction.

## PATIENT-PHYSICIAN COMMUNICATION:
## OVERVIEW AND MANAGED CARE CONTEXT

To set the context for the rest of this chapter, the balance of this section is divided into three brief discussions: one that addresses the relationship between patient-physician communication and outcomes, a second that provides a brief contrast of traditional and contemporary patterns of patient-physician communication, and a third that addresses how the policies and philosophies of managed care have impacted communication between patients and their physicians. The remainder of the chapter separately addresses three important elements of telehealth—telemedicine, email, and the Internet—as having both advantages and disadvantages in managed care settings. We end the chapter with suggestions for future research directions.

### Patient-Physician Communication and Outcomes

The importance of effective communication between physician and patient is well documented (e.g., Emanuel & Dubler, 1995; Roter, 2000), particularly as it relates to outcomes such as patient satisfaction, adherence to treatment, and patient trust. For example, Mechanic (1998a) notes that effective communication "allows the physician to understand the patient's expectations and concerns; to obtain accurate information, thereby facilitating diagnosis . . . and to gain the patient's understanding, cooperation and adherence to treatment" (p. 281). David (1994) argues that physicians' communication skills play an integral role in patient interest and compliance with preventative health procedures, with a straightforward discussion of such issues leading to a higher level of interest and compliance.

Patients report that they are more satisfied when their medical visit includes psychosocial topics than when their visit is restricted to biomedical exchanges (Bertakis, Roter, & Putnam, 1991). Similarly, patient satisfaction has been shown to increase when physicians exhibit a communication style of warmth, supportiveness, and courtesy, and when physicians do not dominate the interaction (Greene, Adelman, Friedmann, & Charon, 1994). Patient satisfaction is taken so seriously by Kaiser-Permanente that patient satisfaction surveys serve as criteria for physician bonuses (Dudley, Miller, Korenbrot, & Luft, 1998).

Arguably one of the most important outcomes of patient-physician communication is trust. For example, patient disclosure is a necessity for accurate diagnosis. Patient disclosure is more likely when trust in the physician exists, as trust encourages open communication (Mechanic, 1998a). Some research conceptualizes trust as relationally defined and more likely to exist in situations where communication is greater, there is an explicitly shared goal for treatment, when a person's autonomy is respected, and when the relationship is viewed as long-term (Thom & Campbell, 1997).

When there is a decline in patient-physician trust, the patient will experience less satisfaction with the medical encounter. Reduced trust also could reduce adherence to treatment recommendations, increase complaints and litigation (Mechanic, 1998a; Thom & Campbell, 1997), and possibly lower health status in general (Thom & Campbell, 1997). Trust between patient and physician also has significant effects on alleviating physician frustration and burnout (Mechanic, 1998a).

## Patterns of Patient-Physician Communication

A variety of excellent research exists addressing patterns of patient-physician communication (Emanuel & Emanuel, 1992; Roter, 2000; Roter et al., 1997; Stewart, 1995). Given the space limitations in this chapter, we review only one of these models from Roter et al. (1997) for three reasons: its currency, its inclusion—in some form—of critical elements of other models, and its empirical soundness.

Roter and colleagues (1997) content analyzed 537 audiotaped patient-physician interviews from 127 primary care physicians. The purpose of their study was to identify patterns of communication styles. Included in the analysis were patient surveys completed after the interview and measuring patient satisfaction with physician's communication (task-directed skill, attentiveness, interpersonal skill, emotional support, and patient-physician partnership). Physicians also completed a survey after each interview that included among other things a measure of visit satisfaction. The analysis yielded five distinct styles "accounting for 95% of the visits and 99% of the physicians" (Roter et al., p. 352). The first style Roter and colleagues label as "narrowly biomedical." This style was characterized by a high level of biomedical talk and verbal dominance by the physician. The level of socioemotional talk was very low (7% for physician and patient combined). Roter et al. state this style is reminiscent of the paternalistic style that was predominant through much of the twentieth century. The paternalistic model, although eroding significantly in the past few decades (Barondess, 1994), has not entirely disappeared.

Physicians who follow the paternalistic style assume the values of the patient are consistent with their values, and there is no assumption on the part of patient or physician that patients should be significantly involved in decisions about their treatment. In this paradigm, patients' interactions with physicians are generally limited to physicians gathering information from them to diagnose their conditions and to reach conclusions about the appropriate treatment (Roter et al., 1997). Makoul (1998) characterizes patients in this paternalistic relationship as "physician-reliant" and looking for directives rather than advice. They play a relatively passive role in the relationship, respecting and bowing to physicians' authority. Due to the biomedical focus of the relationship, paternalistic physicians have characteristically treated patients impersonally (Alpers, 1998).

Roter et al. (1997) label the second pattern to emerge "expanded biomedical." Physicians still dominated this type of interaction but allowed for somewhat more psychosocial input by patients than the narrowly biomedical pattern. In later work, Roter (2000) characterizes this pattern as "in transition" where the possibility of more expression of patient perspective exists; however, the power held by patients is minimal at best. The narrowly biomedical and expanded bio-medical patterns accounted for roughly two thirds of the analyzed visits. Previous research, however, indicates these patterns may not be associated with favorable outcomes. For example, Cecil (1998) found that physician domineer-ingness and patient submission were negatively related to patient compliance. In addition, physician dominance was negatively related to patient satisfaction.

In the third pattern, "biopsychosocial," biomedical discussion is still prevalent but more balanced with psychosocial exchange than in the previously discussed models. There is less dominance by the physician, and patients' "health values and preferences are likely to be mutually negotiated and explored within these exchanges, with implication for patient autonomy, self-understanding, and self-discovery" (Roter et al., 1997, p. 355). In other words, it represents a relation-ship-centered interaction. About 20% of the analyzed visits represented this pat-tern. In this pattern the balance of power tilts more in the patient's favor than in the previous two styles (Roter, 2000).

Biomedical and psychosocial talk by physicians was almost equal in the fourth pattern, labeled by Roter et al. (1997) as "psychosocial." Patients, on the other hand, talked twice as frequently about psychosocial topics as about bio-medical topics and were in more control of the interaction than in any of the pre-viously discussed patterns. As Roter (2000) notes, "this pattern provides an oppor-tunity for in-depth dialogue about the social and emotional implications of the patient's conditions. The physician's role may be friend or therapist, engaging the patient in dialogue about life issues that go well beyond the biomedical circum-stances" (p. 11). This pattern was represented in only 8% of the visits analyzed.

The fifth and final pattern Roter et al. (1997) call the "consumerist" pattern. This pattern is characterized by a high frequency of patient questions and a low frequency of physician questions. Physicians' answers to questions, however, are primarily of a biomedical nature; little psychosocial discussion occurs. Succinctly put, Roter et al. state this is a "down-to-business" pattern. This pat-tern presents a picture of physicians and patients as both active participants in their interactions. Patients are viewed as informed and desiring autonomy when it comes to decisions about their health care. They seek information about treat-ment options and want to exercise choice in selecting the option that fits their needs and values. Physicians are viewed as technical experts, advisers, consult-ants "providing the patient with the means to exercise control" (Emanuel & Emanuel, 1992, par. 9). Their power in this type relationship is through persua-sion (Makoul, 1998); however, it is considerably lower than that of the patient (Roter, 2000). Roter et al. report only 8% of the analyzed visits contained this pattern. Just as the paternalistic nature of the first two patterns ignores patient views, the consumerist pattern lacks appreciation for physician's contribution (Roter, 2000). Roter identifies these biopsychosocial and psychosocial patterns as optimal in establishing an environment of mutuality.

Of particular note in Roter et al.'s (1997) study is the fact that half the physicians in their sample tended toward a particular pattern for most of their visits, however, all of them used more than one pattern. These results provide evidence, however slight, of a movement away from the traditional paternalistic model.

## Managed Care and Patient-Physician Communication

As mentioned earlier, the patient-physician relationship has been significantly affected by managed care as a health delivery system (for a review of the impact of these changes on the patient-physician relationship see Emanuel & Dubler, 1995). Two changes that have pronounced and direct impact on communication between physicians and patients are discussed here: (a) the changing roles of both patient and physician and (b) time constraints imposed on the medical interview.

*Changing roles.* In managed care settings, primary care physicians serve patients in their general care and also act as "gatekeepers," determining and coordinating patients' referral to specialists and receipt of diagnostic tests (Goold & Lipkin, 1999; Thom & Campbell, 1997). They are both agents representing the profitability interests of managed care organizations and medical professionals whose long-time dedicated charge has been to patient health care. These responsibilities put physicians in the role of "double agent." For example, Degnin (1999) states "managed care organizations place limits on what physicians may order for patients. Even where there are no explicit limits, there are often financial or punitive incentives for PCPs [primary care physicians] to limit care" (p. 19). Such practices increase doubt in patients' minds about whether the physician is acting in the patients' best interest (Angell, 1993). This suspicion can affect the way patients interact with physicians (Mechanic, 1998b).

Whereas managed care policies may serve useful purposes in coordinating daily activities, task completion, and cost reduction, it is equally true these structural regulators lead to depersonalized relationships and mindless communication. As related to the patient-physician relationship within managed care, Siegler (1993) notes that guidelines "do not necessitate much communication between doctors and patients" (p. 466).

As demands for productivity increase in managed care organizations, physicians will have less and less time to devote to building or maintaining relationships with patients (LaPuma, 1994). Recent research indicates physicians who participate in managed care plans do in fact distance themselves from patients, willingly or unwillingly (Shapiro, Tym, Gudmundson, Derse, & Klein, 2000). All physicians licensed in Wisconsin in 1995 were surveyed about their arrangements with managed care. Of the approximately 2,500 responses, Shapiro et al. note half "indicated that they have changed their clinical behavior since participating in managed care" (p. 75). One behavior in particular that was changed as a result of the managed care structure was spending a comfortable amount of time with patients, "a restriction that may well inhibit maintenance and nurturing of their patient-physician relationships" (p. 79).

*Time constraints.* Some research has indicated in the managed care structure the patient-physician relationship is formalized in ways that limit both communication between the patient and physician and the development of a trusting relationship between them. For example, one of the standards against which physicians' performance is judged is time spent with each patient. Considering the volume of patients seen by most physicians coupled with efficiency concerns, it seems unlikely that physicians' have much incentive to actively listen to patients (e.g., ask open-ended rather than or in addition to closed-ended questions) or to spend time encouraging and answering patient questions. This suggestion is doubly disturbing when considered in light of research that identifies physicians as poor listeners (Epstein, Campbell, Cohen-Cole, McWhinney, & Smilkstein, 1993).

Time constraints imposed by the structure and practice of managed care (e.g., restrictions on the length of office visits) have received substantial criticism with regard to the effects of such constraints on patient-physician communication. For example, Siegler (1993) notes that to develop the kind of relationship that leads to trust, confidence and stability, time is required; time to communicate, discuss and negotiate patient preferences with physician advice regarding the patient's medical condition. Similarly, imposing time constraints on patient-physician interactions blocks effective communication, increasing the possibility of confusion (Gold, 1999), and decreasing satisfaction for both physician and patient (Mechanic, 1998a).

The implications of policies that limit physician time with patient may be more severe than loss of patient trust and dissatisfaction on the part of both patient and physician. For example, Levinson, Roter, Mullooly, Dull, and Frankel (1997) compared primary care physicians who have had less than two malpractice claims filed against them with those who have had two or more claims filed. Those with less than two claims spent more time with patients in routine visits (18.3 minutes) than did those with two or more claims (15 minutes). In addition, Levinson et al. note "the length of routine primary care visits did contribute to predicting the malpractice claims status of primary care physicians" (p. 558). These findings are consistent with those of previous research indicating malpractice suits are associated with patients feeling rushed by their physician in routine visits (Beckman, Markakis, Suchman, & Frankel, 1994).

In summary, physicians and patients have adopted a variety of communication patterns that are apparent in their encounters. These patterns are reflective of the internal and external shifts in their relationship described earlier and have implications for important outcomes of the communication. Managed care policies related to structure and mission have contributed to the shifting roles of patient and physician in ways that may not be altogether healthy for the relationship. In particular, time constraints imposed by administrative policies have created barriers to effective communication and also threaten to reduce outcomes such as patient satisfaction and trust.

We turn our attention now to a more in-depth look at three aspects of telehealth to discover the extent to which they will both help and hinder communication between patients and physicians.

## TELEMEDICINE AND PATIENT-PHYSICIAN COMMUNICATION

One technology that has received a great deal of attention is "telemedicine," which is generally defined as the delivery of health services at a distance. New emerging technologies have opened up opportunities for patient-physician interaction to go beyond face-to-face interaction and into the realm of mediated interaction. There is some speculation in the medical literature, communication literature, and the popular press on how mediated communication will alter the patient-physician relationship, but there is little agreement beyond the assertion that telemedicine is different than traditional face-to-face encounters (Miller, 2001). This section will examine the influence of telemedicine on patient-physician communication and will discuss the benefits of using telemedicine as well as the barriers preventing its widespread adoption.

### Definitions

Telemedicine was first developed in the 1960s and until recently has been used primarily by the U.S. Military (Darkins & Cary, 2000; Kuszler, 1999; Long, 1998). However, new technologies have made it more widely available to the public and also more difficult to define. "Tele-" means operating at a distance, so "telemedicine" is the practice of medicine over distances (Darkins & Cary, 2000; Miller, 2001; Terry, 1999; Vyborny, 1996) and usually involves the use of telecommunications technology to assist in the delivery of health care (Whitten, 1997). In the broadest definition of the term, telemedicine could include the use of telephones or facsimile machines to transmit health information or may be narrowly defined to include two-way interactive video and audio systems that allow transmission of a patient's image as well as diagnostic data sent over a video link (Caryl, 1997; Charles, 2000; McCarthy, 1995; Silverman, 2000).

Regardless of how it is defined, telemedicine usually involves four basic characteristics: (a) the geographic separation of patient and provider during the clinical encounter or between two providers collaborating on the patient's behalf; (b) the use of telecommunication or computer technology to enable, facilitate, or enhance the interactions between the parties; (c) the development of protocols and normative standards to replace those of traditional face-to-face contact; and (d) an infrastructure to support the telemedicine technology (Kuszler, 1999).

As satellite technology becomes more financially accessible to the private sector, telemedicine is becoming an integral part of health care delivery in many different settings. Telemedicine is most often used for one of three main tasks: (a) to supply additional information to aid in decision making, (b) for collaboration between physicians for the management of patients at a distance, and (c) for remote sensing of diagnostic equipment at a distance, such as transmission of electrocardiogram and pacemaker signals over telephone lines (Kuszler, 1999).

Patient-Physician Communication Via Telemedicine

In a survey of over 1,000 articles on telemedicine, Roine, Ohinmaa, and Hailey (2001) found that the majority of studies on the effectiveness of telemedicine focused on either psychiatry or radiology, rather than "traditional" medical encounters and most available literature referred only to pilot projects and short-term outcomes. In many cases, the efficacy of the application was tested, rather than its effectiveness. Although studies of patient-physician communication in telemedicine are scant, some studies have found that technology does not hinder the communication process and may even help it in some cases.

*Comparisons to face-to-face encounters.* Although traditional patient-physician communication has typically taken place in a doctor's office or hospital, new technologies have provided patients and physicians with the opportunity to communicate in other ways. Some scholars argue that the mediation of communication will be more problematic than face-to-face due to the "filtering out of cues" (e.g., Culnan & Markus, 1987) and that some of the richness, subtlety, and complexity of the patient-physician communication may be lost (Collins & Sypher, 1996). Other scholars have argued that nonverbal cues are present in all forms of mediated communication, regardless of whether the participants can even see each other (Stoner, Burgoon, Bonito, Ramirez, & Dunbar, 1999; Walther, 1996), and that meeting face-to-face provides too much extraneous information, so the "filtering out of cues" may help the interactants remain task-focused and less distracted by irrelevant nonverbal details (Burgoon et al., in press).

Face-to-face interaction differs from video-teleconferencing in that face-to-face is typically easier (Burgoon et al., in press), more spontaneous, free-flowing, and faster-paced whereas video-teleconferencing is more formal, has longer conversational turns, and more explicit turn-taking (Street, Wheeler, & McCaughan, 2000). In addition, despite some claims that the mediated context has the potential to eliminate status cues (Lea & Spears, 1995), other research has found that mediation perpetuates the status differences between physicians and patients (Saunders, Robey, & Vaverek, 1994). This point is illustrated in a study of telemedical consultations of a physician and patient with a remote specialist, where Street et al. found that the specialist was the most dominant actor and, along with the primary physician, accounted for the majority of the talk (53%) while patients were the least active participants, accounting for only 23% of the total utterances. They also found that the primary physician and the specialist gave each other more information than they gave the patient. Although the purpose of the teleconsultations was ostensibly to ask the specialists for advice, these behaviors could function to make the patient feel excluded or unimportant, thus reducing their overall satisfaction with their care, adherence to treatment regimens, and overall successful disease management (Street et al., 2000).

Video-consultations, although physically distant, can also create a psychological sense of distance between doctor and patient. Even the highest quality connections available have pictures worse than a normal television set and have short delays in voice and picture that result in stilted and awkward conversations (Aarnio, Lamminen, Lepisto, & Alho, 1999; Holtan, 1998; Loane et al., 1998). In addition, direct eye-contact is impossible due to the fact that interactants are seeing each other on a screen, which causes some patients to feel a lack of connection and immediacy with their physicians (Holtan, 1998). Physicians report that although they believe they can build rapport with patients via telemedicine, reading nonverbal cues such as facial expression and body language is problematic due to the lack of bandwidth available (Gelber & Alexander, 1999). The lack of the connection between remote providers and patients is demonstrated by Holton (1998). In teleconsultations with specialists, she noted that none of the patients she interviewed mentioned the specialists by name—they referred to a specialist as "he," or "the expert"—while they often referred to their physically present physicians by their surname or first name.

Beyond the physical distance, another thing that distinguishes telemedicine from face-to-face encounters is the fact that instead of having only two individuals in the encounter (physician and patient), there are now at least three with the addition of a specialist or a consultant whose advice is being sought, as well as technical personnel who may be present at both ends (Callahan, Hilty, & Nesbitt, 1998; Street et al., 2000). This situation creates a "hybrid" of mediated and face-to-face communication that differs from either context alone and "increases the likelihood of uncertainty, frustration, and unmet expectations with respect to who controls the encounter, what information is of importance, and who is responsible for making decisions" (Street et al., 2000, p. 46). It might also affect the patient's willingness to reveal sensitive personal information as nonmedical professionals are not obligated under the same ethical codes as physicians to retain patients' confidentiality (Callahan et al., 1998). Maintaining privacy in telemedicine is a serious concern—see Blair, Bambas, and Stone (1998) for a more detailed review of privacy issues relating to telemedicine.

The three-way communication between patient, physician, and remote specialist creates new types of communication patterns even beyond the various permutations identified in dyadic communication by Roter et al. (1997). Holtan (1998) identifies four such triadic "frames" in telemedicine. The first frame is called the "personal consultation" in which the specialist has the medical expert role and the general practitioner (GP) has an emotional, supporting role and helps the patient communicate with the specialist. The second combination, called the "impersonal consultation" focuses on the dialogue between the patient and specialist where the GP is an outsider in the consultation, reduced almost to the role of camera operator. The third type, "bureaucratic consultation," is one in which the communication occurs nearly exclusively between the GP and the specialist because the specialist is only consulted to re-affirm the GP's diagnosis. The specialist is viewed as an outsider, both medically and socially, and patients do not see the teleconsultation as necessary. In the final type, the "care-needed consultation," the GP and the specialist appear as a team, with the GP leading. The dialogue is mostly between the patient and the GP, who serves as a mediator between the specialist and the patient. The amount of control over the encounter felt by the patients differs greatly depending on the frame being used. Holtan found that in both the personal and care-needed consultations the patients were active participants, but in the bureaucratic and impersonal consultations, they were relegated to the role of "spectator," which echoes the findings of Street et al. (2000), likely reduces their feelings of connectedness with the remote provider, and may have implications for their satisfaction with the encounter.

*Patient satisfaction.* Collins and Sypher (1996) argue that "patient satisfaction—a decidedly communicative phenomenon—is also strongly linked to well-being" (p. 27), and so is a very important variable to consider when evaluating the effectiveness of patient-physician communication via telemedicine. Many studies have been conducted on this issue in recent years and few have reported any patient discomfort with using the technology. For example, Loane et al. (1997) found that patients were neither embarrassed nor uncomfortable about using the technology to consult a dermatologist and Whitten, Mair, and Collins (1997) found that elderly patients did not experience any excitement or worry about using telenursing, nor did they have difficulty using it. In McConnell, Steed, Tichenor, and Hannon's (1999) study of 21 telecardiology encounters, the patients reported that they were able to communicate adequately with the physician via telemedicine in all 21 cases. Further, no patients reported having any difficulty in seeing or hearing the physician and none reported feeling embarrassed or uncomfortable because of the telemedicine context of the examination (McConnell et al., 1999). Additionally, some studies have reported that patients are quite satisfied with the quality of the video available in teleconferencing (Aarnio et al., 1999; Loane et al., 1997).

Surveys that directly measured patient satisfaction have found similar results. Cancer patients have reported they were satisfied with seeing their oncologist using interactive videoconferencing, at least on an occasional basis (Allen & Hayes, 1995), and other patients seeing a variety of specialists including psychiatry, dermatology, orthopedics, and nutritional counseling, are satisfied with telemedicine as a means of health care delivery (Aarnio et al., 1999; Callahan et al., 1998; Harrison, Clayton, & Wallace, 1999; Huston & Burton, 1997; Mekhjian, Turner, Gailiun, & McCain, 1999; Pederson & Holand, 1995). All of these studies examined telemedicine for the purpose of consulting a specialist, however, and so more studies must be conducted before assuming patients would be equally satisfied with seeing their primary-care physician via telemedicine.

Benefits of Telemedicine

There are important benefits of telemedicine including increased access to physicians, decreased cost over traditional face-to-face encounters, and improved communication in the patient-physician interaction. A brief description of these is offered here.

*Access to physicians.* One of the obvious benefits of telemedicine is the availability of physicians to those who would not normally have access to physicians face-to-face. One application has been for patients in rural areas who do not have access to health care providers, particularly specialists. Telemedicine allows them access to specialty care previously unavailable in their area (Silverman, 2000; Whitten, 1997). Many states also use telemedicine to provide medical care to prisons where security and transportation costs hinder the use of face-to-face consultations. Similarly, the U.S. military has used telemedicine to bring medical expertise closer to those injured in battle without risking injury to health care personnel (Darkins & Cary, 2000). Home health agencies and providers also use interactive video links to enhance care for home-bound patients (Kuszler, 1999). Although telemedicine is often touted as a solution to patient shortages, it should not be seen as a replacement for physicians, and the dangers of having non-physicians play a larger role in medical treatment must be acknowledged (McCarthy, 1995).

Telemedicine also allows for the quick dissemination of information across long distances, which may be extremely important in the tracking and prevention of infectious diseases and when health problems necessitate quick intervention (Daley, 2000). This is especially important for rural physicians who are often isolated from colleagues who can provide a second opinion (Caryl, 1997; Daley, 2000). Additionally, telemedicine allows rural physicians to continue their medical education without the need for traveling long distances (Caryl, 1997).

*Cost.* The use of telemedicine is often justified based on its cost savings in transportation and unproductive travel time that is avoided and the reduction in specialty staff that must be employed at a single facility (Caryl, 1997; Darkins & Cary, 2000; McCarthy, 1995; Moore, 1998). For example, some health care delivery systems that treat prison inmates, such as the University of Texas Medical Branch, say that telemedicine saves them as much as 25–29% primarily due to avoided transportation and increased efficiency in the length of the consultation (Darkins & Cary, 2000; Moore, 1998). Although the initial start-up costs for telemedicine equipment are high, some estimates say the U.S. could reduce health costs in the long-run by as much as $36 billon when savings are considered not only in transportation and productivity increases, but also in more accurate diagnoses and reducing the length of hospital stays for patients who can be monitored at home (Daley, 2000; Greenberger & Puffer, 1989). These estimates of cost savings must be viewed cautiously, however. Roine et al. (2001) argue that "cost-effectiveness" is often assumed without any scientific evidence and there are few studies that directly compare the cost of telemedicine to traditional care directly in controlled experiments.

Despite the cost savings and improved access to physicians, telemedicine's acceptance is growing rather slowly—it has not "exploded" into the health arena as it was once projected to do (Davis, 1998). This may be due to the attitudinal, financial, and legal barriers that telemedicine faces. Attitudinal barriers are addressed below as they are most closely related to the focus of this chapter. For discussion of the financial barriers to implementing telemedicine, readers are referred to Daly (2000), Long (1998), Nagy (1994), and Wakefield, Kienzle, Zollo, Kash, & Uden-Holman (1997). For discussion of the legal barriers to implementation of telemedicine please see Blair et al. (1998), Caryl (1997), Silverman (2000), and Vyborny (1996).

## Attitudinal Barriers to Telemedicine

Many physicians are reluctant to use telemedicine because it is a new and as yet unproven technology (Nagy, 1994). Surveys of rural physicians and hospital administrators have demonstrated that the physicians and hospital decision makers possess a very a limited awareness of telemedicine, particularly whether is it effective, cost-effective, and reliable (Kane, Marken, Boulger, Crouse, & Bergeron, 1995; Wakefield et al., 1997; Whitten & Franken, 1995), and even rural physicians familiar with the technology are doubtful of its usefulness, effectiveness, and cost-effectiveness (Tilford, Garner, Strode, & Bynum, 1997). Even in urban settings, few hospitals have telemedicine programs, and physicians frequently express concerns about its reliability (McCarthy, 1995).

The physicians' concerns may not be unfounded. Phillips et al. (1996) warn that little work has been done to test the diagnostic accuracy of telemedicine in dermatology but Loane et al. (1997) demonstrated that improving the camera quality can reduce the number of missed and incorrect diagnoses. McConnell et al. (1999) compared telecardiology with face-to-face cardiology examinations and found that telecardiology resulted in a missed diagnosis in 2 of 21 patients. They argue that this is not statistically significant and may have more to do with the physicians than the telemedicine itself. They conclude that "telemedicine was reasonably accurate and did not miss any clinically important findings" (p. 160). However, more work needs to be done before any generalizations are made about the diagnostic accuracy of telemedicine. The lack of data on the accuracy of telemedical examinations has resulted in its use primarily reserved for psychiatry and non-emergency follow-up examinations (McCarthy, 1995).

Physicians may also be fearful of the new technology. It is possible that a provider, lacking experience with the new technology or technique, may fail to use it in an optimal fashion or may even misread the data, information, or image because of unfamiliarity with the telemedicine system. Like any other medical tool, it will require skill and practice for the physician to use it adeptly (Kuszler, 1999). When physicians become familiar with the technology, they may become more comfortable with it. A study of pediatricians in Georgia showed that physicians who were reluctant to use telemedicine at first were comfortable with seeing new patients via teleconference once they became more experienced with telemedicine (Karp et al., 2000).

The patients' lack of knowledge about telemedicine may prove to be another attitudinal barrier to face. Surveys in both Canada and the U.S. on attitudes toward telemedicine have demonstrated that fewer than a third of the population even knows of the existence of telemedicine or that video-teleconferencing can be used to conduct medical tests and make diagnoses (Brick, Bashshur, Brick, & D'Alessandri, 1997; Martin, 2001). Only educating physicians and patients about the uses of telemedicine and training physicians to implement it can help erode these attitudinal barriers.

Patient-Physician Trust

Integral to the patient-physician relationship is trust. When patients trust their physicians, they are more likely to communicate effectively with them and are more likely to follow their directions and report satisfaction when their encounters (Mechanic, 1998b; Roter & Hall, 1992; Thom & Campbell, 1997). In addition, trust is important for reducing anxiety and increasing a patient's sense of being cared for, which in turn may improve a patient's sense of well-being and improve functioning (Thom & Campbell, 1997). Expression of affect or emotion, both positive and negative, by physicians and patients is also related to reporting of better functional status and subjective evaluations of health by patients at follow-up. It is possible that active engagement of the physician reinforces the patients' confidence in their ability to manage their disease and increases their trust that the physician can help them heal (Kaplan, Greenfield, & Ware 1989).

The question, then, is can trust be established when physician and patient do not meet face-to-face? In general, physical proximity promotes psychological closeness, and physical distance conveys psychological distance. Moreover, physical proximity creates a sense of mutuality, of connection, common ground, and shared understandings that should heighten already existing positivity and truth biases and promote higher levels of credibility, trust, and influence (Burgoon et al., in press). If physical separation between physician and patient retards this ability to establish rapport or trust, then patient satisfaction and well-being may be irreparably impaired (Blair et al., 1998). In addition, if the patient is seeing the physician remotely, then the nurse or other nonphysician may become the primary caregiver in the patient's locale and so may also need to work to establish trust with the patient on their own.

Contrary to this logic, however, Miller's (2001) review of communication variables in telemedical encounters revealed that, in general, patients said it was indeed possible for them to establish rapport with physicians who were not physically present, especially when visual cues were provided through the mediated channel such as in video-teleconferencing. This is consistent with much of the other literature comparing mediated and live interactions, some of which has found that mediated channels can even exceed face-to-face communication in its ability to engender trust (e.g., Burgoon et al., in press; Walther, 1996). Walther (1996) hypothesizes that this is due to the fact that when faced with a lack of information about a conversational partners, we assume things about them to "fill-in-the-blanks" and actually create a "hyperpersonal" fantasy of them that exceeds how they are in reality. Thus, we may even trust our mediated physicians more than the ones we see face-to-face. We await future research comparing telemedicine to traditional medicine that may answer this question.

## PATIENT-PHYSICIAN COMMUNICATION VIA ELECTRONIC MAIL

Electronic mail is widely described as one of the most promising communication technologies in medicine for its potential to transform twenty-first century patient-physician relationships (Menduno, 1998; Neil, Mainous, Clark, & Hagen, 1994; Spielberg, 1998). In health care, email is used to accomplish administrative tasks such as appointment scheduling and answering questions about medical coverage. Increases in email use for patient consultations, diagnosis, and managing treatment, however, reflect the willingness of both physicians and patients to test the applicability of email technology in the most intimate patient-physician interactions (Borowitz & Wyatt, 1998). Ease of use and the rapid, direct access to physicians and patients afforded by email make it a tempting substitute for face-to-face communication; yet at what cost to patient care? Despite the growing integration of email by physicians in the delivery of patient care, the implications of email use on the patient-physician relationship and their communication has not been widely examined or tested.

Researchers caution that email is cited as much for the problems it presents to patient-physician communication as for its promise (Mandl et al., 1998; Spielberg, 1998, 1999). Echoing these sentiments, Herman and Abenstein (2001) question whether the increased access to physicians afforded by technology necessarily means improved care for patients.

> Does the ability of technology to make this communication possible make this communication necessary or even desirable? Should the technical ability to communicate with each other at any time make it mandatory that we do so? When does the ability for instant communication cease to be helpful and become a distraction to patient care? Is there a point at which patient care is compromised rather than enhanced? (p. 8)

These questions draw our attention away from the characteristics and capabilities of particular media to refocus on the implications of their use, or the lack thereof, for the patient-physician relationship and, ultimately, the quality of patient care. Using these questions as a guide, this portion of the chapter will provide an overview of email use in medical interactions and examine how electronic mail technologies are being used by patients and physicians and the consequences of their use for the communication between them. The concerns both parties have about email relative to issues of privacy and trust and their effects on the patient-physician relationship and communication will also be addressed.

Email and the Patient-Physician Relationship

Electronic mail, championed for its fast, asynchronous communication, has already become an important tool in the delivery of health care. Although patients have driven the use of email in their interactions with physicians, email has transformed and improved communication among physicians and between physicians and hospitals, pharmacies, and insurance industry representatives (Spielberg, 1998). Proponents of email use contend successful communication in health interactions should improve the patients' understanding of the diagnosis and increase adherence with therapeutic recommendations and interventions of the physician (Borowitz & Wyatt, 1998). Early adopters of email contend the technology does this and more. According to Mandl, Kohane, and Brandt (1998), email opens avenues for improved public access to health care, it generally increases physician outreach to patients, and dramatically increases the involvement of patients in their own care. The unique advantages of email to patients include convenient, direct, constant access to physicians and confirmation that messages are received (Kane & Sands, 1998).

As noted previously, email is lauded as a good means of accomplishing nonurgent tasks such as appointment scheduling, handling patient questions about medical benefits, refilling prescriptions, and communicating lab results (Mandl, Kohane, & Brandt, 1998). However, recent applications of email technology reveal that it can be used in more complex medical interactions including consultations and diagnosing and managing patient treatment (Borowitz & Wyatt, 1998). Borowitz and Wyatt report 90% of patients who use email to communicate with their physicians relay important and sensitive medical information, the kind that is particularly helpful in the more complex consultative interaction. These findings are consistent with research on email use in corporate settings where email is often used and praised for accomplishing complex, important tasks. For example, Rice, Grant, Schmitz, and Torobin (1990) found that email is used either by itself or combined with other media to accomplish complex tasks. Using multiple media to facilitate patient education and care has long been a practice in health care interactions. In the case of email use, physicians and patients who may initially send and receive electronic messages may use a follow-up call from the physician for further clarification if an office visit is deemed unnecessary to complete the consultation.

Guidelines for Email Use

In 1998, *The Journal of the American Medical Informatics Association* (JAMIA) published the first guidelines for the clinical use of electronic mail with patients. The taskforce assigned to the job defines patient-provider electronic mail as "computer-based communication between clinicians and patients within a contractual relationship in which the health care provider has taken on an explicit measure of responsibility for the client's care" (Kane & Sands, 1998, p. 104). Online discussion groups and public support forums that physicians might participate in, but do not constitute a contractual relationship with a specific patient, do not fall under the purview of the JAMIA guidelines.

The JAMIA guidelines address two aspects of the delivery of medical care: effective interaction between the physician and patient and the observance of medicolegal prudence (e.g., privacy, confidentiality, accurate medical record-keeping). Both areas represent the concerns patients and physicians have for whether the quality of their interactions and adequacy of case management can be maintained, let alone improved, in an electronic environment. The set of guidelines for using email to support effective medical interactions will be discussed in some detail here in relation to physicians' and patients' communication concerns. The guidelines for email use with regard to medicolegal and administrative issues will be discussed at the end of this section of the chapter in light of patients' and physicians' concerns for privacy and threats to patient trust in physicians.

The JAMIA taskforce concluded email is most effectively used when the physician and patient negotiate certain aspects of electronic communication in relation to medical care. Due to space constraints, only those guidelines that address patient-physician communication that, if violated, may call into question the integrity of the patient-physician relationship are reviewed. Kane and Sands (1998) indicate the following aspects of email use should be negotiated in advance with patients to inform them of office email policies and norms, as well as to determine whether email should be used in future interactions and for what purposes.

*Turnaround time.* The timeliness of physicians' responses to patients' emails is a major concern of patients (Neil et al., 1994). Physicians should clearly indicate the messaging culture of the office or clinic and communicate how quickly they will respond to messages and on what criteria message response times are based. For example, the context of the patient's message will often drive more expedient responses. Urgent requests may get a reply the same day or the following day from their physician. Non-urgent questions about the results of a routine exam may be emailed a response within 48 hours of receiving the message.

*Privacy.* A large portion of the JAMIA guidelines for clinical email use are dedicated to issues of confidentiality and maintaining the privacy of patients (Kane & Sands, 1998). The task force indicates that certain aspects of privacy should be negotiated with patients and other information about how physicians will handle the privacy concerns of patients should be available to them in written form. Physicians should indicate whether email addressed to their private account will be read only by them or whether messages will be triaged by the office or nursing staff. In addition, patients should be asked under what circumstances a physician may share their email message, such as when consulting with another physician or nurse.

*Permissible transactions and content.* The extent of action permitted over email and that can be expected using email should also be established with patients. Whether email will be used to refill prescriptions, to dispense medical advice, manage a treatment regimen, test results, and release records should be agreed upon by physician and patient. Kane and Sands (1998) cite Stanford University Medical Clinic's forbidding of discussions about HIV status, mental illness, and workers' compensation claims in email as examples of what might be considered taboo topics.

*Automatic reply to incoming messages.* All incoming messages from patients should be responded to using an automatic reply to confirm receipt of the email, indicate the response policy, and direct patients to alternative contact information such as a phone number. Automatic replies are especially important given the value patients place on being able to have direct access to physicians, thereby circumventing inadequate messages left with office staff and the practice of "telephone tag" (Neil et al., 1994).

Patient Perspectives on Email

Kassirer (2000) indicates that of the approximately 37 million people who use the Internet to find health-related information, most report they are interested in contacting their physician by email. That more patients are taking an active role in managing their own health in the information age should not be surprising. But the trepidation on the part of most physicians to adopt email in their interactions with patients is surprising. Regardless of their reasons for not jumping on the technology bandwagon, physicians' adoption of email is being driven by a cyber-savvy patient population and increasing consumer demand for the instantaneous communication capabilities it affords (Ferguson, 1998; Spielberg, 1998).

Using email to reach one's physician is so desirable that in one survey of online health seekers, one third of the respondents said they would probably switch doctors if they could communicate with them by email (Kassirer, 2000). Visionaries predict medical interactions of the future, where electronic communication will be routine, will set extraordinary patient expectations for speed, access, and convenience, and allow self-care to burgeon as private residences become the center for health management (D'Amaro, 1998). This not-so-distant future may suit those patients who welcome greater involvement in health inter-actions and dismay others who desire the more traditional doctor-centered rela-tionship with physicians mentioned earlier in the chapter (Roter et al., 1997).

In a study of email-using patients in a university-based family practice facili-ty, patients cited speed, convenience, utility for managing simple problems, effi-ciency, improved documentation, and avoidance of telephone tag as positive characteristics of email (Neil et al., 1994). The fact that email is never busy and does not require the recipient to be present to receive the message is cited as another advantage of using this technology (Spielberg, 1999). However, patients worry about the timeliness of a physician's response to a message sent electron-ically. "If email were monitored on a timely basis . . . it would greatly enhance communication between patient and physician. It could be a mechanism for receiving prompt advice/information without the inconvenience of telephone interruptions" (Neil et al., 1994, p. 270). Acknowledgment of the benefits of email use in medical interactions appears to be widespread. For example, empir-ical findings from a recent survey of California consumers' use and rating of sources of health care information indicate that of the 1,007 adults surveyed, 46% report using email "often" to communicate with their own doctors and nurs-es. The study also found physicians and health care providers were more trusted sources for health information than any other source, including the Internet (Pennbridge, Moya, & Rodrigues, 1999).

Kassirer (2000) warns that essential elements of the patient-physician rela-tionship such as an understanding of patients' needs and personal preferences will be lost if email is used in lieu of face-to-face interactions instead of as sup-port for them. He argues the intensely personal, repeated interactions with patients that gradually result in the development of a trusting relationship cannot be replicated and are compromised by electronic exchanges. He also notes that email messages lack context and nonverbal cues that are helpful in diagnosing and determining treatment options for patients. However, patients do not seem to share the same concerns or perceive the same limitations of email in developing trusting relationships with their physicians, at least not to the extent described by Kassirer.

## Patients' Privacy Concerns

Patients must realize that if they have Internet and email access at their place of employment, their coworkers or employers could have access to their incom-ing messages. Systems managers can read and disseminate any message sent along a system. Even when email is received at home, the patient's spouse or children may have access to their email account (Mandl et al., 1998; Seeman & Seeman, 1999; Sherman & Adams, 1999). Spielberg (1999) warns that people might also refrain from making medical decisions about their health care for fear the email may be misdirected or mishandled and reveal the personal thought process of health treatment decision making to unforeseen people.

Patient doubts over the confidentiality of electronically communicated medical information can have dire health consequences extending beyond the degree of trust patients have or do not have with their physicians. For example, a 1977 U.S. Supreme Court case evaluated whether a computerized public health database, which included identifiable health information pertaining to prescription drug use, violated individuals' privacy interests. The plaintiffs argued that decisional privacy ought to be invoked because the knowledge alone that one's medical information is readily available in a computerized database creates a genuine concern that causes some people to decline needed medication or care (Spielberg, 1999). Similarly an even stronger argument can be made for the protection of patient-physician email.

The JAMIA guidelines for email use in clinical settings advise clarifying with office staff how email messages will be handled or managed by physicians to address patients' privacy concerns and communicating this information to patients (Kane & Sands, 1998). Given that privacy, confidentiality, and maintaining the integrity of the patient-physician relationship is a grave concern for patients with regard to technology use in medical encounters, open, direct communication about how email will be used and what precautions will be taken should alleviate those concerns.

## Physician Perspectives on Email

Even when a patient has regular face-to-face contact with his or her physician, it can be difficult for meaningful communication to take place. Appointments are often difficult to get at the last minute, and patients can feel rushed when there are many other patients waiting. If a patient forgets the dose of the medication, or wants to ask a quick follow-up question after an appointment, he or she must often wait for another appointment or leave phone messages and wait for them to be returned. To reduce patients' frustration, many physicians have started to use email, although no reliable or consistent data on the total number of physicians who use email to interact with patients exists to date. Increasingly though, physicians are using email to increase contact with their patients in less time, make follow-ups to clinical visits easier, and eliminate phone tag (Ferguson, 1997).

Physicians who use email find that patients are very willing to use it as an alternative to phone messages. They find that they can send several emails in the time it takes to make one phone call (Mangan, 1996; Neill et al., 1994). Email can be more efficient than the telephone partly due to the tendency of users to cut to the chase in their written messages (Grove, 1998). In one study of patient-physician email use, the physician indicated that although half of his roughly 800 patients use email, the only ones he hears from regularly are a handful of chronically ill patients. In less than two hours he is able to answer the 20 to 30 messages he gets from patients each week (Mangan, 1996). Another physician in a separate study praised email for enhancing his ability to "keep in contact with patients and, in the long run, deliver better patient care in less time" (Spicer, 1999, p. 38). Physicians cite the ability to follow up face-to-face or telephone interactions with patients to clarify advice and the ability to easily distribute health education materials to patients as reason for adopting email. In addition, they say it allows them to forego unnecessary, lengthy patient visits because email consultations are sufficient to adequately answer patient questions and handle patient referrals to specialists (Borowitz & Wyatt, 1998).

Still many physicians are reluctant to use email because of their lack of technical skills, lack of institutional support, and physicians' fears of being "flooded" by patient messages (Ferguson, 1997; Mandl, Kohane, & Brandt, 1998). Email overload is a valid concern. Whittaker and Sidner (1995) warn that the inability to effectively manage communication during overload means lost information and reduced responsiveness with negative outcomes for productivity. For physicians, reduced responsiveness and low productivity means low quality care for patients, which will carry with it dire consequences in medical settings.

Time constraints dominate discussions of barriers to physician acceptance of email (Spielberg, 1998, 1999). Physicians' perceptions that answering patient emails will cut into their tight schedules even further poses a major roadblock to the wide acceptance of this technology. The asynchrony of email (i.e., users do not need to be in the same place at the same time) is viewed as a drawback rather than a benefit to some doctors who imagine email messages piling up in their inboxes like the stacks of paperwork on their desks.

Katz and Rice (2001) remind us of another groundbreaking technology that transformed patient-physician relationships: the telephone. These authors give a brief history of the telephone "to show the context of email and how it may be oversold by those who think it will be a panacea for patient-physician communication" (p. 424). Despite being accepted much more rapidly than email has been, similar comparisons can be drawn between the telephone and email. When the telephone was introduced to the patient-physician relationship, privacy was of utmost concern (Spielberg, 1998). The same can be said for email. A large portion of the JAMIA's guidelines for clinical email use is dedicated to how physicians can maintain the confidentiality of email messages, demonstrating how this perceived barrier can be overcome (Kane & Sands, 1998). Yet, Katz and Rice (2001) contend physicians have skillfully moderated patient access to them by refusing to give out a home phone number, using sophisticated messaging systems, and hiring answering services. Old habits die hard, they argue, and physicians will not see the intrusions and confidentiality concerns of email as being any different from those of the telephone. "Hence, we are skeptical about the promise that email will be a welcome and often-used addition to the doctor's black bag" (Katz & Rice, 2001, p. 424). Skeptics, argues Kassirer (2000), ignore the power of economic and social pressures brought to bear by a cyber-savvy patient population to bring about change. Already, patients are driving physician adoption of email at increasing rates and enticements to belong to electronic networks initiated by physician and patient groups, health plans, and integrated delivery systems are prevalent.

Physicians' Privacy Concerns

Physician skeptics who are weighing whether to use email should know they can take advantage of new technology to reduce confidentiality concerns. Current encryption methods can technically overcome privacy concerns (Seeman & Seeman, 1999), and doctors can use programs such as the new technology called "public key cryptography" in which users encrypt messages using "keys" that designate them as either public or private (Mandl et al., 1998). To avoid malpractice suits and prevent confidentiality breeches, another option for physicians is to avoid sending confidential material or making diagnoses electronically and reserve email for patient education, appointment reminders and follow-ups, and more general information (Sherman & Adams, 1999). Given the overwhelming evidence that email can improve patient care (e.g., Ferguson, 1997; Mandl et al., 1998; Mangan, 1996; Seeman & Seeman, 1999; Spicer, 1999), confidentiality issues should not deter physicians from pursuing it as an option in their practices. As one physician observed, when used properly, "the reality is that email communication is much safer than phone messages written on little slips of paper that pass through many hands and end up in the trash" (Mangan, 1996, p. 155).

In grappling with the complex privacy issues posed by new medical communication technologies, the legal system has historically been steadfast in its protection of patient-physician communication (Spielberg, 1998). In one such case the centrality of medical communication and importance of its privacy was acknowledged in the dissenting opinion by a Justice Blackmun who indicated "the doctor-patient dialogue embodies a unique relationship of trust . . . [and therefore,] we have guarded so jealously the doctor-patient dialogue from governmental intrusion" (Spielberg, 1999, p. 280). However, legal protection of personal medical information from government access affords medical patients and health-information consumers only partial protection.

THE INTERNET AND PATIENT-PHYSICIAN COMMUNICATION

It should come as no surprise that as use of the Internet has increased, it has become an important source of health care information (Johnson & Ramaprasad, 2000; Pennbridge, Moya, & Rodrigues, 1999), and some say a major source of such information (Aspden, Katz, & Bemis, 2001). By one estimate, health care information dominates a quarter of the Internet (Blum, 2001), and the number of estimated health-related sites ranges from 10,000 (Lowes, 1997) to 100,000 (Kolata, 2000). Medical journals are now available online and are frequently accessed by the public. For example, more than 250,000 people access the *New England Journal of Medicine* online each week, only 25% of whom are subscribers (Campion, Anderson, & Drazen, 2001). Recent physician surveys indicate it is not uncommon for patients to present them with medical information obtained on the Internet (Canadian Medical Association, 2000).

The movement toward increased patient autonomy (Mechanic, 1998a) at least partially explains increasing public interest in health-related information found on the Internet. Other related explanations exist, however. Kassirer (2000) argues that patient and physician dissatisfaction with the current health care delivery system of managed care has been a catalyst for the increased patient use of the Internet. Whatever the reasons behind the exploding interest, patient-physician communication centered on information gathered on the Internet will affect the relationship in both positive and negative ways (Goldsmith, 2000; Kassirer, 2000). There is much to be learned about how patients and physicians negotiate this information in reaching decisions about patient care.

A caveat about the direction of our discussion in this section is in order before we go further. Reeves (2000) argues that among the many functions of the Internet are information, communication, and interaction. Our focus in this section is primarily on the information function within the context of the patient-physician relationship, that is, how information retrieved from health-related Internet sites influences patient-physician communication. The communication and interaction functions are equally deserving of attention (e.g., direct-to-consumer advertising, cybermedicine, online support groups and chatrooms) but do not fit within our primary focus in this chapter. That said, we proceed by first discussing the distinct advantages to the patient of Internet information followed by sources of physician resistance to Internet use by patients. Next, we address what is known about the negotiation of Internet information between patients and physicians. Finally, an overview of what the future of Internet use by patients and physicians may mean to their relationships and interactions is provided.

### Patient Internet Use

One of the most important advantages to patients of the vast array of health-related information on the Internet is that it has the potential to empower them. As Goldsmith (2000) notes, the Internet "strengthen[s] the consumer's role in relation to practitioners and health care institutions, and . . . create[s] a powerful new tool to help people manage their own health risks more effectively" (par. 57). The health-related information derived from the Internet can potentially change lives (Reeves, 2000) and increase self-confidence (Ferguson, 1996). Armed with more information, patients may find it easier to confront their doctors (Chew, 2001), to speak with more authority, and to have a greater sense of control in selecting strategies to deal with their illnesses (Reeves, 2000).

Because the Internet is accessible 24 hours a day, seven days a week, patients can search the Internet at their convenience (Reeves, 2000). For patients who desire to do so, Internet information can help them prepare for visits with their doctor, enabling them to formulate questions and analyze their concerns prior to their health interview. Provided patients have a willing physician, and that the Internet information they have gathered is accurate and relevant to their health issues, this information potentially encourages discussion between patient and physician that helps them jointly sort out the best choices for the patient. Being a more informed patient won't balance the scale of knowledge between physician and patient but "it will enable patients to begin their dialogue with physicians at a much higher level and provide them with leverage to influence the care process" (Goldsmith, 2000, par. 27).

Recent research (Aspden, Katz, & Bemis, 2001) indicates that patients' response to Internet information may represent one of two models. They may use the information in conjunction with continuing to see their doctor, following what Aspden et al. call an "adjunct" model. Alternatively, they may use the information to increase personal management of their own health, subsequently limiting contact with their physicians. This latter "self-service" model, as it is labeled by Aspden et al., at one extreme places patients in full charge of their health, using Internet information to diagnose and treat themselves. Clearly, there are limits to the effectiveness of this strategy that relate to the patients' ability to understand and analyze complex medical information.

## Sources of Physician Resistance to Patient Internet Use

Physician resistance to Internet use by patients has been much publicized. The sources of this resistance fall primarily into three categories: (a) potential loss of expert status, (b) limited time with patients, and (c) varied patient preparation and information processing ability.

*Potential loss of expert status.* With the increased availability of health-related information on the Internet and accessible through other media (e.g., magazines, TV), physicians have lost their status as the primary patient source of health care information (Gotten, 2001). This loss has coincided with structural changes associated with the managed care model that have reduced physicians' traditional autonomy and authority in caring for patients. Some doctors cope with this loss by discouraging patients from using Internet information, thereby trying to reestablish themselves as the primary source of medical information (Miller, 1998). Although such efforts may appear to protect their expert status, they seem futile given that doctors cannot know everything available on a given medical topic (Lowes, 1997), particularly given the pace at which medical information evolves today. In sharp contrast to this view, Lowes argues that Internet information derived from patients can actually save physicians time—time traditionally devoted to teaching patients about their illness. In addition, it may also supplement their knowledge. Being updated by patients on current medical news for some physicians, however, may be a difficult pill to swallow, particularly if they are uncomfortable sharing their expert status with well-informed patients (Goldsmith, 2000).

In the instances described above it seems unlikely physicians will readily accept the use of the Internet by their patients. Pessimism about this acceptance, and thus its impact on patient-physician communication, was recently voiced by Street and Piziak (2001) who note that the Internet is an "area where we do not see revolutionary prospects for improvement in . . . patient-physician communication. Long before the advent of the Internet, physicians were complaining about patient intrusion into their attempt to minister to the welfare of their patients" (p. 423).

There is room for optimism about Internet influence on patient-physician communication. Recent research indicates physicians who use the Internet are generally supportive of the patients seeking information on it, support recommending relevant Internet sites to patients for their review, and do not believe they should remain neutral about the information patients obtain from the Internet (Aspden, Katz, & Bemis, 2001). Additional evidence indicates physicians may not have to worry about losing their status as an expert, or at the very least, a trustworthy consultant. In a recent survey of 1,003 Californians (407 of whom had Internet access), 78% of overall respondents (and 75% of those who have Internet access at home) said that physicians and health care providers were their most trusted health information sources. The Internet was ranked fifth overall as a trustworthy source (ranked third by those with home Internet access). In addition, 70% of the overall respondents said they would be likely to consult their physician or health care provider for medical information in the future (Pennbridge et al., 1999).

*Limited time with patients.* Although the cost consciousness of managed care has yielded a variety of economic benefits to medical organizations, some of those benefits have come at the expense of increased time pressures on physicians (Kolata, 2000). Kassirer (2000) describes physicians' dilemma in this way: "Physicians are dissatisfied with large patient loads, burdened with administrative tasks, frustrated by reporting requirements, and angry about losing control of patient care decisions" (par. 2). These conditions mean they have less time to devote to the patient-physician relationship (Holtz, 1998; LaPuma 1994).

It is little wonder that under these conditions, even physicians who promote the development of well-informed patients may wince when patients arrive armed with pages of Internet health care information. Still other physicians may resent them (Goldsmith, 2000). Mittman and Cain (2001) capture this scenario well:

> Physicians are both threatened and fascinated by the Web. Many understand the value of having well-informed patients and the role the Internet can play in educating their patients. At the same time, they are concerned about losing control over the interaction with their patients. In a normal 10-minute office visit, they have trouble answering all the questions of a patient armed with 400 pages printed from the Internet. (p. 59)

The prevalence with which patients arrive at their doctors' appointments with

Internet information is increasing steadily (Kolata, 2000). Some of this information is not as specific as patients would like it to be (Mechanic, 1998a); thus patients seek their physicians' help in relating it to their own health care needs. More often than not physicians wonder how they will find time to sift through and make sense of these mounds of material (Kassirer, 2000), particularly when they find it difficult to even keep up with their subscribed professional reading.

*Varied patient preparation and processing ability.* Not all patients are created equal. Whereas some may spend time preparing for a doctor's visit (e.g., locating relevant information about their illness or treatment) and processing what they've learned from experience as well as from research (e.g., developing a set of questions for their physician and treatment options), others will arrive either unprepared or willing to let the physician carry the burden of any decision making about their health care. Lowes (1997) argues educated patients are preferable to uneducated ones but also acknowledges not all patients are capable of analyzing their health condition.

Johnson and Ramaprasad (2000) identify two types of patients based on the degree to which they process information about their health care. "Informed" patients merely possess information but they are unable to put it to use to improve their health care. They seek the help of their physician in doing so. Alternatively, "understanding" patients possess information about their health care, process it, and are capable of contributing substantially to the success of their treatment. From the brief descriptions of these two types of patients offered by Johnson and Ramaprasad, we assume either kind of patient is capable of seeking information, though the "informed" patient may not have the focused research skills of the "understanding" patient.

Given the array of health information available on the Internet, even the "understanding" patient will probably need occasional help in making sense of information gathered and in knowing when to stop collecting information. For example, "people can process and use only a limited number of variables. However, when asked, consumers will often say they want more information rather than less" (Hibbard, Slovic, & Jewett, 1997, p. 397). Similarly, there is no guarantee that physicians—as well trained and well read as they may be—are capable of taking into account all relevant scientific knowledge and successfully integrating it with their knowledge of each specific patient's condition (Weed, 1997).

To some degree physicians may be experiencing some confusion about the extent to which patients want to be, and should be, involved in making their health care decisions. As Orvell et al. (1995) note: "Physicians have taught for years that when they treat themselves they have a fool for a patient, yet we now believe that patients should take more responsibility for their own care" (par. 9).

*Amount and quality of health care information on the Internet.* It is impossible for physicians to stay current with the enormous amount of health care information generated monthly (Goldsmith, 2000) or to assess its credibility. There is reason for concern about the quality of this information (Goldsmith, 2000; Gotten, 2001), its accuracy (Mechanic, 1998a; Reeves, 2000), and the degree to which it is counterproductive (Mechanic, 1998a). In a recent study, 58% of physicians surveyed had concerns about the trustworthiness of Internet information (Aspden, Katz, & Bemis, 2001). Other research indicates doctors worry that Web sites reflect information not approved by authoritative sources or information that is simply wrong (Widman & Tong, 1997). Although efforts are being made to develop mechanisms ensuring the quality and accuracy of Internet health care information (e.g., Fried, Weinreich, Cavalier, & Lester, 2000), currently there is no way to completely ensure erroneous information does not appear on the Internet.

Despite the vast amount of information available on the Internet and the concern about its credibility, there is evidence that physicians are to some extent benefiting from its inclusion in interaction with patients. For example, in one study 33% of the physicians surveyed reported their interactions with patients were more effective as a result of the inclusion of Internet information (Aspden, Katz, & Bemis, 2001).

In summary, although information patients obtain on the Internet may pose a threat to physicians' traditional expert status, there is some evidence they remain the most trusted source of medical information with the Internet trailing behind. The limited time they have available to spend with patients (particularly those in managed care health organizations) is stressed when patients confront them with health information from the Internet, information with which they may be unfamiliar and have little or no time to process in the health care interview context. Some patients are better prepared to discuss this information than others. Those who merely access the information and present it to their physicians are not likely to be viewed as favorably as those who have read and processed the information and come prepared with a list of relevant questions associated with it. Finally, physicians are concerned about the amount of health-related information available on the Internet and its trustworthiness.

Patient-Physician Negotiation of Internet Information

It is not likely that the movement toward patient involvement in health care decisions is going to abate. It is highly likely, however, that patients will continue to use the Internet as a source of health care information and do so in increasing numbers. They are currently better informed than ever before and will continue to expect their physicians to help them interpret information they get online (Kassirer, 2000) and to form more participatory relationships with them (Mechanic, 2000). Thus, it makes good sense for patients and their physicians to negotiate how Internet information will be used in their interactions (Gotten, 2001). Miller (1998) underscores this point, arguing that the law of informed consent requires it.

To some extent this negotiation has already begun. There are physicians who not only welcome information presented by their patients, but also see it as a way to increase their own knowledge base (Johnson & Ramaprasad, 2000). Some physicians assume the important responsibility of directing patients away from poor quality information and to reliable sources (Landro, 2000) that are easy to read (Lowes, 1997). For example, Pal (2000) selects Internet information that may be useful to patients and makes it accessible on a Web site. Physicians report they should take a proactive role when it comes to guiding patients in the selection and use of health care information obtained on the Internet (Aspden, Katz, & Bemis, 2001). Physicians in one study expressed strong support for patients seeking their feedback before acting on information retrieved from the Internet, and for warning patients about inaccuracies of Internet information (Aspden, Katz, & Bemis, 2001). Providing this feedback is easier to do if physicians have taken the time to surf the Web to explore what their patients are reading, a tactic advised by Landro (2000). To date, however, physician survey data indicates mixed (Aspden, Katz, & Bemis, 2001) or low levels (Canadian Medical Association, 2000) of support for doing so.

It appears that although some physicians may see the benefit of discussing Internet information with their patients, they are not yet ready to share with patients Internet information they themselves retrieve. In a recent study of 2,800 physicians conducted by the Canadian Medical Association (2000), whereas 84.2% reported patients have at least occasionally presented them with medical information obtained on the Internet, a large number reported they never (64.3%) or only occasionally (22.8%) give information to patients they have retrieved on the Internet.

Negotiating the use of health care information from the Internet may be difficult in some cases. For example, not all physicians have flexible time schedules that allow them to devote the necessary time and attention to fully discuss patient questions and concerns about Internet information (Johnson & Ramaprasad, 2000). This scenario becomes more complex when the physician is unfamiliar with the information provided by the patient. Physician and patient stress can be eased in this situation by the physician admitting to the patient he or she either does not have time currently to discuss the information or is not familiar with it. In either case, agreeing to review the information and discuss it at a prescribed date and time via appointment or phone call lets the patient know he or she is not being dismissed and that the physician takes the request seriously (Dudley, Falvo, Podell, & Renner, 1996).

It is not difficult to imagine scenarios where physicians will not agree with conclusions patients have reached from the Internet information they have gathered, and hence disagree on treatment as well. Patients may decide to seek a new physician if the dispute is not resolved to their satisfaction. Physicians may be ill equipped to handle such disputes given that until recently negotiation and conflict management skills were not taught in medical schools (Darkins & Cary,

2000). Mechanic's (2000) observations about similar disputes between physicians and patients over patients' desire for prescription drugs seen in direct-to-consumer (DTC) drug advertisements may be applicable here. He suggests that the most important mechanism holding the relationship together under circumstances such as these is the "strength of the patient-physician relationship and the patient's belief that the physician will not allow him or her to be harmed" (par 17).

The established communication pattern between patient and physician is another factor that will likely influence their negotiation of Internet information use. Physicians who prefer a paternalistic or doctor-centered approach will not be as likely to welcome patients' introduction of health care information from the Internet into care and treatment discussions as physicians who prefer a patient-centered approach (i.e., desiring and valuing patient involvement in decision making regarding their health). The patient-centered approach appears to be more versatile in its effectiveness than the doctor-centered approach. For example, Krupat et al. (2000) found that incongruence of patient and doctor styles does not necessarily lead to patient dissatisfaction. Patient-centered doctors styles (e.g., solicits patient input) led to patient satisfaction even when the patient's orientation was one of preference for a doctor-centered relationship (e.g., leaving decision making up to the doctor). When paired with a paternalistic physician, however, patients who desired involvement in the decision-making process were less satisfied. Thus patients who expect to be involved in active discussion with physicians about the use of Internet information in making their health care decisions will be most satisfied with a physician who appreciates that level of interaction.

### The Internet and the Future of Patient-Physician Communication

Darkins and Cary (2000) provide a view of the future where physicians, equipped with sophisticated databases and remote analysis techniques, will no longer feel the need to project the image of experts who know everything. Instead they will feel quite comfortable acknowledging when they are unsure and subsequently seeking a second opinion, perhaps online. Patients in this futuristic view will be comfortable with physicians' roles as supportive decision-making experts. Whether this view will become a reality remains to be seen.

Although health-related information obtained by patients on the Internet poses challenges for patient-physician interactions, there is evidence that physicians are responding to the challenge. Both patient and physician must be responsible for ensuring the use of reliable information, although it appears physicians may be expected to take the lead in this regard. Patients will need to be well prepared for office visits where they wish to discuss information retrieved over the Internet, factoring in the limited time most physicians have available for each patient and using that time wisely. Both physician and patient will need to examine their established communication pattern to determine the extent to which it supports discussion of Internet information.

## DIRECTIONS FOR FUTURE RESEARCH

The intersect between patient-physician communication and the internal and external change forces in which it is caught up represent significant research opportunities for communication scholars. Perhaps the most immediate need is in the area of applied research addressing the extent to which technology may be used effectively in patient-physician communication. This is particularly true with regard to patient-physician email correspondence. Our review of the literature indicates the available information on this topic is currently more anecdotal than empirical. There is still much to learn, such as under what circumstances this is the most appropriate and effective mode of communication between patient and physician. In addition, given the prevalence of health-related information available on the Internet, it is critical that researchers address not only how patients access and evaluate such information, but also the extent to which they successfully negotiate use of that information with their primary care physician.

It seems clear that those physicians who are not already literate in Internet use will need to become literate. It is difficult to converse with patients about the Internet without having experience in navigating it (Aspden, Katz, & Bemis, 2001; Lowes, 1997). Beyond this literacy, however, the literature offers some reasonable suggestions to help physicians effectively manage patient Internet use. For example, patient history forms might be updated to include where patients obtain health-related information, and the extent to which they use the Internet for such information, to assess the credibility of the information they refer to in health consultations (Gotten, 2001; Lowes, 1997). Also, physicians might encourage patients to share relevant Internet information with them, but do so with boundaries attached. Lowes (1997) suggests physicians request that patients fax or email relevant articles a week prior to their scheduled appointment, allowing ample time for review. The number of articles should be limited to two per appointment and the patient should be notified in advance that if the discussion goes over the allotted time for the appointment, there will be an additional charge. If additional time is not an option, the patient should also be told this in advance. These suggestions speak to the manner in which physicians negotiate time constraints with the inevitability of patient Internet use and provide an additional area of further research.

Telemedicine, as well as email and patient Internet use, however, will continue to pose concerns for time constraints experienced by physicians. For example, the use of telemedicine will only exacerbate physicians' existing time constraints as the "organizational cost of consulting remote patients may place limits on the length of the interaction. With less time available, stress is placed on efficiently gathering appropriate medical information—perhaps at the expense of the relationship-building that is so important to the patient's sense of well-being" (Collins

& Sypher, 1996, p. 42). Future research addressing technology use in medical interactions must consider how that technology constrains patient-physician communication and what strategies both parties use to overcome those constraints.

As researchers in health care organizations, we must remember to view the extant literature with a critical eye. Many articles have been written touting the benefits of technology for physicians and patients, but this is often assumed without any scientific evidence, and there are few studies that directly compare the care given by physicians who use technology, such as telemedicine, to traditional care directly in controlled experiments (Roine et al., 2001). For example, in a comprehensive review of the patient-physician communication literature in telemedicine, Miller (2001) found that approximately 80% of the research findings favored telemedicine. These findings must be viewed somewhat skeptically, however, because many of the studies' authors are those with a vested interest in seeing telemedicine succeed, such as health care providers who work with telemedicine or even the creators of telemedicine programs. Often, neutral parties wishing to conduct fair evaluations of a new technology are denied access to it. One colleague of the authors wished to evaluate the telemedicine program at the medical school associated with her university and was told by the Telemedicine Director that she would not be allowed to conduct this research for fear that the evaluation would not be positive and could have repercussions for the telemedicine program's funding.

At a panel of the 2001 National Communication Association convention, one discussion topic that arose was the need for collaboration between organizational communication scholars and health communication scholars. The interface between patient-physician communication, managed care, and technology is ripe for such joint research interests. A few overlapping areas of research come to mind, such as organizational justice and stakeholder perspectives. With regard to organizational justice, Mechanic (2000) addresses the tension between the traditional conceptualization of medical professionalism and current managed care organizational structures. He calls for "a new professional ethic . . . [that] acknowledges physicians' responsibility to allocate resources but to advocate on behalf of patients within this framework, depending on a clear structure of procedural justice" (par. 4). Organizational communication scholars (e.g., Deetz, 1992; Mumby, 1988) have explored justice issues of power and authority in organizations from a critical perspective and provide a springboard from which to begin examination of managed care core policies and procedures that undermine physician authority and influence honest and ethical communication with patients. In particular, the social implications of mediated communication between patient and physician and its consequences for the delivery of medical care are of utmost importance. On a related note, stakeholder research could provide the opportunity to explore further how patients and physicians (both stakeholders in managed care organizations) negotiate their roles, particularly with regard to the use of email and Internet information.

As with any new technology, telehealth must be integrated into the existing health care system before it can be effectively utilized by patients and physicians to improve health care delivery. Wootton (2001) makes the point that the main problem in telehealth is not a lack of technology, rather, it is the organizational problem of how to take advantage of the technology. Research by communication scholars can do much to inform the effective integration of technology into health care delivery systems and its effect on patient-physician communication. Thus, educating providers and physicians about the communication implications of new technology should remain a high priority.

## REFERENCES

Aarnio, P., Lamminen, H., Lepisto, J., & Alho, A. (1999). A prospective study of teleconferencing for orthopaedic consultations. *Journal of Telemedicine and Telecare, 5,* 62–66.

Allen, A., & Hayes, J. (1995). Patient satisfaction with teleoncology: A pilot study. *Telemedicine Journal, 1,* 41–46.

Alpers, A. (1998). Justice Blackmun and the good physician: Patients, populations, and the paradox of medicine. *Hastings Constitutional Law Quarterly, 26*(1), 41–58.

Angell, M. (1993). The doctor as double agent. *Kennedy Institute of Ethics Journal, 3*(3), 279–286.

Aspden, P., Katz, J. E., & Bemis, A. E. (2001). Use of the internet for professional purposes: A survey of New Jersey physicians. In R. E. Rice & J. E. Katz (Eds.), *The internet and health communication: Experiences and expectations* (pp. 107–120). Thousand Oaks, CA: Sage.

Barondess, J. A. (1994). The doctor's dilemma: Whom to serve? *Journal of the Royal Society of Medicine, 87*(Supp. 22), 31–34.

Beckman, H. G., Markakis, K. M., Suchman, A. L., & Frankel, R. M. (1994). The doctor-plaintiff relationship: Lessons from plaintiff depositions. *Archives of Internal Medicine, 154,* 1365–1370.

Beisecker, A. E. (1988). Aging and the desire for information and input in medical decisions: Patient consumerism in medical encounters. *Gerontologist, 28,* 330–335.

Bensing, J. M., Verhaak, F. M., van Dulmen, & A. M., Visser, A. P. (2000). Communication: The royal pathway to patient-centered medicine. *Patient Education and Counseling, 39,* 1–3.

Bertakis, K. D., Roter, D., & Putnam, S. M. (1991). The relationship of physician medical interview style to patient satisfaction. *Journal of Family Practice, 32*(2). [Online]. Available: http://infotrac.galegroup.com.

Blair, P. D., Bambas, A., & Stone, T. H. (1998). Legal and ethical issues. In S. F. Viegas & K. Dunn (Eds.), *Telemedicine: Practicing in the information age* (pp. 49–60). Philadelphia: Lippincott-Raven.

Blum, J. (2001). Creating a cyber doctor-patient relationship. *American Medical News, 44*(29), 21. [Online]. Available: http://www.ncbi.nlm.nih.gov.

Borowitz, S. M., & Wyatt, J. C. (1998). The origin, content, and workload of e-mail consultations. *Journal of the American Medical Association, 280*(15), 1321–1324.

Brick, J. E., Bashshur, R. L., Brick, J. F., & D'Alessandri, R. M. (1997). Public knowledge, perception, and expressed choice of telemedicine in rural West Virginia. *Telemedicine Journal, 3*(2), 159–171.

Burgoon, J. K., Bonito, J. A., Ramirez, Jr., A., Dunbar, N. E., Kam, K., & Fischer, J. (in press). Testing the interactivity principle: Effects of mediation, verbal and nonverbal modalities, and propinquity in decision-making interactions. *Journal of Communication.*

Callahan, E. J., Hilty, D. M., & Nesbitt, T. S. (1998). Patient satisfaction with telemedicine consultation in primary care: Comparison of rating of medical and mental health applications. *Telemedicine Journal, 4*(4), 363–369.

Campion, E. W., Anderson, K. R., & Drazen, J. M. (2001). A new web site and a new policy. *New England Journal of Medicine, 344*(22), 1710–1711. [Online]. Available: http://content.nejm.org.

Canadian Medical Association (2000). More net-savvy MDs surfing the web. *Canadian Medical Association Journal, 163*(5), 590. [Online]. Available: http://www/cma/ca/cmaj/vol-163/issue-5/0590.htm.

Caryl, C. J. (1997). Malpractice and other legal issues preventing the development of telemedicine. *Journal of Law and Health, 12*. [Online]. Available: http://wb.lexis-nexis.com/universe.

Cecil, D. W. (1998). Relational control patterns in patient-physician clinical encounters: Continuing the conversation. *Health Communication, 10*(2), 125–149.

Charles, B. L. (2000). Telemedicine can lower costs and improve access. *Healthcare Financial Management, 54*(4), 66–69.

Chew, P. H. (2001). Patient empowerment. *British Medical Journal, 322*, 1472. [Online]. Available: http://infotrac.galegroup.com.

Collins, B., & Sypher, H. (1996, April/May). Developing better relationships in telemedicine practice. *Telemedicine Today, 4*, 27, 42.

Culnan, M. J., & Markus, M. L. (1987). Information technologies. In F. M. Jablin, L. L. Putnam, K. H. Roberts, & L. W. Porter (Eds.), *Handbook of organizational communication: An interdisciplinary perspective,* (pp. 420–443). Newbury Park, CA: Sage.

D'Amaro, R. (1998, September 5). Checkup 2020. *Hospitals and Heath Networks,* 18–20.

Daley, H. A. (2000). Telemedicine: The invisible legal barriers to the health care of the future. *Annals of Health Law, 9*. [Online]. Available: http://wb.lexis-nexis.com/universe.

Darkins, A. W., & Cary, M. A. (2000). *Telemedicine and telehealth: Principles, policies, performance, and pitfalls.* New York: Springer.

David, A. K. (1994). Challenges in personal and public health promotion: The primary care physician perspective. *American Journal of Preventive Medicine, 10* (Supp. 3), 36–38.

Davis, S. H. (1998). What's holding up the telemedicine explosion? *Telephony, 234*, 66–73.

Deetz, S. (1992). *Democracy in an age of corporate colonization: Developments in communication and the politics of everyday life.* Albany: State University of New York Press.

Degnin, F. D. (1999). Between a rock and a hard place: Ethics in managed care and the patient-physician relationship. *Managed Care Quarterly, 7*(2), 15–22.

Dudley, T. E., Falvo, D. R., Podell, R. N., & Renner, J. (1996). The informed patient poses a different challenge. *Patient Care, 30*(16). [Online]. Available: http://infotrac.galegroup.com.

Dudley, R. A., Miller, R. H., Korenbrot, T. Y., & Luft, H. S. (1998). The impact of financial incentives on quality of health care. *Milbank Quarterly, 76*(4), 649–686.

Emanuel, E. J., & Dubler, N. N. (1995). Preserving the patient-physician relationship in the era of managed care. *Journal of the American Medical Association, 273*(4). [Online]. Available: http://infotrac.galegroup.com.

Emanuel, E. J., & Emanuel, L. L. (1992). Four models of patient-physician relationship. *Journal of the American Medical Association, 267*(16). [Online]. Available: http://infotrac.galegroup.com.

Epstein, R. M., Campbell, T. L., Cohen-Cole, S. A., McWhinney, I. R., & Smilkstein, G. (1993). Perspectives on patient-doctor communication. *The Journal of Family Practice, 37*(4), 377–388.

Ferguson, R. (1996). *Health online.* Reading, MA: Addison-Wesley.

Ferguson, T. (1997 November/December). Health care in cyberspace: Patients lead a revolution. *Futurist, 31*(6), 29–33.

Ferguson, T. (1998, October 21). Digital doctoring—Opportunities and challenges in electronic patient-physician communication. *Journal of the American Medical Association, 280*(15), 1361–1362.

Fried, B. M., Weinreich, G., Cavalier, G. M., & Lester, K. J. (2000). E-health: Technologic revolution meets regulatory constraint. *Health Affairs, 19*(6), 124–131. [Online]. Available: http://proquest.umi.com.

Gelber, H., & Alexander, M. (1999). An evaluation of an Australian videoconferencing project for child and adolescent telepsychiatry. *Journal of Telemedicine and Telecare, 5*(Supp. 1), 21–23.

Gold, M. (1999). The changing US health care system: Challenges for responsible public policy, *Milbank Quarterly, 77*(1), 3–37.

Goldsmith, J. (2000). The internet and managed care: A new wave of innovation. *Health Affairs, 19*(6), 42–56. [Online]. Available: http://web.lexis-nexis.com/universe.

Goold, S. D. & Lipkin, M. (1999). The doctor-patient relationship: Challenges, opportunities, and strategies. *Journal of General Internal Medicine, 14*(1), S26–S33.

Gotten, S. R. (2001). Implications of internet technology for medical sociology in the new millennium. *Sociological Spectrum, 21*(3). [Online]. Available: http://stvgw8.epnet.com/ehost.

Grove, A. S. (1998). The X factor: Impact of information technology on economic growth and medical care. A piece of my mind. *Journal of the American Medical Association, 280*(15), 1294(1). [Online]. Available: http://www.proquest.umi.com.

Greenberger, M., & Puffer, J. C. (1989). Telemedicine: Toward better health care for the elderly. *Journal of Communication, 39*(3), 137–144.

Greene, M. G., Adelman, R. D., Friedmann, E., & Charon, R. (1994). Older patient satisfaction with communication during an initial medical encounter. *Social Science & Medicine, 38*(9), 1279–1288.

Harrison, R., Clayton, W., & Wallace, P. (1999). Virtual outreach: A telemedicine pilot study using a cluster-randomized controlled design. *Journal of Telemedicine and Telecare, 5*, 126–130.

Herman, D. C., & Abenstein, J. P. (2001). Communication technology, patient safety, and the patient-physician relationship. *Mayo Clinic Proceedings, 76*(1), 7–8.

Hibbard, J. H., Slovic, P., & Jewett, J. J. (1997). Informing consumer decisions in health care: Implications from decision-making research. *Milbank Quarterly, 75*(3), 395–414.

Holtan, A. (1998). Patient reactions to specialist telemedicine consultations—A sociological approach. *Journal of Telemedicine and Telecare, 4*, 206–213.

Holtz, W. E. (1998). Consumer-directed prescription drug advertising: Effects on public health. *Journal of Law and Health, 13*(2), 199. [Online]. Available: http://www.ncbi.nlm.nih.gov.

Huston, J. L., & Burton, D. C. (1997). Patient satisfaction with multispecialty interactive teleconsultations. *Journal of Telemedicine and Telecare, 3*, 205–208.

Johnson, G. L., & Ramaprasad, A. (2000). Patient-physician relationships in the information age. *Marketing Health Services, 20*(1), 20–27. [Online]. Available: http://proquest.umi.com.

Kane, J., Marken, J., Boulger, J., Crouse, B., & Bergeron, D. (1995). Rural Minnesota family physicians' attitudes toward telemedicine. *Minnesota Medicine, 78*, 19–23.

Kane, B., & Sands, D. Z. (1998). Guidelines for the clinical use of electronic mail with patients. *Journal of the American Medical Informatics Association, 5*, pp. 104–111.

Kaplan, S. H., Greenfield, S., & Ware, J.E. (1989). Assessing the effects of patient-physician interactions on the outcomes of chronic disease. *Medical Care, 27*(3), S110–S127.

Karp, W. B., Grigsby, R. K., Swiggan-Hardin, M., Pursley-Crotteau, S., Adams, L. N., Bell, W., Stachura, M. E., & Kanto, W. P. (2000). Use of telemedicine for children with special health care needs. *Pediatrics, 105*, 843–847. [Online]. Available: http://wb.lexis-nexis.com/universe.

Kassirer, J. P. (2000). Patients, physicians, and the internet. *Health Affairs, 19*(6),115–123. [Online]. Available: http://proquest.umi.com.

Katz, J. E., & Rice, R. E. (2001). Concluding thoughts. In J. E. Katz & R. E. Rice (Eds.), *The internet and health communication: Experiences and expectations* (pp. 417–429). Thousand Oaks, CA: Sage.

Kolata, G. (2000). Web research transforms visit to the doctor. *Pediatrics, 106*(2), pA46. [Online]. Available: http://infotrac.galegroup.com.

Krupat, E., Rosenkranz, S. L., Yeager, C. M., Barnard, K., Putnam, S. M., & Inui, T. S. (2000). The practice orientations of physicians and patients: The effect of doctor-patient congruence on satisfaction. *Patient Education and Counseling, 39*, 49–59.

Kuszler, P. C. (1999). Telemedicine and integrated health care delivery: Compounding malpractice liability. *American Journal of Law & Medicine, 25*(2/3), 297–327. [Online]. Available: http://wb.lexis-nexis.com/universe.

Lambert, B. L., Street, R. L., Cegala, D. J., Smith, D. H., Kurtz, S., & Schofield, T. (1997). Provider-patient communication, patient-centered care, and the mangle of practice. *Health Communication, 9*(1), 27–43.

Landro, L. (2000). Patient-physician communication: An emerging partnership. *Annals of Oncology, 11*, 53–56.

LaPuma, J. (1994). Anticipated changes in the doctor-patient relationship in the managed care and managed competition of the Health Security Act of 1993. *Archives of Family Medicine, 3*(8), 665–671.

Lea, M., & Spears, R. (1995). Love at first byte? Building personal relationships over computer networks. In J. T. Wood & S. Duck (Eds.), *Understudied relationships: Off the beaten track* (pp. 197–233). Thousand Oaks, CA: Sage.

Levinson, W., Roter, D. L., Mullooly, J. P., Dull, V. T., & Frankel, R. M. (1997). Patient-physician communication: The relationship with malpractice claims among primary care physicians and surgeons. *Journal of the American Medical Association, 277*(7), 553–559.

Loane, M. A., Bloomer, S. E., Corbett, R., Eedy, D. J., Gore, H. E., Mathews, C., Steele, K., & Wootton, R. (1998). Patient satisfaction with realtime teledermatology in Northern Ireland. *Journal of Telemedicine and Telecare, 4*, 36–40.

Loane, M. A., Gore, H. E., Corbett, R., Steele, K. Mathews, C., Bloomer, S. E., Eedy, D. J., Telford, R. W., & Wootton, R. (1997). Effect of camera performance on diagnostic accuracy: Preliminary results from the Northern Ireland arms of the UK Multicentre Teledermatology Trial. *Journal of Telemedicine and Telecare, 3*, 83–88.

Long, J. D. (1998). TeleHealth and direct health care delivery: An introduction. In M. L. Armstrong (Ed.), *Telecommunications for health professionals: Providing successful distance education and telehealth* (pp. 187–203). New York: Springer.

Lowes, R. L. (1997). Here come patients who've "studied" medicine on-line. *Medical Economics, 74*(2). [Online]. Available: http://infotrac.galegroup.com.

Makoul, G. (1998). Perpetuating passivity: Reliance and reciprocal determinism in patient-physician interaction. *Journal of Health Communication, 3*, 233–259.

Mandl, K. D., Kohane, I. S., & Brandt, A. M. (1998). Electronic patient-physician communication: Problems and promise. *Annals of Internal Medicine, 129*(6), 495–500.

Martin, S. (2001). Public ignorant about telemedicine, survey finds. *Canadian Medical Association Journal, 164*(7), 1035–1038.

McCarthy, D. (1995). The virtual health economy: Telemedicine and the supply of primary care physicians in rural America. *American Journal of Law & Medicine, 21*. [Online]. Available: http://wb.lexis-nexis.com/universe.

McConnell, M. E., Steed, R. D., Tichenor, J. M., & Hannon, D. W. (1999). Interactive telecardiology for the evaluation of heart murmurs in children. *Telemedicine Journal, 5*(2), 157–161.

Mechanic, D. (2000). Managed care and the imperative for a new professional ethic. *Health Affairs, 20*. [Online]. Available: http://web.lexis-nexis.com/universe.

Mechanic, D. (1998a). Public trust and initiatives for new health care partnerships. *Milbank Quarterly, 76*(2), 281–302.

Mechanic, D. (1998b). The functions and limitations of trust in the provision of medical care. *Journal of Health Politics, Policy and Law, 23*(4), 661–686.

Mechanic, D., & Schlesinger, M. (1996). The impact of managed care on patients' trust in medical care and their physicians. *Journal of the American Medical Association, 275*(21), 1693–1697.

Mekhjian, H., Turner, J. W, Gailiun, M., & McCain, T. (1999). Patient satisfaction with telemedicine in a prison environment. *Journal of Telemedicine and Telecare, 5*, 55–61.

Menduno, M. (1998, November 5). Prognosis: Why internet technology is the next medical breakthrough. *Hospitals and Health Networks*, 28–35.

Miller, F. H. (1998). Health care information technology and informed consent: computers and the doctor-patient relationship. *Indiana Law Review, 31*(4), 1019–1042.

Miller, E. A. (2001). Telemedicine and doctor-patient communication: An analytical survey of the literature. *Journal of Telemedicine and Telecare, 7,* 1–17.

Mittman, R., & Cain, M. (2001). The future of the internet in health care: A five-year forecast. In R. E. Rice & J. E. Katz (Eds.), *The internet and health communication: Experiences and expectations* (pp. 47–74). Thousand Oaks, CA: Sage.

Moore, M. (1998). Cost analysis of telemedicine consultations. In S. F. Viegas & K. Dunn (Eds.), *Telemedicine: Practicing in the information age* (pp. 229-244). Philadelphia: Lippincott-Raven.

Mumby, D. (1988). *Communication and power in organizations: Discourse, ideology, and domination.* Norwood, NJ: Ablex.

Nagy, K. (1994). Telemedicine creeping into use, despite obstacles. *Journal of the National Cancer Institute, 86,* 1576–1578. [Online]. Available: http://wb.lexis-nexis.com/universe.

Neill, R. A, Mainous, A. G., Clark, J. R., & Hagen, M. D. (1994). The utility of electronic mail as a medium for patient-physician communication. *Archives of Family Medicine, 3,* 268–271.

Orvell, B., Rockefeller, R. G., Price, R. B., Reynolds, J. T., & Kassirer, J. P. (1995). The next transformation in the delivery of health care. *New England Journal of Medicine, 332,* 1099–1100.

Pal, B. (2000). Internet helps communication between doctors and patients. *British Medical Journal, 320.* [Online]. Available: http://infotrac.galegroup.com.

Pedersen, S., & Holand, U. (1995). Tele-endoscopic otorhinolaryngoloical examination: Preliminary study of patient satisfaction. *Telemedicine Journal, 1,* 47–52.

Pennbridge, J., Moya, R., & Rodrigues, L. (1999). Questionnaire survey of California consumers' use and rating of sources of health care information including the Internet. *Western Journal of Medicine, 171,* 302–305. [Online]. Available: http://infotrac.galegroup.com.

Phillips, C. M., Murphy, R., Burke, W. A., Laing, V. B., Jones, B. E., Balch, D., & Gustke, S. (1996). Dermatology teleconsultations to Central Prison: Experience at East Carolina University. *Telemedicine Journal, 2,* 139–143.

Reeves, P. M. (2000). Coping in cyberspace: The impact of internet use on the ability of HIV-positive individuals to deal with their illness. *Journal of Health Communication, 5* (Supp.), 47–59.

Rice, R. E., Grant, A. E., Schmitz, J., & Torobin, J. (1990). Individual and network influences on the adoption and perceived outcomes of electronic messaging. *Social Networks, 12,* 27–55.

Roine, R., Ohinmaa, A., & Hailey, D. (2001). Assessing telemedicine: A systematic review of the literature. *Canadian Medical Association Journal, 165*(6), 765–772.

Roter, D. (2000). The enduring and evolving nature of the patient-physician relationship. *Patient Education and Counseling, 39,* 5–15.

Roter, D., & Hall, J. A. (1992). *Doctors talking with patients/patients talking with doctors: Improving communication in medical visits.* Westport, CT: Auburn House.

Roter, D. L., Stewart, M., Putnam, S. M., Lipkin Jr., M., Stiles, W., & Inui, T. (1997). Communication patterns of primary care physicians. *Journal of the American Medical Association, 277,* 350–357.

Saunders, C. S., Robey, D., & Vaverek, K. A. (1994). The persistence of status differentials in computer conferencing. *Human Communication Research, 20,* 443–472.

Seeman, M. V., & Seeman, B. (1999). E-psychiatry: The patient-psychiatrist relationship in the electronic age. *Canadian Medical Association Journal, 161*(9), 1147–1149.

Shapiro, R. S., Tym, K.A., Gudmundson, J. L., Derse, A. R. & Klein, J. P. (2000). Managed care: Effects on the patient-physician relationship. *Cambridge Quarterly of Healthcare Ethics, 9,* 71–81.

Sharf, B. F. (1988). Teaching patients to speak up: Past and future trends. *Patient Education and Counseling, 11,* 95–108.

Sharf, B. F., & Street, R. L., (1997). The patient as a central construct: Shifting the emphasis. *Health Communication, 9*(1), 1–11.

Sherman, L., & Adams, M. (1999). Patients and email: Technology means increased confidentiality concerns. *Wisconsin Medical Journal, 98*(3), 66–67.

Siegler, M. (1993). Falling off the pedestal: What is happening to the traditional doctor-patient relationship? *Mayo Clinical Proceedings, 68,* 461–467.

Silverman, R. D. (2000). The changing face of law and medicine in the new millennium. *American*

*Journal of Law & Medicine, 26.* [Online]. Available: http://wb.lexis-nexis.com/universe.

Smith, R. C., Marshall-Dorsey, A. A., Osborn, G. G., Shebroe, V., Lyles, J. S., Stoffelmayr, B. E., Van Egeren, L. F., Mettler, J., Maduschke, K., Stanley, J. M., & Gardiner, J. C. (2000). Evidence-based guidelines for teaching patient-centered interviewing. *Patient Education and Counseling, 39,* 27–36.

Spicer, J. (1999). Getting patients off hold and online. *Family Practice Management, 6*(1), 34–38.

Spielberg, A. R. (1998). On call and online: Sociohistorical, legal and ethical implications of email for the patient-physician relationship. *Journal of the American Medical Association, 280*(15), 1353–1359.

Spielberg, A. R. (1999). Online without a net: Patient-physician communication by electronic mail. *American Journal of Law and Medicine, 25,* 267–295.

Stewart, M. A. (1995). Effective patient-physician communication and health outcomes: A review. *Canadian Medical Association Journal, 152,* 1423–1433.

Stoner, G. M., Burgoon, J. K., Bonito, J. A., Ramirez, A., Jr., & Dunbar, N. (1999, May). *Nonverbal cues in mediated communication.* Paper presented at the annual conference of the International Communication Association, San Francisco.

Street, R. L., Jr., & Piziak, V. K. (2001). Improving diabetes care with telecomputing technology. In R. E. Rice & J. E. Katz (Eds.), *The internet and health communication: Experiences and expectations* (pp. 287–308). Thousand Oaks, CA: Sage.

Street, R. L., Wheeler, E. J., & McCaughan, W. T. (2000). Specialist-primary care provider-patient communication in telemedicine consultations. *Telemedicine Journal, 6*(1), 45–54.

Terry, N. P. (1999). Cyber-Malpractice: Legal exposure for cybermedicine. *American Journal of Law & Medicine, 25.* [Online]. Available: http://wb.lexis-nexis.com/universe.

Thom, D. H., & Campbell, B. (1997). Patient-physician trust: An exploratory study. *Journal of Family Practice, 44*(2), 169–176.

Tilford, J. M., Garner, W. E., Strode, S. W., & Bynum, A. B. (1997). Rural Arkansas physicians and telemedicine technology: Attitudes in communities receiving equipment. *Telemedicine Journal, 3*(4), 257–263.

Vyborny, K. M. (1996). Legal and political issues facing telemedicine. *Annals of Health Law, 5.* [Online]. Available: http://wb.lexis-nexis.com/universe.

Wakefield, D. S., Kienzle, M. G., Zollo, S. A., Kash, J. B., & Uden-Holman, T. (1997). Health care providers' perceptions of telemedicine services. *Telemedicine Journal, 3*(1), 59–65.

Walther, J. B. (1996). Computer-mediated communication: Impersonal, interpersonal, and hyperpersonal interaction. *Communication Research, 23,* 3–43.

Weed, L. L. (1997). New connections between medical knowledge and patient care. *British Medical Journal, 315,* 231–235.

Whittaker, S., & Sidner, C. (1997). Email overload: Exploring personal information management of email. In S. Kiesler (Ed.), *Cultures of the internet* (pp. 277–295). Mahwah, NJ: Erlbaum.

Whitten, P. S. (1997). Telemedicine in Kansas: Using technology to bring healthcare to rural areas. In B. D. Sypher (Ed.), *Case studies in organizational communication* (pp. 297–311). New York: Guilford Press.

Whitten, P. S., & Franken, E. A. (1995). Telemedicine for patient consultation: Factors affecting use by rural primary-care physicians in Kansas. *Journal of Telemedicine and Telecare, 1,* 139–144.

Whitten, P. S., Mair, F., & Collins, B. (1997). Home nursing in Kansas: Patients' perceptions of uses and benefits. *Journal of Telemedicine and Telecare, 3,* 67–69.

Widman, L. E., & Tong, D. A. (1997). Requests for medical advice from patients and families to health care providers who publish on the World Wide Web. *Archives of Internal Medicine, 157*(2). [Online]. Available: http://infotrac.galegroup.com.

Wootton, R. (2001). Recent advances in telemedicine. *British Medical Journal, 322*(7312), 557–561.

# CHAPTER CONTENTS

• Introduction                                      367

• Cognition                                         370

• Language Development                              373

• Communication Competence                         374

• Relationship Change Across the Lifespan          378

• Capturing Change in Lifespan Communication       381

• Epilogue                                          382

• References                                        385

# 11   Lifespan Communication

JON F. NUSSBAUM
*Pennsylvania State University*

LORETTA L. PECCHIONI
*Louisiana State University*

DOREEN K. BARINGER
AMANDA L. KUNDRAT
*Pennsylvania State University*

Lifespan communication researchers investigate the changes in relevant communication perceptions, behaviors, and interpersonal relationships across the entirety of our lives. Borrowing from the pioneering work of behavioral researchers in our sister disciplines of psychology, sociology, anthropology, and human development, communication researchers utilizing the lifespan perspective to guide their investigations have produced a significant amount of literature throughout the past three decades. This article reviews several significant areas of lifespan communication research related to cognition/social cognition, language development, communication competence, relationship change across the lifespan, and the longitudinal design best suited to capture age-related, intraindividual change. The article concludes with a discussion of how communication scholars can embrace this perspective and the type of knowledge that can be gained once the perspective guides research inquiries.

T he lifespan developmental approach toward understanding and explaining human behavior has become accepted and quite popular in our sister disciplines of psychology, sociology, anthropology, and human development and family studies (see Bigner, 1994; Hareven, 1978; Mosher, Youngman, & Day, 1999; Schwebel, Maher, & Fagley, 1990; Smith, 1990; and Stevenson, 1994 for applications in these fields). Communication scholars borrowing heavily from the pioneering efforts within these complementary disciplines began to speculate several decades ago that a lifespan approach may be a useful metaperspective addressing our interpersonal behavior (Knapp, 1978; Nussbaum, 1989). The research that has followed the original exhortations of Knapp, Nussbaum, and

Correspondence: Jon F. Nussbaum, Department of Communication Arts and Sciences, Pennsylvania State University, University Park, PA 16802-5201; email: jfn5@psu.edu.

*Communication Yearbook 26*, pp. 366–389

others, to incorporate lifespan notions into our communication investigations, has produced an impressive literature that focuses upon not only differing interactive behaviors as we age, but also on the numerous changes in the communicative functions and meanings of our behaviors as we manage and negotiate our lives.

The basic premise of any lifespan developmental approach that investigates human behavior is that potential for development extends throughout the lifespan. This simple statement represents a radical shift away from theorists, perhaps best represented by Piaget (1954, 1959, 1972), who were quite certain that development accelerated rapidly throughout childhood, followed by brief stability and then decline throughout the remainder of life. To this day, the majority of research within Developmental Psychology, for instance, concentrates on the very early years of our lives implicitly suggesting that the most important and interesting events of our existence occur in these early years. Lifespan developmentalists, on the other hand, do not consider any age, neither the first 12 years of life nor the last 12 years of life, to hold supremacy in regulating the nature of development (Baltes, Smith, & Studinger, 1992), although these researchers generally agree that the rates of development vary across the lifespan.

Taking a lifespan perspective allows us to examine dynamic changes coupled with strategies to maintain stability throughout an individual's life or throughout the life of an interpersonal relationship. The level of analysis may be the individual, the relationship, or society. From a more psychological approach (where the term lifespan is most commonly used), researchers focus on changes in the individual as she or he ages. From a more sociological, anthropological, or family studies approach (where the term "life course" is more commonly used), researchers focus on the relationship as it changes over time, or social and cultural expectations for individuals and relationships as they change over time, including historical times.

Five assertions of the lifespan perspective, as put forth by Baltes (1987), are helpful in understanding this perspective and any significance this perspective has for the discipline of Communication. First, the lifespan perspective rejects commonly accepted notions of almost universal decline as we age. An enduring myth of aging in our society is that each one of us who is past the age of 12 is in a constant state of decline. As a consequence of this thinking, people believe that, whether it is our ability to think, to run, to work, or to be interpersonally competent, we will perform better at age 20 than at age 50 than at age 70. Communication researchers rarely address the possibility that competent communicators may exist at any age or that our ability to function competently in human interaction may not only be quite different at various points in our lifespan, but may actually improve as we age.

Second, "considerable diversity and pluralism is found in the directionality of changes that constitute development. The direction of change varies by category of behavior" (Baltes, Smith, & Staudinger, 1992, p. 25). Development throughout our lives may progress on a number of different factors at a number of differing speeds. For instance, the development of mental abilities is not always perfectly in sync with the development of physical abilities and these may change over time. For example, a professional golfer who was excellent at age 30 does not necessarily dominate the senior professional tour for golfers over 50. In a similar manner, our interpersonal competencies may not emerge until numerous life experiences have shaped our expectations and reactions. In fact, many interpersonal competencies may not emerge at all until later in our lives, particularly as we develop greater social knowledge and understanding. Environmental influences (such as culture, historical times, and social networks) have a significant impact upon each of our relational lives. These influences are often not predictable nor do they affect each of us in the same way. Even siblings with similar genetic and environmental influences may assign different meanings and respond very differently to the same event. Family communicative patterns dramatically change when new family members are added or deleted from our interactive space. Intimacy comes and goes. The direction and intensity of our numerous relational trajectories are far from linear throughout our lives. Although this complexity may seemingly obscure our predictive models, an understanding of the diversity inherent within development should help us to capture the reality of our interactive lives, and the meanings people assign to their life experiences.

Third, development is best viewed as a gain-loss dynamic. Certain abilities do indeed decline over the lifespan. However, other abilities will increase in their effectiveness and efficiency. Communication may be one area of human behavior in which gains can outweigh declines. In addition, Nussbaum, Pecchioni, Robinson, and Thompson (2000) present a very compelling case that communication competencies may help to overcome numerous cognitive and physical limitations that are age-related. Communication technologies may also function to turn a loss into a gain for many of us. Just as eyeglasses have provided a simple eloquent solution to age-related vision loss, new technologies are aiding those who suffer from hearing loss, mobility issues, and memory disorders, and they afford us the ability to contact another individual at anytime, anywhere in the world. Technological advances, however, are not the only means through which we balance gains and losses. Older individuals who have developed strong social support networks have access to more options for managing physical declines and thus maintain a sense of control over their everyday lives (Cicirelli, 1992; Collopy, 1988; Pecchioni & Nussbaum, 2000; Rook, 1995).

Fourth, there is much intra- and interindividual diversity as we develop throughout the lifespan. Communication researchers would be wise to keep in mind communication-related variability not only within each individual from moment to moment during interactions, but also the variability that exists within and between individuals across time. Each of us will possess differing levels and types of competencies given specific interaction. For example, some individuals may manage one-on-one interactions very competently, whereas they perform very poorly in public speaking settings or vice-versa. Nor do these competencies need to always be utilized to their fullest potential, depending on factors such as motivation, fatigue, needing to balance numerous demands on time and attention, and so forth. In addition, these competencies may change quite dramatically as we age. Intraindividual change across the lifespan does not equate to interindividual change across groups of differing ages. Changes across groups of differing ages are called cohort effects, which exist because different groups of similarly aged people pass through varied historical and cultural times. For example, the current cohort of elderly were adolescents and young adults during World War II whereas the Baby Boomer generation were adolescents and young adults during the Vietnam War. These differing experiences frame a cohort's attitudes and expectations in different ways. Therefore, comparisons of different age groups need to account for cohort differences. Communication researchers need to address the significant individual differences that affect our interactive behavior and any consequences these individual differences have as we develop across time.

Finally, the person and the environment reciprocally influence one another. As mentioned previously, each of us are not only situated within specific and unique sociocultural contexts, but we also actively influence these contexts in very dramatic ways. Our cultural and societal expectations, for example, are not "out there" to be handed to us as a given, but are shaped by our interactions and willingness to adapt or challenge these expectations. Communication scholars are especially "burdened" with a responsibility to incorporate environmental influences, such as existing relationships, culture, the physical environment, and past history, into our explanations of interpersonal communication. It matters when, where, and with whom we are discussing a certain topic.

The lifespan perspective, as put forth by Baltes (1987) and adopted by Nussbaum (1989), Nussbaum et al. (2000), and Williams and Nussbaum (2001), does not specify any particular theory of human behavior as the most useful explanation or description of human development. Instead, this perspective attempts to frame change across the lifespan as an essential ingredient in any attempt to capture the nature and functions of the communication process. The remaining pages of this manuscript will address several significant issues in communication that can and should be viewed within the lifespan perspective. The final section of this article will look toward the future and point communication scholars to fertile areas of future investigation.


## COGNITION

Cognition is generally recognized as the study of how people acquire knowledge (Haslett & Samter, 1997). If the knowledge that is being acquired concerns the interface of human thought processes and human interaction, then researchers have classified these specific cognitive processes into the domain of social cognition (Knapp & Miller, 1994). Although this distinction between cognition and social cognition may be useful for some social scientists, we suggest that all internal thought processes that involve the storage, use, and retrieval of knowledge probably play some role in our ability to communicate effectively with another human being. Nussbaum, Hummert, Williams, and Harwood (1996) clearly state that cognitive processes must be considered in any attempt to fully understand our interactive behavior. That being stated, the question for lifespan communication scholars becomes whether our cognitive processes change over time and if they do, how these cognitive changes are in any way causal or related to communicative changes over time.

Haslett and Samter (1997), relying on well over 50 years of research by cognitive psychologists and communication scholars, present a convincing case that the first five years of life are replete with massive advances in our cognitive abilities. No one would attempt to refute the argument that normal growth in the first years of life is highlighted by significant and meaningful gains in our ability to store, retrieve, and use information. In addition, Haslett and Samter (1997) link these advances in cognitive abilities to a child's ability to communicate effectively. Once again, it has become an accepted fact of social science that a normal child's ability to store, process, and retrieve information increases with age, ultimately leading to increases in ability to communicate effectively. In turn, the child's ability to use language appropriately and communicate effectively increases with his or her cognitive processing ability.

Although young children do exhibit tremendous gains in their cognitive functions, these abilities do not decline until advanced old age. Schaie and Hofer (2001) reviewed the current status of longitudinal studies being conducted in psychology and aging. The overwhelming evidence from these longitudinal studies point to the changing nature of our cognitive abilities across the lifespan. Stated simply, these investigations show that our cognitive abilities demonstrate impressive gains in early life, followed by relative stability throughout our midlife, followed by a slow decline in late life, until a rapid decline is recorded past the age of 80. Cognitive psychologists and communication scholars have also studied the cognitive processes of older adults (Howard, 1983). Numerous investigators have attempted to document the decline of our working memory, processing speed, and retrieval issues as we age beyond 65 years of age (see Nussbaum et al., 1996, for a brief review of the basic findings of this research). Most of these declines have relatively little consequence for functioning and interaction until the decline becomes quite pronounced (Schaie, 1996).

Cognitive processing, however, is not just a matter of speed, but includes many different domains, such as intelligence, memory, problem solving, decision making, everyday coping, and social intelligence. Intelligence is not a simple factor, but consists of several domains including not only processing speed, but also information processing, working memory, memory structures, and semantic knowledge (Schaie, 1996). Individuals continue to develop in their thinking and problem solving abilities across the lifespan, however, they may choose different strategies with age (Smith & Baltes, 1990). When examining the problems of everyday life, older individuals are more likely to base decisions on prior experience, whereas younger individuals spend more time collecting relevant data because they have fewer personal experiences upon which to draw (Willis, 1996). These different styles might lead to intergenerational conflict as each group will have a different approach for solving the same problem. Due to the greater potential for having more experiences as we age, older individuals generally have more social knowledge than do younger individuals (Blanchard-Fields & Abeles, 1996). For example, younger individuals experiencing their first life crisis are not likely to have the same level of coping strategies for managing these events as do older individuals. Older individuals are more likely to understand that crises arise in life, but these events can be managed and survived successfully, adopting a "this too shall pass" attitude. In summary, older individuals do exhibit declines in processing speeds, but often exhibit more complex processing structures based on years and number of experiences.

It should also be noted that the declines observed in later life are much more pronounced within interindividual change (cross sectional comparisons, i.e., comparisons made between younger and older adults) versus intraindividual change (change within the same individual measured over some period of time) due to cohort differences, which often reflect educational and social expectations and experiences. For example, older adults perform more poorly on paper and pencil tests because they have not used this method for years. Training in test-taking reduces the measured differences between age cohorts (Schaie, 1996). Sometimes, differences in performance reflect instrumentation bias. As noted previously, younger and older individuals use different problem solving strategies. If the instrument used to measure problem solving ability favors one group's strategy over the other's, then age group comparisons will be inherently biased. In addition, programmatic research by Hummert (1990, 1994a, 1994b), Giles and Williams (1994), and Ryan (1991) throughout the 1990s have emphasized the importance of studying stereotyping and the possible effects that these negative and positive stereotypes have upon our communicative behavior. Levy's (1996) work shows that exposure to negative stereotypes of aging worsens older individuals' memory performance whereas exposure to positive stereotypes of aging improves their performance. Exposure to stereotypes, however, does not affect memory processing among young adults. Therefore, exposure to stereotypes of aging have real consequences for older individuals.

The empirical evidence is quite clear that our cognitive abilities change quite dramatically across the lifespan. After initial tremendous gains, this change may be rather slight for some individuals and rather impressive for others. These changes are obviously influenced by pathologies, such as mental retardation and dementia. Nevertheless, the basic foundation of our ability to communicate effectively, our cognitive processing capability, changes as a function of time (age).

## LANGUAGE DEVELOPMENT

In much the same way that cognitive scientists have concentrated their research efforts at the beginning and at the end of the lifespan, linguists, sociolinguists, developmental psychologists, and communication scholars have placed great emphasis on the developmental gains of language within children and on the decline of language abilities in old age. Haslett and Samter (1997) have written several informative chapters on the precise nature of change in our language abilities during the first few years of life. From prelinguistic development, to speech pronunciation, to our first words, to semantic development, to syntactic development, the fundamental process of language acquisition that occurs within the great majority of normal humans has been well researched.

Of special note for the understanding of the development of language within childhood is an ongoing controversy centering on the degree the environment impacts our ability to acquire language. Haslett and Samter (1997) point to numerous theoretical perspectives that incorporate discussions of why children show such variability in their language skills. The most plausible explanations for this variability focus upon both innate causes and environmental constraints. A child with the normal genetic predispositions to acquire language who has been placed into a rich, linguistic environment will have a greater chance of developing superior language abilities. Recent research has pointed to the physiological basis of social cognition as well (Frith & Frith, 2001). Thus, some interaction between internal brain functioning and environmental richness must be causing variability in language development. Nevertheless, it is universally accepted that language does develop across time and that the major developmental stages for language acquisition occur early in life.

Nussbaum et al. (1996) have reviewed the significant literatures that address language in later life. Investigations by Kemper (1992), Light (1990), Ryan (1991), and numerous others have found some declines in our syntactic and discourse processing abilities as we age. Name retrieval has been shown to be more of a problem for older adults when compared to individuals who are much younger (Cohen, 1994). In addition, numerous longitudinal studies have pointed to significant declines in verbal fluency, vocabulary, and verbal performance as we age past 70 (Schaie & Hofer, 2001). These declines in language performance have consequences for interaction as others feel the need to step in and help the older individual with problems. This potentially leads to greater frustration for the older participant, sometimes resulting in the become frustration and avoidance of interaction altogether, thus reducing the interactive lives of older individuals.

Communication scholars who have studied language in later life have emphasized the style component of language much more than the structural component. Coupland, Coupland, and Giles (1991) use communication accommodation theory to explain and describe how interactions with older adults often demand and result in adaptive language use. The adaptation can take the form of overaccommodating to the perceived needs of the older interactant (e.g., speaking louder and slower) or underaccommodating to these interactive needs (e.g., shutting off topics of conversation). In either case, the use of language has been shown to be a significant and complex factor in the overall communicative milieu of older adults (see Williams & Nussbaum, 2001, for an extensive review and commentary of research utilizing communication accommodation theory in an older population).

Jacobs (1994) has written a quite extraordinary chapter that reframes the study of language away from "the technical structural interests of sentence grammarians" to the use of the term discourse to describe an effort to study the uses of language or the structure of language in interaction. This reframing from language to discourse can serve to move communication scholars to consider discourse as a lifespan developmental phenomenon. The view of "linguistic communication as a process of strategic design and constructive influence" (Jacobs, 1994, p. 225) presupposes that all discourse, at all points in the lifespan, is a very dynamic and ever changing activity. Whereas the research on language development has produced very clear results that the early years of our life are critical to normal development and that the later years may be a period of decline in certain language abilities, the process of discourse as an ever present, developing, interactive ability throughout our lifespan can connect these two extreme points in the lifespan. The middle years of life may be a period of learning and fine-tuning our discourse abilities to enhance the effectiveness of our interactions. These discursive abilities lead to the topic of communication competence.

## COMMUNICATION COMPETENCE

Communication scholars have produced an impressive volume of literature that concentrates upon communication competence. Spitzberg and Cupach (1984), Duran (1989), and Parks (1994) have attempted to bring some conceptual clarity to the numerous definitions of and approaches toward communication competence that populate the literature. For our purposes in this article, communication competence is defined as "the degree to which individuals satisfy and perceive that they have satisfied their goals within the limits of a given social situation without jeopardizing their ability or opportunity to pursue their subjectively more important goals" (Parks, 1994, p. 595). This definition of communication competence limits our discussion to very specific, small encounters. It also emphasizes a mastery over the social skills that will accomplish clearly thought out interactive goals. Communication competence in any social context cannot be achieved without the more fundamental competencies that control cognition and language behavior. Thus, the developmental processes that inhibit or manage cognition and language will also have a significant impact upon our ability to accomplish our social goals.

Parks (1994) presents a hierarchical control model as an attempt to organize the literature and research findings within the general domain of communication competence. The nine levels in this model capture the competencies that an individual may possess in any given interaction (The levels are: intensity, sensation, configuration, transition, sequence, relationship, program, principle, and system concept). From an ability to coordinate specific muscle groups, to an ability to incorporate concerns of others, to an ability to translate self-concepts into principles of social interaction, all of us are quite active participants in the construction of communication competence.

The important issues facing lifespan developmentalists include how these communication competencies discussed above develop across the lifespan. Do all of the competencies outlined by Parks (1994) develop simultaneously? Do certain communicative competencies have critical periods within which they develop and, if these particular competencies do not develop during this restricted time frame, do they never develop or develop in a retarded manner? Do some competencies serve us much better at specific stages in life? Are there gains and declines in competencies throughout the lifespan?

Haslett and Samter (1997) separate the development of communication competence for young children into two domains: the development of verbal communication and the development of communication knowledge. From birth until five years, children progress through several stages in their abilities to communicate verbally. From accomplishing complex expressive exchanges very shortly after birth, to participating in interactive routines from 2–12 months, to producing single words around 14 months, to initiating and sustaining conversational topics at around the age of five, to checking message accuracy and adequacy after age five, the development of verbal communication skills remains one of the most fascinating processes in human behavior.

These verbal communication skills, however, must be coordinated and adapted before the child can utilize them appropriately in social settings. "The ability to communicate effectively involves a complex cognitive assessment of the communication task, the interactants, and the social setting" (Haslett & Samter, 1997, p. 131). The development of communication knowledge also progresses through various stages. A child begins to recognize others as separate from him- or herself and that others have a potential for social interaction shortly after birth. At 12 months, children begin to recognize the qualities of others that make the other a unique individual. After one year, children develop the knowledge that family members are different from peers, and that friendship and authority are relational qualities. In addition, children begin to recognize that certain behaviors are appropriate because of contextual constraints. The developmental processes that simultaneously "permit" the child to incorporate effective verbal communication skills and communicative knowledge enable the child to communicate with some level of competence.

Stohl (1989) studied the relationship between attributes of children's social networks and the development of perceived communicative competence. Stohl (1989) reasoned that certain attributes of a child's social networks (size, diversity, interconnectedness) may affect the content and form of a child's social experience and thus affect the development of communicative competence. Children attending day care averaging 52 months old participated in the study. Results revealed the children with more network members and who participate in more communicative activities and special outings are perceived by their teachers to be more communicatively competent. The fact that a certain level of competence must be required to form and to engage in interaction within a large, diverse, interconnected social network indicates that children with effective communicative competencies at a very young age act in ways to reinforce these competencies and have a greater likelihood to develop more sophisticated communicative competencies as life progresses because of their social networks. These findings are congruent with Frith and Frith (2001), mentioned previously, who found that children in a richer linguistic environment have a greater chance of developing superior language abilities.

Cappella (1994) has written about the management of conversational interaction both in infancy and adulthood as a significant communicative competency. According to Cappella, the management of conversations involves at least two distinct processes. First, conversational management "implies that a person intentionally seeks to alter the content, tenor, or events of a conversation toward some preordained end" (Cappella, p. 380). The second sense of conversational management involves control over the more microscopic events such as gaze and gesturing during interaction. This coordination of numerous cognitive, verbal, nonverbal, and relational processes that must occur to successfully manage a conversation are presented as the essential characteristic of interpersonal interaction. Although Cappella does not frame his chapter within the lifespan developmental perspective, he implicitly suggests that the management of conversation is just as important for children as it is for adults and that the process of mutual influence may indeed be different for children when compared to adults. In other words, the competencies that are required to manage conversations are very much dependent upon cognitions, language skills, and environmental influences that change dramatically across the lifespan.

Children must also learn how to manage topic transitions in conversation (Drew & Holt, 1998). Children learn to use figures of speech in order to introduce a new topic, summarize a topic of conversation, make transitions to new topics, and terminate current topics. In this process, children demonstrate their understanding of conversation as a turn-taking system and that they understand the rules of conversation (Hawes, 1998). To be competent communicators, children must learn conversational mores, devices and properties, such as greetings, questions and answers, accounts, invitations to provide corrections, stories, paraphrasing, gossiping, visiting, politeness, and many other conversational skills (Hawes, 1998). However, just because children are the focus of these studies does not imply that older individuals can not and do not learn to improve on their own conversational skills throughout life.

One area of communicative competency skills that has received considerable attention in communication relates to cognitive complexity and perspective taking. Although these studies are not framed in a lifespan perspective, they are inherently developmental in nature. Cognitive complexity deals with the number and variety of constructs that an individual has in order to generate meaning about individuals, relationships, and situations. Individuals who are more cognitively complex have a greater number of constructs to draw upon, and their constructs are more abstract in nature than are the constructs of less cognitively complex individuals. Individuals who are more cognitively complex are better able to take into consideration the other person and adapt their messages to fit the situation. In a classic study, Clark and Delia (1977) demonstrated the developmental nature of cognitive complexity as children demonstrated increased abilities to adapt their messages to the receiver. They found that children in kindergarten and first grade made unelaborated requests; second through fifth graders made personal need arguments; sixth through ninth graders made need arguments, but had minimal counterarguments; and tenth to twelfth graders made benefit arguments, negotiated, made elaborated need arguments, and were able to make counterarguments. Older children were better able to take the perspective of the other and to adapt their messages to the individual listener, therefore exhibiting greater sophistication in their interactive strategies. The development of more sophisticated persuasive strategies has also been examined by O'Keefe (1988) who found that more cognitively complex individuals are more likely to use more sophisticated message design logics, that is, they generate messages that achieve the speaker's goals while attending to the needs of the listener as well.

Cognitively complex individuals also demonstrate greater communicative competence when using comforting messages (Burleson, 1994), in maintaining relationships (Burleson & Samter, 1994), and in organizational settings (Sypher & Zorn, 1986). In each of these settings, cognitively complex individuals are better able to adapt their messages to the needs of the listener and, therefore, are more effective at achieving both their own and the listener's goals. Although most studies on the development of cognitive complexity focus on children's development, none of these studies makes a convincing argument that cognitive complexity cannot be further developed in later years. As individuals have more experiences and opportunities to have their assumptions challenged, they may indeed become better able to take the perspective of the other, to become more cognitively complex, and, ultimately, to become more effective communicators.

An additional communicative competency that has received some attention from communication scholars is the management of interpersonal conflict across the lifespan (Bergstrom & Nussbaum, 1996; Pecchioni & Nussbaum, 2001; Sillars & Zietlow, 1993). It is reasoned, within these studies, that interpersonal conflict is to some extent defined by the various disagreements contextualized by lifespan circumstances. Dunn and Slomkowski (1992) specifically address how children develop greater social understanding through conflict episodes. Through these interactions, children learn the difference between self and other, that others have feelings and desires, social rules for interactions, social categories for others (e.g., friend vs. non-friend), and develop social strategies for managing the complexities of interaction with others. Studies by communication scholars with adult participants (Bergstrom & Nussbaum, 1996; Pecchioni & Nussbaum, 2001; Sillars & Zietlow, 1993) suggest that not only do older adults prefer solution-oriented, cooperative conflict styles when compared to the more confrontational styles of younger adults, but that participants within marital relationships or parent-child relationships do indeed modify their conflict strategies dependent upon the "maturity" of the relationship. These findings suggest that life experiences can influence and ultimately change how we manage our interpersonal conflicts.

In summary, communicative competence is inherently a developmental process. By learning as children, through our interactive environments, the rudiments of interaction (such as verbal and nonverbal skills and their coordination, turning taking and topic management), we learn to take the perspective of others and adapt our messages accordingly so that our own and our interactive partners' goals are achieved, especially in persuasive and conflict situations. Individuals who are more cognitively complex are more competent communicators, performing more effectively across a number of situational settings. These communicative skills continue to be developed, fine-tuned, and adapted to situations throughout the lifespan.

## RELATIONSHIP CHANGE ACROSS THE LIFESPAN

The great majority of research that has utilized the lifespan communication perspective has investigated the changing nature and functions of numerous family, friend, and professional relationships (see Noller, Feeny, & Peterson, 2001; Nussbaum & Coupland, 1995; Nussbaum et al., 2000; Williams & Nussbaum, 2001, for excellent literature reviews on numerous lifespan relationships). This research has emphasized the necessity to study relationship change across time to truly understand and describe our relational behavior. Although the study of relationships is by no means an undeveloped field of inquiry, and numerous theoretical advances have been outlined to help us better understand interpersonal relationships, nevertheless, the authors of this article maintain that a rich explanation of any ongoing relationship must be situated within the history of that relationship. Most relationship scholars ignore the lifespan perspective, even when they examine relational trajectories, turning points, and historical changes in relational definitions. Numerous family relationships, friendships, and professional relationships develop over the course of our lifespans. It is not unreasonable to expect that the very nature and function of these relationships change just as we change over time.

The parent-child relationship is an excellent example of developmental change from childhood (Haslett & Samter, 1997) through midlife (Putney & Bengtson, 2001) into old age (Cicirelli, 1981; Fingerman, 2001; Pecchioni & Nussbaum, 2001). Not only do we negotiate the level of closeness with our parents throughout our entire lifespan, but, more importantly, we develop through several critical power transformations that have significant impact upon our well being. It is universally accepted that good parenting is associated with adult control over just about every aspect of a child's life. This control, however, does not last past adolescence and is often reversed in late life (Williams & Nussbaum, 2001). Once a child reaches adulthood, parents perceive a shift in their responsibilities for the child, but still maintain a role as parent (Bleiszner & Mancini, 1987). Parent-child relationships often undergo a number of changes in relational dynamics as they undergo changes in their lives; for instance, when the child leaves the parents' home, when the child gets married or becomes a parent, and when the parents divorce, retire, or experience health crises (Kaufman & Uhlenberg, 1998). How family members manage these transition points depends, to some extent, on the history of their relationship. Because of these inherent developmental processes, the caretaker role of the parent develops from that of total care in all aspects of life to a stable provider of comfort to that of advice-giver in many parent-child relationships until the adult child becomes the primary caregiver for a fragile parent. The successful negotiation of these multiple changes in power across the lifespan is thought to be a fundamental factor in our ability to successfully adapt to the numerous difficulties each of us must cope with in life (Nussbaum et al., 2000).

The sibling relationship is another excellent example of developmental change across the lifespan (Cicirelli, 1980, 1983, 1991; Cicirelli & Nussbaum, 1989). The closeness trajectory of siblings is typically viewed as a progression from closeness in early life, distance in middle life, and back to closeness in later life. During childhood, siblings are likely to coreside for extended periods of time. Living in the same residence leads to a large number of shared experiences that continue to provide meaning to the relationship throughout their lives (Borland, 1989; Cicirelli, 1991). Sibling rivalry is highest during these periods of coresidence, but tends to subside greatly once they leave the parental home (Ross & Milgram, 1992). Siblings, while maintaining some level of constant contact, must raise their own families in mid-life and often live in distant communities. The intimacy fueled by physical attachment growing up in the same household fades as family priorities change from family of origin to family of procreation. Once the siblings enter middle and old age, they are often faced with the caregiving challenges of their parents, the death of a spouse, and fewer responsibilities within their own nuclear family. During middle and later life, siblings often reconnect with each other and strengthen their attachment bonds because they understand each other's lives, values, and attitudes. The sibling relationship is a remarkable case of enduring lifespan closeness, even though the very nature of the relationship changes quite dramatically.

Patterson, Bettini, and Nussbaum (1993) reasoned that the friend relationship should evidence dramatic change throughout the lifespan similar to the changes uncovered in numerous family relationships. Children define a friend as a play-mate and are relatively fickle about maintaining friendships (Dunn & Slomkowski, 1992). Someone with whom a child has recently had a fight is "no longer a friend," but this person may again fall into the friend category when the disagreement has been resolved or forgotten. Samter (1997) provides an excep-tional description of how children enact the friendship role and how our com-municative behavior accomplishes the friend relationship in childhood. It is interesting to note that Samter (1997) is quite clear that doing friendship is dependent upon the cognitive, language, and communicative developmental processes that are the hallmark of individual development across the lifespan. The nature and definition of friendship often changes in adolescence and contin-ues throughout adulthood as the topics of conversation change, the role of play is replaced with other shared activities, and individuals are able to maintain rela-tionships despite geographic separations (Rawlins, 1995; Wilmot & Shellen, 1990). Bleiszner and Adams (1992), Mathews (1986), and Rawlins (1982) have each written about the nature and critical importance of our friend relationships and friendship networks later in our lives. Nussbaum et al. (2000) go so far as to speculate that the friend relationship has not only been overlooked as an essen-tial component of our ability to successfully age, but may be just as important as family relationships we assume to be the key to our well-being in later life because they serve very different but important functions in our lives. As Rook (1995) has argued, during a crisis family can bring our emotional state back to a baseline level; friends, however, are the only ones who can bring us above that baseline level.

The study by Patterson et al. (1993) was based upon the notion that friendship scholars had not captured the developmental processes that work to change the definition of friendship as we age. Not only does friendship function differently throughout our lives, but the way we understand the nature of friendship changes throughout our lifespan. Results from the investigation asking younger and older adults to describe their understanding of friendship revealed that older adults had a much more complex and multidimensional "grasp" of the friend relationship. These cognitive perceptions of the more complex nature of friendship for older adults fit very nicely into the changing functions of friendship as we grow older. Young adults have difficulty establishing friendship as more than a "best friend" phenomenon. Older adults were able to distinguish their best friend with whom they grew up, from best friends with whom they had worked throughout most of their lives, from best friends with whom they now enjoy activities at the retire-ment villages. Each of these different sets of best friends were perceived to be close and to be important components of a rich and full life. Younger adults did not conceptualize different levels or different groupings of best friends. They only reported those friends with whom contact was ever present. Patterson et al. (1993) concluded that a more complex understanding for doing friendship develops over the lifespan to better serve our needs as we age. The very nature of friendship changes in functionally effective ways as we age.


## CAPTURING CHANGE IN LIFESPAN COMMUNICATION

The ability to design and to conduct an empirical investigation that captures communicative change across the lifespan is a rather complex task. The majority of lifespan research conducted by social scientists has tested interindividual change with the use of various cross-sectional, age-comparative designs. Individuals of differing ages are tested at one point in time and comparisons are made between the various age groups. In lifespan communication, studies have typically involved college students (young adults) compared to their parents (mid-life adults) compared to their grandparents (older adults). This simple design has produced numerous, impressive results that have "hinted" at capturing lifespan change. However, cross-sectional designs cannot assess change over time and are very limited in their ability to reveal causal influences in causal processes (Alwin & Campbell, 2001).

"There is a virtual consensus among quantitative social scientists that one of the most productive approaches to the study of aging and human development involves the collection and analysis of longitudinal data" (Alwin & Campbell, 2001, p. 22). Hofer (2001), among others, has been a very strong advocate for longitudinal designs, while attempting to convince social scientists interested in studying the process of developmental change not to utilize cross-sectional, age-comparative designs. The temptation to attribute true measurement of intraindividual change to the results of cross sectional investigations that measure only interindividual change is often too much to overcome.

Rudinger and Rietz (2001) have identified five rationales for the utility of longitudinal research within behavioral development. First, as has been noted above, a longitudinal design provides direct identification of intraindividual change. To our knowledge, no long-term longitudinal data investigating communication competence or relationship change across the lifespan has been published. Thus, no valid statement can be made at this point as to whether individual competencies actually change or precisely how they change across the lifespan. Second, a longitudinal design can identify interindividual variability in intraindividual change. Communication behavior within any one individual or relationship may not change in ways predicted by group parameters. Schaie and Hofer (2001) have pointed to numerous examples of interpretations of data based upon cross-sectional designs that are quite different than the data from longitudinal studies have indicated. For instance, cross-sectional data has always predicted a sharp decline in memory and in intelligence as we age past 70. These sharp declines are not found when studying the results of individual change patterns within longitudinal investigations.

Third, certain processes, such as most of the communication phenomena that we study, are quite complex and may require knowledge about many separate "variables" occurring simultaneously. Longitudinal designs allow for the discovery of structural changes across numerous variables. Fourth, the determinants of intraindividual change across the lifespan may not always be a simple, continuous process. Communication competencies or relationship redefinition may occur in spurts of development during certain critical points in our lifespan. Language skills emerge during childhood whereas the competencies to utilize these skills may emerge much slower at later points in the lifespan, if at all. Finally, the communicative behaviors being studied across the lifespan may be similar within an individual but may be attributable to combinations of causal sequences that are quite different. Different communication competencies can be achieved at the same time in the lifespan by very different means.

These five rationales for utilizing longitudinal designs help to answer the important theoretical issues of the lifespan perspective outlined at the start of this article. The typical statistical procedures utilized to test longitudinal hypotheses in the majority of the longitudinal studies now being conducted attend to mean differences (*t*-tests, [M]ANOVA, and various nonparametric procedures). Rudinger and Rietz (2001) present a very compelling case for social scientists interested in studying change within time-bound processes to consider linear structural equation modeling (SEM). The basic analysis of longitudinal data within SEM involves variances and covariances rather than mean structures. "Most of the conceptual problems associated with longitudinal aging research are solvable with SEM" (Rudinger & Rietz, 2001, p. 47). Numerous psychometricians and experts in research methodologies are advancing our understanding of SEM and soon should solve the rather complex statistical-mathematical issues that prevent SEM from being accepted more readily within the discipline of Communication (McArdle, 1998; McArdle & Nesselroade, 1994).

## EPILOGUE

The lifespan communication perspective emphasizes the study of change in communication phenomena. Whether a communication scholar is interested in the ability of individuals to process, store, and retrieve information, the development of verbal and nonverbal behavior, the ability to communicate competently with another human being in any context, or the nature and function of friend or family relationships, an understanding of change in each of these processes across the lifespan is thought to enhance our ability to describe, explain, and predict any specific communicative process.

The study of individual change across the lifespan has only been a focus of investigation for social scientists since the 1960s. Yet, the results produced by these investigators have created an enormously rich theoretical and methodological heritage. Communication scholars have recently adopted the lifespan perspective and are beginning to add in significant ways to the knowledge base of human behavior. Adopting the lifespan perspective has forced communication scholars to rethink numerous fundamental assumptions advanced in the theoretical foundations of our discipline. In addition, methodologies that capture change have had to be developed, learned, and executed.

Returning to the five assertions of the lifespan perspective outlined in the introduction of this article helps focus in on the types of knowledge about communicative behaviors and processes that still need attention. The first assertion states that humans do not experience inevitable decline during adulthood. Communication scholars need to examine communication skills and competencies across the lifespan and even ask whether the same set of skills and behaviors demonstrate competency at all stages of life. Whereas developmental psychologists have based too many of their theories of intelligence and cognition upon research findings using samples of children, communication researchers have used too many college-aged subjects to generate and test their theories of communication.

The second assertion states that the direction of change is pluralistic. Communication scholars need to examine the emergence of competencies across the lifespan. Because individuals respond differently to similar events, communication scholars need to examine the underlying mechanisms that lead to these differing assignments of meaning and the consequences of these differences. Because relational trajectories are not linear, that is, closeness does not develop steadily along a straight line, but rather in bursts of intensity through a series of events or exchanges, examining how and why relationship development changes across the lifespan would deepen our understanding of the role others play in our lives.

The third assertion states that individuals gain and lose abilities in a dynamic fashion. Abilities, once developed, may not be retained if not practiced. Communication scholars need to examine how individuals compensate for losses, while continuing to develop new or greater competency in other areas.

The fourth assertion points to the diversity of intra- and interindividual abilities. Communication scholars need to examine how and why an individual may exhibit varying ability within an interaction or across contexts and how these abilities change over time as the individual develops new competencies or deals with specific losses. In addition, what is defined as competent at one point in history may no longer be considered competent in the next generation, so these changes over historical time need to be examined as well.

The fifth assertion states that the individual and his or her environment mutually influence each other. Communication scholars need to examine how these entities mutually influence each other and whether and how an individual can "overcome" a "bad" environment.

Combining these five assertions points to the complexity of human interaction, but also allows us to focus our attention on critical aspects of life. By applying the lifespan perspective to communication phenomena, we can address a

variety of new, complex questions. We can examine the role of cognition and language development as well as their interrelationships as we age. Do we
"become" apprehensive about public speaking because we had a (or several)
negative experience(s)? Does a set of experiences reinforce a positive or negative view of our "self"? Do we become more or less competent in interactions as
we achieve success or experience failure in interaction? Do communication constructs that have been operationalized based on college student samples continue to be appropriate, effective, or accurate for other age groups? Are the meanings we assign to experiences the same or do they change throughout the lifespan? It was stated previously: It matters when, where, and with whom we are discussing a certain topic. Unpacking this statement raises several questions that
should be addressed in any lifespan study. Who are the participants? What characteristics (e.g., age, gender, personality traits, experiences, etc.) do they possess
that may impact on the nature of their interaction? Do the participants have a
prior history with one another and do they anticipate an ongoing one as well?
Does the topic at hand have relational importance for these interactions? For
example, is this an issue that has generated conflict or greater feelings of closeness in the past? Has the meaning of the topic changed for the interactants over
time? Where are they having this conversation (e.g., at home, in the car, at the
mall, at dinner or church, in their therapist's office)? What cultural and social
expectations (e.g., gender roles, roles of family members and friends) are they
operating under? What are their historical times? How does the historical time
effect all of the above? Although answering all of these questions may seem
daunting, acknowledging the importance of the wide range of factors that impact
on any given interaction will enable researchers to move our understanding of
human communication forward. By using sophisticated research designs and
data analysis, we are more likely to account for the complexity inherent in these
dynamic processes.

Applying the lifespan perspective to communication research endeavors
should not simply focus on answering a set of complex, yet specific questions,
but should also incorporate the perspective into our theoretical conceptualizations as well. The lifespan perspective does not specify any theory of social
behaviors as a "best" explanation of development. Rather, the lifespan perspective forces any particular theorist to contemplate the possibility of change and to
discuss how change might affect the postulates of that theory. Communication
theorists have become accustomed to giving some attention to active, dynamic
processes, but have not addressed how these dynamic processes experience fundamental change as the result of the passage of time. Communication scholars
need to identify the underlying mechanisms that drive change. The possibility
that communicative perceptions or behaviors may not be consistent across the
lifespan and that these changes may significantly alter the validity of certain theoretical assumptions is problematic for many current communication theories
which ignore these issues.

Once communication scholars have incorporated change into theory, these same researchers must learn how to recognize, test for, and interpret change. Longitudinal designs must begin to replace cross sectional designs. Sophisticated structural equation models will have to be developed to test for the nature of that change. The skills needed to master these complex techniques are not easily learned. Scholars will have to leave their comfort zone of "methodological space" to venture across campus and engage developmental methodologists as students once more.

K. Warner Schaie, a professor of human development and psychology at Pennsylvania State University, is a pioneer and excellent model of a scholar who has made a career out of the study of change when no such investigations existed. The Seattle Longitudinal Study (Schaie, 1996) began as a cross-sectional doctoral investigation of adult intelligence. After some initial work that included learning how to fund research by writing grants and fellowships, Schaie proposed and has conducted a longitudinal investigation of change in adult intelligence that has lasted for over 40 years. Every seven years data are collected and new information is learned about changes in intelligence.

Communication scholars must do what Schaie has done. We must invest our intellectual time and energy in multiyear, longitudinal designs. We must convince funding agencies that the study of lifespan change within communicative behavior is just as important as the study of intellectual change across the lifespan. Finally, we must convince ourselves that to fully understand communication phenomena, we must study the dynamic process of lifespan change.

## REFERENCES

Alwin, D. F., & Campbell, R. T., (2001). Quantitative approaches: Longitudinal methods in the study of human development and aging. In R.H. Binstock & L. K. George (Eds.), *Handbook of aging and the social sciences* (pp. 22–43). San Diego, CA: Academic Press.

Baltes, P. B. (1987). Theoretical propositions of life-span developmental psychology: On the dynamics between growth and decline. *Developmental Psychology, 23,* 611–626.

Baltes, P. B., Smith, J., & Studinger, U. M. (1992). Wisdom and successful aging. In T. B. Sonderegger (Ed.), *Nebraska symposium on motivation: Psychology and aging* (pp. 123–167). Lincoln: University of Nebraska Press.

Bergstrom, M. J., & Nussbaum, J. F., (1996). Cohort differences in interpersonal conflict: Implications for older patient-younger care provider interactions. *Health Communication, 8,* 233–248.

Bigner, J. J. (1994). *Individual and family development: A life-span interdisciplinary approach.* Englewood Cliffs, NJ: Prentice-Hall.

Blanchard-Fields, F., & Abeles, R. P. (1996). Social cognition and aging. In J. E. Birren & K. W. Schaie (Eds.), *Handbook of the psychology of aging* (4th ed., pp. 150–161). San Diego, CA: Academic Press.

Bleiszner, R. & Adams, R. G., (1992). *Adult friendship.* Newbury Park, CA: Sage.

Bleiszner, R., & Mancini, J. (1987). Enduring ties: Older adults' parental role and responsibilities. *Family Relations, 36,* 176–180.

Borland, D. C. (1989). The sibling relationship as a housing alternative to institutionalization in later life. In L. Ade-Ridder & D. B. Hennon (Eds.), *Lifestyles of the elderly: Diversity in relationships, health, and caregiving* (pp. 205–219). New York: Human Science Press.

Burleson, B. (1994). Comforting messages: Significance, approaches, and effects. In B. Burleson, T. Albrecht, & I. Sarason (Eds.), *Communication of social support* (pp. 3–28). Thousand Oaks, CA: Sage.

Burleson, B., & Samter. W. (1994). A social skills approach to relationship maintenance. In D. Canary & L. Stafford (Eds.), *Communication and relationship maintenance* (pp. 61–90). San Diego, CA: Academic Press.

Cappella, J. N. (1994). The management of conversational interaction in adults and infants. In M. L. Knapp & G.R. Miller (Eds.), *Handbook of interpersonal communication* (2nd ed., pp. 380–418). Thousand Oaks, CA: Sage.

Cicirelli, V. G. (1980). Sibling relationships in adulthood: A life span perspective. In L. W. Poon (Ed.), *Aging in the 1980's* (pp. 455–462). Washington, DC: American Psychological Association.

Cicirelli, V. G. (1981). *Helping elderly parents: The role of adult children.* Boston: Auburn House.

Cicirelli, V. G. (1983). Adult children's attachment and helping behavior to elderly parents. *Journal of Marriage and the Family, 45,* 815–823.

Cicirelli, V. G. (1991). Sibling relationships in adulthood. In S. K. Pfeifer & M. B. Sussman (Eds.), *Families: Intergenerational and generational connections, part two* (pp. 291–309). New York: Hayworth Press.

Cicirelli, V. G. (1992). *Family caregiving: Autonomous and paternalistic decision making.* Newbury Park, CA: Sage.

Cicirelli, V. G., & Nussbaum, J. F., (1989). Relationships with siblings in later life. In J. F. Nussbaum (Ed.), *Life-span communication: Normative processes* (pp. 283–297). Hillsdale, NJ: Erlbaum.

Clark, R. A., & Delia, J. (1977). Cognitive complexity, social perspective-taking, and functional persuasive skills in second-to-ninth-grade students. *Human Communication Research, 3,* 128–134.

Cohen, G. (1994). Age-related problems in the use of proper names in communication. In M. L. Hummert, J. M. Wiemann, & J. F. Nussbaum (Eds.), *Interpersonal communication in older adulthood: Interdisciplinary theory and research* (pp. 40–57). Thousand Oaks, CA: Sage.

Collopy, B. J. (1988). Autonomy in long term care: Some crucial distinctions. *Gerontologist, 28*(Supp.), 10–17.

Coupland, N., Coupland, J., & Giles, H., (1991). *Language, society and the elderly.* Oxford, UK: Basil Blackwell.

Drew, P., & Holt, E. (1998). Figures of speech: Figurative expressions and the management of topic transition in conversation. *Language in Society, 27,* 495–522.

Dunn, J., & Slomkowski, C. (1992). Conflict and the development of social understanding. In C. U. Shantz & W. W. Hartup (Eds.), *Conflict in child and adolescent development* (pp. 70–92). Cambridge, UK: Cambridge University Press.

Duran, R. L. (1989). Social communicative competence in adulthood. In J. F. Nussbaum (Ed.), *Life-span communication: Normative processes* (pp. 195–224). Hillsdale, NJ: Erlbaum.

Fingerman, K. (2001). *Aging mothers and their adult daughters: A case of mixed emotions.* New York: Springer.

Giles, H., & Williams, A. (1994). Patronizing the young: Forms and evaluation. *International Journal of Aging and Human Development, 39,* 33–53.

Hareven, T. K. (1978). Introduction: The historical study of the life course. In T. K. Hareven (Ed.), *Transitions: The family and the life course in historical perspective* (pp. 1–16). New York: Academic Press.

Haslett, B. B., & Samter, W. (Eds.). (1997). *Children communicating: The first 5 years.* Mahwah, NJ: Erlbaum.

Hawes, L. C. (1998). Becoming other-wise: Conversational performance and the politics of experience. *Text and Performance Quarterly, 18,* 273–299.

Hofer, S. (2001, September). *Longitudinal studies of aging: Past, present, and future.* Presentation to the Gerontology Center colloquium. University Park: Pennsylvania State University,

Howard, D. V. (1983). *Cognitive Psychology: Memory, language, and thought.* New York: Macmillan

Hummert, M. L. (1990). Multiple stereotypes of elderly and young adults: A comparison of structure and evaluations. *Psychology and Aging, 5,* 182–193.

Hummert, M. L. (1994a). Physiognomic cues to age and the activation of stereotypes of the elderly in interaction. *International Journal of Aging and Human Development, 39,* 5–20.

Hummert, M. L. (1994b). Stereotypes of the elderly and patronizing speech. In M. L. Hummert, J. M. Wiemann, & J. F. Nussbaum (Eds.), *Interpersonal communication in older adulthood: Interdisciplinary theory and research* (pp. 162–184). Thousand Oaks, CA: Sage.

Jacobs, S. (1994). Language and interpersonal communication. In M. L. Knapp & G.R. Miller (Eds.), *Handbook of interpersonal communication* (2nd ed., pp. 199–228). Thousand Oaks, CA; Sage.

Kaufman, G., & Uhlenberg, P. (1988). Effects of life course transitions on the quality of relationships between adult children and their parents. *Journal of Marriage and the Family, 60,* 924–938.

Kemper, S. (1992). Language and aging. In F. I. M. Craik & T. Salthouse (Eds.), *Handbook of aging and cognition* (pp. 213–270). Hillsdale, NJ: Erlbaum.

Knapp, M. L. (1978). *Social intercourse: From greetings to goodbye.* Boston: Allyn Bacon.

Knapp, M. L., & Miller, G.R. (Eds.). (1994). *Handbook of interpersonal communication* (2nd ed.). Thousand Oaks, CA: Sage.

Levy, B. (1996). Improving memory in old age through implicit self-stereotyping. *Journal of Personality and Social Psychology, 71,* 1092–1107.

Light. L. L. (1990). Interactions between memory and language in old age. In J. E. Birren & K. W. Schaie (Eds.), *Handbook of psychology and aging* (pp. 275-290). San Diego, CA: Academic Press.

Mathews, S.H. (1986). *Friendships through the life course: Oral biographies in old age.* Beverly Hills, CA: Sage.

McArdle, J. J. (1998). Modeling longitudinal data by latent growth curve methods. In G. A. Marcoulides (Ed.), *Modern methods for business research: Methodology for business and management* (pp. 359–406). Mawah, NJ: Erlbaum.

McArdle, J. J., & Nesselroade, J. R. (1994). Using multivariate data to structure developmental change. In S. H. Cohen & H. W. Reese (Eds.), *Life-span developmental psychology: Methodological contributions* (pp. 223–267). Hillsdale, NJ: Erlbaum.

Mosher, R. L., Youngman, D. J., & Day, J. M. (Eds.) (1999). *Human development across the life span: Educational and psychological applications.* Westport, CT: Praeger.

Noller, P., Feeney, J. A., & Peterson, C., (2001). *Personal relationships across the lifespan.* East Sussex, UK: Psychology Press.

Nussbaum, J. F. (Eds.). (1989). *Life-span communication: Normative processes.* Hillsdale, NJ: Erlbaum.

Nussbaum, J. F., & Coupland, J., (Eds.). (1995). *Handbook of communication and aging research.* Mahwah, NJ: Erlbaum.

Nussbaum, J. F., Pecchioni, L. L., Robinson, J. D., & Thompson, T. L. (2000). *Communication and aging* (2nd ed.). Mahwah, NJ: Erlbaum.

Nussbaum, J. F., Hummert, M. L., Williams, A., & Harwood, J. (1996). Communication and older adults. In B. Burleson (Ed.), *Communication yearbook 19* (pp. 1–48). Thousand Oaks, CA: Sage.

O'Keefe, B. (1988). The logic of message design: Individual differences in reasoning about communication. *Communication Monographs, 55,* 80–103.

Parks, M. R. (1994). Communication competence and interpersonal control. In M. L. Knapp & G. R. Miller (Eds.), *Handbook of interpersonal communication* (2nd ed., pp. 589–618). Thousand Oaks, CA: Sage.

Patterson, B. R., Bettini, L., & Nussbaum, J. F., (1993). The meaning of friendship across the lifespan: Two studies. *Communication Quarterly, 41,* 145–160.

Pecchioni, L. L., & Nussbaum, J. F. (2000). The influence of autonomy and paternalism on communicative behaviors in mother-daughter relationships prior to dependency. *Health Communication,* *12,* 317–388.

Pecchioni, L. L., & Nussbaum, J. F. (2001). Mother-adult daughter discussions of caregiving prior to dependency: Exploring conflicts among European-American women. *Journal of Family Communication, 1,* 133–150.

Piaget, J. (1954). *The construction of reality in the child.* New York: Basic Books.

Piaget, J. (1959). *The language and thought of the child.* New York: Free Press.

Piaget, J. (1972). *The psychology of intelligence.* Totowa, NJ: Littlefield-Adams.

Putney, N. M., & Bengtson, V. L., (2001). Families, intergenerational relationships, and kinkeeping in midlife. In M. E. Lachman (Ed.), *Handbook of midlife development* (pp. 528–570). New York: Wiley.

Rawlins, W. K. (1995). Friendships in later life. In J. F. Nussbaum & J. Coupland (Eds.), *Handbook of communication and aging research* (pp. 227–257). Mahwah, NJ: Erlbaum.

Rawlins, W. K. (1982). *Friendship matters: Communication, dialectics, and the life course.* New York: de Gruyter.

Rook, K. S. (1995). Support, companionship, and control in older adults' social networks: Implications for well-being. In J. F. Nussbaum & J. Coupland (Eds.), *Handbook of communication and aging research* (pp. 437–463). Mahwah, NJ: Erlbaum.

Ross, H. G., & Milgram, J. I. (1992). Important variables in adult sibling relationships: A qualitative study. In M. E. Lamb & B. Sutton-Smith (Eds.), *Sibling relationships: Their nature and significance across the lifespan* (pp. 225–249). Hillsdale, NJ: Erlbaum.

Rudinger, G., & Rietz, C., (2001). Structural equation modeling in longitudinal research. In J. E. Birren & K. W. Schaie (Eds.), *Handbook of the psychology of aging* (pp. 29–52). San Diego, CA: Academic Press.

Ryan, E. B. (1991). Normal aging and language. In R. Lubinski (Ed.), *Dementia and communication: Clinical and research issues* (pp. 84–97). Toronto, Canada: B. C. Decker.

Samter, W. (1997). Doing friendship. In B.B. Haslett & W. Samter (Eds.), *Children communication: The first five years* (pp. 208–235). Mahwah, NJ: Erlbaum.

Schaie, K. W. (1996). Intellectual development in adulthood. In J. E. Birren & K. W. Schaie (Eds.), *Handbook of the psychology of aging* (4th ed., pp. 266–286). San Diego, CA: Academic Press.

Schaie, K. W., & Hofer, S. M., (2001). Longitudinal studies in aging research. In J. E. Birren & K. W. Schaie (Eds.), *Handbook of the psychology of aging* (pp. 53–77). San Diego, CA: Academic Press.

Schaie, K. W., & Hofer, S.M. (2001). Longitudinal studies in aging research. In J. E. Birren & K. W. Schaie, (Eds.), *Handbook of the psychology of aging* (pp. 53–77). San Diego, CA: Academic Press.

Schaie, W. K. (2001, September). *Longitudinal studies and the early predictions of risk for dementia.* Presentation to the Gerontology Center colloquium. University Park: Pennsylvania State University.

Schwebel, J., Maher, C. A., & Fagley, N. S. (Eds.). (1990). *Promoting cognitive growth over the life span.* Hillsdale, NJ: Erlbaum.

Sillars, A. L., & Zietlow, P. H. (1993). Investigations of marital communication and lifespan development. In N. Coupland & J. F. Nussbaum (Eds.), *Discourse and lifespan identity.* Newbury Park, CA: Sage.

Smith, A. D. (1996). Memory. In J. E. Birren & K. W. Schaie (Eds.), *Handbook of the psychology of aging* (4th ed., pp. 236–250). San Diego, CA: Academic Press.

Smith, J., & Baltes, P. B. (1990). A life-span perspective on thinking and problem-solving. In M. Scwebel, C. A. Maher, & N. S. Fagley (Eds.), *Promoting cognitive growth over the life span* (pp. 47–69). Hillsdale, NJ: Erlbaum.

Smith, R. M. (Ed.). (1990). *Learning to learn across the lifespan.* San Francisco: Jossey-Bass.

Spitzberg, B. H., & Cupach, W. R., (1984). *Interpersonal communication competence.* Beverly Hills,

CA: Sage.

Stevenson, M. R. (Ed.) (1994). *Gender roles through the life span: A multidisciplinary perspective.* Muncie, IN: Ball State University.

Stohl, C. (1989). Children's social network and the development of communicative competence. In J. F. Nussbaum (Ed.), *Life-span communication: Normative processes* (pp. 53–78). Hillsdale, NJ: Erlbaum.

Sypher, B. D., & Zorn, T. (1986). Communication-related abilities and upward mobility: A longitudinal investigation. *Human Communication Research, 12,* 420–431.

Williams, A., & Nussbaum, J. F. (2001). *Intergenerational communication across the life span.* Mahwah, NJ: Erlbaum.

Willis, S. L. (1996). Everyday problem solving. In J. E. Birren & K. W. Schaie (Eds.), *Handbook of the psychology of aging* (4th ed., pp. 286–307). San Diego, CA: Academic Press.

Wilmot, W. W., & Shellen, W. N. (1990). Language in friendships. In H. Giles & W. P. Robinson (Eds.), *Handbook of language and social psychology* (pp. 413–431). Chicester, UK: Wiley.

# AUTHOR INDEX

## A

Aamio, P., 337, 338, *359*
Abel, E., 243, 244, 245, 246, 247, *259*
Abeles, R. P., 372, *385*
Abenstein, J. P., 342, *361*
Abercrombie, N., 302, *321*
Abraham, R., 204, 205, 208, 212, 214, 216, 219, *226*
Abrams, M. L., 135, *153*
Abramson, J. B., 143, *153*
Abzug, R., 252, *259*
Acker, L. E., 92, 104, 105, *106*
Acker, M. A., 104, 105, *106*
Adams, D. B., 172, *192*
Adams, L. N., 341, *361*
Adams, M., 346, 349, *363*
Adams, R. G., 379, 380, *385*
Adams, W., 185, *191*
Adelman, R. D., 330, *361*
Adkins, L., 178, *191*
Adler, P., 312, *321*
Adorno, T. W., 128, *153, 155*
Afifi, W. A., 80, 82, 104, *106*
Airaksinen, T., 236, *259*
Albarran, A. B., 134, *153*
Alberts, J. K., 105, *107*
Albrecht, T. L., 79, 93, *106, 108*
Aleman, C. G., 7, *35*
Alexander, A., 142, 151, *154, 157*
Alexander, H. E., 183, *191*
Alexander, M., 337, *360*
Alho, A., 337, 338, *359*
Allen, A. 338, *359*
Allen, M., *108*
Alpers, A., 331, *359*
Altheide, D. L., 173, *191*
Althusser, L., 169, *191*
Alwin, D. F., 381, *385*
Alwitt, L. F., 147, *153*
Amenta, E., 165, *199*
Amrhein, P. C., 16, *32*
Andersen, J. F., 102, *107*
Andersen, P. A., 71, 77, 78, 79, 80, 81, 83, 88, 89, 90, 102, 104, 105, 107, *111*
Anderson, A., 234, *259*
Anderson, C. M., 72, *107*
Anderson, D. R., 138, 147, *153*

Anderson, J. A., 129, 136, *153*
Anderson, K. R., 349, *360*
Anderson. R., 75, 108, 310, *321*
Andrews, G., 72, 73, 77, 96, *111*
Andrusiak, P., 6, *35*
Ang, I., 137, 151, *153*
Angell, M., 333, *359*
Angleitner, A., 92, *114*
Antos, S., 14, *35*
Applegate, J. L., 37, 40, 41, *67*
Arnold, R. D., 162, *191*
Arrington, A., 38, *67*
Arrington, C., Jr., 177, 180, *191*
Asai, M., 27, *35*
Asante, M., 305, *321*
Ashforth, B. E., 212, *226*
Ashley, A., 27, *33*
Aspden, P., 349, 351, 352, 354, 355, 357, *359*
Atkin, D. J., 134, *153*
Aupperle, K. E., 248, *259*
Austin, J. L., 15, *32*

## B

Bachrach, P., 169, 171, 186, *191*
Baker, L. W., 232, *259*
Baker, R., 300, *321*
Bakken, L., 84, *107*
Balch, D., *363*
Balin, J. A., 23, *34*
Ball-Rokeach, S. J., 133, *153*
Baltes, P. B., 368, 370, 372, *385, 388*
Bambas, A., 337, 340, 341, *359*
Baratz, M. S., 169, 171, 186, *191*
Barbato, C. A., 73, 74, 77, 78, 81, 83, 84, 97, 107, *113*
Barber, B., 233, 238, *259*
Barber, B. K., 72, 73, 84, 104, 106, *109*
Bargmann, C. I., 91, *108*
Barker, S. F., 232, *259*
Barnard, K., 328, 356, *361*
Barnes, B., 186, *191*
Barnes, J. H., 258, *265*
Barnes, M., 85, *108*
Barnes, M. K., 79, *107*
Barney, R., 254, 256, *259*
Baron, R. A., 215, 218, *227*
Barondess, J. A., 331, *359*

Barr, D. J., 23, *34*
Bartlett, R., 180, *191*
Bashshur, R. L., 341, *359*
Bates, J. E., 91, 92, *109*
Bauer, R., 165, 185, *191*
Baumgartner, F. R., 162, 164, 166, 167, 180, 182, 183, 184, 185, *192*, *196*
Baumrind, D., 40, 41, 63, *67*
Bavelas, J. B., 7, *32*
Baxter, B. L., 239, *259*
Baxter, L. A., 47, 67, 94, *113*
Bayles, M. D., 232, 233, 234, *259*
Bayon, C., 72, 73, *116*
Beard, C. A., 164, *192*
Beatty, M. J., 91, *107*
Beckman, C., 212, *228*
Beckman, H. G., 334, *359*
Beisecker, A. E., 329, *359*
Bell, D., 175, *192*
Bell, N., 21, *32*
Bell, R. A., 73, 89, 105, *107*
Bell, W., 341, *361*
Bellah, R. N., 55, *67*
Bemis, A. E., 349, 351, 352, 354, 355, 357, *359*
Benford, R. D., 170, 174, 175, 185, *192*
Bengtson, V. L., 72, 92, 112, 113, 379, *388*
Bennett, W. L., 170, 173, *192*, 283, *294*
Bensing, J. M., 328, *359*
Bentley, A. F., 164, *192*
Berelson, B., 131, 132, *153*, *156*, 273, *294*
Berger, B. K., 179, 180, 182, 183, 184, 191, *192*
Berger, P., 37, *67*
Bergeron, D., 340, *361*
Bergstrom, M. J., 377, 378, *385*
Berkowitz, D., 171, 172, *192*
Berkowitz, L., 120, 147, *155*
Bernays, E. L., 239, 243, *259*
Berry, J., 313, *321*
Berry, J. M., 164, 165, 166, 167, 179, 182, 184, 185, *192*
Bertakis, K. D., 330, *359*
Best, P., 87, *109*
Bettini, L., 380, *387*
Bigner, J. J., 367, *385*
Billig, M., 301, 307, *321*
Biocca, F. A., 130, 147, *153*
Birnbaum, J. H., 185, *192*
Bissland, J. H., 232, 239, 241, 257, *259*
Bivins, T. H., 232, 234, 236, 239, 241, 257, *259*
Black, A., 7, *32*
Black, J., 254, 256, *259*
Blackmore, S., 271, *294*
Blair, J. D., 252, *264*
Blair, P. D., 337, 340, 341, *359*
Blanchard-Fields, F., 372, *385*
Bleiszner, R., 379, 380, *385*
Bliss, T. J., 178, *192*

Bloomer, S. E., 337, 338, 340, *362*
Blum, J., 349, *359*
Blumer, H., 127, *153*
Blumler, J., 120, 132, *155*
Blumler, J. G., 132, *153*
Bly, B., 23, *34*
Blyskal, J., 173, 178, 186, *192*
Blyskal, M., 173, 178, 186, *192*
Boatright, J. R., 251, *259*
Bock, D. G., 82, *112*
Boer, F., 99, 104, 105, 106, *107*
Bonito, J. A., 338, 341, 342, *359*, *364*
Bontempo, R., 27, *35*
Bookin, H., 14, 15, *33*
Booth-Butterfield, M., 76, 79, 107, *109*
Bordon, S. L., 250, 258, *260*
Borland, D. C., 379, *386*
Bornman, E., 315, 316, *322*
Borowitz, S. M., 342, 343, 348, *359*
Bosk, C. L., 169, 171, 173, *196*
Bostdorff, D. M., 244, 252, 253, *260*
Botkin, D., 85, 93, 97, 104, 105, 106, 107, *114*
Bottery, M., 241, *260*
Boulger, J., 340, *361*
Bourhis, R., 313, *321*
Bovet, S. R., 234, 239, *260*
Bowen, S. A., 254, 254, 255, *260*
Bowen, W. G., 248, *260*
Bowers, J. W., 78, *111*
Bowlby, J., 93, *107*
Boynton, L. A., 235, 242, 244, 247, *260*
Braam, G. P. A., 186, *192*
Bradac, J., 314, *322*
Bradford, L., 315, *323*
Bradley, M. M., 138, *156*
Brady, H. E., 167, *200*
Brandt, A. M., 342, 343, 346, 348, 349, *362*
Breed, W., 250, *260*
Brennan, S. E., 32, *32*
Brenner, D. J., *197*
Brenner, S. N., 185, *192*
Bresnahan, M., *34*
Brewer, W., 16, *35*
Brick, J. E., 341, *359*
Brick, J. F., 341, *359*
Brody, R. A., 281, *296*
Broom, G. H., 237, 238, 239, 240, 251, *260*
Broome, B., 315, *321*
Brosius, H., 172, *192*
Brousseau, P. L., 258, *260*
Brown, L. B., 77, 96, *112*
Brown, P., 4, 6, 20, 25, 26, *32*
Brown, R., 7, 22, 23, *32*
Browne, N., 125, *153*
Browne, W. P., 166, *192*
Bruess, C. J. S., 78, *107*
Bryant, J., 120, 133, *153*

Buchholz, R. A., 177, 178, 179, 180, 181, 182, 185, 186, *192, 198*
Budd, J. F., Jr., 235, 258, *260*
Buerkel-Rothfuss, N. L., 105, *107*
Buhrmester, D., 72, 75, 78, 104, 105, 106, *112*
Buller, D. B., 77, 82, 83, *108*
Buller, D. K., 102, *107*
Bumpus, M. A., 248, *261*
Burgoon, J. K., 71, 74, 76, 77, 82, 83, 90, 95, 102, 104, 107, 108, 109, 338, 341, 342, *359, 364*
Burke, W. A., *363*
Burleson, B., 377, *386*
Burleson, B. R., 79, 93, 106, *108*
Burns, J., 138, *153*
Burton, D. C., 338, *361*
Buss, D. M., 85, 91, *108*
Bynum, A. B., 340, *364*

**C**

Cacciari, C., 14, *32*
Cacioppo, J. T., 141, *157*
Cai, D., 7, 26, *34*
Cain, M., 352, *363*
Callahan, E. J., 337, 338, *359*
Calver, H. N., 238, *260*
Cameron, G. T., 173, *193*, 233, 237, *264*
Campbell, B., 331, 333, 341, *364*
Campbell, R. T., 381, *385*
Campbell, T. L., 334, *360*
Campion, E. W., 349, *360*
Canadian Medical Association, 349, 355, *360*
Canary, D. J., 73, 78, 98, 102, *108*
Canas, F., 72, 73, *116*
Cancian, F. M., 85, *108*
Cantril, H., 130, *153*
Cappella, J. N., 271, *294*, 376, *386*
Carbaugh, D., 315, *321*
Carey, J., 137, *153*
Carey, J. L., 235, *260*
Carey, J. W., 144, *153*
Cargile, A., 314, 318, *322*
Carroll, A. P., 248, *259*
Cary, M. A., 327, 328, 329, 335, 339, 355, 356, *360*
Caryl, C. J., 335, 339, 340, *360*
Casmir, F., 312, *321*
Castiglia, P. T., 72, 75, 84, 89, 92, 94, *108*
Cater, D., 165, 180, *193*
Cavalier, G. M., 354, *360*
Cecil, D. W., 332, *360*
Cegala, D. J., 328, *362*
Center, A. H., 231, 237, 238, 239, 251, *260*
Chadwick, R. F., 236, *260*
Chaffee, S. H., 37, 42, 44, 52, 61, 68, 125, *154*

Chamoto, S., 277, *294*
Charles, B. L., 335, *360*
Charon, R., 330, *361*
Charters, W. W., 126, 127, *154*
Chase, W. H., 177, 180, 181, 182, *193, 196*
Chen, L., 222, 228
Cheney, G., 185, *193*, 244, 247, 249, 250, 251, 253, *260*
Chew, P. H., 350, *360*
Choi, S., 26, *34*
Chomsky, N., 170, *196*
Chovil, N., 7, *32*
Christensen, A., 38, 51, *67*
Christians, C., 247, *260*
Cicirelli, V. G., 369, 379, 379, *386*
Ciesla, J. R., 248, *261*
Cigler, A. J., 166, 167, 182, 183, 184, *193*
Cissna, K. N., 75, *108*
Clark, C. L., 47, *67*
Clark, H. H., 3, 7, 13, 19, 20, 22, 23, *32*
Clark, J. R., 342, 344, 345, 346, 347, *363*
Clark, R. A., 377, *386*
Clawson, D., 180, 183, 184, 185, *193*
Clayton, W., 338, *361*
Cobb, R. W., 162, 169, 171, 172, 173, 174, 175, 177, 180, 181, 184, 186, *193, 198*
Cobley, P., 125, 137, *154*
Coe, B. J., 178, *193*
Cohen, B. C., 171, *193*
Cohen, G., 373, *386*
Cohen, J., 58, 59, *67*
Cohen, P., 58, 59, *67*
Cohen-Cole, S. A., 334, *360*
Coleman, L. M., 79, *108*
Collier, M., 315, 316, 320, *322*
Collins, A. M., 140, *154*
Collins, B., 338, 338, 357, *360*
Collopy, B. J., 369, *386*
Commission on Public Relations Education, 237, *260*
Compton, M. V., 72, 83, *108*
Condit, C. M., 253, *260*
Condit, D. M., 253, *260*
Condor, S., 301, 307, *321*
Connell, S., 234, *264*
Connine, C. M., 14, *35*
Conway, M. M., 183, 184, 185, *193*
Cook, E. T., 213, 214, *226*
Cooper, M. R., 179, 180, 181, 182, 185, 186, *197*
Cooper, M. W., 235, *260*
Corbett, R., 337, 338, 340, *362*
Corman, S. R., 105, *107*
Costanza, R., 84, *108*
Coupland, J., 373, 378, *386, 387*
Coupland, N., 373, *386*
Cousino, K. R., 177, *195*
Cowles, M. G., 186, *193*

Cox, E. O., 73, *112*
Crable, R. E., 176, 177, 184, *193*
Crain, E. C., 215, 227
Crawford, K. G., 182, *193*
Crouse, B., 340, *361*
Csikszentmihalyi, M., 139, 142, 147, *156*
Culnan, M. J., 338, *360*
Cummings, E. M., 92, 93, *108*
Cunningham, J. L., 97, 99, 104, 105, 106, *114*
Cupach, W., 315, *322*
Cupach, W. R., 374, *388*
Curran, J., 124, 137, *154*
Curtin, P. A., 173, *193*
Cutlip, S. M., 173, *193*, 237, 238, 239, 251, *260*
Cvancara, K. E., 47, 48, 63, *68*
Cyert, R. M., 240, *261*

**D**

Dahl, D., 16, *35*
Dahl, R. A., 164, *193*
Dahms, L., 104, 105, 106, *114*
Dainton, M., 72, 73, 98, 102, *108*
Dale, E., 127, *154*
D'Alessandri, R. M., 341, *359*
Daley, H. A., 339, 340, *360*
D'Amaro, R., 345, *360*
Daniel, J., 315, *322*
Danielian, L., 171, *193*
Darkins, A. W., 327, 328, 329, 335, 339, 355, 356, *360*
Dascal, M., 3, *32*
David, A. K., 330, *360*
Davies, M., 204, 205, 208, 213, 214, 218, 227
Davis, D., 29, *32*
Davis, D. K., 284, *295*
Davis, J. T., 205, 219, 229
Davis, S., 169, 175, *193*
Davis, S. H., 340, *360*
Dawkins, R., 271, *295*
Day, D. V., 215, 227
Day, J. M., 367, *387*
de Bono, M., 91, *108*
de Sola Pool, I., 165, 185, *191*
Dearing, J. W., 145, *154*, 171, 172, *193*, *198*
Decker, F. K., 232, 235, *261*
Deetz, S., 358, *360*
DeFleur, M. L., 126, 133, *153*, *154*, 237, *263*
Degnin, F. D., 333, *360*
DeGregorio, C., 184, *193*
Dejoie, R. M., 241, *264*
Delaney, P., 72, 73, *112*
Delia, J., 377, *386*
Delia, J. G., 37, 40, 41, 67, 209, 214, 227
Deluga, R. J., 215, 227
Demaris, O., 166, 185, *193*
Deming, W. E., 250, *261*

Dempsey, G. R., 145, *157*
Denise, T. C., 255, *261*
Dennis, E. E., 126, *154*
DePaulo, B. M., 79, *108*
Derber, C., 166, 177, 184, 185, 186, *193*
Derlega, V. J., 76, 78, 84, *108*
Derrida, J., 135, *154*
Derse, A. R., 333, *363*
DeVito, J. A., 104, 105, 106, *108*
Dexter, L., 165, 185, *191*
DiCioccio, R. L., 89, *115*
Dickie, R. B., 185, 186, *193*
Diesing, P., 301, *322*
Diggs, R. C., 23, *35*
Dilenscheider, R. L., 241, *261*
Dillman, L., 95, *110*
Dindia, K., *108*
Dinerman, H., 132, *156*
Dionisopoulos, G. N., 184, *194*
DiPaolo, M., 214, 218, 228
Dolin, D. J., 79, *109*
Domhoff, G. W., 166, 167, 179, 180, 184, 185, *194*
Donaldson, J., 234, 244, *261*
Dopkins, S., 16, *32*
Douglas, W., 178, 184, *196*
Dowdy, S., 84, 104, *110*
Downs, V. C., 72, 73, 83, *109*
Dozier, D. M., 240, *260*, *261*
Drazen, J. M., 349, *360*
Drechsel, R. E., 246, *261*
Drew, P., 376, *386*
Drozd, B., 27, *33*
Dubler, N. N., 328, 330, 333, *360*
Duck, S., 79, *107*
Dudley, R. A., 330, *360*
Dudley, T. E., 355, *360*
Duffy, E. A., 248, *260*
Duhe, S. F., 173, *194*
Dull, V. T., 334, *362*
Dunbar, N., 338, *364*
Dunbar, N. E., 338, 341, 342, *359*
Dunn, D. G., 134, *157*
Dunn, J., 377, 380, *386*
Duran, R. L., 374, *386*
Dutton, J. E., 177, 180, *194*, 218, 220, 227
Dye, T. R., 166, 179, *194*

**E**

Eberly, M. B., 71, 83, 84, *109*
Eberly, M. D., 71, 99, *111*
Eco, U., 125, *154*
Edelman, M., 170, 184, 185, *194*
Edwards, D., 301, 307, *321*
Eedy, D. J., 337, 338, 340, *362*
Einsiedel, E., 284, 285, *296*
Eismeier, T. J., 179, 183, 184, *194*

Ekman, P., 214, 227
Elder, C. D., 162, 169, 171, 172, 173, 174, 175,
     177, 180, 181, 184, 186, 193
Ellemers, N., 314, 324
Ellul, J., 170, 175, 194
Elmendorf, F. M., 180, 194
Elwood, T. D., 53, 67
Emanuel, E. J., 328, 330, 331, 332, 333, 360
Emanuel, L. L., 331, 332, 360
Emmers-Sommer, T. M., 78, 108
Entman, R. M., 170, 173, 174, 175, 194
Epstein, E. M., 164, 194
Epstein, R. M., 334, 360
Erikson, E., 314, 322
Ervin-Tripp, S., 21, 32
Esrock, S. L., 251, 261
Estrada, G., 145, 156
Etzioni, A., 232, 261, 321, 322
Evans, D. M., 183, 184, 185, 194
Evans, P. B., 65, 194
Ewen, S., 243, 244, 261
Ewing, R. P., 176, 177, 178, 180, 181, 185, 194

F

Fagley, N. S., 367, 388
Falvo, D. R., 355, 360
Faulkner, S., 78, 108
Feeney, J. A., 378, 387
Fenno, R. F., 183, 194
Fenton, M., 237, 261
Ferguson, D. A., 134, 154
Ferguson, T., 345, 347, 348, 349, 350, 360
Ferris, G. R., 215, 229
Fiebig, G. V., 209, 210, 227
Fiedler, F. E., 206, 227
Fineman, H., 143, 154
Fineman, S., 204, 205, 216, 217, 219, 221,
     222, 224, 227
Fingerman, K., 379, 386
Fischer, J., 338, 341, 342, 359
Fish, S., 137, 154
Fisher, S. G., 74, 79, 109
Fiske, A. P., 73, 109
Fiske, J., 137, 149, 154
Fiske, S. T., 141, 154
Fitch, K., 315, 322
Fitch, K. L., 25, 32
Fitzpatrick, K., 234, 235, 236, 239, 241, 251,
     255, 258, 265
Fitzpatrick, K. R., 257, 261
Fitzpatrick, M. A., 37, 38, 42, 43, 44, 45, 46,
     47, 48, 50, 51, 52, 53, 56, 57, 58,
     60, 61, 63, 64, 65, 67, 68, 78, 87,
     104, 105, 106, 109, 112
Flaherty, L. M., 82, 109
Flam, H., 206, 227

Flores, L., 316, 322
Floyd, K., 71, 72, 75, 76, 77, 78, 83, 84, 85, 88,
     89, 95, 97, 105, 106, 109, 111, 112
Foa, E., 87, 114
Foa, E. B., 75, 80, 81, 87, 88, 89, 95, 97, 100,
     101, 111
Foa, U., 87, 114
Foa, U. G., 75, 80, 81, 87, 88, 89, 95, 97, 100,
     101, 111
Forbes, P. S., 239, 261
Fotiou, A., 174, 175, 200
Foucault, M., 124, 154
Fowler, L. L., 183, 194
Fox, J., 99, 104, 105, 106, 114
Fox, K. F., 178, 194
Franco, B., 72, 73, 116
Frandsen, K. D., 82, 113
Frankel, R. M., 334, 359, 362
Franken, E. A., 340, 364
Frederick, H. H., 275, 295
Frelick, L., 78, 114
Frendreis, J. P., 166, 194
Fried, B. M., 354, 360
Friedman, 166, 171, 181, 197
Friedman, M., 248, 261
Friedmann, E., 330, 361
Friedson, E., 239, 261
Friesen, W. V., 214, 227
Fromkin, D., 124, 154
Frost, P. J., 218, 220, 227
Fry, D., 151, 154
Fry, D. H., 151, 154
Fulford, K. W. M., 236, 261
Funkhouser, G. R., 145, 154, 282, 295
Furio, B. J., 77, 113
Furnham, A., 211, 228
Fussell, S. R., 22, 23, 34

G

Gailiun, M., 338, 362
Gaines, S. O., Jr., 72, 73, 75, 81, 83, 85, 87, 88,
     90, 97, 101, 109, 110
Galambos, L., 167, 194
Gallant, L. M., 222, 228
Gallois, C., 314, 324
Gallois, S., 314, 318, 322
Gandy, O. H., Jr., 171, 172, 178, 181, 182, 184,
     185, 195
Gane, M., 301, 307, 321
Gans, H., 145, 154
Gans, H. J., 172, 173, 195
Gantz, W., 283, 295
Garbrah-Aidoo, E. R., 171, 195
Gardiner, J. C., 328, 364
Gardner, H., 207, 227
Garner, W. E., 340, 364

Gaudet, H., 131, *156*
Gaunt, P., 181, *195*
Gaylin, W., 91, 93, *110*
Geddes, K., 210, 221, *228*
Geher, G., 204, 206, 214, *228*
Geiger, S., 140, *154*
Gelber, H., 337, *360*
Gelfand, M. J., 26, *34*
Gerbner, G., 129, *154*
Gerbner, G. L., 129, *154*
Gergen, D. R., 248, *261*
Gernsbacher, M. A.,
Gerrig, R. J., 32, *32*
Gerstenzang, M. L., 84, 96, 100, *110*
Getz, K. A., 163, 182, *195*
Ghanem, S., 145, *154*
Gibbs, R. W., 14, 19, 20, *32*
Gibbs, R. W., Jr., 3, 4, 12, *32*
Giddens, A., 124, *155*, 256, *261*
Gildea, P., 14, 15, *32, 33*
Gilder, G., 143, *155*
Giles, H., 314, 318, *322, 324*, 372, 373, *386*
Gilman, A., 7, *32*
Gilsdorf, J. W., 238, *261*
Ginsburg, G. P., 22, *35*
Gitlin, T., 129, *155*, 169, 172, *195*, 291, *295*
Glaser, K., 258, *262*
Glazer, N., 313, *322*
Glenn, R. B., 105, *112*
Glover, S. H., 248, *261*
Glucksberg, S., 4, 12, 14, 15, *32, 33*
Godbold, L. C., 126, *157*
Godwin, R. K., 171, 184, *195*
Goffman, E., 4, 6, 27, *33*
Gold, M., 334, *361*
Goldman, E. F., 243, *261*
Goldsmith, D., 79, 93, *106*
Goldsmith, D. J., 79, *108*
Goldsmith, H. H., 16, *32*
Goldsmith, J., 350, 351, 351, 352, 353, 354, *361*
Goldstein, R., 147, *158*
Goleman, D., 203, 204, 205, 209, 210, 214,
    217, 221, 226, *227*
Goold, S. D., 333, *361*
Gordon, A. D., 247, *261*
Gordon, M., 303, *322*
Gordon, M. T., 285, 291, *296*
Gore, H. E., 337, 338, 340, *362*
Gore, K. E., 105, *107*
Gorham, J. S., 77, *113*
Gotten, S. R., 351, 354, 357, *361*
Gottman, J. M., 221, *227*
Gough, H. G., 95, *110*
Graell, M., 72, 73, *116*
Graesser, A. C., 6, 16, *33*
Graff, G., 301, 306, *322*
Gramsci, A., 291, *295*

Grant, A. E., 343, *363*
Gray, J. A., 91, *110*
Gray, P., 309, *322*
Grayer, A. R., 28, *34*
Greeley, A., 313, *322*
Green, V. A., 72, *110*
Greenberg, B. S., 283, *295*
Greenberg, M. T., 213, 214, *226*
Greenberger, M., 340, *361*
Greene, M. G., 330, *361*
Greenfield, S., 341, *361*
Greening, D. W., 178, 181, *195*
Greenwald, M. K., 138, *156*
Grefe, E. A., 166, 180, 181, 182, 184, 185,
    186, *195*
Grenzke, J. M., 184, *195*
Grice, H. P., 3, 4, 5, 13, 14, 18, 22, 25, 27, 29, *33*
Grigsby, R. K., 341, *361*
Gross, G., 243, 245, 250, *261*
Gross, L., 129, *154*
Grove, A. S., 347, *361*
Gruenfeld, D. H., 28, *33*
Grunig, J. E., *195*, 234, 240, 241, 242, 251,
    252, 254, 257, *261*
Grunig, L. A., 240, *261*
Grunwald, H., 303, *322*
Gudmundson, J. L., 333, *363*
Gudykunst, W., 26, *33*
Guerrero, L. K., 71, 79, 80, 81, 88, 89, 102,
    104, 105, *107*
Gunn, G. W., Jr., 81, *110*
Gurevitch, M., 120, 124, 132, *154, 155*
Gustke, S., *363*

## H

Habermas, J., 128, *155*, 255, *261*
Hacker, A., 305, *322*
Hagel, R. C., 248, *261*
Hagen, M. D., 342, 344, 345, 346, 347, *363*
Hailey, D., 338, 340, 358, *363*
Hainsworth, B. E., 177, *195*
Hainsworth, R. E., 177, 181, *195*
Hale, J. L., 74, 102, *108*
Hall, E., 312, *322*
Hall, E. T., 90, *110*
Hall, J. A., 341, *363*
Hall, R. L., 183, 184, *195*
Hall, S., 136, *155*, 169, 170, 171, *195*
Halldorson, M., 6, *35*
Hallin, D. C., 170, 171, 175, *195*
Hamada, T., 223, *227*
Hamm, A. O., 138, *156*
Hammersley, M., 301, 316, *322*
Han, A., 16, *35*
Hannon, D. W., 338, 340, *362*
Hansen no kain giin wo keigo, 268, *295*

Hara, K., 26, *33*
Harden, J., 258, *262*
Hareven, T. K., 367, *386*
Harlos, K. P., 221, *227*
Harris, F. R., 166, 180, 182, 185, 186, *195*
Harris, N. G. E., 233, 234, 236, 254, *262*
Harrison, R., 338, *361*
Harrison, S., 84, *108*
Harrison, S. L., 237, *262*
Harrison-Speake, K., 104, *110*
Harwood, J., 371, 373, *387*
Haslam, N., 87, 100, *110*
Haslett, B. B., 370, 371, 373, 375, 379, *386*
Hastie, R., 6, *33*
Hatfield, J. D., 248, *259*
Hawes, L. C., 376, *386*
Hayes, J., 338, *359*
Hayry, H., 234, *262*
Hayry, M., 234, *262*
Healey, J. G., 73, 89, 105, *107*
Hearn, J., 221, *227*
Heath, R., 178, 184, *196*
Heath, R. L., 177, 178, 181, 184, *195*, *196*, 243,
        244, 248, 249, 250, 251, 252, *262*
Hecht, M., 315, *322*
Hecht, M. L., 71, 87, 104, 105, 106, *111*
Heclo, H., 165, *196*
Hedge, R., 316, *322*
Heffner, J. A., 250, *262*
Hegarty, W. H., 248, *262*
Heilbrun, A. B., Jr., 95, *110*
Heinz, J. P., 181, *196*
Heisel, A. D., 91, *107*
Hellmann, D. C., 269, *295*
Henderson, A. S., 72, 73, 77, 96, *111*
Herbst, S., 172, *196*
Herman, D. C., 342, *361*
Herman, E., 170, 171, *196*
Herman, E. S., 170, *196*
Herrenkohl, R. C., 250, *262*
Herring, P., 164, 167, 182, 185, *196*
Hertog, J. K., 169, 174, *196*, *197*
Hesse, M. B., 237, *262*
Heyman, S., 26, *33*
Hibbard, J. H., 353, *361*
Higgins, E. T., 53, *68*
Hilgartner, S., 169, 171, 173, *196*
Hill, A., 269, 283, *296*
Hill, M., 258, *262*
Hilty, D. M., 337, 338, *359*
Himes, D. P., 249, *262*
Hirsch, J., 147, *158*
Hirsch, P. M., 129, *157*
Hochheimer, J. L., 125, *154*
Hochschild, A. R., 209, 210, 211, 212, 215,
        216, 221, *227*
Hofer, S., 381, *386*

Hofer, S. M., 371, 373, 381, *388*
Hoggart, R., 136, *155*
Hojnacki, M., 166, 181, 182, *196*
Holand, U., 338, *363*
Holland, J., 84, 96, 100, *110*
Hollender, M. H., 84, 104, *110*
Holt, E., 376, *386*
Holtan, A., 337, *361*
Holtgraves, T., 29, *32*
Holtgraves, T. M., 4, 7, 9, 10, 11, 12, 13, 18,
        19, 20, 21, 22, 24, 25, 26, 27, 28,
        29, 30, *33*, *34*
Holtz, W. E., 352, *361*
Hong, Y., 126, *157*
Horkheimer, M., 128, *155*
Horton, D., 120, *155*
Horton, W. S., 23, *34*
Hovarth, A., *34*
Howard, D. V., 371, *387*
Howard, N., 220, *227*
Hughes, E. C., 233, *262*
Hula, K. W., 166, 181, 185, *196*
Hummert, M. L., 371, 372, 373, *387*
Humphrey, R. H., 212, *226*
Hunt, M. A., 166, 182, 184, 186, *199*
Hunt, T., 257, *261*, *262*
Hunter, J. E., *34*
Huston, J. L., 338, *361*
Huston, T. L., 74, 75, *110*
Hyson, M. C., 92, 104, *110*

I

Iggers, J., 236, 244, *262*
Ikei, M., 277, *295*
Imahori, T., 315, *322*
Inman, C. C., 105, 106, *115*
Inn, A., 311, *324*
Innis, H., 143, *155*
International Association of Business Com-
        municators, 238, *262*
Inui, T., 331, 332, 333, 337, 345, *363*
Inui, T. S., 328, 356, *361*
Isen, A. M., 215, 218, *227*
Ishida, O., 277, *295*
Ito, Y., 285, 291, *295*
Iyengar, S., 145, *155*
Iyer, P., 304, *322*

J

Jablin, F. M., 209, 210, *228*
Jackson, J., 232, 233, 236, 238, *262*
Jackson, P., 231, 235, 237, 238, 239, *260*, *262*
Jackson, S. E., 177, *194*
Jacobs, D. C. D., 166, 180, 181, *196*
Jacobs, S., 374, *387*

Jacobson, N. S., 221, 227
Jacobvitz, R. S., 142, 157
Jacoby, T., 306, 322
Jaggar, A. M., 219, 220, 227
Janis, I. L., 126, 156
Javidi, M., 72, 73, 83, 109
Jay, M., 128, 155
Jeffres, L. W., 134, 153
Jenkins, J. M., 72, 73, 75, 79, 81, 90, 91, 92, 93, 112, 205, 207, 214, 228
Jensen, A. D., 102, 107
Jerry, D., 72, 83, 90, 112
Jewett, J. J., 353, 361
Jieikan no honne, 280, 295
Jo, E., 120, 147, 155
Johnson, D., 72, 83, 90, 112
Johnson, G. L., 349, 353, 355, 361
Johnson, M. L., 80, 82, 104, 106
Johnson, O. V., 232, 265
Johnson, P., 314, 322
Jones, B. D., 171, 180, 181, 183, 184, 185, 190, 192, 196
Jones, B. E., 363
Jones, B. L., 177, 180, 181, 196
Jones, E., 314, 318, 322
Jones, S. E., 80, 104, 110
Jones, W., Jr., 184, 196
Jorgensen, P. F., 102, 107
Jucker, A. H., 11, 34
Judd, L. R., 241, 243, 251, 252, 262
Judson, G. T., 250, 262
Jurgensen, J. H., 234, 235, 262

K

Kahneman, D., 141, 158
Kakegawa, T., 277, 295
Kam, K., 338, 341, 342, 359
Kane, B., 343, 344, 345, 347, 348, 361
Kane, J., 340, 361
Kankoku no nihon bunka kaiho, 270, 295
Kanto, W. P., 341, 361
Kaplan, S. H., 341, 361
Karp, W. B., 341, 361
Kash, J. B., 340, 364
Kashima, Y., 26, 34, 310, 325
Kasser, S. J., 180, 196
Kassirer, J. P., 329, 345, 346, 348, 349, 350, 352, 353, 354, 361, 363
Katz, E., 120, 128, 132, 146, 150, 155, 156
Katz, J. E., 348, 349, 351, 352, 354, 355, 357, 359, 361
Kaufman, G., 379, 387
Keenan, E. O., 25, 34
Keiser, K. R., 184, 196
Kellar-Guenther, Y., 105, 107

Kelleher, K., 72, 104, 105, 110
Kellerman, J., 110
Kellner, D., 129, 136, 155
Kemper, S., 373, 387
Kendall, P. L., 131, 155
Kepplinger, H., 172, 192
Kerestes, G., 71, 92, 110
Kerlinger, F. N., 60, 61, 62, 68
Keysar, B., 14, 15, 23, 32, 34
Kienzle, M. G., 340, 364
Kim, C., 16, 32
Kim, K. S., 26, 33
Kim, M. S., 7, 23, 26, 33, 34, 35
Kim, U., 26, 34
Kim, Y., 302, 310, 311, 313, 315, 318, 323
Kim, Y. Y., 311, 318, 322, 323
Kimball, D., 182, 196
Kimboko, P. J., 73, 112
Kingdon, J. W., 172, 176, 184, 185, 186, 196
Kirkman, B. L., 250, 262
Kitayama, S., 209, 227
Kittross, J. M., 247, 261
Klapper, J. T., 120, 124, 155
Klein, J. P., 333, 363
Knapp, M. L., 73, 75, 77, 78, 79, 86, 95, 105, 106, 110, 367, 370, 387
Knoke, D., 165, 182, 185, 196, 197
Knopoff, K., 212, 228
Koblinsky, S. A., 93, 110
Kochman, T., 315, 323
Koerner, A. F., 46, 47, 48, 50, 51, 52, 53, 57, 59, 63, 68, 126, 157
Koester, J., 90, 111
Kohane, I. S., 342, 343, 346, 348, 349, 362
Kohler, W., 140, 155
Kolata, G., 349, 353, 361
Kolko, G., 166, 196
Korenbrot, T. Y., 330, 360
Korten, D. C., 166, 184, 185, 186, 196
Kosicki, G. M., 171, 176, 196, 198
Kotulski, D., 85, 97, 110
Kourany, R. K., 84, 104, 110
Kowalski, R., 23, 34
Koyano, W., 72, 110
Kramer, M. W., 209, 210, 227
Krauss, R. M., 22, 23, 34
Krcmar, M., 47, 65, 68
Kreuz, R. J., 6, 35
Krippendorff, K., 150, 155
Krizek, R., 315, 323
Krone, K. J., 209, 210, 215, 222, 223, 227, 228, 229
Kruckeberg, D., 235, 241, 258, 262
Krugman, H., 138, 139, 155
Kruml, S. M., 210, 221, 228
Krupat, E., 328, 356, 361

Kubey, R., 139, 142, 144, 147, 148, 150, *155, 156, 157*
Kultgen, O., 233, 234, 239, *262*
Kunda, G., 217, 222, 223, *229*
Kurogi, A., 315, *325*
Kurtz, S., 328, *362*
Kusche, C. A., 213, 214, *226*
Kuszler, P. C., 335, 336, 339, 340, *361*
Kuterovac-Jagodic, G., 71, 92, *110*
Kuubaku Hinan no Ketsugi, 268, *295*
Kyoryoku hoan no genten wo miushinauna, 281, *296*
Kyudan subeki bunka hakai, 293, *296*

L

Labacqz, K., 233, 236, 237, *262*
Laczniak, G. R., 236, 254, 255, *262*
LaFrance, M., 76, *112*
Laing, V. B., *363*
Laird, J. D., *110*
Lakoff, R., 11, *34*
Lalljee, M., 22, *35*
Lamb, R., 22, *35*
Lambert, B. L., 328, *362*
Lamminen, H., 337, 338, *359*
Lampert, M., 21, *32*
Landau, R., 92, 104, *110*
Landro, L., 355, *362*
Lang, G. E., 284, *296*
Lang, K., 284, *296*
Lang, P. J., 138, *156*
Langer, E., 141, 142, *156*
LaPuma, J., 333, 352, *362*
Larimer, L. V, 258, *262*
Lariscy, R. A. W., 233, 237, *264*
Lasorsa, D. L., 145, *156*
Lasswell, H. D., 126, *156*
Latham, E., 164, *197*
Laumann, E. O., 165, 181, 185, *196*
Lazarsfeld, P. F., 128, 131, 132, *155, 156*
Lazarus, R. S., 209, *228*
Lea, M., 336, *362*
Lear, J. C., 6, *35*
Leatham, G. B., 7, *35*
LeDoux, J. E., 91, *110*
Lee, B. W., 235, *263*
Lee, J., 209, 210, *228*
Lee, W., 126, *157*
Leech, B. L., 162, 164, 166, 167, 180, 182, 183, *192*
Lefcoe, D., 72, 78, *114*
Leiber, L., 84, 96, 100, *110*
Leichty, G., 240, *263*
Leichty, G. B., 251, *261*
Leigh, R. D., 245, 246, 247, *263*
Lemert, J. B., 172, *196, 197*

Lemieux, R., 105, 106, *110*
Lepisto, J., 337, 338, *359*
Lesly, P., 239, *263*
Lester, K. J., 354, *360*
L'Etang, J., 235, 241, 242, 243, 244, 247, 248, 249, 251, 252, 253, 254, 255, 257, 258, *263, 264*
Leutwiler, T. J., 47, 65, *68*
Levin, S. T., 147, *153*
Levine, A., 300, *323*
Levinson, S., 4, 6, 20, 25, 26, *32*
Levinson, S. C., 15, 24, *34*
Levinson, W., 334, *362*
Levitan, S. A., 179, 180, 181, 182, 185, 186, *197*
Levy, B., 372, *387*
Levy, C. S., 242, *263*
Levy, M. R., 130, 133, *156*
Levy, S. J., 125, *156*
Lewis, J., 110, 137, *156*, 306, *323*
Lewis, R. J., 84, *108*
Liden, R. C., 215, *229*
Liebes, T., 146, *156*
Liederman, G., 72, 75, 85, 100, 102, *111*
Light, L. L., 373, *387*
Lind, M., 310, *323*
Lindenberg, S., 72, 75, 77, 95, *112*
Link, T. G., 206, *227*
Linsky, M., 166, 180, 181, 185, 186, *195, 197*
Lipkin, M., 333, *361*
Lipkin, M., Jr., 331, 332, 333, 337, 345, *363*
Lippmann, W., 126, *156*
Lipsitz, N. E., 242, *265*
Livingstone, S. M., 152, *156*
Lloyd, S., 250, *263*
Loane, M. A., 337, 338, 340, *362*
Loevinger, L., 241, *263*
Logan, J. E., 248, *261*
Long, J. D., 335, 340, *362*
Long, N. E., 291, *296*
Loomis, B. A., 166, 167, 182, 183, 184, *193*
Lopez, F. G., 93, 94, *111*
Lorch, E. P., 147, *153*
Loury, G., 303, *323*
Lowenthal, L., *156*
Lowery, S. A., 237, *263*
Lowes, R. L., 349, 351, 353, 355, 357, *362*
Lowi, T. J., 165, 181, *197*
Lucca, N., 27, *35*
Luckmann, T., 37, *67*
Luft, H. S., 330, *360*
Lukaszewski, J. E., 234, 235, *262*
Lull, J., 137, *156*
Lumsdaine, A. A., 126, *156*
Lusterman, S., 177, *197*
Lustig, M. W., 90, *111*
Lyles, J. S., 328, *364*
Lyotard, J., 135, *156*

# M

MacDonald, K., 72, 73, 79, 81, 90, 91, 93, 106, 111
Mackinnon, A., 72, 73, 77, 96, 111
Macrosson, W. D. K., 74, 79, 109
Madsen, R., 55, 67
Maduschke, K., 328, 364
Maesaka, T., 278, 296
Magleby, D. B., 183, 197
Magnusson, P., 249, 263
Maher, C. A., 367, 388
Mahoney, F. X., 250, 263
Mainous, A. G., 342, 344, 345, 346, 347, 363
Mair, F., 338, 364
Majone, G., 171, 185, 186, 197
Makoul, G., 331, 332, 362
Malbin, M. J., 184, 197
Mancini, J., 385
Mandl, K. D., 342, 343, 346, 348, 349, 362
Manke, M. L., 71, 111
Manne, H. G., 248, 263
March, J. G., 240, 261
Marcuse, H., 128, 156
Margulis, S. T., 76, 78, 108
Markakis, K. M., 334, 359
Marken, J., 340, 361
Markus, M. L., 336, 360
Marshall, L. J., 47, 65, 68
Marshall-Dorsey, A. A., 328, 364
Marston, J., 236, 237, 239, 263
Marston, P. J., 71, 87, 104, 105, 106, 111
Martin, J., 212, 228, 315, 320, 323
Martin, M. M., 71, 72, 73, 75, 81, 82, 83, 84, 107, 113
Martin, S., 341, 362
Martinez-Pons, M., 205, 219, 228
Martinson, D. L., 243, 244, 263
Marton, J., 92, 104, 105, 106
Maslow, A. H., 75, 111
Masuda, M., 310, 323
Mathes, R., 273, 296
Mathews, C., 337, 338, 340, 362
Mathews, S. H., 380, 387
Mathias-Riegel, B., 72, 73, 111
Matsumoto, G., 310, 323
Matsumoto, Y., 26, 33
Mayer, J. D., 204, 205, 206, 207, 208, 214, 215, 216, 218, 228
Mayo, C., 76, 112
McBride, G., 255, 263
McCabe, M. P., 83, 85, 111
McCain, T., 338, 362
McCammond, D. B., 235, 263
McCarthy, D., 335, 339, 340, 362
McCaughan, W. T., 336, 337, 338, 364
McCauley, T., 311, 323

McCombs, M., 145, 156, 157, 171, 198, 284, 285, 296
McCombs, M. E., 145, 157, 172, 197
McConnell, G., 164, 165, 197
McConnell, M. E., 338, 340, 362
McCroskey, J. C., 91, 107
McCubbin, H. I., 50, 68
McDaniel, E., 90, 111
McDaniel, S., 71, 111
McDonald, D., 147, 158
McDonald, M., 258, 263
McDowell, B., 232, 263
McElrath, D., 72, 78, 114
McFarland, A. S., 164, 165, 197
McGuire, W. J., 124, 138, 157
McHale, S. M., 99, 104, 105, 106, 107
McIlwraith, R. D., 142, 157
McKoon, G., 16, 34
McLaughlin, T., 248, 249, 263
McLeod, D. M., 169, 174, 196, 197
McLeod, J. M., 37, 42, 44, 52, 61, 68
McLuhan, M., 143, 157
McQuaid, K., 177, 180, 182, 183, 184, 185, 197
McQuail, D., 126, 157
McWhinney, I. R., 334, 360
Mead, G. H., 22, 23, 35
Mechanic, D., 328, 330, 331, 333, 334, 341, 350, 354, 356, 358, 362
MeElreath, M. P., 254, 257, 258, 263
Megalli, M., 166, 171, 181, 197
Megwa, E. R., 197
Mehrabian, A., 102, 111, 114, 204, 205, 219, 228
Mekhjian, H., 338, 362
Menduno, M., 342, 362
Meng, M., 177, 195
Meredith, G., 310, 323
Merton, R., 131, 156
Messerschmidt, J. W., 220, 228
Mettler, J., 328, 364
Metts, S., 76, 78, 108, 111
Meyer, P., 234, 236, 244, 247, 263
Meyrowitz, J., 144, 157
Middleton, D., 301, 307, 321
Milbrath, L., 165, 182, 184, 197
Milgram, J. I., 379, 388
Miliband, R., 165, 197
Mill, D., 71, 72, 99, 111
Mill, J. S., 245, 255, 263
Millar, F., 74, 77, 78, 111
Miller, E. A., 335, 341, 351, 354, 358, 362
Miller, G. R., 76, 111, 370, 387
Miller, R. H., 330, 360
Millerson, G., 233, 241, 263
Mills, C. W., 124, 157, 164, 169, 175, 180, 197
Milton, J., 245, 263
Mitchell, N. J., 165, 166, 185, 186, 197
Mittman, R., 352, 363

Miyahara, A., *34*
Mizruchi, M. S., 166, *197*
Moise, L., 313, *321*
Molotch, H. L., 285, 287, 291, *296*
Monroe, A. D., 281, 282, *296*
Monsour, M., 104, 105, 106, *111*
Montemayor, R., 71, 83, 84, 99, *111*
Moore, D. G., 177, 178, 179, 180, 186, *197*
Moore, M., 339, *363*
Morgan, J. M., 222, 223, *228*
Morgan, M., 129, *154, 157*
Morgan, N., 311, *323*
Morley, D., 136, *157*
Morman, M. T., 71, 72, 75, 76, 88, 89, 97, 109, *111*
Morris, E. K., 93, 104, *111*
Morris, W., 75, *111*
Morrison, C., 178, 183, *197*
Morton, L. P., 173, *198*
Mosher, R. L., 367, *387*
Moskowitz, G. B., 16, *35*
Moss, E. K., 232, *263*
Mottet, T. P., 102, 103, *111*
Mount, E., Jr., 241, *263*
Moya, R., 346, 349, 352, *363*
Moynihan, D., 313, *322*
Mucciaroni, G., 165, 171, 181, 185, 186, *198*
Mukerji, C., 129, *157*
Mulac, A., 314, *322*
Mulholland, T., 139, 147, *157*
Mullet, J., 7, *32*
Mullooly, J. P., 334, *362*
Mumby, D., 358, *363*
Mumby, D. K., 212, 217, 220, *228*
Munsterberg, H., 130, 146, 147, *157*
Murphy, P. E., 236, 254, 255, *262*
Murphy, R., *363*
Murstein, B. I., 72, 83, 85, *111*
Myers, J. L., 16, *32*

N

Nadin, M., 124, *157*
Nages, N. R., 237, *263*
Nagy, K., 340, *363*
Nakayama, T., 315, 320, *323*
Namazi, K., 311, *323*
Narvaez, M., 72, 83, 90, *112*
Nass, C., 138, *158*
Negroponte, N., 143, *157*
Neill, R. A., 342, 344, 345, 346, 347, *363*
Nelson, B., 313, *324*
Nelson, B. J., 183, *198*
Nelson, C. J., 183, *197*
Nelson, R., 232, 233, 253, *263, 264*
Nelson, R. A., 177, *196*
Nelson, R. L., 181, *196*

Nesbitt, T. S., 337, 338, *359*
Neuendorf, K. A., 134, *153*
Neuman, W. R., 143, *157*
Neustadtl, A., 180, 183, 184, 185, *193*
Newcomb, H., 129, *157*
Newhagen, J., 140, *154*
Newman, L. N., 184, *198*
Niemeyer, J. A., 72, 83, *108*
Nimmo, D. D., 162, *198*
Nishida, T., 26, *33*
Nix, T. W., 252, *264*
Noelle-Neumann, E., 129, *157*, 269, 271, 273, *296*
Noller, P., 38, 40, 41, 68, 78, 104, 105, 106, *111, 112, 378, 387*
Nordquist, V. M., 72, 75, 76, 77, 93, 94, 104, 105, 106, *114*
Novak, M., 312, *324*
Nunns, S., 249, *264*
Nussbaum, J. F., 367, 369, 370, 371, 373, 374, 377, 378, 379, 380, *385, 386, 387, 388, 389*
Nwachukwu, S. L., 258, *265*
Nygren, T. I., 248, *260*

O

Oatley, K., 72, 73, 75, 79, 81, 90, 91, 92, 93, 112, 205, 207, 214, *228*
Oberman, W. D., 182, *198*
O'Connell, B., 249, *264*
Ohaeri, J. O., 32, *32*
Ohinmaa, A., 336, 340, 358, *363*
O'Keefe, B., 377, *387*
O'Keefe, B. J., 209, 214, *227*
O'Keefe, D. J., 209, 214, *227*
Olasky, M., 235, *264*
Olcott, W., 249, *264*
Oliver, J. M., 72, 73, *112*
Oliver, R. L., 73, 95, 104, 105, 106, *112*
Ollenburger, J., 181, *195*
Olson, A. T., 233, *264*
Olson, M., 164, *198*
Orbe, M., 316, *324*
Ormel, J., 72, 75, 77, 95, *112*
Ortony, A., 14, *35*
Orvell, B., 329, 353, *363*
Osborn, G. G., 328, *364*
Ota, H., 314, 318, *322*
O'Toole, J. E., 178, *198*
Ottensmeyer, E., 177, 180, *194*
Owen, W. F., 84, *112*

P

Paek, T., 23, *34*
Page, B. B., 233, *264*

Page, B. I., 145, *157*, 172, *198*, 281, *296*
Page, J., 310, *324*
Pal, B., 355, *363*
Paletz, D., 283, *294*
Paletz, D. L., 283, *296*
Palmer, M. T., 104, 105, *114*
Palmeter, J. G., 93, *110*
Palmgreen, P., 132, *157*
Paluszek, J., 237, 239, *264*
Pan, Z., 176, *198*
Paradice, D. B., 241, *264*
Parenti, M., 313, *324*
Parker, G., 77, 96, 112, 250, *265*
Parks, M. R., 78, 84, 109, 112, 374, 375, *387*
Parrott, T. M., 72, 92, 112, *113*
Parsons, P. H., 234, 240, *264*
Parsons, R. J., 73, *112*
Parsons, T., 169, *198*
Patterson, B. R., 380, *387*
Patterson, J. M., 50, *68*
Patterson, M. L., 77, 83, *112*
Patton, D., 101, *112*
Pearce, D., 104, 105, 106, *114*
Pearce, K. J., 82, *109*
Pearce, W. B., 22, 23, *35*, 78, 85, *112*
Pearson, D., 104, 105, *106*
Pearson, J. C., 78, *107*
Pearson, R., 240, *264*
Pecchioni, L. L., 369, 370, 377, 378, 379, 380, *387, 388*
Pedersen, S., 338, *363*
Penaloza, L. J., 126, *157*
Pennbridge, J., 346, 349, 352, *363*
Perloff, R. M., 283, 285, *296*
Perreault, S., 313, *321*
Perry, J. T., 215, *227*
Perse, E. M., 73, 74, 77, 78, 81, 83, 84, 97, 107, 113, 134, 151, *154*, *157*
Peterfreund, S. P., 255, *261*
Peterson, C., 378, *387*
Peterson, R. A., 134, *157*
Peterson, T., 243, 244, 245, 246, 247, 250, *264*
Petracca, M. P., 167, 182, 184, 185, *198*
Petrides, K. V., 211, *228*
Petronio, S., 76, 78, 108, 314, *324*
Petty, R. E., 141, *157*
Pfau, M., 126, *157*
Pfetsch, B., 273, *296*
Phillips, C. M., *363*
Phillips, N., 97, *117*
Piaget, J., 368, 387, 388
Pieczka, M., 241, 242, *264*
Pierce, J., 222, 223, *228*
Pinder, C. C., 221, *227*
Piper, A., 141, 142, *156*
Pires, M. A., 181, *198*
Piziak, V. K., 352, *364*

Plotke, D., 177, 181, 185, *198*
Plumb, M. M., 84, 96, 100, *110*
Podell, R. N., 355, *360*
Pokrywczynski, J., 178, *199*
Pollock, P. H., 179, 183, 184, *194*
Polsby, N. W., 181, *198*
Poole, I., 143, *157*
Porter, W. M., 253, *264*
Post, J. E., 177, *198*
Postiglione, G., 303, 310, *324*
Postman, N., 143, *158*
Potterfield, T. A., 250, *264*
Poulantzas, N., 165, *198*
Powell, J. L., 82, *112*
Powers, R., 309, *324*
Powers, W. G., 105, *112*
Prager, K. J., 72, 75, 77, 78, 104, 105, 106, *112*
Pratt, C. B., 234, 236, 237, 238, *264*
Pratt, J., 167, *194*
Pratt, S., 315, *324, 325*
Prescott, J. W., 72, 73, 96, 98, *114*
Preston, L. E., 177, *198*
Price, R. B., 329, 353, *363*
Pritchard, D., 172, *198*
Protess, D. L., 171, *198*, 285, 291, *296*
Prudhoe, C. M., 92, 104, *110*
Public Relations Society of America, 238, *264*
Puffer, J. C., 339, *361*
Pursley-Crotteau, S., 341, *361*
Putnam, L. L., 212, 217, 220, *228*
Putnam, S. M., 328, 330, 331, 332, 333, 337, 345, 356, *359, 361, 363*
Putney, N. M., 379, *388*

**Q**

Quillian, M. R., 140, *154*
Quinn, W. H., 72, 73, *112*

**R**

Rabinow, P., 135, *158*
Radke-Yarrow, M., 92, 93, *108*
Radley, A., 301, 307, *321*
Radway, J., 120, 137, *158*
Rafaeli, A., 212, 216, 225, *228, 229*
Raftery, M., 72, 73, *112*
Ramaprasad, A., 349, 353, 355, *361*
Ramirez, A., Jr., 336, 341, 342, *359, 364*
Ranney, M., 241, *264*
Ratcliff, R., 16, *34*
Rawlins, W. K., 380, *388*
Rayburn, J. D., II, 132, *157*
Reamer, F. G., 242, *264*
Red Lion Broadcasting, 244, *264*
Reddon, J. R., 78, 101, 112, *114*
Reeb, A., 72, 73, *112*

Reeck, D., 232, 233, *264*
Reed, B. S., 234, *264*
Reeder, H., 71, *111*
Reeder, H. M., 83, *112*
Reese, S. D., 145, *156*, 174, 176, *198*, 232, *265*
Reeves, B., 138, 147, *158*
Reeves, P. M., 350, 354, *363*
Regan, P. C., 72, 83, 90, *112*
Reid, L. N., 178, *199*
Reis, H. T., 78, *112*
Reiss, D., 37, *68*
Renfro, W. L., 177, 181, *198*
Renner, J., 355, *360*
Rentner, T. L., 232, 239, 241, 257, *259*
Reynolds, J. T., 329, 353, *363*
Reynolds, R., 14, *35*
Ribeau, S., 315, *322*
Rice, R. E., 343, 348, *361*, *363*
Richmond, V. P., 77, 102, 103, 111, *113*
Rietz, C., 381, 382, *388*
Riker, W. H., 171, 181, 185, 186, *198*
Ritchie, D. L., 42, *68*
Ritchie, L. D., 37, 38, 42, 43, 44, 45, 46, 52, 56, 57, 58, 60, 61, 64, *68*
Robers, T., 104, 105, 106, *111*
Roberts, M., 146, *158*
Roberts, R. D., 204, 205, 208, 213, 214, 218, 227
Roberts, R. E. L., 73, 92, *113*
Roberts, R. M., 6, *35*
Robertson, R. R., 16, *32*
Robey, D., 336, *363*
Robinson, J. D., 369, 370, 378, 379, 380, *387*
Rochefort, D. A., 181, *198*
Rockefeller, R. G., 329, 353, *363*
Rodrigues, L., 346, 349, 352, *363*
Rogers, C. R., 75, *113*
Rogers, E. M., 145, *154*, 171, 172, *193*, *198*
Rogers-Millar, L. E., 74, 77, 78, *111*
Roine, R., 336, 340, 358, *363*
Rojecki, A., 175, *194*
Roloff, M. E., 95, *113*
Roman, R. J., 16, *35*
Romano-White, D., 71, 72, 99, *111*
Romig, C., 84, *107*
Rommetviet, R., 22, 23, *35*
Rook, K. S., 369, 380, *388*
Root, M., 309, *324*
Rorty, R., 302, 306, *324*
Rosaldo, M. Z., 25, *35*
Rosen, B., 250, *262*
Rosenfeld, L. B., 82, *113*
Rosengren, K. E., 132, *158*
Rosenkranz, S. L., 328, 356, *361*
Rosenthal, R., 143, *158*
Ross, H. G., 379, *388*
Rossides, D., 303, *324*
Roter, D., 328, 330, 331, 332, 341, *359*, *363*

Roter, D. L., 331, 332, 333, 334, 337, 346, *362*, *363*
Rothenberg, L. S., 183, *198*
Rothschild, M., 147, *158*
Rubin, A., 134, 142, *158*
Rubin, R. B., 71, 72, 73, 74, 75, 77, 78, 81, 82, 83, 84, 89, 97, 109, 113, *115*
Rubin, Z., 85, 101, 102, *113*
Rudinger, G., 381, 382, *388*
Rueschemeyer, D., 65, *194*
Russell, A., 72, *113*
Russell, A. W., 23, *35*
Russell, L., 78, *114*
Ryan, A., 306, *324*
Ryan, C., 170, 174, 185, 186, *198*
Ryan, E. B., 372, 373, *388*
Ryan, M., 243, 244, 251, 252, *262*
Ryan, M. H., 178, 180, 181, 182, 186, *198*

S

Sabato, L. J., 166, 183, 184, *198*
Sacks, H., 6, 11, *35*
Saenz, R., 310, *321*
Sahlins, M., 311, *324*
Saiko, 270, *296*
Salamon, L. M., 166, *198*, 248, *264*
Salisbury, R. H., 163, 167, 181, *196*, *198*, *199*
Sallot, L. M., 173, *193*, 233, 237, *264*
Salmon, C. T., 178, *199*
Salovey, P., 204, 205, 206, 207, 208, 214, 215, 216, 218, *228*
Salt, R. E., 104, *113*
Salvador, M., 72, 73, *116*
Sam, D., 313, *321*
Sampson, E., 302, *324*
Samter, W., 370, 371, 373, 375, 377, 379, 380, *386*, *388*
Sanders, D. L., 177, 178, 179, 181, 182, 184, 185, 186, 187, *199*
Sanders, K. R., 162, *198*
Sanders, R. E., 25, *32*
Sands, D. Z., 343, 344, 345, 347, 348, *361*
SantoDomingo, J., 72, 73, *116*
Sapolsky, R. M., 72, *113*
Sarason, I. G., 79, *108*
Saunders, C. S., 336, *363*
Saussure, F., 125, *158*
Savage, G. T., 252, *264*
Sawaya, R. N., 177, 180, *191*
Scala, R. P., 248, 249, *264*
Scarisbrick, D., 105, *113*
Schaie, K. W., 371, 372, 373, 381, 385, *388*
Schaie, W. K., *388*
Schallert, D., 14, *35*
Schattschneider, E. E., 164, 167, 171, 180, 181, 183, 185, *199*

Schegloff, E., 6, 11, *35*
Schick, T. A., 240, 241, *264*
Schlesinger, M., 328, *362*
Schlozman, K. L., 164, 167, 180, 181, 182, 183, 184, 185, 186, 190, *199, 200*
Schmertz, H., 178, 184, *199*
Schmidt, C., 83, *113*
Schmitz, J., 343, *363*
Schmuhl, R., 236, 245, 246, 247, *264*
Schneider, M., 185, 186, *199*
Schober, M. F., 23, *35*
Schoenhofer, S. O., 104, *113*
Schofield, T., 328, *362*
Schrader, D. C., 53, *67*
Schramm, W., 117, 124, 127, 131, 137, 146, *158*
Schriftgiesser, K., 182, 186, *199*
Schudson, M., 129, *157*
Schultz, C. L., 72, *113*
Schultz, N. C., 72, *113*
Schunk, D., 7, 13, *32*
Schutz, W., 72, 74, 75, 77, 78, 82, 86, 89, 92, 100, *113*
Schwartz, S., 99, 104, 105, 106, *114*
Schwarz, N., 5, *35*
Schwebel, J., 367, *388*
Schweller, K., 16, *35*
Scott, A. M., 166, 182, 184, 186, *199*
Scott, D., 180, 183, 184, 185, *193*
Searle, J. R., 15, 16, 20, 25, *35*
Seeman, B., 346, 349, *363*
Seeman, M. V., 346, 349, *363*
Segrin, C., 50, *68*
SeiffgeKrenke, I., 83, *113*
Senecal, S., 313, *321*
Senso to shimbun, 276, 277, *296*
Sethi, S. P., 178, 182, 184, 185, *199*
Shaiko, R. G., 183, *194*
Shamir, J., 234, *264*
Shapiro, I. S., 177, 183, *199*
Shapiro, R. M., 84, 89, 98, *113*
Shapiro, R. S., 333, *363*
Shapiro, R. Y., 145, *157*, 172, *198*
Sharf, B. F., 328, *363*
Sharkey, W. F., 23, *35*
Sharp, E. B., 185, *199*
Sharp, S. M., 78, 85, *112*
Sharpe, M. L., 239, *264*
Shaw, D. L., 145, *157*, 172, *197*
Shebroe, V., 328, *364*
Shellen, W. N., 380, *389*
Shepsle, K. A., 172, *199*
Sherman, L., 346, 349, *363*
Shimada, E., 310, *325*
Shin, H. C., 7, 26, *34*
Shoemaker, P. J., 232, *265*
Shreve, C., 97, 104, 105, 106, *114*
Shrum, L. J., 141, *158*

Shuler, S., 210, 211, 212, *228*
Shuntich, R. J., 84, 89, 98, *113*
Shuter, R., 223, *228*
Sias, P. M., 210, *228*
Sidner, C., 348, *364*
Sieb, P., 234, 235, 236, 239, 241, 251, 255, 258, *265*
Siebert, F. S., 244, *265*
Siegfried, J. J., 166, *198*
Siegler, M., 333, 334, *363*
Signorielli, N., 129, *154, 157, 158*
Silk, L., 177, *199*
Sillars, A. L., 377, 378, *388*
Silverman, R. D., 335, 339, 340, *363*
Silverstein, M., 92, *113*
Simmons, K. B., 104, 105, *114*
Simon, E. P., 94, *113*
Sims, H. P., Jr., 248, *262*
Singer, J. L., 138, 139, 140, *158*
Singer, M., 6, 16, *33, 35*
Skinner, E. R., 59, *68*
Skocpol, T., 165, *194, 199*
Skolnik, R., 249, *265*
Slama, K. M., 78, 85, *112*
Slater, M. D., 178, 181, 182, *200*
Slater, M. R., 59, *68*
Sloan, D. K., 222, *228*
Slomkowski, C., 377, 380, *386*
Slovic, P., 353, *361*
Slugoski, B., 22, *35*
Small, A., 164, *199*
Smilkstein, G., 334, *360*
Smith, A. D., *388*
Smith, D. H., 328, *362*
Smith, G. D., 240, *260*
Smith, G. L., 93, 104, *111*
Smith, J., 241, *265*, 368, 372, *385, 388*
Smith, M. A., 185, *199*
Smith, R. A., 166, 182, 183, 184, 185, 186, 187, *199*
Smith, R. C., 328, *364*
Smith, R. M., 367, *388*
Smitherman-Donaldson, G., 315, *322*
Smolowe, J., 309, *324*
Snell, W. E., Jr., 85, 98, *113*
Snow, D. A., 170, 174, 175, 185, *192*
Snow, R. E., 206, *228*
Socall, D., 21, *34*
Sollie, D., 97, 104, 105, 106, *114*
Solomon, D. H., 71, 78, 85, 88, *113*
Sorauf, F. J., 183, 184, *199*
Southern Poverty Law Center, 307, *324*
Spanier, G., 72, 101, *113*
Spears, R., 336, *362*
Sperber, D., 21, *35*
Spicer, C., 256, *265*
Spicer, J., 347, 349, *364*

Spielberg, A. R., 342, 343, 345, 346, 347, 348, 349, *364*
Spitzberg, B. H., 374, *388*
Sprecher, S., 78, 105, *114*
Springston, J., 240, *263*
Srull, T. K., 21, *34*
Stachura, M. E., 341, *361*
Stafford, L., 73, 98, 102, *108*
Staiti, C., 250, *265*
Stankov, L., 204, 205, 208, 213, 214, 218, *227*
Stanley, J. M., 328, *364*
Stanton, F. N., 132, *156*
Steed, R. D., 338, 340, *362*
Steele, B., 254, 256, *259*
Steele, K., 337, 338, 340, *362*
Steinberg, M., 76, *111*
Stern, L. A., 95, *110*
Stevenson, M. R., 367, *389*
Steverink, N., 72, 75, 77, 95, *112*
Stewart, M., 331, 332, 333, 337, 345, *363*
Stewart, M. A., 331, *364*
Stiles, W., 331, 332, 333, 337, 345, *363*
Stiles, W. B., 47, *68*
Stocker, C. M., 99, 104, 105, 106, *107*
Stoffelmayr, B. E., 328, *364*
Stohl, C., 376, *389*
Stone, D. A., 162, 173, 181, 182, 185, 191, *200*
Stone, T. H., 337, 340, 341, *359*
Stonequist, E., 313, *324*
Stoner, G. M., 336, *364*
Strage, M., 21, *32*
Stratmann, T., 184, *200*
Street, R. L., 328, 336, 337, 338, *362*, *363*, *364*
Street, R. L., Jr., 352, *364*
Strelau, J., 92, *114*
Strode, S. W., 340, *364*
Strouse, J. C., 287, 290, *296*
Stuart, B. J., 72, *114*
Studinger, U. M., 368, *385*
Suarez, S. L., 181, *200*
Suchman, A. L., 334, *359*
Sudo, Y., 268, *296*
Sullaway, M., 51, *67*
Sullivan, A. J., 240, *265*
Sullivan, W. M., 55, 67, 135, *158*
Sung, K. T., 72, *114*
Suro, R., 310, *324*
Sutton, R. I., 212, 216, 217, 225, *228*, *229*
Suzuki, K., 277, *296*
Swain, S., 84, 89, 105, 106, *114*
Swanson, C. L., 178, 180, 181, 182, 186, *198*
Swidler, A., 55, *67*
Swiggan-Hardin, M., 341, *361*
Sypher, B. D., 210, 211, 212, *228*, 377, *389*
Sypher, H., 336, 338, 357, *360*
Szalay, L., 311, *324*

**T**

Tajfel, H., 314, *324*
Talbert, J. C., 184, 185, *196*
Tapscott, D., 143, *158*
Taylor, C., 300, *324*
Taylor, M., 258, *265*
Taylor, S. E., 141, *154*
Tedlow, R. S., 247, *265*
Telford, R. W., 340, *362*
Terry, N. P., 335, *364*
Teske, P., 185, 186, *199*
Teske, R., 313, *324*
Theus, K. T., 240, *265*
Thiagarajan, S., 250, *265*
Thom, D. H., 331, 333, 341, *364*
Thomas, D. L., 72, 73, 84, 104, 106, *109*
Thomas, M., 315, *322*
Thomas-Brown, A. M., 72, *114*
Thompson, T. L., 369, 370, 378, 379, 380, *387*
Thor, C. G., 250, *263*
Thornton, M., 301, *324*
Thorson, E., 147, *158*
Tichenor, J. M., 338, 340, *362*
Tierney, J. T., 164, 167, 180, 181, 182, 183, 184, 185, 186, 190, *199*, *200*
Tilford, J. M., 340, *364*
Tillman, M. P., 78, *114*
Ting-Toomey, S., 26, *33*, *35*, 315, *325*
Tipton, S. M., 55, *67*
Tirpok, A., 257, *262*
Titone, D. A., 14, *35*
Tolich, M. B., 211, 216, *229*
Tong, D. A., 354, *364*
Torobin, J., 343, *363*
Townley, K. F., 85, 93, *107*
Trabasso, T., 6, 16, *33*
Tracy, K., 209, 210, *229*
Tracy, S. J., 207, 209, 210, 221, 223, *229*
Trapnell, P., 97, *117*
Traub, J., 305, *325*
Triandafyllidou, A., 174, 175, *200*
Triandis, H., 26, 26, *35*, 310, *325*
Triandis, H. C., 90, *114*
Trotta, M. R., 76, *107*
Truax, G., 180, *196*
Truitt, R. H., 237, *263*
Truman, D. B., 164, 186, *200*
Tsuda, Y., 303, 305, 317, *325*
Tsukamoto, M., 277, 278, *296*
Tuchman, G., 172, *200*
Tuerkheimer, A., 72, 83, 85, *111*
Tupling, H., 77, 96, *112*
Turner, J., 301, 314, *324*, *325*
Turner, J. L., 87, *114*
Turner, J. W., 338, *362*
Turner, L., 223, *228*

Turner, S. E., 248, *260*
Tusing, K. J., 126, *157*
Tversky, A., 141, *158*
Twardosz, S., 72, 75, 76, 77, 85, 93, 94, 97, 99,
   104, 105, 106, 107, *114*
Tym, K. A., 333, *363*

U

Uden-Holman, T., 340, *364*
Uehara, E. S., 87, 95, *114*
Uhlenberg, P., 379, *387*
Uleman, J. S., 16, *35*
Umphrey, D., 134, *153*
Updegraff, K. A., 99, 104, 105, 106, *107*
Useem, M., 166, 167, 177, 180, 182, 183, 185,
   186, *200*

V

Vaillant, G. E., 205, 219, *229*
Van Dijk, T., 301, *325*
van Dulmen, A. M., 328, *359*
Van Egeren, L. F., 328, *364*
Van Leuven, J. K., 178, 181, 182, *200*
Van Maanen, J., 217, 222, 223, *229*
Vanderveken, D., 16, *35*
Vangelisti, A. L., 73, 74, 75, 77, 78, 79, 86, 95,
   105, 106, *110*
Vasquez, G. M., 258, *265*
Vaux, A., 79, *114*
Vaverek, K. A., 336, *363*
Vawter, L. K., 238, *261*
Vega, B. R., 72, 73, *116*
Verba, S., 167, *200*
Verbrugge, L. M., 72, 75, 77, 95, *112*
Verhaak, F M., 328, *359*
Vibbert, S. L., 176, 177, 184, 185, *193*, 244,
   247, 249, 250, 251, 252, 253, *260*
Villard, K. L., 72, 73, 74, 76, 77, 78, 80, 81,
   82, 85, 86, 87, 90, 95, 98, 104, 105,
   106, 111, *114*
Villareal, M., 27, *35*, 310, *325*
Vincent, G., 164, *199*
Visser, A. P., 328, *359*
Vitell, S. J., 258, *265*
Vogel, D., 167, 177, 184, 185, 187, *199, 200*
Volosinov, V. N., 136, *158*
Voloudakis, M., 71, 75, 76, 77, 78, *109*
Vyborny, K. M., 335, 340, *364*

W

Wagner, R. K., 206, *229*
Wakefield, D. S., 340, *364*
Waldron, V. R., 207, 209, 210, 211, 216, 222,
   223, *229*
Walker, A., 238, *265*

Walker, C. A., 74, 79, *109*
Walker, J. L., 172, 180, 181, 182, *200*
Walker, J. L., Jr., 165, 180, 181, 185, *200*
Wallace, D., 72, 73, 96, 98, *114*
Wallace, D. H., 72, 84, 85, 92, 96, 98, 104,
   105, 106, *114*
Wallace, P., 338, *361*
Wallen, K., 85, *114*
Walters, J., 104, 105, 106, *114*
Walther, J. B., 336, 342, *364*
Waltzer, H., 178, *200*
Wanta, W., 145, *158*
Ward, A., 301, *325*
Ware, J. E., 341, *361*
Waring, E., 72, 78, *114*
Waring, E. M., 78, 101, 112, *116*
Waterman, R. W., 166, *194*
Watson, J., 269, 283, *296*
Wayman, F. W., 183, *195*
Wayne, S. J., 215, *229*
Weaver, D., 232, *265*, 284, 285, *296*
Weaver, D. H., 145, *157*
Webb, N. J., 252, *259*
Webster's New Collegiate Dictionary, 75, *114*
Weddle, K., 97, 104, 105, 106, *114*
Weed, L. L., 353, *364*
Weimann, G., 134, *158*
Weinberg, D. J., 106, *114*
Weingast, B. R., 172, *199*
Weinreich, G., 354, *360*
Weisinger, H., 203, 204, 205, 217, *229*
Weiss, A., 250, *265*
Weiss, R. S., 87, *114*
Weisz, G., 72, 78, *114*
Welfel, E. R., 242, *265*
Westenberg, P. M., 99, 104, 105, 106, *107*
Westmyer, S. A., 89, *115*
Whannel, P., 136, *155*
Wheeler, E. J., 336, 337, 338, *364*
Whipple, L. J., 76, 80, 82, 85, 86, 87, 90, 104,
   105, 106, *114*
White, N. P., 255, *261*
White, O. F., 250, *265*
Whitehead, C. J., 252, *264*
Whitehead, L. C., 92, 104, *110*
Whitney, P., 16, *35*
Whittaker, S., 348, *364*
Whitten, P. S., 335, 338, 339, 340, *364*
Widman, L. E., 354, *364*
Wiebe, R. H., 167, *200*
Wieder, L., 17, *325*
Wiener, M., 102, *114*
Wiggins, J. S., 97, *115*
Wilcox, C., 180, 185, 186, *200*
Wildermuth, N. L., 72, *110*
Wilkinson, C. A., 104, 105, 106, *115*
Willer, R. W., 178, *199*

Williams, A., 370, 371352, 373, 374, 378, 379, *386*, *387*, *389*
Williams, R., 124, 145, *158*
Williams, T. M., 142, *159*
Williams-Whitney, D. L., 16, *35*
Willis, F. N., 104, *110*
Willis, S. L., 372, *389*
Wilmot, W. W., 380, *389*
Wilson, A., 218, 220, 227
Wilson, D., 21, *35*
Wilson, G., 166, 167, 178, 184, 186, *200*
Wilson, S. R., 7, *35*
Windahl, S., 130, 133, *156*
Winkleman, M., 234, *265*
Winstead, B. A., 84, *108*
Wittenberg, E., 183, *200*
Wittenberg, E., 183, *200*
Wohl, R. R., 120, *155*
Wolf, J. F., 250, *265*
Wolf, K. M., 131, *155*
Wolfe, A., 306, 308, *325*
Wolfinger, R., 313, *325*
Wolpe, B. C., 183, *200*
Wood, J. T., 83, 87, 107, 106, *115*
Woodall, W. G., 77, 82, 83, *108*
Woodward, K., 300, *325*
Woollacott, J., 124, *154*
Wootton, R., 337, 338, 340, 358, *362*, *364*
Worline, M. C., 218, 220, 227
Wren-Lewis, J., 151, *159*
Wright, D. K., 232, 233, 234, 235, 238, 239, 243, 244, 250, 251, 258, *265*

Wright, J. R., 183, 184, *200*
Wright, L. K., 72, *115*
Wright, P. H., 78, 85, *112*
Wright, R., 143, *159*
Wu, W., 232, *265*
Wyatt, J. C., 342, 343, 348, *359*
Wyer, R. S., Jr., 28, *33*
Wylie, F., 233, 237, 238, 239, *265*

Y

Yamaguchi, S., 26, *34*
Yamamoto, S., 269, 271, 272, 275, 292, *296*
Yang, J. N., 7, 13, 20, 26, *34*
Yang, V. S., 126, *157*
Yarborough, E., 80, 104, *110*
Yeager, C. M., 328, 356, *361*
Yoon, H., *34*
Yoon, Y. C., 26, *33*
Youn, S., 134, *159*
Young, R., 316, 317, *325*
Youngman, D. J., 367, *387*
Yuki, M., 26, *34*

Z

Zahn-Waxler, C., 92, 93, *108*
Zakia, R., 124, *157*
Zietlow, P. H., 377, 378, *388*
Zillmann, D., 120, 133, *153*
Zollo, S. A., 340, *364*
Zom, T., 377, *389*
Zweigenhalf, R., 310, 325

# SUBJECT INDEX

Locators annotated with *f* indicate figures
Locators annotated with *t* indicate tables

## A

ABC, *see* Accredited Business Communicator
Acceptance, 75, 340
Accessibility, 350
Accreditation/licensing, 238–239
Accredited Business Communicator (ABC), 238
Accredited in Public Relations (APR), 238
Acculturation, 311
Accuracy, 340, 354
ACI, *see* Affectionate Communication Index
Acquaintance relationships, 74–79, *see also* Relationships
Adaptations, 311, 312–313
Adjacency pairs, 6, 11
Adjunct model, 351
Adjustment process, 23
Adolescent Prosocial Behavior Inventory (APBI), 99
Adolescents, 40, 83, 313–314
Adult discount, 127
Adults, 83, 371, 379, *see also* Adolescents; Children
Advertisers, 170
Advertising, 125
advocacy, 178
AEFO, *see* Affectional Environment in the Family of Origin
Affection and Autonomy Index, 95
Affection, interpersonal relationships
  factors influencing communication
    communicator, 81–86
    compatibility and reciprocity, 86–87
    context or situation, 89
    culture, 89–91
    nature of relationship, 87–89
    relational partner, 86
  influence of biology and environment in pattern development, 91–94
  many and varied, 80
  measurement as need or behavior, 95–103
  positive regard in all types, 74–79
  significant role, 72–73
  social exchange theories that explain communication, 94–95

underlying dimension, 73–74
Affectional Environment in the Family of Origin (AEFO), 96
Affectional History Questionnaire (AHQ), 96
Affectional Interaction Scale (AIS), 100
Affectional Needs and Behavior Scale (ANBS), 100
Affectionate Communication Index (ACI), 97
Affiliations, 88
Affinity, 77
Affirmative action, 306
African Americans, 134, 223, 303–304
Afrocentricity, 305
Age of Enlightenment, 245
Agenda setting, 273
  theory, 145–146
Agenda studies, 171–173
Aggression, 217
Aging, 368
Agreeableness, 81
AHQ, *see* Affectional History Questionnaire
AIS, *see* Affectional Interaction Scale
Alliance, 187
Altruism, 77
Alzheimer's disease, 83–84
Ambiguity, 29–30
American News Magazine, 281
American Society of Newspaper Editors, 245
ANBS, *see* Affectional Needs and Behavior Scale
Anglo Americans, 310
Animistic connotation, 272
ANOVA, 58
Anticommunist ideology, 171
Anti-elite newspapers, 268
Antigovernment newspapers, 268
Anti-Japanism, 270
Antimodernist view, 128
Antiwar *kuuki*, 278–283
Antiwar newspapers, 268
Anxiety, 52–53, 341
APBI, *see* Adolescent Prosocial Behavior Inventory
Apparent self-disclosure, 76
Approach/avoidance behaviors, 91
Appropriateness rules, 90
APR, *see* Accredited in Public Relations
*Asahi*, 279–280

Asian Indians, 316
Asians, 89–90, *see also* Individual entries
Assertives, 16, 22
Assimilation ideology concept, 313
Assimilationism, 303–304, 308
Assimilationism–integrationism, 310–312
Athens, 267
Attachments, 87–88, 93, 94, 379
Attentional inertia, 147
Attitudes, 39, 340–341
Audience
    active, 130–138
    active/passive, 138–146
    method and conceptual bias, 150–152
    need for synthesis, 152–153
    passive, 124–130
    problem, 118–124
Authoritarian parenting, 40, 63
Authoritative parenting, 63
Autonomous emotion management, 214
Autonomy, 239–241, 349

B

Behavior Indicants of Immediacy Scale (BII),
    102
Behavior
    affection measurement, 97–100
    communication of affection, 75–77
    family communication patterns, 41, 47–52
    human and lifespan communication, 367
    many and varied of affection, 80
    problems correlated with reading other's
        emotion, 214
Beliefs, 39, 41, 46, 256
Belongingness, 75
Berkeley, California, 268
Best friends, 380
Bias
    audience activity–passivity, 150–152
    family communication patterns, 43, 57, 60
Bicultural identity, 314
Big five factors, 92
BII, *see* Behavior Indicants of Immediacy
    Scale
Bilingual education, 304, 309
Biology, affectionate communication patterns,
    91–92
Biomedical/expanded biomedical pattern,
    331–332
Biopsychosocial patterns, 332
Birmingham school, 136–138
Black-White marriages, 310, *see also* African
        Americans; Caucasians
Boredom, 133
Bounded emotionality, 212
Brazilians, 310

Buddha statues of Bamian, 293–295
Bullet theory, 125–126
Bullies, 221–222
Bureau of Applied Social Research, 130–132
Bureaucratic consultation, 337–338
Bureaucrats, 180
Burnout, 221
Business organizations, political role/influence
    focus and communication research agenda,
        187–198
    framing: the symbolic construction of
        public policy issues, 173–176
    identifying social issues and influencing
        agendas, 171–173
    literature: political science perspectives,
        163–167
    managing issues and public policy
        involvement, 176–179
    overview of communication perspectives,
        167–169
    policy process in cultural context, 169–171
    propositions regarding economic power,
        179–186
    suggestions for communication research
        agenda, 187–191

C

CAE, *see* Current Affectional Experience
Cancer patients, 338
Caregivers, 73, 93
Caring, 77, 98
CAs, *see* Communication apprehensives
Caucasians, 134
Central route processing, 141–142
Change, lifespan communication, 381–382
Charities, 248–249
Children
    affectionate behavior communication, 83,
        92–93, 99–10
    family communication patterns, 39, 43, 66
    lifespan communication, 371, 373, 375 380
    Payne Fund studies, 126, 128
Chinese, 223 270
Cinema studies, 125
Citizens, safeguarding, 245
CIS, *see* Conversational indirectness scale
Civil Rights movement, 312
Class theorists, 165
Climate of opinion, *see Kuuki*
Clinton, President Bill, 306
Closeness, 78
Cluster analysis, 57, 75
CMC, *see* Computer-mediated communication
Coalitions, 166, 179, 181, 185
Co-cultural theory, 316
Code of ethics

press and social responsibility theory, 245, 247
professionalism, 233–236
Cognition, 12, 13, 370–372
Cognitive ability, 206
Cognitive appraisal, 209
Cognitive complexity, 377
Cognitive development, 41
    theory, 140–141
Cognitive engagement, 147
Cognitive/psychological approaches, 140–142
Cognitive representations, 64
Cognitive structures, 41–42
Cohesion, 50, 149
Cohort effects, 370
Collection action theory, 164–165
Collective action frames, 174–175
Collectivism, 26, 27
Collectivistic cultures, 90
Columbine High School, 221
Comfort, 341, *see also* Telehealth
    messages, 377
Commission on Freedom of the Press, 245
Commissives, 17
Communalism, 90
Communication apprehensives (CAs), 82
Communications
    accommodation, 373–374
        theory, 314–315, 318
    affectionate, *see* Affection, interpersonal
        relationships
    apprehension, 53
    emotional intelligence measurement, 205
    facilitator, 240
    family patterns, 44–45, 46
    orientation, 207
    patient–physician patterns, 330, 331–333
    political role/influence of business
        organizations, 180, 181
    researchers
        agenda suggestions, 187–191
        future and Revised Family
            Communication Patterns,
            64–65
        political role/influence of business
            organizations, 185
        theories of communication and future
            needs, 383–385
    technician, 240
    technology, 329
Communications Patterns Questionnaire
    (CPQ), 51
Communicator, 81–86
Community, 219–220
Compassion, 218, 220
Compatibility, 86–87
Competence, communication

lifespan, 369, 374–378
    pluralistic families, 44
Compliance, 182
Compromise, 170
Computer-mediated communication (CMC), 82
Computers, 134–135, *see also* Internet;
    Telehealth
Concept-orientation, 42, 43
Confidentiality, 346–347, 349
Confirming behaviors, 49, *see also* Behavior
Conflict
    academic conceptions of ethnic identity,
        316, 318
    family communication patterns, 49, 50–52,
        63
    political role/influence of business
        organizations, 170, 180
Conflict avoidance, 39
Conflict strategies, 377–378
Conformity orientation, family communication
        patterns
    behavior outcomes, 47–50
    conversation orientation correlation with
        RFCP, 54–56
    validity, 60
    different perspectives as function of family
        role, 57, 58*t*
    dimensions of family communication, 39–40
    discrete family types and continuous
        dimensions, 58–59
    family types and conflict, 52
    pluralistic families, 44
    psychosocial outcomes, 52–53
Congressional debates, 182
Consensual families, 44, 48*t*, 52
Consistency, 149
Constitutive rules, 211
Construct validity, 62, *see also* Validity
Consultations, 251, 343, 347
Consumerist pattern, 332
Content analysis, 287–288, 289*f*, *see also*
        Public opinion surveys
Content validity, 60, *see also* Validity
Context
    communicating affectionate behavior, 89
    emotional intelligence, 208, 214, 222–223
    processing conversational implicatures, 14
    processing speaker meaning, 26–27
Control, 119, 222
Convenience, electronic mail, 342, *see also*
        Electronic mail
Conventionality, 19–20
Conversation orientation, family
        communication patterns
    conformity orientation correlation, 54–56
    different perspectives as function of family
        role, 57, 58*t*

dimensions 39
discrete family types and continuous
    dimensions, 58–59
validity, 60
Conversational implicatures
    coordinating perspective and communica-
        tion of speaker meaning, 22
    processing
        conventionality, 19–20
        generalized, 14–17
        overview, 12–14
        particularized, 17–19
        status and interpretation, 20–22
Conversational indirectness scale (CIS), 26
Conversational management, 376
Conversational maxim, 4–5, 6, 7, 27
Cooperative principle (CP), 4
Coping, 217
Corporate executives, 183
Corporations, social responsibility, 247–251,
    *see also* Business organizations,
    political role/influence
public relations, 251–252
Cost, telemedicine, 339–340
Counseling, 204
Countervailing group power concept, 165
Courtroom testimony, 28–29
CP, *see* Cooperative principle
CPQ, *see* Communications Patterns Questionnaire
Credibility, 169, 175, 353–354
Criteria, 290–291, *see also Kuuki*
Criterion validity, 61, *see also* Validity
Critical theory, 128–129
Critical thinking, 131
Cross-generational studies, 310
Cues, 336, 341–342, *see also* Telehealth
Cultivation theory, 129
Cultural context, 169–171
Cultural control, 217–218
Cultural imperialism, 317
Cultural studies, 136–137, *see also* Audience
Cultural values, 55
Cultural variability, 25–27, 30
Culture, 89–91, 223
Currency, 353–354
Current Affectional Experience (CAE), 98
Curriculum, 237
Cynicism theory, 271

D

*Dallas*, 146
Danger, 292, *see also Kuuki*
DAS, *see* Dyadic Adjustment Scale
Daughters, 92
Decision making
    family communication patterns, 39, 44, 45, 55

code of ethics and professionalism, 234
corporate social responsibility, 249–250, 251
public relations, 254–256, 257, 258
organizational and emotional intelligence,
    220
Deep acting, 212
Defect conditions, 186
Democracies, 143–144, 161–162, 244
Denial, 28
Deontology, 254, 257
Depression, 52–53
Development, 72, 368–369, *see also* Lifespan
    communication
Diagnosis, 340, 349
Diagnostic framing, 174
Dignity, 254
Dimensions, emotional intelligence, 207, 208*f*
Dimensions of Relational Message Themes, 102
Directive readings, 21, 22
Directives, 17, *see also* Conversational
    implicatures
Direct-to-consumer advertising (DTC), 356,
    *see also* Advertising
Disclosure, 330, *see also* Telehealth
Discourse abilities, 374
Discourse theory, 255
Dispositional inference, 16, *see also* Inference
Dispreferred turns, *see* Preferred/dispreferred
    turns
Dissatisfaction, 334, *see also* Telehealth
Distance, sense, 337
Diversionary viewing, 134
Dominance, 221, 222, 332
Dominant coalition, 242, *see also* Coalitions
Double agent role, 333
DTC, *see* Direct-to-consumer advertising
Duty, 254, 255
Dyadic Adjustment Scale (DAS), 101

E

*E Pluribus Unum*, 303, *see also* Ethnic identity,
    academic conceptions
Early adopter effect, 134–135
Economic currencies, 80, 82
Economic power
    for-profit organizations and political role, 164
    political influence relations
        outcome propositions, 184–186
        strategy propositions, 179–181
        tactics propositions, 181–184
Economic resources, 185
Education, 134, 341, 353
EEG, *see* Electroencephalogram studies
Efficiency, 347, *see also* Telehealth
Egocentric bias, 22–23, 25, *see also* Bias
Elaboration likelihood model, 141

Elders, 73
Electroencephalogram (EEG) studies, 139
Electronic age, 143
Electronic mail, 342–349
Elites, 128–129
Elitist views, 164, 166–167
Email, *see* Electronic mail
Embarrassment, 339
   episodes, 23
Emotion work, 211
Emotional dissonance, 212, 217, 221
Emotional intelligence, organization
         communication
   context, 222–223
   dimensions, 208–211
   discussion, 224–226
   exploring moral dimension, 219–222
   other-experienced/expressed dimension,
         213–219
   self-experienced/expressed dimension,
         209–213
Emotional labor, 211–212, 217
Empathy, 49–50, 214–215
Employee, 215
Encryption methods, 349
Enforcement, 235, *see also* Public relations
         ethics
Engagement, 119
English Canadians, 310
English language, 317
Enlightenment rationalist thinking, 124
Enmeshment, 87
Environment
   affectionate communication patterns, 89,
         92–94
   lifespan communication, 370
   monitoring, social responsibility, and
         public relations, 252
Environmental policy, 174
Environmentalists, 175
Epideictic rhetoric, 252–253
EQ test, 213
Equality, 302, 304–305
Ethical conduct, 236
Ethics dimension, 207, 208*f*
Ethnic identity, academic conceptions
   conceptual grounding, 301–302
   focus, 300–301
   identity polemics, 318–319
      classical liberalism, 302–309
      ideological messages, 309–317
      social engagement and social
         responsibility, 319–321
Ethnicity, affectionate behavior, 83
Ethnography, 315, 319
European Americans, 223
Evolution, 235, 268–269

Excellence model, 257
Excuses, 24
Expectancy violations, 90
   theory, 95
Expectancy-value theory, 132
Expectations, family communication patterns, 53
Experience/expressed dimension, 207, 208*f*
Experienced emotions, 209–210, 215–216
Experienced/expressed emotions, 210–212
Expert prescriber, 240
Expert status, 351–352
Expertise, 183
Expressed emotions, 210
Expressives, 16
External publics, *see* Internal/external publics
Externals, 240
Extraversion, 81
Extremists, 306–307
Extroversion, 92
Eye contact, 337
Eye movements, 139

F

Face management, speaker meaning
   comprehending, 29
   coordinating perspective and
         communication, 24, 25
   reply interpretation, 5–12
Face threatening, 11, 12, 18, 24
Face validity, 97, *see also* Validity
Face-to-face (FtF) communication, 82,
         336–338
Family communication patterns (FCP)
   changes, 369
   dimensions, 38–42
   methodological issues, 54–62
   outcomes, 46–54
   revised, 42–48
Family types
   communication behaviors during normal
         conversation, 48*t*
   conflict and communication patterns,
         50–52
   discrete and continuous dimensions, 57–59
   marital types relation, 46
   psychosocial outcomes, 53–54
   Revised Family Communication Pattern
         instrument, 44–45
Father, 92
Favoritism, state-sponsored, 304
FCP, *see* Family communication patterns
Feedback, 355
Feeling, affection as, 75, 81
Female–female relationships, 89, *see also*
         Relationships
Feminine emotions, 211

Figurative meaning, 14
Films, 147, 149
FIRO, *see* Fundamental Interpersonal Relations
    Orientation theory
Follow-up calls, 343
*Fortune 500* companies, 178, *see also* Business
    organizations
FR, *see* Frame of reference
Frame of reference (FR), 47
Frames, 185–186
Framing
    communication research agenda, 188, 190
    processes and symbolic construction of
        public policy issues, 173–176
    social conditions and political role/
        influence of business
        organizations, 168
Frankfurt School, 127, 146
French Canadians, 310
Friendships, 88, 380
FtF, *see* Face-to-face communication
Fundamental Interpersonal Relations
    Orientation (FIRO), 80, 100
    theory, 74

### G

G protein-coupled receptor, 91
Gain-loss dynamic, 369
Gender, 49, 84
General practitioner (GP), 337–338, *see also*
    Telehealth
Generalists, 240
Generalized implicatures, 14–17, 30
Genetics, 91–92
Genuine emotion, 212
Genuine self-disclosure, 76
Goals, 82–83, 175, 216
Goodness of fit, 179
Good-will gestures, 251
Gough–Heilbrun Adjective Check List, 96
Government, 173, 246–247
    opinion, 287–288, 289f, *see also Kuuki*
GP, *see* General practitioner
Grand theory, 132–133
Grass-roots campaign, 179, 180
Greeks, ancient, 271
Gricean Model, 4–5, 13, 14
Group identity, 304–305
Group satisfaction, 72
Guidance-obtaining relationship, 88
Guidelines, electronic mail, 344–345
Gulf War, 278–281

### H

Haitians, 311
Health care agencies, 339

Health/disability, 83–84
Hearers, 23, 24
Hearst, William Randolph, 275
Hegemony, 129, 272
Heterosexual couples, 89–90
Heuristic processing model, 141
Heuristic rules, 211
Hierarchal organization, 40
Hierarchical control model, 375
Hirohito, Emperor, 276
Hispanics, 89–90, 134, 310
History
    family communication pattern, 42
    *kuuki* phenomena
        antiwar, 278–283
        jingoism, 274–278
        justice, 283–285
Hitler, Adolph, 276
Homogenization theory, 144
Hutchins Commission report, 246–247
Hypodermic theory, 125–126

### I

IAS, *see* Interpersonal Adjective Scale
ICM, *see* Interpersonal Communication
    Motives
Identification
    emotions, 214, 215
    media and active/passive audience,
        146–147
    political role/influence of business
        organizations, 168
    viewers of soap operas, 118
Identity, 329
Identity conflict, 316
Identity negotiation, 315
Ideological circle, 308f, 309
Ideological messages, 309–317
Ideological shift, 299
Idioms, 15, 19
Idiosyncratic characteristics, 83–86
Illocutionary force of utterance, 15, 16, 17
IM, Issues management
Image building, 251
Immediacy, 79–80
Immigrants, 303
Impersonal consultation, 337, *see also*
    Consultation
Impression management, 215
Independent relationships, 45, 46, *see also*
    Relationships
Indirect communication, 3–4, 5, 10, *see also*
    Communication
Indirect meaning, 19, 24
Indirect reply, 10–11
Indirect requests, 20

Indirectness, 26, 27
Individual identity, 303
Individual motivation, 271
Individual variability, 25–27, 30
Individualism, 26, 27
Individualistic cultures, 90
Indochinese, 311
Industrial Revolution, 232, 245
Infants, 93–94
Inferences
    comprehending speaker meaning, 29
    particularized implicatures, 18
    processing conversational implicatures,
        13–14, 15, 16
    status/interpretation, 20
Influence, concept, 190–191
Information
    telemedicine, 339, 349, 350, 351
    indirect requests and literal/nonliteral
        meanings, 13
    political role/influence of business
        organizations, 182
Information processing, 139, 372
Information subsidies, 172, 185
Informed patient, 329, 353
Ingroup–outgroup, 307
Inner states, 76
Inoculation effect, 126
Instrumental perspectives, 177
Instrumental viewing, television, 134, 142
Instrumentalists, 165
Integrationism, 305–306
Integrity, 347
Intelligence, 204–205
Intelligence quotient (IQ), 206
Intensity, opinions, 288, 290
Intentions, public relations, 254
Inter/intraindividual diversity, 369–370
Interaction adaptation theory, 95
Interactional component, emotional
        intelligence, 205
Interactions
    affectionate communication, 93
    family communication, 39, 42, 45
Interactivity, family communication patterns, 64
Interchange compatibility, 86
Intercultural identity, 312
Interest-group studies, 164
Intergenerational exchange, 39, 42
Interlocking relationships, 166, 180, see also
        Relationships
Intermarriage, 310
Intermedia consonance, 273
Internal organization change, 181
Internal/external publics, 249, 250, 252
Internals, public relations, 242
Internet, 347, 349–356, see also Telehealth

Interpersonal Adjective Scale (IAS), 97
Interpersonal Communication Motives (ICM), 97
Interpersonal conflict, 377–378, see also Conflict
Interpersonal relationships, 72–74, 77, see also
        Relationships
Intersubjectivity, 64
Intimacy, see also Relationships
    affection relation, 78
    relationships, 73–79
    styles and gender, 84–85
Intimacy currencies, 80, 82
Involvement, 126, 147–148
Iraq, 278
Iron triangles, 165
Issue ads, 178, 184
Issue networks, 165
Issues management (IM)
    influence internal business policy, 179
    political role/influence of business
        organizations, 168, 180
    social responsibility and public relations,
        251–252
    steps, 176
    use by business organization, 177
Italian Americans, 310

**J**

*James Bond* novels, 125
JAMIA, *see* Journal of the American Medical
        Informatics Association
Japan, 268–269, 310, *see also Kuuki*
Jewish Americans, 271, 310
Jingoism
    *kuuki* phenomenon, 274–278
    what is *kuuki*, 271, 274
Joking, 217
Journal of the American Medical Informatics
        Association (JAMIA), 344
Journalism, 277
Judgment speeds, 8
Justice, 283–285, *see also Kuuki*

**K**

Kaifu, Prime Minister, 278–280, 281
Kantian ethics, 254
Key to socialization, affection as, 72
Keysar model, 23
King, Martin Luther, Jr., 306
Kinships, 88
Knowledge, 232, 236–238, 355
Korea, 26, 270, 311
Ku Klux Klan, 307
*Kuuki*
    measurement, 285–291
    modern history phenomenon

antiwar, 278–283
  jingoism as, 274–278
  justice, 283–285
  what is, 269–274

**L**

Laboratory studies, 151
Laissez-faire families, 45, 48*t*, 63
Language, 311
  development, 373–374
Latinos, *see* Hispanics
Learned behavior, 91, *see also* Behavior
Legislation, 184, *see also* Government
Lexical decision task, 17
Liberal Democratic Party (LDP), 279
Liberalism, 302–309
Libertarian philosophy, 245
Liberty, 245
LDP, *see* Liberal Democratic Party
Life cycles, 178
Lifespan communication
  capturing change, 381–382
  cognition, 370–372
  communication competence, 374–378
  language development, 373–374
  overview, 367–370
  relationship change, 378–381
Likert scale, affection measurement
  as behavior, 98
  as need, 95, 96, 97, 100
Liking, 78
Liking Scale, 101–102
Literacy, 357
Literal/nonliteral meaning
  comprehending speaker meaning, 4, 30
  processing conversational implicatures, 13,
    19, 21
Literature, 163–167
Llongot speech acts, 25, *see also* Speech acts
Lobbies, political role/influence of business
    organizations, 164, 165–167, 180,
    182–183
  formation, 187
Longitudinal studies, 381–382
Love, 78
Love Scale, 85, 101–102
Love, Sex, and Intimacy Questionnaire, 97–98

**M**

Magic bullet theory, 118
Mainstreaming, 303
Male–male relationships, 89, *see also*
    Relationships
Managed health care, 328, 333–336, *see also*
    Telehealth
Manager, 215

Managerial control, 216–217
Manchurian incident, 276–278
Manipulation, 221
Manuchurian Incident, 268, *see also Kuuki*
Marginalized communities, 316
Marginalized groups, 220
Marital relationships, 74, *see also* Relationships
Marital types, 45–46
Market economic theory, 170, 175
Marking, 11
Marxists, 165
Masculine Behavior Scale (MBS), 98
Masculine Role Inventory (MRI), 98
Mass effect, 131
Mass hysteria, 274
Mass media
  *kuuki*
    agenda-setting, 273
    antiwar, 278–281
    justice, 283–285
    opinions and measurement, 287–288,
      289*f*
    Nixon misdeeds and intensity of opinions,
      288, 290
Mass society, 124
MBS, *see* Masculine Behavior Scale
MCR, *see* Mindful channel repertoire
Meaning, 124–125, *see also* Audience
Meaning structures, 136–137
Means–end reasoning, *see* Reasoning process
Measurement, *kuuki*, 285–291
Media
  political role/influence of business
      organizations, 170
  studies, 120, 121–122*t*, 123*f*
Media dependency theory, 133
Median split technique, 55, 60
Medical decision making, 329, 335, *see also*
    Decision making; Telehealth
Medicolegal prudence, 344
Meiji period, 272
Messages, 23, 44, 126
Meta-analysis, 85
Metaphors, 15, 19
Methodological issues
  bias in audience activity–passivity,
      150–152
  family communication patterns, 54–62
  –idealogical systems, 320
Mexican Americans, 310, *see also* Hispanics
Middle-class, 308
Military, 339
Mindful channel repertoire (MCR), 134
Minorities, 309, *see also* Ethnic identity,
    academic conceptions
Misinterpretations, 317
Misunderstanding, 86–87

Mobil oil, 178
Mobilization potency, 175
Monsanto, 173
Mood, 81
Moral character, 205
Moral dimension, 219–222
Moral rectitude, 251
Morality, 207, 208f
Most Important Problem Surveys, 172
Motivation, relevance violation, 8–9
Motivational framing, 174
Motivational state, 81–82
MRI, see Masculine Role Inventory
Multicollinearity, 56
Multiculturalism, 300, 306
Multidimensional theory, 314–315, 318
Multiple linear regression, 56, 58
Mutual understanding, 252
Myers-Briggs Type Indicator, 81

N

Naïve theory of affection, 94
Narcotizing dysfunction, 131
Nation of Islam, 307
National/local policy, setting, 164
Need, 95–97, 100
Negative emotions, 209, 210
Negative information, 24, see also Information
Negative state remark, 19–20
Nematodes, 91
Neo-Nazis, 307
New Black Panthers, 307
News coverage, 172
Newspapers, 287
    surveys, 281
Nixon, Richard, 28, 283, 291
Nonmonetary assets, 184
Nonphysican health care providers, 328
Nonprofit organizations, 237, 248, see also
    Business organizations
Nonrepresentative samples, 60
Nonverbal behavior, 80, 104–105, 106, see
    also Behavior
Nonverbal communication, 80, see also
    Communication
Normative theory, 257
NPY receptors, 91

O

Obligations, 255
Office visits, 356, see also Telehealth
Opinion, 24, 46, see also Public opinion
Opinion situations, 7, 9
Opposite-sex relationships, 88–89, see also
    Relationships
Organizational culture, 217–218, 223

Organizational image, 241
Organizational problems, 203
Organizations, 208, 211–212, see also
    Business organizations
Orienting reflex, 138–139
Originator compatibility, 86
Other's expressed emotions, 208, 216–218
Other-experienced/expressed dimension,
    213–219
Outcome propositions, 184–186
Outcomes
    family communication patterns, 46–54, 63
    patient–physician communication, 332–333
Outlaw emotions, 219, 220
Overload, electronic mail, 348, see also
    Electronic mail; Telehealth

P

PACs, see Political action committee
Pacific War, 275–278
Pair-bond relationship, 88
Paper & pencil tests, 372
Parasocial interaction, 118
Parental Bonding Instrument (PBI), 96
Parent–child relationships, 72, 87–88, 92, 379,
    see also Relationships
Parents, 43, 66–67, see also Family
    communication patterns
Particularized implicatures, 17–19, 30, see also
    Conversational implicatures
Partisanship, 185
Passive spillover effect, 142
Paternalistic pattern, 356
Paternalistic style, 331, see also Telehealth
Patient-centered care (PCC), 328
Patient–physician relationships, 343, 345–346,
    354–356, see also Relationships
Patriot movements, 307
Payne Fund studies, 126–128
PBI, see Parental Bonding Instrument
PCC, see Patient-centered care
PCP, see Primary care physicians
PE, see Presumption of experience
Peers
    affectionate communication, 94
    control of public relations, 240
    corporate social responsibility, 250
    family communication patterns, 45, 54
Perception, biased, 43, see also Bias
Performance, 212, 215, 373
Perlocutionary act, 15
Permissible transactions/content, 345
Permissive parenting, 41, 63
Personal consultation, 337, see also Consultation
Personal information requests, 7, 8, 9, see also
    Information

Personal interest, 40
Personal space, 40
Personal style, 81
Personal success, 207, 208*f*
Personality, 81
Perspective, communication
   competence, 377
   family members, 56
   speaker meaning, 22–25
Persuasive strategies, 377
Philips Petroleum, 253
Photoplays, 148
Physical proximity, 341
Physician access, 339, *see also* Telehealth
Physicians, 347–348, *see also* Electronic mail;
   Telehealth
Planned Parenthood, 253
Plays, 147–148
Plural elitism, 165
Pluralism, 304–305
Pluralism–integrationism, 312–315
Pluralism–separatism, 315–317
Pluralist theory, 164
Pluralistic families, 44, 48*t*, 52
Policy-agenda-building model, 177
Policy decisions, 274
Policy makers, 175–176
Policy venues, 185
Politeness, 6–7, 13, 20, 22
Political action committees (PACs), 165–167,
   178, 183–184
Political culture, 274
Political influence, 187, 189*f*
Political leaders, 273, 281
Political theories, 163–167
Positive regard, 75
Poststructuralism, 135
Power, 20
Power approach, 241–242
*PR NewsWire*, 188
Preference organization, 10–12
Preferred/dispreferred turns, 11
President McKinley, 275
Press, social responsibility, 244–247, *see also*
   Mass media
Press framing, 176
Presumption of experience (PE), 47
Primary care physicians (PCP), 333, *see also*
   Telehealth
Primates, 93
Priming effect, 10, 12, 147
Print media, 178, *see also* Mass media
Prisons, 339
Privacy
   electronic mail and patient–physician com-
     munication, 343, 346–347, 349
   guidelines in use, 344–345

   face-to-face encounters versus
     patient–physician
     communication, 337
Problem solving, 94, 372
Problem-solving process facilitator, 240
Productivity, 216, 333, 349
Professional specialists, 180
Profitability, 249
Prognostic framing, 174
Promise, 15, 16
Propaganda, 131
   model, 170
Protective families, 44–45, 48*t*
PRSA, *see* Public Relations Society of America
Pseudo-environments, 126, *see also* Environment
Psychanalytic theory, 146
Psychological acculturation model, 313
Psychological approach, emotional
     intelligence, 204–205
Psychological closeness, 341
Psychophysiological approach, 138–140
Psychosocial outcomes, 52–54, *see also* Outcomes
Public access, 343
Public hearings, 184
Public interest, 185, 244, 254
Public key cryptography, 349
Public opinion, 172, 178, 269
Public opinion surveys
   differing academic conceptions of ethnic
     identity, 309
   *kuuki*, 281–282, 286–288, 289*f*
Public policy
   concept of influence/role of business
     organizations, 167
   involvement and managing issues, 176–179
   research on framing, 176
   symbolic construction, 173–176
Public relations, 178, 181
Public relations ethics
   decision making, 254–256
   implications, 256–259
     summary, 253–254
   professionalism
     accreditation and licensing, 238–239
     autonomy, 239–241
     body of knowledge, 236–238
     code of ethics, 233–236
     concept and characteristics, 232–233
     power approach, 241–242
     public service, 241
     summary of implications, 242–243
   social responsibility, 251–253
     characterization, 243–244
     corporate, 247–251
     the press, 244–247
Public Relations Society of America (PRSA),
   235, 238

Public service, 241
Pulitzer, Joseph, 275

**Q**

Q-implicatures, 15
Quantity maxim, 25, 27, 28
Question–reply sequence, 11, 12, 18
Quota systems, 306

**R**

Radio, 127
Rapport, establishment, 337, 341–342, *see also*
        Telehealth
Rational interactions, 25
RDI, *see* Relational dimension inventory
Reaction, audience, 119
Reader response theory, 137
Reading, 148–149
Reading emotion, 214–215
Reading other's emotions, 218
Reading time, 18, 20
Reality, 129
Reasoning process, 11
        means–end, 24, 25, 30
Reciprocal compatibility, 86
Reciprocity, 76, 87, 95
Reconciliation, 305–306
Redundancy, unintended 28
Reflexive intention, 27
Reframing, 210, *see also* Frames; Framing
Regulations, 187, 247
Regulative rules, 211
Regulatory behavior, 49, *see also* Behavior
*Reiki*, 269–270
Relation maxim, 10, 18 30
Relational currencies, 80
Relational dimension inventory (RDI), 45, 61
Relational harmony, 77
Relational partner, 86
Relationship-centered interaction, 332
Relationships, *see also* Individual entries
        changes across the lifespan, 378–381
        communicating affectionate behavior,
                87–89
        outside and conformity orientation in
                family communication, 40
Relevance violation, speaker meaning
        comprehending, 30
        face management and reply
                        interpretation, 6, 7, 8–10
        coordinating perspective and
                        communication, 24, 25
Reliability, 60, 286–287, 340
Remote control device, 134
Remote sensing, 336

Reply, 10–12, 345
Reply interpretation, 5–12
Requested information, 24, 25, *see also*
        Information
Requests for action, 20
Resiliency, 53–54
Resistance, physician, 351–354
Resonance, frames, 175
Resource theory, 95
Resources, 40, 80
Respect, 254
Responses, similar/predictable, 149
Revised Family Communication Pattern
        (RFCP) instrument, 42–46
Rewards/punishment, 217
RFCP, *see* Revised Family Communication
        Pattern (RFCP) instrument
Right-wing media groups, 170–171
Risks, affection communication, 76
Ritualized viewing, television, 142
Rituals, 78–79
Rivalry, sibling, 379
Role Behavior Test, 97, 101
Role playing, 84
Roles
        changing in managed care, 333
        family, 56–57, 58*t*
Roll-call votes, 184
Romantic relationships, 51–52, *see also*
        Relationships
Rorschach test, 130
Rules, 90, 254–255
Rural physicians, 399
Russo-Japanese War, 270, 277

**S**

Salience, 175, 181
Same-sex relationships, 88–89, *see also*
        Relationships
Sarcasm, 23
SAT scores, 214
Satellite technology, 335
Satisfaction, patient, 330, 338
Scalar implicatures, 15
Schedules, 40
Scholarly journals, 238
Scientific rationalization, 170
        theory, 175
SE, *see* Source of experience
Security, 87–88
Self-construals, 26
Self-disclosure, 7, 9, 76, 85
Self-esteem, 92
Self-estrangement, 212, 221
Self-expressed/experienced emotions, 208,
        209–213

Self-monitoring, 240, 249
Self-orientation, 47–50
Self/other dimension, 207, 208*f*
Self-regulation, 40
Self-reporting questionnaire, 44
Self-response questionnaires, 209
Self-service model, 351
SEM, *see* Structural equation modeling
Sentence verification, 18, 21
Sentences, 3
Separate relationships, 45, 46, *see also*
    Relationships
Separatism, 306–307
SES, *see* Socioeconomic status
Sex, 83, 84
Sex composition, 88–89
Sexual intercourse, 85
Sibling relationships, 379, *see also* Relationships
Sibling Relationship Inventory (SRI), 99
SIIEG, *see* Social Interaction Inventory for
    Exchanges of Giving
Sino–Japanese War, 275–278
Skinheads, 307
Social cognition, 370–371
theory, 140, 141
Social context, 21, 134, *see also* Context
Social engagement, 319–321
Social exchange theories, 94–95
Social goals, 374, *see also* Goals
Social identity theory, 314
Social intelligence, 204, 206–207
Social Interaction Inventory for Exchanges of
    Giving (SIIEG), 101
Social interactions, 94, *see also* Interactions
Social issues, 171–173
Social knowledge, 372
Social movements, 174
Social networks, 376
Social norms, 273
Social phenomena, 271
Social problems, 169–170, 173
Social production function theory, 95
Social psychological theory, 273–274
Social responsibility, 319–321
    historical background, 243–244
    public relations professionals
        corporate, 247–251
        press, 244–247
        public relations, 251–253
Social science, 318–319
Social support, 50, 79, 90
Social support networks, 369
Socialization, 41, 72
Society, 232
Socioeconomic status (SES), 86
Sociological studies,
Socio-orientation, 42, 43

Somatosensory Index of Affection, 96
Somatosensory Index of Human Affection, 96
Source of experience (SE), 47
South Africa, 316
Spanish–American War, 274–275
Speaker, comprehending meaning
    coordinating perspectives in
        communication, 22–25
    face management and reply interpretation,
        5–12
    Gricean model, 4–5
    individual and cultural variability in
        processing, 25–27
    processing conversational implicatures
        conventionality, 19–20
        generalized, 14–17
        overview, 12–14
        particularized, 17–19
        status and interpretation, 20–22
        unintended inferences, 27–29
Speaker meaning, *see* Speaker, comprehending
    meaning
Speaker status, 20–21
Speech act theory
    locus of meaning and active audience, 137
    processing conversational implicatures, 15,
        16–17, 18, 19
Speech acts, 47, 49
Spiral of cynicism, 273
Spiral of silence, 272–273
theory, 129–130, 269, 271
Spirit, 270–272
Spirit of justice, 283–283
SRI, *see* Sibling Relationship Inventory
Stakeholders, 249, 252
Standards
    concept of professionalism, 232, 233
    enforcement and professional code of
        ethics, 234
    Hutchins Commission and social
        responsibility of press, 246–247
    public relations professionals, 239, 256
Standing, 169
State regulations, 239, *see also* Government
Statistical analysis, 58–59
Statistical analysis software, 56
Status equality, 304–305
Status quo, 220
Status/interpretation, 20–22
Stereotypes, 372
Stimulus-response approach, 125–126
Storytelling, 119–120
Strategies
    influence on agendas by economic
        producers, 172–173
    political role/influence of business
        organizations, 168

Strategy propositions, 179–181
Stress, 133, 221, 311
Structural equation modeling (SEM), 56, 382
Structural linguistics, 135, *see also* Audience
Structuralism, 125, *see also* Audience
Structuralists, 165
Structuration theory, 256
Subordinates, reading other's emotion, 215
Success, 205, 215, 219
Supportive communication, 41, *see also*
  Communication
Suppression, emotions, 210
Supreme Court, 244
Surface acting, emotional labor, 212
Symbolic interactionism, 143, 144
Symbolic structures, 173–174
Synactic processing, 373

T

Tactic propositions, 181–184
Taisho Democracy, 277, 278
Taliban, 293–294
Teaching, 221
Teasing episodes, 23
Technician–manager dichotomy, 240
Technology/culture, 142–145, *see also*
  Audience
Teleconsultations, 336–337
Telehealth
  characterization, 327–329
  directions for future research, 357–359
  patient–physician communication
    electronic mail, 342–349
    internet, 349–356
    overview and managed care, 330–335
    telemedicine, 335–342
Telemedicine, *see* Telehealth
Telenursing, 338, *see also* Telehealth
Teleology, 255, 257
Telephone, 348
Telephone tag, 347
Television, 133, 139, 142
Television age, 143
Temperament, 91–92
*Terebi Asahi*, 280
Terrorist bombing, 267–268
Terrorizing, 221, 222
Test-retest reliability, 60
Test taking, 372
Text processing research, 6
Thematic Apperception Tests, 130
Theories of the sign, 124–125
Theory of conversational implicature, 4
Theory of linguistics/semiotics, 124–125
Thinking, deactivation by television, 143
Threat, 126, *see also* Audience

Tiananmen Square incident, 270
Timber interests, 175
Time
  patient–physician communication,
    334–335, 348, 352–353, 357
  political role/influence of business
    organizations, 168
Tojo Hideki, Prime Minister, 276
Topic changes, 5, 24, 376
Top-tier officials, 183
Total Quality Management (TQM), 250
Touching, 80, *see also* Affection, interpersonal
  relationships
TQM, *see* Total Quality Management
Traditional family structure, 39–40
Traditional managers, 240
Traditional relationships, 45, 46, *see also*
  Relationships
Training, 236, 237, *see also* Public relations
  ethics, professionalism
Trends, *kuuki*, 286–288
Triadic frames, 337, *see also* Frames; Framing
Triadic power, 165
Tripolar *kuuki* model, 290–291
Trust, 330–331, 334, 341–342
Trustworthiness, 204
Turnaround time, 344
Two-dimensional model, 74
Typology, family, 38

U

Understanding, emotion, 214
Understanding patients, 353
Unintended inferences, 27–29
United Nations Peace Cooperation (UNPC)
    Bill, *see also Kuuki*
  Gulf War, 278–280, 281
  intensity, 290
  measurement, 288, 289*f*
Universal Accreditation Program, 238
UNPC, *see* United Nations Peace Cooperation
    Bill
Us-and-them mentality, 306–307, 319
Uses and gratification model, 132–135
Utilitarianism, 255, 256
Utterance, 15, 17, 21

V

Validity
  emotional intelligence, 207
  family communication patterns, 43, 49,
    60–62
  processing speaker meaning, 23
Values, 39, 331, 254–255
Values advocacy, 252

Variability, processing speaker meaning, 25–27, 30
Verbal Approach/Avoidance Survey, 102
Verbal behavior, 80, 105, 106, *see also* Behavior
Verbal response mode (VRM), 47
Verbal skills, 375
Verbs, 16–17
Video-teleconferencing, 336, *see also* Telehealth
Vietnam War, 282, 287
Violations, code of ethics, 235–236
Violence, 129
Voting, 166
VRM, *see* Verbal response mode

### W

*Wall Street Journal, The*, 173
*War of the Worlds*, 130–131
War spirit, 278, 282
Waring Intimacy Questionnaire (WIQ), 101

Warmth, 79, 90, 92
*Washington Post*, 283
Watergate scandal, 283–285
Well-being, psychological, 72–73
Well marker, 11, 12
Wilhelm, II, Kaiser, 276
WIQ, *see* Waring Intimacy Questionnaire
Withdraw-demand, 63
Words, meaning, 3
Work experience, 211
Work relationships, 88, *see also* Relationships
World Trade Centers, 267, 293
World War II, 276–277, 280

### Y

*Yomiuri*, 279–280

### Z

*Zeitgeist*, 271, *see also Kuuki*
z-scores, 57

# ABOUT THE EDITOR

WILLIAM B. GUDYKUNST is a professor of speech communication and a member of the Asian American Studies Program Council at California State University, Fullerton. His work focuses on developing a theory of interpersonal and intergroup effectiveness that can be applied to improving the quality of communication and explaining cross-cultural differences in communication. Gudykunst is the author of *Bridging Differences* and *Asian American Ethnicity and Communication*, as well as co-author of *Culture and Interpersonal Communication*, *Bridging Japanese/North American Differences*, *Ibunkakan Komyunikeishon: Beyondo Ansahtenti* (Intercultural Communication: Beyond Uncertainty, with Tsukasa Nishda), among others. He has edited or co-edited numerous books including *Communication in Japan and the United States*, *Handbook of International and Intercultural Communication*, *Theories of Intercultural Communication*, *Intergroup Communication*, and *Communication in Personal Relationships Across Cultures*, among others. Gudykunst is a fellow of the International Communication Association.

# ABOUT THE CONTRIBUTORS

DOREEN K. BARINGER is a doctoral candidate in communication at The Pennsylvania State University. She is currently a research assistant and editorial assistant for the *Journal of Communication*. Her research interests are in lifespan and instructional communication, and her work has been published in *Communication Theory* and *Communication Education*.

BRUCE K. BERGER is associate professor in the Department of Advertising and Public Relations at the University of Alabama. His research, which focuses on business influence on public policy and on organizational rhetoric, has appeared in the *Journal of Public Relations Research, Journal of Employee Communication Management,* and a number of trade publications. Prior to his doctoral studies, Berger was a public relations executive at the Upjohn Company and later Whirlpool Corporation, where he was responsible for public affairs and issues management in the U.S. and Europe.

LOIS A. BOYNTON is an assistant professor at the School of Journalism and Mass Communication at the University of North Carolina at Chapel Hill where she teaches public relations. Her research interests focus on public relations and ethics. She has presented papers at national conferences and had two articles published on public relations topics.

DEBBIE S. DOUGHERTY is an assistant professor of communication at the University of Missouri, Columbia. Her research interests are in the area of organizational communication with an emphasis on power in organizations, especially as it pertains to emotions, gender, and sexual harassment. Her current research includes theorizing feminist standpoint epistemologies in organizations, the role of emotion in feminist standpoints, the discursive construction of power as domination during airline acquisition, and the gendered constructions of sexual harassment-related power. Her research has been published in *Management Communication Quarterly, Journal of Applied Communication Research, Women's Studies in Communication,* and *Qualitative Research Reports in Communication*.

NORAH E. DUNBAR is an assistant professor of Communication Studies at California State University, Long Beach. Her research interests are in the area of interpersonal communication with an emphasis on interpersonal dominance, nonverbal communication, relational power, and deception.

MARY ANNE FITZPATRICK is the Kellett WARF Professor of Communication and Deputy Dean in the College of Letters and Science at the University of Wisconsin, Madison. Her research and teaching focus on interaction in social and personal relationships with a special emphasis on marital and family relationships. She is a past President of the International Communication Association and recipient of the ICA Career Productivity Award in 2001.

RUTH M. GUZLEY is an associate professor and graduate coordinator of communication at California State University, Chico. Her research interests are in the areas of organizational communication and health communication, with a particular focus on physician-patient relationships in managed care contexts.

STEPHANIE A. HAMEL is a Ph.D. candidate, assistant instructor, and internship coordinator in the Department of Communication Studies at the University of Texas, Austin. Her research interests are in the area of organizational communication and include the social consequences of mediated communication, organizational justice, and communication concerns of the public and nonprofit sectors.

JAMES K. HERTOG is associate professor in the School of Journalism and Telecommunications at the University of Kentucky. He has authored book chapters and articles in a variety of mass and political communication journals, including *Communication Research, Journalism and Mass Communication Quarterly,* and *Journalism & Mass Communication Monographs.* His current work emphasizes media coverage and the framing of social protests groups, political parties and candidates, and military and political events.

THOMAS HOLTGRAVES is a professor of psychology at Ball State University. His primary research program has investigated the social factors involved in the production and comprehension of language, including research on social psychological variables affecting how speakers phrase their remarks, as well as the manner in which social psychological variables affect how hearers comprehend, remember, and interpret remarks. He is the author of *Language as Social Action: Social Psychology and Language Use* (Erlbaum).

ITO YOUICHI is a professor in the Department of Policy and Management at the Shonan Fujisawa campus of Keio University and a researcher in the Institute for Communications Research in Tokyo. He served as a board member-at-large of the International Communication Association (ICA, 1997–2000) and the International Council of the International Association for Media and Communication Research (IAMCR, 1988–1996). He has served as vice president of the Political Communication Section of IAMCR (1992–present) and of the International Political Science Association (IPSA, 1998–present). He was the founding editor of the *Keio Communication Review* (1980–1996).

YOUNG YUN KIM is a professor of communication at the University of Oklahoma. Her research addresses issues of communication in cross-cultural adaptation of immigrants and sojourners, multicultural organizations, and domestic interethnic relations. Her books include *Becoming Intercultural, Communication and Cross-Cultural Adaptation, Theories in Intercultural Communication* (co-edited with W. Gudykunst), and *Communicating With Strangers* (with W. Gudykunst, 3rd ed.), among others.

SPIRO KIOUSIS is an assistant professor of public relations at Iowa State University. His primary research interests are in political communication and new communication technologies.

ASCAN F. KOERNER is an assistant professor of speech communication at the University of Minnesota. His research focuses on the cognitive bases of relationships and their influence on interpersonal communication, including message production and message interpretation. His research has appeared in *Communication Studies, Communication Theory,* and *Human Communication Research.*

KATHLEEN J. KRONE is an associate professor of communication studies at the University of Nebraska, Lincoln. Her research and teaching interests are in the area of organizational communication with special emphasis on emotion, conflict/ negotiation, and gender. Her current research projects include studies of conflict management in Chinese-U.S. joint ventures and turning points in community consensus building. Her research on emotion has been published in *Management Communication Quarterly, Emotion in Organizations* (2nd ed.), and *Journal of Applied Communication Research.*

ROBERT KUBEY is director of the Center for Media Studies and an associate professor at Rutgers University. For Erlbaum he has edited *Media Literacy in the Information Age,* co-authored *Television and the Quality of Life,* and co-edited a series of research volumes on media education.

AMANDA L. KUNDRAT is a doctoral student in communication at The Pennsylvania State University. Her interests include health communication across the lifespan and organizational communication. Currently she is an instructor of small-group communication and a research assistant.

JON F. NUSSBAUM is a professor and associate head of the Department of Communication Arts and Sciences at The Pennsylvania State University. He has published eight books and over 60 refereed articles and book chapters concentrating on lifespan communication. He was a Fulbright research scholar (United Kingdom) for the 1991–92 academic year, is a fellow in Adult Development and Aging (Division 20) of the American Psychological Association, and currently serves as the editor of the *Journal of Communication.*

DONG-JIN PARK is a doctoral candidate in the College of Communication at the University of Alabama. His current research projects and dissertation work focus on the uses and benefits of new information and communication technologies in the policy process, and how and to what extent corporate public relations practitioners use new technologies to attempt policy influence.

LORETTA L. PECCHIONI is an assistant professor of communication at Louisiana State University. Her research focuses on interpersonal relationships across the lifespan, including adult mother-daughter relationships, family caregiving, and the role of grandparent-grandchild relationships in the development of aging stereotypes. She is co-author of *Communication and Aging* (2nd ed.) and has published articles in the *Journal of Social and Personal Relationships, Health Communication, Journal of Communication, Communication Reports, Journal of Family Communication,* and *Journal of Gerontology: Social Science.*

SUE D. PENDELL is associate professor of speech communication at Colorado State University, where she teaches interpersonal, intercultural, nonverbal, and small group communication. After many years of service in faculty and university governance and doing training and development programs internationally, she is returning to research with a cross-cultural focus on affection in interpersonal relationships.

PAUL POWER is vice president of research at King World/CBS Enterprises and a Ph.D. candidate in the Rutgers School of Communication, Information, and Library Studies. His primary research interests are diffusion of emerging communication technologies and consumer behavior.